LETTERS OF

RALPH VAUGHA WILLIAM

1895–1958

LETTERS OF RALPH VAUGHAN WILLIAMS 1895–1958

Edited by Hugh Cobbe

OXFORD
UNIVERSITY PRESS

Great Clarendon Street, Oxford OX2 6DP

Oxford University Press is a department of the University of Oxford.
It furthers the University's objective of excellence in research, scholarship,
and education by publishing worldwide in

Oxford New York

Auckland Cape Town Dar es Salaam Hong Kong Karachi
Kuala Lumpur Madrid Melbourne Mexico City Nairobi
New Delhi Shanghai Taipei Toronto

With offices in

Argentina Austria Brazil Chile Czech Republic France Greece
Guatemala Hungary Italy Japan Poland Portugal Singapore
South Korea Switzerland Thailand Turkey Ukraine Vietnam

Oxford is a registered trade mark of Oxford University Press
in the UK and in certain other countries

Published in the United States
by Oxford University Press Inc., New York

First published 2008

British Library Cataloguing in Publication Data

Data available

Library of Congress Cataloging in Publication Data

Data available

Typeset by SPI Publisher Services, Pondicherry, India
Printed in Great Britain
on acid-free paper by
Biddles Ltd., King's Lynn, Norfolk

ISBN 978–0–19–925797–3

1 3 5 7 9 10 8 6 4 2

THIS VOLUME IS DEDICATED
WITH DEEP AFFECTION AND GRATITUDE
TO THE MEMORY OF THE LATE

URSULA VAUGHAN WILLIAMS

15 MARCH 1911–23 OCTOBER 2007

FOREWORD

In Vaughan Williams's letters you will not find the personal confessions and the insights into creative processes that illuminate Elgar's correspondence. He refused to discuss his music with anyone except his very closest friends. In the following pages there are only a few comments on the 'meaning' of his works. 'Of course music has a meaning', he wrote in 1957, 'but I think that can only be expressed in terms of music. I know that some people try to narrow the effect of music to something visual or verbal. To my mind, when they do so they make a horrible mess of it.' That forthrightness characterizes Vaughan Williams's letter-writing throughout his life. We see him through his letters as loyal friend, champion of causes, spokesman for his professional colleagues, encourager of the young, and defender of his faith in the increasing individuality of English music, something to which he had devoted his life. He never undertook any task or joined any committee unless he was prepared to devote time and energy to it, whether it was collecting wartime salvage, promoting new music, obtaining the release from internment of alien musicians, or finding a way though the tangled affairs of the English Folk Dance and Song Society.

The most personal glimpses occur in his letters to his cousin Ralph Wedgwood dating from his marriage to Adeline Fisher in 1897. His descriptions of their honeymoon visit to Berlin are racy and vivid and illustrate his keen sense of humour and of the ridiculous. It is to Ralph (Randolph) Wedgwood that he confesses that 'you know I always have preferred soft scenery to stern uncomfortable scenery. I can admire it but I can't really enjoy it.' His affection for Wedgwood shines through, and it is no surprise that he should have dedicated *A Sea Symphony* to him since he regarded it as his best work to that date (an accolade he later bestowed on the *Tallis Fantasia*). Reticent as he usually was about his own music, he was always strongly opinionated about other people's. Thus, to the critic Edwin Evans in 1903 about his song 'Tears, idle tears' 'I have an idea that it is more "modern" (in the narrow conventional sense) than some of my other stuff. But I am no judge of this because music which to me seems thoroughly old-fashioned (e.g. some of Strauss) I am told is the "ne plus ultra of modernity" – and other music which seems to me to be at the heart of the real spirit of the age (some of Brahms for instance) I am told is old-fashioned – so I am, apparently, no judge.' In his taste in music he was very much a man of his time. He had no use for Strauss and his generation of late Romantics—although he was more interested in Mahler than he ever let on—and Stravinsky and Schoenberg meant nothing to him. Berg's *Wozzeck* was another matter. He had listened to a broadcast in 1945 and went to the Covent Garden production in 1952. Like so many of his pronouncements, what he wrote to Hubert Foss should be taken with a pinch of salt, especially as we cannot see the teasing twinkle in his eye: 'up to the present Berg has merely bored me – but I went to a bit of a rehearsal the other day and I was so intrigued by the stage that I did not bother to listen to the music: which perhaps is the best way of listening to it, and what the composer meant.'

Although he may have given the impression of having a cavalier attitude to his own music, his 1910 letter to Harold Child, librettist of *Hugh the Drover*, shows how exactly he visualized it before a word or a note had been written and it is a surprise to find him citing Mozart's *Così fan tutte* and Puccini and Charpentier as models. Many of the letters show his concern for its accurate presentation and his diligence in undertaking any task, demanding to know exactly what was required for the masque *Pan's Anniversary* in 1906. He certainly did not subscribe to Holst's belief that 'if a thing is worth doing, it's worth doing badly'. When he was first approached by Mrs W. Hadley in 1906 for incidental music for *The Pilgrim's Progress*, he accepted 'if you can provide me with a string orchestra of *first-rate* amateurs & *3 or 4 professionals* to keep the thing going'. In 1933 when a performance of his Piano Concerto was planned in Strasburg, he reminded the soloist Harriet Cohen: 'If you find that [Hermann] Scherchen has an incomplete or inadequate orchestra, you will refuse to play the concerto won't you?' Witness, too, his detailed instructions about the woodwind in *A Sea Symphony* sent in 1911 to the Bristol conductor Arnold Barter (the start of a long and touching friendship). He did not attend the performance but Barter's report on it made Vaughan Williams 'wish that the work was 1000 times better than it is – I know so well now the weak places – & the places where I didn't do what I wanted to – & the places where I did not follow my real impulses – but some silly considerations came in the way (I imagine that all composers suffer from this) – I wish I c^{d} do it all over again now!' About this date he was disillusioned with the state of English orchestral playing. Writing to Ernest Farrar on this subject, he added: 'About Wood & the promenades (which by the way I except from the above condemnation) I don't know how to get at him – except by a yearly bombardment – I've done so nearly every year for the last 8 or 9 years & he has *twice* taken notice of me.'

His disparagement of his own work was in no way mock-modest. He genuinely feared falling below his own standards and after the death of Holst, on whose judgement he placed such high value, he had second thoughts about releasing works for performance (I remember his threatening to tear up each of the last three symphonies!). Yet although he played his new works through to a 'jury' of a few close colleagues, he usually took no notice of their criticisms. Explaining in 1924 why he would not be a candidate for the Professorship of Music at Cambridge University, he wrote to a supporter: 'People will not realise what an appallingly illiterate person I am – both in ancient and modern music... I look forward now that I can drop some of my outside work to trying to really learn the job of a composer – which I have as yet failed to do – before I am too old to do anything.' Some of the 'outside work' was conducting the Bach Choir, which he handed over, with valuable practical advice, to Adrian Boult. He is on record as saying he disliked his Piano Concerto; and his alleged remark about the Fourth Symphony—'I don't know whether I like it, but it's what I meant'—is supported by various comments on it in his letters, e.g. to Boult in 1934: 'The bits I have shown to people they do not like – Gustav [Holst] heard it all in an early version on 2 pftes – & was puzzled by most of it & disliked the rest.' To Arthur Bliss in 1935 a fortnight after the first performance: 'I have my ups & downs – sometimes I hate it. I'm glad you like the slow mov^{t} best – you know that I owe two enormous last moment improvements entirely to you. What I sh^{d} really like to do is to have composition lessons from you – I usually have my scoring vetted by G[ordon] J[acob] – & with you to put the stuff right you might between you make a composer of me yet.' To Elizabeth Trevelyan in May 1935: 'I quite got to like it myself in the end. The first rehearsal was unimaginable chaos. But the orchestra [BBC Symphony] & Adrian worked like Trojans for 4 rehearsals – & things gradually cleared themselves – chiefly owing to Adrian's *real* insight.' In 1951, after Finzi had expressed doubts about the cantata *The Sons of Light*, he responded: 'if this is really second-rate it had better be put out of its misery by the vet... The funny thing is that (1.) I got excited and liked it while I was doing it and thought the tunes very good. But when I heard them they all seemed to be still-born. (2.) The part I liked best is part I, especially the horses of the sun, and this is the part which most people seem to like least. (3.) The chorus seemed tame and bored, but to excuse the work on these grounds is like a bad workman complaining of his tools. What really worries me is that this flop, if it is one, has made me lose my self-confidence. For the last two months I have been writing away hard, and thinking it all very good, but now after this interval, I am sure I shall say "Am I deceiving myself? and losing my power of self-criticism?"'

The Fourth Symphony, begun in 1931, is one of his works that have provoked controversy about its possible 'meaning'. Although there were precedents in earlier works (*Sancta Civitas, Piano Concerto, Job*), its dissonance and violence took listeners by surprise and after the first performance in 1935 some writers linked this to the Nazi and Fascist threats to the peace of Europe. Vaughan Williams denied this, writing to his old friend Robert Longman in 1937: 'I am not at all sure that I like it myself *now* – all I know is that it is what I wanted to do *at the time.* I wrote it not as a definite picture of anything external e.g. the state of Europe – but simply because it occurred to me like this . . . a thing just comes – or it doesn't – usually doesn't – I always live in hope, as all writers must, that one day I shall "ring the bell" – in younger days when one thought one was going to do the *real thing* each time and each time discovered one hadn't done it, one said hopefully "next time" – but when one touches on 65 one begins to wonder.' Of course, as he admitted, a listener can provide his own 'meaning' and the composer may subconsciously reflect another meaning. Some detected a self-portrait in this symphony, perhaps reflecting his frustrations over Adeline's long years as an invalid. But it seems most likely that its genesis was a purely musical attempt to show that one could write a 'wrong-note' symphony in the format of Beethoven's Fifth. More problems arose with the Sixth Symphony (1944–7), some of which began as unused film music. He wrote confidentially to Frank Howes, music critic of *The Times*, objecting to his description of the work as a 'War Symphony' as though that was its official title. The music certainly invites a programmatic interpretation, with menacing martial music and a finale suggesting a post-atomic Waste Land. He told Longman that 'he had no conscious idea *whatsoever* of doing this', but Longman thought he realized he had done this quite unconsciously. He wrote to me that the nearest one could come to the 'meaning' of the finale was Prospero's 'We are such stuff as dreams are made on and our little life is rounded by a sleep'; and he liked Rutland Boughton's description of the movement as 'an agnostic's *Paradiso*'.

Throughout his life Vaughan Williams helped other composers by encouragement, criticism, and financial aid, sometimes all three. Gerald Finzi was one such protégé and it is interesting to find him writing to Sir Ivor Atkins, one of the Three Choirs Festival conductors, in 1932, sending him '2 Psalms by the young composer Britten aged 18 about which I spoke to you. I have only now persuaded him to make a second copy . . . I have only told Britten that I wanted a copy to show to someone.' Writing in the same year to Anne Macnaghten suggesting composers for her concerts, he said: 'You ought [to] get into touch with Benjamin Britten – I believe he has a str 4tet. I don't know it – but his orchestral & choral things are fine.' He later wrote admiringly of Britten's *A Boy is Born*. Yet Aldeburgh persists in believing that Vaughan Williams in some way obstructed Britten at the Royal College of Music. In truth he shared Britten's view of the RCM, as he wrote in a letter to his cousin Peter Montgomery in 1930, advising him on music as a career and whether to study abroad: 'I know, to my sorrow, how lamentably unthorough the R.C.M is & how badly in need of improvement, & these foreign conservatoires look very imposing *on paper* – but so does the RCM – and we have no proof that the reality abroad comes up to the advertized advantages any more than the R.C.M. After all nearly all the musicians of note in England have done most of their study at home – the people who study abroad seem to come to nothing.' Another aspect of his attitude on helping composers can be found in his reply to the critic Ernest Newman, who felt that the composer Ernest Bloch was unduly neglected in Britain. Vaughan Williams disagreed and added: 'I always feel, when I see the public declaration that a composer is "unduly neglected" that there is something suspect about him. Such a declaration, I believe, creates *distrust*, e.g. the strong prejudice created against Van Dieren by the unwise propaganda of some youthful enthusiasts.'

The letters throw light on his political views. In the 1940s he was enthusiastic about Federal Union, a forerunner of the European Union, although this appeared to contradict his opinions about the individuality of English art. To describe him as a Left Wing Socialist, as some have done, is wide of the mark. He was a liberal of the old school but not in a party sense. His attitude to the General Strike in 1926 was illuminating. He supported the miners but feared it was developing into a class war '& I don't feel at all inclined to side with my own class (though I suppose that at a pinch I should)...have the side of revolution any scheme for the better government of the country to offer if they were victorious? I doubt it...But I cannot deny the right of an Oxford undergraduate to go and unload fish if the man whose job it is refuses to do so. Also I cannot deny the duty of the gov^t to see that people do not starve if the food is to be had...The simplest thing for a man of my age is to do nothing.' He told the Communist composer Alan Bush in 1939 that 'I hold all political opinions to be good or bad according to the nature of the people who hold them'. He explained to Rutland Boughton in 1952: 'The truth is, I think, that when I am with Conservatives I become socialistic and when I am with Socialists I become true blue Tory...Ever since I had a vote I have voted either Radical or Labour except once, after the last War, when I was so disgusted by what I considered the mean tricks of the Labour party in forcing an election. I voted Labour in the last election though in my heart of hearts I wanted the Tories to get in, but the old spirit of opposition crept up and with all the County shouting for the Tories I determined to be on the other side . . . I believe in freedom and that is why I will not be bullied by Nazis, Fascists and Russians.'

A brief foreword can convey only a tithe of the subjects covered by these letters. Of course there are omissions, mainly because no letters exist, for example there is nothing about the practicalities of folk-song collecting, nothing about the lessons with Ravel, and, most significantly, nothing about the 1914–18 War except the poignant note to Holst in 1916: 'I sometimes dread coming back to normal life with so many gaps – especially of course George Butterworth . . . out of those 7 who joined up together in August 1914 only 3 are left.' And there is nothing about his personal life—only a few letters to Ursula. But the portrait of a generous, full-scale personality, a servant of his art in every aspect of it, capable of waspishness and blind prejudice, is vivid. Here is his attitude to money, confided to his accountant when he was setting up the RVW Trust to help other musicians : 'I am not interested in money, except as a means of not having to think about it, and though naturally, I do not want to have too little, I should feel equally burdened if I had too much . . . the payment of income and surtax has never been a worry to me, and I have always found it possible to live on the income which remained.' And how delightful to discover that he opposed a new translation of the Bible, that he had often thought of setting Edward Lear's *The pobble who has no toes*, 'one of the most mysteriously romantic poems I know', and that he knew how to put the BBC in its place. Thanks to the sensitive and erudite editing and annotation by Hugh Cobbe, we discover a different Vaughan Williams, more complex and fascinating than some might have suspected. But the music should have told us that already.

Michael Kennedy

PREFACE

THE task of collecting the letters of Vaughan Williams was entrusted to me by Ralph Vaughan Williams's widow, Ursula, in 1989. The object was to trace letters wherever they might now be, transcribe them, and organize the transcriptions into an electronic database, now comprising some 3,300 letters, from which they could be published. The general purpose of the undertaking was to enable readers to form a view of the composer and his personality through direct contact with his communications with others, as it were by eavesdropping. The selection that is published in this volume represents between a fifth and a quarter of the complete collection but has been designed to provide as full a self-portrait of VW in his own words as possible. It is hoped that the book will also complement existing basic works on the composer, notably Ursula's own biography of her husband and Michael Kennedy's study of his music. The extant letters span his whole active life from 1895 until his death in 1958.

The project enjoyed the strong support of the late Ursula Vaughan Williams from the outset. She readily authorized the publication of any documents in her or her husband's copyright and, through the Vaughan Williams Estate, provided support in terms of equipment and practical assistance. It will become clear that this volume is not only a tribute to a great man in celebration of the fiftieth anniversary of his death, but every bit as much a tribute to Ursula, who not only cared for VW in the later years of his life but after his death did so much and so constantly to further the cause of his music. For the project, she was indefatigable in urging private owners of letters not only to make them available to me for transcription but also to deposit them for preservation in the British Library, where a considerable collection has built up as a result.

The task, however, could not have been carried out without assistance and encouragement from many other people. First of all is Michael Kennedy, a close friend of the composer after the war who not only made his large collection of letters available and gave it to the British Library but has also read the complete text of this volume and contributed a Foreword. My predecessor as Head of Music at the British Library, Oliver Neighbour, a keen admirer of the music, has also read everything and commented on it. Between the two they have averted many a faux pas on my part. Eric Downing, a Director of the Vaughan Williams Estate at the time, provided much help in the early stages when the project was being set up. Others who have allowed me to call on them at every stage were the late Howard Ferguson in Cambridge and Roger Savage in Edinburgh. My employer until 2002, the British Library, was invariably supportive of my work, especially by granting a three-month sabbatical term in 1996 to work on the project; my Director, Alice Prochaska (now University Librarian at Yale), was constantly encouraging and used her good offices in setting up arrangements for the publication of this volume. Merton College, Oxford kindly granted me a Visiting Research Fellowship in Hilary term for my 1996 sabbatical through the good offices of the Warden, Dame Jessica Rawson, and Edward Olleson, Fellow of the College; this provided an opportunity to go through the Music Department archive at Oxford University Press. The Press was very cooperative and provided access without hindrance—I am very grateful to those with whom I have had dealings there over the years: Andrew Potter, David Blackwell, Simon Wright, Evelyn Hendy, Peter Foden, and student interns Sally Robson and Rose Potter, who did much photocopying for me.

A group of younger friends have helped in practical ways: Duncan Hinnells, at the time a postgraduate student at St Catherine's College, Oxford, was very helpful during my term there; Eric Saylor spent a year at the British Library in 1999 on a Fulbright Scholarship and devoted a proportion of his time to helping me with transcriptions and annotations. My colleague, and immediate successor as Head of Music Collections, Chris Banks (now University Librarian at Aberdeen), was ever helpful in keeping me in touch with relevant new acquisitions once I had left the department, and my retired colleague, Arthur Searle, also Librarian of the Royal Philharmonic Society, took a close interest from the start. Jennifer Doctor, now of the University of York, was especially helpful in connection with material concerning VW's women pupils and also the BBC. Bruce Phillips read much of the text and has been particularly helpful about John Ireland. Stephen Connock, Chairman of the RVW Society, has used his contacts to point letters in the direction of the project and also provided opportunities for me to report on progress at relevant gatherings of the society. Alain Frogley, one of the leading VW scholars of the present generation, has shared information with me about collections of letters which he has come across in his own work and has advised on other matters, such as the Shakespeare Prize.

Finally, I have five other personal thanks to record: my niece Rose Cobbe helped with some of the transcription in the early stages; however, the person who has carried the heat and burden of the day on that front is Jane

Parrott, who eventually became very practised at reading VW's scrawl. As the project gathered momentum, Nicolas Bell, Curator of Music Manuscripts at the British Library, became a tower of strength on matters of detail and style and has been, as a mutual friend put it, my faithful Achates. Then there has been Dr Bonnie Blackburn, my copy-editor, whose stalwart eagle eye has averted many a disaster and who has also provided the indexes. Above all there is she who has lived with the project since the first day and who has been the source of so much sage advice and encouragement throughout, my wife Katherine.

Beyond these major debts of gratitude I must acknowledge the help provided by many individuals and institutions who have offered help on particular matters or who have provided photocopies: Richard Abram (EMI), Alan Aldous, the late Felix Aprahamian, Stephen Banfield, Paul Banks, Richard Barber, BBC Information and Archives, Caversham (Jeff Walden), Birmingham City Archives, Catherine Bishop, Anthony Boden, Daniel C. Braden, Bristol University Library, Britten–Pears Library, Aldeburgh (Christopher Grogan), the late Geoffrey Bush, Arthur Butterworth, Gerry Byrne, Cambridge University Library (Richard Andrewes, Patrick Zutshi), Jane Caplan, Carnegie United Kingdom Trust (Elizabeth East), Michael Clifford, Colin Coleman, Columbia University Library (Kenneth Lohf), Shirley Corke (niece of Frances Farrer), Helen Corkery, Cornell University Library (James Cassaro), Lisa Cox, Liane Curtis, George Dannatt, Jennifer Doctor, Mrs Ivan Dowling, Vernon Duker, Vera Duncan (*née* Kantrovitch), Rudolf Elvers, Christopher Finzi, Fitzwilliam Museum, Cambridge, Lewis Foreman, Dorothy Fraser, Helen Fry, Richard Garnett, Robin Goldsbrough, Barrie Greenwood, the late Jean Hadley, Andrew Herbert, Anthony Hodge, Joyce Hooper, Jacqueline Hope Wallace, the Houghton Library at Harvard University (Leslie Morris), the late Michael Hurd, Robin Ivison, Rolf Jordan, Frank P. Jung, The Rowe Music Library, King's College, Cambridge (Margaret Cranmer), the late Iris Lemare, Library and Archives Canada (Maria Calderisi, Marlene Wehrle), Diana McVeagh, Nadine Marshall, Peter Mason, David Matthews, Simona Middleton (*née* Pakenham), Jerrold Northrop Moore, Keith Mullinar, National Library of Australia (Graeme Powell), National Library of New Zealand (Jill Palmer), New York Public Library (Susan Sommer, David Shepherd), Adrian Officer, Rachel O'Higgins, the late Diana Oldridge (*née* Awdry), Julian Onderdonk, the Pierpont Morgan Library (J. Rigbie Turner), Claire Rauter, Royal Academy of Music Library (Katharine Hogg, Bridget Palmer), Royal College of Music Library (Pam Thompson, Christopher Bornet, Paul Andrews, Peter Horton), Malcolm Smith, Diana Sparkes, Renée Stewart (former Secretary, Leith Hill Musical Festival), Jeanne Strang, Rosamund Strode, Margaret Stubbs, Alice Sumsion,

Hazel Sumsion, Surrey History Centre, Laurence Taylor, Malcolm Taylor (Cecil Sharp House), John Thompson in New Zealand, Katharine Thomson, Jean Treves, the University of St Andrews Library (Christine Gascoigne), Ted and Jean Uppman, John Walthew, Shaun Ward, Peter Ward Jones, Martin Wedgwood, the late Dame Veronica Wedgwood, Michael White, Nicholas Williams (Stainer & Bell), Yale University Library (Richard Boursy, Ken Crilley, Stephen Young), Adrian Yardley, and the late Percy Young. There may be those who have been inadvertently omitted; to them I apologize wholeheartedly.

H.M.T.C.

September 2007

ACKNOWLEDGEMENTS

ALL letters of Ralph, Adeline, and Ursula Vaughan Williams are printed by courtesy of the Estate of Ursula Vaughan Williams. Letters in the archives of the Carnegie United Kingdom Trust, held in the Scottish Records Office, are printed by kind permission of the Trust. Letters of Gerald Finzi are printed by courtesy of Christopher Finzi. Letters of Adrian Boult and Steuart Wilson are printed by courtesy of Anne Powers. Letters of Ernest Irving are printed by courtesy of Echo Irving. The letter of Edwin Evans (no. 128) is printed by courtesy of Central Music Library Ltd. The letter of Michael Tippett (no. 424) is printed by courtesy of Meirion Bowen. The letter of Sir John Barbirolli (no. 670) is printed by courtesy of the late Lady Barbirolli. The letter of John Ireland (no. 633) is printed by courtesy of the Trustees of the John Ireland Trust. The letter from Jean Stewart (no. 422) is printed by kind permission of her daughters, Alison Hadley, Nicola Mulligan, and Maggie Tomkins. The letter of Benjamin Britten (no. 756) is printed by courtesy of the Britten–Pears Foundation. Letters and documents held in the BBC Written Archives Centre are printed by kind permission of the BBC. Letters in the Cambridge University Library are printed by permission of the Syndics of Cambridge University Library. Letters in the archives of the OUP Music Department are printed by permission of the Secretary to the Delegates of Oxford University Press (which also owns the copyright in nos. 382 and 635). The reproduction of the portrait of Vaughan Williams by Gerald Kelly on the dust jacket was kindly made available by the Trustees of the National Portrait Gallery. In one or two cases every effort has been made to trace the present administrators of particular copyrights but without success.

CONTENTS

LIST OF ABBREVIATIONS

AVW	Adeline Vaughan Williams
BL	The British Library
BPL	The Britten–Pears Library, Aldeburgh
BRL	Birmingham Reference Library
CGLE	*The Cambridge Guide to Literature in English* (Cambridge, 1988)
CW	Michael Kennedy, *A Catalogue of the Works of Ralph Vaughan Williams*, 2nd edn. (Oxford, 1996). Works are cited by year and number within the year, as given in *CW* (e.g. 1958/2), or by page.
EFDSS	The English Folk Dance and Song Society
EH	*The English Hymnal*
FTFN	*Finzi Trust Friends Newsletter*
Grove 5	*Grove's Dictionary of Music and Musicians*, 5th edn., ed. Eric Blom (London, 1954)
HR	R. Vaughan Williams and Gustav Holst, *Heirs and Rebels: Letters Written to Each Other and Occasional Writings on Music*, ed. Ursula Vaughan Williams and Imogen Holst (London, 1959)
IWWM[12]	*International Who's Who in Music*, 12th edn. (Cambridge, 1990)
LHMF	Leith Hill Musical Festival
LGFHF	*Letters of Gerald Finzi and Howard Ferguson*, ed. Howard Ferguson and Michael Hurd (Woodbridge, 2001)
New Grove	*The New Grove Dictionary of Music and Musicians*, ed. Stanley Sadie (London, 1980)
New Grove II	*The New Grove Dictionary of Music and Musicians*, 2nd edn., ed. Stanley Sadie and John Tyrrell (London, 2001)
New Grove Opera	*The New Grove Dictionary of Opera*, ed. Stanley Sadie (London, 1992)
NM	Ralph Vaughan Williams, *National Music and Other Essays*, 2nd edn. (Oxford, 1987)
OUP	Oxford University Press
PR	Ursula Vaughan Williams, *Paradise Remembered: An Autobiography* (London, 2002)
RCM	Royal College of Music
RVW	Ursula Vaughan Williams, *R. V. W.: A Biography of Ralph Vaughan Williams* (London, 1964)

RVWPB	John E. Lunn and Ursula Vaughan Williams, *Ralph Vaughan Williams: A Pictorial Biography* (London, 1971)
PRMA	*Proceedings of the Royal Musical Association*
SPGS	St Paul's Girls' School
UVW	Ursula Vaughan Williams (previously UW)
UW	Ursula Wood
VW	Ralph Vaughan Williams
VWD	*Vaughan Williams in Dorking: A Collection of Personal Reminiscences of the Composer Dr. Ralph Vaughan Williams O.M.*, ed. Celia Newbury, Local History Group of the Dorking and Leith Hill Preservation Society (Dorking, 1979)
VWP	Lewis Foreman (ed.), *Vaughan Williams in Perspective* (London, 1998)
WVW	Michael Kennedy, *The Works of Ralph Vaughan Williams*, 2nd edn. (London, 1980)
WWVW	Roy Douglas, *Working with Vaughan Williams: The Correspondence of Ralph Vaughan Williams and Roy Douglas*, rev. and enlarged edn. (London, 1988)

INTRODUCTION

COMPOSERS communicate with their audiences through the medium of their music. At one level the audience needs to know nothing about the personality of the composer or the facts of his or her life in order to enjoy the music (or otherwise), since the music speaks for itself. However, musical enjoyment engenders curiosity, which initially can be satisfied by well-informed programme notes, but which soon encourages background reading. In recent years the growth of interest in, and the enjoyment of, the music of Ralph Vaughan Williams has created a thirst for more information about the composer and his music. The three studies written in VW's lifetime by Hubert Foss, Percy Young, and Simona Pakenham were followed by two fundamental works published in tandem in 1964: his widow Ursula's biography *R. V. W.* and Michael Kennedy's study of the music in *The Works of Ralph Vaughan Williams*, which had as an appendix a catalogue of the works (which has since been published separately). Both writers were close to the composer and present him to the reader through the filter of their own perception, and in both cases the personality of the writer is as evident as the personality of the subject. The same year saw the publication of *National Music*, a collection of VW's own major published writings, where the filter was of course VW himself.

The present volume of over 750 letters (between a fifth and a quarter of the surviving corpus) is intended, like the music, to present no barrier between the reader and the composer. With the exception of a few written to newspapers and the like, the letters were not written for publication but to communicate directly with one person at one time. As such, each letter is as it were a single piece in a mosaic which as a whole provides a pen-picture of the writer in his own words. It is hoped that the volume will join the other two works in giving the composer's admirers a fundamental insight into the man behind the music.

The compilation of the collection of letters from which the present volume is drawn has had its challenges, but nonetheless has benefited from the age in which the subject lived—it would not be so straightforward to do the same for a contemporary figure. The possible means of communication between human beings have proliferated and the role of the letter written on paper with an address at the top, stamped, and put in a post box has largely been swept aside by the use of the telephone, which is ephemeral, and more recently e-mail, which is only rarely preserved. When the standard means of personal communication was the letter many people carefully kept their incoming correspondence—though VW himself, sadly, was an exception and discarded his letters once they had been dealt with. Where the recipient was a person of some note, collections of correspondence have found their way into libraries and county record offices and are now grist to the mill of biography and historiography; the British Library, for example, is an active collector of musicians' correspondence for that very purpose. In sum, letter-writing played a more central role in everyday life in the first half of the last century than it does now and the letters which were written provide a ready means of understanding the personality of the writer.

The project to collect the texts of the letters of Vaughan Williams has amassed some 3,300 letters so far, which is probably no more than 20 per cent of the letters he actually wrote when one considers the number of letters that someone of VW's professional standing and longevity was likely to need to write each week or even each day. This is not a surprising conclusion. They are now to be found in a wide variety of locations, either in repositories or in private hands. Naturally most are in the United Kingdom, but there are significant numbers in the United States and some in France, Australia, New Zealand, and elsewhere.

The basic work of collecting texts for the project was greatly facilitated by Ursula's preparation for her biography. OUP, her publisher, put out a call asking owners of letters from VW to lend them so that they could be photocopied and returned. The resulting photocopies went to Ursula and have remained in her files ever since. The transcripts of these thus provided a spine to which the many other letters which came to light afterwards (typically those in public institutions) could be attached, so creating as far as possible a single chronological sequence.

The editing of this corpus of letters presented a number of technical challenges of which the first was VW's notorious handwriting. Up until the First World War his hand was reasonably legible, but thereafter reading it relies increasingly on long familiarity or the eye of faith. Some of his letters in the files at OUP, for example, have been provided with interlinear pencil transcriptions to ensure that those who really needed to know the contents could read it. For the present editor early training at the British Library in the methodical deciphering of difficult scripts was invaluable and in the end only the most recalcitrantly scrawled words remained elusive. VW himself was of course well aware of his illegibility, possibly accounted for by the fact that he was naturally left-handed but had been firmly taught to write with his right hand, and dictated many of his letters on business matters to his first wife Adeline, second wife Ursula, or his secretary, Rachel Fardon, to be either written out in their more legible hands or typewritten.

When writing in his own hand VW seems to have felt that anything indicating a date was an unnecessary adjunct to the document: if one is lucky there is simple day of the week ('Wed' or 'Thur') or at most a day and a month ('10 Jan')—years are given very rarely. The thought that in years to come someone might try to set all his letters in a single chronological order would have struck him as ludicrous and probably rather distasteful (he did not even see much point in keeping his manuscripts once a work had been published, but was happy to give his autograph scores to friends as presents—it was Ursula who rounded them up after his death and ensured that they were preserved for posterity in the British Library). At any rate, an aspect of the work which has been most challenging (and pleasurable) has been the detection needed to establish a working date for every letter in the corpus. In this various kinds of external evidence have been helpful: first and foremost there is any dating that *is* given (a simple day of the week and nothing else certainly presents a challenge but can often be fixed by judicious use of a calendar for the year in question combined with indications from the contents of the letter; then supplying a year to the day and month may not be too difficult). A further indicator is the address from which the letter is written—although this can really only provide a fairly broad indication since VW lived at only three addresses during the greater part of his working life: 13 Cheyne Walk from 1905, The White Gates at Dorking from 1929 (with a change of headed writing paper in or about April 1935 when 'From R. Vaughan Williams' was added in print above the die-stamped address, possibly reflecting the fact that the VWs had bought the freehold of the house in 1933 and now saw it as a permanent home), and 10 Hanover Terrace from 1953. During the war years VW used any spare scrap of paper rather than headed writing paper, but sometimes, happily, the scrap in question was the back of a dated incoming letter (and such scraps are amongst the few incoming letters to survive because of VW's habit of disposing of letters the moment he had dealt with them). Fortunately, many recipients kept their letters from VW in their envelopes so that postmarks have been a prime aid to dating. Finally, for letters written in Adeline's hand, the unfortunate progression of her rheumatoid arthritis, especially towards the end of her life, and its effect on her handwriting can occasionally give some general idea of a date that is otherwise absent, for she went on indomitably supporting her husband as an amanuensis to a very late stage.

If there is no internal evidence, the modern editor has a great advantage over his predecessors. Advances in indexing and keyword searching capability in word-processing programs have made it easier to supplement an editor's often imprecise memory by finding in an ever increasing database letters that may relate to the one in hand and thus throw light on its date. Sheer juxtaposition in the chronological series will often shoot down a bright first guess. In this connection a cautionary experience happened in the case of Harriet Cohen. Ursula's files contained a number of photocopies of letters to her which were tentatively dated. Following Cohen's death in 1967 her voluminous correspondence was reserved from use at the British Museum for a considerable number of years. When it eventually became available, the postmarks of the originals (which were still in their envelopes) showed that the tentative dates were sometimes wide of the mark. Dates assigned by guesswork do need to be treated a little cautiously. Indeed only as this book was going to press did the correct date of no. 167 become clear.

VW's orthography has created dilemmas. He wrote quickly and sometimes thoughtlessly—punctuation other than the odd dash is often lacking and the physical end of a line or the edge of the sheet of paper is often a substitute for a full stop, and his spelling can be erratic. The question for the editor arises whether to correct *lapsus calami* and add appropriate punctuation silently, or relentlessly to present the documents as they lie before him, with a myriad of intrusive footnotes simply saying '*sic*' and of square brackets enclosing single commas, full stops, or question marks. It has been felt that, if the letters presented here are to provide a portrait of the composer in his own words, it is important to remove as many visual obstacles between writer and reader as possible without at the same time running any risk of misrepresentation. Consequently, small matters such as punctuation have been silently corrected and only misspellings that seem to contribute to the pen-picture have been retained (usually marked *sic* in the text to give reassurance that they are not an undetected misprint). Footnotes have been added where it is anticipated that the reader will feel the need of information external to the letter itself to better understand the context of the original, but it is hoped that the danger of drowning VW's text in a sea of annotation has been avoided.

For the most part the present selection has been limited to letters written by, rather than to, VW, and where relevant letters to him are extant (such as in the OUP archive) they are summarized in footnotes. However, an exception has been made where inclusion of an incoming letter seems to the editor to add materially to the overall picture. As a matter of principle all the letters written by VW in the collection are presented in their entirety though irrelevant parts of incoming letters are on occasion omitted.

To turn from the physical characteristics of the corpus to the content: As one might expect, the chronological coverage is not even—the survival rate has appeared to increase in line with VW's own standing. For the 1890s just sixty-eight letters survive, mainly to his family and to close Cambridge friends, above all to his cousin Ralph Wedgwood, to whom he was especially close. VW went off to the First World War a young up-and-coming composer; he came back a composer of truly national stature and by the end of the 1920s he was already the second most eminent composer in the country after Elgar, and after Elgar's death in 1934, the most eminent. The growth in his reputation is reflected in the number of letters preserved for each decade:

1900–9	109
1910–19	144
1920–29	232
1930–39	768
1940–49	872
1950–58	1,039

That what has survived is a small fraction of what there may have been is borne out by the fact that of the 3,300 or so letters some 1,450 are written to just fifteen correspondents. In rough chronological order of first letter these include: Ralph Wedgwood (80), Gustav Holst (60), Gerald Finzi (170), Ursula Wood (later Vaughan Williams) (120), and Michael Kennedy (150). Unsurprisingly, there are some 300 letters in the files of OUP, his publisher, and a further 162 in the BBC Written Archives Centre at Caversham. In addition to the major correspondents mentioned above there are some eighty or so who received significant numbers of letters: pupils such as Elizabeth Maconchy, Douglas Lilburn, Frederick Page, Cedric Thorpe Davie, and Ina Boyle, all of whom assiduously kept his encouraging letters; fellow composers such as Arthur Bliss, John Ireland, Cecil Armstrong Gibbs, Granville Bantock, and Benjamin Britten, and especially younger composers who benefited from his friendship and on occasion his helping hand such as Arthur Benjamin, Michael Tippett, Elisabeth Lutyens, Anthony Scott, and of course Gerald Finzi; there were also eminent conductors and soloists who regularly performed his works, for instance Adrian Boult, Harriet Cohen, Henry Wood, and John Barbirolli. On a different plane but no less important to him were the devoted local choral conductors, for whom he was a constant source of encouragement, such as Arnold Barter and Herbert Byard in Bristol and Katharine Thomson in Birmingham; and, among the many concerned with music performances at Dorking, Margery Cullen, Isidore Schwiller, George

Parker, and Adine O'Neill. Collaborators such as Harold Child (librettist of the *Hugh the Drover*), Evelyn Sharp (librettist of *The Poisoned Kiss*), Michael Mullinar, Roy Douglas, and Robert Müller-Hartmann are all represented, as are his colleagues in the folk movement, Lucy Broadwood, Cecil Sharp, and Maud Karpeles. Music critics such as Edwin Evans, Ernest Newman, A. H. Fox Strangways, Herbert Thomson, Percy Scholes, and Frank Howes all appear along with the authors of books about him: Hubert Foss (who had been his publisher at OUP), Percy Young, and Simona Pakenham (on all of whose scripts he refused to comment other than to correct factual errors). There are a legion of replies to letters from admirers, which are always courteous and appreciative, and letters written to the fellow great and good and to the press when there was a battle to be joined—such as the supplanting of the Authorized Version of the Bible; the internment of foreign musicians early in the war; or bad behaviour by the BBC towards the Third Programme or Alan Bush. It is, however, unfortunate that a major strand in his musical life is unrepresented in the extant letters—his work for Percy Dearmer on the first edition of *The English Hymnal*, which in its own way made as indelible a mark on British musical life as any of his own compositions. Some of the tunes he wrote for it have become very widely used in churches throughout the world. However, some letters survive connected with the 1933 revision of *The English Hymnal* and with his editing of *Songs of Praise* and *The Oxford Book of Carols*.

The corpus of his letters in general, and in particular the present selective publication, which has been carefully chosen so as to reflect the characteristics of the full database (including its chronological organization), is intended to serve the purposes of scholarship at different levels: individual letters can provide information as to what the composer was doing where, when, and with whom, or what works were performed on what dates, and matters of that nature. At a deeper level we can gain insights into his opinions on a wide range of matters: politics, people, religion, and music—mostly other than his own. Ursula has said that he found writing music 5 per cent inspiration and 95 per cent the pure slog of putting notes on paper: the slog is indeed apparent from the letters but the inspiration remains a secret inner chamber into which the reader is never admitted. At the deepest level, though, the corpus provides the observer with as vivid a cumulative picture of the man as we are likely to be able to achieve, a picture which must illuminate our understanding of his music.

The breadth of his vision, his largeness of mind, his willingness to seek the opinions of others on his music, his concern for justice and the well-being of his friends, his lack of preoccupation with his own interests, and his clear sense of what he regarded as right and wrong mark him as one who stood towering above many less public-spirited contemporaries. In this context we can see the mind that wrestled with large and deep questions in his nine symphonies. He was fortunate that the financial resources arising from his Wedgwood background were sufficient for him to be able to pursue composition with an unwavering determination to the end of his life, and at the same time to enable him to give a helping hand to fellow musicians less fortunate than himself, but those resources were not so great as to insulate him from the reality of hard and committed work.

Some of the letters in this volume have already seen the light of day: in *Heirs and Rebels* of 1959, in which Ursula Vaughan Williams and Imogen Holst published the correspondence of VW and Gustav Holst (but which did not contain all the VW letters to Holst and omitted some parts of those it did include), in *R. V. W.* (for which so many were collected), in Michael Kennedy's *The Works of Ralph Vaughan Williams*, and in more recent publications; but the great majority are published for the first time. No apology is made for printing some letters again, since the import of a letter appearing simply in the context of other letters written at about the same time will be different from where it is quoted within a text to illustrate a point the author is making.

It is in the context of the general reassessment and growth in popularity of Vaughan Williams's music in recent years, following comparative neglect in the years immediately following his death, that the publication of his letters seems timely—yet in one sense the time will never be ripe, for inevitably letters will continue to come to light (some of the letters in this volume have been discovered only shortly before going to press). For that reason the database containing the collection from which the present letters have been drawn will remain in being so that any newly discovered letters can be added to it. Meanwhile, it is hoped that the selection here published will illuminate the personality of one of our greatest twentieth-century composers, and, using words of Michael Kennedy, help those who did not know him personally but who appreciate the rich humanity of his music to experience the strong personal magnetism and influence of 'an extraordinary ordinary man'.

1

Earliest Letters (c.1895) to the Outbreak of the First World War: 1895–1914

FEW letters written by Vaughan Williams survive from his school days, his youth at Leith Hill Place, his first period at the Royal College of Music, or indeed from his undergraduate days at Cambridge; this is not surprising since there would have been little incentive to keep ephemeral letters at such a time—VW's later stature was not in the least foreseen, even by doting female relations of the older generation. However, even if no personal documents remain for posterity, the friendships established by VW at Cambridge and at the RCM were, as often happens, ones which lasted far into his adult life. Constant references to mutual friends occur in letters to his Cambridge contemporaries, above all in his lifelong correspondence with his second cousin Ralph Wedgwood. Wedgwood, whom VW invariably called by his family nickname 'Randolph' (and after whom he named the tune he composed for the hymn 'God be with you till we meet again', no. 524 in *The English Hymnal*), remained one of the closest of VW's friends outside the musical world, and at Cambridge and in the years immediately afterwards was probably the closest of all his friends. The series of letters from VW which their friendship engendered provides a personal commentary on events in VW's life told, at least in the earlier years, with a sardonic humorous twist, typical of his friends among the Cambridge Apostles. This is particularly noticeable in the letters in which VW regaled Wedgwood with an account of his life in Berlin during his honeymoon in 1897–8.

Wedgwood was reading Moral Science and was elected to the Apostles (more properly called the Cambridge Conversazione Society) in 1893. Other close friends were also members: G. E. Moore, the philosopher, G. M. Trevelyan, the historian, and his elder brother, Robert Calverley Trevelyan, the poet and translator, all of whom figure in VW's correspondence throughout his life. Much has been written about the brilliance of the Apostles and, given his family connections with the Darwins and the friendship with the Maitlands, it is possibly surprising that VW himself does not appear ever to have sought election to the society. But VW's inner driving force, before, during, and after his time at Cambridge, was music, despite the fact that he was reading history, and the aims of the Apostles would not have felt deeply relevant to him. Certainly, once he had graduated in 1895 he quickly returned to the RCM (where he had already spent two years after Charterhouse studying composition with Hubert Parry before going up to Cambridge in 1892) for a further year to continue his composition studies, this time with Charles Villiers Stanford.

If Wedgwood was his closest Cambridge friend, the friendship VW established with the contemporary he now met at the RCM, Gustav von Holst, was even deeper, since their meetings could take place in VW's inner musical space, where even his friendship with Wedgwood could not venture. In Holst he found a friend with shared musical sympathies which enabled them to provide to each other mutual support in what concerned them most closely, tempered by balanced criticism. VW tended to address Holst as 'V' until, in order to obtain an appointment with the YMCA to direct music in internment camps in 1918, Holst relinquished the 'von' element in his surname by Deed Poll. Their mutual dependence combined with VW's characteristic determination to help Holst in any way he could is evident throughout their correspondence. By and large VW's friendship with Wedgwood was more social in character—the most musical feature of it was perhaps VW's dedication to him of *A Sea Symphony*.

The most important legacy from his student days, ahead of his friendships with Wedgwood and Holst, was of course his devotion to Adeline Fisher, the daughter of Herbert Fisher, a barrister and formerly private secretary to the Prince of Wales. The Fishers and the Vaughan Williamses were acquainted but the impetus for Ralph and Adeline's friendship probably came from their encounters at the house of Frederic Maitland in Downing College (he was Downing Professor of the Laws of England), where Ralph was often a visitor while at Cambridge. Maitland was married to Florence, Adeline's older sister, and Adeline was a regular guest, taking part either on the cello or the piano in the music-making that happened there. She was one of eleven children and was also a cousin through her Aunt Julia of Virginia and Vanessa Stephen, and it was at the Stephens' house that Ralph proposed to Adeline and was accepted by her in June 1897. The Fishers were a close-knit family whose members kept in constant touch with each other (for example, to the end of her life Adeline wrote almost every day to her sister Cordelia), and it has been suggested that VW decided to spend the honeymoon in Berlin, following their marriage on 9 October 1897, not only in order to broaden his musical experience (Stanford had urged him to go to Italy to immerse himself in a less intense form of opera, but for VW at this stage the attraction of Wagner and Germanic culture generally was more powerful) but also to counteract the omnipresence of Adeline's family.

VW spent a year at the RCM after Cambridge and then, either for the experience or for the salary (£50 per annum), took up an appointment as organist at the church of St Barnabas, South Lambeth. He did not enjoy the work, though there were clearly aspects of it, such as choir training and the music-making generally, which were very useful for his musical development, and the experience would have stood him in very good stead when in 1904 he undertook the musical editorship of *The English Hymnal*. However, if he did not enjoy being an organist, the church certainly seems to have valued his ability, for the vicar offered to hold the post open for him while he was abroad in Berlin and VW accepted the offer. VW hoped that Holst might be appointed by the vicar to substitute for him during his absence and so wrote to Holst with advice on his application; however, in the end the job went to John Ireland. In accordance with his undertaking VW took up his duties again on his return in April 1898 but resigned the following year with a sigh of relief, giving up the one salaried post he was ever to hold. It had become clear to him that all he wanted to do was to be a composer and he was fortunate that his circumstances made it possible.

The framework for their life in Berlin was provided by VW's studies with Max Bruch, recommended to VW by Heinrich von Herzogenberg, Professor of Theory and Composition at the Berlin Hochschule für Musik, to whom he had been given an introduction. At the end of his studies Bruch wrote a warm recommendation of him both as a composer and as a director of music societies and church choirs. A stream of letters to Wedgwood describes the newly-weds' social life. His description of going to see the play *Die versunkene Glocke* is a good example. They were also able to add to their circle of close friends while in Berlin, for at the same time René Gatty, brother of VW's Cambridge friends Nicholas and Ivor Gatty (no letters from VW to Nicholas or Ivor have come to light), was there and had found them lodgings in Eichhorn Strasse near the Potsdamer Platz. A firm friendship was established, a measure of which was that in 1904 VW, worried about Gatty's health, insisted on sending him some money to enable him to go to the best doctor. For her part, Adeline did her utmost to place René's poetry in suitable London publications.

After their return to London from Berlin by way of Dresden in April the need to establish themselves in their own living quarters led to a series of addresses: 16 North Street and 5 Cowley Street followed in quick series until February 1899, when they moved into 10 Barton Street. They stayed there until 1905, when the purchase of 13 Cheyne Walk gave them a home which lasted until they moved to Dorking in 1929. As they settled back in London two strands of VW's musical life become evident: his preoccupation with folk song and the development of his own music.

Correspondence with the pioneer folk song collectors Lucy Broadwood and Cecil Sharp, often about the English Folk-Song Society, of which they were all three founder members, stemmed from VW's growing interest in the nature of folk song and his concern, shared with fellow enthusiasts such as Broadwood and Sharp, that since the oral tradition was in danger of dying out it was urgent to collect songs in a systematic manner while that was still possible. His interest in folk song was not entirely disinterested, for he felt that it had something profound to offer his own music; indeed it eventually contributed an element which helped him define his own voice.

Having completed his formal studies in music, VW now needed to set about a task he found uncongenial, but vital if he was to make his name—the promotion of performances of his music and of himself as a composer. He undertook this in a diffident way, not because he lacked confidence, for musically he always knew clearly what he wanted to achieve, but because it went completely against his character to be 'pushy'. His letter to Edwin Evans of 1903 is a good example of gentle diffidence, with an underlying determination to get vital information across. The same applies to his letter to Herbert Thompson, in which he set out to brief the music critic of the *Yorkshire Post* in advance about *A Sea Symphony*, shortly to receive its first performance at the Leeds Triennial Festival in 1910. Two years earlier VW had felt the need for some further guidance from a more experienced composer and arranged for himself and Adeline to spend just under three months in Paris while he studied with Maurice Ravel. An introduction was provided by Michael-Dmitri Calvocoressi, the French and later English critic. The effect of his lessons with Ravel on VW's musical style (apparent, for example, in *On Wenlock Edge*) is a matter of discussion, but a concrete result of this time in Paris was a friendship with the French composer which continued for a decade and more.[1]

VW's letters (with the possible exception of no. 63) may not admit us into his intellectual inner sanctum and allow us to witness the birth pangs of his music, but the genesis of many works is surrounded by a plethora of practical arrangements to which letters bear witness. In particular while

[1] Letters from Ravel to Ralph and Adeline are in the British Library, Add. MS 50360. Some are printed in translation in *RVW*, e.g. on pp. 102–3.

major works creep up on us unawares, we do find correspondence concerning lesser commissions which bore seeds for the future: the first was a commission to arrange music at short notice for a performance of Ben Jonson's masque *Pan's Anniversary* at Stratford in April 1905; the second was one to arrange music for a dramatization by Mrs W. Hadley of *The Pilgrim's Progress* to be given at Reigate Priory in December 1906. Finally, in 1911 he accepted a commission to write incidental music for a number of Greek plays, apparently at the request of Isadora Duncan and her brother, about which he was in correspondence with Gilbert Murray. This was possibly as a result of his having written incidental music to *The Wasps* for a production at Cambridge in 1909. None of this music is published, but in general his willingness to write incidental music led in one direction to an important strand in his output which culminated in his music for such films as Powell and Pressburger's *49th Parallel* in 1941 and, above all, for Charles Frend's *Scott of the Antarctic* in 1948, the precursor to *Sinfonia Antartica*. In the case of the incidental music for *The Pilgrim's Progress* it led in another even more important direction, since it set a train of thought going in his mind that remained with him through further incidental music, his fifth symphony, and eventually to the 'morality' *The Pilgrim's Progress* produced at Covent Garden in 1951.

The correspondence with his Cambridge contemporary Edward Dent about planning a concert entirely of his own works at Cambridge in 1910 has the same characteristics—diffidence combined with a clear idea of what he wanted to achieve. As we have seen, VW's inner musical world was an intensely private place into which very few were welcome. It is thus no surprise that, almost unnoticed in the surviving correspondence, VW had quietly moved forward from a group of early works, still mostly unpublished, to blossom into an established figure with masterpieces such as *Songs of Travel*, *Toward the Unknown Region*, *On Wenlock Edge*, *A Sea Symphony*, *Fantasia on a Theme by Thomas Tallis*, and finally *A London Symphony* to his credit. All these works have retained their place in the standard repertory to the present day. In his letters he doesn't talk of the composition of these pieces (other than occasionally of how long that process took) but presents them as faits accomplis, perhaps with some remarks on how they should be performed (as in his letter about *A Sea Symphony* to the conductor of the Bristol Philharmonic Society, Arnold Barter). He himself felt by 1914, with the clouds of war gathering, that he was only then finding his voice. As he says to Dent: 'I am very glad you like it [*A London Symphony*] – I feel myself that I am perhaps beginning to emerge from the fogs at last.'

1. To G. E. Moore[1]

[1895?]

Leith Hill Place
Nr Dorking

Dear Moore

Thank you very much for your letter. I should be very much pleased to enter into such an arrangement as you suggest with your sister.[2] The examination I have passed is supposed to certify my knowledge of 4 and 5 part counterpoint and fugue as well as harmony and all kindred subjects. I learned fugue under Bridge[3] and, at Cambridge with Charles Wood,[4] who to my mind had the most intelligent idea of what a fugue should be, of any counterpoint teacher I know. I think I may say that as far as knowledge goes I feel quite competent to teach fugue and kindred subjects but I ought to say that I have never given a lesson on it in my life. The irregularity would not matter to me in the least. With regard to terms I must find out what the 'trade-union' rate is i.e. what it is usual for young men at the beginning of things to charge in like circumstances as I do not know.

The summary then is that I take, I think, a more intelligent view of counterpoint and fugue than many people would, but I have had no experience of teaching.

If your sister wishes for someone more experienced write to me again and I will try and recommend someone.

I stay here till the 6th when I return to 46 Vincent Square.

Yours always
R. Vaughan Williams

[1] G. E. Moore (1873–1958), the philosopher and author of *Principia Ethica* (1903). He was to spend the rest of his life in Cambridge.

[2] Possibly the oldest of Moore's four sisters, Annie Harriette, who had been at Cambridge at the same time as Moore and VW; see Levy, *Moore*, 47.

[3] Sir (John) Frederick Bridge (1844–1924), organist of Westminster Abbey and professor at the RCM.

[4] Charles Wood (1866–1926), university lecturer in harmony and counterpoint at Cambridge; in 1924 he briefly succeeded Stanford as Professor of Music, to be succeeded in turn by Edward Dent.

2. To Gustav Holst[1]

[?1896[2]]

Thanks awfully for the photograph. I will send you one when I get one if funny. You ought to have been taken astride your trombone – & I am going to be taken perched on an organ pipe.[3]

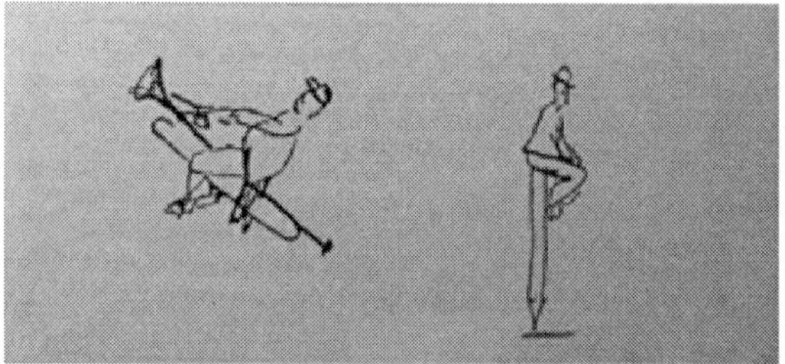

[1] Printed in facsimile as frontispiece to *HR*, dated *c.*1895.
[2] Filed by UVW in this year.
[3] The drawing is a sardonic allusion to the fact that Holst earned extra money by playing the trombone in seaside bands while VW's first job was as organist at St Barnabas, South Lambeth.

3. To Ralph Wedgwood

[just after 10 June 1897[1]]

Dear Randolph

Thank the Lord you're not Sanger[2] but something as much better as the Sun is to a halfpenny dip;[3] and so that you think that it is possible for people to care for each other and when they do find it out they ought to tell each other – That is what Adeline Fisher and I have done and we have agreed to marry.

There now you have my news – take a long breath and then read on.

She is two years older than I am; you know, I think, that for many years we have been great friends and for about the last three I have known my mind on the matter.

It is sometimes said that when a person is going to be married his relations with his friends alter – do not let this be so in this case because she cannot hold *more* the first place than she has done before with me because that is impossible and you and I have never been greater friends than we are now – may I think so at all events – and now you and she will be cousins and great friends too.

Write to me and give me your blessing.

You and Adeline must meet as soon as possible.

Yours always
Ralph Vaughan Williams

P.S. I saw Felix[4] the other day and he wished me to assure you of his esteem and affection.

[1] The date of their engagement.

[2] Charles Percy Sanger, a fellow Apostle with Wedgwood.

[3] A cheap candle.

[4] Arthur Felix Wedgwood (1877–1917), youngest brother of Ralph Wedgwood. He was a civil engineer specializing in the purchase and recovery of wrecks; he wrote amongst other works *The Shadow of a Titan* (London, 1910). See also Gwen Raverat, *Period Piece*, 233–5, where there is an account of the brothers' visits to the Darwins while undergraduates at Cambridge.

4. To Ralph Wedgwood

[later June 1897]

Dear Randolph

I am quite ashamed for not having written to you long ago.

I can't tell you what your letter was to me in fact I won't try to – but only thank you for it over and over again – but I must stick to business or I shall get sentimental and that would be 'perfectly horrid'.

When are you going to be in London? Also my people send me a message to say how much they want to be honoured by a visit. Do try & come Friday if poss: then we could be there and you would meet your second cousin-in-law to be, two such people as you ought to meet as soon as possible.

Yours affectionately and always
Ralph Vaughan Williams

5. To Gustav Holst[1]

[July 1897]

Dear V.H.

Its awfully hard to know what you had better do. I don't think the communication[2] business would matter – as a matter of fact I always did it when there was choral communion because I thought it looked picturesque as I had a hood and went up first and was generally part of the show – all the same he will probably ask you 'what your position as a churchman is and whether you will do your best to promote the reverent conduct of the service' to which I answered that I was broad (not physically) and thought everyone right to do the sort of praying that suited them best – and that I would do my best etc. This is a very useful evasion. I suppose you consider me very wicked to have done all this but I consider it more important to take every chance of improving one's talents (?!?) than to save one's soul. Again the Vicar will not be back till Sunday, when he comes I will tell him that if he wants you he must close with you at once – put off signing your agreement as long as you can.

My dear V.H. I wish to goodness I could offer you anything more definite than this – I *cannot* do anything like promise you will get it as the Vicar is quite mad. Only I will do my best – only I am not at all sure that Crouch End in the hand is not worth S[t] Barnabas in the bush.

I want you for Wed 4th at 7.0 THURSDAY 5th at 8.15. You must do Thursday or you're no good and Sunday 8th. Will 30/0[3] be enough for the whole show?

By the way I promised the Vicar that you would produce a testimonial from Stanford![4] Also a word from Hoyte[5] would be good also Parry and above all if possible Parratt[6] – the Vicar is very great on testimonials. Also your last Vicar would be good also a good character one from somebody – I gave him two! besides musical ones.

Yours in esparation[7]
R. Vaughan Williams

[1] Not included in *HR* but printed in *RVW*, 50.

[2] Communication is used here by VW in the sense of taking communion at Eucharist.

[3] i.e. 30 shillings.

[4] Sir Charles Villiers Stanford (1852–1924), composer, teacher, and conductor. He was Professor of Composition at the RCM from 1883, where he taught both Holst and VW, and was Professor of Music at Cambridge from 1887 until his death.

[5] William Stephenson Hoyte, organist of All Saints', Margaret Street and Holst's organ teacher at the RCM.

[6] Sir Walter Parratt (1841–1924), organist of St George's Windsor and Professor of Organ at the RCM, where he had taught the instrument to VW. He was Master of the King's Musick, 1893–1924.

[7] Presumably the opposite of 'desperation'; however the 'esparation' was misplaced since the post went not to Holst but to John Ireland (Short, *Holst*, 33).

6. To Laura Vaughan Williams[1]

[July 1897]

Dear Aunt Laura

I think that important steps taken by even the most insignificant members of a family should be communicated to the other branches of that family.

I am therefore writing to tell you that Adeline Fisher and myself have agreed to marry. I suppose it would be customary in a letter like this to refer to my good fortune in achieving so much good, and how little worthy I am but this is too obvious, so I will say nothing about it.

I will only ask you and Uncle Roland to wish me as well as I hope you will.

Yours very sincerely
Ralph Vaughan Williams

[1] The wife of VW's uncle, Sir Roland Vaughan Williams, a Lord Justice of Appeal.

7. To Fredegond and Ermengard Maitland[1] [September 1897]

Leith Hill Place
Nr Dorking

Dear Gaga and Vuff

I wrote you a letter last week but I tore it up; so then I thought I would write to you from here; so that you might see where to write me a telegram whenever you want to. Adeline and I think you might like to see some designs for my trousseau.

The first pattern represents my wedding suit, the general colour is puce the spots being of a sandy colour the boots to be light blue with red heels.

Pattern 2 represents a good working suit for everyday wear being made of good strong material with plaid stockings.

Two other pictures are supposed to be guesses of what I shall look like when I come back from Germany – I don't know which is the most likely to be true.

And last of all two pictures of a giraffe one by Adeline and one by me; the head of my one is wrong, but the tail is better than Adeline's. I want to see the new monkey of which also I will give you a picture and end up.

This is not much like a monkey.

R Vaughan Williams

[1] See *RVW*, 51, where this letter is printed. The two girls were nieces of Adeline, daughters of Frederic and Florence Maitland whom VW would have met often during his Cambridge days when he was a frequent visitor to their home in Downing College.

8. To G. E. Moore

[mid-October 1897]

Leith Hill Place
Nr Dorking

Dear Moore

Did Trevy[1] tell you that I wanted Blake or was it unconscious cerebration (I don't mean that) which lead [*sic*] you to send me the beautiful book which arrived this morning. It seems a sort of insult to write and thank you as that is what I am doing to such quantities of unangenehm people (I put that word in to show you that I know some German – I doubt if it does so); but I must try and put on paper how good it is to receive a present like yours in the midst of a wilderness of social duties.

I am also going to spoil this letter by some business; your sister has not sent me any work for a long time – I have quite lost count of how many more lessons I owe her. Also I am going to Berlin – so I suggest that she should send the rest of her work to

E. H. Jones Esq[2]
10 Ashley Road
Hornsey Rise
London N

whom 'I can confidently recommend' and I will arrange with him; but if she prefers to go on with me of course I can perfectly work it from Berlin, only the transit will take some time.

Yours very sincerely
R. Vaughan Williams

[1] G. M. Trevelyan.

[2] Evlyn Howard-Jones (1877–1951), one of VW and Holst's circle at the RCM and later a successful pianist.

9. To *The Musician*[1]

27 October 1897

October 27, 1897

A LETTER FROM BERLIN

The chief musical event here during the last week has been a most noteworthy performance of the *Ring des Nibelungen* at the Opera. Berlin is one of the few towns where the Trilogy can be heard complete; every instrument indicated in the score is found in the orchestra (with the exception, of course, of the six harps in *Das Rheingold*, which are unnecessary except under the peculiar conditions at Bayreuth); and, above all, there are no cuts. It is only necessary to hear the work as it was intended to be heard, to be assured that even 'cuts of discrimination' are artistically impossible. I defy anyone, unless he be an incurable *impresario*, to point out any part of the *Ring* which can be omitted without destroying not only the dramatic continuity but even the sense of the whole. I do not mean to say Wagner's want of conciseness is not a distinct artistic fault; it is unfortunate that he lacked that faculty of self-criticism which would have led him to revise and compress his work – that would have been to have repainted the picture – the managers' mutilations are holes cut in the canvas.

The great features of last week's performance were the Wotan of Van Rooy[2] and the Siegfried of Kraus.[3] Both acted intelligently, and were dignified in presence; moreover, their powerful voices remained strong to the end, and they sang in tune and without vibrato. Dramatic intelligence is often found among German opera-singers, qualities of voice are too often thought unnecessary. Lilli Lehmann, as Brünnhilde was as good as ever, and her performance was especially interesting, as this was her first appearance at the Berlin opera after an absence of many years.

Weingartner was the conductor, so that an admirable rendering was inevitable, though some of his tempi were rather original; the tone of the brass was particularly fine.[4]

It is only for the sake of varying the monotony of praise that I mention one small blot in the performance, which was that the various atmospheric phenomena were not always arranged for the right musical moment. Thus, in the second act of *Gotterdammerung*, the sun was already mirrored in the Rhine while the bass clarinet was still at the grey of dawn. This, however, is a very minor matter, and was the only instance of a lack of intense artistic sincerity which marks all German dramatic and musical performances. Until this spirit inspires English performances, in spite of our vaunted superiority of technique and tone-quality, we shall never achieve such good results as the Germans, even though individually they are sometimes raucous and clumsy.

Why, for instance, do we never hear a real choral or orchestral pianissimo in England? Because each performer is thinking of himself and not of the general good; it is a case of 'each for himself and the devil take the softest'. The German, on the other hand, never aims at producing a hearable sound when alone, but sinks himself in the whole with excellent results. This artistic earnestness was very noticeable at a most interesting performance of Brahms's *Requiem*, given lately by the members of the Hoch-Schule. The defects in the raw material were obvious; nevertheless the true spirit was there, and the rehearsals had evidently been numerous and intelligent, so that the music was made to mean much more than can be imagined by those who frequent only the London concert-rooms. This occasion also served to display Dr. Joachim in a light new to Englishmen; in England we know him only as a performer and composer, but there is a third function in which he is almost equally distinguished – that of conductor.

R. Vaughan Williams

[1] This report appeared in *The Musician*, vol. 1, no. 25, p. 464, dated 27 Oct. 1897. *The Musician* was launched in 1897 and did not survive beyond the end of the year.

[2] Anton van Rooy (1870–1932).

[3] Ernst Kraus (1863–1941).

[4] Felix Weingartner (1863–1942).

10. To Ralph Wedgwood — 29 November 1897

[Berlin] 29.XI.97

Dear Randolph,

You must send the article directly it comes out – it is good getting something into print isn't [it] – and you must get to work and write a book. Either 'Retrogression and Riches' or else a 'History of wages and profits in the house-holding industry from the earliest times to the present date'. What magazine is your article in, and how much are they going to give you for it? By the way I think it was an absolute insult of the general manager to say you were doing exceedingly well – even to X[1] (how is X by the way? I haven't heard of him for a long time – in fact had almost forgotten his existence). He ought rather to have asked you how he was getting on.

Tonight has been very eventful because we had reis-suppe ('Selbst-geschmiedet') for supper. You make it out of the enclosed[2] stuff and boil it for 40 minutes. I mixed mine with Liebigs extract which made it better I think, though opinions vary. We are going to give a dinner party:

Menu

Consommé – au ris à la Liebig
'Reissuppe' au naturel
Entrée: Oeufs à l'aurore (la raw)
Roti Eier à la Scramblée
avec Roggenbrod

Entremets Rogenbrot à la beurre
Pfeffer-kuchen en rien
Kuchen ohne Maass
Hors d'Oeuvres: Oeufs Bouillé
Dessert: Preiselbeeren in Honij
Thée à l'infusoire
Cigarettes et Pipes

'Dieu Sauve la Reine'
Wine list
Tea
Cocoa (Blookers entire)

By the way in a later number of the 'Musician' you will find a chatty 'Letter from Berlin'.[3] Today I have sent off another. I believe still that the stone at the top of the arch is called the key stone.

Don't tell anyone this

I must now relate a most humiliating episode. We had an introduction from the Diceys[4] to Frau von Helmholtz of 12 Rauch Strasse; as usual the houses were numbered so that you couldn't tell which was which and what appeared to be No 12 was a corner house, and the only entrance was in Drake Strasse round the corner and was labelled 3. After much perturbation we decided that this was the only possible place. So we asked for Frau V.H. and left our cards. Next day we had a letter saying there must be a mistake as the writer did not know the Diceys, signed Clara Goldberger!!!

We have just spilled some ink on the table cloth and are trying to get it out with boiling. A. is just wishing you were here to help – this is after reading your article which has come. I at present have only read half of it and we discussed it over tea.

All this spilling of ink is the result of supping at Fredrichs in the Potsdamer Strasse and drinking 'Champagner Bowle' followed by Hock. All this because it isn't any of our birthdays. I could if I wish explain how you were entirely wrong in your conclusions from the mileage averages – but 'why throw pearls before a – statistician' (Browning – as they say in the sixpenny novels).

Your questions made me feel that we aren't getting full good out of Berlin, but I really can't read these awful german[5] newspapers – we just get all our Berlin news out of the Morning Post. We are however studying the german drama. The other day we went to an Echt-modern drama by Hauptmann called 'Die versunkene Glocke' all about a Glocken-gieser and an elfisches wesen called Rautendelein and an 'Elementer-geist' called Nickelman and a Waldschrat[6] – in fact all the dramatis personae of Hans Andersen talking Ibsen as hard as they could. But I think 've'y faine' – especially when our fat german master had explained us the cultural 'idée' which is that man must always come to grief if he tries to do an 'Uebermenschliche Werke' – that is to say he must stop at home with his wife and family and not go off with Rautendelein and build a temple to the sun on the top of a mountain.

The Italian pictures here are nearly all disappointing and touched up and look german – except a beautiful little Raffaelius del Garbo – and the Angelico last judgement, of which Jerome Dakyns[7] used to have a bit. Is it a replica and is the real article in Florence? I feel impelled to go on 'by the way what is the origin of that term in English architecture'.

You must always come to us every evening when you are in London and we will send over to the nearest cookshop for dinner, as of course we shall be having nothing but Reis suppe.

You will be glad to hear that Max Bruch has asked me to his at homes 'in ze Englisch staile' and said he hoped I should be as successful as I was courageous. We do use the tea basket[8] for our tea, only we have now invested in another lamp.

Have you been to Milan – is it possible in winter?

Yours affec[ntely]
R. Vaughan Williams

[1] The identity of 'X' is not clear.

[2] VW apparently enclosed a sample.

[3] Wedgwood appears to have seen *The Musician* of 13 Oct. 1897, which contained an article by VW entitled 'The Romantic Movement and its Results'. VW's *Letter from Berlin* appeared in the issue for 27 Oct. and is printed above, no. 9.

[4] Albert Venn Dicey, Vinerian Professor of English Law at Oxford and colleague of Adeline's brother-in-law Frederic Maitland, Professor of the Laws of England at Cambridge.

[5] VW spells 'german' without an upper case G throughout this letter.

[6] Gerhart Hauptmann's symbolist drama *Die versunkene Glocke* had first opened on 2 Dec. 1896 in the Deutsches Theater, Berlin. Rautendelein is correctly 'ein elbisches Wesen', Nickelman is correctly 'Nickelmann, ein Elementargeist', and Waldschrat is a 'faunischer Waldgeist'. The play concerns Heinrich, a bell-founder, who leaves his wife, Magda, and his children to live on the mountain with Rautendelein, with dire results for all concerned. See Pamela Reilly's introduction to her edition of the play (Oxford, 1956).

[7] Henry Graham Dakyns, one of the group at Cambridge which included VW, Ralph Wedgwood, R. C. Trevelyan, G. E. Moore, and the brothers Crompton and Theodore Llewellyn Davies. See Levy, *Moore*, 53, 57.

[8] Presumably a wedding present. A tea basket comprised a kettle, spirit lamp, and other accessories for the making of tea.

11. From Max Bruch 5 February 1898

5 February 1898

My dear Williams

I have written the 'Zeugnis' in German; if you send it to London, you must add an English translation.

Yours truly
M.B.[1]

Herr Ralph Vaughan Williams, der im Winter 1897–98 die unter meiner Leitung stehende Akademische Meisterschule für musikalische Composition besuchte, ist ein sehr guter Musiker und ein talentvoller Componist. Er verdient, allen Musikgesellschaften, Kirchenchören etc. warm empfohlen zu werden.[2]

Dr Max Bruch. Mitglied der Königl. Akademie der Künste. Berlin 5. Februar 1898.

[1] Max Bruch.

[2] Mr Vaughan Williams, who in the winter of 1897–8 took part in the academic master class in musical composition taken by me, is a very fine musician and talented composer. He deserves to be warmly recommended to all music societies, church choirs, etc.

12. To Ralph Wedgwood [February 1898]

Eichhorn Strasse 6.II
Berlin IV

Dear Randolph

Do write and tell me some news of Felix. I only heard about it all in a letter from home this morning – You must have thought me so brutal to write to him just ordinary when he was so ill – but then I hadn't heard anything about it. Tell me when he will be able to care for receiving letters and I will write him another – if he likes getting letters – I don't think we ever sent the promised packet of Knorrs suppe – I think we had now better defer it till we get back – which will be soon. You must manage to be in London then and we will all go to Ozners[1] or Gatti's[2] and I think to Galts music hall afterwards. I am sure it would amuse and instruct Adeline very much.

You will be glad to hear that Max Bruch considers I am a 'guter musiker und ein Talentvoller Componist'[3] and that I have 've-ry o-riginaal ideeas' but my harmonies are 'rather too originell'; in fact I meet with much more encouragement – this is of course only for your ears who know that I write things and not for Moore for instance – who would think it ridiculous – You may tell him however that all the living germans I have heard in Berlin are most feeble folk – it seems to me that the future of music lies between England and Russia but first the Russians must try to give up being original and the English being imitators – I very much believe in the folk tune theory – by which I don't mean that modern composing is done by sandwiching an occasional national tune – not your own invention – between lumps of '2d the pound' stuff – which seems to be Dvorak's latest method. But that to get the spirit of his national tunes into his work must be good for a composer if it comes natural to him, in which case it doesn't matter if what he writes occasionally corresponds with some real 'folk tune' – All this because in the last thing I wrote for Bruch I used a bit of Welsh tune as my 'Haupt Thema' – unacknowledged of course, – but then 'I made it my own'.

I never answered you about the Wagners. I think in acts is best – but I would much rather you settled – because I should like the idea that every detail in it came entirely from you—that makes the beauty of a present.[4]

We went to a most wonderful dinner party the other day – all professors – the two 'hauptsaches' were

(a) The food and drink which kept on going after dinner in this order 9.30–11.30:
 Cigars, coffee, liqueurs*[see note], belegte brod, caviar, sweets, beer, tea.
(b) The subjects which I discussed with the most brilliant professors of the Berlin university in this order 9.30–11.0:
 α. In German: Bach, Wagner, classical, romantic, Shelley, Keats, the Puritans, the influence of religion on art, Browning, Rossetti, Swinburne, lodgings.
 β. In English: The Riviera, Coleridge, Wordsworth, Oxford, Prigs, German art galleries, Fra Angelico.

Adeline sends you her love,

Yours affec[ntely]
Ralph Vaughan Williams

*Note. Have you ever made a practice of liqueurs? If not you have neglected your opportunities like I have. This must be rectified at our next festlichkeit together.

[1] A restaurant.

[2] A well-known restaurant near Covent Garden.

[3] See no. 11.

[4] As a wedding present Wedgwood had given VW a series of scores of Wagner operas. VW is referring to the question of how they should be bound up.

13. To René Gatty[1]

[3] March 1898

Eichhorn Strasse 6.II
Berlin IV

March 1898

Dear R.A.G.

Please come as soon as you can. My wife and I want you to come and stay here till you find something as there is a small room in the house of which the present owner is away so that it is empty – I hope you got our wire. I'm awfully keen to hear about your heart – why not come today? or if not tomorrow.

Yours always
R. Vaughan Williams

P.S. I didn't know you were in Germany.

[1] René Gatty, writer, brother of Ivor and Nicholas Gatty. Adeline VW copied out his poems and acted as a sort of London agent on his behalf, sending them to the periodicals. He suffered indifferent health. Unfortunately, no letters from VW to his brothers Nicholas or Ivor have come to light. Nicholas Gatty's manuscripts are in Exeter University Library but the collection includes no correspondence. René's letters from VW are preserved in Birmingham Central Library.

14. To René Gatty

[31 March 1898][1]

[Weber's Hotel
Dresden]

Dear Herr Gattoy [*sic*]

I am just writing to say that Dresden is not a Reizendes Dörf - chen but that there has been a good lot of Donnerwetter about today, you may be surprised to hear that we said to our waiter 'wir werden ein fläsche champagner haben' to which he replied 'Ah! Champagner' and brought Rothwein at 2pf the bottle which I aptly described as a 'guter reiner wein'.

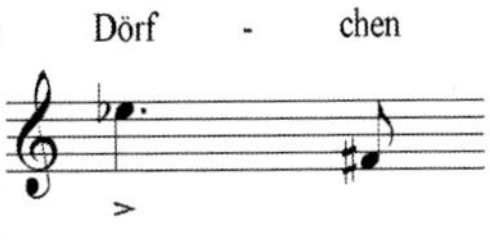

We can't make out this hotel has anything to do with 'Der Freischutz' but Paderewski stays here so that it has some musical reputation. They are doing 'Die Neunte Symphonie' at the opera concert on Sat. & Othello on Sunday evening.

Sat. morning

Another mood now prevails – it is still raining but we are just going off to the pictures to admire the San Sisto[3] – or not as the case may be.

Yours always & affectionately
R. Vaughan Williams

[1] Date of receipt. This letter is printed in *RVW*, 53.
[2] i.e. 'charming little village'.
[3] The San Sisto Madonna by Raphael in the Zwinger Gallery at Dresden.
[4] Opening of the Piano Sonata in A minor, D845 by Schubert.

15. To René Gatty

4 May 1898

16 North St
Westminster

Received: 4th May 1898

Dear Herr Gattoy

I haven't written to you for an age, so now I will begin by saying that I heard from Nicholas[1] the other day. Meine Frau lasst dich herzlich für deine colossal-schöne Briefe Danken – there that's just to show that I haven't forgotten my German(?).

Let me congratulate you on being a Stud: Phil:[2] but you might have told us what sort of lectures you go to? What sort of music has been going on & what have you been to? We've been to very little here – one Sunday afternoon – rather poor performance – Schumann 2nd symphony & Tchaikowski 'casse noisette' suite.

Have you seen anything of the Schratt[3] or Bruch? And also if you see or hear anything of an English Musiker called Hulton tell me. I am sending you an account of the battle of Atbara[4] which is rather good. The Spanish war is pretty dull stuff with no fighting. Spain does want a few unmediaeval ideas shoved into her badly. Talking of America have you read 'The Portrait of a Lady' by Henry James – there [are] whole chunks of detatched Schein[5] in it.

How odd to think of you still pacing the Podzdamer[6] Platz and exclaiming 'Donnerwetter ein reizendes gesicht'[7] as some schönes Mädchen passes you – or going on to Schultheiss[8] and saying 'Ha – Champagner'. I am also sending you some German stamps which we have found.

Yours always
Ralph Vaughan Williams

[1] René Gatty's brother.

[2] Studiosus Philosophiae, i.e. a student of Philosophy.

[3] Leo Schrattenholz (1872–1955), at this time a student in the Königliche Hochschule für Musik in Berlin studying, like VW, under Max Bruch. He remained as a teacher and eventually became a professor there.

[4] The battle of Atbara had just been fought on 8 Apr. in the Second Sudan War. This passage is quoted in *RVW*, 54.

[5] The reference is probably a private joke. In a letter to Gatty from Dresden Adeline VW adds a PS: 'I hope you will admire the envelope that Weber [they were staying at the Hotel Weber] provides us with. Is there any detachment of the Schein about it?'

[6] i.e. Potsdamer.

[7] 'By Jove, what a charming face'.

[8] Schultheiss is an old and well-known brewery company in Berlin, which owned a chain of bars and restaurants.

16. To Ralph Wedgwood

[May or June 1898]

X

Dear Randolph

Just as I was seriously contemplating letting my full juiced Collins waxing over mellow drop in a silent Autumn night[1] – those candles arrived and now I am seriously in doubt whether I am writing a Collins or writing to thank you again for them which their 'real presence' impels me to do; I am also flabbergasted with the effort of compressing into my limited range of experience both how awfully jolly (and amusing and instructive) it was being with you at W Hartlepool and how beautiful the candlesticks are and how good it was of you to have them packed up and how unkind it was of us to refuse to take them with us one in each hand. They make such a blaze in our room that we decided on the spot to spend the sum of £1–0–0 (one pound) on dark blue linen hangings – as we can't repaper.[2]

I feel this is very inadequate expression of all I want to say – but I know you'll understand and not only read between the lines but also in the little blank space marked X at the beginning of this letter as it seems a pity to leave that unoccupied.[3]

We have not done much exciting since we came back but a certain amount of work – I have thoughts of going in for my Mus: Doc: in January – but this must be a secret in case I fail; it makes me feel very young still going in for examinations when you have probably forgotten what an examination is; it makes me feel as if I was still on a toy bicycle while you were on in safety.

When are you coming to London? Do leave those shear-legs[4] for 48 hours sometime (Sunday is unreckoned in this computation as it is not a working day) and we will go and have Asti Spumante & Crème de Menthe at Odones or Gatti's or the Café Royal. I suppose you won't be in Leeds on the 7th or 8th of Oct: as we are going there for 2 days of the festival – rather sporting nicht wahr – which is the best line to go by M.R. or G.N.R.?[5] I have just had a letter from Amos[6] in which he announces himself as being on the crest of a wave of contentment and expounded a theory of life which was very pretty but I didn't know what it meant. He also has got himself much disliked by his slighting references to the successes of Our Brave Soldiers in Avenging the Hero Gordon – also by saying that he prefers the brave barbarian to the Christian cad.[7]

R.V.W.

[1] VW is parodying lines from the third stanza of the Choric Song in Tennyson's *The Lotos-Eaters*: 'The full-juiced apple, waxing over-mellow, / Drops in a silent autumn night.' He once told Michael Kennedy he thought these lines the most beautiful in English poetry. A 'Collins' is a letter of thanks for hospitality.

[2] The candlesticks were Ralph Wedgwood's wedding present to Ralph and Adeline. They had been visiting Wedgwood at West Hartlepool, where he was working for the North Eastern Railway concerned with the docks, in order to collect them.

[3] This is presumably an allusion to the fact that the VWs were on the move—they took up residence at 5 Cowley Street on 30 May.

[4] For loading and unloading goods wagons.

[5] The Midland Railway and the Great Northern Railway both provided services to Leeds, one from St Pancras and the other from King's Cross.

[6] Maurice Amos (1872–1940) was a member of VW and Wedgwood's Cambridge circle and became an eminent lawyer, mainly practising as a judge in Egypt. He was knighted in 1922 and, following his retirement from Egypt in 1925, he was made a KC in 1932.

[7] A reference to the recent victory at Atbara in the Sudan in which the Mahdi's forces were defeated by an Anglo-Egyptian force under Herbert Kitchener—it was seen as revenge for the murder of General Gordon at Khartoum in 1884.

17. To Ralph Wedgwood

[May 1898][1]

5, Cowley Street,
Westminster.

Dear Randolph

I feel a beast – I never write to you – but then you never write to me – I always mean to write to you but I don't – and I never see you and we are becoming perfect strangers – and you mustn't think that because I'm married I don't hate not seeing you just as much – it makes it worse because there are now two of us who want you and never have you.

All this splenetic outbust means in plain language that I'm jealous of Trevy – he came here today – ate a large tea and then announced with the utmost satisfaction that he was going to see you at West H'Pool[2] – I almost pulled his nose off.

Why don't we ever go to you or why don't you ever come to us – of course opulent freelances like Trevy can go off any minute like a pop-gun.

Is it any good trying for Whitsun week[3] – we've thought of going to Holland with my mother but we'd give up this if you'd come (only we decide tomorrow) – well enough of this – only do come as soon as you can – you know I'm tied by the leg to my work here – not that I have to work hard but I have to be here. I'm afraid we chivied you rather too much your last visit but we won't do that again – do try and give me a chance of cutting out Trevy.

(I am scolding Ralph for writing like a spoilt child – he is now going to ask a question w^h interests me very much – A)[4]

Has your report[5] gone off yet – as you promised – and has it made you a name as you said it would—and what name has it made you?

I have become an 'Associate of the Royal College of Music' in two subjects Theory and composition and 'am allowed to affix to my name the letters A.R.C.M.'. Also my name appeared yesterday on a programme – in an obscure corner of a programme of a second rate performance of a first rate play might be seen – 'The orchestra will perform the following selection' – and then among numerous other things

Scenes-de Ballet[6] .... Williams

That's all – but its just a crumb to keep me going.

Thursday

I think Whitsun week is no good because we may have to take my mother to Holland which will be very good for her and there may be no-one else to do it. But do come – and we will bicycle about the city all night and all sorts of things. How about the week after Whitsun?

Have you heard from Amos lately? I forget whether I wrote to him last or he to me.[7]

Yours $affec^{ntely}$
R. Vaughan Williams

Adeline sends her love.

1 Clearly before no. 18.
2 West Hartlepool.
3 Whit Sunday was on 29 May.
4 This sentence in AVW's handwriting.

[5] Presumably a report on some railway matter.
[6] Very possibly this is the student composition *Tunes 'for a ballet'*, *CW* 1891/3.
[7] Printed in part in *WVW*, 397.

18. To Ralph Wedgewood

[early June 1898][1]

Oakrest
Burley
Ringwood
Hants

Dear Randolph,

I am writing in this extraordinary fashion not because of any decadent desire for originality but because 'Oakrest' in spite of its beautiful name (of this more later) doesn't possess any blotting paper so that I wish to get as large a surface as possible before making it illegible by blotting it.[2]

The name of this house is misleading for it is a new little house built by the former proprietor of the queens head Burley (I mean 'queens head'[3]) in a most delightful and unfrequented village in the new forest where we came for Whitsuntide (how I hate that termination -tide) since by a shameful neglect of my duties we have managed to get the whole inside of a week (Holland is no longer on the carpet[4]).

I was glad to get your letter; it poured oil on to all my sore places[5] and I wanted to sit down and write you a whole diary straight off but somehow I thought I'd wait for the new Forest and write there. We have a plan in store which is as follows: I have got before October to write a thing called a degree exercise[6] which will take all my time till then but in-as-much-as such work can be best done in a quiet country place we are thinking of getting as many weeks off as possible and taking a small oak-rest in a part of the country which shall possess (a) bracing air (b) quiet surroundings (c) hills (d) valleys (e) good bicycling roads (f) beautiful forest walks (g) trees (h) heaths (i) fens (j) downs (k) a river (l) nobody we know (m) salt marshes (n) good food (o) good drains (p) no waiters (q) a bathing place (r) shops where one can get pens (s) shops where one can mend bicycles (t.u.v.w.x.y.z) a lot of other things. Will you come and stay with us and make that our holiday together this year?[7]

You asked me for news – but really my life has been uneventful ('happy is the nation' etc[8]). You see your work (the practical part of it) is interesting while mine in the practical part consists of playing hymns & swearing at choir boys.

[later]

The rest of this letter is packed up so I must go on here. The New Forest is a most wonderful place. We've had it grey and wet and fine and green and its always beautiful – not one of your hard stern places where you feel you must discuss high themes but a warm comfortable beauty – though very wild – enourmous [*sic*] heaths and then beech & oakwoods and jolly little rivers and brooks and marshes and an air that makes your strength as the strength of ten (-nyson).[9]

I heard today that you are doing a tour with Mr Gibb[10] inspecting Irish railways & that Trevy comes after that – You didn't tell us of this, and that reminds me that I spoke very harshly of Trevy [in my] last letter, but you must understand that I was speaking of Trevy not as a person but as a cause – because I like him very much – I hear he is going to bicycle to Hallsteads[11] and arrive in nothing but his shirt.

Adeline and I had a quarrell [*sic*] over the meaning of part of your letter, and not having the original to refer to couldn't settle it. I said you meant to give us a Sunday in June (if possible) and a slice of week when we had our holiday. Adeline held that the word 'or' should be substituted for the word 'and'. We fervently hope that I am right. You mustn't think that from the complaining tone of some of my letters that I don't like my work. First you must remember that I don't consider organism my work.

My work is writing (the other is only money making and for the sake of doing something praktisch which I think every one should do – I know you agree with me) and I've been more active at writing and got on more in the last 18 months than ever before.

London

We met Crompton[12] at a concert the other day – it touched me very much his going to a 5/0 place all by himself out of pure love of music – He was most active also in rescuing a fainting lady and nearly pulled all her clothes off in trying to carry her out single-handed.

Tuesday

I haven't yet told you about Lymington – I always imagined that Lymington was a small and unpleasant watering place – but it is in reality a delightful and very sleepy little town which happens to be by the Solent and to look across to the Isle of Wight – here comes in another of my delusions: I always imagined that the Isle of Wight was a gimcracky kind of a place but what we saw of it was a magnificent stretch of downs and white cliffs – Don't think me degenerate in my likes but you know I always have preferred soft scenery to stern uncomfortable scenery. I can admire it but I can't really enjoy it. I know that shows a craven spirit but I can't help it. My heart goes through the same manoeuvres as Wordsworths when he saw a rainbow when I see a long low range of hills – I suppose this comes from being born in Surrey S.W.[13]

I am now working at my degree exercise now – I'm going to write a mass[14] – they're such fine words and you get such good climaxes out of them. I think I told you all this before – but this letter has been going for a week – I find it a very good plan to just write anything down as it occurs to me.[15]

[1] Pencil note on letter. VW refers to it being Whitsuntide (Whit Sunday was 29 May in 1898), but a later instalment is on Cowley Street paper. The VWs were moving into 5 Cowley Street at about this time.

[2] VW is writing across the whole sheet of the paper and not on the first side after folding it, which was normal in that period.

[3] i.e. to emphasize that he is referring to a public house.

[4] i.e. sur le tapis, though they went to Amsterdam and Haarlem later on that year in August. The idea of going to Holland for Whitsun was alluded to in no. 17.

[5] A reference to the somewhat bitter observations in no. 17.

[6] See below.

[7] This holiday did not materialize.

[8] An allusion to the saying 'Happy is the nation that has no history'.

[9] An allusion to the lines in Tennyson's *Sir Galahad*: 'My strength is as the strength of ten, / Because my heart is pure.'

[10] Possibly a senior colleague on the North Eastern Railway.

[11] The house of Wedgwood's mother near Stoke-on-Trent.

[12] Crompton Llewellyn Davies; see *RVWPB*, 18.

[13] VW's allusion is to Wordsworth's poem of 1802 'My heart leaps up when I behold a rainbow in the sky'. His remark about being born in Surrey is a wry one, since he knew perfectly well he had been born at Down Ampney in Gloucestershire.

[14] See *CW* 1899/F.

[15] Printed in part in *WVW*, 396. Either the letter ends here or the remainder does not survive.

19. To René Gatty

18 July 1898

Received: 18 July 1898

Lieber Herr Gattoy,

Leider habe ich absolut Deutch zu sprechen vergessen, überhaupt aber wunsche ich sehr Ihnen erzahlen welche vergnügen wir haben von dem nichola'schen quatuor gehabt.[1] Es war am letzten Freitag im Saal des 'Royal College of Music' am Studenten-vortrag ausgeführt.

Die Erste Satz war ganz gut aber vorzüglich war das Andante – eine ganz neue melodie wirklich mit höchster Empfindung gefüllt – das Scherzo auch war ausserordentlich gut und sehr gut für die Instrumenten geschrieben als auch war alles.

Die Variationen waren nicht so gut – aber vielleicht waren sie ziemlich schlecht gespielt – und das fuga-finale war wunderschön. Ich sende hierzu ein Zettel.

Wie gehts mit Ihnen und mit Herrn Grimson? Mit viel vergnugen hören wir dass Sie kommen bald nach England zurück auch haben wir eine sehr freundschaftliche einladung zu Hooton Roberts mit vielen Freuden empfangen;[2] können Sie vielleicht mit uns einige tage in London wohnen während ihren Reise nach Yorkshire. Verzeihen bitte das ich habe 'Sie' statt 'Du' geschrieben.

Ihr ergebener
R. Vaughan Williams[3]

[1] i.e. a quartet by René's brother, Nicholas Gatty, friend and contemporary of VW.

[2] Hooton Roberts was the home of Gatty's parents. The invitation was for 15 Aug. (as we know from a letter of 3 Aug. to Gatty from AVW).

[3] 'Dear Mr Gatty, Unfortunately I have completely forgotten how to speak German, but I do want to tell you how much pleasure Nicholas's quartet has given us. It was played last Friday in the Hall of the Royal College of Music at a student concert. The first movement was quite good but the andante was excellent – a completely new melody really full of the greatest feeling – the scherzo was also extraordinarily good and very well written for the instruments, as indeed was it all. The variations were not so good – but perhaps they were not very well played – and the fugue finale was beautiful. I am sending a programme herewith. How are you and Mr Grimson? We are very glad to hear that you will soon be coming back to England; we have received with great pleasure a very warm invitation to Hooton Roberts. Can you perhaps stay with us for a few days in London on your way to Yorkshire? Please excuse me having written 'Sie' instead of 'Du'. Yours sincerely R. Vaughan Williams.' A different and incomplete translation is given in *RVW*, 54.

20. To Gustav Holst[1]

[late July 1898]

Hawgoods Temperance Hotel
Bramber
Sussex

Dear V.H.

This isn't really a hotel but a refreshment room and tea gardens with apartments attached. We stay here anyway till Friday and perhaps a week more. I think it is a good place for work. I have done 4 pages of full score today which is rather good for me.[2]

We have just come from a most magnificent evening walk – first a sunset seen from the downs – then blue twilight then stars and nearly losing our way and then home.

Do send me some more of your adorable programmes – I laughed out loud for a whole day over that one. I do hope your hand is really better – your looking glass style[3] is magnificent.

I spent Sunday and Saturday evening with Howard Jones[4] and we walked about and sat on gates till 12 p.m. and talked about music and organs and success and other incongruous subjects. He wants you to write to him but

I explained that your hand was too bad. He is very much excited over playing to D'Albert.[5]

I will write to Gatty about Granville-Whitman (no I mean Walt-Bantock)[6] – Gatty's variations were badly played and splendidly reviewed.[7]

Yrs
R.V.W.

[1] Not included in *HR*.

[2] This was probably either for the mass written for his Mus. Doc., *CW* 1899/F, or the Serenade for small orchestra in A minor, *CW* 1898/1.

[3] i.e. of handwriting with the left hand? Holst had persistent neuritis in his right arm.

[4] Evlyn Howard-Jones. See no. 8.

[5] Howard-Jones went to study with Eugen d'Albert after finishing in the College.

[6] It is not clear what the link between Walt Whitman and Granville Bantock was that gave rise to this joke.

[7] At a concert in the Royal College. See no. 19.

21. To Gustav Holst[1] [1898[2]]

19 Second Avenue
Brighton

Dear V.H.

Thanks so much for your letter – your left hand[3] is most admirable – but does it mean that your hand is still bad – you never said anything about it – this is very wrong of you – I feel pretty stupid today because though it is the sabbath I have been scoring my Mass[4] all day (it is now 4.30) I am approaching the end of the Credo.

Having now been to sleep for 10 minutes I can continue.

Did I ever tell you of my final talk with Stanford in which we agreed that if I *added* a short movement in E major in the middle & altered the Coda the thing might stand – I had already got an extra movement in E major which I had cut out!

Walküre does sound fine on a Brass band doesn't it. I used to hear a German brass band do it at one of the Earls Court exhibitions. When you come back to London – mind you come to see us *directly* you get back. I am going to take my mother to Birdlip next week.[5] I wonder if you will be at Cheltenham by any chance, I think I shall come over and see (if I have an opportunity) whether you are there – also if I can remember where you live. Have you been writing anything or is your hand t[oo] bad – why not try looking glass music?

This took me 1/4 hour![6]

Have you expedited round Lincolnshire at all – but I expect you just want to sit still between your shows.[7] I am sorry for your [being] stuck up in that God-forsaken place, can't you get a *band*master's place somewhere[?] wouldn't that be good – you ought to be able to get one easily after all your experience.

I think H.J.[8] must have gone abroad by now – he was going some time soon I know. Well it will be good when we all meet again in London.

I always thought that working hard in London was bad enough but working hard when you're on a nominal holiday is the devil.

Yours
R.V.W

I will give you 2[d] if you can play this on the trombone.

[1] Printed as Letter I in *HR*.

[2] This letter is dated 1897 in *HR* but was clearly written after his and Adeline's return from Germany at a time he was completing his mass for the Cambridge Mus. Doc. examination, which he sat in Mar. 1899.

[3] Holst suffered from neuritis in his right arm. See no. 20.

[4] The work which VW submitted for his Doctorate at Cambridge, *CW* 1899/F.

[5] Possibly to stay in the George Hotel, which, in a letter not included in the present selection, he recommended to G. E. Moore.

[6] The music is Wagner's 'Siegfried' motif as found in his Funeral March (*Götterdämmerung*, Act III) written backwards.

[7] Holst was playing the trombone in the orchestra of the Carl Rosa Opera Company.

[8] Evlyn Howard-Jones, who was due to go and study with Eugene d'Albert in Berlin. See no. 20.

22. To Ralph Wedgwood [1898?[1]]

Werden Sie nach Leith Hill Platz Sonnabends gehen oder nicht? (German)[2]

R.V.W.

[1] i.e. shortly after the VWs' stay in Germany.

[2] 'Shall you go to Leith Hill Place on Sunday evening or not?'

23. To Ralph Wedgwood

[early 1899]

Hotel Victoria
Prag

Dear Randolph,

My natural pedantry nearly led me to call this place 'Praha' which the Bohemians call it. I don't suppose that you knew we were out of England. But firstly Mother gave us £50 to go abroad with, secondly I was out of employment,[1] thirdly there seemed no chance of your ever coming to London, fourthly we have just taken a house,[2] so that we decided now was the time for action. We first went to Berlin to keep up with the influential people there and incidentally heard some music; then we spent a night in Dresden and now we are in this most delightful place, where everybody talks Czeckish and Dvořak's operas are performed at the national Bohemian theatre – we are going to one tonight which is called 'Cert a Kača' which the waiter tells us means 'the Devil and the Kitty'.[3]

I feel awfully national just now – though I have just written an article against 'national' music which no magazine has thought fit to accept.

Monday

We went to the opera – all the part of it which dealt with Bohemian village life was tremendously good. But when we got down to Hell and there were people being put into cauldrons by devils it got very dull – and much of the music was bagged from the 'Niebelheim' in Wagner's 'Rheingold'. When we get home I am going to make a really strenuous effort to get work to do without returning to organism which I do not want to do even if any parson would have me which I doubt. I hear from Felix that you have had a rise* – but this I am afraid means that you won't stalk York Station in a top hat with a gold band.[4] We are trying to learn Czeckish out of a 'Polyglot Sprachlehrer' which we bought for 25 Kreuzers – tonight we are going to a 'Theatre de Varietés' to hear a bohemian band we hope.[5]

Yours affec[ntely]
R.V.W.

*Nothing fishy is insinuated.

[1] VW had just resigned as organist at St Barnabas, South Lambeth.

[2] Ralph and Adeline signed a lease on 10 Barton Street in late Dec. 1898 and moved in in Feb. 1899 (see *WVW*, 44).

[3] i.e. *The Devil and Kate*.

[4] i.e. as Stationmaster. Wedgwood had joined the North Eastern Railway. He subsequently became General manager of it and its successor, the LNER.

[5] Printed in *WVW*, 396, assigned to Apr. 1898. However, this cannot be correct since this trip took place after they had taken the lease on the house in Barton Street.

24. To Ralph Wedgwood

[February 1899[1]]

My dear Randolph

You must not think that I can do anything but admire your outbreak of military spirit—what else can anybody have now – if for no other reason to try and prevent all the best men in England being mown down. Besides Chamberlain has got us into this damned mess and we've all got to do our best to get ourselves out of it – besides we've got to win, whatever the disgusting beginnings of this horrible business may be we've *got* to win it now – thems my sentiments.[2]

I won't insult you by pressing the truism how much braver you are sticking it here than rushing off to the cape – but what I do want to know is what is the peculiar magic of a real fight – if you want to see men heroically risking their lives you've only got to look round Hull itself – if you want to risk your own you have only to do what you are doing now in which occupation it seems to me you must be risking your life every minute. If you want to see – no this is all pedantic but still I cannot persuade myself what there should be about a fight which should put it on a different level from every other experience – You have never seen Everest but you know Hellvellyn and have got the best of the bargain.

Your letters do me good. Ever since I finished my degree exercise I've been doing precious little except write some articles which have none of them been accepted – I have written trivial but brilliant essays on the following subjects

1. How to play Brahms
2. A school of English music
3. The soporific finale
4. Bach & Schumann

I am now writing a longer & more solid one on 'The Words of a Musical Drama'. This task has been much interrupted by getting into the house of which more later. I am also going to write two more on 'Palestrina & Beethoven' and 'A precursor of Wagner'. Then I am going to get an introduction to the reader of Smith Elder and send him the lot as a small book – when he returns it I shall send it round to several others, and having finally failed in this desperate attempt to get a living I shall take to composing symphonies.[3]

Adeline will tell you a lot about the house. It's most of it white wood and green blinds – I expect we were done in the premium we paid but I don't mind about that as we wanted this kind of house and we had the money about and we prefer to spend it that way and not (say) on dinner parties. The only other thing to say about it is that it contains a spare room with a bed and that Hull is not very far from London.

Yours affectionately
R. Vaughan Williams

[1] References in the letter to the new house (in Barton Street) make it clear that this was written soon after moving into Barton Street in Feb. 1899.

[2] VW's attitude to the Boer War (that it was a mess that the politicians had got into but, once under way, had to be prosecuted energetically so as to get out of it successfully) was the same to each of the two World Wars in later years. 'Them's my sentiments' is a phrase taken from Thackeray, *Vanity Fair*, ch. 21.

[3] All the essays referred to (except 'A precursor of Wagner') were published in the first three issues of *The Vocalist* (Apr.–June 1902). See *CW*, 282.

25. To Gustav Holst[1]

[about December 1900]

My dear V.

You'll think me a very 'destructive' critic – as I have scratched out most of your lines.[2]

I think the whole scheme of the verses is bad:

(1) I should like it to be sung by the girl her self not let that old heavy father give tongue again – would not this be very effective if she sang it softly as if to herself – then stopping where the song breaks off and asking her father.

Now with regard to the scheme itself – you must not make the darkness so 'tief-sinnig' the 'Land of eternal night' means death and nothing else – you must (as far as the legend itself is concerned) treat the darkness as simply a curious natural phenomenon which had the results which you are about to relate. Secondly you must make the possession of the lamp much more important.

Thirdly you *must* quite remodel the part where it says he couldn't get into the garden with his lamp – making it more *emphatic* – why not say that he met a porter* at the gate who said 'throw away your lamp you will have no use for it in the garden – unless you throw away your lamp you may not enter'.

Now about the style – it is much too loose – do be more careful to say just what you mean and no more. If I were in your place I should read Malory and old ballads and only use words that were used by them. If you use odd words like 'hight' (by the way I can't make sense of that line) you *must* make the rest correspond in style; otherwise it will read like Corder's translation of Wagner.

E.g.

why say 'all safe' when you might say 'safe' and many other cases. I like your tune extraordinarily (I obeyed you implicitly) except the third line ('a lamp he carried'). The first line is I suppose in the Phrygian mode, the 2nd and third certainly modulate and imply harmonies.

(By the way to hark back I don't like 'no ending hath that story'; it implies not that the end is torn out but that it goes on for ever.)

I don't quite approve of your martial bit – in itself it is very nice – but surely while the stage issue is vague, you might put in a lot of little bits as she looked at the various legends – not only one – and even then it is a kind of miniature painting which is only suitable in a comic opera (e.g. Meistersinger Act I, Eva's remarks about the three Davids or David's recitation of the various 'tones').

I like all the music and voice parts very much. The leading up to the legend is very good – the last two bars are quite beautiful.

I am keeping the music to show to N.G.[3] when he comes back. H. Jones[4] is gone back to Berlin.

There

Yrs
R.V.W.

N.B. (I mean P.S.) Thanks very much for the shortbread which I hope refers allegorically to your short further absence.

*Not a railway porter.

[1] Printed as Letter V in *HR*.
[2] Holst was writing his own libretto for his opera *The Youth's Choice*, H60.
[3] Nicholas Gatty.
[4] Evlyn Howard-Jones.

26. To Gustav Holst[1] [?1901]

My Dear V.

I am ashamed at not having written to you before. I will first thank you for the 'Ave Maria'[2] which I still think beautiful as I always did. I have [been] playing it over and pointing out its beauties to a cousin of mine who sings in the Magpies[3] and have persuaded her to take an interest in it.

I admire 'Sita'[4] very much – I had some criticisms however to make but I can't remember what they are – and to tell you the truth I feel too lazy tonight to find the drawer where I have put it away.

I think the chief criticism was levelled against the dressing up device – which seems to me rather mechanical and not quite 'rein menschlich' enough. Also it is not quite 'inevitable' enough to fit in with the fatalistic nature of the rest of the plot.

I am alone in my glory at present and likely to be so for some time as my wife is at Brighton looking after her invalid brother[5] and I don't know when she'll be able to leave him.

I have to go to Barnet twice a week now which is an awful nuisance.[6]

Yrs
R.V.W.

[1] Printed as Letter VI in *HR*.
[2] H49.
[3] His cousin Diana Massingberd sang in the Magpie Madrigal Society. See Short, *Gustav Holst*, 40.
[4] Holst's opera in three acts, Op. 23 (H89).
[5] Hervey Fisher.
[6] VW was apparently teaching at a girls' school there.

27. To Gustav Holst[1]

[?1901][2]

You did tell me about the 'Ave Maria': didn't I refer to it? I meant to. I've finished my 'Bucolic Suite'[3] and written a song and made a rough copy of the score of the Trombone thing[4] and finished a volume of Purcell[5] and am starting another orchestral thing called a 'Sentimental Romance'.[6]

That Glasgow critic is a blasted fool and condemns himself out of his own mouth.

My dear V. I meant to have said a lot more but I can't somehow so will compress it all into a comprehensive 'Bless you'.

Yours always
R.V.W.

[1] Printed as Letter VII in *HR*.
[2] The start of this letter is missing.
[3] See *CW* 1900/1.
[4] VW is possibly referring to *Heroic Elegy*, *CW* 1900–1/1, completed in Jan. 1901, which has a prominent part for trombones.
[5] *The Works of Henry Purcell*, Purcell Society, 15: *Welcome Odes*, Part I, published in 1905; vol. 18, Part II, was published in 1910.
[6] *HR* suggests *Symphonic Rhapsody* (*CW* 1904/3).

28. To Ralph Wedgwood

[early 1902]

10 Barton St
Westminster

Telegraphic address:
Williams 'Gaolways' London[1]

My dear Randolph

You are really magnificent! We were glad to get your letter and are very grateful to the pay-bills for not coming in till 9.15.[2]

I've not very much to chronicle except that I've sold my soul to a publisher[3] – that is to say I've agreed not to sell songs to any publisher but him for 5 years. And he is going to publish several pot boiling songs of mine – that is to say not real pot boilers – that is to say they are quite good – I'm not ashamed of them – as they are more or less simple and popular in character. They are to come out in a magazine called 'The Vocalist' and then to be published at 1/0 – which is a new departure – and I'm to get a penny halfpenny on each copy—so you see I'm on the high road to a fortune.[4]

I'm going to lecture on Wagner at Cheltenham next week! and perhaps go on to Merthyr Tydvil (where is it?) to lecture also – on what subject I don't know yet!

I should like to penetrate to Middlesbrough and see the factory chimneys – I'm not sure that I like them so much as I used to – my idaeal [*sic*] of scenery at present is a long low valley this sort of shape [curved line] – all arable and ploughed fields – and just one or two trees. Nevertheless we must come some time, though A is so tied at present as her sister is staying with us for a long period which makes it rather difficult to get away.

I will leave Adeline to tell you about Crompton's pony and how Theodore[5] was run away with – He often comes in here now – I don't know why he is so depressed – he says it's rheumatism or the political situation.

Fancy Dakyns[6] having succumbed – I have been meaning to write to him – in fact I'll do so tonight.

Yrs affectionately
Ralph Vaughan Williams

[1] Having set up house at Barton Street in Feb. 1899, the VWs were clearly feeling short of money; the address implies he felt he was on his way to the debtors' prison!

[2] Perhaps by a later post?

[3] The Vocalist Co., publishers of *The Vocalist*.

[4] The following songs appeared in the first volume (1902) of *The Vocalist*: 'Linden Lea' (*CW* 1901/1); 'Blackmwore by the Stour' (*CW* 1902/4); 'Whither must I wander' (*CW* 1902/6); 'Boy Johnny' (*CW* 1902/7); 'If I were a Queen' (*CW* 1902/8). On the first issue see *WVW*, 50. The five-year agreement would appear not to have been as rigorous as VW implies, since a number of songs written in the immediately following years were published by other publishers, notably Prowse and Boosey; see *CW*, pp. 17–27. Publications by VW in *The Vocalist* petered out after 1905. This passage is printed in *WVW*, 397.

[5] Crompton and Theodore Llewellyn Davies.

[6] Henry Graham Dakyns (see no. 10 n. 7). This possibly is a reference to his becoming engaged.

29. To Lucy Broadwood[1]

Postmark: 24 July 1902

Dear Miss Broadwood

Can you help me on the subject of Scottish songs? I want to say a few words in the course of a lecture on Folksongs, on the subject of Scottish songs – There won't be time to say much on the subject – but I have chosen 3 points

(i) The difference if any between gaelic or highland (are they the same?) and lowland songs. Is there any sharp dividing line between these? What is a characteristic specimen of each kind – I've spent 3 days in the museum and found nothing to help me.

(ii) The pentatonic scale. What is the best example of a pentatonic tune? (*not* a modern imitation like 'Ye banks and Braes')

(iii) The modulation (say) from G minor to F. and back. I am pretty well set up on this subject and have chosen 'Adew Dundie' (out of the Skene M.S.[2]) as my example.

I shall be very grateful if you will help me.

Yrs very truly
R. Vaughan Williams

P.S. I wish you would do for the Scottish songs what you have done for the English – these Malcolm Lawsons and people make me ill![3]

[1] Lucy Broadwood (1858–1929) was a keen student of early music, as an associate of Arnold Dolmetsch, and a founder member of the English Folk-Song Society. Like Cecil Sharp and VW himself, she was a pioneering collector of folk songs.

[2] In the National Library of Scotland, Edinburgh.

[3] VW is thinking of *Songs of the North, Gathered together from the Highlands and Lowlands of Scotland*, ed. A. C. Macleod and H. Boulton, first published in 1885, for which the music was arranged by Malcolm Leonard Lawson, a prolific writer of drawing-room songs. The publication eventually ran to three volumes.

30. To Lucy Broadwood

postmark: 2 October 1902

Little Parkhurst
Abinger Common
Dorking

Dear Miss Broadwood

Thank you so much for your kind letter. I am so glad you think my accomp: suitable. Isn't it a fine tune? It comes out of 'Böhme'[1] where there are about 1000 more.[2]

By the way while we are on the subject of my little efforts, have you seen 'Willow-wood'? and candidly what do you think of it? Especially as regards whether it will come off (with pf: accomp) in a *large hall*.[3]

I believe there is some chance of M^c^Innes singing it at the Broadwood concerts, and I can't make up my mind whether to nip things in the bud.[4] I feel it is very important that I sh^d^ not make a fiasco my first venture with Mr Leslie and his colleagues. You did give me a copy of the 'Folk-song' journal – it is a delight to me every day – I am using 'poor Mary' and 'Young serving man' at a lecture I give in Bournemouth next week. I have also largely quoted from your preface. I hope you do not mind.[5]

Yrs very truly
R. Vaughan Williams

[1] Franz M. Böhme, *Altdeutsches Liederbuch* (Leipzig, 1877).

[2] See *WVW*, 53: '[VW's] arrangement of an old German Volkslied, "Entlaubet ist der Walde" [*CW* 1902/5], had been sung by Campbell McInnes in November 1902.' VW had presumably sent his arrangement for Broadwood to look at.

[3] *Willow-Wood*, cantata for baritone or mezzo-soprano solo and orchestra or pianoforte accompaniment (*CW* 1903/3). Lucy Broadwood could not have seen any published form of the work (the vocal score was not issued until 1909); possibly VW thought she might have seen a manuscript score.

[4] The work was indeed first performed on 12 Mar. 1903 by Campbell McInnes and Evlyn Howard-Jones.

[5] In fact Broadwood agreed to illustrate one of VW's lectures at Bournemouth; see *RVW*, 63.

31. To Edwin Evans[1]

[about June 1903]

10, Barton Street,
Westminster.

Dear Mr Evans[2]

I was born 1872
Went to Trinity College Cambridge 1892–95.
Studied R.C.M. 1890–2 and 1895–6.
Berlin 'Akademie der Kunste' (Max Bruch) 1897.

Paris 1907–8[3]

While at Cambridge I studied counterpoint with Charles Wood.[4]

I have been an organist but have got over that now.

My 'most important works' are

String 4^{tet} (1897)

Serenade for Small orchestra (1898) (Bournemouth 1901)

5^{tet} for Pf^{te}, violin, cello, clarinet and Horn (1898 performed by Mr Clinton in 1901)

'The Garden of Proserpine' (Swinburne) for sop: solo chorus & orchestra (1899)

Bucolic Suite for orchestra (1900) (Bournemouth 1902)

Heroic Elegy & Triumphal Epilogue for orch: (1901–2)

Symphonic Rhapsody (after a poem by Christina Rossetti) (1901–3)

Fantasia for Pf^{te} and orchestra (1896–1901)

'Willow wood' for Baritone and orchestra (1902–3) (done with Pf^{te} at Broadwood Concert 1903)

'The Solent' Orchestral impression (1902–3)

I am sending you another song – in case you come to look at it – I have an idea that it is more 'modern' (in the narrow conventional sense) than some of my other stuff.[5] But I am no judge of this because music which to me seems thoroughly old-fashioned (e.g. some of Strauss) I am told is the 'ne plus ultra of modernity' – and other music which seems to me to be at the heart of the real spirit of the age (some of Brahms for instance) I am told is old-fashioned – so I am, apparently, no judge.

Are you going to include a composer Gustav von Holst in your list? He is to my mind a very fine composer and he is English in spite of his name – he has written a lot of orchestral music and two 'musick-dramas'. His address is

Gustav von Holst
162 Shepherds Bush Road
W

Yours very truly
R. Vaughan Williams

[1] Edwin Evans (1871–1945), a music critic who took a particular interest in contemporary British music.

[2] Evans published an article on VW in the *Musical Standard* on 25 July 1903; see *WVW*, 55 ff. This letter was written to provide him with necessary information.

[3] This is an extraneous annotation in another hand, perhaps made by Evans himself a few years later.

[4] See no. 1 n. 4.

[5] Almost certainly 'Tears, idle tears', *CW* 1903/1, since Evans refers to this in his article and notes its 'leanings towards modernity'; see *WVW*, 56.

32. To Ralph Wedgwood[1]

Postmark: 24 September 1904

10, Barton Street,
Westminster.

My Dear Randolph

I'm not going to write you a long letter, you will be knowing what I feel for you and for all of you much better than if I was to try and put it in words.

I know that your love for Cicely and her love for you is something so great that I have often felt that I could scarcely realize what it meant when I have watched you speaking of her, or her speaking of you.

Dear Randolph I won't say any more to you, and please forgive me if I have said too much already.[2]

Yours affectionately
Ralph Vaughan Williams

[1] Addressed to him at Hallsteads, Penrith.

[2] The letter was written by VW after the death of Wedgwood's sister, Cecily Frances, on 22 Sept. 1904. Cecily had married Maj.-Gen. Sir Arthur Wigram Money, KCB RA on 26 Dec. the year before. For details of Wedgwood's family see *Burke's Peerage* under both the Barony and Baronetcy of Wedgwood. Cecily's name is spelt thus in Burke but given VW's referring to Cicely and the fact that Wedgwood's daughter was christened Cicely Veronica, this may be an error in the publication.

33. To René Gatty

[?1904[1]]

10 Barton S[t]
Westminster

My Dear R.G.

You *must get well* by hook or by crook.[2] Now I consider that between friends and especially between musicians there is a kind of freemasonry which binds us all together like a happy family and makes it the duty of each one of the 'bund' not to stand aloof from the rest when he may give them the opportunity of showing him the value of their friendship. Remember that it's not only for yourself that you've got to get well and not even only for your family but it's for all your friends; you *owe it them* as a proof of any affection you have for them to neglect no opportunity of putting them out of anxiety. You owe it them not to disappoint the expectations we have all formed of your doing something big some day. Therefore please do not despise the little we can do but just receive it and so prove the strength of our friendship. You know that we'd all make you well ourselves if we could – but we can't so we must do it by proxy.

For Heaven's sake do go away from the *cheap*, *incompetent*, *dishonest* quack who has been doing his best to *keep you in his clutches*; and go to the *best* doctor in Berlin and *stick to him* – please use what the postman will bring for that purpose.

Yours always
R.V.W.

P.S. I've just had your letter and the poem. Thank you so much for both – but *do* come home for your holiday. I'm sure it will set you right.

[1] The VWs moved to 13 Cheyne Walk in 1905.
[2] The nature of René Gatty's illness is not clear.

34. To F. W. Evans[1]

6 March 1905

10, Barton Street,
Westminster.

March 6th 1905

Dear Sir

I am much obliged to you for your letter. I found it a little difficult to gather what you intended to ask me; but I think you intended to offer me the engagement to write and arrange the music for the forthcoming Masque, provided that we could come to terms as to fee. Of course this entirely depends on how much there is to be done. Glancing through the Masque hurriedly there appears not to be much and as you say that your funds are limited I suggest a fee of £12.12.0[2] in return for which I will provide the necessary music (if it is about the amount I imagine) and give you the right of performing it on April 24th at Stratford on Avon: but I shall retain my property in the work and shall be able to dispose of the copyright as I like. Also all expenses such as copying parts etc. to be defrayed by you.

It is a work that I should be very interested to undertake and I do not want the question of terms to be an obstacle, but I just point out that you have given me very little time in which adequately to prepare the music and if I find myself pressed for time I might have to call in help. I would of course be *responsible* for all the music and would promise that all should be well done.

Will you kindly tell me exactly what is expected of me – how long and elaborate the various dances are to be and what *number* and *quality* of *soloists* chorus and orchestra I am to expect.

I hope that there will be a good *professional* orchestra. Also I ought to consult with the stage-manager before I set to work on the music.

Kindly let me have all particulars.

Yours faithfully
R. Vaughan Williams

[1] F. W. Evans was Hon. Sec. to the Poet's Birthday Celebrations Special Committee of the Stratford-upon-Avon Shakespeare Club. He had written to William Barclay Squire, the Superintendent of the Music Room at the British Museum, asking for his advice on music for the planned revival of Ben Jonson's masque *Pan's Anniversary* to be given on the following 24 April. On 2 March Squire wrote to him saying that he could find none of the original music extant at the Museum, pointing out that about twelve pieces of music would need to be written, copied, and rehearsed very quickly. He suggested that he approach either VW or Nicholas Gatty. He described VW as a 'very rising and able young man, who is especially interested in English folk-music' and felt that he would approach the music in the right spirit. Finally he offered to bring him together with either composer at his office in the Museum. Evans clearly opted to approach VW. VW's music for *Pan's Anniversary* is *CW* 1905/4. VW himself conducted the first performance, which was given in the open air at the back of the old Shakespeare Memorial Theatre in Stratford.

[2] i.e. 12 guineas.

35. To F. W. Evans

9 March [1905]

10, Barton Street,
Westminster.

March 9th

Dear Sir

I am in receipt of your letter of this morning. I am willing to write the music for the masque and will accept a fee of £5–0–0 – not indeed as a payment, for I think you realize that this in no way represents the work to be done – but to repay me for any expense that I may be put to in preparing the music. The copying of the parts etc to be undertaken by you. Only I must insist that the music must be as adequately performed as the short time you have allowed for preparation admits of.

If I am to prepare the music I must be responsible for it *all* – therefore I shall undertake the dances as well as the rest.

I do not yet understand whether the orchestra is to be amateur or professional & what instruments I am to expect. Also I *must* know how many voices there are to be in the chorus – also how good they are. All this makes a great difference to the kind of music I shall write. Also what kind of dances are going to be danced – Are they to be old dances – such as Pavanes or Galliards or will they be invented in accordance with my music? You do not tell me how much has been already prepared. Perhaps it will save trouble if I enclose a list of questions with spaces for your answers. May I impress upon you that time is very short & that I want to get to work at once.

I am

Yours faithfully
R. Vaughan Williams

Enclosure:

List of Questions

(1) Is the work to be performed on a stage or out of doors.
(2) What preparations have already been made.
(3) What is the size and capability of the chorus? Mention some work they have lately been performing.
(4) Is the orchestra to be amateur or professional
(5) Of what instruments does it consist?
(6) Are the three soloists soprano, mezzo-soprano or contralto?
(7) Has any particular dance been chosen for the 'Antimasque of the Boeotians' and of the 'Thebans'
(8) Is the 'main dance' to be a single short dance or a whole ballet consisting of several dances?
(9) Who is directly responsible for the production of the masque? Can I be put in communication with him?

36. To F. W. Evans

14 March [1905]

10, Barton St
Westminster
S.W.

March 14th

Dear Sir

I am much obliged for your letter. Two points suggest themselves to me

(1) I think it a great mistake to have the masque out of doors – as far as the music is concerned, as it will *not be heard* out of doors.
(2) Could not the orchestra be strengthened by some more *good* string players – it is hardly adequate as it stands.

I find it very difficult to work on the music without consulting with the *stage-manager* as to where music will be wanted and how much – also whether any action goes on during the choruses etc. Is it likely that any of the committee will be coming up to London soon & c^{d} come & talk with me about it. The time is getting so short and I don't see how it is all to be learnt in time. I have already written most of the music for the hymns but I am working in the dark. On the next page I am writing down the various points with queries where I want instruction.

(1) I shall write a short prelude to the whole work.
(2) Entrance of the 2 nymphs – these lines are, I presume, *spoken* not sung – is this so?
(3) 'Loud Music' – Does this accompany a change of scene. If so how long does it take.
(4) Antimasque of the Boeotians – Do the morris dancers have their own instruments or am I to arrange them for the orchestra? Also are they wedded to their tunes? I know many traditional English dance tunes which are much finer than those you mention and might be substituted. But I do not mind about this.
(5) Has any particular kind of dance been settled on for the 'entry' of the Masquers after Hymn I?
(6) 'Here the revels' – what does this consist of?
(7) I propose writing some music to be played after the last speech.

Yours faithfully
R. Vaughan Williams

37. To Ralph Wedgwood

postmark: 12 November 1905

Dear Randolph

In moving house we came upon several of your early letters – what enormous screeds we used to write to each other then![1] I suppose as one gets more & more to do and more & more interested in one's own bee-line one has less to say even to one's greatest friends – or perhaps one can cram more into a few words than one used to – at all events I'm afraid my handwriting is as illegible as ever.

You must come and see the new house soon. I've got a grand study in the attic with a grand view of the river and a bridge and 3 great electric light chimneys and a sunset

[sketch showing Chelsea Bridge, sunset and the chimneys of Lots Road Power Station]

Then I've also got a roll top desk a writing table & a new piano so I ought to do!

What do you think of the change of address cards?

Thank you so much for the cutting – send the full report as I couldn't understand the cutting.

We've got Crompton[2] & Harry[3] coming to dinner on Thursday.

What news of Felix[4] – I wonder if one feels inspired to write music & poetry in the wilds or whether the discomfort is too great?[5]

Yrs affectionately
RVW

[1] The VWs had moved to 13 Cheyne Walk on 1 November.
[2] Crompton Llewellyn Davies.
[3] Possibly Henry Dakyns, on whom see no. 10 n. 7.
[4] Felix Wedgwood was presumably abroad, engaged in either an engineering or a salvage project.
[5] Printed in part in *WVW*, 398.

38. To Ralph Wedgwood[1]

postmark: 1 April 1906

13 Cheyne Walk
S.W.

Dear Randolph

The elegant Swainson's[2] address is Westminster Mansions Great Smith St Westminster S.W – but I don't know the number – let him choose you a piano. I'm sure he will get you a nice one – I'm so glad you are getting a boudoir grand – you will find it makes all the difference.

I'm so sorry Harford[3] & the songs were a frost – he certainly does sing them very well at times – *within his limits* of course and one must always remember that if a singer really did what Moore,[4] say, can do in your sitting room – it would make no *impression at all* in a large room – therefore a different point of view has to be started from altogether – and it is only *the very best* people who can produce the same effect on a large scale – by different means – that Moore can in a small room.

Q.E.D.

It will be splendid to meet in June when the Dearmers cease from troubling and the Athelstans Rile no more.[5]

Yours very affectionately
Ralph Vaughan Williams

[1] Addressed to him at 6 Osborne Road, Newcastle on Tyne.
[2] Not identified.

[3] Francis Harford, a bass who performed VW's songs widely in the early years of the 20th c.

[4] G. E. Moore, VW's friend at Cambridge. In later years VW used to recall Moore singing Schubert after Hall.

[5] A reference to the end of his work as Music Editor of *The English Hymnal*, whose editors were Percy Dearmer and Athelstan Riley. The allusion is to Job 3: 17: 'There the wicked cease from troubling and there the weary be at rest.'

39. To Gustav Holst[1]

[July 1906]

The Warren
Meldreth
Cambs

My Dear V.

It was nice to open y[r] parcel and find my initials over your pieces[2] – I don't know what you owe to me – but I know all I owe you – if I ever do anything worth doing it will be greatly owing to having such a friend as you 'at my command' as the folk-songs say, always ready to help and advise – and some-one whose yea is always yea & nay, nay – which is a quality one really wants in a friend and so seldom gets.

I do thank you from the bottom of me – because I know that you don't do these things unless you mean them.

I've just finished scoring the 2nd movement of the ocean.[3]

Yrs
RVW

[1] Printed as Letter XIII in *HR*.

[2] *Two Songs without Words* for orchestra, Op. 22, H88.

[3] i.e. of *A Sea Symphony*. Partly quoted in *RVW*, 78.

40. To Ralph Wedgwood

[about 1 August 1906[1]]

O my dear Randolph

I am so glad – I've thought so much lately about your lonely life – & c[d]nt bear to think of it – I knew this was what you wanted – of course everyone does – but you especially. You have everything to make a wife happy for ever & ever – and you have everything in you which cries out for it – I noticed this especially in you last time but I didn't know it had taken such a definite shape.[2]

How bad of you to put me off the scent – talking about thin ice – when you were fully intending to tumble all the time!

Of course we shall like your heroine 1st off – any one who is in love with you & with whom you are in love – what more?

& now I must say – though you won't like my doing so – that I consider that the woman who has won you – well there I can't say what I mean but you know – and you can read between the lines – because I'm not saying anything I want to – and I'm boring you fearfully with this long screed – you call Adeline and me your best friends – and I can't say what it means to me to have you say that – and I am exercising a best friend's privilege to the full.

I do want to see her so – & I hear much about her – I'm glad she's so young – only sorry she's not 17 – I hope you'll be married at once – I know you'll be happy with a young wife.

By the way Mrs Urquhart takes a most tender interest in you & asked me the other day if you were engaged! – when I said 'no' she immediately began making plans for you & I believe has even gone so far as to ask over the mother of 'Lily' (photograph on the mantelpiece) to hold pour-parler with me – I'm afraid it will be a queer show then if she ever hears – and she's not strong.

I would venture to send a message to Iris (may I call her so?) if I dared so if I may you can invent one from me – you will do it so much better than I shall!

Goodbye happy dear Randolph

Bless you

This is quite illegible but my hand shakes from excitement.[3]

Yours

R.V.W.

[1] This letter must have been written shortly before 3 August. See no. 41.

[2] Wedgwood had become engaged to Iris Pawson; they married later in the year on 24 October.

[3] Printed in part in *WVW*, 397–8.

41. To Ralph Wedgwood

Postmark: 6 August 1906

My dear Randolph

It's ridiculous of me to write to you again – but I can't help it. It warmed the cockles of my heart to see you so happy on Friday[1] – you always do everything in the best way – and I couldn't imagine you different from what I saw you that evening. The more I think of that photograph the more I realize 'la séduction mème' – Do marry at once and don't wait that beastly 3 months – let all your knowledge of each other come after marriage & not before – that is so much better. Besides she'll be 20 before you've been married a month as it is.

My vicarious engagement goes on its usual course – I couldn't sleep Friday night & I can't work – I took a long walk yest[erday] – the same nearly which you & I took – we are fated to meet Cantabs there – I met – Snoodler White! – but he didn't recognize me.

Ever yrs
RVW

[PS on envelope]
I'm so delighted you met A. in Victoria Street.

[1] 3 Aug., the date before which no. 40 must have been written.

42. To Mrs W. Hadley

[?September 1906]

13 Cheyne Walk
S.W.

Dear Madam

Please forgive my delay in answering your letter. I shall be delighted to arrange & invent some music for the 'Pilgrim's Progress' – if you can provide me with a string orchestra of *first-rate* amateurs & *3 or 4 professionals* to keep the thing going. I see you mention Miss Waterhouse as one of the amateur players – every player should be *at least* as good as she and have had *experience* in playing *in orchestras*.[1]

You will kindly let me know as soon as you can exactly where music will be wanted & where it accompanies business about how long it will last.

I am returning the copy to Miss Ouless so perhaps she will kindly let me have a copy. I have one or two suggestions to make:

(1) I must have a few words – just a sentence or two – for the singing of the angels – something which can be repeated often, like 'alleluia'.
(2) I think it better to have a *real* folksong for the shepherds and not 'He that is down' – also the pipe will be impractical unless we have wind in the orchestra – also it will not be a duet but a solo.
(3) C[d] not the delightful 'Who w[d] true valour see' from part II of P.P. be introduced – possibly the song during the arming of Xtian.[2]

Yrs truly
R. Vaughan Williams

[1] Mrs W. Hadley and Miss E. U. Ouless had made a dramatization of *Pilgrim's Progress*. For the music provided by VW see *CW* 1906/5. It was first performed on 1 Dec. 1906 at Reigate Priory. Subsequent performances were given in the Imperial Theatre on 16 Mar. 1907 and in Lincoln's Inn Hall on 12, 13, and 14 Mar. 1908. See also *RVW*, 87, where the performance is erroneously dated 1909.

[2] It was. VW had recently included this hymn as 'He who would valiant be' in the newly published *English Hymnal*, set to a folk song collected at and called after *Monks Gate*.

43. To Ralph Wedgwood

postmark: 5 October 1906

13 Cheyne Walk

My dear Randolph

It is delightful to get a letter from you – especially one asking me to do anything for you – I've looked through 'Hilf mir Schwester'[1] I see no reason why the *whole song* sh^d^ not be adapted for the organ – but the bit at the end after the voice stops (is that what you mean by 'wedding march'?) is only about 3½ bars – rather too short by its self.[2]

I should love to go and beard that brute at St Margaret's with you. I advise you to make out a *complete* programme of all the music you'd like played and tell him to play that and *nothing else* – otherwise he'll play muck and make everybody sick – think of all your favourite music and I'll select from it what will go on the organ – most *pianoforte music* of the slower kind and *songs* all make nice organ pieces.[3]

I'm just back from one day at the Birmingham festival—I started at 6.30 a.m. got in two concerts and got back at 5.30 a.m. – I just saw Mrs Stephens for one moment – she was so nice & came across & spoke to me – I have it on my conscience that I said that nobody sang well at the 'Kingdom' except Miss Foster – I ought also to have included Miss Nicholls who sang beautifully also. Do tell her if you see her.[4]

Yrs
RVW

P.S. I've just heard that I'm going to see Iris at last! A. went to call on her yesterday and asked her home to tea here tomorrow and we hear now that she can come – that will be splendid.

[1] 'Hilf mir ihr Schwester', no. 5 of Schumann's song cycle about love and marriage, *Frauenliebe und -leben*, Op. 42.

[2] Wedgwood's wedding was to take place on 24 Oct. 1906.

[3] The organist at St Margaret's Westminster at this date was Reginald Goss-Custard FRCO.

[4] Mrs Stephens has not been identified. VW had attended the first performance of Elgar's *The Kingdom* and is referring to Muriel Foster and Agnes Nicholls. The visit is not mentioned in *RVW*.

44. To Mrs W. Hadley

18 October [1906]

13 Cheyne Walk
S.W.

Oct 18th

Dear Mrs Hadley

Pilgrims Progress Music[1]

(1) Opening dance
– enclosed The music may be repeated as often as required by the dance

(2) Flower Girls song
I have chosen for this ''Tis young men and maidens all' from English Country songs (Cramer & Co) *page 58*. I want only the following verses sung 1, 2, 3, 4, 5.
or less if that is too much

(3) Men's quartett
– I have not been able to find a suitable arrangement of 'Down among the dead men' – but I hope to in a day or two.

(4) Strolling musicians song
– enclosed –
I want this scene in the following order
To *open* with the mens 4tett – then cries of 'a song a song' – then some dialogue as the following might follow

Musician 'What shall I sing you'

A man 'sing us a song about Robin Hood'

The crowd 'yes a song about Robin Hood'

Then follows the musicians song – as this is a very long ballad – I have only written out a few verses – and when he gets to the end of these – I thought he could be *interrupted* by the entrance of the prisoners etc

(5) Arming of Faithful. I enclose the tune for 'He who w^{d} valiant be' – perhaps you c^{d} get someone to make some more copies according to the number of singers – only a few singers will be wanted – perhaps just a quartett. The music is from the 'English Hymnal' published by Froude[2]

(6) Shepherds song – enclosed

All the songs are to be sung *without accompaniment* – the accompaniments I have put are only to help the singers when practising.

Will you kindly distribute the music to the performers & when they have learnt it we will have a rehearsal – but it's no good having one too early – as they w^{d} only forget it again.

Will you also give me a date by which you want the music for the tableaux?

Yrs very truly
R. Vaughan Williams

[1] See *CW* 1906/5.

[2] i.e. Oxford University Press—Henry Froude was printer to the University. *The English Hymnal* had been published earlier in the same year.

45. To Cecil Sharp

[November 1906]

13 Cheyne Walk

Dear Sharp

I'm most fearfully sorry about the report (I have lost my copy but I suppose you refer to the sentence about the Board of Education).[1]

I'm afraid it was largely my fault – what happened was as follows – I first suggested that the clause be omitted – but was overruled – then I *think* we modified it a little and finally having got it into shape Fuller Maitland[2] turned to me and said 'Do you think Mr Sharp will approve of it as it now stands?' and I having carefully considered it said 'Yes I think he w^{d}'. Because I honestly think that it does as worded say exactly what you think i.e. that the idea as expressed in the recommendations is good but that it is only so if it is 'consistently carried out'.

Does this not represent exactly what you think? Do you think it worth while making a protest – every body knows what your views are, and before protesting do consider very carefully whether it does not put your view?

After all the FSS general meeting is such a hole & corner affair that it seems hardly worth disturbing them in their slumbers – you have the ear now of all the important people & will be able to do what you want in the teeth of the FSS people.

If you move anything move for *deletion* not alteration – in the former I c^{d} vote with you; in the latter – as I helped to pass it – I obviously c^{dnt}.[3]

Yrs
R. Vaughan Williams

[1] This letter arose from the Folk-Song Society's response to a report from the Board of Education (*Suggestions for the consideration of teachers*, urging the use of national and folk songs as the basis for teaching singing in schools) which had been formulated in Sharp's absence at a meeting in July 1906. Cecil Sharp wrote to Lucy Broadwood on 20 Nov. 1906 saying he had only just read the report and was considering action. He attacked the report on the grounds that it made no distinction between genuinely

traditional folk songs and songs which were merely national and popular, but not traditional. However, the Folk-Song Society continued to support the report and this led to the publication of Sharp's own *English Folk-Song: Some Conclusions* in 1907 and his breaking away from the FSS to form the English Folk Dance Society in 1911, which eventually merged with the Folk-Song Society in 1932. VW described the episode in his article on Cecil Sharp in the *Dictionary of National Biography*, 1922–30 (London, 1937), 762. On the whole episode see Fox Strangways and Karpeles, *Cecil Sharp*, 58–62.

[2] J. A. Fuller Maitland (1856–1936), influential music critic, writer, and music editor, notably of the *Fitzwilliam Virginal Book*.

[3] Sharp accepted VW's proposal for deletion rather than amendment and sent his motion to Lucy Broadwood on 25 Nov. A copy of a speech apparently made by VW at the ensuing meeting survives at Cecil Sharp House in the Vaughan Williams Memorial Library, Cecil Sharp Correspondence, Box 4, Folder J.

46. To the Folk-Song Society [?November 1906]

I think that the 1st paragraph on p. 5, namely that dealing with the B.O.E.[1] needs modification and I should like to propose a resolution on this subject.

But 1st I ought to explain that I am myself a member of the Ctee and was present when the report was drafted. At the time I wished the paragraph to be omitted but when the rest of the Ctee considered this impossible I accepted the [paragraph] believing it to represent the views of the Ctee as expressed by them in a letter which they sent to the B.o.E. Namely that they welcomed the idea of teaching folk-songs in schools but considered that the board was not consistently carrying out the scheme which they enunciated – that is what I understood the paragraph to mean.

I now find however that this sentence is capable of an entirely different construction; indeed I find that several people to whom I have shown it take it for granted that it means *unreserved* approval of the board's scheme, and that the words 'consistently carried out' refer not to the B.o.E. itself but to school teachers and others to whom their suggestions are addressed.

Now the views of your Ctee are not at all this but are, as I understand, approval of the B.o.E's general idea but disapproval of their failure to distinguish between the folk-song and other classes of song, and their failure to include more genuine folk-songs in their list of recommended songs.

This was the substance of a letter sent by this Ctee and signed by our president to the B.o.E.

In such a very important matter as this I feel that there should be no ambiguity. Therefore I for one and I hope other members of his Ctee shall be very glad if the society will give us this opportunity of reconsidering this section of our report.

I should also like to add that we are the Folk Song Society – and that therefore however pleased we may be at the general improvement in music contemplated by the board we ought to confine ourselves to the folk song question and that any mention of any class of song known as 'national' should be omitted as being outside our province and as leading to confusion between those two very distinct classes of music.[2]

[1] Board of Education.

[2] This letter is the draft of a speech to be made to a General Meeting of the Folk-Song Society. See Fox Strangways and Karpeles, *Cecil Sharp*, 58–62. VW's motion to the meeting was not carried and the eventual consequence was the establishment of the English Folk Dance Society.

47. To Ralph Wedgwood

6 January 1907

On Board S.S. Wakool[1]

Jan 6th 1907[2]

Dear Randolph

You will be surprised to see this address – I hope Adeline has already written to you as she said she was going to do. The fact is I am on my way to Canary to see my sister in law—we all felt that someone ought to go – and none of her brothers could – I was free and wanted a holiday – so I started off. Adeline ½ settled to come with me – but was frightened at what might happen if she left home for so long. I expect I shall enjoy it very much. Its certainly, a most lazy life being on a steamer. There is a certain bit of the deck 80 times up and down [of] which means a mile so we can tell exactly how much exercize [*sic*] we are getting also I'm getting a good deal of reading done. Tom Jones (for the 2nd time) and a book about hypnotism and Shakespeare's historical plays & a lot of Browning. Yesterday we passed about 6 miles from C. Finisterre & the mountains in the N.W. of Spain – I thought of you & wondered what mountains they were. Fine arid looking mountains.

It is a small boat going eventually to Australia – we have only 16 salooners on board – a very dull & shoddy crew – I wish you were here to get something out of them – I can't – I can't even flirt with the ladies – There's only one who is *possible* from this point of view – and she is fearfully dull – also she much prefers the chief engineer who tells long stories about the various idiosyncracies of various passengers. But it's very jolly and extraordinary getting gradually into summer – today the sun was actually too hot & we sat out on deck under umbrellas.

I had a dream about you last night that you and I were staying in a house together & we were out for a walk & I heard a folk-song being sung by some school children – we went on for our walk (it was somewhere in the north of England among hills) & on our return I enquired in the school & found that the children had learnt it from an old man in the village (he had some funny name but I can't remember it) – and that the old man knew some more – 'some of them beauties' – so then I said 'You go home and start off in your motor & I will wait here' – but then I suddenly found, what I hadn't realized before, that I might come with you – so I gave up my folk-singing – then somehow suddenly Adeline was with us and she & you & the chauffeur got in & made a trial trip – then you came back for me and I & the chauffeur got in behind and *you* drove – & I woke up.[3]

I believe there are wonderful volcanic mountains at Grand Canary which I intend to climb up – I shall have about 13 or 14 days there – I am supposed to be back on the 30th to conduct an amateur orchestra at Cardiff through my Bucolic suite – but I've told them perhaps I shall not be there.[4]

Give my love to Iris – when shall we see you in London

Yours affectionately
Ralph

The whole company discussed Marie Corelli last night – & [I] realised for the 1st time what it meant to be really out of it. The young man who is going out to be governor at Fort Jameson started it by saying she was his favourite author – his brother objected that she was too far fetched – but he said all good plays and novels *were* far fetched. Then the chief engineer chimed in. *He* said that M.C's work had lasted when that of other chief women novelists (Sarah Grand & 'Iota'[5]) had not. The general opinion seemed to be that 'Sorrows of Satan' and 'Mighty Atom' were not *quite* nice – (Indeed the dressy young lady who is going to the Cape to be married and is very high church went so far as to say that they were 'profane' casting down her eyes) – But the general opinion was 'Thelma' & 'Romance of two worlds' were 'very interesting' – indeed the parson said that one of them had made him think! Which, if true, is indeed a very big testimonial.[6]

RVW

[1] VW was going to Grand Canary, where Adeline's brother-in-law, Frederic Maitland, had died while on holiday for his health. VW was to help his sister-in-law pack up and escort her and the two daughters home. See *RVW*, 78. It is odd that VW does not mention the circumstances of the visit, i.e. Maitland's death—but perhaps he knew Wedgwood was aware of that.

[2] VW wrote the year as 1906 in the original, a common mistake in the first few days of the New Year.

[3] This dream reflects the novelty of the motor car at this time.

[4] This performance of the *Bucolic Suite*, *CW* 1900/1, is mentioned by in *CW*, p. 11.

[5] 'Sarah Grand' was the nom de plume of Frances Elizabeth McFall (1862–1963) and 'Iota' the nom de plume of Kathleen Manningham Caffyn (whose novels were published between 1894 and 1916).

[6] The novels by Marie Corelli (1864–1924) which are mentioned were published as follows: *Thelma* in 1887, *A Romance of Two Worlds* in 1886, *The Sorrows of Satan; or the Strange Experiences of One Geoffrey Tempest, Millionaire* in 1895, and *Mighty Atom* in 1896. The letter is printed almost complete in *WVW*, 398–9.

48. To Ralph Wedgwood

[?summer 1907]

Temple Elfande[1]

Dear Randolph

I see that Adeline is writing to Iris so this inspires me to write to you and thank you for your card. I had to read between the lines of it and found out you were having a good time. We have had a funny summer holiday as my Brother in law Hervey (Fisher) has been very ill – but is nearly well now & we expect to go back to London on Wed: or Thurs:

But it's been an opportunity to do a lot of 'quiet work' – and incidentally I have really finished my magnum opus which I told you I was beginning years ago (at York)[2] – when you said I wasn't to do any more Stevenson but something healthy in fact you said 'Be a man – don't be a cad' (G. Robey[3]) – This is all about the sea and is for every conceivable voice & instrument & takes over an hour to perform – so I suppose it will now go into its drawer and remain there for ever.

We had Curle[4] here for a night lately (just after he had been with you) & he gave us a marvellous account of how he had bicycled 14 miles in an hour at night with a punctured tyre & his lamp always going out & various other mishaps – do you think this is true? – but I'm not sure whether it was after visiting you or after some other visit.

Write to me when you have time and tell me all about Germany. Did you go up the Brenner-Thal after all or not. I presumed from your card that you had been at or near Salzburg part of the time.

Give my love to Iris & to Randolph II.

Yrs
R.V.W.

[1] A house to the east of Capel, south of Dorking.

[2] In no. 64 and again in a published programme note of 1913 VW said that he started *A Sea Symphony*, dedicated to Wedgwood, in 1903 and that the first sketch was complete in 1907 (though at this point its working title was *The Ocean*). It was well under way in 1906; see no. 39. The work was to be the subject of much further revision before eventual performance at Leeds in Oct. 1910.

[3] VW refers to a catchphrase of George Robey, the music hall comedian, 1869–1954. He was knighted in 1954 not long before he died.

[4] Richard Curle, friend of the Wedgwoods and husband of Adeline's sister Cordelia. See Levy, *Moore*, 274.

49. To Frederick Delius

26 October [1907]

13 Cheyne Walk
Chelsea, S.W.

Oct. 26

Dear Mr Delius

I hope you will not think I am making a very audacious request – I should so much like to show you some of my work. I have had it in my mind (and especially now that I have heard your beautiful concerto) that I should profit very much by your advice & if you saw my work you might be able to suggest ways in which I c[d] improve myself – either by going to Paris or not.[1] Have you ever any time to spare – and if you have would you allow me to come and see you. I don't know if I ought to ask this on so slight an acquaintance.

Yours vy truly
R. Vaughan Williams[2]

[1] VW had heard a performance of Delius's Piano Concerto a few days earlier.

[2] Printed in *WVW*, 89, where it is misdated 24 October.

50. To Michael Calvocoressi

[November 1907]

13 Cheyne Walk
London S.W

Cher Monsieur

Selon votre tres aimable invitation j'ecris de vous prevenir que j'espere me trouver à Paris le soir de Jeudi le douze Decembre; et je me ferai l'honneur de vous faire visite le jour prochain si cela ne vous gênera pas.

Mon addresse sera Hotel de l'Univers et du Portugal, Rue Croix des Petits champs.

Agreez mes salutations sinceres[1]
Ralph Vaughan Williams

P.S. This is my best attempt to write a letter in French – I hope it is fairly correct.

R.V.W.

[1] This letter, though addressed to Calvocoressi, is in fact a draft of a letter to Ravel sent for C's approval. The accents omitted by VW throughout the letter have not been restored. See *RVW*, 79, where it is printed.

51. To Michael Calvocoressi [December 1907]

Hotel de L'Univers et du Portugal
Rue Croix des Petits Champs

Dear Mr Calvocoressi

I must write you one line to thank you for introducing me to the man who is *exactly* what I am looking for. As far as I know my own faults he hit on them all exactly & is telling me to do exactly what I half feel in my mind I ought to do – but it just wanted *saying*.[1]

I have got Antar and have set to work on him.[2] It is awfully kind of you to have been present at the lesson – it was such a help

Yrs very truly
R. Vaughan Williams.[3]

[1] VW had begun his lessons with Maurice Ravel.
[2] i.e. Symphony No. 2, *Antar*, by Rimsky-Korsakov.
[3] Printed in *RVW*, 80.

52. To Gustav Holst[1] [January 1908]

My Dear V.

Do you really think that because your work has been crowned with the disfavour of Joseph Bennet,[2] that my & other people's labours, in scratching out your mistakes is made any the more or less worthwhile? – The point is that it's a big work & naturally anything one does to help on that is not wasted.

I'm sorry (a) that you haven't got £500, (b) that you are not promised a performance – perhaps these are rather important side issues but they *are* side issues – the real, important thing is that you have *not* been put in the awful position when 'all men speak well of you'[3] – Think, the awful stigma to have gone through life with a prize opera on your back – almost as damning as a mus: doc:

I'm glad on the whole that you are 'highly commended' – because it probably means that *one* judge (perhaps Stanford?[4] – or Percy Pitt?) did really know a good thing when they saw it – and it may be practically useful as far as performance goes.

P. Greene[5] has written me a very silly letter saying he doesn't like your songs & has sent them back to me – they are at 13 Cheyne Walk.

To return to the opera

I don't know that even my faith in you w[d] have been quite strong enough to have stood the shock of approval by J. Bennet.

So after all, at the expense of worldly advantages, you've saved your honour.

Perhaps you think it's too serious a matter to joke about – well, I know it is – but then after all the *most* important thing is that you've written a big work and that you aren't in the awful position of being continually praise[d] by those whose opinions & methods you despise in every way.

Yrs
RVW

Dear Mr Von Holst

I am sorry that your opera has not been chosen – but I always felt here that the best one could/would not get the prize.

A.V.W.

1 Printed as Letter XIV in *HR*.

2 Holst had entered *Sita* for the Ricordi Prize and had failed to win it by a narrow margin. See Short, *Holst*, 72. Bennett was one of the judges. The others were Charles Stanford, Percy Pitt, and Tito Ricordi.

3 Luke 6: 26.

4 According to Short, *Holst*, loc. cit., Stanford was said to have disliked *Sita* intensely.

5 Harry Plunket Greene, bass/baritone and son-in-law of Hubert Parry. See *New Grove*.

53. To Michael Calvocoressi

[early March 1908]

13 Cheyne Walk
Chelsea
London S.W
(my English address)

Dear Mr Calvocoressi

We were both so sorry not to be able to see Mrs Calvocoressi and yourself before leaving Paris. I called on you on Sunday but had not the pleasure of finding you at home – I hope you received the music all right. I cannot thank you enough for all your hospitality and kindness to me and *especially* in introducing me to Ravel – who has helped me and taught me more than I imagined was possible.

By the way I sent Ravel some money today – the final payment – and as I was in a great hurry I am not sure that I sent the correct sum – could you possibly find out and if it was *not* let me know

We hope very much to see you in London when you next come here.

Yrs very truly
R. Vaughan Williams

54. To E. J. Dent

[November 1908[1]]

13 Cheyne Walk,
S.W.

Dear Dent

Please forgive my not answering your nice letter before.

I think the league[2] is just what people make it – if good people join it will be a good thing – if only bad people – then its not worth considering.

The prospectus is only in the rough and has many faults – but these can be improved. As to your remarks on the cttee – Delius was one of the starters & was put on the ctee for that reason—many of the other names are only names (Wood for example – by the way I don't at all share your objections to him) – because unfortunately to attract people one has to put all the 'official' people on – there are also one or two unknown real useful people such as Harry Evans who runs a big choral society at Liverpool and has made the Matthew Passion into a safe draw. Parry was approached – but unfortunately in the wrong way – one evening when he was in one of his bad tempers – and he was, I believe, very abusive – but wrote and apologized afterwards & wanted to join – & I hope will soon. I am very sorry his name is not on and I feel that we ought to try for it (By the way, this is private of course).

Thank you so much for your invitation – I sh[d] so much like to come sometime.

Yours sincerely
R. Vaughan Williams

[1] Written shortly after sending Dent a prospectus for the Musical League on 11 November.

[2] The Musical League, founded in 1909. See *WVW*, 95. The main event during its short existence was a Festival at Liverpool in Sept. 1909.

55. To Ralph Wedgwood

[?1909]

13 Cheyne Walk
S.W.

My Dear Randolph

I send you herewith your own especial goat which has just come out.[1]

It is my best work I believe up to the present – and so however feeble it may be I love to think of it with your initials at the top – it c[d] have no better fate.

How splendid to think of you being at Cambridge Sat: week. Give my love to Iris.

Yrs
RVW

[1] The 'especial goat' (presumably in the sense of not being a sheep) was the vocal score of *A Sea Symphony* (dedicated to Wedgwood), just published. The first edition was published by Breitkopf & Härtel in 1909.
[2] Printed in part in *WVW*, 400.

56. To Ruth Charrington[1]

[January 1909[2]]

13 Cheyne Walk
S.W

Dear Miss Charrington

We were so sorry to have missed you this afternoon.

About the orchestra – I sh[d] like to undertake it again very much if people are keen enough to go on.[3] It is really too bad of Mrs Farrer[4] not to have taken any steps – she definitely told me she was going to send a circular round to members saying she was going to give it up – and I thought it w[d] be a good plan to do this & test the keenness of the members – and if they were keen someone else w[d] start it.

Now if you really want to restart it – I suggest your writing to Mrs Farrer & ask her if she intends carrying it on (you might if you felt inclined point out how awkward it is having put off things so late) and if she does not want to go on with it ask her to send you all the details about members – subscriptions etc. Then start quite afresh. Call a meeting of prominent members (Miss Stack's address is 17 Rutland Gate S.W. Miss Scott Moncrieff 11 Cheyne Walk is very keen) and reorganise yourselves – elect a secretary, librarian and treasurer and settle who you will ask to conduct you. Some of the members may suggest trying a new conductor – in which case I will if I may give my blessing and hope I shall be asked to hear the first concert – any way I think I can get you some new members.

If you ask me to conduct you again I shall make one or two conditions

(a) That there be at least 20 violins, 4 violas & 5 cellos at all events members 'on paper'
(b) That of these there be at least 4 *first rate players* who are prepared to play 2nd violin

Forgive me this enormous letter – because perhaps you aren't thinking of taking it on at all

Yrs sincerely
R. Vaughan Williams

[1] A cellist who had played under VW in the *Pilgrim's Progress* music at Reigate Priory in 1906 and in other charity concerts subsequently. She was the daughter of Mrs Hadley by her first marriage and lived with her.

[2] According to note by recipient on original.

[3] The orchestra society is clearly that which played in the concert conducted by VW at the Passmore Edwards Settlement on 10 Mar. 1907, since many of the names in this and subsequent letters occur in the list given in the programme of that concert preserved in the British Library, Add. MS 70937A.

[4] Mrs Noel Farrer, who is listed in the 10 Mar. concert programme as playing the first violin.

57. To E. J. Dent

[?January 1910]

13 Cheyne Walk
S.W.

Dear Dent

Your letter fills me with intense pleasure – coupled with considerable alarm – it is nice of you all to think of and consider – and it quite overwhelms me – but the idea of a one-man show (except of course when the 'one man' gives it himself when there is a kind of 'Don't shoot the composer, he's doing his best' feeling about[1]) does alarm me. However after your letter and such an invitation it is not for me to say no.

Now as regards programme – you say 'Of course the quartet'[2] – but I must confess that hardly anyone except me likes it – and I don't want to put off people who were so nice about the 'Wasps' and all you people who are arranging this by producing something ~~you will~~ most people (apparently) loathe. Don't you think you had better consult someone whose judgement you value & who was at my concert before you put it in. – In a way I should like to have it in, as I still like it myself – or perhaps have the two middle movements – but that w^d not do – as it w^d mean bringing down the Schwiller 4^tet[3] especially for that which is absurd – otherwise I w^d suggest my 5tet with Pfte & C. Bass[4] – but that w^d mean an extra player & therefore more expense.

As for songs Francis Harford sings H. of Life[5] – but we oughtn't to make the programme too depressing – I sh^d think a good musician like Carey[6] c^d get up anything – and you might prefer to have him. The Schwiller 4^tet were £21–0–0 for my concert but that was special as they had 15 rehearsals or more – now they know it they ought to be less. Marmaduke Barton plays the p^fte part of my 5^tet better than anyone else.

Once again I can't say anything to tell you how touched I feel by all this.

On re-reading this letter I find I have discussed this matter as if it was settled – but I fully realize that it is only in the air and that prudent counsels may still prevail – But whatever the upshot is, it won't make any difference to my pleasure in the fact that the idea was ever thought of.

Yours very sincerely
R. Vaughan Williams

P.S. I find I have said nothing about dates – anything suits me – ~~perhaps~~ I am actually in Cambridge towards the end of Feb: lecturing on Folk-songs *can it be on the same* date.

[1] An adapted quotation from Oscar Wilde's *Impressions of America*: 'Don't shoot the pianist!'

[2] String Quartet in G minor, *CW* 1908/9.

[3] The quartet led by the violinist Isidore Schwiller, which had taken part in the first performance of *On Wenlock Edge*, *CW* 1909/1. He led the Leith Hill Musical Festival orchestra for many years.

[4] Quintet in C minor for pianoforte, violin, viola, violoncello, and double bass, *CW* 1903/13. Although VW withdrew the work later, it was eventually published, with UVW's agreement, in 2002.

[5] *The House of Life*, *CW* 1904/9.

[6] Clive Carey (1883–1968), baritone singer and opera producer.

58. To E. J. Dent

[January 1910]

13 Cheyne Walk
S.W.

Dear Dent

I have delayed answering your last letter because I was thinking things over.

Now (a) would you very much like to have *Carey* – I hardly know his singing but c^{d} easily arrange a programme with him and the Schwiller 4^{tet} – and I trust your judgement entirely or (b) are you keen on having my new 'Shropshire Lad'[1] cycle – which I consider my best recent work. This however necessitates Gervase Elwes.[2] However if you thought of this I should like to guarantee the expense of him myself – partly because he was very kind in doing a concert with me (which practically meant singing at my concert for nothing) and I feel I owe him something.

Of course the difficulty about him is that he is very busy and w^{d} have to be engaged some time before hand.

Now, there is another point. I had a queer letter from Schwiller the other day saying that the *C.U.M.S.*[3] were perhaps going to ask his 4^{tet} down! This doesn't seem likely – but I mention it for what it is worth as in case it is true you might not care to have them also.

If you settle on the p^{fte} 5^{tet} w^{d} *you* play the pfte part?

I think (apart from the singer) we ought to manage the 4tet and 5tet for 30 guineas. The Schwiller 4tet w^{d} (I hope) be £4–4–0 & the C. Bass another £4–4–0.

I am sending you herewith two great works![4]

(1) Sea Symph. is I hope my magnum opus – it has taken me about 6 years to do.[5]
(2) W. Wood[6] was started also years ago but was finally revised this year.

Yrs
RVW

[1] i.e. *On Wenlock Edge*.

[2] Gervase Elwes (1866–1921), the English tenor who started singing professionally in 1903 following a period in the diplomatic service. He had given the first performance of VW's *On Wenlock Edge* in the Aeolian Hall on 15 Nov. 1909.

[3] Cambridge University Musical Society.

[4] The vocal scores of both works had been published by Breitkopf (London) in 1909.

[5] *A Sea Symphony* was undoubtedly VW's largest and most ambitious work to date and has remained one of his best-known works ever since. It was first performed at Leeds on 12 Oct. 1910, some months after the probable date of this letter.

[6] *Willow-Wood*, conversely, was very much neglected after its early performances and was not seriously revived until it was recorded in 2005.

59. To E. J. Dent

[January 1910]

13 Cheyne Walk
S.W.

Dear Dent

Thank you very much for your telegram – I at last today got definite answers from Elwes and the Schwiller 4tet – Elwes can come all right – but the miserable 2nd violin of the Schwiller 4tet goes off on the 21st for a month's tour – so *they* are no good – and I don't think any other 4tet c^{d} possibly get it up in time. The Langley-Mukle 4tet have got the score and think they are going to rehearse it but I doubt if they c^{d} ~~play it~~ get it up in time and I don't know how they play.

But if you still thought of a concert and wanted it this term ~~we c^{d}~~ and w^{d} do without the *quartet* we c^{d} do my pfte quintet (double bass and no 2nd violin) & a scratch 2nd violin w^{d} be all rght to accompany the Elwes songs.

Or we c^{d} do without Elwes and have (say) the 5tet, House-of-life and odd songs. Failing this the only thing to do is as you suggest and put off till the May term – or perhaps give up altogether – I shall quite appreciate it if you think this is the best plan.

Perhaps you had better wire if you still think it better not to have it this term. Elwes can manage any time up to beginning of March.

Yrs
RVW

60. To E. J. Dent

[towards end of March 1910]

13 Cheyne Walk
S.W.

Dear Dent

Thank you very much for yr letter – yes high pitch.[1]

Elwes will sing 3 songs in his final group (I think that is enough, don't you – the 5tet is 30 minutes, the 4tet about 25, the song cycle 20 & his group about 10 – total 1 ho. 25 mins *actual music*).

The names are

(a) Claribel (1896)
(b) The sky above the roof (1909)
(c) The roadside fire (1904)[2]

– We've decided on the last not because it's very good but I think that people must have *one* that they are likely to find bearable.

It's funny how great minds differ – I was tremendously moved by Orpheus[3] – & came away thinking it the finest opera in the world – (except the last act which is dull except the trio) and just the *kind* of opera I sh[d] like to write. I admit the singing was bad – & if you don't like old Mary of course you *don't* like her & Viola is a gawkish amateur – but I saw what c[d] be done with opera (for the 1st time) with real rehearsal & an attempt to illustrate every moment in the music – and I thought it was awfully successful – & the dance & staging was wonderful – quite modern of course – but if the music can bear it why not? & that girl who danced – I had no idea it was possible to express so much emotion by means of the arms & legs – but I do not care for Ballings[4] conducting – he distinctly over played it.

Yrs
RVW

[1] i.e. for tuning the piano.

[2] The dates given by VW are the dates of publication. 'Claribel' (see *CW* 1899/C) was written around the turn of the century, 'The sky above the roof' (a setting of a translation of Verlaine's poem 'Le ciel est par-dessus le toit') was written in 1908, and 'The roadside fire' was one of the *Songs of Travel* written in 1904.

[3] VW had been to a production of Gluck's *Orfeo* in English at the Savoy Theatre staged by the mezzo-soprano Marie Brema. 'Old Mary' was 54 at this time but the production was widely admired.

[4] Michael Balling (1866–1925), German conductor.

61. To E. J. Dent

[April 1910]

Dear Dent

I enclose copy of S.Lad with words as I want them.

Claribel is the Tennyson

I send a copy of 'The Sky' for words

I don't see why you sh^{d} bother about putting up the players – it w^{d} rather bore your friends to have to entertain orchestral players wdnt it? I shd think they c^{d} find their way to some little pub cdnt they – but of course its not for me to put them off a good thing!

They *are* going to rehearse at Cambridge in the afternoon.

Yrs
RVW

62. To E. J. Dent

[April 1910]

13 Cheyne Walk
S.W.

Dear Dent

Letterbox 2

Is it the large or small Guildhall you are using?[1] If it is going to be a small crowd – wdnt it be possible at the last minute to change to the *small* Guildhall – & be a nice family party instead of a ½ empty room? It will not harm the music a bit – but of course you know best.

Yrs
RVW

[1] For the concert on 6 May.

63. To Harold Child[1]

[about 15 July 1910][2]

Hotel Latemar
Karersee
Botzen
Tirol
Austria

Dear Mr. Child.

(I hope I spell your name right – I've never seen it written!)

First I want to thank you very much for being so kind and sympathetic and apparently actually anxious to cooperate in this operatic venture.

Secondly to remind you that if our scheme ever comes to anything then it will never get past pen on paper – for I see *hardly any* chance of an opera by an English composer ever being produced, at all events in *our* lifetime – does this make any difference to your entering into the scheme?

Thirdly, this is the letter which I promised with my ideas on the particular kind of opera I had an idea we might cooperate on – please forgive the extreme length. I have a lot of nebulous ideas as to how an opera should be made which I have tried to work out on a small scale by myself – but have come to the conclusion that what I must try and do first is to get some practical knowledge of the stage* and for this purpose I want to try my hand at an opera on more or less accepted lines – preferably a *comedy* – to be full of tunes, and lively, and one tune that will really *come off*:

*I have already found this to a very small extent in some incidental music to plays.

(I'm sorry for talking about myself such a lot but it is inevitable!)

This fitted in with another idea of mine which was to write a musical, what the Germans call 'Bauern-Comedie' – only applied to *English* country life (real as far as possible – not sham) – something on the lines of Smetana's 'Verkaufte Braut'.[3] For I have an idea that an opera written to *real* English words – with a certain amount of *real* English music and also a *real* English subject might just hit the right nail on the head.

As regards the form – *not* Wagnerian and not altogether Mozartian – but more the Mozartian with some of his squareness taken away – perhaps a certain amount of the Charpentier–Puccini conversational methods thrown in – but this is all vague and I sh[d] like to fit in with your ideas.

Only I think the whole thing might be *folk-songy* in character – with a certain amount of real ballad stuff thrown in.

I will now put down some ideas as to scenes I have – which may possibly be useful *in case they happen to fit in with any ideas of yours* – otherwise please discard them absolutely.

(1) Opening scene, a fair with all the paraphernalia – merry-go-round, cake-stalls, shooting-gallery, fat-woman 'Show to life guardsman' – a ballad-monger, small boys with whistles, etc. etc. An opening chorus and scene – (not a set chorus 'the chorus sing the praise of a good glass of beer') but ejaculations in fragments on a sort of symphonic basis, with lavender cries, people shouting out what they have to sell, etc. and the ballad seller singing bits of ballads – all leading up to a climax when

a prize fight is announced – the village champion enters his name (scene between him and his young lady?). No challenger appears till at last a stranger rides (or walks up) (possibly a gypsy – see one of the opening chapters of Borrow's I Zincali*[4])

Defeat of the village champion – heroine feels inclined to transfer her affections to the stranger – disgust of the village hero.

*I am not sure however whether it is in the nature of things for a gypsy to run off with a non-gypsy – which I suppose wd be the inevitable conclusion perhaps the stranger might be some purely fanciful character?

(2) Then would possibly follow a plot to down the stranger by the village hero and his boon companions – possibly a scene late at night in the village inn (or just outside it). The village hero and his friends go out at night intending to come back early in the morning to have their revenge – which is somehow triumphantly frustrated by the stranger who when morning comes rides (or perhaps drives in his little cart) off with the heroine before the whole village and the discomfited village hero.

But before this climax is reached I have an idea for another scene (which will I think fit in with the above) viz.

(3) Early in the morning (still dark) the stranger comes in singing a ballad (see 'Sweet Europe' in Sharp's 'Folk Songs from Somerset') which brings the heroine to the window – there follows a scene in which they arrange to go off together (or whatever they *do* arrange). This starts quietly and conversationally and gradually works up to a duet 'appassionato' in which the ballad tune (and possibly part of the words) has a large share – the stranger then goes off, the heroine shuts her window and the dawn gradually comes (empty stage). As soon as it is a little light the Mayers are heard in the far distance – coming back with their branches of May and singing – they gradually get nearer and nearer and fill the stage and the full light gradually comes.[5]

But after all it is *you* who are to write the play, not me – these ideas are only to be taken for what they are worth.

Or perhaps you want to write something quite different either

(a) all music,
(b) with dialogue,
(c) with melodrama,

perhaps a gay sort of comedy, like Cosí fan Tutte – with purely formal square-cut numbers, or a purely fantastic opera or an English subject of quite a different nature (e.g. The Mayor of Casterbridge).

By the way, I have no objection to the structure being more or less formal & conventional – as I like duets, trios, quartets or even quintets – I think all opera has to be conventional (or perhaps I should say *not* realistic).

As regards the relationship of words and music – there are I think three grades

(1) Dry recitative, in which the pure facts are set forth
(2) 'arioso' or 'scena' in which the emotional growth of the drama can be set out
(3) Lyrical sections – which, dramatically, should be pure points of repose (corresponding to such passages as Hamlet's soliloquies or 'O Romeo, wherefore art thou Romeo.')

The story should not be told in lyrical moments – and one must always remember that it is *always* difficult to take the logical meaning of a sentence in when it is sung.

Out of the way words and elaborate phraseology does not do in a lyric – because they are in themselves an attempt to supply the decorative element which the music is there to supply.

I think that is all – slow–long tableaux – or long dramatic pauses are always good, as the music takes a long time to speak, much longer than words by themselves – in fact, one wants purely musical effects in an opera just as one wants purely poetical effects in a drama. I have put down all that occurs to me – but please don't consider any of it as of *any* importance.

I am here for about a month,

Yrs very tr[uly]
R. Vaughan Williams.

[1] Harold Child (1869–1945), writer and theatre critic. He regularly contributed leading articles to *The Times*. *Hugh the Drover*, CW 1924/1, was his only opera libretto.

[2] This letter is the first of a series written to Harold Child about the opera, which is printed substantially complete as Appendix I in *RVW*, 402–21. These letters are unusual in the corpus of VW's letters in that they, and in particular the present letter, give more evidence about the artistic genesis of a work than in any other case. According to the diary of Adeline VW's mother, they left on holiday on 10 July and returned on 8 Aug., so the date of the letter would be about 15 July after arrival in the Dolomites. That the year was 1910 is confirmed by VW's remarks on the origins of the opera to Percy Scholes in no. 132.

[3] Smetana's opera *The Bartered Bride* has some similarities to *Hugh the Drover*, in its village setting and core theme of the conflict between a marriage arranged for the heroine by her family and one dictated by the heroine's own inclinations.

[4] A reference to the section 'The English Gypsies' in George Borrow's Introduction to his *The Zincali, or An Account of The Gypsies in Spain* of 1841 (source of the challenge that occurs in Act I of *Hugh the Drover*: 'The best man in England for twenty pounds!').

[5] The outline plot which VW proposes to Child is, broadly speaking, that to which the opera was eventually written. For an outline of the plot in its later form, which VW sent to Percy Scholes, see no. 132, and for some changes made as the first production at the RCM was being prepared, see no. 143.

64. To Herbert Thompson[1] [about September 1910]

13 Cheyne Walk
S.W.

Dear Mr Thompson

I will tell you all I can. I think it best to put down any thing that occurs to me and then you can select anything out of it which you want.[2]

(1) With regard to the name 'Symphony' – I use the word because the treatment of the words is symphonic rather than dramatic – that is to say the words are used as a basis on which to build up a decorative musical scheme. I have therefore felt justified in repeating the words a good deal – especially in the 1st movement.

(2) As regards your enquiry about 'significance of tunes' – I can only think of two –

(a) the harmonic progression which starts the work & comes again pp. 6. 47. 49 (letter E). 56. 62 (letter F.) 87. etc

(b) the phrase

which is part of the opening theme and comes again several times in the 1st & last movements.

These two themes (for no particular reason) seem to suggest the sea to my mind![3]

(3) As regards its history – it has been gradually growing in my mind for about 7 years – The sketch was completed in 1907[4] and revised and scored

in 1908 and 9 – When the festival Ct^{ee} accepted it last year it had another clean up & finally during the last 6 months I have been revising the full score which meant re-copying most of it.

I don't know from your letter whether you want my 'general' history – but in case you do:

I was born in 1872. General education Charterhouse School & Trinity College Cambridge – musical education R.C.M. & also with Charles Wood at Cambridge – also 6 months in Berlin with Max Bruch.

For some years I was organist at a church in South London.

I am sending a copy of the vocal score with a few indications – c^{d} you kindly return it when you have done with it as it is the only one I have.

Yrs vy ty
R. Vaughan Williams

P.S. The full score is now being copied – otherwise I sh^{d} have been delighted to send it you.

[1] Herbert Thompson (1856–1945) was for fifty years the music critic for the *Yorkshire Post*. This letter is printed in full as no. 36 in Foreman, *From Parry to Britten*, 41–2.

[2] Thomson had apparently been commissioned to prepare the programme notes for the first performance of *A Sea Symphony*, *CW* 1909/3, which was to take place on 12 Oct. at Leeds Town Hall.

[3] See VW's programme note of 1913 printed in *CW*, p. 53, where he draws attention to the same two themes.

[4] In fact it seems that a full score was complete—see no. 39, where he tells Holst that he has finished scoring the second movement of the Ocean, and no. 48, where he reports to Wedgwood that his 'magnum opus' is really finished.

65. To E. J. Dent

[early 1911[1]]

13 Cheyne Walk,
S.W.

Dear Dent

Do you remember René Gatty who was up in our time – I expect you do. He has been for some years Reader in English at Prague University – he is now homesick & has given up his job & is coming back to England – he will therefore be out of a job – do you think there is any chance of work for him at Cambridge – he knows German like English & Bohemian to a certain extent also – I wondered if there was any opening for a teacher of languages at Cambridge – he w^{d} also be good at Librarians' work – He w^{d} be a great assett [*sic*] to your town & he is a very good & keen musician (also by the way a *first rate* composer in the light style – & I think may still one day make his mark that way) – He is a delightful person & a genius in his way & worth helping to keep in England.

Yrs very truly
R. Vaughan Williams

[1] From context.

66. To Arnold Barter[1]

[about 11 March 1911]

13 Cheyne Walk
Chelsea, S.W.

Dear Mr Barter

I learn from Breitkopfs that your performance of my Sea Symphony is coming off very soon now – I didn't know it was so soon[2] – & I have been so busy that I have not been able to make the orchestral arrangement of the scherzo – perhaps you are not doing the whole of the work – I have no objection to that as I have said on the title page.[3] I find that B&H[4] have not finished copying the score – so there is only my copy to conduct from – which I am afraid from frequent revision is very untidy by now.

I am afraid some of the orchestra passages are very hard and are made worse by the *disgraceful* parts which B&H have provided – do blow them up about it if you find difficulties – they may then be persuaded to have some new copies made.

I have cued in the bass clarinet, 3rd flute, 2nd oboe, E♭ clarinet & contra-fag. parts – so direct your players to play those cues if you have not those instruments.

If there is no 2nd oboe, the cor anglais must play off the *special part* provided for the purpose – also the 2nd flute if there is no 3rd flute – if there is no bass clar the 2nd bassoon must play off the special part *except in No 3 (scherzo)*.

I have just been conducting a performance at Oxford so I venture to make one or two suggestions gained from my experience there.[5]

– I also send a copy of the revised vocal score – the voice parts of which correspond with the full score – however the old voice parts fit with the orchestral parts all right except in those few pages of the last movement which I believe B&H have sent you.

Suggestions

p. 3.	Poco animando each entry of the theme in the bass (ie p. 4 bar 2 & 7) to be *slightly* quicker than the last
p. 5. bar 1	start beating 2 in the bar

p. 7. start the allegro *steady* but get *rather* brighter at p. 9. 2nd score

p. 13. the animando starts 4 bars after M.

p. 23. poco animando sh^{d} be poco *animato* – i.e. a little quicker & *then* steady time.

p. 25. andante – make the soprano solo come *on* the first beat & not just after, as they have a habit of doing.

p. 35. *no need* to get any quicker at the 'piu mosso'

p. 36. Tempo del principio – slow off a bit in the 3 bars preceding the baritone entry.

p. 45. letter Hh. I have taken out 'meno mosso' as the tempo is really about the same though it *sounds* slower.

p. 66 score 2 'largamente' not too slow – but tightly.[6]

p. 81 start as slow as you like – but get a *shade* quicker at the tenor entry 'covered all over'.

p. 85 beat 4 here.

p. 87 Poco animando start beating 2 here.

p. 91 4 bars after H, the C should be ¢, i.e. continue to beat 2.

p. 95 the baritone solo must be rather *slower* than ♩ = ♩ so get rather slower 5 bars before he comes in (this is marked in the full score).

p. 106 Allegro – the metronome mark is *too quick* here.

p. 112 $\frac{2}{2}$ do not make too much of the allargando etc – a steady 2 in the bar is the only safe way of beating this.

p. 112 Allegro agitato *not* too quick

p. 113. Choruses have great difficulty over these passages – the chorus part *may be omitted* until they all come in to the last bar of p. 115.

on page 115 'animato' *disregard this*

Yrs very truly
R. Vaughan Williams

[1] Conductor of the Bristol Philharmonic Society chorus and orchestra. His main job was as an employee of W. D. & H. O. Wills, the tobacco company. He remained a friend of VW until the end of VW's life.

[2] The performance was given on 26 Apr. 1911.

[3] This is something of a conundrum. In *WVW* (p. 98) MK refers to an allegation made by Hugh Allen that the Scherzo was omitted at the first performance in Leeds, because it was found too difficult by the Festival Chorus. On the other hand the reviews by Herbert Thompson and others refer to that movement being sung, so Allen's statement appears to have been a *canard*, but one to which the implication of VW's statement that the orchestration of the Scherzo was not yet complete lends some support.

[4] i.e. Breitkopf & Härtel.

[5] The Oxford Choral Society and the Oxford Bach Choir 'with Dr Allen's orchestra and professional wind from London Symphony Orchestra' had given a performance of *A Sea Symphony* conducted by

VW on Wednesday, 8 Mar. 1911. The soloists were V. Salvin and Campbell McInnes (who had also sung the baritone solo in the first performance at Leeds). A notice that appeared in the *Oxford Times* on 11 Mar. is interesting with hindsight: 'Does Dr. Williams's music increase the vivid impression of the words? This is the supreme question, the final test, and only a favourable answer can justify the setting of them to music. Dr. Vaughan Williams is one of our most earnest and gifted composers, and his setting of "Toward the Unknown Region" had led us to expect a considerable measure of success in a work of similar profound motive, and we were not disappointed. In parts the work receives an impressive and illuminative setting, increasing the effect of the words, and charming as pure music; while in others there is a striving after an ideal setting, which is not realised. The work is over-scored and the orchestration is in parts singularly ineffective . . . The work is one of great difficulty, both for chorus and orchestra, even in some parts well-nigh impossible, although it had been somewhat simplified since its first production. Bearing this point in mind, we must allow that the performance was good; at the same time it was far below the standard the local societies have accustomed us to. Dr. Allen and his devoted forces have literally slaved at the work, though dispirited by its excessive difficulty, and then only achieved moderate results.'

[6] Perhaps *lightly*.

67. To Gilbert Murray[1]

25 April [1911]

13 Cheyne Walk
Chelsea, S.W.

April 25th

Dear Professor Murray

I do not know whether you are at all interested in the work of Mr Cecil Sharp in collecting and spreading the knowledge of our traditional folk-songs & dances.

I venture to write to you about this because a movement is on foot to present a petition to the Prime Minister to make him a grant from the civil list.

Mr Sharp has, as I daresay you know, discovered and made accessible an immense mass of English traditional art – poetry, music & dancing – of which we were, a few years ago, entirely ignorant, and his discoveries are not only of great antiquarian and scientific interest but of vital artistic value besides being educationally very important.

To do this work Mr Sharp has given up time which might have been spent in remunerative work and the expense of travelling about the country and finding material is considerable – of course his publications bring in a little – but this is an entirely inadequate return for his outlay. Besides this Mr Sharp is always willing to lecture for little or no remuneration, and this willingness is taken full advantage of! If his work is to continue some means of support must be found.

If you consider that Mr Sharp's work is of sufficient importance and interest would you be so very kind as to sign the petition.

We have already obtained the signatures of most of the folklore experts besides musicians like Sir C.V. Stanford; we are represented on the literary side by Hardy, Masefield & others.

Yours very truly
R. Vaughan Williams

[1] Gilbert Murray (1866–1957), Regius Professor of Greek at Oxford.

68. To Arnold Barter

29 April 1911

13 Cheyne Walk
Chelsea, S.W.

Received: Apr. 29/11

Dear Mr Barter

When I received your letter this morning I thought that I could read between the lines and guessed that the performance of my 'Sea Symphony' had been quite first rate. This guess of mine is now corroborated[1] by the testimony of a niece of mine of whose musical judgement I have a very high opinion, and who has heard the work both at Leeds and Oxford – she was present at your performance on Wednesday and says it was the nicest performance she has heard – 'The chorus so fresh and lovely in its tone—the band small but so good and the whole thing so spontaneous and vigorous.'[2]

Now, first I want to thank *you* for all the immense labour and thought you have expended over the work, and for using all that musical capacity and insight, which I know you must possess, to secure such a fine rendering.

Secondly I want you kindly to convey my very best thanks to the choir for their splendid determination to give a new work the very best possible chance. I know from bitter experience how hard the work is, and I know what self denial all those extra rehearsals must have entailed. I only hope that the success of their efforts has been some reward to them.

And thirdly I must thank your orchestra who behaved like true artists in giving an extra rehearsal and thus contributing so much to the total success.

It is a great pleasure and encouragement to feel that my work has given pleasure to you and your performers. I hope I may one day have the pleasure of hearing your choir sing.

I thought that the two soloists you chose were quite excellent.

Thanking you once again

I remain yours very truly
R. Vaughan Williams[3]

[1] The version printed in *RVW* erroneously reads 'confirmed' here.
[2] UVW (*RVW*, 96) suggests that the niece in question was Ermengard Maitland.
[3] The letter is printed complete in *RVW*, 96.

69. Postcard to E. J. Dent

postmark: 17 June 1911

13 Cheyne Walk
S.W.

I send this in case you happen to be in London.

A few composers are coming here to smoke next Monday evening (June 19th) 8.30 onwards – any chance of seeing you?

R. Vaughan Williams
13 Cheyne Walk
S.W.

70. To Ernest Farrar[1]

postmark: 8 July 1911

13 Cheyne Walk
Chelsea, S.W.

Dear Farrar,

I am very glad to hear from you again – I will do my best to answer all your questions.

a) 'Five Mystical Songs' is published by Stainer & Bell.
b) I don't think I *could* write Church Music, but there's no telling what one may not do as senile decay sets in – I certainly am coming more & more to the conclusion that concert music is *beastly* – that what we want is music for an occasion – a ceremony or a cause! – but I expect I am too old to change my methods now.

About Wood & the promenades (which by the way I except from the above condemnation) I don't know how to get at him – except by a yearly bombardment – I've done so nearly every year for the last 8 or 9 years & he has *twice* taken notice of me. I believe, however, that Speyer has weight, if you know him.[2]

Do come and see me when you are in London and *bring some of your things*. I hardly know anything of yours except the Rossetti which I liked very much.[3]

Yrs
R. Vaughan Williams.

[1] Ernest Farrar (1885–1918), composer and organist, at this time in South Shields. Like VW he had been a pupil of Stanford and Parratt.

[2] Henry Wood was the musical figurehead of the Promenade Concerts inaugurated at the Queen's Hall, recently built in 1895 by Robert Newman, and remained so until his death in 1944. Sir Edgar Speyer, a wealthy banker and patron of music of German extraction, had been behind the construction of the first tube railways in London and was Chairman of the Queen's Hall concerts from 1902 and regularly bailed out the Promenade concerts. He was a friend of Elgar. Despite being a baronet and a Privy Councillor, anti-German sentiment forced him to leave London for New York in 1914 and he never returned. See Leanne Langley, 'Building an Orchestra, Creating an Audience', in Doctor and Wright (eds.), *The Proms*, 62.

[3] *The Blessed Damozel*, Op. 6, for chorus and orchestra.

71. To Cecil Sharp

[July 1911]

13 Cheyne Walk
S.W.

Dear Sharp

I can't tell you how much your letter has delighted me – indeed I feel so excited I can do no work this morning. I had been in fearful dumps ever since the list came out in the paper and your name not there!

But don't give me the credit! The real prime movers are (1) Mrs Hanway – who *started* the whole idea & got together the necessary facts about your public work. (2) Sir L. & Lady Gomme who actually approached the authorities.[1] I wish you c^d have seen the document we sent in to the prime minister – it was the most remarkable collection of distinguished names I have ever seen – about 30 in all – and I am certain many more w^d have signed if they had been asked only we were advised that with such a list we need go no further. I cannot remember them all but here are a few of them: Lord Alverstone, Baring-Gould, Thomas Hardy, [James] Frazer, E. V. Lucas, Gilbert Murray, C. V. Stanford, Edward Elgar, Plunket Greene, Henry J. Wood, J. Masefield etc. (By the way this is *private* because they do not know that *you* know they have signed). You see you have admirers in all sorts of unexpected quarters![2]

I sh^d like to come awfully – but I am in the middle of a great work[3] & unless I get stuck in it I don't want to leave it – especially as I *have* to go away for the week-end. I want to hear your criticisms on Wenlock awfully.

Yrs
RVW

[1] Lady (Alice) Gomme had co-operated with Sharp and VW in 1910 and 1911 on the 'May Day Revels' scene in the Coronation 'Pageant of London' organized at the Crystal Palace by Sir Lawrence Gomme in 1911.

[2] VW had been instrumental in obtaining a Civil List pension of £100 p.a. for Sharp in recognition of his work on folk song and dance. See Fox Strangways and Karpeles, *Cecil Sharp*, 85, where a portion of

this letter is printed unattributed to VW. VW's letter to Gilbert Murray seeking support for the proposal is no. 67.

[3] *A London Symphony.*

72. To Gilbert Murray

[early October 1911[1]]

13 Cheyne Walk
S.W.

Dear Professor Murray

It will be a great pleasure to me to call on you when I come to Oxford & talk about Greek play music.

May I say how much it has distressed me to hear those wonderful lines in Elektra and your other plays mauled about by (as it seems to me) quite the wrong kind of musical setting.

Whether I shall be any use in suggesting anything more suitable I do not know – but anyway it will be a great pleasure to me to hear your opinion on the subject.

I shall be in Oxford on November 16th & 17th – w[d] either of these days suit you?[2]

Yours very truly
R. Vaughan Williams

[1] Clearly this letter precedes the following one, which is firmly dated.

[2] On this correspondence see Wilson, *Gilbert Murray*, 169 ff.

73. To Gilbert Murray

12 October [1911]

13 Cheyne Walk
S.W.

Oct 12th

Dear Professor Murray

Thank you very much for your kind letter and for all the much too kind things you say in it. Of course there is nothing I should like better than to be associated in such a production as you foreshadow – however problematical it may be.

I have had several shots at some Electra music and have found the task much harder than I thought – I cannot make up my mind what *sort* of music w[d] be the best and naturally until I can do that the music itself refuses to come. However your letter has excited me so that I believe my imagination is beginning to work. I should much like to have a talk with M[r] Duncan[1] & am writing to him – I believe that if he has any very definite ideas it might set me moving.[2]

Yours very sincerely
R. Vaughan Williams

[1] Augustin Duncan, the actor.
[2] On VW's incidental music for *Electra*, *Bacchae*, and *Iphigenia in Tauris* see *CW* 1911/4.

74. To Gilbert Murray

6 November 1911

13 Cheyne Walk
S.W.

Nov. 6. 11

Dear Professor Murray

I am getting on slowly with some Greek Play music – I have done two Electra choruses & am finishing two Bacchae choruses and have notes for several more. I have had several interviews with the Duncans – but no one seems to know what is wanted exactly – I wish I did. The problem gets more insoluble the more I work on it. I tried setting them in the way I suggested to you – a sort of chant without any accompaniment – but it did not seem to work altogether – I have tried other parts in a more operatic method – the result is rather a mixture – the only way I think will be a sort of trial performance of some of the music when it is ready. I can't hope to satisfy you & Miss Duncan and Augustine (who wants the choruses spoken!).[1]

I want to ask you a lot about the Bacchae choruses – whether *all* the big choruses should be sung throughout – or whether part spoken [–] & what bits sh[d] be murmured & what parts declaimed.

Are you ever in London – c[d] we meet – if not c[d] I come & see you in Oxford one day[?]

Yours very truly
R. Vaughan Williams

[1] Isadora Duncan and her brother, Augustin. See Wilson, *Gilbert Murray*, 170, where part of this letter is quoted.

75. To Ernest Farrar

[31 December 1911[1]]

13 Cheyne Walk
S.W.

Dear Mr Farrar,

Please forgive my delay in answering your letter. I looked out a score to send you and found it required some revision – I will send it off tomorrow – on the whole I am sending you more than one in case you find anything you would care to put down on your programme viz

1) Two Impressions for small orchestra (These have cor anglais, but I have cued it in as you will see).[2]
2) Overture to Aristophanes 'Wasps'.
3) Fantasia on a theme by Tallis for *string orchestra*. (This, I think, is the best thing I have done).

It's awfully good of you to think of doing something of mine. I'm very glad to think of you getting conducting, it's the best kind of composition lesson, I think.[3]

I wish I could have heard your songs but hope to do so in London soon.

As to instrumental music – it's a very difficult problem finding a publisher. I think Novellos might be worth trying, or Schotts, or of the small people, Larway or Goodwin and Tabb.

Are you coming south at all? Look me up if you do so.

Yours very sincerely,
R. Vaughan Williams

P.S. Of course don't hesitate to say if my things aren't suitable.

[1] The letter is postmarked 12.15 am 1 January 1912 and must therefore have been written on 31 Dec. 1911.

[2] Possibly *CW* 1903/12, *Burley Heath* and *The Solent*, although the former work is incomplete in the surviving manuscript.

[3] Farrar was to conduct the annual concert of the South Shields Orchestral Union on 27 Mar. The advertised programme included 'Orchestral impression' by VW, perhaps *In the Fen Country*, *CW* 1904/4, or *Harnham Down*, *CW* 1904/6.

76. To Cecil Sharp [1911]

Dear Sharp

I can't get over my shame in not having acknowledged your present[1] – & when you have done me the great honour (*I mean this*) to put my name at the head of it my only reason is (its no excuse) that I thought I *had* done so – & I suppose my brain was in this sloppy condition because I was working up to 2, 3 & 4 in the morning trying to finish some work.

Its a fine book – I've always loved carols – I remember a time when, if I said 'carol' it could get no spark out of you – now, as usual you have gone ahead and left me in the lurch.[2]

A. Introduction – I'm glad you've said something about those 'village organist' carols because there is something remarkable and quite unlike anything else about them – a tune like 'Christians awake'* is a truly national thing – though it has nothing to do with folk-song.
B. I've always noticed what a peculiar atmosphere the *major* carol tunes have (e.g. II. Bitter withy III. Cherry Tree (1) VII Holly & Ivy XI Come all you worthy XII Sunny bank (1)) (sons of Levi also fine but a *different atmosphere*).
C. Other fine modal tunes are Little room (what splendid words), Truth sent from above, 12 Apostles, New Year's carol.
D. I especially like your accomps to Bitter Withy, Cherry Tree (1), Holly & Ivy, On Xmas night, Come all you worthy, Little room (I intend to crib the opening bar one day[3]).

It was a good meeting last night[4] & Whitings speech conclusively proves their unanimity – for if anything was calculated to put off the waverer it was that – the majors speech came like a draught of fresh air after it.[5]

I have a message from Mrs Leather[6] to say she is teaching her boys some of your carols.

Good luck

Yrs
RVW

P.S. I am sending you Butterworths songs
*The best specimen of that class

[1] *English Folk-carols* (London, 1911).

[2] Note added here by Maud Karpeles (?) on original: 'This is significant MK'.

[3] VW used some of the carols mentioned here in the *Fantasia on Christmas Carols*, *CW* 1912/6, first performed at Hereford in 1912. The work was dedicated to Sharp.

[4] Possibly of the Committee of the recently formed English Folk Dance Society.
[5] The nature of the meeting is not clear.
[6] Ella Mary Leather, with whom VW had collected folk songs in Herefordshire earlier in the year.

77. To E. J. Dent [March 1912]

Dear Dent

Many thanks for your letter – I wish I could come to hear the Marlowe Society – This is the busiest time of the year – I am off on Monday to the Isle of Man (if I ever get there!) to judge. I was awfully interested in the Spaniard's views – I wonder if he was one of the 30 or 40 people who were introduced to me after the concert[1] – They were all very nice and friendly and complimentary – there was a party after the concert in the shop of a music publisher called Mathot – champagne flowing like water.

Have you ever heard of a composer called Eric Satie – Ravel has, apparently discovered him – he was doing all the Debussy tricks in 1887 before D. was interested. – They are not much in themselves but are interesting as fore-runners.

V. D'Indy on Brahms is interesting – I sh[d] say just the same of D'Indy himself.

Yrs
R. Vaughan Williams

[1] Possibly the performance of *On Wenlock Edge* in Paris on 29 Feb. 1912; see *RVW*, 102–3.

78. To Lucy Broadwood postmark: 22 January 1913

Dear Miss Broadwood

I bought Moffatt and Kidson's book at your bidding[1] – I am afraid I am not very enthusiastic about it. There are some good tunes in it – but most of those I know already – the others, most of them, do not strike me much – but perhaps this is owing to the arrangements, which in most cases seem to me entirely inadequate (but more of this later). It seems to me that Moffatt has *no* feeling for the folk-dances – he is much better at the minuets and gavottes (except of course the *appalling* arrangement of a minuet '11th of September'). Also I don't think Kidson (if he made the selection) has an ear for a good tune. He probably thinks that every thing which appears in an old printed book is good.

It is a pity that he has so often chosen neither the earliest printed nor (this is more important) the finest version of a tune. e.g.

A la mode de France of which there is a much finer version in Playford in the minor (1650 edition).
Staines Morris[2] (see Playford 1650).
Ten Pound Lass (of which there is a slightly better version in Playford 1650). This version is apparently 'early 18th century'.
Amaryllis ('17th century') This may be an earlier version than Playford (1670) but is certainly not so good.
Goddesses (1650) see Playford's version same date.
Dull Sir John (see Playford 1650).

Of course I can only speak of the ones I happen to know from the reprints, which you of course know, in Sharp's 'Country Dances'[3] – but it makes one wonder about the whole collection.

I have just been reading your letter again as I see you speak of 'composed' originals which have been lately collected as folk-stuff. I have looked through carefully & have found none yet – with the possible exception of 'Princess Royal' (surely Kidson doesn't think that because he finds a tune printed in an old book it must have been 'composed' by someone and was not a (probably mutilated) transcript of a traditional tune!)

As regards P. Royal the statement about 'O' Carolan does not seem to me to go for much[4] – and by the way if the magnificent traditional version of this tune from Bampton (I think) & elsewhere are 'corruptions' then long live corruptions! (By the way is the tune in the 9th symphony a corruption of that in the choral Fantasia?[5])*

*Also it wd be impossible to dance any of the versions I know of the P.R. *dance* to this tune because it has not that splendid slow movement. (Is this a serious book on how to dance or is it only a collection of tunes – it seems neither one nor the other.)

Also it must be remembered

(1) that because a tune is printed in an old book it is no proof that it is not traditional
(2) collectors of folk-dances know well that they are occasionally danced to 'composed tunes' (see Sharp 'English Folk dance airs' introduction[6])

I am afraid any dancing enthusiast would be frightened off the book at the out set by those terrible ogling young women who are supposed to be dancing a country dance – & to any one who does not already know I shd be afraid to recommend the book in case they sh[d] think *that* had any thing to do with country dancing.

I see that K & M are not responsible for the photographs but Miss M Chaplin – she ought to be ashamed of herself! Still K & M might not have allowed them to go in – but perhaps they were under the thumb of a publisher.[7]

Kidson's preface is very nice as far as it goes – but I doubt if any one c[d] learn the dances from his description – he says nothing about the steps except that they may be learned from a dancing master – I wonder which!!

Indeed I am puzzled as to whether this book is meant seriously to instruct people in dancing or not (most of the best dances are not described only the tunes given) – if *not* it ought to be so stated.

And many of the tunes are *not easy* – Chelsea Reach e.g. w[d] be *impossible* to play at the pace it ought to go for the dance – & the cadence to the end of line 3 entirely spoils the tune from the dancing point of view – It is v. instructive to compare this setting with Sharp's delightful and very *danceable* setting in his newest book – Moffatt evidently has no feeling for these tunes & I w[d] say has never seen a country dance.

I must say I am amazed at your praising the accompaniments – anything *more* out of keeping, more banal and more helplessly amateurish (with a few exceptions) I don't think I have ever seen – I am sure if I had met the tunes I already know & love in these versions I sh[d] have passed them over.

Do you really admire Mad Robin with its start more or less in style & then that helpless tum-tum at bar 4 & the A & M[8] harmonies at 4th bar from the end (indeed there is hardly anything but the conventional polka accomp: in many of the settings) or the setting of the Staines Morris or the 'vamping' chorus in Del Caro's Hornpipe (see 3rd bar from end) or 'Buttered Pease' unspeakable! or 'Harly Bush fair'

And the score of easiness does not excuse them because easy & artistic accompaniments with *some* feeling for the character of the tune are to be found frequently nowadays.

I am afraid this is more to blame than praise – perhaps I was led to expect too much from your letter – to make up I will transcribe some of the notes I have scribbled by the side of the Tunes:

Fox & geese	fairly good
E.O.	fairly good
Hampstead Heath	fairly good
Bouree	good
Maids Morris	fairly good
Saraband	fairly good

Bright & airy	good tune bad setting
Canst thou not	good
Marionettes	fairly good
Kent Jig	good tune – but bad setting (impossible to dance to)
Cheshire Rounds	fairly good
Newmarket Downfall	good
Cockle Shells	good tune – setting *abominable*
Rigadon	good tune
The Maids	good

I think that 10 years ago as a pioneer book this might have been useful – But now that we have books like Sharps 'Country Dances' selected by a man with a real feeling for the fine tunes and a real musical sense (nearly always) & fitting character in the settings & above all a knowledge of the dances – a book like this seems rather useless.

Yrs very truly
R. Vaughan Williams

[1] *Dances of the Olden Time arranged for the Pianoforte by Alfred Moffat with an Essay on Old English Dancing... by Frank Kidson* (London, 1912).

[2] 'Stanes' Morris' in the book.

[3] Cecil Sharp, *Country Dance Tunes Collected and Arranged by C. J. Sharp*, sets 3 and 4 (London, 1911).

[4] The note reads: 'Although difficult to determine its exact origin it is highly probably that "The Princess Royal" was composed by Carolan, the Irish harper.'

[5] VW refers to the main theme of the last movement of Beethoven's Ninth Symphony, which had similarities to a theme in the Choral Fantasia, Op. 80.

[6] Preface to Sharp's *Folk-Dance Airs* (London, 1909).

[7] The photographs of which VW is complaining are of rather mannered dancers in various forms of 'quaint' costume and are described as having been 'prepared under the direction of Miss Nellie Chaplin, London'.

[8] i.e. *Hymns Ancient & Modern*.

79. To Cecil Sharp

[July 1913]

Gasthof Ampezzo
Toblach Tirol

Dear Sharp

I've had it on my mind some time to write to you on the general policy of the E.F.D.S.[1] – & this Paris business has made me think of it more – I don't know any of the ins and outs of it – & I quite imagine that the putting off of the 1st performance was quite unavoidable & was no ones fault – about that as I say I can say nothing as I know nothing – but it has brought home to me what I have felt for some time – that we are rather too prone to a policy of *hurry* & I can't help feeling that a more hum-drum method – though it might lose us a certain amount – w^d in the long run be the better for us – I feel so strongly that truth is great and will prevail – & that the 'hurry' policy – which I believe is largely due to the fear that the false will get in first is unnecessary – because even if people do see the wrong first it won't prevent those who are capable of it seeing the right *afterwards*.[2]

I've seen three instances of it

(1) The extra show we gave at the Kingsway theatre (which I believe you were against)
(2) The Paris performance – which anyhow would have been better for some more preparation.
(3) The question of dancing in the Parks – I had a talk with Helen Karpeles[3] the other night – she told me how M. Neal had been approached and was going to organize dancing – & seemed to think we ought to step in now inspite of having refused before – But I pointed out to her that we had decided in committee it was *not* a good thing to do – and if that was so it *still remained* not a good thing to do in spite of Mary Neal.[4]

I know the value of impetuosity as a driving force – but I feel that in this society we've got enough impetuosity to drive us any distance – what we want is a touch of the north-midland, lower-middle-class, unitarian, Wedgwood prudence which I imagine I was put on the c^{tee} to represent.

I wish I was going to see you all at Stratford this time – we shall be back in the beginning of August – and I might manage to run down for a night.[5]

Yrs
R.V.W.

P.S. I have no particular address for the next three weeks – but shall probably be at Cortina in rather less than a week

address Poste Restante
Cortina d'Ampezzo
Tirol
Austria

P.P.S. I never thanked you for, I believe, recommending me to Barker[6] – to write music for the Millionaire in Park Lane – I liked Barker v. much – & it gave me a lot of good experience – also helped to pay for all this![7]

[1] The English Folk Dance Society, founded in 1911.

[2] The Society had arranged a series of demonstrations of English folk dances in Paris on 13 and 14 June 1913.

[3] Sister of Maud Karpeles, first Secretary of the EFDS and wife of Douglas Kennedy, Sharp's successor as director.

[4] Mary Neal, founder of the Espérance Society, which laid less emphasis than Sharp's EFDS on authenticity of performance and purity of tradition in folk dance. She had advocated the teaching of Morris dancing en masse to crowds in the London parks.

[5] From 1911 onwards an August 'vacation school' of folk dances and song was held annually at Stratford-upon-Avon under the supervision of Cecil Sharp and the EFDS, which coincided with an annual season of drama mounted by Frank Benson's company in the Shakespeare Memorial Theatre there. VW was Benson's musical director for the August season in 1912, as he was for the (purely theatrical) season of April–May 1913. See *RVW*, 150–1.

[6] Harley Granville-Barker (1877–1946), the playwright and theatrical producer.

[7] The 'millionaire in Park Lane' was Philip Sassoon, who mounted a private performance in 1913 of Maeterlinck's *Death of Tintagiles*, produced by Granville-Barker with incidental music by VW (*CW* 1913/6). See *RVW*, 108. Barker and Sharp were both members of the Fabian Society and had been in correspondence about Barker's 1912 production of *A Winter's Tale*.

80. To Ralph Wedgwood

postmark: 1 August 1913

Dear Randolph

I will meet you at 6.0 p.m. at Waterford on September 3rd – I shd have liked to have seen the Wicklow Mtains where the Neo-Kelts come from—but I dare say Munster (is it?) will be v. good – How about making for the coast of 'Connacht' which is also very neo-Kelt. I like walking v. much – but will bring my bicycle – only I'm afraid my old machine won't go quick enough for you – only I'm afraid my legs won't either so its much of a much-ness. Will the mountains require naily boots (I have some!)[1]

And shall I bring my rück-sack?

Yrs
R.V.W.

[1] This trip to Ireland with Ralph Wedgwood is not recorded in *RVW*. His reference to the gentleman from Killaloe in no. 83 implies that they did indeed strike over towards the west coast.

81. To Arnold Barter

December 1913

Hotel-Suisse
Ospedalette-Ligure

Dec. 1913[1]

Dear Mr Barter

I cannot thank you enough for your long and interesting letter – it only makes me long all the more to have been there[2] – and to wish that the work was 1000 times better than it is – I know so well now the weak places – & the places where I didn't do what I wanted to – & the places where I did not follow my real impulses – but some silly considerations came in the way (I imagine that all composers suffer from this) – I wish I c^{d} do it all over again now!

You say that you know me through my work – & I really believe you *do* – for you told me all the things I wanted to hear – especially about the two factory-girls.

Thank you once again – I do hope we shall have an opportunity of meeting in the flesh one of these days.

Please send me your annual report when it comes out, as you have kindly done before.

Yrs sincerely
R. Vaughan Williams

P.S. I thoroughly agree with you about those *dreadful* string parts – I am quoting what you say to B&H.[3]

[1] Date noted in the hand of the recipient. The letter seems to have been written after that to Barter of 19 Dec. Perhaps written about 30 Dec.

[2] i.e. at their performance of *A Sea Symphony* which VW very much regretted not having been able to attend.

[3] Breitkopf & Härtel.

82. To Athelstan Riley[1]

11 February 1914

Hotel Suisse
Ospedaletti Ligure
Riviera
Italy

February 11 1914

Dear Riley

I return your articles which interested me very much.

I've only two remarks to make & they'd not practically affect your writings at all.

i) With regard to 'Northrop' it is much too grand for the appendix – how it got there in the early stages of the book when we had a rule only to put one tune (i.e. *our choice*) with the text – and all second strings with the appendix – afterwards we broke the rule – & dreadful things like 'St Gertrude' got into the text.[2]

ii) It is not true of *quite* modern music that it is bounded by the tune in 2 minor modes – indeed the most characteristic harmony is an extension of the truly modally conceived harmony. The so-called 'modal' harmony of the Palestrina school is not truly modal at all – its character and beauty depend largely from the fact there is a half-way house between modal & major-minor. But taking 'modern' to mean between Beethoven–Schubert & Wagner you are quite correct.

Yours sincerely
R. Vaughan Williams

[1] Riley had been a member of the editorial committee of *The English Hymnal*. Transcript kindly provided by Stephen Connock.

[2] 'Northrop' was included in *The English Hymnal* (Appendix, no. 8) as an alternative tune to Hymn 30, 'While shepherds watched their flocks by night'. VW retained a strong affection for the tune; see no. 705. 'St Gertrude' is of course Arthur Sullivan's tune for 'Onward Christian soldiers', which had been reluctantly included in the main body of the hymn-book as an alternative tune for the hymn.

83. To Ralph Wedgwood

postmark: 14 February 1914

Hotel Suisse
Ospedaletti Ligure
Riviera
Italy

Dear Randolph

How good of the gentleman of Killaloe to send me Lecky – It will make me all the more prepared to volunteer (if they'll have me) on the side of law and order when the fight comes.[1]

We are here for our healths – & my brother-in-law[2] fell ill the first fortnight & is so still & Adeline is not much the better for it – I am very well – but then I was never ill – And the opera is nearly finished[3] – I come back in March – but I hope they will stop on.

I heard of you in Switzerland – good fellow that you are – among the nobs. This is a very jolly place – with fine walks up in the mountains – I bathed when we first came and shall probably bath[e] again soon – So I've sampled 3 seas in 1913 – Adriatic, Atlantic & Mediterranean.

Tomorrow I go a motor drive in to the mountains with some of my smart friends – ahem – Give my love to Iris & all[4]

Yrs
RVW

R L Wedgwood Esq
Stonefall Hall
Harrogate
Yorks
Inghilterra

[1] VW seems to have been contemplating serving in Ireland in some capacity. The book sent may have been W. E. H. Lecky's *A History of Ireland in the Eighteenth Century*, which had appeared in a new edition in 1892 in five volumes. A trip to Munster and Connaught had been planned for September the previous year (see no. 80). Or possibly there is no Irish connection and this refers to the oncoming Great War.

[2] Hervey Fisher.

[3] *Hugh the Drover*, *CW* 1924/2. Writing to Percy Scholes in 1921 he said that the 'Vocal score was completed 1914 (May)' (see no. 132).

[4] Printed in part in *WVW*, 401.

84. From George Butterworth[1]

28 March 1914

43 Colville Gardens
Bayswater W.

March 28 1914

My dear Ralph

Among all the debauch of last night's congratulations and mutual pattings on the back, I really had nothing much to add, but should now like to tell you how frightfully glad I am that you have at last achieved something worthy of your gifts (I refer to the work & its performance jointly, for after all a work cannot be a fine one until it is finely played – and it is still possible that the Sea Symphony & the Mystical Songs may turn out equally well – but at present they are not in the same class).[2]

I really advise you not to alter a note of the Symph: until after its second performance (which is bound to come soon) – the passages I kicked at didn't bother me at all, because the music as a whole is so definite that a little occasional meandering is pleasant rather than otherwise. As to the scoring, I frankly don't understand how it all comes off so well, but it does all sound right, so there's nothing more to be said.

One practical result is that you have turned the Ellis concerts from a doubtful into a certain success and I hope he will announce another series *soon*, & perhaps start a guarantee fund.[3]

Meanwhile here's to Symph no 2![4]

Yours
George B.

[1] This letter is one of a group passed from Butterworth's stepmother to her grandson A. J. Croft, whose widow, Margaret Croft, presented them to the Bodleian Library. A. J. Croft was administrator of the Butterworth Trust, of which VW was a Trustee.

[2] *A London Symphony* had received its first performance the night before.

[3] His own Idyll, *The Banks of Green Willow*, had been given at an earlier concert on 20 March.

[4] This letter was partially quoted by VW in his memoir about Butterworth included in a memorial volume privately printed by his father in 1918.

85. To E. J. Dent

[about 1 April 1914]

Leith Hill Place,
Nr Dorking.
13 Cheyne Walk
S.W.

Dear Dent

I don't know which of the two alternatives I hope is the true one. Because (A) I admire your judgement extremely but (B) I value your friendship even more – so if the two are in conflict I should not know which to choose – but let us hope that you are right & the two are compatible – & that I may trust and be grateful for the judgement which approves of the symphony[1] & the friendship which has led you to write and tell me so. I am very glad you like it – I feel myself that I am perhaps beginning to emerge from the fogs at last.

I am glad you admire George's stuff[2] – I believe he is going to be very great man – if indeed he is not so already.

Now I have something on my conscience – about two years ago you wrote to me about a young & struggling musician whom you asked me to invite to see me – at the time I was going away & c[d] do nothing – then I lost his name & address (Brixton I think) & have done nothing since – I feel thoroughly ashamed – can I do anything now?

Yrs
R. Vaughan Williams

[1] *A London Symphony*, which had received its first performance on 27 March. See *CW* 1913/5.

[2] George Butterworth.

2

From the Beginning of the First World War until the Move to Dorking: 1914–1929

IN 1914 VW felt himself emerging 'from the fogs' in terms of his development as a composer, but other fogs, of war, were gathering around his world even as he was writing that to Dent. These would profoundly affect his own path forward as well as doing much to destroy the world in which he had grown up. He himself does not seem to have questioned the reasons for going to war but rather like his contemporaries, especially the younger ones, he wanted 'to do his bit' despite being 41 years old when war was declared and thus above military age. A further measure of VW's resolve to contribute physically to the war was how much he ignored the promptings of friends such as his teacher Hubert Parry, and went against his personal determination to devote himself to writing music, which war service would make impossible. His first step at the outbreak of war was to join the Special Constabulary of the Metropolitan Police Service operating in the locality of his house at Cheyne Walk; but this did not provide the challenge he was looking for and by the end of the year he had enlisted as a Wagon Orderly with the Royal Army Medical Corps.

There were some musical loose ends to be tied up, especially regarding *A London Symphony*, which had received its first performance in March. The full score had been sent to Germany in July (either to Fritz Busch to consider for performance or to Breitkopf & Härtel to consider for publication, since that firm had already published *Willow Wood*, *Toward the Unknown Region*, and *A Sea Symphony*) and was probably irrecoverable. However the orchestral material was to hand, so George Butterworth, who had written so encouragingly about the symphony after its first performance, organized a small group of friends (including Edward Dent and Denis Browne, a fellow pupil of Charles Wood and Alan Gray) to assist VW in reconstructing the full score from the parts. The letters to Dent provide a record of his part in this act of solidarity, which VW later acknowledged by not only reading and commenting on Dent's book on Mozart operas but also by doing his best to help obtain the Cambridge chair of music for him when it became vacant in 1924 following the death of Sir Charles Stanford.

It is through letters written to Holst and other friends that we have glimpses of VW's wartime experiences, but only glimpses. We get an idea of his frustration at the time spent being trained—he was not sent abroad until June 1916, eighteen months after enlisting. As he wrote to Dent, 'I expect you are doing more for your King and Country than I am – indeed you can't be doing less'. However, we do learn that VW engendered music wherever he found himself, for example by forming a choir amongst his fellow soldiers. He was aided and abetted by his comrade-in-arms Harry Steggles, who would later contribute a valuable account of serving alongside VW to the 1959 commemorative issue of the *RCM Magazine*. After service in France and then in Salonika VW returned to England in August 1917 to train for a commission in the Royal Garrison Artillery. He passed out in November and was sent to France in March 1918, after courses at Lydd and at Bordon, to be stationed near Rouen. After the armistice his unit set out for Germany and eventually VW was attached to the Headquarters of the First Army at Valenciennes as Director of Music, the first formal acknowledgement by the Army of his abilities as a musician. Demobilization followed in February.

As an ambulance driver, VW had seen the full horror of the Western Front and it is not in the least surprising that he had not been able to do any composing during the war; even if he had had the time or the privacy that he needed to do it the exigencies of the moment would always have been too pressing to allow it. For example, in 1917 he firmly told the Carnegie Trust, which had agreed to publish *A London Symphony* in the Carnegie Collection of British Music, that it must not be printed without thorough revision by him and this would have to wait until after the War. Similarly, the opera he had completed in vocal score in 1914, *Hugh the Drover*, had to remain on ice until he picked it up afterwards to 'polish its face'. The only major work which appears to have been slowly emerging from his experiences during the war was *The Pastoral Symphony*, as we learn from a letter to Ursula Wood written much later, in 1938. It was therefore a challenge to pick up his pen again after four years' absence and to find his place in a musical world which no longer contained such great friends as George Butterworth. The letters he sent Butterworth's father, Sir Alexander Kaye-Butterworth, after George's death demonstrate his sense of loss as well as the closeness of their friendship—Butterworth was as important to him as Ralph Wedgwood or Gustav Holst, and, as with Holst, VW remained fiercely loyal to his memory for the rest of his life. We do not have the body of letters to record their friendship that we do for others, but an indication is the fact that, until his marriage to

Ursula in 1953 made new arrangements necessary, VW planned to leave all his copyrights and royalties to the Butterworth Trust, of which he was a long-time Trustee. Having changed his will, he and Ursula, having the example of the Butterworth Trust before them, set up the R.V.W. Trust instead, which continues to provide support for young composers to the present day.

The first thing VW needed after his return in February 1919 was some peace and quiet (he was demobilized and ceased to draw pay at this point, but appears to have remained in the Reserve, at least until his application for promotion to Lieutenant in October 1920 was turned down on grounds of his age and general untidiness). He was now 46 years old and was probably content that Adeline had taken furnished rooms on the Norfolk coast in order to care for her invalid brother Hervey. From mid-1919 until Hervey's death in May 1921, VW's letters are often written from a series of houses with nautical names in Sheringham, and this sojourn surely provided the respite he needed to pick up the threads of composition again. There was the revision of *A London Symphony* for publication, the preparation of the full score of *Hugh the Drover* from the vocal score completed in 1914, the final revision of *The Lark Ascending*, also written in 1914 (destined to become one of his most popular works), and, most important, the development of his ideas for the new symphony, of which he completed the score in June 1921. VW had gone off to war as a young 42-year-old considered an up-and-coming bright light amongst English composers with two symphonies behind him. He returned from the war aged 46, having crossed the threshold into middle age and become transformed by time and survival into something of a senior statesman in a much altered musical world. He was asked to become a professor at the RCM by its new Director, his old friend Hugh Allen; he was invited in late 1919 to become Conductor of the Handel Society Choir and then, in 1921, of the Bach Choir; his opinion was sought by the Carnegie Trust on music submitted for possible publication by composers of the younger generation. When Arthur Fox Strangways, the music critic, founded and edited the new journal *Music & Letters* in 1920, the first issue contained as a frontispiece a portrait of Elgar by William Rothenstein, while the second had a portrait of VW by the same artist, thereby demonstrating the critic's view of the hierarchy in British music at the time.

A further sign of VW's post-war eminence, now reinforced by the successful first performance of the *Pastoral Symphony* in January 1922, was an invitation from the American philanthropist Carl Stoeckel to conduct the first American performance of the symphony with the New York Symphony Orchestra at the music festival he had founded at Norfolk, Connecticut. We may surmise from his letters home that this visit was the first time, and possibly the last, that VW and Adeline felt under an obligation to endure a surfeit of well-meant hospitality, albeit mitigated by the excitement of new sights and experiences.

After their return, we can see VW absorbed in his work with the London Bach Choir and in particular with his first encounter as a conductor with Bach's St Matthew Passion, a work which meant more to him than perhaps any other and to which he brought so much of his own emotion as to inspire his audiences both in London and in later years at Dorking. However, it was in this context that the composer ran for the first time into the quagmire of authentic Baroque performance practice, which was already becoming a matter of argument and crusade. He remained convinced for the rest of his life that the niceties of Baroque practice should be subsidiary to the overall emotive effect of great works, such as the Bach Passions, and that the effect of a harpsichord, for example, was too puny in the context of a large-scale choir in the Queen's Hall. With newer music, though, he was able to provide support to colleagues he admired: he programmed a new work of Gustav Holst, *Ode to Death*, to be performed twice in the same concert.

VW's immersion in choral music at this time, both at the Leith Hill Musical Festival (in which his sister, Margaret, was deeply involved and of which he was the conductor from its foundation in 1904 until after his eightieth birthday in 1953), and with the Bach Choir in London, determined the main thrust of the works which were now appearing regularly: the haunting Mass in G minor, his one-act 'pastoral episode' *The Shepherds of the Delectable Mountains*, his operas *Hugh the Drover* and *Sir John in Love*, and his oratorio *Sancta Civitas* (which became his favourite amongst his choral works). All were vocal, whether involving soloists or chorus or both. Even some primarily instrumental works, such as the *Pastoral Symphony* and *Flos Campi*, had parts for voices singing wordlessly. If one also remembers that at this time he was also continuing the work begun with *The English Hymnal* in 1905, with his collaboration with Martin Shaw on *Songs of Praise* published in 1925 and the *Oxford Book of Carols*, published in 1930, we can form a picture of VW as a composer who has learnt that he can most effectively engage with his audience through the medium of the human voice.

We find him concerned about the community in a political sense—he was torn in two directions by the General Strike of 1926 and uncertain how he should react, if at all. VW certainly had socialist tendencies, which led him firmly to join the army in the ranks and usually to vote against the conservative governments in elections. He was never at all extreme in his politics, but there is already a sense that he was sufficiently sure of himself to take a line on what he felt was right, regardless of what others might think. This was evident in his determination to serve in the First World War.

He also felt that he owed it to the musical community to take his duties as a Professor of Composition at the RCM seriously for the sake of the younger generation. He took great trouble with his pupils, and went to great lengths to support them, when he was not certain himself as to what their next move should be, by consulting others, such as Edward Dent. Long after they had moved on he would continue to do his best to obtain performances for them. In this period we encounter two of his pupils, who preserved his letters assiduously: the Irishwoman Ina Boyle and especially Elizabeth Maconchy, who remained a close friend for the rest of his life. Two other regular correspondents make an appearance at this time: Gerald Finzi was not his pupil but an admirer who was having lessons with R. O. Morris, VW's brother-in-law. He would regularly ask VW to look at his compositions and the two formed a close and mutually beneficial bond which lasted until Finzi's death thirty years later. Diana Awdry became an honorary 'niece' (VW enjoyed being an 'uncle' figure to young ladies he found attractive) and having been an enthusiastic visitor to the Leith Hill Musical Festival she sought VW's help in launching a similar event at Stinchcombe in Gloucestershire, her own stamping ground. Over the years she continually sought VW's advice about competition music and, like Finzi, carefully kept all the letters VW sent her.

In the background Adeline wrote many of VW's business letters for him, since her handwriting was very much more legible than his, and took a keen and critical interest in all his doings. At the same time she continued to provide a focal point for her brothers and sisters, especially for her sister Cordelia, to whom she wrote in an idiosyncratic but affectionate shorthand most days. However, she had long suffered from arthritis and, despite trying many possible remedies, she had decided to accept it as a cross to be borne. A fall in 1927, which left her in a plaster cast for a long period, brought home the fact that 13 Cheyne Walk with its stairs was not ideal and so they went scouting the land for a suitable house which would be easier for Adeline but still reasonably accessible to London. In 1928 we find letters being written from a variety of houses in and around Dorking, which was near VW's old home, Leith Hill Place, and the centre of the Leith Hill Musical Festival. They eventually found a bungalow to rent called 'Chote Ghar' and moved in in October 1929, having changed the name to the altogether less imperial 'The White Gates'. They had spent twenty-four years at 13 Cheyne Walk and would spend twenty-two years together in their new house.

VW was now 57 years old and established as the leader of British music second only to Elgar, who had long since almost ceased to compose. Indeed it is known that VW was considered for the post of Master of the King's Musick when the vacancy had last arisen in 1924, since he was thought 'to be the most representative of British music', but, wisely, the post was offered to Elgar (if it had been offered to VW, he would almost certainly have turned it down since he was never comfortable with obligations, except those to people who mattered to him). In another respect too he had become settled: his music down to 1925 had been published by a variety of publishers, notably Breitkopf & Härtel, Stainer & Bell, Boosey & Co, and J. Curwen & Sons. In that year he happened to approach the newly formed music department of the Oxford University Press (the publisher with which he had worked on *The English Hymnal*) to see if they would be interested in publishing *The Shepherds of the Delectable Mountains*. The work was accepted, and so began a relationship that would last until the end of the composer's life. It was never enshrined in any contract but was based on a 'gentleman's' understanding that VW would offer any new work to OUP before offering it to anyone else. As we have seen, VW loathed promoting himself or his music; this arrangement with OUP meant he would no longer have to do so.

86. To Edward Dent

[September 1914]

13 Cheyne Walk
S.W.

Dear Dent

I am so much touched by your offer – but I really don't know if I should accept – why sh[d] you spoil your holiday – I do feel inclined to accept in fact – if the performance for the beginning of November in Edinburgh is not put off.[1]

Would you do a bit of it? The difficulty is there is only one set of wind parts. Would you, say, copy in the string parts of the slow movement – I c[d] send you a set of string parts & plenty of music paper & a very complete small score by Toye[2] which w[d] guide you as to how to space it out.

If you really do offer to do this you would be doing a great service not only to me but to a young musician called Coles who was to have copied the score – He wanted to enlist (home service) & being married didn't know if he could so Von Holst & I have arranged to keep his job warm & I have advanced him the money he w[d] have made over my score – he to take it out in other copying later – less any of the score which you did. I should, with your leave, consider written off his debt to me.[3]

But really ought you to do it? I can't express how much I feel your even offering to do it.

Yrs
R. Vaughan Williams

[1] This refers to the collaborative reconstruction of the full score of *A London Symphony*, *CW* 1913/5, from the orchestral parts by VW aided by a group of friends (Edward Dent, Denis Browne, and George Butterworth). The original score had been sent to Germany either to Fritz Busch to consider for performance (as VW told MK) or to Breitkopf & Härtel to consider for publication, since they had already published *Willow Wood*, *Toward the Unknown Region*, and *A Sea Symphony* (as VW told UVW), and was now considered irretrievable. See *RVW*, 113–14 and *CW*, p. 68. VW eventually gave the reconstructed manuscript to Adrian Boult, who was much involved in the later development of the symphony, and he eventually presented it to the British Museum Library (now the British Library). The performance in Edinburgh which created the need for a new full score was given by the Scottish Orchestra conducted by the composer in the Usher Hall on 30 Nov. 1914. The performance is not noted in Lloyd, 'A London Symphony: Early Versions'.

[2] Geoffrey Toye (1889–1942), who had conducted the first performance of *A London Symphony* on 27 Mar. 1914 at the Queen's Hall.

[3] Cecil Coles (1888–1918), a young Scottish composer and friend of Gustav Holst, was killed while serving with the Queen's Victoria Rifles in 1918.

87. To E. J. Dent

[about 1 October 1914[1]]

13 Cheyne Walk,
Chelsea, S.W.

Dear Dent

With many misgivings as to whether I ought to send the string parts of slow movement of my symph – with (I think) enough music paper & the short score. If you want more music paper send me a card.

The score consists of

Fl: I & II	Trumpet I.II.	Cellos (divisi)
Fl. III	Trombone I & II	C. Bass
Ob I.II	Trombone III & Tuba	
Cor ang:	Timpani	
Clar I & II	G.C. & piatti	
Bass clar	Jingles[2]	
Fag I & II	1 Harp part (2 players)	
Contra fag	v. I	
Cor I.II	v. II	
Cor III.IV	violas (divisi)	

I saw Denis Browne[3] yesterday & he thought I might be some possible use to you looking through your book – of course if I could do anything in that way I should be proud.[4]

Yrs
RVW

[1] After no. 86.

[2] i.e. triangles, which imitate the jingle of a cab in the second movement.

[3] Composer, conductor, and organist at Guy's Hospital, killed at Gallipoli in 1915 (see *RVW*, 112, 421). He had taken part in the *Wasps* in 1909—see also no. 90.

[4] *Mozart's Operas: A Critical Study*, which had been published the year before. Dent took up VW's offer to read and comment on it. See no. 91 below.

88. To Herbert Howells

postmark: 9 October 1914

13 Cheyne Walk
Chelsea, S.W.

Dear Mr Howells

I shall be delighted to make your acquaintance – & will write to you again as soon as ever I can see my way to some free time.

Yours sincerely
R. Vaughan Williams

89. To E. J. Dent

[c.10 October 1914]

13 Cheyne Walk
Chelsea, S.W.

Dear Dent

Very many thanks for the score – my last letter was sent off before your parcel arrived – the score is really beautiful – it seems a shame to be adding percussion in another handwriting.

The wind parts will be at liberty in a day or two & I will send them along as [soon] as I can with the score – we can [do] this work simultaneously.

Yrs
R.V.W.

90. To E. J. Dent

[c.12 October 1914]

13 Cheyne Walk,
Chelsea, S.W.

Dear Dent

I won't attempt to thank you any more – but am sending you the short score of no IV & some more music paper. I think that that is best to do – as there is only 1 set of wind parts from which my wife & I & occasionally Denis Browne are copying I & II – then later on we can put in the string parts of I & II & release the wind parts for you to put in as much as you like of.

The score of no IV is
Fl. I II
___ III
Ob: I II
Cor angl
Cl. I & II
B. Clar
Fag I II
C. Fag
Horns I & II
___ III & IV
Trumpets I & II
Cornets I & II
Trombones I & II
Trombone III & Tuba
Timpani

Δ[le] & S. Drum[1]
G.C. & Ptti
Tam Tam
Harp
Strings

Yrs
R. Vaughan Williams

[1] i.e triangle and side drum.

91. To E. J. Dent

[November 1914]

13 Cheyne Walk
S.W.

Dear Dent

I've now finished your book[1] – & I do congratulate you on it most heartily. I now want you to write a book called 'Further discussion of the things I hadn't time to say in my Mozart book' & sh[d] consist of

(1) a further discussion of the language of music with regard to nationality – whether in the musical language there are varieties of dialect – the English, the German, the French etc
(2) With regard to folk-song & the composer – an elaboration of what you say about it *not yet* being our national language – whether in the course of years it may become so & whether[2] if it does whether any good will accrue – At present your paragraph leads me to suppose that you do *not* believe in the F.S.[3] as a good influence but

  (a) perhaps you don't mean this
  (b) if you do it may quite possibly be the truth any way a book from you on the subject w[d] be most valuable.

(3) elaborate p. 411 starting 'It is indeed this very remoteness' – that seems to me the basis of all technical instruction & I always urge my few pupils to found their technique *entirely* on Palestrina, Bach, Mozart & then build up for *themselves*.

Thank you again.

Yrs
R.V.W.

[1] *Mozart's Operas: A Critical Study* (1913).
[2] 'whether' is repeated in original.
[3] i.e. folk song

92. Notice as Sergeant in the Special Constabulary[1]

24 November [1914]

13 Cheyne Walk
S.W.

Nov 24th

(1) The South Fulham Constitutional Club 163 New King's Road has offered the use of its rifle range free except for the price of ammunition to members of our Company Showing their Warrant Cards every evening from 7.30 to 10.30 pm.
It is hoped members will avail themselves of this as it is proposed to arrange shooting competitions between the various companies.
(2) Arrangements have been made to take a photograph of the Chelsea Company on Sunday Dec: 6th at 12 noon.
It is hoped that all members will attend on that date at the Station Yard of the Chelsea Police Station.
(3) Cars carrying bright head-lights are not to be stopped but their N° is to be reported to the Superintendent.
(4) Any Constable making a report in the Post Note book must see that a copy of that report reaches the Sergeant or a Sub Inspector before 10 am the next morning.
(5) If you were on duty at the Opening of Parliament will you kindly let me know.

R. Vaughan Williams
Sergt.

[1] VW joined the Special Constabulary at the outbreak of War on 29 July 1914 and had become a Sergeant by 29 August. By the end of the year he had joined the R.A.M.C. See *RVW*, 115, 116. This letter was sold at Sotheby's on 21 Nov. 1990, lot 387.

93. From Hubert Parry

19 January 1915

Royal College of Music
Prince Consort Road,
South Kensington,
London, S.W.

Jany 19. 1915

My dear old V.W.

I am not altogether surprised, but I am thoroughly bothered. It's a most awkward situation! I have written to Major Darwin and hope to see him tomorrow & discuss this matter further.[1]

As to your enlisting, I can't express myself in any way that is likely to be serviceable. There are certain individuals who are capable of serving their country in certain exceptional and very valuable ways, and they are not on the same footing as ordinary folks who if they are exterminated are just one individual gone and no more. You have already served your country in very notable and exceptional ways and are likely to do so again; and such folks should be shielded from risk rather than exposed to it.

We may admit the generosity of the impulse, and feel – I will not say what.

Yours affectionately
C. Hubert H. Parry[2]

[1] The nature of the matter to which Parry refers is uncertain. Major Darwin is referred to again by Parry in no. 102 below, where he calls him 'your dear old Uncle'. As VW's mother had no brothers he may have been an uncle of hers and thus a brother of Caroline Darwin.

[2] The greater part of this letter is printed in *RVW*, 117.

94. To E. J. Dent

postmark: 24 May 1915

B.W.T.A. Soldiers' Recreation Rooms,
Friends' Meeting House,
Saffron Walden,
Essex.

From 2033 P^te R.V. Williams
2/4th London Field Ambulance

Dear Dent

I shall be delighted to do what I can for Peter[1] – I know *no* one of importance in America but I am writing him a testimonial – on this paper!

Don't you think it would amuse you to come over on your bicycle to see me one day. I'm usually done by 4.0 – & its only 14 miles – I *can't* come & see you because its out of bounds! I billet at 29 Bridge Street about the 3rd cottage on the right as you enter the town from Cambridge.

I expect you are doing much more for your King & Country than I am – indeed you can't be doing less.

Yrs
R.V.W.

P.S. Cecil Forsyth[2] is in America – wd it be worth your while to write to him – I will try & get his address if you think it is a good plan.[3]

[1] Dent had presumably asked VW to provide an introduction in America for a pupil or friend clearly known to VW.

[2] Cecil Forsyth (1870–1941), author of *Orchestration* (London and New York, 1914). He worked for the music publisher H. W. Gray in New York which represented Novello's in America until 1937. See *New Grove*.

[3] The PS is written on the envelope.

95. To Constance Machray 5 April [1916]

April 5th

Dear Connie

I add a word to Harrys to thank you very much for Easter remembrances and to give mine in return to you & all of you especially your mother who was always so kind to me at Bps Stortford.[1] I hope Nellie gets on with her music – I shd like to hear – just to remind you of Harry & the old times I will quote you this

Yrs
R. Vaughan Williams

[1] VW and Harry Steggles were billetted with the Machray family in Bishops Stortford from May 1915 until early 1916, when they were moved to Sutton Veny in Wiltshire. See *RVW*, 119–20. There was much music-making in the Machray household, not all of it serious, as is clear from the musical quotation.

[2] The tune has not so far been identified.

96. To Gustav Holst[1]

[June 1916]

Sutton Veney

Dear V.

We are on the eve – all packed & ready – I can't say more – write to me occasionally, my wife will give you the address.[2]

Your letter about Thaxted was splendid[3] – I sometimes feel that the future of musical England rests with you – because every Paulina[4] who goes out, & for the matter of that every Morleyite will infect 10 others & they in their turn will infect 10 others – I will leave you to make the necessary calculation.

Good luck to you – I feel that perhaps after the war England will be a *better* place for music than before – largely because we shan't be able to buy expensive performers etc. like we did. I wish I c[d] have been there – perhaps next Whits: – who knows?

I read your letter over & over again, it was so inspiriting – we don't take music as part of our every day life half enough – I often wish we could all migrate to some small town where there could really be a musical community – London is impossible from that point of view.

Goodbye & good luck

Yrs
RVW

[1] Printed as Letter XVIII in *HR*.

[2] His unit embarked for France on 22 June; see *RVW*, 120.

[3] See Short, *Holst*, 138. From this year it became usual for a group of Holst's pupils at Morley College and St Paul's to come to Thaxted, where the Holsts had a cottage, for a weekend of music, formal and informal, over Whitsuntide, which this year was on 10–12 June. For a full account see ibid. 138–9.

[4] i.e. ex-pupil of St Paul's Girls' School, where Holst was Director of Music.

97. To Gustav Holst[1]

[late June 1916]

Dear V.

I should v. much like to have news of you – I wish I c[d] write you an interesting letter – but one is hardly allowed to say anything. However I am very well & enjoy my work – all parades & such things cease. I am 'Wagon orderly' and go up the line every night to bring back wounded & sick on a motor ambulance – this all takes place at night – except an occasional day journey for urgent cases.

Write & let me know all the news – I hear from my wife that all Thaxted is still singing Bach.[2]

Did you see that Rutland Boughton applied for exemption on the grounds that he was doing work of national importance at Glastonbury![3]

I suppose I shall make you very angry with what I am about to say and I can't put it just as I mean – but I feel strongly that what you are doing at Thaxted is the *real* thing of which Boughton's vapourings at Glastonbury are the sham imitation – you know the slosh that Buckley talked in his book about an 'artistic community' – well like all rotten ideas it is the sham of something real – and this is what I believe you've got – amen.

Yrs
RVW

[1] Partially printed, omitting references to Boughton, in *RVW*, 120–1. Not included in *HR*.

[2] The Whitsuntide weekend had included a performance of Bach's Mass in A.

[3] Boughton, with Reginald Buckley and Christine Walshe, had founded the Glastonbury Festival in 1914 with the idea of creating a commune of artists around the performance of 'choral drama' written by him. The best-known was *The Immortal Hour*. The Festival lasted until 1927, but Boughton did not escape military service.

98. To Alexander Kaye-Butterworth — 16 August [1916]

Aug 16th

Dear Sir Kaye Butterworth[1]

I hope you will not mind my writing to you about George – you know how my wife and I loved and admired him – but I feel it would be impertinent of me to write to you more about this.[2]

But I feel I may write to you about his music – at first one can only think of all the possibilities locked up in him and of the great things one knew he had it in him to express. I think I know of no composer whose music expressed his character more exactly – all the strength and purpose in him – the determination to be and to say exactly what he meant and no other.

One cannot believe that all these possibilities which were in him are wasted. At all events there is all the beautiful music he has already written – that remains with us as something imperishable. But even that still bigger music which was still unfulfilled in him one cannot believe is lost – it *must* have its influence on the world somehow – from the very fact that it existed locked up in his mind.

Yours sincerely
R. Vaughan Williams

[1] VW seems to be confused as to how to address his old friend's father, but got it right in the following letter.

[2] George Butterworth [George Sainton Kaye-Butterworth] had been killed in action on 4 Aug. This letter is preserved in an album of papers concerning the death of his son compiled by Sir Alexander Kaye-Butterworth, now in the Bodleian Library.

99. To Alexander Kaye-Butterworth

[4?] September [1916]

Monday Sept

Dear Sir Alexander

Thank you very much for your kind letter – I felt quite overwhelmed that George should have left what amounts to nearly all his compositions to me – I feel it a great responsibility but one that I would not be without for anything.

As regards publication – one would like to publish the whole of that all too small list as a permanent memorial to him – but this is probably impracticable – If a selection is to be made I should suggest the 'Shropshire Lad' Rapsody [*sic*] the 'Banks of Green Willow' and the beautiful Henley songs.

The music would all need to be carefully revised and edited (not of course with a view to any alteration but to correct the inevitable errors which occur in the m.s. of all pieces) – This I should want to have the privilege of doing myself – but I feel you may wish to have the music published *soon* and there is no knowing when I shall be back in England and able to undertake the revision. The only other man to whom I could imagine the work being entrusted is Allen[1] – it w^d be a great disappointment to me not to do it – but failing that it w^d be great satisfaction to me, and I imagine to you, for it to be undertaken by such a wonderful musician and one who loved George and knew and honoured his music so well.

Yours sincerely
R. Vaughan Williams

1 Hugh Allen, a contemporary of VW's at Cambridge. At this time he was Choragus at Oxford, and also Conductor of the London Bach Choir, but in 1918 he became Professor at Oxford and succeeded Hubert Parry as Director of the RCM.

100. To Gustav Holst[1]

21 October 1916

Saturday Oct 21st

Dear V.

I was most touched by your letter. I've indeed longed to be home in many ways during the last month – but in other ways I should not like to come home for good till everything is over or in some other normal way.

Remember me to all the Morleyites and wish them good luck from me – & I shall think of all your schoolgirls on all saints day.

I sometimes dread coming back to normal life with so many gaps – especially of course George Butterworth – he has left most of his MS to me – & now I hear that Ellis[2] is killed – out of those 7 who joined up together in

August 1914 only 3 are left – I sometimes think now that it is wrong to have made friends with people much younger than oneself – because soon there will only be the middle aged left – & I have got out of touch with most of my contemporary friends – but then there is always you & thank Heaven we have never got out of touch & I don't see why we ever should.

Goodbye.

Yrs
RVW

[1] Printed as Letter XIX in *HR*.

[2] F. B. Ellis, promoter of a series of concerts of modern orchestral music, in which the first performance of *A London Symphony* was given, conducted by Geoffrey Toye.

101. To Gustav Holst

5 December 1916

Field Service Post Card

Dec 5th 1916

I am quite well
Letter follows at first opportunity
A Merry Xmas
R.V. Williams

102. From Hubert Parry

26 February 1917

Royal College of Music
Prince Consort Road,
South Kensington,
London, S.W.

Feb[ry] 26. 1917

My dear Vaughan Williams

I have been wanting to write to you for eversolong [*sic*], but the apparent difficulty of finding out where you were just sufficed, on top of being always rather busy, to stop my taking any opportunity to get under way. Now your dear old Uncle, Major Darwin, suggests, what I ought to have thought of long ago, that I might get a letter through by asking your wife to forward it – and so late as it is I won't forego letting you know how splendidly I thought the 'Sea Symphony' came off at the Bach Choir Naval Concert at Queens Hall. Allen[1] took any amount of trouble with it and it's worth it – and they all got into the spirit of it splendidly. I daresay you remember how enthusiastic everyone was when they did it before and how they had you up and shouted with pleasure. It was quite the same this time and it does the public credit that they have found out what a splendid work it is – quite one of the finest and most genuine and characteristic things that has been achieved in late years – so great and big!

[....][2] you to write something more in the strange conditions you must be in now – What experiences they must be! Perhaps you will extract something out of them! I should so like to have news of you.

Your sincere friend
C. Hubert H. Parry

[1] On Hugh Allen see no. 99 n. 1.

[2] Passage illegible because of being on a worn and stained fold—probably the letter had been carried around in VW's pocket for some time.

103. To the Carnegie United Kingdom Trust from AVW

9 April [1917]

13 Cheyne Walk
S.W.3

April 9th

Dear Sir

I am forwarding your letter to my husband who is at Salonika.

I am sure that he will feel much gratified at the honour which the Carnegie United Kingdom Trustees have done him in deciding to publish his work.

Believe me

Yours faithfully
Adeline Vaughan Williams

[1] The Carnegie United Kingdom Trust had chosen *A London Symphony*, CW 1913/5, for inclusion in their Carnegie Collection of British Music published by Stainer & Bell.

104. To the Carnegie United Kingdom Trust

25 July [1917]

6 Phene St[1]
London S.W.3.

July 25

Dear Sir

I have just returned from abroad and have received your kind letter with regards to my 'London symphony'.[2]

Owing to absence from home I was unable to revise the score before I sent it in.

It is absolutely essential that it should be thoroughly revised before printing and, owing to my military duties I see no chance of being able to do this during the War. In these circumstances would you still wish me to send the score to Messrs Stainer and Bell and to sign the agreement?

Yrs faithfully,
R. Vaughan Williams

A. L. Hetherington Esq

[1] Possibly the house of Bruce and Elena Richmond, where VW stayed immediately after his return from Salonika; see *RVW*, 125.

[2] VW had returned from service with the R.A.M.C. at Salonika in order to train as an officer in the Royal Garrison Artillery.

105. To Gustav Holst[1]

4 August [1917]

Y.M.C.A.
H.M. Forces on Active Service

Aug 4

Dear V

I wish we could have met again – but I was bunged off here all in a hurry – so I'm *in* it now – though we don't really start work till Monday – no leave till the middle of the course – about 2 months – it seems a fairly free and easy place at present – but a good deal of stupid ceremonial – *white gloves* (on ceremonial parades) (N.B. I believe there is a war on). I sh[d] have loved another long talk with you. Our hut-orderly is a funny little chap called Smith who has played with all the 'worm'[2] sort of orchestras (violin) all over the place, he was at the R.C.M. 12 years ago and knows Schwiller.[3]

My address is

Cadet R. Vaughan Williams,
3 Section 'H' Company,
No. 2 R.G.A. Cadet School,
Maresfield Park,
Uckfield,
Sussex.

Yrs
RVW

[1] Printed in *RVW*, 126–7, but not included in *HR*.

[2] A reference to the White Viennese Band, conducted by Stanislas Wurm, in which Holst had played trombone.

[3] The violinist Isidore Schwiller. See no. 57 n. 3.

106. To the Carnegie United Kingdom Trust 23 September [1917]

13 Cheyne Walk
S.W.3

Sept 23rd

Dear Sir

I fear there is *no* chance of my being able to revise my symphony for a long time to come. However, I do not think that the revisions will make much difference to the *size* of the work (if anything it will be shorter) so I am sending the score to Messrs Stainer & Bell so that they may give their estimate.[1]

Yrs faithfully
R. Vaughan Williams

[1] VW progressively made cuts and alterations in all movements of *A London Symphony* except the first, both now and subsequently, until the final version was established in 1933. See *CW* 1913/5 and Stephen Lloyd, 'Vaughan Williams's *A London Symphony*'.

107. To the Carnegie United Kingdom Trust 1 October [1917]

13 Cheyne Walk
S.W.3

Oct 1st

Dear Sir

I am afraid I cannot have made my letter clear – I certainly intended to say that I was sending my score, at your request, to Stainer & Bell for an *estimate* only *not* for engraving – It w^d be quite impossible to make the revisions on the printed score, they must be made in the M.S. But as it will make very little difference to the number of pages & notes it can well be estimated for quite well in its present state.

But perhaps to make it all clear I had better repeat what I have already written that I *cannot have it printed* until I have had an opportunity of revising it; as there appears to be no chance of my being able to do the revision until the war is over perhaps your ct^ee w^d rather I withdrew the work altogether.

Yrs truly
R. Vaughan Williams

108. To Sir Alexander Kaye-Butterworth

2 December 1917

RA Mess
Hut Town
Lydd.

Dec 2nd 1917

Dear Sir Alexander

I am sending a few words which I have tried to write about George – I wish it was more worthy – if you w^{d} care to do so please use part or all of it as you think best.[1] I am sorry it is in pencil but pens and ink are hard to come by here.

I am enclosing George's letter from which I quote – I feel you may care to keep it.

Cecil Sharp is still in America. I wish he c^{d} have written something.

Yours sincerely
R. Vaughan Williams

One of my most grateful memories of George is connected with my 'London Symphony'. Indeed I owe its whole idea to him. I remember very well how the idea originated. He had been sitting with us one evening talking, smoking & playing (I like to think that it was one of those rare occasions when we persuaded him to play us his beautiful little Pianoforte piece 'Firle Beacon'). At the end of the evening just as he was getting up to go he said in his characteristically abrupt way 'You know, you ought to write a symphony'. From that moment the idea of a symphony – a thing which I had always declared I would never attempt – dominated my mind. I showed the sketches to George bit by bit as they were finished – and it was then that I realised that he possessed, in common with very few composers, a wonderful power of criticism of other men's work and insight into their ideas and motives.

I can never feel to[o] grateful to him for all he did for me over this work – and his help did not stop short at criticism. When Ellis suggested that my symphony should be produced at one of his concerts I was away from home and unable to revise the score myself and George together with Ellis and Francis Toye undertook to revise it and to make a 'short score' from the original – George himself undertook the last movement.[2]

There was one passage which troubled him very much – but I could never get him to say exactly what was wrong with it – All he would say was 'It won't do at all'. After the performance he at once wrote to tell me he had changed his mind – He wrote

'A work cannot be a fine one until it is finely played – and it is possible that [other ~~of my music~~ works] may turn out equally well . . . I really advise you not to alter a note of the Symph: until after its second performance . . . The passages I kicked at didn't bother me at all because the music as a whole is so definite that a little occasional meandering is pleasant rather than otherwise. As to the scoring, I frankly don't understand how it all comes off so well, but it does all sound right, so there's nothing more to be said.'[3]

Another musical meeting ground for George and myself was the English Folksong for which he did so much and which did so much for him. It has often been my privilege to hear him improvise harmonies to the folk-tunes which he had collected, bringing out in them a beauty and character which I had not realised when merely looking at them. This was not merely a case of 'clever harmonisation', it meant that the inspiration which led to the original inception of these melodies and that which lay at the root of Butterworth's art were one and the same and that in harmonising folk-tunes or using them in his compositions he was simply carrying out a process of evolution of which these primitive melodies and his own art are different stages.

When I first knew George's compositions the traces of that individuality which was so pronounced later on were, indeed, to be found – but hindered and checked to a certain extent by the influence of Schumann & Brahms and partly by what may be described as the 'Oxford manner' in music – that fear of self-expression which seems to be fostered by academic traditions.

It was the folk-song which freed Butterworth's art from its foreign surroundings. To George Butterworth the folk-song was a means of freedom which enabled him to throw off the fetters which hindered his earlier efforts and formed a nucleus which focussed his hitherto vague stirrings after those things at which he really aimed. It is certain that his study of folk-song coincided with the development of his real musical self. To him the folk-song as a basis of musical inspiration was not merely 'playing with local colour' – his most beautiful composition the 'Shropshire Lad' for example or the Henley songs[4] have no direct connection with any folk-tune – but their influence was no less clearly to be seen than in the 'Idylls' in which he definitely took folk-music as the thematic basis.[5] Indeed he could no more help composing in his own national idiom than he could help speaking his own mother-tongue.

R. Vaughan Williams

[1] George Butterworth's parents were compiling a memorial volume, *George Butterworth 1885–1916* (York and London, 1918), printed for private circulation. See no. 84.

[2] VW was in Italy at Ospedaletti.

[3] This passage, taken from the text published in the memorial volume, is printed in *RVW*, III. Butterworth's original letter is no. 84 above.

[4] His rhapsody *A Shropshire Lad*, of 1912, and *Love blows as the wind blows*, a cycle of four settings of poems by W. E. Henley for voice and string quartet, of 1914. The reference to 'playing with local colour' was a phrase inspired by Rosa Newmarch and tended to be used by VW in connection with artistic nationalism.

[5] *Three English Idylls* of 1911 and *The Banks of Green Willow* of 1913.

109. To Cecil Sharp

28 December [1917]

22 Marina
St Leonards-on-Sea

Dec 28th

Dear Sharp

I've lately been spending some delightful hours over your American book[1] – a wonderful collection – of course I've only studied them 'dry' – i.e. just looking at them as I've no piano or any instrument here – and one misses many beauties that way.

My favourite I think at present is 'The False Young Man' (94A).

I was much interested in the first tune to 'Lord Randal' – because I trace a slight family resemblance to the now well known Somerset Tune – which has always puzzled us so much.

I was so sorry to hear of your illness and do so much hope you are well again now – only go slow, we can't afford to have you breakdown – it wastes time in the end. As for me – I came back from Salonica last August to try my hand at another trade – Artillery – I wondered if I was crazy to start an absolutely new subject at my age – However after 5 months of pretty strenuous work I have passed my exams & am now on leave awaiting my 'pip' – what they will do with me then I have no idea.

We had a sight of Charlie last time we were in London – it was good to see him well again after all he has been through – or nearly well though of course altered.

Well – to our next meeting & all our best wishes for the new year

Yrs ever
R. Vaughan Williams

[1] C. J. Sharp and O. D. Campbell, *English Folk-songs from the Southern Appalachians* (London, 1917).

110. To Adrian Boult

29 February [1918]

R.A. Mess,
St. Lucia Barracks,
Bordon, Hants.

Feb 20th

Dear Boult

In all the hurry of Monday I never had an opportunity of thanking you

(1) for doing my symph
(2) for giving such a fine performance – it really was splendid – you had got the score right into you & through you into your orch:[1]

May I say how much I admired your conducting – it is real *conducting* – you get just what you want and *know* what you want – and your players trust you because they know it also – I heard many expressions of admiration from both audience and performers (von Holst & A. Hobday[2] among others) – of course your [*sic*] an experienced conductor by now & your power is well known to many – but to me who have been out of music for 3 years it was new – good luck to you – I look for great things in the future when such musical ability and such public spirit go hand in hand

Yrs sincerely
R. Vaughan Williams[3]

[1] Boult had given a performance of *A London Symphony* at the Queen's Hall on 18 Feb., after which VW made some revisions which were incorporated in a performance again by Boult on 18 Mar. 1918 in the Queen's Hall, at which time VW was in France. See *WVW*, 144.

[2] Alfred Hobday (1870–1942), the viola player who gave the first performance of the *Four Hymns*, *CW* 1914/2, in 1920. See *Grove* 5.

[3] Printed in Moore, *Music and Friends*, 27.

111. To Adrian Boult[1]

[24 February 1918]

Leith Hill Place
nr. Dorking

Sunday

Dear Boult

Thank you very much for your letter – I sh[d] be proud for any part of the L.S.[2] to be done again by you – but you certainly musn't cut about your programme for it – especially not the 'Shropshire Lad' which ought to be heard everywhere as often as possible.[3]

I agree with you that the last movement & possibly the scherzo of my symphony are too long – but it is re-writing they want – I do not think that mechanical cutting – however skilfully done w[d] be satisfactory.[4]

Why not do the 1st movement only? It stands fairly well by itself.

I fear I shall be far away on March 18th as I am down for overseas – & may leave any day now.[5]

Yours very sincerely
R. Vaughan Williams

[1] Part of the original (from 'especially not "The Shropshire Lad"') is in UVW's file for 1945 with another letter to Boult of that year. The top of this letter is supplied from the text published in Moore, *Music and Friends*, 28. However, the date suggested there by Moore (3 Mar. 1918) is a few days too late since according to *RVW*, 128 VW left for France on 1 March. The date should probably be Sunday, 24 February. Boult gave concerts in Liverpool during the First World War.

[2] *A London Symphony*, *CW* 1913/5. See no. 110 n. 1.

[3] George Butterworth's Rhapsody of this name, written in 1912.

[4] By the time of the performance on 18 Mar. VW had cut some ten minutes of the symphony. Further changes were made before the score was published in 1920 and then more before the third revision was performed by the London Philharmonic Orchestra under Thomas Beecham in 1934 and published *c.*1936. Details are set out in *CW*, pp. 68–71. A recording of the long first version of the symphony was eventually made and released in 2001.

[5] VW was sent to France on 1 Mar. 1918 as a Lieutenant in the Royal Garrison Artillery. He had previously been to France as a Private in the R.A.M.C. in 1916.

112. To E. J. Dent

26 February [postmark: 1918]

13 Cheyne Walk
Chelsea, S.W.3.

Feb 26th

Dear Dent

I was talking to my brother-in-law H. A. L. Fisher (minister of education)[1] on Sunday – He thinks he could get a sum of money to start English opera – Now he has been talking with P. Greene[2] & Beecham & sucking in their ideas – I am very anxious he should hear the ideas of the younger generation & suggested that you w[d] be the person to give him these. He w[d] very much like to have a talk with you about it – Could you find time when next you come to London to make an appointment with him? Now is the time to strike!

His address

R[t] Hon: H. A. L. Fisher
43 Grosvenor Road

Westminster
S.W.1

I'm off to France on Friday!

Yrs
R. Vaughan Williams

[1] Herbert Fisher at this time held a cabinet post as President of the Board of Education. He was MP for the combined universities.
[2] Harry Plunket Greene; see no. 52 n. 5.

113. To Mrs Turner[1] 11 May [1918]

May 11th

Dear Madam

I was very glad to receive your letter and am happy to be able to tell you that your husband is all right again.

I consider it the duty of every officer to do all he can for the welfare of those under his command; I have been in the camps myself and know what a hard life it is.

I hope that before long we shall all be back with our families and that this dreadful separation will be over.

Yours truly
R. Vaughan Williams
2/Lt R.G.A.[2]

[1] Mrs Turner sent this letter to RVW in 1954. At first he disclaimed ever having written it!
[2] Royal Garrison Artillery. See *RVW*, 125. VW had passed out in Nov. 1917 and was now stationed near Rouen.

114. To Gustav Holst[1] [summer 1918]

Dear V.

I've not written to you ever since I came out this time (nor for the matter of fact you to me). But I keep posted up in all your doings & I see your letters.

I wonder if you will go to Holland – I sh[d] feel more inclined for the naval job myself – but still there is the 3rd alternative I hope, of your stopping at Morley – when all this is over it will I believe [be] the people who've kept the lamp alight who will count as the heroes.

The war has brought me strange jobs – can you imagine me in charge of 200 horses!! That's my job at present – I was dumped down on to it straight away, and before I had time to find out which were horses and which were wagons I found myself in the middle of a retreat – as a matter of fact we had a very easy time over that – only one horse killed so we were lucky.

At present I am down near the sea undergoing a 'gunnery course' – more of a rest than anything else but it's given me an opportunity of learning something about my gun (among other things.) Having been trained entirely as a 6" Howitzer man I've been bunged into a 60^{pdr}!

I wish I c^{d} have been at Thaxted – but that will all come after the war – I sh^{d} be very sorry for you to leave Morley & Thaxted and all that – but it w^{d} be interesting to see if you have established a tradition & if it will carry on without you.

Let me have a letter when you can. What are you writing?

Yrs
RVW

address 2/Lt RVW R G A
141 Heavy Bty
B E F
France

[1] Printed as Letter XX in *HR*.

115. To Gustav Holst[1] 12 December 1918

12.12.18

Dear Gustav,

I was so glad of your letter – what troubles you are having – I only hope you'll get refunded some time – luckily you don't depend on the army for it. I wonder what Island you are at – I was at Milo for one day & bathed in the bay – I don't know Gallipoli – it was Taranto where I landed. I am still out here – slowly trekking towards Germany, not a job I relish, either the journey or its object. I've seen Namur and Charleroi and was disappointed in both – every village we pass is hung with flags and triumphal arches 'Gloire à nos vainqueurs' etc.

We usually march about 10 Kilos or more a day & rest every 4th day – it's a tiresome job watering & feeding horses in the dark before we start (though I must confess that there being 8 subalterns in this Bty my turn of turning out early for this only comes once a week). Then usually 2 or 3 wagons stick fast in the mud at the 1st start off & worry & delay ensues, & finally when one get's to one's destination one has to set up one's horse lines and find water and fill up nose bags etc. and if *this* has to be done in the dark it beggars description. So you see there's not much music-writing going on at present. But I've started a singing class and we are practising Xmas carols and 'Sweet and Low'.

Yrs
RVW.

[1] Printed in *RVW*, 131; not included in *HR*.

116. To L. J. Pollard

3 February 1919

3/2/19

111840 Gnr. Pollard has permission to use organ in Lecture hall.[1]

R. Vaughan Williams
2/Lt

[1] At this time VW was Director of Music, First Army, B.E.F., France, based at Valenciennes, and on the point of being demobilized. Pollard was anxious to find an organ to play and VW had heard of this one. See *RVW*, 131–2.

117. To Margaret Longman[1]

6 June 1919

10 Madingley Road
Cambridge[2]

6/6/19

Dear Miss Longman

Please forgive my being so slow in answering – I feel much drawn towards your scenario – & music, I feel, might quite possibly occur to me for it one day – but one can never be certain – so if you know of anyone else meanwhile who wants to set it straight away he (or she) had better do so. Meanwhile have you a more detailed scheme that I could see.[3]

One or two points occur to me – I think the whole thing ought to be quite short & in one scene – one c^{d} I think arrange this by conventionalising the whole thing and having a double (or triple) stage each one a few steps higher than the other – on the lowest stage w^{d} be the magician in his little hut – on the middle one the young woman would come on and dance – on the highest one w[d] be the trees where the voice is.

Also I don't quite like the owner of the voice finally *appearing* – it will take away the mystery – I think it c[d] be suggested by a bright light or something of that kind.

I must say once again what enormous pleasure your singing gave me and everyone last Saturday.

Yrs very sincerely
R. Vaughan Williams

[1] 'A singer who often assisted VW by providing the illustrations when he lectured on folk song' (see *RVW*, 105).

[2] The home of E. J. Dent, which the VWs took periodically.

[3] The scenario, by Margaret Longman and Angela Hubbard, was entitled *The Voice in the Wood*: 'Through many thousands of years a Voice has been heard singing in the Wood, but no man has ever seen the singer . . .'. It is clear from no. 158 that VW made a start on the music for this ballet but soon abandoned the project, finding it uncongenial. He used some of the music in the *Pastoral Symphony*.

118. To William Rothenstein[1]

22 August 1919

Northern Lights
Sheringham
Norfolk[2]

22/8/19

Dear Rothenstein

Very many thanks for your kind letter. My plans are so vague that I don't like to make any promises to be at any particular place at a particular time.

All I can suggest is that when you happen to be in London you should let me know of any times that are convenient to you – But I quite see that that would be a most awkward arrangement for you & know you w[d] prefer to drop it altogether.[3]

Yours sincerely
R. Vaughan Williams

[1] Professor of Civic Art at Sheffield University, to which post he was appointed by VW's brother-in-law Herbert Fisher, the university's Vice-Chancellor.

[2] AVW had taken rooms in Sheringham for the benefit of her brother Hervey's health and the VWs spent much time there until his death in May 1921. See *RVW*, 133.

[3] Printed in *RVW*, 134. Rothenstein had been commissioned to make a drawing of VW for publication in the second issue of *Music & Letters*. The first issue had contained a drawing by Rothenstein of Elgar.

119. To Philip Webb[1]

7 November 1919

Northern Lights
Sheringham
Norfolk

7/11/19

Dear Webb

Thank you very much for your letter. I sh^{d} like above all things to accept the conductorship of the Handel if initial difficulties c^{d} be overcome. The great (& indeed only) one is that I am obliged to be out of London (5 hours by rail) for the next few months.[2]

I shall have, however, probably to come up to London once a week during this time – W^{d} it be possible for me to take the choir on Thursdays & have someone else at present for the orchestra – as I do not see how I can manage twice a week regularly – But I quite understand that you will probably prefer to have someone who can do the whole job from the start & w^{d} also be more on the spot at other times than this out of the way place.

But I am *most anxious* to have the honour of conducting you and very much hope that some arrangement can be made to tide me over what I hope is only a temporary absence from London.

When do you propose to start?

Yrs sincerely
R. Vaughan Williams

[1] P. G. L. Webb was Secretary of the Handel Society from its inception.

[2] The Handel Society, founded in London in 1882 for the performance of his lesser-known oratorios, was being revived after the War. VW conducted it until he became Musical Director of the Bach Choir in 1921, when he was succeeded by Eugene Goossens; see *RVW*, 139. The society had approached Adrian Boult and Allen Gill before VW but both had declined.

120. To William Rothenstein

25 December [1919]

The SUN-DIAL
Sheringham
Norfolk
(note new address)

Dec 25

Dear Rothenstein

Many thanks for your kind letter. Indeed it was an honour to sit to you & I only feel guilty (though in all innocence) of taking up so much of your time.

I am very glad to think you are coming back to London.[1]

Yrs very sincerely
R. Vaughan Williams

[1] Rothenstein had been appointed Principal of the Royal College of Art.

121. To C. E. Sayle[1]

14 March 1920

The SUN DIAL
Sheringham
Norfolk
(note new address)

14/3/20

Dear Sayle

The one person who really started the Fairy Queen ball rolling (after old Shedlock[2] who discovered it and published it in the Purcell Soc) was G. T. Holst who gave, I believe, the first performance (in concert form) since Purcell's time.[3]

He (Holst) is musical director at Morley Working Men's College – and directly Shedlock's edition came out he decided to put his people to work on it – they all worked like slaves – copying all the parts (there was no Novello 8vo edition then) – and rearranging and transposing certain numbers to fit the very limited capabilities of the performers. The result was a really remarkable performance – I was fresh from this performance & it was ringing in my ears when I met Dent & he was discussing what they sh[d] do as a sequel to the Magic Flute – I at once said 'Why don't you do the Fairy Queen' – & that is all I had to do with it.

I saw two performances at Cambridge (Sat. aft and evening) & was quite bowled over.

Yours ever
R. Vaughan Williams

[1] Charles Edward Sayle (1864–1924), Assistant Librarian at Cambridge University Library and poet.

[2] J. S. Shedlock (1843–1919), pianist and writer on music. Mainly well known for his Beethoven studies, he edited *The Fairy Queen* for the Purcell Society (vol. 12, 1903).

[3] In fact Shedlock had organized a concert performance in 1901 of 'a liberal selection of the music', so Holst's was not the first modern performance. See a review in *Athenaeum*, 22 June 1901, p. 798. Holst's 1911 performance certainly contained more of the music than Shedlock's in 1901.

122. To the Carnegie United Kingdom Trust 15 December 1920

Opinion, as member of assessment panel for the Trust's 'Scheme for the publication of musical compositions', on Chamber Rhapsody no. 2 by Arthur Bliss

Received: 15th December 1920

This piece seems to me to have a rare and classical sense of beauty – and indicates a healthy departure from the rather heavy romanticism of much that has been sent in. It breaks fresh ground and as such it ought to be encouraged.

I know it has weak points – a certain squareness & a tendency to shut the music into water-tight compartments 2 bars long. But it has certainly great beauty of theme, harmony & colour.

As to the voices, I also do not like voices without words – but I think this is a prejudice – there is no doubt about the exquisite beauty of the combination of voices & instruments (I have heard the work). **A** in my opinion.[1]

[1] The other members of the panel were Henry Hadow and Dan Godfrey. Hadow disapproved of the wordless voices and felt the work didn't have much substance and awarded a C, though he was prepared to consider a B. Godfrey agreed with Hadow about wordless voices but felt that the composer would 'certainly come to the front' and that the work should be considered. The eventual verdict was positive and the work was published in the Carnegie Collection of British Music as *Rhapsody for Flute, Cor Anglais, String Quartet, Bass and Two Voices—Soprano and Tenor* by Stainer & Bell in 1921. VW's views about wordless voices changed—as is evident from the wordless mixed chorus in *Flos Campi* (*CW* 1925/5).

123. To Ralph Wedgwood [?early April 1921[1]]

'Mainsail House'
Sheringham
Norfolk

My Dear Randolph

It was such a pleasure to see your handwriting again after all these years. – I've been thinking so often about you – how somehow we were each waiting for the other to move first – I was quite near you once at Montreuil but I was too shy to call on you under the circumstances.

Adeline went out this morning & interviewed the nice landlady she knows of – she has not got her *best* rooms vacant – they are all quite nice – but this sitting-room and bed room face *north* (N.B. North is sea-wards here) & there is also a bed room on the top floor which faces south. Adeline is writing all this to Iris.

The address is

Mrs Jenkinson
The Little House

South St
Sheringham

Now do let us try & arrange a meeting before long – Wed; & Thurs: are my nights in London in term time – are they ever yours? We have just moved into a new furnished house with the above appalling name.

Give my love to Iris & Adeline sends you hers – why not come down yourself & settle Veronica in?

Yours
R.V.W.

[1] Cicely Veronica Wedgwood, Wedgwood's daughter, born in 1910 and at this time 11 years old, was to spend some time at Sheringham. VW reported on the visit in a letter (not included in the present collection) to Wedgwood on 30 April. Veronica later became Dame Veronica Wedgwood, the historian.

124. To Mrs W. Hadley

14 August 1921

Leith Hill Place
Dorking

14/8/21

Dear Mrs Hadley

Have you by any chance got a copy of a song I wrote for 'Pilgrims Progress' years ago 'Who so dwelleth' – If not it is not a bit important – but if you have w^d you lend it me to copy – I will return it to you (that is to say if you want it back – which perhaps you will not).[1]

I often think with pleasure of those 'P.P' times

Yrs sincerely
R. Vaughan Williams

[1] VW was starting work on *The Shepherds of the Delectable Mountains*, CW 1922/6, of which this is the opening section. See no. 42.

125. To Vally Lasker

22 December 1921

13 Cheyne Walk
S.W.3

22/12/21

My Dear Miss Lasker

Your letter about the Bach choir has only just been found – It was addressed all right but got hidden. How hard you must have thought me not to thank you for it.

Which I do now most heartily – I value encouragement very much – I confess I was rather pleased myself.[1]

Yrs very sincerely
R. Vaughan Williams

[1] VW became conductor of the Bach Choir in 1921 and his first concert—a programme of Bach cantatas—had taken place on 14 Dec. See *RVW*, 140. Vally Lasker, a music teacher at St Paul's Girls' School and a colleague of Gustav Holst, was to become a great friend.

126. To the Carnegie United Kingdom Trust 18 January 1922

13 Cheyne Walk
S.W.3

18/1/22

Dear Colonel Mitchell

I returned the document signed.[1]

As regards the schedule – I think it advisable to leave the question of fee vague – that is to say – I do not wish to charge a fee at present – but I want to retain the *right* to do so & the am[t] cannot be stipulated for in an extreme case I might wish to make it prohibitive.

Yrs sincerely
R. Vaughan Williams

[1] The document was the Agreement covering publication of *A London Symphony*.

127. From Lucy Broadwood 29 January 1922

3[c] Montagu Mansions
W.

Jan. 29. 1922

Dear Ralph,

Thank you a million times for the gorgeously beautiful Symphony you gave us on Thursday.[1] I hope that some of our joy returned, reflected, to you, and that to have the 'old Philharmonic' shouting & waving to you across the dour bust of Beethoven was a happy thing, and a funny thing too, for you. The one regret that I have is not to be, at such times, a young thing at a musical college – with young ears and enough training to understand the modern idiom. Now and then I find a new musical nut very hard to crack, and now & then I know that certain things which I apprehended with some effort were easily and absolutely understood by the younger listeners & those more accustomed to hearing quite new things. Now I am longing to quickly hear your splendid Symphony again. The trumpet stirred me desperately – and how finely it was played! And surely the voice was perfection?[2]

It was funny that I was describing to my cousin here (who is musical, but not strong enough to go to concerts) the effect of your music in this Symphony. I said that the stuff suggested granite rocks, heather, lichens, & great open spaces etc. to me. Next day Mr Collis (wasn't it?) writes of tufts of grass & moss etc.[3] So you see, you *must* be a painter in sound!

This has been hurriedly scrawled amongst interruptions, & it ill expresses my deep delight and admiration & enjoyment.

My love to Adeline, please,[4]

Yrs most sincerely
Lucy E. Broadwood.

[1] *Pastoral Symphony*, *CW* 1921/13, had received its first performance on 26 Jan. at the Queen's Hall with the orchestra of the Royal Philharmonic Society conducted by Adrian Boult.

[2] Flora Mann.

[3] H. C. Colles, Chief Music Critic of *The Times*, contributed an unsigned notice on 28 Jan. and then a signed piece on Saturday, 4 Feb. entitled 'Three symphonies: Vaughan Williams' progress—the influence of Walt Whitman'.

[4] Printed for the most part in *RVW*, 140.

128. From Edwin Evans[1]

8 May 1922

May 8th, 1922.

My dear Vaughan Williams,

If I thought that your view of this affair was representative I should obviously have declined the compliment very promptly.[2] But do you think seriously that there is behind it any suggestion of rewarding me for praise given? From conversations that I have had, I have gathered a very different impression altogether – that the proposed tribute was less to the journalist than to the fellow worker. I should be very sorry to think that it had anything to do with the opinion I have formed of any individual composer's work. When I began my work exactly twenty years ago the cause of modern music in general and of modern British music in particular was an unpopular one, and I see in this affair a recognition of the fact that I took upon myself to share its unpopularity. It has many friends now, but it has gratified me exceedingly to discover that a few people have long memories. You must remember that I have paid a heavy price for having from the beginning associated myself with the workers. The prizes of journalism go not to those who join crusades, but to those who voice the opinion of the majority. These, who were hostile or apathetic when the public was hostile or apathetic, are now as well disposed to you all as the public has since become. Even so, glaring instances of opportunism still occur, as when a certain critic found 'The Planets' uninteresting and disappointing at a first hearing but, when its success was assured, pronounced it to be the most remarkable music heard that year. I cannot look from this point of view at anything that means as much to me as music does. The result is that no prominent or well-paid post has ever come my way. In confidence I may tell you that my receipts from the Pall Mall Gazette for the first quarter of this year averaged 33/– weekly. And you suggest that I should look to audiences or publishers for reward having fought the battle of composers! How aloof you are from the world you live in! Reflect a little upon that figure, and upon the fact that I have never possessed private means, and you will recognise that the work I have done in these years would, in any other walk of life, have brought me at least material security, instead of which my life to-day is more precarious than it has ever been, and that simply because I placed certain things which are dear to you and to me before all else. And you think that I would accept payment for such praise as it has been my privilege to give whilst pursuing this ideal! The model I have kept before me is Stassoff in his relation to the Five Russian Nationalists,[2] but he at least had security in material things. Further, you speak of me merely as a critic. Do you believe that my work has been so limited? Think of the list of performances that have resulted from my initiative. Have you not heard that I have sometimes been a friend to composers in other and more helpful ways than those of a journalist? It distresses me to have to speak of my record like this, and I assure you that I have never in my life done so before, but it has pained me very much to think that you believe that I would accept any compliment in such a spirit as your letter describes. If you have any reason for believing that this is the idea which has prompted your confreres to take this course, I trust that you will let me know, so that I can make quite clear what I feel on the subject.[3]

Yours cordially
[Edwin Evans]

[1] See no. 31.

[2] Vladimir Stasov (1824–1906), who coined the phrase 'The mighty handful' for Balakirev, Borodin, Cui, Rimsky-Korsakov, and Musorgsky.

[3] The occasion of this letter was either Evans's nomination as Chairman of the British Section of the newly founded International Society for Contemporary Music or the proposal to hold a dinner in his honour, which in fact took place on 21 Jan. 1923 at Pagani's. Many composers were present but not, apparently, VW. See the obituary piece on Edwin Evans in the *Musical Times* (Mar. 1945).

129. To Edwin Evans

[11 May 1922]

13 Cheyne Walk
S.W.3

Thursday

Dear Evans

I fear I have hurt your feelings – & I suppose it c^{dnt} be helped – I dislike doing so very much – because you know that I admire all the work you have done so much

I hope however you will give me the credit

(a) of being honest
(b) of having taken the least agreeable and more difficult course – Because obviously the easiest and pleasantest thing for me w^{d} have been to have gone in with the rest, or if I did not, to say nothing about it, in which case neither you nor anyone else w^{d} have noticed the omission.

What the opinion of the promoters are I do not know – but I cannot see that a *composer* c^{d} possibly make a presentation to a *critic* (among other things) without the obvious inference being drawn – (that we are publicly thanking you for praising us).

By the way I did not say that the public etc *w^{d}* recognize you but that they were the people who *ought* to recognize you since it is, at all events theoretically, for their sake not for ours that you have propagandized – so I still feel that much as I feel that your work ought to be publicly recognized that[1] it is emphatically *not* the composer who can promote it.[2]

Yrs very sincerely
R. Vaughan Williams

[1] Word repeated in original.
[2] See no. 128.

130. To Gustav Holst[1]

[about 5 June 1922]

Plaza Hotel
New York

Dear Gustav

I have now seen (a) Niagara (b) the Woolworths Building and am most impressed by (b) – I've come to the conclusion that the Works of Man terrify me more than the Works of God – I told myself all the time that N'ga was the most wonderful thing in the world – & so it is – especially when you get right under it – but I did not once want to fall on my knees & confess my sins – whereas I can sit all day & look out of my windows (16 floors up) at the sky scrapers (this kind of thing –)

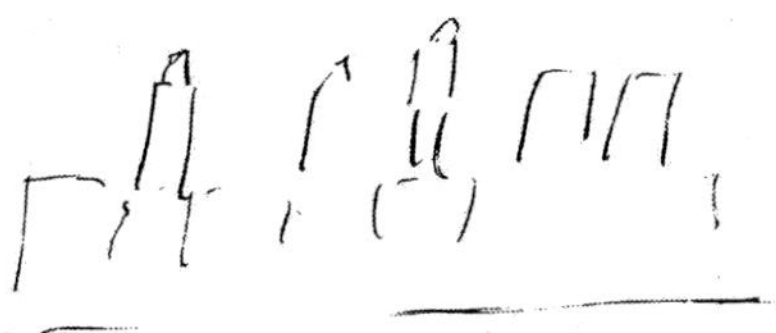

By the way my millionaire has put us up at *the* swaggerest Hotel in N.Y. – our landing was like a sort of very nice night mare – waited in dock on the ship for 3 hours to pass the immigration officer – then we came down the impossibly steep gangway into a dusky shed out of which there gradually loomed (a) Stockel's secretary (a pretty young woman in blue) (b) H. W. Gray[2] (c) Forsyth – Then as we moved off I heard 'Ralph' shouted out – & there outside the barrier were the Longmans![3] Then 2 niggers bundled our luggage down a chute – we were whirled off in a taxi & up 16 floors in an elevator – to a *suite* of rooms with *2 bath rooms* with this wonderful view all over N.Y. – then whirled down again into a sort of cathedral where we had supper (chicken salad – (oh the American food – it's beyond powers of expression)). Then at 11.0 – just as we were going to bed the GREAT MAN and HIS WIFE appeared – very nice & simple. But I never want a patron – it's too wearing.[4]

I've come to the conclusion that N.Y. is a good place but wants hustling badly – the busses are slow & stop wherever you like – Broadway is I believe easier to cross than High Street Thaxted[5] – I've had two rehearsals of 1¼ hours as yet – I think I shall need all I shall get – I've got two more – many of the players are v. good but the back desks of the fiddles are not v. good – & Trombones have not much beef about them.

Just off to Norfolk Conn. now. I address this to the *house* which I hope is right (No I won't because I can't remember the number).

Give my love to all my pupils if you see them.

Love
RVW

[1] Not in *HR*. Printed with omissions in *RVW*, 142.

[2] Head of the firm which represented Novello & Co in the US. On the firm and on Cecil Forsyth see no. 94 n. 2.

[3] Robert and Dorothy Longman. Robert Longman was a member of the publishing family and a keen member of the Bach Choir of which VW was now the conductor. Robert and, until her death, Dorothy remained close friends.

[4] Carl Stoeckel, son of Gustav Stoeckel, the first Professor of Music at Yale, was Patron of the Festival at Norfolk, Connecticut, where VW was to conduct the first American performance of the *Pastoral Symphony*.

[5] Where Holst had a cottage.

131. To Cordelia Curle from Adeline Vaughan Williams[1]

14 June [1922]

The Plaza
Fifth Avenue

June 14th

Beloved Boo

We have come here for 1 night from Boston. Mr Stoeckel still sticks to us & pays everything! Today we say goodbye to him & go to the Atwaters – we shall have 4 days with them – Then the Berengaria again. Its cool after the thunderstorms.

There is a very good kind of melon here the canterlope & you cut it in half take out the seeds & then it is filled up with pink ice cream. Mr Stoeckel loves sight seeing & the cafe life – Lunch at 1 spreads itself out till 3 or 4! Ralph is feeling restive & says he now knows how Mozart & his contemporaries felt living under a patron.

This will probably be the last letter you may get – we ought to be home by June 26th if we have a good passage – Shall we see you on yr way to Devonshire? Any how we will meet.[2]

Yr
A

Love to Ad.[3]

[1] Cordelia Curle was the youngest of Adeline's three sisters, with whom Adeline kept up an almost daily correspondence.

[2] Two passages printed in *RVW*, 144.

[3] Cordelia's son, Adam.

132. To Percy Scholes

13 July [1922]

From R. Vaughan Williams
Wheatfield
Tetsworth
Oxon[1]

July 13

Dear Scholes

Re my opera

(a) *Is it finished*. Vocal score was completed 1914 (May). Full score June–Aug 1920. The only thing not ready yet is the title which will *probably* be –

'Hugh the Drover'
(or Love in the Stocks)

A Romantic Ballad opera in 2 acts
Text by Harold Child music by R. Vaughan Williams

(b) *Is any performance arranged*. No: but possibly the Patrons' Fund are going to try through a scene or two.
(c) *What is the nature of the work*. In 1910 I was introduced to Harold Child (whose books you doubtless know and also his work in the Times Lit: Sup.) and asked him to write me a libretto for an opera which should be a sort of English parallel to Smetana's 'Verkaufte Braut'. I stipulated that it should hinge round a scene from Borrow's 'Zincali'[2] which describes a gypsy and a prize fight, also I wanted to introduce the Fowlmere 'May Day Song' which I had lately heard. Also I suggested (or between us we evolved) that the form, situations etc should be conventionally operatic as it was our first shot. (As a matter of fact it is not at all conventional except superficially as that would be impossible for H. C. but he did his best.)

I call it a ballad opera because it is frankly in song and ensembles with recitative in between – I meant to use a lot of traditional tunes – as a matter of fact I have used very few.

Plot

Scene a Cotswold village.
Period 1800–12 about.
Time Monday morning April 30 & early Tuesday morning May 1st.

Act I A fair in progress. The chief feature of which is the *Showman* who exhibits a dummy of Napoleon for cock-shies. Then a ballad singer who sings 'Tuesday Morning' (F.S. from Somerset). Enter *Mary* (heroine, soprano) – bursts into tears on hearing the words 'I'm to be married on Tuesday morning' – obviously she is to be married & it makes her unhappy. She is comforted by Aunt Jane (conventional operatic contralto).

Enter *Constable* (Mary's father) & *John* the butcher (her lover) who upbraids her for being unhappy the day before her marriage – He tries to take her arm – she refuses – general scrimmage interrupted by entry of Morris Men who sweep the whole crowd off the stage except Mary & Aunt Jane – Aunt Jane sings the joys of domesticity but Mary seems to prefer a 'free life under heaven' (we used to imagine we liked that kind of thing before the war when we had not experienced it).

Meanwhile *Hugh* the Drover (Hero – Tenor) has entered unseen – he enters into conversation (much against Aunt Jane's will) & gradually fascinates Mary with his description of the joys of the road. Meanwhile Aunt Jane who disapproves of the proceedings at last goes off to fetch the Constable (Mary's father) to put a stop to things. This gives an opportunity for the first

Grand Duo

Interrupted by entry of Aunt Jane & Constable. A short cursing match between Hugh & Constable then enter Showman and chorus announcing that John the Butcher will fight all comers for £20. Hugh accepts the challenge but the prize is to be the hand of Mary.

(big ensemble)

They fight – 3 rounds – & John is knocked out. Acclamation from the crowd but John & the Constable after a secret consultation denounce Hugh as a french spy – consternation – The crowd immediately turn against Hugh – He is seized and marched off – Mary faints in Aunt Jane's arms.

Curtain

Act II

Early morning of May 1st. – Clock strikes four. Hugh is sitting in the stocks in the market place. Sounds of revelry from the pub. John and his friends come out very drunk on their way to go out & gather the May blossom – They abuse Hugh & tell him the soldiers are coming to fetch him to Gloster gaol. They go off & enter Mary softly – She has stolen her father's keys and lets Hugh out – They agree to fly together.

(Grand Duo no 2)

As they are escaping a light appears in the Constable's house. He is heard shouting (This the critics will say is a crib from Meistersingers – so I make you a present of it beforehand).

Hugh and Mary crouch behind the stocks & cover themselves with his big cloak – Enter Constable – Aunt Jane – all seems well & they go off again. The Dawn gradually breaks. Hugh 'Now my love 'tis time'. They start again to escape. This time they are stopped by the distant sound of the May-horn.

Hugh 'What are we to do'

Mary 'Obey me get back into the stocks & I will get in also'

They both sit in the stocks covered completely by Hugh's cloak. John's voice heard off stage singing the May Song.

> 'A branch of May I've brought to you
> And at your door it stands'

Enter John and chorus – and sing below Mary's window. No answer – Constable enters 'Where's my daughter' – general ensemble during which John discovers that Hugh is not alone.

'Why there's a girl with him – here goes for a kiss'

Mary throws off the cloak 'Mary'! general shout

Constable 'Here John how do you feel about managing a trull like that.'

John Marriage – certainly not – but perhaps some other arrangement!

General indignation from the chorus – a grand scrimmage interrupted by the sound of a bugle & dawn. Enter Sergeant & Squad.

Sergeant 'Where is the spy'?

Hugh comes forward wrapped in his cloak

Sergeant 'Take off your cloak' 'Why – this is no spy – This is my old friend Hugh the drover – well – I won't go back empty handed. We'll take that butcher there & make a soldier of him'.

Exeunt soldiers dragging John with them.

Constable who has been much impressed with the proceedings goes up to Hugh & invites him to settle down & marry Mary.

Hugh. 'No not this quiet respectable life for me – Mary will you come on the roads with me?'

Mary 'Yes'.
Hugh 'Now for the road again
The blessed sun & rain
Come Mary by my side
So the Drover claims his bride'

Exeunt. Constable tries to stop them but Aunt Jane prevents him
'They're not for us nor for our quiet days
Life calls these lovers out to wilder ways'

Curtain.

R.V.W.

[1] Cordelia Curle's house, where the VWs spent their summer holiday in 1922 as house-sitters while Cordelia and her son Adam were in France. See *RVW*, 145.

[2] George Borrow, *The Zincali* (1841). See no. 63 n. 4.

133. To Ina Boyle[1]

postmark: 15 February 1923

13 Cheyne Walk
S.W.3

Tel: Kensington 2551

Dear Miss Boyle

I c[d] see you on Saturday Feb 3rd at 10.0 if that w[d] suit you.

Yrs sincerely
R. Vaughan Williams

P.S. I see you ask my terms they are £1–1–0 an hour[2]

[1] Ina Boyle (1889–1967), Irish composer and an early pupil of VW. She came to London sporadically for lessons.

[2] i.e. 1 guinea an hour.

134. To Vally Lasker

postmark: 10 March 1923

Dear Miss Lasker

Thank you very very much.[1]

They all love it & worked at it – & so they can triumph over the absence of throat resonance!

Yrs
RVW.

[1] Vally Lasker had written to VW on 8 Mar. about his first performance of the St Matthew Passion with the Bach Choir: 'Let me thank you from the bottom of my heart for the greatest spiritual & musical experience I have ever had in my life. I cannot talk of last night's experience as a performance, because that is just, thank Heaven, what it never was. It was rather a manifestation of the spiritual powers & understanding of one man permeating the whole of choir & orchestra & soloists & audience, making the Queens Hall into a true palace of worship without any of the outward trappings of one. I never thought such a thing possible & it never has been before. It rested with you to bring home to us the ideal & to make the singing & playing for once worthy of the music & its creator. I don't congratulate you, but I congratulate myself & us all for being born in the same generation as you.'

His teacher, Charles Stanford, had also written on the same day: 'You will forgive me for sending you a word of congratulation on last night's performance of the Bach. It was so dignified & pious (*not "pi"*) all through: & the points were so exactly what J.S.B. meant. The only things I felt were that the Trumpet was out of the picture! & for me, the Jesus was too emotionally sung. I remember the greatest in it, Stockhausen, & the only moment when he was emotional was "Eli, Eli", which made it doubly thrilling! But this is only my own view, with which you may or may not agree. Meantime, I say thank you very heartily – & after all my great ancestor W.S.B [William Sterndale Bennett] was the father of doing it here at all!'

135. To Lucy Broadwood postmark: 3 April 1923

Dear Miss Broadwood

If I only just say 'thank you' it means that I can't say all I sh^d like to – But I remember years ago at St George's Square when I was v. raw how you shewed me Purcell & Bach & many things I did not know & as to Folksong – it was you who 1st introduced me to it.[1]

Yrs very sincerely
R. Vaughan Williams

[1] VW had recently conducted Bach's St Matthew and St John Passions with the Bach Choir for the first time and LB had presumably written warmly about a performance. See *RVW*, 48.

136. From Margaret Vaughan Williams 11 October 1923

Leith Hill Place
Nr. Dorking

Thursday Oct: 11th 1923

My dear old Ralph –

Your Birthday when you receive this – I can only say many many happy returns and years of your and Adelines life together – such a perfect one between you two and such a very dear son to me. This very ungrammatical sentence expresses what I have to say to you two dear Children.[1]

M.J.V.W.

[1] Printed in *RVW*, 153.

137. To William Rothenstein

21 October 1923

13 Cheyne Walk
SW3

21/10/23

Dear Rothenstein

Thank you very much for your most interesting series of portraits.[1] One advantage the artist has over the musician is that he is obliged to study human nature & get into contact with other interesting minds.

I feel proud, though slightly embarrassed, at being in such distinguished company.

Yours sincerely
R. Vaughan Williams

[1] William Rothenstein, *Twenty-four Portraits with Critical Appreciations by Various Hands . . . Second Series*, published by Chatto & Windus in 1923. The first series had been published by Allen & Unwin in 1920.

138. To Gerald Finzi[1]

17 November 1923

17/11/23

Dear Mr Finzi

As far as I am concerned, with pleasure. But please ask Mrs Leather as well. Address –

Castle House,
Weobley
R.S.O.
Herefordshire.

By the way perhaps I ought to tell you that I also have used the tune in a choral work published by Stainer and Bell.[2]

Yours sincerely
R. Vaughan Williams

[1] English composer (1901–56).

[2] Gerald Finzi had asked for permission to use 'The truth sent from above' as the basis for his Christmas carol *The Brightness of this day* (later published by Stainer & Bell in 1925). VW had collected the tune at King's Pyon, Herefordshire, with Mrs Ella Mary Leather in Aug. 1909 (see *CW*, p. 274) and had used it as the opening tune in *Fantasia on Christmas Carols* (*CW* 1912/6). The permission granted by VW and Mrs Leather is duly acknowledged in the score of Finzi's work. Finzi's reply is drafted on the bottom of the original: 'Dear Dr Williams, V. many thanks. Of course I know you have used the tune, but the thing is so slight that I did not think it worth while apologising for doing the same. Yours sincerely Gerald Finzi.' This letter marks the start of a lifelong friendship.

139. From Karl Straube[1]

5 December 1923

Leipzig
Dorotheenplatz 1 [ix]

Dez 5th 1923

Dear Sir

I had the honour and great pleasure of bringing out your Mass in G minor in St Thomas's Church Leipzig, if I should be not wrong, as first performance in Germany.[2]

The work made a very deep impression on the whole audience, indeed has made your name popular in Leipzig, the musicians were fascinated and the 'connoisseurs' of music over-powered by the beauty of the composition; we all have to bring thanks to you, for giving us this refined masterpiece of musical art.

Sincerely yours
Karl Straube.

[1] Kantor of St Thomas's Church, Leipzig.

[2] The performance of the mass, *CW* 1922/5, had been on 16 November. A letter from Kenneth Curwen of 7 Aug. 1923 survives explaining that copies of the mass had had to be sent in effect *gratis*, though they had received a note for 5,000 marks, which he suggested VW keep as a memento (it is still in UVW's papers). Straube had written to Curwen: 'I find the mass very beautiful; it possesses the charm and the finished form which have always been the hall mark of the best English music. Especially the "Sanctus" must sound well, and make a deep impression. I am very keen to hear how it will sound when sung by a German choir. Could you not come to Leipzig for the performance? As you have English pounds, it would mean very little expense to you. I shall let you know the date, as soon as it is fixed.'

140. To Gustav Holst[1]

31 December [1923]

Dec 31.

N.B. This is not a new years letter tho' it sounds like it.

Dear Gustav

I won't have you talking about 'bother' – there is no necessity for you & me to talk about such things – but in this case I am *going* to say what a wonderful experience it was for me & all of us learning your wonderful music – which got better & better as we went on. It was a tussle I admit – but from the 1st they loved it – & I know of no other work which I shd have *dared* to make a choir slog so at – There – you must bear with me so far.[2]

Now as to the awful news about Keats – I hoped I shd have seen Isobel & Imogen[3] at the EFDS yesterday & hear it was found – do send me a card.[4] As to my scoring it *must* go to the copyist today – as the show is Jan: 21 – so it must take its chance[5] – I think if I go away at all I shall go by the sea for a day or two to try & get rid of my cold – Today I go to Middlesboro' for an Eisteddfoddd(dd)

Yrs
RVW

[1] Printed in part as Letter XXIV in *HR*.
[2] VW had conducted the London Bach Choir in the first performance of the *The Ode to Death*, Op. 38, H144 (played twice) and also the *Short Festival Te Deum*, H145, at the Queen's Hall on 19 December. Holst had written (*HR*, Letter XXIII, p. 60) thanking him and suggesting a contract to conduct every first performance he got for the next ten years.
[3] Holst's wife and daughter.
[4] A reference perhaps to the manuscript draft of Holst's *Choral Symphony*, settings of poems by Keats and referred to by Holst sometimes as the 'Keats Symphony', which had been completed during the autumn of 1923. See Short, *Holst*, 218.
[5] Though it is not certain, VW may be referring to the orchestral version of *On Wenlock Edge*, *CW* 1909/1, which was prepared around this time.

141. To Cedric Glover[1]

[April 1924]

13 Cheyne Walk
SW 3

Dear Mr Glover

I once heard a Bach performance with harpsichord throughout (in Queens Hall) & it sounded intolerable in a large place – I think a harpsichord & a small organ is ideal for the recitatives (as they do at Amsterdam) – but this is out of practical politics – & who is to play it? Also the harpsichord by itself at once gives an 'antiquarian' flavour to the music which we want to avoid at all costs. I do not propose to use the pfte in the choruses except to strengthen the bass in one or two places.

And we must remember that the modern violin oboe & horns are as about as remote from the instruments of Bachs time as the pfte is from the harpsichord.

As to the figuring in the confiteor and other places – it does not follow that because Bach did not mark them he did not want them (see Schweitzer[2])

I think Bach probably wrote no solos for viola because no one c^d play it – his viola parts look like this – I rather like the viola in the agnus.

I am having some of the recitatives done on the organ

But please bring it up at the C^tee I am quite open to argument[3]

Yrs sincerely
R. Vaughan Williams

P.S. On Bach's instrumentation generally read Schweitzer – Do you remember Allens[4] magnificent trombones at the end of the mass.

P.P.S. The harpsichord is all right with a small band & small choir – but 350 in Q. Hall!

[1] A member of the Bach Choir who was later a neighbour in Dorking. He played the viola in the LHMF orchestra and was Treasurer of the Royal Musical Association, 1949–62.

[2] Albert Schweitzer's *J. S. Bach, le musicien-poète* (Leipzig, 1905) had been published in an English translation by Ernest Newman as *J. S. Bach* in 1911 and re-issued in 1923.

[3] VW was to conduct Bach's B minor Mass for the first time on 13 May at the Queen's Hall; see *RVW*, 154. VW remained convinced about the ineffectiveness of the harpsichord in performances of the mass and the Passions to the end of his life, in the face of the growing trend towards the use of authentic instruments. This letter is printed in *RVW*, Appendix II, p. 427.

[4] Hugh Allen, VW's predecessor as conductor of the Bach Choir.

142. To E. J. Dent

[before 5 June 1924]

Lemons Cottage
Abinger Common, Dorking
Surrey[1]

Dear Dent

I hope you won't mind me butting in on the subject of the Cambridge Professorship. I hear a report that you do not propose to stand for it. I hope this is not true.[2]

I admit that what the authorities *ought* to do is to offer it you *without* your applying. But I believe they are so hide bound that they will not go outside their custom, which is only to consider those who have applied.

I feel it so very important for music in England that you should have the position – in fact if I may make so bold I think it is your *duty* to offer yourself.

So I very much hope that you will give in to the prejudice of these people to the extent at all events of a formal letter to the effect that you wish to stand for the post.

I realize that if by any chance they did appoint someone else (and of course there is no lengths of foolishness to which a committee cannot go) you w[d] feel in an unpleasant position – But I do feel that we ought to give *them the chance* of doing the right thing –

Yrs ever
R. Vaughan Williams

[1] Home of Olive Heseltine, sister of H. A. L. Fisher's wife, Lettice.

[2] The chair of music at Cambridge had fallen vacant following the death of Charles Stanford on 29 Mar. 1924.

143. To Humphrey Procter-Gregg[1]

[June 1924]

Dear Procter Gregg

I *can't* stomach our Mike being made drunk & put in the stocks. – He seems to me a poetical character & it w[d] leave a decided nasty taste in the mouth to have him made drunk & made a fool of – he ought to be outside the action. It will to my mind entirely spoil the memory of his entry in Act I.[2]

On the other hand I am willing to give up Aunt Jane – So shall we compromise on the *Turnkey*

– he could either (1) come out very drunk with the other roysterers & fall asleep by the stocks (or any where else)

or (2) we could have a modified version of the present interruption when the constable looks out of the window – Aunt Jane c^{d} come out then & see Mary & be silenced by her by a few words

A. J. (softly) Mary here?

Mary (whispers) don't give me away

A. J. aloud to constable (who has remained up stairs) 'All's well'

Constable. 'Hullo where's that damned turnkey – come along sir & watch the spy – Jane come in & give me my night-posset' (exit Aunt Jane)

Enter Turnkey very drunk from the pub sits down & sings a ridiculous song

'Watching a spy
makes me feel dry' etc

– He falls asleep

Hugh 'Now, now my love 'tis time' – they are about to start when they are confronted by Aunt Jane – 'Now you people what's all this about'

Then your ensemble (with modifications)[3]

Yrs
R. Vaughan Williams

[1] Head of the Opera Department at the RCM and Stage Manager and designer of their first productions of *The Shepherds of the Delectable Mountains* and *Hugh the Drover* and producer of *Sir John in Love*.

[2] Mike is the Ballad Seller in *Hugh the Drover*. The action in question takes place in Act II of the opera.

[3] In the final version of the opera Mike neither appears drunk nor is put in the stocks.

144. To E. J. Dent

postmark: 5 June 1924[1]

13 Cheyne Walk
Chelsea, S.W.

Dear Dent

I've written to the V.C.[2] with great pleasure – you are the one person I want to see in that post. You've never had your deserts yet. I hear a rumour (confidential) that they may appoint C.W.[3] and offer you a readership. – I do hope you w^{d} pocket the insult & and accept it, if this be so – Because, to my mind, you w^{d} then be professor *de facto* tho' not *de jure* – & it w^{d} be splendid for Cambridge.[4]

Yrs very sincerely
R. Vaughan Williams

[1] Addressed to Dent at Hotel Passage, Prag and redirected thence to Frankfurt o/M, Hospic Schweizerhof.

[2] The Vice-Chancellor, Sir Albert Charles Seward (1863–1941), Master of Downing College.

[3] Charles Wood, who was indeed appointed Professor on this occasion. Dent became Professor two years later in 1926 following Wood's death in July of that year. See also no. 146 to T. H. Marshall, in which VW explains why he himself had not stood for the post.

[4] If a readership was offered, Dent did not accept it but remained in London until he succeeded Wood.

145. To Ralph Wedgwood

23 June 1924

23.6.24[1]

Dear Randolph

I know you don't care about titles – But you must allow your friends to feel pleased when your work is recognized.[2]

Yrs affectionately
R. Vaughan Williams

Don't answer of course

[1] Date in hand of recipient.

[2] Wedgwood had received a knighthood in the birthday honours in recognition of his work as General Manager of the LNER.

146. To T. H. Marshall[1]

16 September 1924

As from 13 Cheyne Walk
SW3

9/16/24[2]

Dear Mr Marshall

Thank you very much for your letter. I did not stand for the post[3] entirely because I thought (and still think) that I am not a 'fit and proper person'. People will not realise what an appallingly illiterate person I am – both in ancient and modern music – nor have I had more than a very little experience of teaching and organising. My whole life has been taken up (in the intervals of earning my living) with trying to become a composer – & I look forward now that I can drop some of my outside work to trying to really learn the job of a composer – which I have as yet failed to do – before I am too old to do anything.

To take up an important work, for which I am entirely unprepared, at the age of 51 wd become an appalling prospect. In order to carry out the conditions of teaching organising (which people like Dent w[d] take in their stride) I should have to go back to school & learn it all up – this wd take all my time & goodbye to all my private work.

The one thing I feel I c[d] do fairly adequately, conducting the C.U.M.S.[4] etc is already being very well done – and I cd not interfere with it. Don't think I am being selfish in this – for the very reason which makes me not want to undertake it, would also, obviously, make me a very bad professor.

To put it shortly – at my time of life I've got to settle whether with the rest of what remains to me I am to write or to teach – I want (rightly or wrongly) to write – I can't do both – also for the same reason I am a bad teacher.

I wrote (I believe at your original suggestion) to the V.C.[5] on behalf of Dent – This in itself prevents my now standing myself. I have also had a very kind letter from Stewart[6] – wd you mind showing him this rigmarole – as it will answer him as well as you.

I am sorry for delay in answering – but I am away from home this week.

Yours very sincerely
R. Vaughan Williams

[1] T. H. Marshall was, at the time of this letter, a Prize Fellow at Trinity College, Cambridge, and a keen amateur musician, and thus served on the Committee for the election to the Chair of Music. Subsequently he became Professor of Sociology at the London School of Economics and Director of Social Sciences at UNESCO. He died in 1981.

[2] This American arrangement of the date is unusual for VW. It is possible he just wrote 24 and Marshall added 9/16 in front of the figure.

[3] The Chair of Music at Cambridge—Charles Wood was appointed on this occasion. Dent succeeded him in 1926.

[4] Cambridge University Musical Society.

[5] See no. 144 to Dent on the subject of his standing for the Professorship.

[6] H. F. Stewart, French scholar and Fellow of Trinity College.

147. To Percy Scholes

21 September 1924

13 Cheyne Walk
Chelsea, S.W.3

21/9/24

My dear Scholes

I'm sorry – but why should you inflict Mrs Coates' bosh on an unoffending public?

Her screed was entirely unauthorized – & did a lot of harm in U.S.A.[1]

Up to the present I've managed to keep it out of England – I don't mind Finale so much[2] – but would rather not have it – it spoils your otherwise excellent article – but really Mrs Coates is rather too much for me.

By the way, the 'interpolation' you mention (p. 8?) is really the beginning of the recapitulation – it almost exactly reproduces the section of the 1st part beginning

(I cannot verify as I have no copy here) and so goes right on to the 2nd subject.[3]

Yrs
R. Vaughan Williams

[1] Madelon Coates, wife of the conductor Albert Coates, had written some notes on *A London Symphony* based on pictures which VW had told her and her husband (apparently rather reluctantly) that he had had in mind while composing the work. When VW saw what she had written he was unhappy but she claimed he had allowed her to publish the notes in America. He was certainly anxious that they should have no circulation in England. Scholes had asked Mrs Coates for permission to use her notes in his *Second Book of the Gramophone Record*; this she gave him but warned him that she expected VW would be unhappy about it. Scholes told her that he would send VW his piece in proof but would be careful not to annoy him.

[2] Presumably Coates's note on the last movement.

[3] The passage quoted by VW occurs at letter G in the first movement.

148. To E. J. Dent

[January 1925]

13 Cheyne Walk,
S.W.

Dear Dent

Many thanks for your letter. I feel much honoured at being selected to represent England at the next Festival.[1]

As regards conducting – I sh[d] think if Talich[2] feels a sympathy with the work & w[d] like to do it – he had better do so. Failing him Adrian or Malcolm Sargent (who conducts it at the Phil: in April).

As regards the 'Rondels' Steuart is the man for them if possible.[3]

Yours very sincerely
R. Vaughan Williams

[1] The *Pastoral Symphony* was to be given at the ISCM Festival in Prague. Adrian Boult eventually conducted the work. See no. 150 and *RVW*, 158–9.

[2] Vaclav Talich (1883–1962), principal conductor of the Czech Philharmonic Orchestra 1919–41.

[3] *Merciless Beauty*. Three rondels for high voice, with accompaniment for string trio (2 violins, 1 violoncello) or pianoforte, *CW* 1921/11. 'Steuart' is the tenor Steuart Wilson, the dedicatee of *Four Hymns*, *CW* 1914/2.

149. To E. J. Dent

13 January [1925]

13 Cheyne Walk
S.W.3

Jan 13

Dear Dent

I had a letter from Steuart[1] the other day – he seems to be getting on 1st rate. Don't you think he ought to have another 6 months? I send another contribution to the fund.

I'm v. sorry if I am foolish about the internat:[2] – But I can't face sending in works to be 'sat on' – I've never done so (since I was quite young)* – If anyone honours me by asking to do a work of mine I feel honoured – but I never *ask them*.

Yours very sincerely
R. Vaughan Williams

* An apparent exception is the L. Symphony[3] – but I was under the impression that the Carnegie people were asking to publish it – not that I was sending in for a competition or I sh[d] never have sent it in.
P.S. I have nothing against Ansermet[4] – he was the only adjudicator whose name I knew.

[1] This refers to the aftermath of serious injuries suffered by Wilson in the war, in which he lost a kidney and part of a lung.

[2] Dent was the first President of the International Society for Contemporary Music and asked VW to submit a work to be considered for performance at the ISCM in Prague. VW must have given in gracefully, for the *Pastoral Symphony* was eventually chosen for performance.

[3] *A London Symphony*.

[4] Ernest Ansermet, founder in 1918 of L'Orchestre de la Suisse Romande.

150. To E. J. Dent

postmark: 5 February 1925

Dear Dent

I'm sorry there has been any trouble – I wrote to Talich as you suggested & received a v. nice letter from him saying he was willing (He c[d] not see me) – The next thing I knew was a notice in the Times that a subscription was being got up to provide a British conductor for my work (rather as if I was a 'deserving case'). On my protesting I was told by the secretary[1] that the matter rested entirely in their hands & if I really preferred a foreign conductor & *w[d] give my reasons* (!) they w[d] consider it.

So now I have told them they have got me (and you) into this mess & they must get us out again.

Yrs
RVW

P.S. I don't think there is any good analysis of the P.S.[2]

[1] Of the British Music Society.
[2] *Pastoral Symphony*, *CW* 1921/13.

151. To Robert F. McEwen[1]

postmark: 29 March 1925

My Dear McEwen

I was so much touched by your suggestion about my 'Shepherds' – both the fact of your offer & the way you made it.[2]

But I do not think I ought to accept it – For one thing I think it quite possible that a publisher might accept it in the ordinary course of business – only I am too lazy & too busy to make the necessary effort to approach one. Also I feel that I ought to be able (if necessary) to do this myself out of the ill-gotten gains of such sins of my youth as 'Linden Lea' which becomes every year more horribly popular

But all this does not prevent my feeling grateful to you for such a testimony of friendship and interest.

Yrs very sincerely
R. Vaughan Williams[3]

[1] Robert Finnie McEwen of Marchmont, Berwickshire. VW had stayed with Mr and Mrs McEwen in 1923.
[2] McEwen had offered to finance the publication of *The Shepherds of the Delectable Mountains*, *CW* 1922/6. See no. 157.
[3] Printed in *RVW*, 158.

152. To the Revd Lancelot Bark

30 April [1925]

13 Cheyne Walk
S.W.3

April 30

Dear Mr Bark

Many thanks for your interesting letter. The next musical visitor to Patmos will probably collect my tune as a Greek folk-song![1]

Yours sincerely
R. Vaughan Williams

[1] Canon Bark related the circumstances giving rise to VW's letter in a covering letter to UVW printed in *RVW*, 159–60: he had been music director of an Anglo-Catholic pilgrimage to the Holy Places in 1925 and, on approaching the monastery at Patmos, the whole party of 300 or more sang 'For all the Saints' to VW's *Sine Nomine*. The abbot had asked Mr Bark to write the tune down for their use and had provided vellum and ink for the purpose.

153. To Robert F. McEwen[1]

postmark: 10 May 1925

Dear M^c^Ewen

Thank you so much for sending me your two compositions. I am just off to Prag for the 'Freak' festival.[2]

You may be glad to hear that your interest in the 'Shepherds' has indirectly borne fruit – for it stirred me up to send it to the Oxford Press & they have accepted it.[3]

Yours sincerely
R. Vaughan Williams

[1] See no. 151.
[2] The VWs were attending the ISCM Festival in Prague.
[3] See no. 151. Quoted in *RVW*, 158, 159.

154. To Gustav Holst[1]

[about 1 November 1925[2]]

Dear Gustav

I feel I want to write & put down (chiefly for my own benefit) why I felt vaguely disappointed after the Phil (so you need not read this.) Not perhaps dissappointed [*sic*] – I felt cold admiration – but did not want to get up & embrace everyone & then get drunk like I did after the H of J.[3] I think it is only because it *is* a new work & I am more slowly moving than I used to be & it's got to soak in.[4]

But first I want to set down the bits where I was all there, viz.

The opening (a great surprize to me)

Dorothy's[5] first solo,

The orchestral end of the scherzo

The two lovely tunes in the Finale

Then again I've come to the conclusion that the Leeds Chorus *CANNOT SING* – the Bacchus Chorus sounded like an Oratorio.

As to the Grecian Urn it was *pattered* not sung – No phrasing & no legato. If only the B.C.[6] c^{d} sing in tune or Morley had any tenors we c^{d} show them how to do it.

In the scherzo they made the words sound so *common*.

I couldn't bear to think that I was going to 'drift apart' from you musically speaking. (If I do, who shall I have to crib from?) – & I don't believe it is so – so I shall live in faith till I have heard it again several times & then I shall find out what a bloody fool I was not to see it all first time.

Forgive me this rigmarole – but I wanted to get it off my chest.

Yrs
RVW

[1] Printed as Letter XXV in *HR*.

[2] Holst replied on 11 Nov. (*HR*, Letter XXVI, p. 61).

[3] i.e. *The Hymn of Jesus*.

[4] VW had been to the second performance of the *First Choral Symphony* at the Queen's Hall on 29 Oct. given at a Royal Philharmonic Society concert by the LSO conducted by Albert Coates. On the critical reception of the *Choral Symphony* see Short, *Holst*, 237–41.

[5] Dorothy Silk, the soprano soloist.

[6] The Bach Choir.

155. Memorandum on the General Strike [about May 1926]

A. On the whole I am with the miners in this dispute. I think the owners are incompetent (I hear that the best owners are not in the association and do not take part in the negotiations). I think Baldwin was wrong to stop negotiations on account of the D.M. episode[1] however much provocation he had and even if the T.U.C. did break faith – because the welfare of the country is more important than the morals of the T.U.C.

I mistrust the Churchill–Birkenhead gang in the cabinet & think the attitude of the gov^{t} is largely theirs – and the beastly rag the National Gazette which is trying to inflame evil passions is theirs also.

I think it quite possible that a section of the party will want to be vindictive if the strike continues long and is then broken & will want to reduce wages all round.

Also this is developing into a *class* war & I don't feel at all inclined to side with my own class (though I suppose that at a pinch I should)

B. Isn't our duty to support the govt as such even if in the end it has to resort to armed force? Is it wrong to be on the side of revolution if it came to that? I should not be against revolution by violence in the last resort (I don't think the status quo any thing to be proud of) But before I c[d] do that & envisage the temporary anarchy which would follow I must be fairly certain that a *better* state of things is going to emerge. And have the side of revolution any scheme for the better government of the country to offer if they were victorious? I doubt it.

Is it not in that case our duty to support the gov[t] (however much one dislikes it) and in that case one must go the whole hog & if the govt find it necessary to shoot to go & shoot with them:

This brings me to C.

C. Much as I dislike the govt I mistrust the labour leaders also MacDonald[2] is an unpractical sentimentalist & Cook is an empty wind-bag – & moreover he and many of his colleagues are the paid agents of Trade Unions & are afraid of losing their jobs if they are not continually 'asking for more'. I think the TUC made a great mistake in refusing to budge even a nominal inch in the negotiations.

Also I believe there is some truth in the talk of trade union tyranny, & I think that 'Ca' Canny' is contemptible.[3]

D. I hate the O.M.S. – it accents the class war side.[4]

But I cannot deny the right of an Oxford undergraduate to go and unload fish if the man whose job it is refuses to do so. Also I cannot deny the duty of the gov[t] to see that people do not starve if the food is to be had. Now what is one to do?

The simplest thing for a man of my age is to do nothing.

But one cannot help benefiting by the gov[t] action – one is powerless to refuse the benefits – If one accepts the benefits must not one support the organization which provides them. Once again I don't believe in half hogs in this matter.[5]

[1] The compositors at the *Daily Mail* had refused to set the paper because of a government advertisement appealing for volunteers to assist against the strike.

[2] Ramsay MacDonald, leader of the Labour Party. Arthur James Cook was General Secretary of the Miners Federation of Great Britain.

[3] 'Ca' canny': a Scots expression meaning go cautiously or 'go slow'.

[4] The Organization for the Maintenance of Supplies, which was set up to keep supplies moving in the event of a general strike.

[5] This note setting out his personal dilemma is in UVW's file for 1926 and is summed up by her: 'he was deeply troubled by the political situation and he was in doubt as to what part, if any, he should take when the strike happened' (*RVW*, 162).

156. To the members of the Bach Choir [about 12 June 1926]

MESSAGE FROM THE MUSICAL DIRECTOR.

As I shall not have an opportunity of meeting many of the members of the Bach Choir before next season, I want to tell them of my admiration of the manner in which they carried out our arduous four day festival.[1]

There was present throughout that 'inner fire', (to quote Dr. Straube[2]) that enthusiasm and devotion which are of more value than any amount of technique.

Particularly I wish to thank the Choir for their fine performance of my 'Sancta Civitas' and I want to tell members that I am aware that this performance was the result of much more than our weekly practices.[3]

The performance of the Mass was to my mind a worthy climax to a week of splendid singing.[4]

R. Vaughan Williams,
Musical Director

[1] The Festival was to celebrate the Bach Choir's Fiftieth Jubilee. See *RVW*, 164.

[2] Karl Straube, Kantor of St Thomas's Church, Leipzig, who had given the first performance in Germany of VW's Mass in G minor. See no. 139. He was present at the Festival.

[3] The Choir had given the first London performance of *Sancta Civitas* (*CW* 1925/6) on 9 June.

[4] A performance of Bach's B minor Mass. The letter is printed in *RVW*, 164.

157. To John McEwen[1] postmark: 29 July 1926

13 Cheyne Walk

Dear Mr McEwen

It was a great pleasure to me to receive the copy of the Brahms Clarinet Sonatas from your father's library. Up to the present I have not been able to connect his gift with any particular conversation or other circumstance – but we used to talk about so much music when we met that I think we may have discussed this work.

I am always very sorry that I was not able to send your father a copy of my 'Shepherds of the delectable Mountains'. About two years ago he most generously offered to defray the expense of publishing it. At the time I did not feel that I ought to accept his very kind offer but the indirect result was that I overcame my inertia and offered 'The Shepherds' to a publisher who to my surprise immediately accepted it. The copies have only lately appeared – I wish I could have sent him one.

Yours sincerely
R. Vaughan Williams

[1] John McEwen of Marchmont, Berwickshire, son of Robert Finnie McEwen, who had just died. See no. 151.

158. To Donald Francis Tovey[1]

3 March [1927]

13 Cheyne Walk
Chelsea, S.W.

March 3

Dear Tovey

Thank you very much for your delightful and informative letter.

I wish I could have heard your performance of my P.S.[2] Your analytical programme interested me very much – I didn't know that I was being 'tri-planar'! After all it's only a very slight extension of our old friends the 'added thirds' that we used to learn about in the counterpoint books, but I suppose that, like M. Jourdain I have been talking prose all my life without knowing it.[3]

I only join issue with you on one point – that is the supposed 'rusticity' of the Scherzo – It was far from my mind when I wrote it – To let you into a secret the last two movements have for their material the sketches for a ballet that I was once asked to write but discarded as I found the subject uncongenial.[4] It was something about a voice in a wood and the themes of the scherzo were to have been a dance of oofs and goblins and at the end they all run off[5] – But don't say anything about this because I don't think it a good plan labelling works with programmes. Though a programme may often help the composer and the interpreter may often be helped by making up a programme *of his own* but not a ready-made one by someone else. Forgive this long rigmarole. It is only a roundabout way of saying Thank you very much. I hope we may meet soon.

Yrs sincerely
R. Vaughan Williams

P.S. Your account of E♭ Tpt & its tricks v. interesting. I bought a real E♭ my self – but I find the trumpet players can fake the 'natural' notes.[6]

RVW

[1] Donald Francis Tovey (1875–1940), pianist, conductor, and writer on music, best known for his programme notes collected as *Essays on Musical Analysis* (1935–9). From 1914 he was Reid Professor of Music at Edinburgh University.

[2] Tovey had conducted a performance of both VW's and Beethoven's Pastoral Symphonies by the Reid Symphony Orchestra at the Usher Hall on 24 Feb. 1927.

[3] A reference to the well-known remark by M. Jourdain in Molière's *Le Bourgeois Gentilhomme*, Act II, Scene iv. The programme note was republished in Tovey's *Essays in Musical Analysis*, ii (London, 1935) with additions based on this letter (despite VW's request not to say anything about his source material). However, when writing Tovey misremembered the word 'oofs' as 'oafs' and was so quoted by MK in *WVW*, 205.

[4] VW had been asked to write music for a ballet, *The Voice in the Wood*, to a scenario by Margaret Longman (a singer) and Angela Hubbard (see no. 117). The scenario survives.

[5] VW has in mind Mrs Page's phrase in *The Merry Wives of Windsor*, Act IV, Scene iv, l. 50: 'and three or four more of their growth we'll dress / like urchins, ouphes and fairies, green and white . . .'. At this time VW was working on *Sir John in Love* and this passage was incorporated into Act IV, Scene i of the opera. See *WVW*, 205.

[6] In his note Tovey discusses the E♭ trumpet required for the solo in the second movement and the nature of the seventh note (B♭) in its series of natural harmonics, which VW required (see the note on this quoted in *CW*, p. 90).

159. To Evelyn Sharp[1]

26 July [1927]

The Rew Cottage
Abinger Common
Dorking

July 26th

Dear Miss Sharp

Does Garnett mean 10% of the monies earned by us or earned by our publisher? If the latter there would be practically nothing left for us, in which case our work would be a pure labour of love. I don't mind this but I think it wrong on principle for I consider the labourer is worthy of his hire. Would it in that case be better to drop it altogether[2]

I haven't got very far with it yet for other things have surged up in my mind which it was imperative I should fix before I lost them.

If Garnett means 10% of what *we* earn I should feel inclined to accept that because then if we fail to bring the work to a satisfactory conclusion or to persuade a manager to take it we shall not have paid anything.

I hope to write to you when I have done the job I am on suggesting some alterations & extensions in your 1st Act.[3]

Yrs sincerely
R. Vaughan Williams

[1] Evelyn Sharp was the sister of Vaughan Williams's friend and fellow folk-song collector, Cecil Sharp. She married the writer Henry Nevinson in 1933.

[2] Evelyn Sharp was preparing a libretto for the opera *The Poisoned Kiss* (*CW* 1936/4), whose plot was developed from a short story 'The Poison Maid' from *Twilight of the Gods* by Richard Garnett.

[3] Letters from VW to Evelyn Sharp suggesting alterations to the plot in considerable detail are extant in British Library, MS Mus. 161.

160. To Evelyn Sharp

postmark: 18 August 1927

Dear Miss Sharp

Many thanks for Act II

I think it looks v. good – but have not digested it yet.

Of course after that light satirical 1st Act we mustn't get *too* serious

Another practical point we mustn't have too many *principal* characters – it looks from yr Act II as if the 3 Hobs and the 3 mediums wd have to be principals & not merely superior chorus – this wd make 11 principals & presumably with the Empress in Act III = 12!

If you happen to be stuck up for metres I have been studying 'Polly' & he gets some v. good metres from fitting words to tunes.[1]

So *if* you happened to be stuck up for metres it might be worthwhile looking at the country dances/some of the more musical rhythms ('Mr Isaacs Maggot' occurs to me) – but this is only one suggestion – I don't want you to be fettered in any way – I believe the best method is for me to make hay of your words *after* you have written them (you'll have a fit when you see all the alterations I want to make in Act I)

By the way if you happen to want a song (or duet or trio) of a light rather folk songy character you might consider this metre – as I have at the moment a tune in my head in that metre

V.S.[2]

. . . [page missing]

We've really got to make up our minds whether this is to be a musical comedy or real comic opera. In musical comedy (or ballad opera) the music is purely incidental i.e. the music cd be left out and the drama wd remain intact. In comic opera at certain points (usually the finale) the drama is carried on through the music – the only difference this makes to the librettist is that in certain places the drama goes on in verse & not in prose – & usually in *short* sentences not long songs

In our 1st Act the music is more or less incidental & we may have to strengthen the ensemble [in] places.

– on the other hand I see you have a long musical finale to Act II

– on the other hand I feel that the actual end of Act III ought to be a sort of choral set song.

What a rigmarole

Yrs very sincerely
R. Vaughan Williams[3]

P.S. I am back in London on Sept 1st & we might meet then

[1] *Polly*, a ballad opera arranged by Johann Christoph Pepusch, with libretto by John Gay, written in 1728 but banned by the Lord Chamberlain and not performed until 1777. It was a sequel to *The Beggar's Opera*.
[2] i.e. *Volte subito* or P.T.O. However, the page with the metre is missing.
[3] Printed in part in *WVW*, 199.

161. To Evelyn Sharp

23 September [1927]

13 Cheyne Walk
S.W.3

Sep 23

Dear Miss Sharp

Many thanks for your letter. Certainly close with Mr. Garnett and accept his offer of 15% and I will agree to pay you half of that sum. As you suggest I enclose a formal letter to that effect.

I do not want a regular agreement if you don't. I fear it will be some time before I get on to the opera again as I have so many neglected jobs to do and I may feel it difficult to take it up again – But having once made a start I feel happy about it and if you will have patience with me I feel sure we shall bring it to a successful issue one day.[1]

Yours very sincerely
R. Vaughan Williams

[1] VW was now occupying himself with *Job*.

162. To Evelyn Sharp

[23 September 1927]

Letter No 2[1]

Dear Miss Sharp

This is an addition to ⌊the⌋ enclosed.

Before I write my final letter there are one or two things I want to make clear in my own mind.

I propose – as you know – that we should share equally all the takings, both from music and libretto of our proposed opera – But does Mr Garnett know this? And if he does not *need* he ever know it? Because though I think equal division is the only fair method it is not the usual method. Would it be unfair on Mr Garnett for us to find out what the usual librettist share is and to pay him 15% on that?[2]

We would then make a financial agreement to that effect including an agreement on my part to pay half Mr Garnett's fee and the equal sharing could be done by an informal understanding afterwards –

Does this strike you as underhand?

I don't think so –

Yrs very sincerely
R. Vaughan Williams

[1] This letter was enclosed with no. 161.

[2] Richard Garnett was claiming a share of the royalties since the plot was based on a short story by him. See nos. 159 and 185.

163. To Gwen Raverat

[August 1927[1]]

The REW Cottage
Abinger Common
Dorking

Dear Gwen

I am anxiously awaiting your *scenario*[2] – otherwise the music will push on by itself which may cause trouble later on.

I've got the Wicksteed book[3] – but I'm not going to worry about the left foot & the right foot.

Yours sincerely
R. Vaughan Williams

[1] MK suggests 1928 for this letter (*WVW*, 202) but it is in fact 1927—see no. 159 for a letter written from the same address.

[2] For *Job* (*CW* 1930/5), see *WVW*, 202, where this letter is printed.

[3] Joseph Wicksteed, *Blake's Vision of the Book of Job* (1910). He expounded a view of Blake's symbolism.

164. To Gwen Raverat

[October 1927]

13 Cheyne Walk
Chelsea, SW 3

My dear Gwen

I amused myself with making a sketch of Job – I never expected Djag[1] w[d] look at it – & I'm glad on the whole . . .

– the 'reclame' w^d have been rather amusing – but it really wdnt have suited the sham serious really decadent & frivolous attitude of the R.B.[2] towards everything – can you imagine Job sandwiched in between 'Les Biches' and 'Cimarosiana'[3] – & that dreadful pseudo-cultured audience saying to each other 'my dear have you seen God at the Russian Ballet'.

No – I think we are well out of it – I don't think this is sour grapes – for I admit that it w^d have been great fun to have had a production by the R.B. – though I feel myself that they w^d have made an unholy mess of it with their over-developed calves.

Yrs affectionately
R. Vaughan Williams

[1] It was originally intended that Sergei Diaghilev's Russian Ballet should put on *Job* (see *RVW*, 183).

[2] Russian Ballet, i.e. Ballets Russes.

[3] *Les Biches*, to music by Francis Poulenc, was first given in Monte Carlo by the Ballets Russes in 1924; *Cimarosiana*, to music of Cimarosa arranged by Gian Francesco Malipiero, was first given in 1921.

165. To Gerald Finzi

18 November [postmark: 1927]

13 Cheyne Walk

Nov 18

Dear Finzi

I have been thinking about your Concerto[1] and should like to have another look at it. Can you come round and show it to me one day – any morning except Wednesday. If Tuesday I must go out at 11.30 –

Yours sincerely
R. Vaughan Williams

[1] Finzi's Violin Concerto, which had been first performed by Sybil Eaton with the British Women's Symphony Orchestra conducted by Malcolm Sargent in May 1927. Its second performance was to be given by her in a Bach Choir concert conducted by RVW on 1 Feb. 1928 at the Queen's Hall.

166. To Gerald Finzi

postmark: 2 December 1927

Dear Finzi

Weve [*sic*] fixed up the Concerto now. It only remains for you to write it.[1]

Yrs
RVW

[1] Finzi rewrote one movement and altered much else for the second performance. See McVeagh, *Gerald Finzi*, 51.

167. To E. J. Dent

1 July [1928[1]]

13 Cheyne Walk
S.W.

July 1

Dear Dent

May I ask you for some advice? A composition pupil of mine at the R.C.M. whom I consider very gifted is anxious to go abroad and study music, especially composition, for 6 months, or possibly longer.

I also think it would be very good for her. Who do you consider the best composition teacher in Europe at present? And which centre do you consider the best for a young student to receive a 'finishing' musical education and generally to improve their musical culture. I expect you will say that the two queries are incompatible, in which case we shall have to make a compromise.

Miss Maconchy[2] is just 19 – plays the piano quite well and had has a thorough grounding at the hands of Kitson and Charles Wood. She has – as I say – in my opinion decided inventive powers but is of course at present like all young people going through a new phase every month. At present she has been badly bitten by Bartok and is of course anxious to study with him, but I rather doubt the wisdom of this.

I feel possibly that Respighi or Casella might be good for her – if they ever take pupils. On the other hand neither Rome nor Buda-Pesth would I imagine be good from the point of view of general musical atmosphere and the hearing of plenty of good music etc. Also of course we must consider a place where we could find a nice family for her to live with and so on.

Are Leipzig or Dresden any good nowadays? Prague has been suggested to me – what do you think of that? or I thought of sending her to Ravel but I doubt if he would take any pupils now.

I should be most grateful for your advice. I hope I am not asking too much but I feel I have a certain claim on you in your professorial capacity[3] though I am no longer an undergraduate of your university.

Yrs
R. Vaughan Williams

[1] 1928 is the year in which the VWs left Cheyne Walk for Dorking. The letter is in fact from 1926: See p. 4.

[2] Elizabeth Maconchy studied at the RCM 1923–9 and in fact went to Prague to study with Jirák, though it is not known if this was because of advice from Dent. See *New Grove*.

[3] Dent had been appointed Professor of Music at Cambridge in 1926, having been strongly urged by VW to apply for the post in 1924 following Sir Charles Stanford's death (see nos. 142 and 144).

168. To Gerald Finzi

15 August [1928]

The Old Barn
Holmbury St Mary
Dorking

Aug 15

Dear Finzi

(1) 23rd will suit me very well
(2) Come as early in the morning as you like.
(3) Take a bus at Dorking to Holmbury St Mary & enquire for the footpath up.
(4) But if you want a longer walk you can take a bus to Wotton Manor Farm or Crossways & walk here via Abinger Common
(5) You have been here before
(6) Certainly bring some stuff with you.

Yrs
R. Vaughan Williams

169. To Hubert Foss at OUP

[about 1 October 1928]

Glorydene
St Paul's Road
Dorking

Dear Foss

I have been asked to write a Te Deum for the enthronement of the new Archbp in Cant: Cath: W^{d} you like to see it? It will be ready by Wednesday. But it *must* be out by Nov. 1st – so time presses – I was only asked to do it a 4^{t}-night ago.[1]

Yrs
R. Vaughan Williams

Note Address

[1] The *Te Deum*, *CW* 1928/1, was written for the enthronement of Cosmo Lang as Archbishop on 4 Dec. 1928 at Canterbury Cathedral. Foss replied on 11 Oct. accepting the work for publication. OUP had become VW's regular publisher ever since OUP had accepted *Shepherds of the Delectable Mountains*.

170. To Adrian Boult

14 October [1928]

Glorydene
Dorking

Oct 14

Dear Adrian

Thank you so much for your letter

I know the choir* will make great strides with you. I have already had an enthusiastic account of the first practice.

I enclose a (confidential) list of singers who would do for semi-chorus.[1]

I used to find Lady Gowers a splendid help in arranging the choir-seating for performance discovering semi-chorus singers.

I feel rather diffident about offering advice to such an experienced chorus trainer as you but I will chance my arm & make the following suggestions –

(1) Don't wait to start practice till everybody is ready – or you will never start at all. I always used to kick off at 5–30 sharp however much row was going off at the bargain counter behind the curtain.

(2) Always insist on 2 band rehearsals – the extra rehearsal only costs about £25 which is a drop in the ocean compared with our total loss on each concert. I used to have full rehearsal 4 to 7 the day before the concert, telling the chorus to come at 4–30 or 5 as the case might be – They were very good about it & I got most of the females there by 4–30 & usually had the full chorus there from 5–30 to 6–45 when the band used to disappear & I sometimes kept the chorus on alone up to 7 or later.

Then I had a band rehearsal with soloists & such of the chorus as could turn up at 10 am on the day of the concert.

Yrs
RVW[2]

*I think Bach choir – AMB

[1] VW had given up the conductorship of the Bach Choir on moving to Dorking and Boult had been appointed to succeed him. The footnote asterisked in the letter was added by Boult's wife Ann at a later date.

[2] Printed in Moore, *Music and Friends*, 84.

171. To Lucy Broadwood

30 October [1928]

October 30

Dear Miss Broadwood

Many thanks for your letter.

I wish you had sent your emendations to *me* as I originally asked you – and could you specify your rather vague condemnation of Dearmer's methods? The only one you specify is in the 'Mummer's Carol'. I would point out that the book is for *use* and Dearmer quite rightly (to my mind) went to all the best sources of words and collections and used the best – a few alterations, as you know are necessary (e.g. your revision which you kindly did for me of Mrs Leather's carol about the man who went ploughing on Sunday). I myself think this was quite right.

Also if my memory is correct your own version of the Mummer's Carol in 'English Traditional Songs' is a collection of various versions – In your early version of this carol if I remember right the verse 'when righteous Joseph' did not appear.

To my mind, it makes a much finer whole without it – especially as the verse in question appears in *Carol 41*.

As regards it's being labelled 'Lent' (I thought the poor man would get into trouble over this) the designation does not refer to the *origin* or source but to suitability for practical use – and surely in a poem of which *all* the narrative verses refer *not* to the nativity but to the crucifixion & burial an Editor is justified in suggesting that it is suitable for Lent & Passiontide!![1]

It seems to me that the duty of an editor is to get the best of all versions and put them together – You, as a collector know that it is very seldom one gets a perfect tune and a perfect set of words – Suppose for example you found from one singer a very beautiful version of the tune and from another (or even 2 others) a beautiful version of the words of a ballad – would you not put them together for singing purposes? Is this 'cooking'? If it is may I often sit down to the meal.[2]

Yours sincerely
R. Vaughan Williams

[1] The Sussex Mummers Carol is no. 45 in the *Oxford Book of Carols*, *CW* 1928/2 and had a revised footnote drafted by Lucy Broadwood in reprints.

[2] Broadwood had apparently sent VW some strong criticisms of the newly published *Oxford Book of Carols*. Possibly she was planning a review. VW's reply was originally lost in the post so AVW copied it out from VW's first draft and sent it to her on 7 Nov. with the following covering letter: 'Dear Lucy, You *ought* to have found Ralph's letter in that pile – for he had written. He wrote to you feeling very troubled at your criticisms & his writing was specially illegible so he asked me to copy it – It is so *horrid* to have a

copy but I have done as he asked me but I enclose a page of original script to show you that he did write himself – O how vexatious these printing mistakes are – The next edition must set some things right. Love from Adeline VW'.

172. From Lucy Broadwood [about 1 November 1928]

41 Drayton Court,
S.W.10

Dear Ralph,

I am so sorry ab^{t} your lost letter, which has not reappeared, & for the trouble given to Adeline to transcribe its contents. Please tell her so with many thanks.

In the spring I wrote to you that I was sending Dr Dearmer a list of 'errors' that c^{ld} be easily corrected by the printers & I told you that there was so much more to say that I could not then trouble you (you being very busy and anxious at the time). My allusions must necessarily remain 'vague' for you, as unless I was to annotate the Carol-book page by page & send you the copy you w^{ld} not see what my reasons are based on. But if Dr Dearmer sh^{ld} have kept the letter & fairly long notes which I sent him also, bearing on certain points in his essay and on 'Tomorrow shall be my dancing day', you c^{ld} read them & w^{ld} see that I was not otherwise than definite, tho' I merely touched on two or three of the points which need attention 'en passant': The annunciation verse *is* in *Sussex Songs*. The mummers who came yearly to Lyne always sang it, & I have two copies of the text given to me by two of the mummers separately in which it figures. Years later, I received the other versions. In a few of those the 1st verse was lacking, and other verses had been forgotten.

'Tomorrow shall be my Dancing Day' is, I believe, the most remarkable and important carol that we have (I have shown reasons in my note on it, sent to Dr Dearmer). I connect it with the long-lost 'Acts of John'. The footnote on the carol seems wholly misleading & inadequate.

I can't undertake to write more than a few words ab^{t} other points. But, taking one at random: 'Welcome Summer' (p. 256) where Chaucer's words are wedded to what is called 'an old *Irish Carol tune* slightly altered'. Would it not have been more accurate to say that this is the famous tune 'stolen' (as he himself puts it) 'from an old ballad air "Death & the Lady"' by Carey; and that it is also used in England for a variety of carol-texts, including 'Have you not heard', 'Xmas now is drawing etc.' (see Folk S. Journal, no. 7, pp. 134 to 139, but especially pp. 135 and 137). The Oxford Carol Book version, with its idiosyncrasies, is note for note that on p. 137 of Journal and must surely have been copied from the Journal. It was given to me in 1892 by Mrs Kennedy who had noted it from her Antrim aunt. But the aunt did not sing it to a 'carol' but to 'Death & the Lady'.

I *cannot* think it right to class 'Blow, blow' with its 2 tunes amongst 'carols'.

By the bye, Dr Grattan Flood's Irish carol-tune No. 6 is widely known for the children's ring-game 'Hullabaloo balee! Hullabaloo balay', & I have noted it to that myself. The Czech carol 'The Birds' on p. 212 is an interesting variant of the hackneyed German song, beloved of students, 'Es ritten drei Reiter zum Thore hinaus, a-de!' (thought by the editor of the Neues Wunderhorn to be a tune of the 13th century[1]).

Taking it as a purely 'popular' publication I – whom you have known as a pernickety fogey – should say nothing ab^t the methods of the Carol Book. It was the fact of my having expected something quite different *as coming from the Oxford University Press*: an authoritative book consisting of meticulously-sifted selection of British Carols only, each carol having its complete original text, historical notes, bibliography (partial references are worse than none, often) etc. That shocked me!

[1] This poem was set by Mahler in *Lieder aus der Jugendzeit*, no. 12.

173. To Penelope Spencer[1]

[third week of January 1929]

The Brown House
Cliff Drive
Canford Cliffs
Dorset

Dear Miss Spencer

Many thanks for your letter.

I fear I shall not be able to be in London till *Thursday week* Feb 1 – I hope this will not delay your preparations.[2]

In answer to your questions

(1) The only two boy fairies which are important are the 'Fairy in green' & the 'Fairy in white' who dance with Slender & Caius – If you can persuade them not to be too self conscious, 'boyish' & bumptious certainly have girls.

(2) As to the dances – they also must not be self consciously Hobbley-hoyish & 'Rustic' – neither must they be 'Dainty' – can you strike a happy mean?

There are 4 chief dances in the Act:

(a) At the beginning of Sc. 2 which I imagine to be more a mysterious assembling & dispersal of the characters more than a set dance (b)[3] The dance where the fairies 1st appear to Falstaff

(c) The main fairies dance – Here Slender, Caius, Fenton & Ann have to dance – are you prepared to teach them as well as your trained dancers?

(d) The dance round Falstaff after the fairies have gone – more of a procession than a dance (here also the actors have to dance!)

(e) The final country dance 'Half Hanikin' – I want this to be the real dance belonging to the tune & every one should *finally* join in somehow. (Also a few steps of dance between the verses of the final song).

Yrs ever
R. Vaughan Williams

[1] Penelope Spencer (1901–93) began working for the Royal College of Music in 1923 as Ballet Mistress, a position she held for sixteen years until 1939, and for which she was awarded 'Hon. RCM' in 1928.

[2] Spencer was preparing the dances in *Sir John in Love* (*CW* 1928/3) for its first performance, which took place at the RCM on 21 Mar. 1929.

[3] VW absent-mindedly changed his numeration from (a) to (2) over the page. The alphabetical series is continued here.

174. To Diana Awdry[1]

11 March 1929

13 Cheyne Walk
S.W.3

Received: 11th March 1929[2]

My Dear Diana

I've already told you that I like being bothered when the right people bother (among whom I hope I may be able to count you).

As regards the 'terzetto' my memory is that the scoring is for 'continuo' (i.e. cello & bass) with the harmonies filled up on pfte or organ. I arranged the part for cellos (playing the part) & c. Basses adding a few notes occasionally – with the pfte filling in the harmonies (as it should do at discretion in the whole cantata).[3]

I hope the cello & bass parts have not disappeared out of the parts – I didn't look through them when they last came home.

If they are not there the only thing to do will be to copy the cello part from the *full score* which I sent down with the parts. But you say something about a B. & H.[4] arrangement – if you have that & there is an arrangement of the upper parts for strings there w[d] be no harm in using that – But 'cello, bass & pfte is all that is in Bach's original – Let me know, will you, how it stands?

Now I'm going to bother *you* – when is your performance? Because a man from Broadstairs has asked to borrow them for March 21st & I have told him to ask you to send it direct to him if you have *done with* it by then. Otherwise, of course, he must do without it.

I stupidly forgot your address & you may never get the letter.

His name is

F. E. Fisher F.R.C.O.
Rock Lodge
Stone Road
Broadstairs

C^d you get in touch with him?

Yrs
Ralph Vaughan Williams

1 On Diana Awdry (afterwards Diana Oldridge) see p. 100 above.

2 According to a note in the recipient's hand.

3 It is not clear which Bach cantata he is referring to here.

4 This probably refers to Breitkopf & Härtel, who regularly published Bach cantatas, rather than Boosey & Hawkes.

175. To the Royal College of Music

22 March 1929

13 Cheyne Walk
S.W.

March 22 1929

Miss Elizabeth Maconchy has been my pupil for nearly four years. I have great pleasure in testifying to her industry, good character and power to profit by instruction. She would I feel sure be able to take full advantage of the opportunities provided by the Mendelssohn Scholarship.[1]

Ralph Vaughan Williams

1 Elizabeth Maconchy did not win the Mendelssohn Scholarship, but did win the Blumenthal Travelling Scholarship (see *Grove* v), which enabled her to travel to Prague to study with Jirák in 1930.

176. To Malcolm Sargent

[23 June 1929][1]

13 Cheyne Walk—SW3

Sunday

Dear Sargent

Thank you so much for the tickets on Friday.[2]

It was a wonderful spectacle and I enjoyed it very much. But my present feeling is that 'Hugh' will not do at all as it stands. All the quick action &

dialogue will have to be scrapped and practically a new opera written introducing as much as possible [of] the old music. I feel that this is not impossible, but the question is who is to do it?

After seeing the show on Friday I have fairly definite ideas of what I should like which might not agree with yours. Would it be therefore better – supposing of course that the thing comes off at all – for me to be out of it altogether & the show described as 'arranged by M.S from the opera by RVW'

Supposing I do take it on (of course in cooperation with you) there are certain things I don't want. The ordinary kind of ballet – such as you had in Hiawatha would to my mind be entirely unsuitable – more especially if it was given the ordinary theatrical producer's touch of 'rusticity'.

How about cooperating with the English Folk Dance Society? e.g We could have some real country dances danced by the massed dancers and when the Morris men come in one of their picked teams could dance the Morris dance. And a thing like the Abbot's Bromley Horn dance makes a magnificent spectacle in the Albert Hall as I know by experience. It would correspond to one of your slow processions in Hiawatha. Also, some folk songs in chorus might be well introduced while the crowd was being brought on at the beginning of Act 1.

I think we might usefully co-opt a third partner Gordon Jacob by preference to do the scoring and some of the practical carpentry which he would do much better than me. Anyhow I suggest the following of my music which might be used when additional music was required.

(1) Wasp's Suite (not the overture)
(2) Old King Cole Ballet (these are both Curwen)
(3) Folk Song Suite (Boosey)
(4) March on Sea Songs (Boosey)
(5) Toccata Marziale (Hawkes)
(6) Charterhouse Suite (Stainer & Bell)
(7) Folk dances for Ballet 'Xmas Carol' [*On christmas Night*, *CW* 1926\2]
(8) Music to May Day Pageant [*London Pageant*, *CW* 1911/3]
(9) Music to 'Pan's Anniversary'

These last 3 are in M.S. but I could send them to you if you wish to look at them.

This letter has the appearance of taking the thing as settled but I have only done this from convenience & I know really that everything is vague at present.[3]

Yours sincerely
R. Vaughan Williams

[1] Sargent had written to VW on Monday, 17 June. VW replied the following Sunday, 23 June. Sargent's letter in reply to this letter was sent on Monday, 24 June.

[2] Sargent had invited VW to a performance at the Albert Hall of *Hiawatha* by Coleridge-Taylor and at the same time had proposed that he should adapt *Hugh the Drover* (of which he had conducted the first public performance on 14 July 1924) for performance there the following year, *inter alia* by introducing ballets. VW responds to his various suggestions.

[3] Although the correspondence closes with Sargent planning to proceed with his adaptation with VW's blessing, the project never went ahead.

177. To Rutland Boughton

21 July [1929]

13 Cheyne Walk

July 21

Dear Boughton

After you left Holst & I had a long conversation which is summarized in the enclosed suggestions which I send to you in case they are of any use to you.

Yours sincerely
R. Vaughan Williams

Memorandum of suggestions for Opera scheme of G. H. & R.V.W.

A. *No splash* eg: Mountain Ash festival to start with – The opening performances to be on the same scale as what we propose to continue with. Also *under the same circumstances*. A show by a small company intended for cooperative hall should not be judged by the critics under the circumstances of a London Theatre; therefore the invited 'press' show should take place in the provinces at one of the cooperative halls.

B. Performances, though small in scale, should be as nearly perfect as possible in *quality* – Therefore we do not advise operas which audiences may have seen on a large scale with all the glitter and tinsel of a large crowd and showy costumes etc – There must be no feeling of 'make shift' e.g 2 men & a boy to represent a whole regiment of soldiers. The operas must be chosen with regard to this.

C. We suggest that under a good Director local *amateur* effort might be enlisted in each town visited, to walk on & represent crowds etc even where possible to help in the chorus.

D. We suggest everything on a small scale to start with – No orchestra but only a piano (N.B. a good piano should be bought and carried round – not to depend on the local piano) A company of about 20 – everyone willing to take a hand at everything e.g the principal soprano of Monday would walk on on Tuesday – help mend the costumes on Wednesday and be 'noises off' on Thursday – But everyone of these artists must be first rate and hard working.

E. We suggest as two quite separate propositions that 'The Immortal Hour' is a good opera to start with and that R.B would be the best Director – and to avoid any suspicion that R.B. was made Director and then chose his own work, the work should be selected first and R.B then invited by the C^tee to direct *it* and incidentally any other operas in the repertoire –

F. We suggest a repertoire of not more than 3 operas – beside 'The Immortal Hour' – We suggest Gluck's 'Orpheus' Mozart's 'Cosi fan tutte' Verdi's 'Rigoletto' (Also Stanford's 'Shamus O'Brien' & Holst's 'Golden Goose' ballet – These last 2 added by R.V.W since conversation with Holst)

G. We think it a mistake to pose as 'British' opera – British opera is at present, very naturally, suspect – it will we are sure have to be introduced at first in small doses.[1]

[1] Rutland Boughton had asked for advice about his plan to start a Welsh Festival. The letter and memorandum are printed in full in *RVW*, 176–7.

178. To Diana Awdry

[July/August 1929[1]]

13 Cheyne Walk
S.W.3

My Dear Diana

Shall you be in Worcester on Friday 11th – I come down then for the combined rehearsal so look out for me if you are not otherwise too busy.

As regards comp.[2] music – ours is still in the melting pot – so you *can't* take it.

The Holst Psalms we have never tackled – I've always thought them too hard – but perhaps they are not – anyway choirs love them. I don't care very much for Wood's Veterans[3] & I imagine it is hard.

Otherwise your scheme seems good. We've turned out [the] Basso song and put in Gibbs 'Fol-dol-do' instead & Love on my heart Holst for women instead of the Scarlatti also 'Sleep wayward'[4] was pronounced dull – but it is v. easy.

I suppose you have done the following

Madrigals

Come shepherds (Benet)
Sing we and chant it (Morley)
Fair Phyllis (Farmer)
Camilla fair (5 pts) Bateson
Weep O mine eyes (Benet[5])
Thyrsis sleepest thou (? – pub. Novello)[6]

Partsongs

Cradle song	Ireland
O breathe not his name	Stanford
Since thou O fondest	Parry
Evening scene (diff[icult])	Elgar

Have you done 'Agincourt song' arr for mens voices by Warrell (O.U.P.)[7] it is *splendid*.

Yrs
R. Vaughan Williams

Ask again if you want to know anything else.

[1] According to note in the recipient's hand.
[2] i.e. competition.
[3] *Dirge for Two Veterans*, first performed at the Leeds Festival of 1901.
[4] 'Sleep wayward thoughts and rest you with my love' by Dowland.
[5] i.e. John Bennet, *fl.* 1599–1614.
[6] In fact also by Bennet. Both works are from his *Madrigalls to foure voices*, 1599.
[7] Arthur Sydney Warrell. The arrangement had just been published by OUP as no. 611 in the series Oxford Choral Songs.

179. To Ina Boyle

postmark: 6 October 1929

Printed postcard

CHANGE OF ADDRESS

MR. AND MRS RALPH VAUGHAN WILLIAMS,[1]
THE WHITE GATES,
WESTCOTT ROAD,
DORKING.

Telephone: Dorking 355

[1] It is interesting that in this change of address card VW did not use his title Dr.

3

From the Move to Dorking until the Outbreak of the Second World War: 1929–September 1939

'I'M a country cousin now', wrote VW to Diana Awdry shortly after he and Adeline moved to The White Gates; he now found that he needed to ration his journeys to London and to group appointments around Wednesdays, the day he spent teaching at the RCM. Longer London visits were necessary: for example, he spent much of November 1930 at the Eversleigh Hotel. However, the house in Dorking suited Adeline well so in 1933 they bought the lease and at once set about adding an annexe, staying in London for the two months of the building works. The final symptom of their sense of stability in the house came in 1935 when they added 'From R Vaughan Williams' to the address on their writing paper; hitherto the writing paper could have been used by any subsequent owner should the VWs have decided to move. This change, made about April 1935, has incidentally proved a useful dating tool for otherwise undated letters.

The move came at a time when VW was extremely busy: his opera *Sir John in Love* had received its first performance at the Royal College of Music the previous March and his mind was still occupied with amendments and adjustments for future performances; still in the course of development in collaboration with his cousin, Gwen Raverat, was *Job: A Masque for Dancing*, whose first performance, in a concert version, would take place in Norwich on October 1930; the first and second movements of his Piano Concerto had been completed in 1926, but the final movement remained to be written and was eagerly awaited by Harriet Cohen; he was involved with the enlarged edition of *Songs of Praise*, which would be published in 1931 and be closely followed in 1933 by a new edition of *The English Hymnal* in which the music would be thoroughly revised. Also complete were two operas: the first, *The Poisoned Kiss*, to a libretto by Cecil Sharp's sister, Evelyn, was to give him more trouble and achieve less success (despite having good and tuneful music) than almost anything else he wrote—he would revise it a further three times in his lifetime. The second was achieved far more easily and for many counts as his most effective achievement in the genre: the tragic plot of J. M. Synge's play, *Riders to the Sea*, was possibly a milieu in which he felt more at home than in that of the rather stilted comedy of *The Poisoned Kiss*.

Ahead lay a great deal of further achievement: the next six years were to see the completion of the Piano Concerto and the writing of the Fourth Symphony, *Five Tudor Portraits*, the cantata *Dona Nobis Pacem*, and the piece in honour of Sir Henry Wood's golden jubilee as a conductor, *Serenade to Music*. All these works contributed to the consolidation of VW's stature as the leading figure in English music after Elgar's death in 1934, but in different ways. While the *Five Tudor Portraits* and the *Serenade* were readily approachable, a harsh and percussive character made itself felt in the Piano Concerto, which possibly rather alarmed its dedicatee Harriet Cohen and certainly gave VW some anxiety about the balance between orchestra and soloist. In the Fourth Symphony too, this unfamiliar character took its audience by surprise. Indeed VW himself seems to have been rather taken aback by what had emerged from his labours. When the symphony was tried out on a few friends at a play-through on two pianos there was clearly considerable discussion: 'The bits I have shown to people they do not like – Gustav heard it all in an early version on 2 pftes – & was puzzled by most of it & disliked the rest', as VW wrote later to Adrian Boult. Writing to Arthur Bliss after the first performance, VW admitted that sometimes he hated the work. Many have seen the unsettled atmosphere of the symphony as a reflexion of the increasingly threatening political situation in Europe; others have suggested that the uneasiness came from closer to home and was to do with Adeline's increasing infirmity and the resulting frustration for VW, perhaps arising from an unwelcome need to move to the country. It was certainly a far cry from the music that many associated with the composer of *The Lark Ascending*, tapping an unapparent vein of inner anguish which would again become evident to his audience in *Dona Nobis Pacem*, which was indeed a reaction to events in Europe, and in *Riders to the Sea*.

There had, however, been a pleasant interlude in all this productive work: VW had accepted an invitation to give the fifth series of Mary Flexner Lectures in the Humanities at Bryn Mawr College, Pennsylvania, in October and November 1932. Unlike his American journey in 1922, he was not this time in the pocket of one patron and was more of a celebrity; distinction in one's field was a criterion for choosing the lecturer. Preparing the lectures allowed VW to put into order thoughts, based on his own experience, about the role of folk song in the development of a composer's style in the context of the music of his own country. The lectures were covered in great detail in the college newspaper and gave rise, as an integral part of the arrangement, to his first book, *National Music*, published by Oxford University Press in 1934. This work remained at the core of his literary output.

In the period covered by this chapter some new correspondents enter the arena to join the continuing correspondence with existing friends, colleagues, and pupils. Amongst musicians, a young composer, Cedric Thorpe Davie, came to VW at the Royal College of Music as a pupil after a spell at the Royal Academy of Music, and a warm friendship developed; Thorpe Davie was to spend much of his life at St Andrew's. Better known was Herbert Howells, with whom he had been in touch in 1914 and again in 1924, but it was only in the 1930s that he became a regular correspondent. VW's letter to Howells, written at the time of the death of Howells's son Michael, was especially sympathetic and provides a pointer to VW's own eschatological views: 'I don't think it is really any comfort – indeed "comfort" would be just an impertinence – but I cannot help believing that a life once begun can never really stop – though it has stopped for us – and that there may, after all, be a real joining up some day.'

Elgar and VW were never close friends but encountered each other reasonably regularly, especially at the Three Choirs Festival. Their backgrounds and their music were very different but the signs are that they drew together somewhat in this period. Two letters from VW to the older composer survive: in one VW and a group at the Three Choirs in Gloucester humorously encourage Elgar to write a third symphony; in the other VW asks Elgar's blessing on a forthcoming performance of *The Dream of Gerontius* at the Leith Hill Festival, a letter which Elgar received as he was lying on his deathbed. Elgar's death on 23 February 1934 was the first great loss to English music in that year; the third loss was Frederick Delius, who died on 10 June and whose funeral at Limpsfield Ralph and Adeline attended. However, for VW the irreparable loss of that year was the second, when Gustav Holst died on 25 May.

Holst's death left a void in VW's spirit, so close had been their friendship and so much had he depended on Gustav's advice and encouragement. As he wrote to Holst's widow and daughter: 'My only thought is now which ever way I turn what are we to do without him – every thing seems to have turned back to him – what would Gustav think or advise or do.' VW remained devoted to the cause of Holst's music and his memory for the rest of his life: the first thing he asked of the R.V.W. Trust, which he and Ursula set up in 1956, was to enable a concert of Holst's music to be given by the London Philharmonic Orchestra under Adrian Boult. He never again found someone with whom he could discuss his music as with an equal. He had to rely on the opinions of younger, respectful composers when he wanted advice on new works. Of the younger generation the one who came nearest to filling Holst's role and with whom he formed an especially close friendship was Gerald Finzi.

After the death of Elgar, VW was the undoubted doyen of English music. In 1935 this was recognized by King George V by conferring on him the Order of Merit. Hitherto VW had consistently refused all civil honours, but as Adeline VW put it when writing to her sister Cordelia: 'He had the letter offering it from the King's Sec about 3 weeks ago – he was rather alarmed – but it is the only honour that he could possibly receive that would fit him – so I am pleased and I see that he is.' He felt in some ways that he had possibly betrayed Holst's memory by accepting it but felt that it was as much a recognition of the music profession in general as of himself in particular and therefore should be accepted. The OM remained his one civil honour.

We have seen that, in contrast to the Fourth Symphony, *Dona Nobis Pacem* was a plea for peace responding to the steadily worsening political situation in Europe. He thus found himself in something of a predicament when the Professor of German at Oxford, Hermann Fiedler, approached him in 1937 with the tentative offer of the first Shakespeare Prize, established in the cause of promoting cultural friendship between England and Germany by the Hanseatic Foundation and its founder, the wealthy Hamburg merchant Alfred Toepfer. Again his first instinct was to decline on both personal and political grounds, but again he realized that the prize was offered to him as a representative of British music. He consulted Gilbert Murray and others and, having been reassured (possibly less than honestly) by Fiedler that the prize was not a matter of political propaganda, cautiously accepted. In 1938 he made the journey to Hamburg in some apprehension for the formal award ceremony. All went well and he enjoyed himself, but the prize, 10,000 marks, presented a problem in that it could not be taken out of Germany and his subsequent efforts to make it available for helping refugees seem to have led to a ban on his music by the Nazi regime.

Thus the German political situation directly impinged on VW. At home he was beset by the communist backwash from Russia when Alan Bush approached him to write a piece for the 'Festival of music for the people'. He entered into a lively discussion on what Bush and his fellow communists meant by 'the people' and on the implication that art was being used for political propaganda, a notion that he resisted and resented, just as he had in connection with the Shakespeare Prize.

VW had written a group of important new works in the mid-1930s, as we have seen. His preoccupation in 1937 with the coronation and the Hamburg Shakespeare Prize covers what appears to have been a distinctly fallow creative period. Writing to Gerald Finzi in July of that year he asked for a list of gramophone records or piano arrangements of works of Sibelius (whom he described as THE GREAT MAN in a letter to Cedric Thorpe Davie) because 'being no longer able to compose and having by my mode of life unfitted myself for any useful occupation I think it is time I learnt something about music'. Later, in October, he wrote to Bobby Longman 'I sometimes think I ought to train my mind or my soul or whatever it is by exercises as the Yogis do—but I can never make up my mind to it.' Because of VW's reticence about his composing, it is not entirely clear whether this unproductive period was simply that or whether there was in fact a work in hand that was refusing to come together; if the latter was the case the work very probably was the early stages of his opera on *The Pilgrim's Progress*. However this may have been, the fallow period appears to have extended well into 1938 until, in July, he withdrew from Dorking to a cottage at Stapleford in Wiltshire to see if that would help: 'My private opinion is that I have dried up' he wrote to a friend. Adeline wrote to him there: 'Even if compo doesn't come, the new scenes and the quiet bit will sow the seed.' VW would not have been the first composer to cease composition at the age of 65 or before.

Events, however, conspired to make the wheels turn again. Study of Sibelius surely helped in the new start, perhaps encouraging him to turn the music which refused to come together as an opera into what became the Fifth Symphony instead—certainly music that first appeared in the symphony reappeared in *The Pilgrim's Progress* when it eventually emerged more than a decade or so later. This hypothesis about the symphony's genesis certainly seems to be borne out by the otherwise unexpected decision that the symphony should be 'dedicated to Sibelius without permission' (a dedication which gave Sibelius much pleasure, as he recorded in his diary: 'Yesterday a great moment like a caress from a summer world. Heard the symphony that Vaughan Williams has dedicated to me').

If Sibelius was one factor in unlocking the wheels of composition, a more fundamental stimulus arose from a chance encounter in October 1937 with a young woman who had sent him a scenario for a folk ballet. She was called Ursula Wood. Without question VW was and remained devoted to Adeline, to whom he had been married for forty years, but he was by no means impervious to the charms of young women he came across, as his correspondence with Diana Awdry and Elizabeth Maconchy demonstrates. However, the friendship which sprang up between VW and Ursula Wood was of a different order. She offered him a devoted warmth and admiration which complemented his long-standing partnership with Adeline in a way that re-enlivened his imagination and led to a renewal of his creative energy. Ralph and Ursula did not allow their friendship to threaten either Adeline or Michael Wood, Ursula's husband in the Royal Artillery, nor did it. Adeline must have been aware of Ursula's effect on Ralph, and his on her, but warmly welcomed Ursula into their circle nonetheless. As time went on she knew that Ursula could provide Ralph with companionship at concerts and the like which she, virtually housebound, could not. It was Adeline who remained Ralph's first concern, but it was Ursula who helped release his muse once more. As he wrote to her from his Wiltshire retreat: 'The hermitage is succeeding I think…I have been [for] wonderful walks on the downs – they were perfect – sun, high wind & wonderful July field flowers, the kind I like best.'

It was thus against a background of reinvigorated composing and an enriched emotional life that VW engaged enthusiastically with the problems thrown up by the onset of another war—and in particular with the plight of Jewish refugees from the Third Reich. His involvement with the Dorking & District Refugees Committee led directly to two important friendships (with the Russians Yanya and Genia Hornstein and with Robert Müller-Hartmann) and was to set the course for an important aspect of his contribution to the British war effort.

180. To Diana Awdry

postmark: 16 October 1929

The White Gates
Westcott Road
Dorking

My Dear Diana

Your letter reminds me of delightful afternoons & evenings in Worcester Cathedral, when you took pity on my loneliness and alleviated my cold (but thank heaven I didn't catch it). But you mustn't laugh at my boots – they are for use not for ornament.

Now for business

Don't do the Elgar its *awful* (this in confidence).[1]

Why not a Handel chorus – I haven't got my lists with me – but I remember 'Ye tutelar Gods' & a slow chorus which w^d go with it out of 'Belshazzar'[2] – or 'Sing unto God' from Judas or (quite slow but v. fine) 'Then round about the starry throne' and 'Fixed in his everlasting seat' from Samson.

I sh^d think the Schubert w^d do very well if 4 parts is not too formidable.

I thought you all sang splendidly in my tune – I told Atkins so in a letter & I hope he passed it on.[3]

Do you ever come to London – I'm a country cousin now – but I go up occasionally from Dorking – so we might come across each other.

Yrs
R. Vaughan Williams

[1] i.e. 'Evening Scene', which he had suggested in no. 178.

[2] The Chorus of Babylonians at the opening of Act II, Scene ii of *Belshazzar.* The slow chorus is possibly 'Oh, misery! Oh terror, hopeless grief!', which follows shortly afterwards.

[3] The Three Choirs Festival at Worcester had included a performance of *Sancta Civitas* conducted by the composer.

181. To Michael Mullinar[1]

received: 21 October 1929[2]

The White Gates,
Westcott Road,
Dorking.

Dear Michael

I've just been playing through your song – which I like very much – indeed I think it is too good for the words – which are rather of the 'Mamble' order.[3]

I'm not sure that I like your 'extraneous 9th' at the end – but that's a bug bear of mine as you know

Alas! I fear I can't manage the concert – please thank Mrs Warden very much for her kind invitation – I sh[d] have liked to see you all again so much.

Yrs
R. Vaughan Williams

[1] Michael Mullinar, a young music teacher, composer, and pianist, had been a pupil and became a close friend of VW. VW called upon him regularly in later years to play through the first drafts of compositions in front of a group of friends.

[2] Note in the hand of the recipient, confirmed by the date of publication of the song to which VW refers.

[3] The song was, according to the recipient's son Keith, a setting of 'Tavern', a poem by the American poet Edna St Vincent Millay. The song was published by Augener in 1929. 'Mamble' is an allusion to a poem by John Drinkwater, set to music by various composers, of which the first verse is: 'I never went to Mamble, that lies above the Teme, so I wonder who's in Mamble, and whether people seem who breed and brew along there as lazy as the name, and whether any song there sets alehouse wits aflame.' The first verse of the Millay poem runs: 'I'll keep a little tavern below the high hills' crest, wherein all grey-eyed people may sit them down and rest. There shall be plates a-plenty, and mugs to melt the chill of all the grey-eyed people who happen up the hill.'

182. To Harriet Cohen

The White Gates,
Westcott Road,
Dorking.

1st December 1929

Dear Harriet

I know you'll play it beautifully – no not too quick; & calm but with subconscious emotion – I sh[d] love to hear you play it 1st – but my only day in London is Wed. at the R.C.M. busy morning to night.

But I will come to the concert if I may[1]

Yrs
R.V.W.

[1] Harriet Cohen was to give the first peformance of *Hymn Tune Prelude on 'Song 13' by Orlando Gibbons*, *CW* 1930/3, on 14 Jan. 1930 at the Wigmore Hall. Printed in *RVW*, 181; partially quoted in *CW*, p. 137.

183. To Pablo Casals[1]

29 December [1929]

Shiffolds

December 29

Dear Sir

In preparing my 'Fantasia' I have made a few slight alterations which I am sending you herewith.[2]

Also I am not quite sure about the final cadenza. Perhaps it has not enough technical display. Would you feel inclined to be so very kind as to help me with this?

Yours faithfully
R. Vaughan Williams

[1] Based on a transcript made by H. L. Kirk in the Casals Archive at San Juan in 1973.
[2] *Fantasia on Sussex Folk Tunes* for violoncello and orchestra, *CW* 1929/6, later withdrawn by the composer (though an arrangement for cello and piano was published after his death). Casals was the soloist in the first performance at the Queen's Hall on 13 Mar. 1930.

184. To Harriet Cohen

postmark: 30 January 1930

The White Gates,
Westcott Road,
Dorking.

My Dear Harriet

Alas – the other prelude won't boil – I'm so sorry – perhaps when I am in a calm mood later on & not scoring against time it will materialize.[1]

Yrs
R.V.W.

[1] The proposed companion prelude to *Hymn Tune Prelude on 'Song 13' by Orlando Gibbons*, *CW* 1930/3. Letter printed in *RVW*, 181.

185. To Evelyn Sharp

19 January 1930

The White Gates,
Westcott Road,
Dorking.

Sunday Jan. 19: 1930

Dear Miss Sharp

I feel it is fair that composer and author should share equally. But it is not usual I believe and I don't see why Mr. Garnett should mulct you of a proportion of more than your 'usual' share. Would it be too sharp practice for us to draw up a contract giving you the normal proportion & then a 'secret treaty' by which I paid you over the rest of your half.[1]

Do you think you could discuss this with Mr Thring of the Authors[2] or with his successor?

I do not think that our 'secret treaty' need be a signed & sealed affair, but just an informal understanding unless you prefer it otherwise.

By the way I have no idea what the usual proportion between composer and librettist is – perhaps Mr Thring could tell you.

And, finally I think the whole discussion is academic because I do not suppose that either of us will make any money out of it!

Yours sincerely
R. Vaughan Williams

[1] For earlier discussion of the topic, see no. 159.
[2] i.e. the Society of Authors.

186. To Peter Montgomery[1]

[about June 1930]

The White Gates,
Westcott Road,
Dorking.

Dear Peter

I quite agree with Dent's letter – & I am in the same difficulty as he is about not knowing altogether what your purely technical qualifications are – could you bear a schoolmaster's job? I think it best – because those purely technical achievements do not matter so much & character, education & general culture are very important. But even a schoolmaster has to have a good comprehensive technique & you must decide for yourself whether you have that or w^{d} in a reasonable time be able to acquire it.

I don't think there's any career in *conducting* – no jobs, & lots of very clever young men after them.

As regards study abroad – I venture to think that Dent is too frightened of the foreigner – he is always wondering nervously what the opinion of the foreigner is about us – that does not seem to me to be important (except always insofar as outside opinion is always helpful & stimulating) – if we are to do any good in England for music we must find out the kind & style of music which is best for us – & *not* make our music a weak imitation of foreign models. Of course if your ambition in life is to write like Hindemith or Webern you must go to the source to find out how to do it – But is that the best basis for one's own self-expression?

And to come down to practical things – I don't know much about German & French organists – but I have an idea that men like Darke, Ley & Ball[2] can beat them hollow in style & technique & w^{d} be able to teach & understand the mind of an English pupil. I know, to my sorrow, how lamentably unthorough the R.C.M. is & how badly in need of improvement, & these foreign conservatoires look very imposing *on paper* – but so does the R.C.M. – and we have no proof that the reality abroad comes up to the advertized advantages any more than the R.C.M.

After all nearly all the musicians of note in England have done most of their study at home – the people who study abroad seem to come to nothing.

Composers	Parry, Elgar, Holst, Bax (exceptions are Sullivan & Stanford)
Theoreticians	Tovey & Dent[3]
Organists	Parratt, Lloyd, & the others I have mentioned.[4]

I admit that in violin & pfte it may be different. But even here we have Samuel, Cohen, Hess, Sammons (I believe) & Tertis (I believe).[5]

No my advice is learn your groundwork here (at the R.C.M. I think) because I *know* that any one who really wants to work can ground himself thoroughly at the R.C.M. – the fault of the R.C.M. is that largely for financial reasons it is not able to make short work of the slackers. Then I sh[d] advise 6 months abroad to get new ideas & broaden one's mind generally.

I don't believe that a foreign trained musician will ever be able to teach an English schoolboy.

A school job w[d] give you an opportunity of conducting on a small scale which w[d] lead on to more. W[d] it be a good plan to come & have an 'audition' with some organ or pfte teacher to get an opinion?

As regards going abroad – of course it is easier to settle down to things if you are entirely cut off from your own belongings.

I should love for you to be an active participator in the great job which I am also living for – but the question is the best way. But I think everything points to acquiring *technical command* of both theory & practice whatever you finally decide on.[6]

Our love to all of you

Yrs affectionately
R. Vaughan Williams

[1] A cousin of VW's. His mother, Mary, and his aunt, Diana, had married two Montgomery brothers. His uncle had taken the name Massingberd-Montgomery when his aunt had inherited the Massingberd estate at Gunby. He gave the following account of his relationship with VW in June 1959 in a covering letter sent when he lent his correspondence for copying by OUP:

Dear Sir, In answer to your request for the loan of letters of 'V.W.' I have pleasure in sending you the enclosed, mostly written in the earlier 30s. The most interesting one is on top, written to me just after leaving Cambridge in 1930 and advising me about a musical career. There is nothing of import in the others but I send them for perusal in case there might be some chance remark which can fill in a gap or supply a missing link. My mother (Mary Massingberd) was his cousin and about the same age. Her sister Lady Montgomery Massingberd, is still alive, and as she has many early memories of 'V.W.' I suggested that she should get in touch with you—also. Her address is Gunby Hall, Spilsby, Lincs. Yours faithfully Peter Montgomery

P.S. Some of the letters refer to V.W.'s visit to conduct a concert of his works with the Belfast Philharmonic Society on 17 Feb 1933. He stayed with my parents (now both dead) here [Co. Tyrone] before the concert. P.M.

[2] Harold Darke, Henry G. Ley, and George Thalben-Ball.

[3] Donald Francis Tovey and Edward Dent.

[4] Walter Parratt and Charles H. Lloyd.

[5] Harold Samuel, Harriet Cohen, Myra Hess, Albert Sammons, and Lionel Tertis.

[6] This letter is similar in content to no. 361, written to Lord Kennet about his son's musical education. See *RVW*, 243 n. 1.

187. To Herbert Ellingford[1]

9 December [1930]

The White Gates,
Westcott Road,
Dorking.

December 9th

Dear Mr Ellingford

Many thanks for your interesting letter and the programmes.

I hope very much to have the pleasure of reading your article when it comes out.

Your quotation rather alarms me. I did not know I had been guilty of all that, and feel rather like the gentleman who was terrified to discover that he had been speaking prose all his life without knowing it![2]

Yours sincerely
R. Vaughan Williams

[1] Organist of St George's Hall, Liverpool.

[2] Ellingford had written to say that he had been playing VW's Prelude and Fugue in C minor (*CW* 1930/4) to children in St George's Hall and had written an article around it entitled 'Bach and Vaughan Williams', which he hoped would appear in *The Organ* in 1931. The quotation to which VW refers ends: 'the pronounced effect of the simultaneous use of harmonic opposites which are seen in the foregoing excerpts from Bach are justified by the sound they produce'.

188. To Edwin Evans

[14 December 1930]

The White Gates,
Westcott Road,
Dorking.

Sunday

Dear Evans

Holst has handed me your letter. I need hardly say that I feel much honoured at the idea that the 'Camargo' may care to produce 'Job'.[1]

I will boil down the score to anything in reason (please let me know soon the *largest* orchestra you can put up). I will have it ready by any date (again within reason) that you name.

The only condition as far as I am concerned, and I am sure the mention of it is a mere formality – *that I shall be allowed to veto anything in the production which to my mind does not agree with my music.*

All this as far as I am concerned. But I cannot move without Geoffrey Keynes & Mrs Gwen Raverat who are the prime instigators & have designed the scenery & costumes.

– I am asking Keynes to write to you direct on the matter.[2] One more stipulation – I want the work called a '*Masque*' not a 'Ballet' which has acquired unfortunate connotations of late years to me.

Yours sincerely
R. Vaughan Williams

[1] *Job: A masque for dancing founded on Blake's illustrations for the* Book of Job. Scenario by Geoffrey Keynes and Gwendolen Raverat, *CW* 1930/5. *Job* had received a concert performance at Norwich on 23 Oct. Evans had proposed a staged performance by the Camargo Society, which eventually took place at the Cambridge Theatre on 5 July 1931.

[2] Keynes wrote on 16 Dec. also welcoming the idea that the Camargo Society should mount a production of *Job*. He specified that it be produced by Ninette de Valois and asked that, since VW appeared to have a complex about the word 'ballet', it should be described as a masque.

189. To Gustav Holst[1]

[about 20 December 1930]

The White Gates
Westcott Road
Dorking.

Dear Gustav

I've never written to you since the great night at S.P.G.S.[2] – I somehow thought we should meet & talk it over.

The Organ Concerto[3] is *it*, all right, – there is only one place where I have any doubts – & that is I think where the chorus first enters in harmony; [it] sounds a little bit respectable & out of the picture – I sh^d like very much to talk about that place one day. The organ part is magnificent – I suppose Nora[4] couldn't play it in ~~Oxford~~ Gloucester? I can't think who can sing your soprano solo at the end – Dorothy[5] might manage it – Of course if you say 'impersonal' Sumsion[6] will put a choir boy on to it which will be fatal – Any way you know of course that it mustn't sound in the least like that young woman the other day. (By the way what *is* the matter with her – she seems to have imbibed all the worst faults of the worst RCM style (1) wobble (2) edge on the voice (3) sacrificing words to supposed 'tone' – I noticed that especially in the opera[7] – where she lengthened all her final syllables so as to get 'tone' – with the result that you could hear nothing of the words.[)]

By the way – it was interesting to note that the most obvious amateur of your lot (the schoolmaster) was far the most successful – because he was thinking of his *words* and his *part* all the time and not worrying about his damned tone.

I know the answer to this is that in a larger place he would not be heard – But is there no way of preserving that *natural* singing and yet getting the voice big enough? One thing is that it is *impossible* to get a big tone on English words – & the sooner singing masters recognize this the better – either sing English with a small tone (Plunket Greene) or don't sing English at all (Caruso).

By the way (ii) have you heard the soprano who sings the little bits of solo in the wireless singers[?][8] it is *perfect* – she'd do for your end bit (I am harking back to the organ concerto). I *rather think* she is Nixon a pupil of D. Webb at the RCM – I wonder if the moral is obvious.

The opera gave me quite a new idea – the *concert opera*[:] sit round a table *with copies* & sing with a minimum of action (*no costumes*). I thought it was a perfect representation.

Do you think there's a *little* bit too much $\frac{6}{8}$ in the opera? I wonder if Nigel Playfair[9] would do it at his light opera season – But I daresay you've thought of that.

The one thing I can't yet get hold of is 'Hammersmith' – but you are (like your daughter) a realist & you are almost unique in that your stuff sounds better when it is played on the instrument it was originally written for.

I want very much to have a lesson on 'Riders'[10] soon. I've been revising & rough scoring it.

I wrote to E.E.[11] re: Job but have had no answer.

Yrs
RVW.

[1] Printed with significant omissions as Letter XXXI in *HR*.

[2] On 12 Dec. three new works of Holst has been tried over on the piano at St Paul's Girls' School: *The Wandering Scholar*, Op. 50, H176, *A Choral Fantasia*, Op. 51, H177, and *Hammersmith*, Op. 52, H178. See Short, *Holst*, 294.

[3] i.e. *A Choral Fantasia*—a work with a concertante organ part that had been commissioned for the Three Choirs Festival at Gloucester.

[4] Nora Day, an assistant music mistress at St Paul's Girls' School.

[5] Dorothy Silk.

[6] Herbert Sumsion, organist at Gloucester Cathedral 1928–67. He and his wife Alice became close friends of VW.

[7] Holst's opera, *The Wandering Scholar*, Op. 50, H176, to a libretto by Clifford Bax, first performed in 1934 at the David Lewis Theatre, Liverpool.

[8] The Wireless Singers were a full-time octet of soloists drawn from the Wireless Chorus (later to become the BBC Singers).

[9] Nigel Playfair (1874–1934), actor-manager of the Lyric Theatre, Hammersmith.
[10] *Riders to the Sea*, *CW* 1936/6.
[11] Edwin Evans.

190. To Canon Frederick Dwelly[1]

[1930]

The White Gates,
Westcott Road,
Dorking.

Dear Canon Dwelly

Martin Shaw has shewn me your letter – False accents & ungrammatical pauses are, as you must know, inevitable in hymns where the same tune has to be sung in each verse & hymn word writers *will* indulge in Caesurae (is this the right word?[2]) across the lines. But it surprizes me that when you have passed without comment such things as –

'Teach me to live that I may dread⌒
The grave as little as my bed'

or

'He spake and straight⌒ way the celestial choir'

and dozens of others – and object to this one which (if I remember right) we chose especially because the triple measure goes very far to mitigate the false accents – since it is possible to run on from one line to another without pause – as one *cannot do* in duple time tune.[3]

e.g.

Made lowly wise we pray no more for mi- ra- cle & sign
and if the causal [...][4]

Perhaps you have been misled by the double bars – but these are as you surely know merely indications of the end of the line of words & do not necessarily mean a break – but if it will make you happier we will leave out the double bars after ll.1 & 3. – But it certainly won't make matters work by substituting a duple time tune. It is much easier to vary the accent in this tune than in one with all equal note values.

Of course any congregation w^{d} sing v. 4

the bar lines are only for convenience – of course it w[d] be very nice to have a book with every verse properly 'pointed' – but I fear the library of Liverpool Cathedral w[d] not contain all the volumes which this w[d] entail.

Yours sincerely
R. Vaughan Williams

[1] Frederick Dwelly (1881–1957) was a Canon of Liverpool Cathedral and was to become first Dean in October the following year.

[2] In fact the word VW needs is 'enjambement'.

[3] This letter arises from the enlargement of *Songs of Praise*, which was published in 1932, and concerns hymn no. 575 ('Made lowly wise, we pray no more', by F. L. Hosmer), which is set to a triple-time tune, *Blackbourne*—though with a duple-time tune (*Relief*) given as an alternative.

[4] First lines of vv. 1 and 4.

191. To Percy Dearmer [*c.*1930]

The White Gates,
Westcott Road,
Dorking.

Dear Dearmer

We had already decided long ago (in deference to someone's objection) to exclude the tune 'Covenanters' from the new S.P. Personally I am sorry as I consider it a fine vigorous tune and well suited to the words.

Your correspondent calls it 'Jazz' – but there is no hint of 'Jazz' characteristics in the tune – but perhaps your correspondent uses the epithet 'Jazz' like many people use the word 'Bolshie' to designate anything they disapprove of.

As to its 'origin' I care nothing. If your correspondent enquires closely into the credentials of every tune he admits into his church I fear his congregation will be cut off from all the noblest hymn tunes in the world – is he aware that 'O Filii et Filiae'[1] is adapted from a presumably pagan song in praise of spring 'Vois venir le joli mois'? That 'Innsbruck'[2] was originally a secular song? That the 'Old Hundredth'[3] is an adaptation of a love song? That the splendid solemn 'Helmsley'[4] is probably an adaptation of a stage song (sung by a female actor) 'Where's the mortal can resist me'? That 'Jesu meine Freude'[5] was originally 'Flora meine Freude'? That the tune 'St Theodulph'[6] is first cousin to the dance tune 'Sellenger's Round' – That 'Amsterdam'[7] is similarly derived from a dance tune? These adaptations have always been the principle of every church, and I believe quite rightly – so that the 'Devil may not have all the pretty tunes'.[8]

Otherwise we shall be reduced to the lucubrations of the Rev. J. B. Dykes – doubtless very pious but decidedly anaemic.

However the discussion is an academic one for we have decided, rather unwillingly, to omit the tune.

Yours sincerely
R. Vaughan Williams

[1] *Songs of Praise*, no. 143.
[2] Ibid. no. 57.
[3] Ibid. no. 443.
[4] Ibid. no. 65.
[5] Ibid. no. 544.
[6] Ibid. no. 135.
[7] Ibid. no. 286.
[8] VW took up the subject again in 1958 in a letter to Simona Pakenham (see no. 732), in which he declined to give the sources for the folk tunes he had used in his *Te Deum*.

192. To Harriet Cohen

postmark: 22 November 1931

The White Gates

Dearest Harriet

How can I say 'no' – when such a reward will be mine if I say 'yes'? I shall claim it *to the full* (and the 1580th).[1]

Yrs
RVW

[1] This letter may be a response to a request by Harriet Cohen for the Piano Concerto, of which the first two movements had already been written by this date. See *CW* 1931/3. The reward was 10,000 kisses, the gradual paying off of which became a standing joke in VW's letters to her.

193. To Ina Boyle

postmark: 22 March 1931

The White Gates,
Westcott Road,
Dorking.

Dear Miss Boyle

I'm so sorry I didn't write before. I thought your motets were splendid & v. well sung[1] – It is a pity that the programme led people to think that the *music* as well as the words were traditional. I hope A. Bernard[2] will do something by you.

Many thanks for cheque

Yrs very sincerely
R. Vaughan Williams

[1] The works were the five *Gaelic Hymns*, written by Boyle in 1923–4 and published by J. & W. Chester in 1930. They had just been given their first performance by the Oriana Choir.

[2] Anthony Bernard (1891–1963), founder and conductor of the London Chamber Orchestra. See *New Grove*.

194. To Adrian Boult at the BBC

22 March 1931

The White Gates,
Westcott Road,
Dorking.

Received: 22 March 1931

Dear Adrian

I owe you 2 answers

(1) To your letter of March 10th
I have ½ finished a pfte concerto which Harriet Cohen is to play if she likes it – But (a) it may never be finished (b) I may not like it when it is (c) she may not – so that's that. Please say nothing about this at present.

(2) '*Job*'[1] – with great pleasure – a pfte acc^t is being done and it will be ready soon – Of course I sh^d be pleased if you w^d conduct it – (the score is illegible).

Yrs
R. Vaughan Williams[2]

[1] In fact Boult, although the dedicatee of *Job*, *CW* 1930/5, did not conduct any of the performances noted in *CW*. The piano arrangement was by Vally Lasker.

[2] Printed in Moore, *Music and Friends*, 95.

195. To Diana Awdry

[?March 1931[1]]

The White Gates,
Westcott Road,
Dorking.

O my dearest child to think that you should ever be frightened that I should laugh at you – or that I don't like poetry – or that I shouldn't like to hear it well read. If I really am all that you did *quite right* to hide any amount of truth from me – & I should not be worthy to be your 'particular friend'.

I know I *did* once laugh a little bit about verse speaking – but it was only to tease you – you can't seriously believe that I don't think that poetry together with music & one or two other things make up what is worth having in life (friendship is another) and *of course* I believe really that for people to speak good poetry aloud is often the *only* way to get at its beauty – & even if sometimes they sound rather absurd to jaded prigs like me – what do *we* matter (its just like the folk dancing or choral singing – very often the result is nothing much to hear or see but it *makes* the soul of those who do it – & *that* is what matters). So my darling Diana do forgive me if I have ever seriously laughed at such a sacred thing as artistic self expression.

So please let me share your mind – because your mind is as beautiful as your face and unless you can let me do that you must feel there is something wrong with me – & I don't want you to do that – we must have no 'inhibitions' (as the jargon goes).

It was lovely seeing you even for a little bit – & more lovely to think that we shall be together during fest: week – only ought you really to go to all that expense? It worries me to think that perhaps I have let you in for it.

I had a letter from Saliva[2] apologizing for the Magnif![3] – I have ½ a mind to suggest a small chorus for it – but in that case could I make a special proviso that you were to be in it?

By the way you never told me anything about your visit to Aldershot – I was frightfully interested & want to hear more about it.

Well, goodbye dear Diana, & try to forgive me for ever having laughed at anything you held precious – which is an unforgivable thing to do – & try to believe that I *do* believe in beautiful things & that therefore I believe in you.

Love from
Uncle Ralph

[1] Letter undated and postmark obscure. However, the apology possibly arises from something VW said in a letter he wrote on 6 Mar. 1931: 'Good luck to your festival—what a lot of verse speaking!'

[2] Sir Ivor Atkins was often referred to in VW's circle as 'Saliva'.

[3] Magnificat, *CW* 1932/2, which was to be performed at the Worcester Three Choirs Festival on 8 Sept. 1932. See also no. 211.

196. To Adrian Boult at the BBC[1]

5 April [1931[2]]

The White Gates,
Westcott Road,
Dorking.

April 5

Dear Adrian

Many thanks for your letter – Probably the inchoate (piano) concerto[3] had better stand over and please say nothing about it to anyone as it may all come to nothing.

You ask about neglected master pieces by me. About 20 years ago I had a piece played called 'In the Fen Country'[4] which I rather liked then. I will look it out one day and see whether I still like it enough to submit it for your disapproval.

Yrs
RVW

[1] Printed in Moore, *Music and Friends*, 96.
[2] Note in hand of recipient.
[3] The work was performed by Harriet Cohen under Adrian Boult at the Queen's Hall on 1 Feb. 1933.
[4] VW did in fact later revise the orchestration, in 1935.

197. To Gwen Raverat

12 July [1931[1]]

The White Gates,
Westcott Road,
Dorking.

July 12

Dear Gwen

You have reason to be very proud of yourself for your beautiful realization of Blake – and I was pleased to find that my music seemed to fit in with your scenery and dresses. I hope you felt so too.

I enclose the 'Spectator'[2] in case you have not seen it.

As regards the order of the scenes I am entirely unrepentant. I know that according to the Bible and Blake, following the Bible, that the culminating cause of Job's misery was not the destruction of his flocks in herds – not the burning of his homesteads – not the death of his sons & daughters, but the 'universal and distressing' complaint of boils. This would hardly make a dramatic climax and I am sure we are justified in altering it. And though Job's bad dreams do not actually come in the history but are referred to in Job's lamentation surely we can use them as one of his trials.

Though scientifically perhaps a bad dream is reminiscent practically speaking it is usually prophetic and my idea was that Job's terrible visions in his dreams were realized when he woke by the entry of the Messengers.

Of course if my stage directions could have been faithfully carried out this would have been all much clearer. For the bad dream I wanted a much wilder more macabre dance with the stage full of characters dancing *at* Job instead of the merely grotesque dance we were given. Also during the middle part of my messenger scene there should have been a procession across the back of the stage culminating in the bodies of Job's sons & daughters carried on the shoulders of bearers. (This would I think have given you a great opportunity.) Of course those 3 young men jumping about & catching flies looked ludicrous during that long spell of music. If we cannot have the procession I am cutting a good deal of the music there.

The alteration of the order of the scenes would involve entire re-writing of the music as we could not have the two grotesque dances (bad dream & Comforters) following one on the other – And though I should be quite prepared to alter my music if I felt I was dramatically wrong you perceive I am not so convinced.

One more point – Are the Blake pictures in any particular order? It is true that the messenger picture comes before the boils picture – but in between them comes the picture representing 'And Satan went forth from the presence of the Lord' wh[ich] in the story should of course come much earlier.

Yrs
R. Vaughan Williams

[1] The Camargo Society had put on the first performance of the stage version of *Job* on Sunday, 5 July at the Cambridge Theatre.

[2] Richard Jennings wrote a laudatory review of *Job* in *The Spectator*, 11 July 1931, p. 47. On the design he says 'Mme. Raverat who has designed the scenery and costumes is entirely faithful to [Blake's] surface simplicity. It is a miracle that she has not disappointed or shocked those who know Blake's illustrations.'

198. To Gerald Finzi

postmark: 14 July 1931

The White Gates,
Westcott Road,
Dorking.

Dear Finzi

If you will come to S.P.G.S. (Brook Green) at 5.0 on Friday we are trying through the Concerto (6 hands on 2 pfts)[1] – it sounds like nothing on earth on 2 pftes (not their fault) – but come if you can

RVW

[1] A trial at St Paul's Girls' School of VW's Concerto in C major for pianoforte and orchestra (*CW* 1931/3), to be played by Nora Day, Vally Lasker, and Helen Bidder.

199. To Harriet Cohen

postmark: 14 July 1931

The White Gates,
Westcott Road,
Dorking.

Dearest Harriet

Here it is.[1]

If you don't like it send it back. If you *do* like it I will come and claim my reward.

I had not forgotten about the theatre – But I'm a country cousin now & never in London – & you an international celebrity & never in England – But I *want* it & we *will* do it

Yrs
RVW

[1] Probably the last movement of the Piano Concerto, *CW* 1931/3.

200. To Gwen Raverat

[*c*.20 July 1931[1]]

The White Gates,
Westcott Road,
Dorking.

Dear Gwen

I've been carefully thinking over the 'Job' situation & I don't mind trying the alteration of the order of the scenes (say at the Old Vic[2]) *as an experiment*

– It will only involve (again if we consider it experimentally) a little alteration in the opening and closing bars of the music.

But in this case (indeed in any case) the *dance* must be radically changed – It must be danced *at Job* & not at the Audience & it must be *terrifying* & not comic & I think should have a *fuller* stage & Satan should not I think dance in it. But he should *start* it with a realization of the 'Satan with his torch' + illustration which was absolutely the finest – but it doesn't follow that it makes a good *stage* climax – Also I don't feel inclined necessarily to read into it all that Wickstead & others say that it means. I am only interested in the *picture itself* & the texts with which *Blake* surrounds it.

But this does not solve the difficulty of the messenger scene – It is quite impossible for these 3 dancers to fill out all that music – so either it must be drastically cut or my procession idea must come off. I can't see why it should be absurd if kept vague enough – figures carrying burdens across the back of the stage (after all you see the countryside all in flames & all the refugees must have been hurrying away from the 'devastated area'). I've seen such processions on the stage & I know they 'come off'.

Another problem will be this: The scenes at present are Job asleep – Boils – Job wakes up – Messenger. Shall we start with Job asleep & woken up by the messenger? But then before the 'Boils' he must also be asleep (or at all events lying down) (see illustration) & he can't go to sleep *twice*. Perhaps the opening music might be taken to suggest just calm & not sleep – but it all requires some thought. Would you mind sending this letter (or the substance of it) to Geoffrey Keynes who has written me a kind but reproving letter on the subject (more in sorrow than in anger I think).

Yrs
R. Vaughan Williams

+ I agree that this illustration is probably not realised at all by Ninette.

[1] This letter clearly follows no. 197.
[2] The first performance by Sadler's Wells was to be at the Old Vic on 22 Sept.

201. To Edward Elgar

[9 September 1931[1]]

Millers Green,
Gloucester[2]

Dear Sir Edward Elgar

You said last night that owing to the badness of the Woolworth pencils you could no longer write music. We all want that new symphony & the 3rd part of The Apostles.

Will these pencils of varying softness help?[3]

Yrs affectionately
R. Vaughan Williams
W. H. Reed[4]
R. O. Morris
Alice Sumsion
Emmeline Morris
E. Reed[5]
J. Bailey
Herbert Sumsion

[1] Date suggested in Elgar, *Letters of a Lifetime*, ed. Moore, 440, where this letter is printed. Although the third Symphony was not commissioned by the BBC until Dec. 1932, there had been pressure on Elgar to write it, notably from George Bernard Shaw, for some time before. This letter was written during the 1931 Three Choirs at Gloucester, where both Shaw and Elgar were present: Elgar conducted *Gerontius*, the Violin Concerto, and *Nursery Suite*; VW was there to conduct *Job* and *The Lark Ascending* (*On Wenlock Edge* was also given); while the Morrises were there for the first performance of R. O.'s Sinfonia in C major. Elgar had clearly been urged by those present the previous evening to complete the projected works and had made excuses!

[2] No. 7, the organist's house at Gloucester Cathedral, where Herbert ('John') Sumsion had succeeded Herbert Brewer in 1928.

[3] This letter is discussed in Cobbe, '"My dear Elgar": The Letters of Elgar and Vaughan Williams'.

[4] The violinist.

[5] Eveline Reed, W. H. Reed's wife.

202. To Adrian Boult at the BBC

20 September [1931]

The White Gates,
Westcott Road,
Dorking.

September 20

Dear Adrian

How very nice of you to write. I had no idea you were there – I wish I had seen you.[1]

It would indeed give me great pleasure to hear you conduct 'Job' one day.

While I am writing, I want to make a humble suggestion for what it is worth to the Control department. The controllers seem in concertos and songs to have the old fashioned idea of the soloist first and the rest nowhere. This is especially so at the Proms – for instance at the Bach concert last Friday in 'Schlummert Ein' when the soloist has long holding notes and the orchestra has a beautiful tune against it I heard nothing but the holding note – and similarly in the D Minor Concerto in places where all the themes are in the orchestra & the pfte has only arpeggios I heard nothing but the arpeggios and I do not think this could have been my receiving set because presumably the *relative* values would be the same on any set.

Yrs
R. Vaughan Williams

[1] Probably at the performance of *Job* at Gloucester.

203. To E. J. Dent

[mid-October 1931][1]

The White Gates,
Westcott Road,
Dorking.

Dear Dent

I'm sorry about your young man Glock[2] – but I imagine he was hardly the kind of candidate the ctee had in view – meanwhile what about the Butterworth Trust? Of course it w[d] only be quite a small sum, if he got it, but it w[d] help. The trust has a meeting on Oct 29th – could you send me an account of Glock & I will send it or take it, if I can go, to the meeting.

There may of course be a feeling, which I to a certain extent share, against sending money abroad at this moment – but personally I think this is a justifiable case.

Could I know by the way, if *and when* I shall be wanted to examine at Cambridge again this year.[3]

Yrs
R. Vaughan Williams

[1] The letter clearly precedes no. 207.
[2] William Glock had been Organ Scholar at Gonville and Caius College, Cambridge, and was now studying the piano in Berlin under Artur Schnabel.
[3] VW was to be an external examiner in Harmony.

204. To Harriet Cohen

[late October 1931?]

The White Gates,
Westcott Road,
Dorking.

Dearest Harriet

Here is the concerto

(1) Full score
(2) Pfte solo with indications of orchestra (N.B. if you ever try this on *2 pfte* you must play certain bits in *green ink* which I c^{d} not get on to the 2nd pfte part)
(3) Orchestra arranged for 4 hands (it w^{dnt} go on 2)

These are the only copies in the world!

Yrs
RVW

205. To Evelyn Sharp

6 November 1931

The White Gates,
Westcott Road,
Dorking.

Nov 6 1931

Dear Miss Sharp

I enclose a letter from Hubert Foss of the Oxford Press about our opera.[1]

I don't know what you think about it – or are you tired of the whole thing and would you prefer some arrangement by which you should hand all your work over to me and have no more to do with it except of course as regards appropriate emoluments – if any – ?

Yours sincerely
R. Vaughan Williams

[1] The letter does not survive but OUP did agree to publish the opera, presumably with a number of conditions about the libretto, which was subsequently revised first by Foss's brother, William (*WVW*, 249), and eventually, after VW had bought out Evelyn Sharp's copyright from her executors, by UVW.

206. To Adrian Boult at the BBC

17 November [1931[1]]

The White Gates,
Westcott Road,
Dorking.

November 17

Dear Adrian

H. Cohen wants to propose my Concerto for the Phil and Manchester next season.

As I once offered it to the B.B.C I want to make quite sure that you do not think you have a claim on it – as you could not give it a date when I *did* offer it.[2]

Could I have answer by Thursday when she leaves for America.

Yrs
R. Vaughan Williams

[1] Year taken from context.

[2] See no. 194. Boult asked Kenneth Wright to reply asking VW to keep the first performance for the BBC, which took place under Boult with the BBC Symphony Orchestra at the Queen's Hall on 1 Feb. 1933.

207. To E. J. Dent

[after 2 November 1931[1]]

The White Gates,
Westcott Road,
Dorking.

Dear Dent

I am a fearful nuisance – but there are Phil: rehearsals on Dec 1 & 2 at 2.0 p.m. & as B Cameron is I believe doing 'Job' I ought to be there – but I will write to him & see if he will do it on Tuesday not on Wed:

As regard the Mus. Ass. I will do my best to be present.[2]

Thank you very much for your screed about Glock – one thing surprizes me – you say that he sat for the Mus.B. May 1931 (i.e. last May) & that he failed because his free composition was not approved of though his stodge was good – In that case I must have examined him – & I cannot imagine myself turning down a candidate who had passed in stodge because I did not like his original work – so I can't understand.

Yrs
R. Vaughan Williams

[1] The date of an earlier letter to Dent, not included here, about the arrangements.

[2] Dent was to give a paper to the Musical Association (now Royal Musical Association) entitled 'The Romantic Spirit in Music', which was delivered on 9 Mar. 1933 and published in the *Proceedings of the Musical Association*, 59 (1932–3), 85–102.

208. To Frederick Dwelly[1]

[after October 1931]

The White Gates,
Westcott Road,
Dorking.

My Dear Dean

I need hardly say that I appreciate very much the honour you propose. Nevertheless I feel that such things are really not for me – I have no real connection with anything ecclesiastical & no longer count myself a member of the Church of England.

I drifted into hymns more or less by accident (chiefly to prevent someone else doing it & making a mess of it). Church music will be splendidly represented by Martin Shaw.[2]

Yrs sincerely
R. Vaughan Williams

[1] Dwelly had become the First Dean of Liverpool Cathedral in Oct. 1931 and remained so until his retirement in 1955.

[2] This letter is possibly a response to an informal offer from Dwelly on behalf of the Archishop of Canterbury of a Lambeth Doctorate in Music, a degree conferred on Martin Shaw in 1932 (see *DNB*). It was doubtless offered in recognition of VW's contribution to the *English Hymnal*, *Songs of Praise*, and *Oxford Book of Carols*.

209. To Gerald Finzi

postmark: 4 January 1932

The White Gates,
Westcott Road,
Dorking.

Dear Finzi

We are trying through the sketch of my new symph (2 pfts) at St Pauls G.S. next Wednesday (Jan 6th) at 2.0 P.M. Do come if you can – go to the side entrance (48 Rowan Road) & ask for Gustav or me – & be on time if possible as Gustav does not want to keep the headmistresses bell ringing all afternoon.[1]

Yrs
RVW

[1] Helen Bidder and Vally Lasker were to play through the Fourth Symphony on two pianos at St Paul's Girls' School, where Gustav Holst was Director of Music. See Short, *Holst*, 302.

210. To Ivor Atkins[1]

11 February [1932]

The White Gates,
Westcott Road,
Dorking.

February 11

Dear Atkins

I am sending you herewith the 2 Psalms by the young composer Britten aged 18 about which I spoke to you.

I have only now persuaded him to make a second copy so I fear it is now rather late – but whether you include it or not I should be much obliged if you will look at it and give me your opinion.

I have only told Britten that I wanted a copy to show to someone.

P.S I shall be sending my Magnificat for your perusal in a few days.[2]

[1] Organist of Worcester Cathedral 1897–1950.

[2] The Britten works were settings of Pss. 130 and 150 for chorus and orchestra written while Britten was at the RCM. The final page of the letter with signature is missing. VW sent Atkins the Magnificat on 16 Feb. and it was first performed at the Three Choirs Festival on 8 September.

211. To Gustav Holst[1]

20 March [1932]

The White Gates
Westcott Road
Dorking.

March 20

Dear Gustav

I got the 'Intercession' (through Nora Day). Thank you so much. I like it as much as when you played it to me which is a lot.[2]

I've not had a letter from you – but then I haven't written one so I don't deserve one. But I'm longing for news. Imogen gave me a wonderful letter to read all about your adventures with the Boston Symph[y] orch.[3]

M[rs] Herbert Jones spent the aft. with us the other day – & we both liked her *enormously* – she just sat in a chair after lunch & sang & talked and told us her whole life history. I've been invited to Gregynnogg(?) – & am ½ inclined to go.[4]

Otherwise I have no particular news except that I've written a magnificat for Astra Desmond to sing at the Worcester festival – & that I miss you very much when I want to know how to compose – in [fact] I didn't realize how much you wrote of my music before.[5]

I wonder how you enjoy being led by the nose by an American agent – an agent of Foss's wrote to me and wanted to lead me round America for several months – but I shied off.[6]

I started this letter some days ago & then something intervened & I broke off. I do want to know how America goes – &

have you time for your own work

because I believe the change will produce a great new work from you – but perhaps that will come when you get back – 'emotion remembered in tranquillity' etc.

Did I tell you that I am writing a 'Magnificat' for Worcester Fest? The story is as follows:

(a) When I heard Saliva in G flat at Gloucester last year[7] I wondered if it w[d] be possible to lift the words out of the smug atmosphere which has settled down on it from being sung at evening service for so long. (I've tried hard to get the smugness out, I don't know if I have succeeded – I find it awfully hard to eradicate it.)

(b) Last year at Gloucester rehearsals Steuart[8] (I think) said that it was not quite nice that young unmarried women like Elsie Suddaby should always be singing Magnificats – so Astra Desmond who was there said to me 'I'm a married woman with 4 children why don't you write one for me' – So I promised her if ever I wrote one it should be for her.

Come back soon

Yrs
RVW

[1] Printed with omissions as Letter XXXV in *HR*.

[2] No. 1 of *Six Choruses*, Op. 53, H186, for male voices.

[3] Holst had been appointed Horatio Lamb Lecturer in Composition at Harvard University from Feb. to May 1932 and at the same time had been invited to conduct concerts of his own works beforehand in Jan. by the Boston Symphony Orchestra. See Short, *Holst*, 303 ff.

[4] The sisters Gwendoline and Margaret Davies of Gregynog Hall, near Newtown, Powys, started the Gregynog Music Festival in this year. The Festival, which became known for its associations with VW, Holst, Elgar, and Britten, survived until 1938. It was revived in the 1960s by the University of Wales, which had acquired the Hall after the death of the owners.

[5] *Magnificat* for contralto solo, women's choir, solo flute, and orchestra, *CW* 1932/2.

[6] Duncan Mackenzie of the Oxford University Press, New York, whom Holst had asked to make engagements for him during his visit, at a commission of 20% of the fee. See Short, *Holst*, 302.

[7] VW is apparently referring to a Magnificat in G flat by Ivor Atkins, and possibly means in fact his Magnificat in G published in 1904.

[8] Steuart Wilson.

212. To Ivor Atkins

[about 10 July 1932]

The White Gates,
Westcott Road,
Dorking.

Dear Atkins

I enjoyed my self very much on Thursday – the Benedicite went 1st rate – & I am sure the magnif: will be good – I wonder if the trouble was that the choir was too large? Would a small select choir, say 30 or 40 voices be better – women I think not boys – unless we have one or two boys in to give colour.[1]

As regards 'Quoniam' – I think there is nothing between *complete rescoring* & the original – unless you added 1 desk of viola & 1 desk of cellos to the 2 bassoon parts – to avoid that 'drunken' sound of the 2 bassoons solo.[2]

Allen used to do this I think i.e. horn 2 fag (doubled with 2 v^as^ & 2 cellos) then say 4 cellos & 1 bass playing the bass & the pfte doing continuo where needed. I think if the solo horn could have had a good blow in one of the loud choruses previously.

I will send you the parts at once – also my trumpet parts – because there is one very important place – 1st entry of trumpet in Gloria – I make the trumpets start à 3 – it sounds magnificent – instead of one rather timid trumpet starting by himself (I quote from memory)

then as written

Yrs
R. Vaughan Williams

[1] VW went to Worcester for a night on 7 July to attend rehearsals of his *Benedicite* (*CW* 1929/1) and *Magnificat* (*CW* 1932/2), in preparation for the latter's first performance on 8 Sept. in the Three Choirs Festival.

[2] VW is referring to J. S. Bach's setting of the 'Quoniam tu solus sanctus' from the Gloria in the B Minor Mass, which is scored for horn, two bassoons, and bass continuo.

213. To Gustav Holst[1]

[September 1932]

The White Gates,
Westcott Road
Dorking.

Dear Gustav

I was v. sorry not to see you. But it was wonderful having you on Tues: I feel ashamed of myself sometimes letting you waste all that nervous energy which you ought to be spending on your own stuff over composing my stuff for me – But it's too late to mend now & I can't get on without you, so that's that.

Curwen suggested another publisher before I asked anything![2]

I'm sorry I shan't see Valerie – but I want to meet your brother fearfully & will try to get in first.[3]

I wish we had more talk about you & what really matters & not spent so much time over my damned compos: Your sentence about 'too much alone' puzzles me – but we will discuss it in Dec.

Yrs
RVW

P.S. I send the £5 from my fund for your performances – don't say it comes from that or through me if you can help it.

RVW

[1] Printed with omissions as Letter XXXVII in *HR*.

[2] It is not clear which work VW had offered to Curwen.

[3] Holst's brother, Emil, was an actor working in America under the stage name of Ernest Cossart and VW was to meet him while giving the Mary Flexner lectures at Bryn Mawr. Valerie Cossart was Emil's daughter. The Mary Flexner lectures were published in 1934 by OUP as *National Music*.

214. To Maud Karpeles

[12 October 1932[1]]

Canadian Pacific Steamship Lines
R.M.S. ....

Wednesday

Dear Maud

Here I am on the last day of my sea voyage – I find I'm a *good sailor* – the waves were said to be bigger than they've been for 2 years – & I went to the look out place high up & watched the ship plunging – it was superb – the sun came out occasionally & the huge rollers all blue & green & white were magnificent – otherwise very comfortable but rather dull. Surette was on board but 1st class & he only discovered me today – & I had tea with him in his palace.[2] I land tomorrow & go to Boston on Friday. It was so nice seeing you at the station – I'm reading your jingle book – & like it v. much – I've not tackled the New York book yet. By the way you *must* read 'John Brown'.[3]

Yrs
RVW

[1] Almost certainly this date as his first lecture at Bryn Mawr was the following Wednesday.

[2] Thomas Surette (1862–1941), American composer, organist, and Director of Music at Bryn Mawr.

[3] It is not clear what book VW means. A historical novel by Leonard Ehrlich entitled *God's Angry Man* and based on the life of John Brown was published in 1932.

215. To Gustav Holst[1]

[on or about 21 October 1932]

College Inn
Bryn Mawr.
Penna

Dear Gustav,

Why didn't you tell me that *Una*[2] is here? – I only found out by accident – she is the Light of my Eyes and the Joy of my Heart and my Guardian Angel and has taught me the technique of shopping and gave me a delicious dinner all cooked by herself.

I had a splendid 2 days with the Davisons[3] – they were so nice – while in Boston I went (i) to a football match and (ii) Boston Symph. Orch. – both suffer I think from being too much organized.

I've come to the conclusion that I like *bad* orchestral playing just as I like bad wine – it all sounded *too* easy & smooth. – & lost thrill (e.g. Don Juan opening string passage & the 4 horns – I longed for a bubble from one of the horns).

Tonight I shall hear Phila: orch. and on Monday N.Y. Orch.[4]

I am fairly happy here and everyone is v. hospitable – I went to a music store in Phila: yesterday and was introduced to the Manager – it was just like a chapter out of Martin Chuzzlewit.

Yrs
RVW

[1] Not in *HR*. Mostly printed in *RVW*, 192.
[2] Una Lucas, former head-girl of St Paul's Girls' School (*RVW*, 192).
[3] Archibald Davison, American musicologist (1883–1961). At this time he was Professor of Choral Music at Harvard University; from 1940 to 1954 he was James Edward Ditson Professor of Music there. See *New Grove*.
[4] See no. 216.

216. To Diana Awdry

postmark: 24 October 1932

Bryn Mawr
Penna
U.S.A.

My dear Diana

Did I ever thank you for the lovely book marker – it was dear of you to send it. I'm getting on fairly well here – everyone is v. kind. I've given my first lecture and it seemed quite successful – about 800 people in a large gothic hall 'very English' as they proudly say!

You'll never guess what I did yesterday – I went to a supper party where we all sat round (about 50) and sang Brahms' Requiem – not at all bad. A rich lawyer, a nice rough kind of American, violently keen on Brahms – & told us all Brahms' life history between the numbers – then a very good sup with 'near-beer' and 'near-cider' to drink.

Let me have another letter sometime to cheer me up.

I've heard the Boston Symph: & Philadelphia orch: now I hear the N.Y. orch tonight.

Love from
Uncle Ralph

217. To Imogen Holst

[about 1 November 1932]

College Inn
Bryn Mawr
Penn.

Dear Imogen

Thank you so much for your card – which came, for some reason, a day later than the avalanche.[1] I go to New York on the 12th for 2 nights & will duly pronounce your blessing on it – the chief thing I noticed as I passed through was that the Woolworth B^{dg} is now quite insignificant.

I have to stand up before a class the day after each lecture & be heckled by a crowd of young women – who ask me 'what I meant by' then they refer to their note books – I've come off fairly unscathed up to the present.

Give my love to Vicky if you are still staying with her.[2]

Yrs
Uncle Ralph

[1] i.e. of all the letters of birthday wishes on his 60th birthday on 12 Oct. 1932.

[2] Victoria Reid, later Mrs Leonard Ingrams, with whom Imogen was staying in Scotland.

218. To Maud Karpeles

[about 13 November 1932[1]]

The Biltmore
Madison and Vanderbilt Avenues
New York

Dear Maud

I am for the moment in N.Y. staying surrounded by luxury at the expense of some old friends. I had a wonderful experience at the top of the 'Empire State' first sunset over the river & all the sky scrapers suddenly lighting up. Then all the street lights came out & the moon!

New York looks more classically & tragically beautiful than ever. I've got to come here next week to talk to the E.F.D.S[2] – I thought it was just to be a cosy little affair & now I find they've invited all the musicians of N.Y. & I've got to talk for ¾ of an hour! Too bad. I'm so sorry OUP were such idiots over 'Greensleeves'.[3] I hope its all right now. I think 'Blow the Wind' is a lovely tune beautifully arranged[4] – no diplomacy there!

I start home on Dec 3rd & v. glad I shall be though I've had a good time here.[5]

Yrs
RVW

[1] See no. 217, where VW tells Imogen Holst that he is going to New York on 12 November.

[2] The American branch of the English Folk Dance and Song Society.

[3] Presumably they had claimed copyright and asked for a fee in connection with the tune, following VW's setting of it in *Sir John in Love*, *CW* 1928/3, though the separate publication of his treatment both in a vocal version and in the adaptation by Ralph Greaves, as *Fantasia on 'Greensleeves'*, did not happen until 1934.

[4] 'Blow the wind southerly', later made famous by Kathleen Ferrier's recording.

[5] Mostly printed in *RVW*, 193.

219. To Harriet Cohen

31 December 1932

The White Gates,
Westcott Road,
Dorking.

Saturday 31st December 1932[1]

Dearest Harriet

My cold is well, but now my mother is seriously ill and it *may* be impossible for me to come to London on Monday. I know you will understand if I am not there.[2]

I have written to Adrian & told him that if you both feel that it is over scored anywhere he has *carte blanche* to thin out the orchestration – all he thinks fit. Gustav will, I hope, be there to advise.

I do hope you are better – I know that well or ill you are going to play *beautifully*.

One small point – the 2 bars of Arnold – I like them *slower* (I know Wood takes it quicker) – quite slow & very far off like a dream.[3]

Yrs
R.V.W.

[1] However, the postmark is 5 Jan. 1933, a Thursday, if the envelope attached to the letter is the correct one.

[2] i.e. for the rehearsal of the Piano Concerto which Harriet Cohen was to play under Adrian Boult on 31 January.

[3] There was a quotation from Bax's Third Symphony towards the end of the finale in the first version of the concerto—but this was removed after the first performance (see no. 231). The quotation was an acknowledgement of the close friendship between Bax and her. Partially printed in *WVW*, 236.

220. To Anne Macnaghten

[1932?]

The White Gates,
Westcott Road,
Dorking.

My Dear Anne

How splendid of you to be carrying on with the good work.[1] I have several suggestions:

(1) Dorothy Gow's 4[tet] is good but v. hard still you might try it through & see (she's never heard it yet). Also she has a 'scherzo fugale' for 5 wind instruments – this again would want very expert playing.

(2) Grace Williams – you ought to do her two psalms for contralto & small orch[estra] (Meriel Green would sing them) also the Valse from her ballet – I believe her variations on 'Veni Emmanuel' for str[ing] 4^{tet} are good but I don't know them
(3) Kennedy Andrews has written some lovely songs and fine motets for unnaccomp[anied] voice (chiefly O.U.P.)
(4) Somers Cocks' sonatina for oboe & pianoforte lovely also some v. good songs
(5) Gerald Finzi: Symphony for chamber orchestra also oboe 5^{tet} or concerto – don't know this – also some v. good songs also a v. good choral work with small orch (I forget its name)
(6) David Griffith a very pleasant Fantasy-str[ing]-4tet.
(7) You ought [to] get into touch with Benjamin Britten – I believe he has a str 4tet.[2] I don't know it – but his orchestral & choral things are fine
(8) Helen Hunter Fantasy for string trio I think v. good
(9) I've never heard of Fred Stone[3]

Yrs
Uncle Ralph

P.S. I was so glad to hear your good news of Betty[4]

[1] Anne Macnaghten and Iris Lemare had founded the Macnaghten Concerts Society in 1931 to perform the works of young or little-known British composers. She had written to VW, apparently asking him if he knew of works by these composers which might be performed in her concerts.

[2] String Quartet in D major, written in 1931. Britten revised it in 1974 and it was published in 1975.

[3] VW had encountered most of these composers as pupils at the RCM. Of the number Gow, Williams, Andrews, Somers-Cocks, and of course Finzi and Britten all went on to make a name for themselves in varying degrees. Macnaghten made a note to herself on the verso of the letter: 'Orchestral: G Williams. Contralt – Psalms; Finzi Symphony Write now; Andrews; Haydn Concerto; Write to Britten – what & how long.'

[4] Elizabeth Maconchy.

221. To the Editor of *The Radio Times* 6 January 1933

Dorking

6th January 1933

I notice a curious error in your issue of December 16. In discussing a concert of compositions by Arnold Bax and various continental composers you state that: 'Arnold Bax is clearly in place in this distinguished company'. I take it that the sentence was meant to express that the other composers were not unworthy of a place beside Arnold Bax. Personally I do not consider that most of the names on that programme are worthy to stand beside Bax, but this of course is a matter of opinion.

R. Vaughan Williams.

[The other composers mentioned in the context referred to by Dr. Vaughan Williams were Szymanowski, Schönberg, Conrad Beck, Norbert von Hannenheim, Hindemith, Poulenc and Stravinsky. – EDITOR, The Radio Times][1]

[1] VW was reacting to a notice of a concert of choral and piano music by the composers listed in the Editor's note, to be given on 23 Dec. 1932 on the National Programme by the Wireless Singers and Else C. Krauss, which contained the comment: 'We are not in the habit of ranking our own composers, but Arnold Bax is clearly in place in this distinguished company.'

222. To Adrian Boult at the BBC

23 January 1933

The White Gates,
Westcott Road,
Dorking.

Received: 23 January 1933

Dear Adrian

I hope very much to be at the rehearsal on *Monday* – but I may possibly be prevented.

Now what I am frightened about in this concerto[1] is the *balance*; it may be *overscored* – so if I am not there I give you *carte blanche* to thin out the score all you wish if you do not think the pfte will come through enough (not necessarily *right at the top* all the way through).

I hope Gustav will be at the rehearsal

Yrs
R. Vaughan Williams

P.S. At all events you very likely won't want all the desks of strings playing all the time.

[1] i.e. the Piano Concerto, *CW* 1931/3.

223. To Gustav Holst[1]

[about January 1933]

The White Gates
Westcott Road
Dorking

Dear Gustav

For our sake you must keep well – but for the sake of music you must go on writing canons – so try and combine the two.[2]

I like especially Fields of Sorrow & David's Lament – the two big ones I feel I am going to like – but can't vizualize them yet. I liked the old Trio[3] – but always felt that its being in 3 keys was more seen by the eye than felt by the ear. After all, 'Lovely Venus' depends a lot on the 'natural chord' doesn't it? I don't think I like your notation. After all, key signatures are simply a means of avoiding accidentals – isn't that so? And I believe that on the balance you w[d] get fewer accidentals by putting a christian key signature – & not, incidentally, make unhappy people like me who try to play them on the pfte permanently cross-eyed.

Let me hear them soon – we are perhaps coming to London for a week round Feb 1st.[4]

Yrs
RVW

[1] Printed as Letter XXXVIII in *HR*.

[2] Holst had completed six of *Eight Canons for Equal Voices*, H187, in 1932 during VW's absence in the USA. A further two were added in 1933.

[3] i.e. the *Terzetto*.

[4] VW's Piano Concerto was to be given its first performance by Harriet Cohen at the Queen's Hall on 1 February.

224. To Adrian Boult at the BBC

7 February 1933

The White Gates,
Westcott Road,
Dorking.

February 7 1933

Dear Adrian

I have now sufficiently recovered from the shock of last Wednesday to be able to write to thank you and your orchestra for your beautiful performance.[1] You have made impossible the composer's time-honoured excuse that the work would have sounded all right if it had been properly played – I could not have imagined a better first performance.

I am so sorry that you were not at Mrs Fisher's[2] party after the concert. Some of the guests were invited by me and some by her and we both took it for granted that you were the first person who would be invited by the other. When we discovered our mistake we telephoned wildly to every conceivable address, but in vain.

Yrs
R. Vaughan Williams[3]

[1] Boult had conducted the premiere of the Piano Concerto on 1 Feb. at the Queen's Hall.

[2] Lettice Fisher, wife of H. A. L. Fisher, AVW's brother.

[3] Printed in Moore, *Music and Friends*, 108.

225. To Harriet Cohen

[February 1933]

The White Gates,
Westcott Road,
Dorking.

Dearest Harriet

Thank you so much for your sweet letter & I'm so sorry you've not been well – & that I shan't see you for so long.[1]

I'm so sorry N.Y. doesn't want the concerto – but no one ever does like my stuff the first time – so we must put up with that – also I *can't* push my own stuff – I'm not made that way – & I'm sure I warned you of that when you so sweetly & nobly undertook to play my stuff – so don't worry about my old thing & play them what will give you honour & glory – which is the sincerest wish of your devoted R.V.W.[2]

By the way before you play it again (if you do) let me have good notice as I want to make some alterations – the fugue wants lengthening – & the cadenzas want altering.[3]

Good luck at Vienna & do I still claim my 1065½ or am I in disgrace for writing you a bad concerto?[4]

Love from
RVW

P.S. After all you & I like it & that's all that matters in the long run.

[1] Harriet Cohen was going to be away for some two months from about 20 Feb. on a tour that included Vienna.

[2] She had wanted to give the Concerto with the New York Philharmonic under Bruno Walter, but he had turned down the idea. See Cohen, *A Bundle of Time*, 260, where the letter is printed. She did give it in the Carnegie Hall in Jan. 1934.

[3] Partially quoted in *WVW*, 236.

[4] The only visit to Vienna at this time is mentioned out of sequence in Cohen, *A Bundle of Time*, 174 as taking place in 'spring 1934'.

226. To Elizabeth Maconchy

[about 13 March 1933]

The White Gates,
Westcott Road,
Dorking.

My Darling Betty

What lovely news & how sweet of you to telephone. – I heard all about it in London from Gibbs. Of course you ought to have been 1st – because yours *must* be better than all the others. But still even as it is it is a sign of grace in the adjudicators.[1]

Much Love from
Uncle Ralph

[1] EM had been awarded third prize in the Daily Telegraph Chamber Music Competition for her Oboe Quintet of 1932. The first prize had been awarded to Edric Cundell and second prize to Cecil Armstrong Gibbs.

227. To Keith Falkner[1]

[about March 1933[2]]

The White Gates,
Westcott Road,
Dorking.

Dear Keith Falkner

I meant to have shown you the enclosed songs when I saw you at Belfast – but there was no time. They are for string 4tet but I have had a pfte arrangement made for rehearsal purposes.

They are by an ex-pupil of mine Alex Burnard an Australian & I think there is something in them.[3]

It wd be very kind of you if you could find time to look at them and let me know what you think

If you like I will send you the string 4tet score.

Yrs vy sincerely
R. Vaughan Williams

[1] English bass/baritone singer (1900–94), who had sung the role of the Constable in the first performance of *Hugh the Drover* at the RCM in 1924. He later was professor of singing at Cornell University and in 1960 became Director of the RCM.

[2] VW had been in Belfast to conduct a concert of his works on 17 Feb. 1933. See no. 186 n. 1.

[3] David Alexander Burnard, Australian composer, who studied with VW and Herbert Fryer at the RCM before completing his studies at the University of Adelaide in 1932. The work was *Five Shakespeare Songs* for Baritone and String Quartet, dedicated to VW.

228. To Elizabeth Maconchy

[March ?1933]

The White Gates,
Westcott Road,
Dorking.

Dearest Betty

(Or am I to call you Betsy – I think I prefer Betty as I've always called you that.)

I went to the studio last night – it was lovely – & the *sureness of touch* was wonderful – the 2 slow movements are the best I think – is the first a little *too* 'chip chippy' – & I am old fashioned enough to want a coda to the last movement. I was so dreadfully sorry not to see you – They had shoved on a rehearsal for the Dorking festival that afternoon – which went on till nearly 5.0.

I thought they played v. well – & was a relief after the dreary Schumann – I shall be there on the 30th – good bye dearest Betty

with love from
Uncle Ralph

229. To Vally Lasker

[April 14 1933[1]]

The White Gates,
Westcott Road,
Dorking.

Dear Vally

I heard just now from Mrs O'Neill[2] that Gustav was not so well. So I rung up Ealing – he is better again & Dr Jones does not think he is in danger. There was a haemorrhage but it has now stopped and he is comfortable. The haemorrhage came on early this morning and he was taken to a nursing home in Ealing. Isobel[3] has come up & is now stopping with Miss Jones.

So I think all is going well & they are ringing me up tomorrow morning. I promised to let you know as they cannot get you on the phone.[4]

Yrs
RVW

[1] Note in the hand of the recipient: 'Good Friday 1933'.
[2] Adine, wife of Norman O'Neill, pianist and music mistress at St Paul's Girls' School.
[3] Isobel Holst, Gustav's wife.
[4] Holst was suffering from a duodenal ulcer; see Short, *Holst*, 318.

230. To Gustav Holst[1]

[about 15 April 1933[2]]

The White Gates,
Westcott Road,
Dorking.

Dear Gustav

You are not missing much by being indoors these last few days – Hail & snow – & our poor flowers all bitten by the frost & they were looking so nice – Not that I've wanted to go out much – Festival odd jobs keep me pretty busy the last few days – Faking the 4 horn parts of the Brahms serenade in to 2 parts – I only had to leave out about 12 notes!

I heard the early Ireland sonata (Pfte & violin) the other day – I am ashamed to say I did not know it – the slow movement is really very lovely – the rest a little spoilt by the desire to shine & show he understands the instrument. I wonder how much a composer *ought* to know instrumental technique – do you remember we had a long talk about that last year – of course the deepest abyss of the result of writing 'effectively' is Frank Bridge – but there is a slight *snobbishness* about Ireland's music which worries me if you know what I mean.

[1] Not in *HR*. Lacking final page(s).
[2] *Music Won the Cause* records that Brahms's Serenade in D was given at LHMF this year.

231. To Gerald Finzi

7 July [1933]

The White Gates,
Westcott Road,
Dorking.

Dictated
July 7

Dear Gerald

The following facts are true –

(a) I fell into the brook.
(b) I broke my ancle [*sic*]
(c) I mayn't put my foot to the ground for a month.

But – (a) I have no pain
(b) I am quite well
(c) I was not drunk at the time.

Don't wait to examine those registry steps[1] till my foot is well – but come over one day – both of you – and see us.

I find that Ellen[2] has reported about the steps as follows – There are none.

Mayn't I play the harmonium?[3]

Yrs
RVW

Bob[4] has passed his exam & has a 1st in Mechanics.

AMVW

[1] Gerald Finzi and Joy were to be married at Dorking Registry Office on 16 Sept. GF was concerned that there might be steps into the Office which the VWs might not be able to negotiate because of Adeline's lameness and his injured foot.

[2] According to UVW this was AVW's maid.

[3] i.e. at the wedding.

[4] Robert de Ropp, a distant relative of Adeline's who had returned from Australia after trying to become a sheep farmer. The VWs financed the remainder of his education (UVW). On his stay with the VWs see the chapter entitled 'Gentle Warriors' in his book *Warrior's Way* (Nevada City, 1992), 39–48.

232. To Harriet Cohen

postmark: 22 July 1933

The White Gates,
Westcott Road,
Dorking.

Dearest Harriet

Thank you 1000 times for those lovely flowers & for your dear letter – I am so sorry you have been ill and for the cause of it. It is v. exciting about the concerto but rather upsetting – I meant to have rewritten the last movement to make it better for you – & I kept on putting it off and off till I c^d approach it with a calm mind – now it's got to go once again in its old form. – One slight alteration I think we can make – the 'quotation' at the end of the work does not 'come off' – *we* understand it – but the audience does not. So, I will in the next few days think out a new ending – only about 4 new bars for you to learn.[1]

Much love from
R.V.W.

[1] The concerto was to be given at the Promenade concerts on 22 Aug., with VW conducting. There was a quotation from Bax's Third Symphony towards the end of the finale in the first version of the concerto as an acknowledgement of the close friendship between Bax and Cohen, but this was removed after the first performance.

233. To Elizabeth Trevelyan[1]

23 July [1933]

The White Gates,
Westcott Road,
Dorking.

July 23

Dear Bessy

Thank you so much for writing – I am sitting up for the 1st time. I feel ridiculously well – only I mayn't put my stupid foot to the ground till it is quite healed – I'm not learning any new instrument but luckily a lot of proofs have come in to keep me busy – also I've completed 'plucking the partridge'.[2]

Yrs
RVW

P.S. A fine puff of Ursula & Julian in the 'Evening Standard' yesterday![3]

[1] The Dutch wife of Robert, the elder brother of VW's friend G. M. Trevelyan ('Trevy'). She and Robert lived at The Shiffolds, near Leith Hill Place.

[2] He had thought of learning the clarinet while laid up and Elizabeth Darbishire came to teach him – but by this time, presumably, it had been realized that the enterprise was unlikely to prosper. The proofs were possibly either of the full score of *Job* or of the revised edition (1933) of the *English Hymnal*. The reference to 'Plucking the partridge' is not clear; perhaps it refers to a folk song.

[3] A reference to the marriage of VW's cousin Ursula Darwin to Julian Trevelyan.

234. To Charles Myers[1]

[July 1933[2]]

The White Gates,
Westcott Road,
Dorking.

Dear Dr Myers

Thank you very much for your interesting pamphlet[3] – I did not want to acknowledge it until I had read it *twice*.

I wonder if we pay too much attention to peoples *descriptions* of their reactions to music. After all I suppose musical appreciation is inexplicable in words and some people take refuge in analogies when they try & ~~express~~ describe their sensations & others try & hide them in technical criticism.

I am glad you think that song (at all events) came through excited speech.

I once heard a Gaelic preacher – this is of course a common experience – & when he got excited he recited on a fixed succession of notes

(I am not sure of the pitch)

Now this & the allied formula

is the starting point of many British Folksongs.

E.G.

Bushes and briars

etc.[4]

Forgive this garrulity – but I am lying in bed with a cracked ankle.

Yours sincerely
R. Vaughan Williams

[1] Charles Samuel Myers (1873–1946), Cambridge psychologist and anthropologist with a special interest in ethnic music.

[2] This date is inferred from the reference by VW to his cracked ankle.

[3] The pamphlet was possibly *The Absurdity of Any Mind–Body Relation, etc.*, a lecture which had been published by OUP in 1932.

[4] VW set out the general point made in this letter at greater length in his second Mary Flexner Lecture at Bryn Mawr College in 1932. See *National Music* (1987), 17 ff.

235. To Harriet Cohen

postmark: 3 August 1933

The White Gates,
Westcott Road,
Dorking.

Dearest Harriet

One more word

If you find that Scherchen has an incomplete or inadequate orchestra you will refuse to play the concerto won't you?[1]

Yrs
RVW

[1] Hermann Scherchen, German conductor and pioneer of new music (1891–1966). At this time he was giving up his post as Generalmusikdirektor at Königsberg and moving to Switzerland, where he was director of the Zürich Radio Orchestra. He was planning a performance of the concerto at Strasburg later in the month.

236. To W. W. Thompson at the BBC

15 August [1933[1]]

The White Gates,
Westcott Road,
Dorking.

August 15

Dear Mr Thompson

Many thanks for programme note which I return herewith. I am sorry you thought it necessary to call me 10 minutes early for rehearsal as I am not in the habit of being late for my appointments.

Yours sincerely
R Vaughan Williams

CONCERTO IN C MAJOR, FOR PIANOFORTE AND ORCHESTRA – Vaughan Williams[2]

Toccata – Romanza – Fuga Chromatica
Con Finale alla Tedesca

The Concerto had its first performance at a B.B.C. Concert in February of this year,[3] when Miss Harriet Cohen, to whom it is dedicated, was the soloist, as she is this evening.

The composer has told us that the first two movements were sketched in 1926, and the third in 1930. There are no breaks between the movements.

The first movement is begun by the pianoforte with a swift semiquaver figure in 7-8 measure, characteristic of toccatas, against which the orchestra plays a broad theme soaring upwards. Then follows a figure on the pianoforte, in 3-4, easily recognisable by beginning with a reiterated note. A development of that leads to a spritely, jumping theme, and then the whole is repeated with slight modifications, the pianoforte and orchestra as a rule changing places. After that comes a development of the pianoforte's reiterated note figure, which serves as an accompaniment to a new theme. An extension of the orchestra's 7-8 theme leads to a short recapitulation, and the movement which is quite short, ends with a version of the theme which came just before it, canonically treated by pianoforte and orchestra. A short *cadenza* for pianoforte leads to the *romanza*, whose principal theme is played by pianoforte solo and repeated by the flute accompanied by pianoforte and strings. An additional theme for strings and muted horns and an episode in 3-2 time follows. The opening themes are then heard again, but the movement is interrupted by the trombones, and a few bars of introduction lead to *Fuga chromatica con Finale alla Tedesca*. The subject of the fugue is given out by the pianoforte, and there is a counter-subject, which, like the chief subject, opens with a silent beat. After various episodes a *stretto* on a dominant pedal is reached, built up chiefly on an augmentation of part of the fugue subject with which the subject and counter-subject are combined. A *cadenza* for the pianoforte separates the fugue and the Finale, the subjects of which are the same as those of the fugue, but treated harmonically rather than contrapuntally, and finally there is another *cadenza* for the pianoforte, made up chiefly out of the episode in the slow movement. The *cadenza* ends with a quotation two bars long from a contemporary composer,[4] added 'According to my promise'. Then a few bars of *Allegro* bring the Concerto to an end.

[1] Year taken from context.
[2] The text of the programme note is similar to but not identical with the note printed in *CW*, pp. 138–9.
[3] On 1 Feb. 1933 at the Queen's Hall.
[4] The quotation was from Arnold Bax; see no. 232.

237. To Elizabeth Maconchy

[about 23 September 1933[1]]

Birling Gap Hotel
Sussex

My Darling Betty

It was a pleasure to hear from you after so long – good news about the concerto. I think, as you say, that Hallé seems the best (you *did* send it on to the Freak Fest when Schuloff [*sic*] was on the jury[2]). I will write about it to Hallé when I find out where to write – Harriet will know – By the way dear Betty, don't place too great hopes on this: Harriet gets so enthusiastic & thinks sometimes that because she wants a thing done it *will* be done – but we have to reckon with committees & conductors & all those kind of wild-fowl before a thing really gets through.[3]

I am eager to hear the new 4^{tet}. Alas! its no good your coming over yet – the house at Dorking is being mended & we've got to turn out for 2 months & go to London (11 Roxburgh Mansions, Kensington W) – if you *do* ever come to London remember this.

My love to Billy[4] & a thousand loves to you

from
Uncle Ralph

[1] The VWs were unable to be at The White Gates from Oct. until early Dec. 1933 due to rebuilding work.

[2] Ervin Schulhoff, Czech composer and pianist. The 'Freak Fest' was the ISCM Festival, which VW had attended in Prague in 1925, finding much of the music uncongenial. In 1933 it was in Amsterdam.

[3] VW was in close touch with Harriet Cohen at this time as he prepared a revised version of his Piano Concerto (*CW* 1931/3) and wrote to her on 23 Sept. thanking her for encouraging Maconchy.

[4] William Lefanu, whom Maconchy had married in 1930.

238. To Iris Lemare[1]

postmark: 16 October 1933

The White Gates,
Westcott Road,
Dorking.

My dear Iris

My house is all shut up & I cannot get at anything until December.[2] I don't *think* I've got any band parts of 'Sleepers Wake'[3] – But if by December you've failed elsewhere I will then be at home & will look & see.

Good luck to your concert.

Love from
Uncle Ralph

[1] Iris Lemare (1902–97), founder, in 1931, of the Macnaghten–Lemare Concerts and of the Lemare orchestra. She was the first woman to conduct the BBC SO. VW had provided both encouragement and financial support for the concerts.

[2] The VWs were in London while an annexe was being built to The White Gates.

[3] Bach cantata no. 140, *Wachet auf, ruft uns die Stimme.*

239. To Hubert Foss at OUP

12 November [1933]

11 Roxburghe Mansions
Kensington Court
W.8

Nov 12

Dear Foss

re Greensleeves

I cannot criticize Greaves' arrangement without a copy of the music which I have not by me. But I suggest that if he wants a 'B' to go between the two

'A's' the obvious thing would be the folk-tune 'Lovely Joan' as it appears in the Interlude between scenes 1 & 2 of Act II.[1]

Re Music from Percival

Would you mind keeping this till we decide what to do with it – But meanwhile could you send me the *vocal* score of all 3 scenes to this address? I want to show it to Gordon at the R.C.M.[2]

Yours sincerely
R. Vaughan Williams

[1] OUP had received requests for an arrangement for strings of the Greensleeves music from *Sir John in Love* and had decided to commission Ralph Greaves to make it under VW's supervision. It was published in 1934 as *Fantasia on Greensleeves* and 'Lovely Joan' was indeed used as the central section of the piece.

[2] Robert Percival had produced and conducted six performances, which included the Prologue and possibly the Episode and Interlude from *Sir John in Love* at Bristol Opera School on 30 Oct. 1933; see *CW* 1928/3a. OUP published the new additions in 1936.

240. To Jack Gordon[1]

7 December [1933[2]]

The White Gates,
Dorking.

Dear Gordon

You put your finger on the chief difficulty of my second Interlude (the scene with Fenton, Anne & chorus) the other day when you pointed out that that scene would require a full stage and would thus make practical difficulties coming immediately before the Falstaff–Quickly scene – And you have probably already anticipated the idea which came to me this morning that this Interlude should be the 1st scene of Act II – the 2nd scene would then be the Letter scene and the rest of the act follows as printed.

Am I right in supposing that you would then be able to have a full stage for the Fenton–Anne Scene, followed by a front scene for the Letter Scene during which the stage could be set for the interior of the 'Garter'? This would have the additional advantage of letting the interview of Quickly & Falstaff follow immediately on the Letter Scene as it really should do.

You have probably thought of all this already and I only write to say that I quite approve. It would of course involve writing some new music to take the curtain up on this new beginning of Act II – but this I think could easily be done if you wanted it.

Yrs
R. Vaughan Williams

[1] John Barritt Gordon (1898–1978), educated at Repton, served in the Royal Artillery in 1917–18, matriculated at New College Oxford 1919, and did a short course for returning soldiers in History, graduating in 1921. He was busy at Sadler's Wells in 1930s but apparently not after 1939 or so.

[2] This letter appears to concern amendments to *Sir John in Love* (*Prologue, Episode and Interlude*, *CW* 1928/3a), of which the Prologue had been written for a performance at Bristol in 1933 while the Episode and Interlude appear to have been written for a possible performance at Sadler's Wells in the 1934–5 season, which did not materialize. All three were published by OUP in 1936. The year must be 1933 since VW refers to the matter in a letter to OUP received by them on 4 Jan. 1934. See no. 241.

241. To Hubert Foss at OUP

4 January 1934

The White Gates,
Dorking.

Received: 4th January 1934

Dear Foss

I've just been on the telephone with Jack Gordon – He wants to keep Interlude in its place *after* Act II scene 1 – so the vocal score stays as it is – But he will probably *not* do the prologue – but I hope you will print that all the same as other people may want to do it. *He* has the vocal score when you want it.

Yrs
R. Vaughan Williams

242. To Julian Herbage at the BBC[1]

18 January [1934]

The White Gates,
Westcott Road,
Dorking.

Jan 18

Dear Mr Herbage

Thank you for your letter.[2]

My 'Four Hymns' belong properly to Tenor so I should prefer to have Mr Wilson – their original interpreter.

The solo at the end of the 'Pastoral Symphony' is marked 'soprano or tenor' though it is usually sung by a soprano – But of course I must leave this to you.

As regards the timing of the various pieces I will go through the Hymns and give you an accurate timing. You probably have a timing of the other items.

With regard to the 'Norfolk Rhapsody' there is only one – Nos 2 & 3 were scrapped long ago. I suggest that if we include the 'Running Set' it should come last to make a cheerful end.

Also would it be a good plan to start with the Norfolk Rhapsody, put the Tallis Fantasia second & the 'Four Hymns' immediately after which being in much the same mood as the Fantasia would make a good pendant to it – But again I must leave this to you as an experienced programme maker.

Yours sincerely
R. Vaughan Williams

[1] Julian Herbage (1904–76) had been a member of the Music Department of the BBC since 1927 and at this time assisted Kenneth Wright with programme building.
[2] Herbage had proposed a concert of works by VW.

243. To Edward Elgar

19 February [1934]

The White Gates,
Westcott Road,
Dorking.

Feb 19th

Dear Elgar

I want to tell you how my choirs of the Dorking Festival are loving preparing 'Gerontius' – Greatly daring I suggested it for this year's festival – I had been longing to do it for years, but had thought it too dangerous an experiment as I could not bear to do it badly – Whether we shall do it well I do not know – But if enthusiasm and hard work can achieve anything be sure that it will not lack those.

And it will be one of the great moments in my life when I stand with trembling baton to conduct it – we have good soloists – Astra Desmond, Steuart Wilson and Harold Williams – and we shall think of you – please give us your blessing.[1]

Of course this wants no answer.

Yours affectionately
R. Vaughan Williams

[1] On the performance of *Gerontius* at Dorking, see *RVW*, 197. Elgar was terminally ill at this time and died on 23 Feb., three days after receiving this letter.

244. To Ralph Greaves at OUP

25 February [1934]

The White Gates,
Westcott Road,
Dorking.

Feb 25

Dear Greaves

I have looked through your score which I return – I make one or two suggestions otherwise I think it is very good. Thank you so much for taking so much trouble.[1]

Yours sincerely
R. Vaughan Williams

[1] Greaves had adapted 'Greensleeves' from the opera *Sir John in Love*, *CW* 1928/3, into the *Fantasia on Greensleeves*, *CW* 1934/1.

245. To Adrian Boult

8 April [1934 or earlier]

The White Gates,
Westcott Road,
Dorking.

April 8

Dear Adrian

Thank you very much for a most beautiful and moving performance last Sunday – quite frankly I was rather dreading it because I hadn't heard it since I tried to conduct it myself – and as you know yourself when one has lived in every note of a work one gets rather morbidly sensitive about it. But those opening bars so beautifully slow and yet flowing put me right for the evening and everything followed as it should. I sometimes feel rather jealous that you apparently with one wink of your eye can make those people do things that I couldn't make them do with hours of grind.

The whole thing though of course it wasn't my way was yet a right and good way and absolutely convincing.

I didn't care for the lady at the harpsichord – partly because I could not tell in the least what notes she was playing from my place in the hall, partly because of the unconscionable way she dragged out her cadences when everything pointed to swift action & partly because I imagine it is her fault that Steuart's interpretation is to my mind not so good as it used to be – But after all what I was there for was to hear the choir and they covered themselves with glory.[1]

Thank you very much for your offer of help on the subject on which I wrote to you. I am sure you can help & I will write again soon –

Yrs
R. Vaughan Williams

[1] The letter is apparently about a performance of the St Matthew Passion of J. S. Bach by the Bach Choir with Steuart Wilson as the evangelist.

246. To Gustav Holst[1]

[13 April 1934]

The White Gates
Westcott Road
Dorking.

Friday

Dear Gustav

After promising myself all the year that I would attend *every* rehearsal of the choral symph. I attended *none* – I stupidly went & got a little chill & temperature – nothing bad, but in view of next week & *having* to go to London for rehearsals twice this week, I thought I must take no risks – I was never so disgusted in my life. The wireless behaved pretty well – funnily the scherzo came over best I thought & as far as I can make out they sang that beautifully – & it *was* a relief to hear the urn sung by people who had some idea what the words meant. All except that horrid Lycette woman.[2]

By the way, I wish you would consider taking that last phrase away from the soloist (even Dorothy[3]) and giving it to say 4 of the chorus (just as you have done [with] one or two of the other phrases).

As to the tune its self – I *wholly* liked the Urn for the first time. I'm not sure that it is the Urn – but it's *you*, which is all I know & all I need to know.

The scherzo is what I always thought it was, you at your best.

I am not so sure about the finale – I love the big tune – but some of it seems to be just getting through the words – I wonder if a cut of one or two of the poets would be possible or advisable?[4]

Jelly[5] came & rehearsed the Mendelssohn concerto with my strings yesterday – we had great fun singing the wind parts as a duet.

Yrs
RVW

[1] Printed with omissions as Letter XLI in *HR*.

[2] Holst's *A Choral Symphony* had been broadcast on 11 April. It includes a setting of Keats's *Ode on a Grecian Urn*. The soloist VW refers to was Miriam Licette.

[3] Dorothy Silk.

[4] The finale is, in part, a setting of Keats's *Ode to Apollo*, in which stanzas are addressed successively to Homer, Maro (i.e. Virgil), Milton, Shakespeare, Spenser, and Tasso. Holst did not omit any of them.

[5] Jelly d'Arányi, the violinist, dedicatee, and first exponent of the Violin Concerto in D minor, *CW* 1925/7. See also no. 427 n. 2.

247. To Isobel and Imogen Holst

[25 May 1934[1]]

The White Gates,
Westcott Road,
Dorking.

Dear Isobel & Imogen

My very dearest love to you both. I know you don't want me to say more & I know that you know that he has it & you have it.

My only thought is now which ever way I turn what are we to do without him – every thing seems to have turned back to him – what would Gustav think or advise or do.

But I do believe as you told me that he did not want to go on in this life unless it could be a full one – and perhaps it is a fuller & better one for him now – so it is purely selfish of me perhaps to want it different.[2]

I longed to come straight away & see you when dear Imogen telephoned me this morning – & you know you have only got to say 'come' & I will come at once.[3]

RVW

[1] The day Holst died.

[2] Following the operation for the removal of a duodenal ulcer, it was likely that Holst would have remained an invalid had he survived.

[3] Isobel Holst replied on 3 June: 'Thank you so much for your beautiful letter & for all that you have done for us always. One can't write about these things, but I would like you to know that dear Gustav died quietly & peacefully like a little child, knowing nothing about it. I was with him all the time & he suffered no pain after the operation.'

248. To Harriet Cohen

postmark: 10 June 1934

The White Gates,
Westcott Road,
Dorking.

Dearest Harriet

Many thanks for the M.S. – I *had* got the new cadenza etc – what I had *not* got were the small emendations we made in the figuration at various places – I have now done those by heart as best I can – I hope I've got them right!

Now I must be fair to the OUP. I never said they were going to publish it but that I *hoped* they were going to publish it – a very different thing alas!

Now I also want to be fair to *you* both for the great admiration I have for you & your playing & for the splendid work you are doing for English music – Now how long do you think you ought to have the concerto before it is thrown open by publication or otherwise? I don't know in the least what is right to do. I gave Jelly[1] a 6 month run of my violin concerto – (not that she made much use of it.).

How long did Kreisler keep the Elgar concerto?

Personally I don't think any one else will ever *want* to play it because you and Arnold (and possibly myself) are the only 3 people who like it and as to students – I know you are far too generous to mind [some] student from Birmingham Midland Institute (such as wrote to me the other day) having it to *study* – I don't think there was any question of public performance.[2]

So dearest Harriet – let me know what you think

Yrs
RVW

[1] Jelly d'Arányi; see no. 246 n. 5.
[2] This letter is printed in *WVW*, 237–8.

249. To Adrian Boult at the BBC

27 July 1934

The White Gates,
Westcott Road,
Dorking.

Received: 27 July 1934

Dear Adrian

Several people have expressed surprise to me that the Proms contain no concert devoted to Gustav's music. I have an idea that one of the B.B.C. Autumn Concerts is going to be devoted to his music – am I right in this? And if so may I tell people who ask me why there is no concert of his music at the 'Proms'.

Also you may know that Gustav was planning a symphony of which the scherzo was already finished.[1] I feel this ought to have an important place in next seasons scheme – *not* at a memorial concert (as a sort of pious memorial) but for its own sake at an ordinary concert.

Will it fit in to one of the B.B.C. Wednesdays or shall I write to the Philharmonic?[2]

Yrs
RVW[3]

[1] Scherzo, H192.

[2] Boult did not reply until 16 Aug.: 'I am sorry we have been so long answering your letter, particularly as I gather you want the information for other people. Various circumstances, which are too long to write, but which I will tell you, have made it only possible that our second Concert should contain a memorial to Gustav. We are doing "The Planets" that day, and I hope it will be a worthy performance. Owing to the previous engagement of Myra Hess, who can come on no other date, it is not possible to give the complete programme to his works, but a space is being left in a later Concert for the Scherzo. We certainly should like to have it, though I am always careful to say that we are not out to grasp first performances. If it is of use to other organizations to have the first performance, we are quite content to give the second. This is a matter of principle, but I personally do feel rather selfish and greedy where the Scherzo is concerned. One of our Programme Advisory Committee members mentioned a new Symphony by yourself. I need hardly say we are only too ready to get more information when you feel like giving it to us. ACB.' The Scherzo was first performed by the BBC SO under Boult on 6 Feb. 1935 at the Queen's Hall.

[3] Printed together with Boult's reply in Moore, *Music and Friends*, 116–17.

250. To Adrian Boult at the BBC

[19 August 1934[1]]

The White Gates,
Westcott Road,
Dorking.

Sunday

Dear Adrian

Many thanks for your letter.[2] I am telling Isobel what you say & asking her to write to you. It is of course *she* & not I who have control over Gustav's music.

As regards my symphony I have been writing it for about 3 years now & I believe it is finished.[3] I have made a 2 pfte arrangement & will get that tried through to see if I can bear it. But the situation at present is that some time ago before Sargent[4] fell ill he asked me if I had anything new & I told him about this symphony – whether this amounts to a promise & whether he wants it even if it did I don't know – W[d] you like to get in touch with him?

The bits I have shown to people they do not like – Gustav heard it all in an early version on 2 pftes – & was puzzled by most of it & disliked the rest.[5]

Yrs
RVW

[1] Date noted by recipient on original.

[2] See no. 249 n. 2.

[3] Symphony in F Minor, *CW* 1934/13. The first performance of the symphony was given by the BBC SO under Boult on 10 Apr. 1935 at the Queen's Hall.

[4] Malcolm Sargent.

[5] In particular Holst appears to have criticized some of the earlier ideas for the last movement as being somewhat superficial. VW had responded: 'The "nice" tunes in the Finale have already been replaced by better ones (at all events they are *real* ones). What I mean is that I *knew* the others were made-up stuff and these are not' (*HR*, Letter XL).

251. To Alice Sumsion

[probably 28 August 1934]

The White Gates,
Westcott Road,
Dorking.

Tuesday

Dear Alice

Alas – its now definite I can't come – I'm getting on splendidly but I mayn't move till it is *quite* healed.[1]

Do you know I believe I've not missed a festival for 10 years.

I *was* looking forward to this so. Give my love to John & wish him good luck through all his trials and *my* love to the *Prettiest Girl in Gloucester.*

xxxxxxxxxxxx

I shall claim all those[2] when next we meet.

Love from
RVW

[1] VW had a poisoned abscess on his ankle which had developed from a blister gained, according to UVW, on a long walk in Sussex following Gustav Holst's funeral. It kept him in bed for eight weeks; see *RVW*, 201.

[2] i.e. the kisses represented by the 'x's.

252. To Herbert Howells

postmark: 12 September 1934

The White Gates,
Westcott Road,
Dorking.

Dear Herbert

Thank you so much for your amusing & informative letter.[1]

It was awful missing all the Nymphs[2] of Gloucester – & it was I who was feeling jealous of you and Billy.[3] Did you hear R.O's tune – I particularly wanted to hear that.[4]

I really think I shall be up in a few days – though I don't boast as I've tried 3 times & had to go back. The ridiculous thing is I've been *quite well* but not allowed to move *in case* anything bad should result.

All the result of neglecting a blister. Do you hear that poor Ken Andrews[5] has got TB & has to go off to Switzerland for some months. I shall like to hear (?) very much what you thought of C.B.R's tune.[6]

Yrs
RVW

[1] About the Gloucester Three Choirs Festival.
[2] i.e. all the pretty girls, such as Diana Awdry.
[3] W. H. Reed, whose Symphony for Strings was performed at the Festival.
[4] No work by R. O. Morris is mentioned in Boden, *Three Choirs*, as being performed at the 1934 Festival.
[5] Herbert Kennedy Andrews, Northern Irish composer and music scholar who later settled at Oxford. See *New Grove*.
[6] A setting of Milton's *Ode on the Morning of Christ's Nativity* by Cyril Rootham.

253. To W. W. Thompson (?) at the BBC

23 September [1934]

The White Gates,
Westcott Road,
Dorking.

Sept 23

Dear Sir

I see in the current Radio Times that my 'Fantasia on a theme of Tallis' is described as 'Fantasy' – I hope that in the programme of the Promenade Concert next Thursday you will not make me guilty of this affected word.

FANTASIA please.

Yrs faithfully
R. Vaughan Williams

254. To Adrian Boult at the BBC

[about 16 October 1934]

The White Gates,
Dorking.

Dear Adrian

I want you to hear the [F Min] Symph on 2 pianos *soon* because I want to get down to it & wash its face – Now have you any free dates? Vally and Nora[1] are free after 5.30 on Fridays & Saturday mornings – also *possibly* Thursdays after 6.0 & *possibly* Thursday mornings (Fri or Sat: best) – Could you get Mrs Beckett[2] to ring up & say if any of those days *soon* will be poss for you (Nov 10th is *imposs* for me) – but I hope for something earlier.[3]

Yrs
RVW

[1] VW had written to Nora Day and Vally Lasker on 14 Oct. asking if they would play for the run-through, and the information about their availability must have come in their response.

[2] Gwen Beckett, Boult's secretary.

[3] The run-through had taken place by early Nov. because VW wrote to Bliss on 6 Nov. responding to some comments of his on the symphony which he had clearly heard at the run-through. See no. 256.

255. To Bernard van Dieren[1]

20 October [?1934[2]]

The White Gates,
Westcott Road,
Dorking.

October 20

Dear Mr Van Dieren

I am taking the liberty of writing to you about our common acquaintance John Buckland.[3]

I know how kind and helpful you have been to him and you evidently understand him very well so that before writing to give him any advice I should like to know what you think would be right for him so that our opinions shall not clash. His last letter to me seemed discontented and very emotional. Personally I feel that he ought to try to throw himself more into his work at Fords[4] and not take it for granted that it is a necessary evil – In his last letter he speaks for example of sordid everyday drudgery and talks of his life as being a stereotyped copy for the millions of lives led by our population.

I am very much interested in him, but cannot yet make up my mind whether he has really any musical creativeness – I should be glad to know your opinion about this – I need hardly say that he does not know that I am writing to you and I of course will treat anything you tell me as confidential.

Yours sincerely
R. Vaughan Williams

[1] The composer (1887–1936); see *New Grove*. Van Dieren, who strongly influenced Peter Warlock and his circle, lay rather outside VW's own milieu.

[2] This was the last October before the writing paper was changed and 'From R. Vaughan Williams' was added to the address.

[3] A young friend who had apparently sought VW's advice on making a career in music.

[4] Presumably the motor car manufacturer.

256. To Arthur Bliss

6 November [1934]

The White Gates,
Westcott Road,
Dorking.[1]

Nov 6

Dear Arthur

Thank you very much for your letter[2] – as a matter of fact what you said set me thinking hard with the result that I had already made an alteration – I can't *cut out* that recapitulation of the 2nd subject *slow* at the end – but I have led up to it differently – I realize that that scrabble which I thought w[d] sound brilliant was merely fussy – & the *sudden pp* was wrong – now I have made a more emotional climax and a gradual diminuendo to the soft end. So now we have the 2nd subject for 1st time vigorous led up to by a scrabble & 2nd time soft & slow led *down* to by a dim – I believe that will be all right.

I am going to alter the end of the scherzo – but cannot yet see the right way to do it. I have cut about 10 bars out of the slow mov[t].

I cannot yet see my way to alter the finale & at present it seems all right to me.

You mustn't think your advice has not been valuable because I have not exactly followed it – when I give advice to my pupils I tell them that they can do one of 3 things

(a) accept it blindly – bad
(b) reject it kindly – bad but not so bad
(c) think out a 3rd course for themselves – sound.

Yrs with much gratitude
R. Vaughan Williams

[1] In fact VW was staying in London at this time.

[2] Bliss had attended a play-through of the Fourth Symphony at St Paul's Girls' School by Nora Day and Vally Lasker. VW found his advice sound.

257. To Hubert Foss at OUP

25 December [1934]

The White Gates,
Westcott Road,
Dorking.

Xmas Day

Dear Foss

I agree to your proposals for the division of fees on 'Job'.[1]

Now I want your advice as to my relationships with Mr Keynes and Mrs Raverat. I originally told Keynes to make his own arrangements with you—but apparently he has not done so.[2]

Would this be possible even now? It would be much more convenient to me. ~~I will send him the author's shares on the fees already received which I suppose ought to be 25% for myself and 75% to be divided between the two authors that is on the dramatic fee.~~ I will send him a proportion of my share of the dramatic fees – I suppose that 75% of my share ought to go to the two authors. I do not think I owe them anything on concert – broadcasting–gramophone or hiring fees – What is your opinion on this?

Also ought the authors to have a share of my royalties on the sale of the copies and if so how much? I shall be very glad to know what you think about all this.

Yours sincerely
R. Vaughan Williams

Thank you both so much for the Xmas card

RVW

[1] Foss had written pointing out that no agreement existed between VW and OUP for *Job*, *CW* 1930/5, and setting out a proposed division of performing fees.

[2] The scenario of *Job* was by Gwendolen Raverat, who also designed the scenery and costumes, and her brother-in-law, Geoffrey Keynes. See no. 197.

258. To Elizabeth Maconchy

[February 1935]

The White Gates,
Westcott Road,
Dorking.

Darling Betty

I meant to have written before – but have been so v. busy.

I never said I didn't like Agrippa – but that I liked the overture better – I can't help feeling that in Agrippa – there are certain stravynskyesque [*sic*] clichés which are not really you & are not worthy of you – they rather stood out & prevented my listening properly to the tunes – but I dare say that a 2[d] time the good w[d] come out & the framing fall into its proper background – but still I do feel that you are capable of so much finer *thought* than that Russian Monkey-brain & that you injure your real self by condescending to use any of his monkey-tricks.[1]

– But everyone else (even the Times) seemed to have liked it. So you must forgive the old & ancient uncle for being stupid

Love from
Uncle Ralph

Personally I think that while the English Ballet people simply (in their dancing) do bad imitations of all those discredited old Ballet Russe tricks there is no hope for them & that it is up to you young people to show them the way by your music.

[1] Maconchy's ballet *Great Agrippa, or the Inky Boys*, based on the poem in *Struwwelpeter* by Heinrich Hoffmann, was given at a Macnaghten–Lemare Concert on 4 Feb. 1935.

259. To Arthur Bliss

27 April [1935]

Dorking

April 27

Dear Arthur

Thank you so much – I have my ups & downs – sometimes I hate it. I'm glad you like the slow mov[t] best – you know that I owe two enormous last moment improvements entirely to you.[1]

What I sh[d] really like to do is to have composition lessons from you – I usually have my scoring vetted by G.J.[2] – & with you to put the stuff right you might between you make a composer of me yet.

Yrs
RVW

[1] The Fourth Symphony had been given its first performance on 10 April.

[2] Gordon Jacob, whose advice on orchestration was widely sought. He was consulted regularly by VW.

260. To Elizabeth Trevelyan

[May 1935][1]

From R. Vaughan Williams,
The White Gates,
Westcott Road,
Dorking.

Dear Bessy

It was wonderful of you to write – & I value your opinion very much (not only when favourable!)

I quite got to like it myself in the end. The first rehearsal was unimaginable chaos. But the orchestra & Adrian worked like Trojans for 4 rehearsals – & things gradually cleared themselves – chiefly owing to Adrian's *real* insight.

I am so glad to think that you are well enough to go home tomorrow & hope you are really better – what a trying time you must have had.

Yrs
RVW

[1] According to a note on the original—but more probably Apr. 1935—the fourth symphony was given on 10 April.

261. To Gerald Finzi

postmark: 8 June 1935

From R. Vaughan Williams,
The White Gates,
Westcott Road,
Dorking.

Dear Gerald

Yrs was one of the best letters I have had. Its an awful responsibility to be chosen to 'represent' music – but it w[d] have been false modesty to set up my opinion against that of the authorities.[1]

My love to Joyce & many thanks again.[2]

Yrs
RVW

[1] VW had been awarded the OM in the King's Birthday Honours.

[2] The VWs called Joy Finzi by her full name 'Joyce' until about the time of Gerald's death, when they started using the name used by all the Finzis' friends.

262. To Elizabeth Trevelyan

[June 1935]

The White Gates,
Westcott Road,
Dorking.

Dear Bessie

Thank you so much for writing – you at all events know that as M. Balieff of the Chauve-Souris says 'we artis' arre cheeldren, we laike àpplos – yes'[1]

Yrs
R.V.W.

[1] An allusion to a revue running in London put on by the Chauve Souris company, of which Nikita Balieff was the Director. He made a point of speaking exaggeratedly bad English.

263. To Arnold Goldsbrough[1]

7 June [1935]

From R. Vaughan Williams,
The White Gates,
Westcott Road,
Dorking.

June 7

Dear Arnold

Thank you so very much. You have had more opportunities than most of finding out how little I know about music – so I appreciate your good wishes all the more.

Yours ever
RVW

[1] Arnold Goldsbrough (1892–1964), keyboard player, conductor, and teacher. He was at this time nearing the end of a period as organist of St Martin's-in-the-Fields. Thereafter he founded the Goldsbrough Orchestra, which later became the English Chamber Orchestra.

264. To Imogen Holst

[7th June 1935]

Dear Imogen

I did love your telegram. I do hope Gustav would have thought me right not to refuse – I know he would have (probably did) refused himself – But it seemed right not to.

Love from
Uncle Ralph[1]

[1] Note by Imogen: 'Letter from Vaughan Williams after he had been given the OM.' VW had refused all other honours on the grounds that they involved obligations which he was not prepared to take on.

265. To Gerald Finzi

postmark: 4 July 1935

The White Gates,
Westcott Road,
Dorking.

Dear Gerald

I thought the 'New Years Music' was beautiful – It just gave me the true Hardy spirit (this will very likely make you furious – but I can't help it) – just the sort of melody I have wanted to do all my life & have never brought off.[1]

The orchestration seemed beautifully clear – especially when the trombones come in. *Perhaps* it wants tightening up a little towards the end – just where it dies down to its softest after the climax it seemed to hang fire a little – but that may have been the fault of the radio. They seemed to play it well – though not quite rhythmically enough – we must hear it again soon.

My love to Joyce. I hear that you heard a performance of 'Lot'.[2]

Yrs
RVW

[1] *New Year Music (Nocturne)*, Op. 7, which had been written in 1926.

[2] According to Howard Ferguson, this was a spoof cantata on words from the Bible, written by Cedric Thorpe Davie and Jon Henderson and performed in a Hampstead studio.

266. To Ethel Strudwick[1]

6 July [1935]

From R. Vaughan Williams,
The White Gates,
Westcott Road,
Dorking.

July 6
[dictated]

Dear Miss Strudwick

I tried to see you when I came to school yesterday and, as I shall not be at school again until the 22nd, I think I had better write what I want to say and not wait till then.

I hope I have been some use to you during this past year – I have watched the teaching carefully and I feel strongly that you have a splendid staff of music mistresses who know exactly what is wanted and do not need any extraneous help.[2] Indeed, during my last few visits I have felt quite uncomfortable because there was absolutely nothing for me to do. So I think that you will get on very well without me after this term – and you can have full confidence that the musical side of the work will prosper – I need hardly say that though my official connection with the school will cease that I hope I may still be allowed to remain a friend of the school where I have so many happy memories. And of course if you ever do need any advice or suggestions I shall consider it a privilege to be consulted.[3]

Yrs very sincerely
R. Vaughan Williams

[1] Ethel Strudwick (1880–1954), High Mistress of St Paul's Girls' School, 1927–48.

[2] The mistresses included Nora Day and Vally Lasker, who had become great friends of VW and regularly assisted him.

[3] VW had diffidently agreed to a request from Adine O'Neill (now head music mistress) to help 'keep the flag flying' by supporting the music teachers at St Paul's Girls' School in the year following the death of Gustav Holst; this is not mentioned in *RVW*.

267. To Herbert Howells

postmark: 10 September 1935

From R. Vaughan Williams,
The White Gates,
Westcott Road,
Dorking.

Tuesday

Dear Herbert

I have heard from Marion Scott of your terrible loss.[1]

I know that letters & words can do little at these times – but I felt I must write just to tell you that one of your old friends is feeling for you. I have never had to suffer such a loss as this – but I sometimes try to imagine what it would be to lose one of those who are really ones own.

One feels the futility of all the things one usually sets value on when one is faced with reality.

I don't think it is really any comfort – indeed 'comfort' would be just an impertinence – but I cannot help believing that a life once begun can never really stop – though it has stopped for us and that there may, after all, be a real joining up some day.

Please do not mind my writing to you – though words are such inadequate things.

And *of course* I want no answer

Yrs
R. Vaughan Williams

[1] Herbert Howells's son Michael had died at the age of 9 of poliomyelitis. Howells's *Hymnus paradisi* was written in his memory.

268. To Hubert Foss at OUP

12 October [1935]

From R. Vaughan Williams,
The White Gates,
Westcott Road,
Dorking.

October 12

Dear Foss

I have just received a present of an old print in the shape of a portrait of Elinor Rumming with a mug of ale in each hand.[1]

She is described as the famous ale wife of England and there is a verse underneath connecting her with Skelton's poem. This would be just the thing for a frontispiece of my Choral Suite – But (1) I do not want to delay publication and (2) I do not want to add to the expense of the copy – It is evidently a rare print so I do not want to trust it to the post—but I presume it is in the B.M so if you think it a good plan would it be possible for it to be photocopied from the copy there?[2]

Yours sincerely
R. Vaughan Williams

[1] The vocal score was required by the performers in Norwich by 1 Nov.; however, it was not yet ready by early December. Writing an internal note to the Publisher, Humphrey Milford, on 3 July, Foss reported that he had committed OUP to publishing it and, on the question of the title, observed that VW wished to call the work *Elinor Rumming* after its first movement even though he realized that it would not fit with the other four. Perhaps this was because, according to VW's recollection at this time, the initial suggestion which had come from Elgar had been 'You should make an oratorio out of Elinor Rumming'; see no. 713, although in 1937 VW had told Philip Henderson, whose edition of Skelton he had used, that Elgar had mentioned the possibility of setting the poem himself: see *WVW*, 253–4. Foss seems to have suggested 'A Skelton Suite' but VW rejected this. The eventual title does not seem to have been finally decided by the date of this letter, though it certainly had been by December.

[2] This print was indeed used on the cover of the vocal score of *Five Tudor Portraits*, *CW* 1935/5, published by OUP in 1935.

269. To Evelyn Sharp

[15 May 1936[1]]

The White Gates

Friday

Dear Mrs Nevinson

I dictate this so as to make it more legible!

I don't think we need worry too much about the press. The fact remains that people enjoyed our joint effort very much and some people came three times which would be impossible if they thought too badly either of words or music – One cannot dissociate these two in opera.

But I think we shall both agree that if it is ever done again we shall want to make omissions and alterations both in words & music – Musically I feel inclined to agree with Colles[2] whose letter I enclose – that the end of Act I is scrappy. We might improve that by cutting Dipsacus' ballad and carrying on the entry of the milliners musically right into the finale. I feel that the whole episode of Dipsacus' story is rather long winded, partly owing to the fact that we have to tell it all over twice in dialogue and in song – Also I have always felt and I think have said to you – that the ballad is not quite amusing enough.

In Act 2 I want to cut the journalists and perhaps restore the Hobs first trio. Act 3 suffers from being cut up by too many songs. I think the Empress' song 'When I was young' must go and certainly the chorus 'Out of the dawn' which I only left in out of deference to the C.U.M.S.[3] chorus. The ensemble – I forget its name where the figure of Dipsacus appears on the screen did not come off as it stood – partly because it was sung off stage which was not intended; and I think it is too long. On the other hand we ought to restore 'Love in a hut' – the present dialogue is too obvious a makeshift for the purposes of getting the characters off stage – It gets a laugh I know but one can get a laugh on the stage by any reference to intemperance or profanity.

Now as regards the words – The song texts were in almost all cases quite satisfactory to me. I can think however of two exceptions which have always worried me and which I ought to have mentioned earlier in the day; but I feel so strongly that collaborators have equal rights that I did not like to press the point. Now however, in case there is ever another performance I should be very grateful if they could be altered. One is the line 'upsets the apple cart' and the other 'my father's spell doesn't work very well' which seem to me misfits since they are facetious remarks at purely romantic moments and of course, as such things would, they stuck out very clearly, and perhaps led to the criticism that words and music did not always fit – One single instance of this kind can be spread out into a generalisation.

Now as regards the dialogue –

Most of it seems to bear repeated hearing very well. The low comedy part I now confess alarmed me in cold print but there is no doubt that it got across – But it *is* a question, as someone said to me – whether one would care to hear it *twice*, and I think one ought to be able to do that. So much for quality – as regards quantity I think it still might be cut a bit. (1) The explanations between Angelica & Gallanthus after the duet 'It does not appear'. Are these necessary? Gallanthus says that he is going to warn his master but apparently he does not do so – Is not this a weakness? I should feel inclined to cut all explanations between these two at this point and merely keep the assignation to meet at supper, which would explain Angelica's absence at the critical moment (I think generally all through the opera we have too many explanations about poisons etc).

(2) The scene in Act 3 Empress Angelica and Empress Tormentilla seems to be rather long & clumsy and must they all come out of that bathing hut? Could we not cut the scene with Angelica altogether – I know it makes a

difficulty owing to the necessary explanation about the poison chocs but I believe this could be got over.

We have now heard the opera more or less as we wrote it – If any manager nibbles after it I am prepared to let him have a free hand, reserving only a right of *veto*. Are you prepared to do the same?

Please forgive this long rigmarole.[4]

Let me have Colles' letter back when you have done with it

Yrs
RVW

[1] This letter was clearly written soon after the first performance of *The Poisoned Kiss* (*CW* 1936/4) at the Cambridge Arts Theatre on 12 May 1936. As it doesn't mention the positive notice by Richard Capell which appeared in the *Daily Telegraph* on 17 May, it is to be assumed that it was written on the preceding Friday, 15 May. See *WVW*, 249.

[2] Henry Colles (1879–1943), Chief Critic of *The Times*, 1911–43, and essayist.

[3] Cambridge University Music Society.

[4] On the opera's reception at its first production see *WVW*, 249 ff.

270. To Cedric Thorpe Davie

[June 1936]

From R. Vaughan Williams,
The White Gates,
Westcott Road,
Dorking.

My Dear Cedric

I thoroughly enjoyed your first rate letter – don't fall in love with the daughters as well as the music of the great man.[1]

Give my profound respects to Kilpinen (& to the GREAT MAN if he remembers having once met me)

We must get you a good job when you return

Yrs
RVW

P.S. I listened to Cuchullain – it is *very good*. Waddington liked it.[2]

[1] Thorpe Davie was in Finland (the letter was addressed to him c/o Hinnerichsen, Rehbindervägen 4/7, Helsingfors, Finland). The Great Man is of course Sibelius, but Davie was studying with Kilpinen. The date of this letter must be after 20 May, when we know Davie was still in England from a letter not included in the present collection, and before 2 Aug., when we know he was back (see no. 272).

[2] VW had asked Davie to submit the score of his work *Dirge for Cuthullin* to Sidney P. Waddington, composer and teacher at the RCM, with a view to a possible performance—which it clearly received.

271. To Herbert Howells [?June 1936]

From R. Vaughan Williams,
The White Gates,
Westcott Road,
Dorking.

Confidential

Dear Herbert

I had a talk with Miss Strudwick & Mrs O'Neill yesterday & also with Vally Lasker. I do hope you will see your way to taking over SPGS. We all feel that some new blood is wanted & that there is a danger of the Gustav tradition becoming dry bones & also that Vally & Nora have no *outside standard* by which to judge their work.[1]

– I insisted that you sh[d] be given a free hand & not expected to carry on exactly in the old way if you did not wish to – on the other hand you are the only person who because of your knowledge of the school & your love of Gustav who could at the same time work in well with those who have been so nobly carrying on the great work of Gustav during the last two years. Do go *soon* to Miss Strudwick & talk it over – because she would like so much to be able to announce it on speech day – July 21.

Yrs
RVW

[1] Howells was being invited to become Director of Music at St Paul's Girls' School in succession to Gustav Holst. He accepted the post and retained it until 1962.

272. To Cedric Thorpe Davie postmark: 2 August 1936

From R. Vaughan Williams,
The White Gates,
Westcott Road,
Dorking.

Dear Cedric

Welcome home.

Yes, now the rosy dawn of the 'student life' gives way to the cold hard light of bread-winning as they say in the books – I believe you could if you would do some work for me occasionally – have you got a meticulous pernickety mind? – Or are you an artist? If the *former* you w[d] be just the person to 'vet' my full scores etc to see I haven't done foolish things – I longed for someone like that this summer when I have had to finish two large full scores against time – my copyist is very good & careful – but he has not the courage e.g. to finish an important horn phrase which I forgot during a turn-over.

I should like to see G.G.N. very much – but *not* till the tyrannys [*sic*] of Hereford (Sep 5–12) & Norwich (Sep 23–27) are over past (Oh yes *in between* those 2 dates are possible).[1]

As regards performance I fear the Old Vic is hopeless if they refused H the D (which they *probably* will do) – they will almost certainly (I speak as a fool) refuse an unknown work (unless, indeed, they are tired of old fogies & want young blood) & I think the RCM is more hopeful – Waddington admires Cuthullin very much.[2]

Yrs
RVW

P.S. Send the *vocal* score to me – You know by this time that I can't read a full score.

[1] G.G.N. is *Gammer Gurton's Needle*, an opera based on the anonymous 16th-c. comedy of that title. It was Thorpe Davie's Op. 1. 'Tyrannys' is an allusion to Ps. 57: 1 in the *Book of Common Prayer* ('and under the shadow of thy wings shall be my refuge, until this tyranny be over-past'). The first performance of VW's *Two Hymn-Tune Preludes* for small orchestra, *CW* 1936/7, was being given at Hereford and of *Five Tudor Portraits*, *CW* 1935/5, at Norwich. See *RVW*, 211.

[2] Thorpe Davie's opera apparently remains unstaged. 'I speak as a fool' is another biblical echo, from 2 Cor. 11: 23: 'Are they ministers of Christ? (I speak as a fool) I am more'.

273. To Adrian Boult

[about 22 October 1936]

From R. Vaughan Williams,
The White Gates,
Westcott Road,
Dorking.

Dear Adrian

There seem to be two essentials of great conducting

(1) Faithfulness to the composer
(2) The power of the conductor to express *himself* to the full *at the moment* – to feel himself in the music & the music in himself

I always know I shall get (1) from you but sometimes without (2)

Thank heaven I have never heard from you (II) without (I)[1] – & I know I never shall.

Yesterday we had (1) + (2) – result a great performance & great conducting for which I thank you from the bottom of my heart – and your singers & players too – the chorus were superb – their surety, their words their tone, their phrasing.

The orchestra I knew w^d be magnificent – even our friend the 1st oboe, who seemed to have swallowed a dose of vinegar before the Mozart had evidently corrected it with something more delectable during the interval – You have made me like the old work again & the awkward places seemed to have disappeared by magic.

Things that stick out particularly in my memory are the end of the slow movement the scherzo & the beginning and end of the 'explorers' – though it was really all 'high lights' – Just to show this is not just undiscriminating praise I was occasionally disappointed in the soloists (particularly owing I think to my position) – but the duet in No IV was wonderful even the tiresome man in front of me who was getting bored and fidgetty – hushed down to attention during that.

Thank you again 1000 times.[2]

Yrs
RVW[3]

[1] *Recte* (2) and (1).
[2] This performance of *A Sea Symphony* is not noted in *RVW*.
[3] Printed in Moore, *Music and Friends*, 121–2.

274. To Diana Awdry

[26 December 1936[1]]

From R. Vaughan Williams,
The White Gates,
Westcott Road,
Dorking.

Dear Diana

The lovely Caerphilly is already ½ gone – we love it & I have made my entire meal off it for two evenings – together with some Welsh Butter sent me by a Welsh pupil[2] – so I am becoming quite Welsh look-you! I do hope you have had a calm Xmas – I did only I ate a lot of forbidden things!

I read your letter in the Spectator.

Love from
Uncle Ralph

[1] Obviously written at or about the same time as a letter to Diana Awdrey from Adeline which also refers to the Caerphilly cheese—the year is based on the writing paper, not used until mid-1935.
[2] Perhaps Grace Williams.

275. To Cedric Thorpe Davie

postmark: 23 January 1937

From R. Vaughan Williams,
The White Gates,
Westcott Road,
Dorking.

Dear Cedric

I hear a rumour that you are about to be married – I think you ought to have told your pastor & master – I sh[d] like so much to give you a wedding present – but don't want to worry you with things you don't want. – I suggest some books or music – will you send me some suggestions – a list from which I can choose something I sh[d] like to give you.[1]

Yrs with best wishes
RVW

[1] Davie was to marry Margaret Brown (known as Bruno) on 23 Mar.

276. To Herbert Fisher[1]

[2 February 1937]

From R. Vaughan Williams,
The White Gates,
Westcott Road,
Dorking.

Tuesday

Dear Herbert

My chief feeling is one of great pride that I can call myself a member of the same body as yourself – only in your case it is you who honour any order of which you become a member.[2]

Of course this is not to be answered – you will be receiving thousands of letters.

Yrs
R. Vaughan Williams

[1] AVW's brother, the historian H. A. L. Fisher, Warden of New College, Oxford 1925–40.
[2] Fisher had been appointed a member of the Order of Merit in the New Year's Honours list.

277. To Geoffrey Bush[1]

17 March [1937[2]]

The White Gates,
Dorking.

March 17

Dear Mr Bush

I was very glad to have news of you. I quite agree with you that love & enthusiasm goes a long way to cover technical faults – indeed *without* that the finest technical performance in the world becomes sounding brass and tinkling cymbal.[3]

I will do my best to listen on Tuesday

Yours sincerely
R. Vaughan Williams

[1] Geoffrey Bush (1920–98), composer. No relation to the composer Alan Bush.

[2] Bush's suggestion. He had been brought to see VW by his music master that year and thinks that this was a reply to a follow-up letter.

[3] An allusion to 1 Cor. 13: 1.

278. To Ina Boyle

[3 May 1937[1]]

From R. Vaughan Williams,
The White Gates,
Westcott Road,
Dorking.

Monday

Dear Miss Boyle

Many thanks for your letter & cheque. I think it is most courageous of you to go on with so little recognition. The only thing to say is that it sometimes *does* come finally.

I have given Honorine your very kind message – it would be a delightful visit for her.[2]

Yours sincerely
R. Vaughan Williams

[1] The letter was postmarked 4 May, which was a Tuesday.

[2] Honorine Williamson was a niece of Adeline's brother-in-law R. O. Morris; she had come to live with the VWs, fresh from a domestic science college, in 1928 to help Adeline in the house and with the impending move. She remained a much-loved member of the household for twelve years. Ina Boyle had possibly invited her to visit her in Ireland.

279. To Hermann Fiedler[1]

[July 1937]

Draft

I have never yet accepted a money prize though indeed I have never yet been offered one! And my first inclination is to refuse in spite of the great honour which this offer implies.

But I feel that the honour is offered, not so much to me personally, as to the whole of English musical art. Therefore I must put personal questions on one side.

Indeed this honour to English music is so unprecedented that I want to make sure that it is made only from a desire to recognise art and learning in this country.

Now – though I wish to avoid the personal side of the question I feel bound to explain that I am strongly opposed to the present system of government in Germany, especially with regard to its treatment of artists and scholars.

I belong to more than one English Society whose object is to combat all that the present German *régime* stands for.

Therefore am I the kind of person to whom a German University would wish to offer a prize?

I cannot accept this great honour without satisfying my own conscience that I shall not feel in any way hampered in the free expression of my opinions in accepting it.[2]

[1] Hermann Georg Fiedler (1862–1945) was at this time Professor of German and Fellow of the Queen's College at Oxford and had been instrumental in obtaining the nomination of VW for the Shakespeare Prize. See *RVW*, 217–18. On the complicated background and implications of the whole matter see Frogley, 'Vaughan Williams and Nazi Germany'.

[2] Printed in *RVW*, 217.

280. To Gerald Finzi

[25 July 1937]

From R. Vaughan Williams,
The White Gates,
Westcott Road,
Dorking.

Sunday

Dear Gerald

I am sending the Gurney songs to Foss tomorrow. I have been through them with Herbert[1] and we have both come to the conclusion that 'Blaweary' and 'Ploughman singing' ought to go out anyway.

Further that if Foss thinks the vols to[o] big that 'Kathleen' & 'You are my sky' sh[d] be the first to go – what do you think?

On the other hand if Foss wants 10 songs per vol: then will you select 2 more and send them to him direct? You have done a great work in your copying & editing for which we are all very grateful.

Now another subject

Could you send me a complete list of all gramophone records, pfte duet or solo arrts of Sibelius symphonies. I want these (a) because, as you know, I can't read a full score (b) because, being no longer able to compose, and having by my mode of life unfitted myself for any useful occupation I think it is time I learnt something about music.[2]

We passed through Aldbourne the other day where (a) Hon:[3] bought an ice (b) we failed to spot your house.

My love to Joyce

Yrs
RVW

[1] Herbert Howells.

[2] No major work was written following the coronation in 1937 (though VW may have been trying unsuccessfully to start the opera based on *The Pilgrim's Progress*) until the Fifth Symphony (dedicated 'without permission' to Sibelius), first performed in 1943.

[3] Honorine Williamson.

281. To Gilbert Murray

6 August 1937

From R. Vaughan Williams,
The White Gates,
Westcott Road,
Dorking.

Aug 6th 1937

Dear Professor Murray

I feel it a great shame for you, who hardly know me, to be worried by me on your holiday. But your opinion on the following would be very valuable to me.

A rich Hamburg merchant has, through the university of Hamburg, offered a prize (10,000 marks) to be given, strange to relate, to an English composer. It has been offered to me. The offer has come to me through Professor Fiedler of Oxford. At first I suspected political propaganda but he assures me that it is entirely private and absolutely non-political – that in fact is why music was chosen as one of the subjects. (Similar prizes are being offered to Scandinavia and Holland). I feel that for the sake of my profession I ought to accept such an unprecedented offer. But I want to be reasonably certain that I can do so with clean hands & not, thereby, have my anti-Nazi teeth drawn. I put all these points to Fiedler and he reassured me thoroughly.

Your opinion would be most valuable to me.

Yours sincerely
R. Vaughan Williams

282. To Hermann Fiedler

16 August 1937

From R. Vaughan Williams,
The White Gates,
Westcott Road,
Dorking.

August 16 1937

Dear Professor Fiedler

Please forgive my delay in coming to a decision, but I feel that the great honour which the University of Hamburg asks me to accept is more than a personal matter being in fact a gesture of recognition to the whole art of music in England through me as one of it's [*sic*] representatives. Therefore I found it necessary to consult with others before deciding.

You have assured me that this honour is offered purely in the cause of art by a learned body to a member of the English musical profession; that it implies no political propaganda and that I shall feel free as an honourable man, if I accept, to hold and express any views on the general state of Germany which are allowable to a British citizen.[1]

In these circumstances I have pleasure in cordially accepting the honour offered to me in your letter.

Yours sincerely
R. Vaughan Williams

[1] Printed in *RVW*, 217.

283. Gilbert Murray

16 August [1937]

From R. Vaughan Williams,
The White Gates,
Westcott Road,
Dorking.

Aug 16th

Dear Professor Murray

Thank you very much for your advice which has been most valuable to me.

I have decided to *accept* & have written a letter pointing out that in accepting I take it that (a) No political propaganda are implied (b) That it is merely a gesture of recognition from a learned body to the artists & scholars of England (c) That I shall feel honourably free after accepting to hold & express any views on the state of Germany which are at present allowable to me as a British Citizen.

Yours sincerely
R. Vaughan Williams

284. To Imogen Holst

postmark: 19 September 1937

From R. Vaughan Williams,
The White Gates,
Westcott Road,
Dorking.

Dear Imogen

How dear of you to send me that message.

They played magnificently.[1]

I hope the book goes well.[2]

I have been thinking of two things Gustav once said to me – I don't know if he ever wrote them to any body – I hope he did for they ought to be recorded

1) About 'Aristocracy in art' – art is not for all but only for the chosen few – but the only way to find those few is to bring art to everyone – then the artists have a sort of masonic signal by which they recognise each

other in the crowd – he put it much better than that – but that is the gist.

2) That the artist is born again & starts again afresh with every new work.

Love from
Uncle Ralph

[1] VW had been to Gloucester to conduct a performance of *Dona Nobis Pacem* (*CW* 1936/5) in the Three Choirs Festival at Gloucester. See *RVW*, 215.

[2] Imogen was preparing *Gustav Holst: A Biography*, published by Oxford University Press in 1938.

285. To Hubert Foss

25 October 1937

From R. Vaughan Williams,
The White Gates,
Westcott Road,
Dorking.

Received: 25 October 1937

Dear Foss

Thank you very much

I thought I must accept – though honours from Germany are not what they were.

Yrs
R. Vaughan Williams

286. To Ursula Wood

[October 1937]

From R. Vaughan Williams,
The White Gates,
Westcott Road,
Dorking.

Dear Madam,

Many thanks for your scenario. It seems to me more suitable for miming to accompany a recitation or singing of the ballad. However I am sending it on to Mr Kennedy of the EFDS & see what he thinks.[1]

Yrs Faithfully
R. Vaughan Williams

[1] VW's first contact with Ursula Wood, who was eventually to become his second wife. However, on this occasion the substantive reply came from Douglas Kennedy, Director of the EFSS, who wrote to UW on 19 Oct.: 'Your letter addressed to Dr. Vaughan Williams enclosing the scenario for a Ballet has been forwarded to me. Dr. Vaughan Williams and I have done things in concert before and we have had in mind for some little time the idea of producing a typical English Ballet. Whether the actual story of Clerk Saunders is suitable I am not sure but I should very much like an opportunity to discuss the idea with you.'

287. To Robert Longman

[December 1937[1]]

The White Gates,
Westcott Road,
Dorking.

Monday

Dear Bobby

I spent yesterday in bed – nursing a cold – so I decided to try and answer your long & splendid letter of a long time ago.

Writing in bed was difficult – so now I am copying it out in hopes of making it more or less legible.

(1) I agree with you that all music must have *beauty* – the problem being what *is* beauty – so when you say you do not think my F mi Symphony [is beautiful] my answer *must* be that *I do* think it beautiful – not, that I did not *mean* it to be beautiful because it reflects unbeautiful things because we know that beauty can come from unbeautiful things (e.g. King Lear, Rembrandts School of Anatomy, Wagners Niebelungs etc)

As a matter of fact

(1) I am not at all sure that I like it myself *now* [–] all I know is that it is what I wanted to do *at the time*.
(2) I wrote it not as a definite picture of anything external e.g. the state of Europe – but simply because it occurred to me like this – I can't explain why – I don't think that sitting down & thinking about great things ever produces a great work of art (at least I hope not – because I never do so – & when you state your belief in me, dear Bobby, I feel the completest of frauds) – a thing just comes – or it doesn't – usually doesn't – I always live in hope, as all writers must, that one day I shall 'ring the bell' – in younger days when one thought one was going to do the *real thing* each time & each time discovered one hadn't done it, one said hopefully 'next time' – but when one touches on 65 one begins to wonder.

I sometimes think I ought to train my mind or my soul or whatever it is by exercizes as the Yogis do – but I can never make up my mind to it.

On the other hand I think, sometimes, that I ought not to try to do the greatest thing on earth, which no fellow will understand, but to use my skill, such as I have, for doing useful work. E.g. things for Div:2 kind of people to sing & enjoy (By the way do you know of any good poem which would make into a cantata on the lines of 'The Revenge'[2] – I mean of course not on *Spain* but in form & design)

I think that is all for the present.[3]

Yrs
RVW

[1] Date suggested in a note on the original by either UVW or recipient. In Oct. 1958 Longman wrote a note to UVW on the reverse of the last page: 'You know of course, what he told me about the 6th symphony, when I & all the critics said it represented the dreadful world in which we lived & that the last movement was the completely desolated world of the future. He said that he had no conscious idea *whatsoever* of doing this. I think, however, that he realised that he had done this quite unconsciously.'

[2] The poem by Tennyson, which had been set by Stanford.

[3] This letter is printed in full in *WVW*, 246–7.

288. To the *Musical Times*

February 1938
Dorking

February 1938

Miss Engel Lund's Recital

Sir,

I am really very sorry for 'H. J. K.' The muse of traditional art is notoriously proud and reserved. She has evidently averted her face from H. J. K.'s ardent gaze, so I feel inclined to sympathize with him when he has to console himself in his discomfiture by murmuring, 'Well, perhaps she has not got a face after all'.[1]

He has evidently still to realize the supreme art and also the immense difficulty of that absolute simplicity which Miss Engel Lund has achieved.

At present he reminds me of the schoolboy who said 'I could have written all that Shakespeare stuff myself if I had thought of it'.

Yours, &c.,
R. Vaughan Williams.

[1] 'HJK' had reviewed a recital entitled 'Folksongs of all nations' at the Wigmore Hall by Engel Lund by pointing out that the programme contained a portrait of the singer in a black robe with her face averted and had drawn the analogy that folk songs also were too featureless to enable the singer to demonstrate her talent, and that she would have done better to sing Lieder.

289. To G. E. Moore

8 March [?1938]

From R. Vaughan Williams,
The White Gates,
Westcott Road,
Dorking.

March 8

Dear Moore

I should very much like to look at your son's compositions – both because I am interested in the younger generation and because you and I are old friends – But I should like to do it personally and not merely have his M.S. sent me.[1]

I shall be in Cambridge I expect pretty frequently at the end of April and the beginning of May – but I expect he would be at school then. Alternatively if you and he were in this direction during the holidays it would be very nice to see you here.

I fear I cannot manage March 14. It is kind of your wife and you to invite me.

Yrs always
R. Vaughan Williams

[1] Timothy Moore was born in Feb. 1922. After an interrupted career at Cambridge he became a composer and was a music master at Dartington Hall. He might have been about 16 at the time of this letter.

290. To Hubert Foss at OUP

25 March [1938[1]]

From R. Vaughan Williams,
The White Gates,
Westcott Road,
Dorking.

March 25

Dear Foss,

In answer to your 3 letters.

N°s 1 & 3 re Housman.[2] You may print anything you like. If the biographer[3] comments I think I ought to be allowed my say which is that the composer has a perfect right artistically to set any portion of a poem he chooses provided he does not actually alter the sense: that makers of anthologies headed by the late Poet Laureate[4] have done the same thing. I also feel that a poet should be grateful to anyone who fails to perpetuate such lines as:–

'The goal stands up, the Keeper
Stands up to keep the goal.'

In answer to your letter about P.K.[5] I have had a long talk with Stanford Robinson some time ago and we came to a rough agreement about cuts and omissions in the music. He also told me that he proposed to ask Dunn[6] to revise the libretto for broadcasting. Stanford Robinson distinctly said 75 minutes not 60.

As regards fees we must not kill the goose with golden eggs as we did in the case of my Symphony at Boston. The BBC were very generous over 'Hugh the Drover'!

Lastly – You will perhaps remember that I made an arrangement of my Magnificat for a Dutch Society. With your leave I sent the score & parts direct to them last November – I had no acknowlegement & no word of any kind from them – I wrote again a few weeks ago and again have had no answer. Would you like to do something about it since indeed the material belongs to you – the address is –

C. Engelbrecht
Het Nederlandsch Kamer Orkest
Smidswater 19[A]
Den Haag – Holland

Yrs
R. Vaughan Williams

[1] Year taken from context. Richards's book (see n. 3) was published in 1941; VW's comments were most likely solicited in 1938 or 1939—postal traffic with Holland would no longer have been easy/possible in 1940.

[2] A. E. Housman, poet and author of *A Shropshire Lad*. VW used these texts in his song cycle *On Wenlock Edge* (*CW* 1909/1). Housman was extremely annoyed at VW's omission of two verses in his setting of 'Is my team ploughing?'

[3] F. T. Grant Richards, Housman's biographer.

[4] Robert Bridges had edited an anthology aimed at soldiers in the trenches, *The Spirit of Man: An Anthology in English and French from the Philosophers and Poets, Made by the Poet Laureate in 1915* (London, 1916), of which VW had a copy (see *RVW*, 231).

[5] About a proposal to prepare a version of *The Poisoned Kiss* (*CW* 1936/4) for broadcasting.

[6] Geoffrey Dunn (1903–81), librettist and translator.

291. To Ursula Wood

[about April 1938]

The White Gates,
Westcott Road,
Dorking.

Bellissima Donna senza Misericordia!

I meant to have written long ago, but I wanted to send you those Bullen[1] books – & the bookseller has only just sent them. Then I wanted to write

'Ursula' inside them & a lovely line from Epithalamium, but I do not dare undo the parcel because I should never be able to do it up again; so it goes as it is (I hope it's the books I meant!). Then I wanted to send you a copy of 'The Sky above the roof' (D'un Prison)[2] – but I've not got a copy of that – so the fates are against me.

I loved having your poems – the one about your hair especially; I also like the one about thoughts – I'm not sure about the word 'skull' but I daresay you are right.[3]

The 2 1st verses of the Verlaine[4] seem to me very good – in v. 3 I am not quite sure about 'seduction' – it seems prosaic – but that is perhaps because it has been spoilt by the daily press. Just as you don't like Bridegroom & Bride – in which I quite disagree with you – If we are to give up all beautiful words which are prostituted by the Daily Mirror our vocabulary will be very small.

Think of

> 'The voice of the Bridegroom and the Bride shall be heard no more in thee'[5]

I had a long journey to Liverpool and back the other day & thought a lot about you & Epithalamium. My ideas are crystallizing. One thing: I feel more and more certain the Bride & Bridegroom must not dance – they must move & mime (not too much) to a background of dancing. But I will write more when I have got it more fixed – or perhaps we shall meet – when?

Yours in thrall[6]
RVW

[1] A. H. Bullen, *Lyrics from the Dramatists of the Elizabethan Age*, first published London in 1889, and *Lyrics from the Song Books of the Elizabethan Age*, first published London in 1887.

[2] VW had set a translation by Mabel Dearmer of 'Le ciel est pardessus le toit' by Paul Verlaine (*Sagesse* III. vi) in 1908 (see *CW* 1908/4). UW had also made a translation (now lost).

[3] The poems appeared in UW's first book, *No Other Chance* (Oxford: Basil Blackwell, 1941). The poem about hair is 'When I unplait my hair at night / I touch it as a stranger might'. The 'one about thoughts' is from 'Excavations by moonlight': 'An antler shaped as a pick and the skull that stares at it'.

[4] *Sagesse* I. xxi, which UW had translated in 1933.

[5] *Revelation* 18: 23, words which VW had set in *Sancta Civitas*, *CW* 1925/6, fig. 33ff.

[6] VW's opening and closing allude to stanza 10 of Keats's poem 'La belle dame sans merci': 'La belle dame sans merci / hath thee in thrall'.

292. To G. E. Moore

26 April [?1938]

From R. Vaughan Williams,
The White Gates,
Westcott Road,
Dorking.

April 26

Dear Moore

As I daresay you know we had a visit from Timothy the other day and we liked him so much. He is evidently very musical – Besides looking at his compositions I asked him to play me something and he played me some Chopin very musically and with a kind of dogged determination which showed great strength of character and incidentally reminded me much of his father's playing. His music – though of course still on the simple and small scale, showed a sureness of touch and technical power which I thought remarkable for his age. I wish that many of my pupils at the R.C.M. who are much older had such a grasp. He has evidently been very well taught. It is difficult, of course, to say at present how much original thought there is – one does not expect it, or indeed wish for it, at his absorbent age: but I did see a feeling for beauty and a sense of style. I like best his latest part-song and also his early choral tune of which he now professes to be ashamed, but of which he has no need to be.

He tells me he is keen to write for orchestra and I have suggested to him that he should write something for his school band since when all's said and done the best way of acquiring mastery is the often painful and bitter experience of 'trying it on the dog'.

Yrs
R. Vaughan Williams

293. To Ursula Wood

postmark: 14 June 1938

Atlantic Hamburg
An der Alster 73–79

Midnight—Tuesday

My dear

I meant to send you a picture postcard as you told me to – but after all I want to write a letter.

I've just come from an opera by an Italian composer on the 'Scarlet Letter'. All very gloomy, but I find that I do not thrill when young women are branded with 'A'.[1]

How sweet of you to send the books. The Penguin [is] just what I wanted. I am getting hold of Donne – at first he seems too artificial and quirky for a love poet. My ideal of love poetry are the 2 lines from the ballad

'I'd rather rest
on my true love's breast
than any other where'[2]

(simple, sensuous & passionate?[3]). By the way didn't Donne write some S.S. & P.[4] words which do not appear in this collection

'Ah dear heart why do you rise
The light that shines comes from your eyes
The day breaks not, it is my heart
To think that you & I must part
O stay or else my hopes will die
And perish in their infancy'[5]

By the way I copied out practically the whole of Epithalamium before I left England.

When do we meet again?

Yrs
RVW

[1] VW had been to see *The Scarlet Letter*, an opera by the American composer Vittorio Giannini (1903–66) based on the story by Nathaniel Hawthorne. The opera was first produced in Hamburg and had had its first performance two weeks earlier on 2 June.

[2] Lines from v. 3 of the folk song 'Searching for lambs'.

[3] A phrase from Milton's *Tractate on Education*: '[Rhetoric] to which poetry would be made subsequent, or indeed rather precedent, as being less subtle and fine, but more simple, sensuous and passionate.'

[4] i.e. simple, sensuous, and passionate.

[5] The words of a madrigal by Orlando Gibbons.

294. To the Editor of *The Times* 26 June [1938]

From R. Vaughan Williams,
The White Gates,
Westcott Road,
Dorking.

June 26

Sir,

Your unfavourable notice of a choral work by Willy Burkhard[1] performed at a contemporary music concert at Queen's Hall last Friday prompts me to venture to express my opinion that we have here a remarkable, often beautiful and often deeply moving composition. It seemed to me that evening to stand out amid a waste of arid note-spinning as a genuine and deeply felt expression.

I ought perhaps to add that in case my opinion should cause the composer to lose face among his fellow 'contemporary' musicians that he is fully as capable of inventing lacerating discords as any of them. But these discords seemed to me to come from a genuinely emotional impulse and not from the desire to outshine one's neighbours in hideosity.

I hope that one of our choral festivals will perform this work, having previously revised the present English translation.

Yours faithfully
R. Vaughan Williams

[1] Swiss composer (1900–55). The work was Burkhard's oratorio *Das Gesicht Jesajas*, Op. 41, completed in 1935.

295. To Hermann Fiedler postmark: 26 June 1938

From R. Vaughan Williams,
The White Gates,
Westcott Road,
Dorking.

Sunday

My Dear Professor

Thank you very much for your letter and the copy of the Rektors speech – also for the address of the artist! (By the way Herma tells me that you adopted a niece on your way home) I don't think we will worry about expenses – I had a splendid holiday owing to your goodness to me – & I enjoyed every moment (except the actual ceremony). Do you think I might write to Herr Toepfer?[1] I was so sorry to miss him.

I wish I could have been present when your university paid you a well deserved honour.

Yrs very sincerely
R. Vaughan Williams

[1] Alfred Toepfer, founder of the Hanseatic Foundation, which had established the Shakespeare Prize.

296. To Mary Fletcher[1]

10 July 1938

From R. Vaughan Williams,
The White Gates,
Westcott Road,
Dorking.

July 10, 1938

My Dear Mary

It is most kind of you to have done all this for me – I hope something will result from all my friends efforts but my private opinion is that I have dried up.

Yrs
RVW

[1] The most likely recipient, though the envelope doesn't survive to confirm this. A sister of Dorothy Longman, she had lent the VWs her house at Oare in Wiltshire in July 1924 when VW wished to find a quiet retreat from London where he could write. This time she seems to have been responsible for VW finding Rose Cottage at Stapleford.

297. To RVW from Adeline Vaughan Williams

[12 July 1938[1]]

Tuesday

Dear one

2 letters – and I felt so happy to have them –

Even if compo doesn't come the new scenes & the quiet bit will sow the seed.

All is well with us – a lovely day – Brett spread the hay yesterday – & believes Mr Arthur[2] will take it – It is dry now.

No letters of the right kind to send you. But how ashamed I was to have forgotten to put 'de quoi' in your case – Hon has bought you a pkt of Bromo – what have you done? Smuse paper is so solid.[3]

I send a cheque for pfte

AVW

[1] The envelope is postmarked 14 July 1938. See *RVW*, 222.

[2] The local builder.

[3] Bromo is lavatory paper; 'smuse paper' is of course music manuscript paper.

298. To Ursula Wood

[17 July 1938]

My Dear

I am here in the Wiltshire Downs – & the hermitage is succeeding I think – But I must confess that the other thing has taken precedence of Epithal:. You know I can't do things unless I think I ought to be doing something else. I read right through your letter – so there![1]

I have been [for] wonderful walks on the downs – they were perfect – sun, high wind & wonderful July field flowers, the kind I like best

Love yrs
RVW

[1] The 'other thing' was the work which would eventually emerge as the Fifth Symphony.

299. To Cedric Thorpe Davie

11 August [postmark: 1938]

From R. Vaughan Williams,
The White Gates,
Westcott Road,
Dorking.

Aug 11

Dear Cedric

I was very glad to hear from you – Yes please use my name

I hope you are *writing* – I know you have little time & its disheartening work – But the only thing to do is to *peg away* & hope for the best – if it doesn't hit the nail on the head *this* time always hope that it will *next* time – you are young & there will be lots of next times for you – when you get old like me & you hate what you have written you suddenly realise that perhaps there *won't* be a next time.[1]

I am so sorry Bruno has not been well – Give her my love (on both cheeks) & tell her she shall certainly have a photograph when I can find one.

Yrs
RVW

[1] VW is speaking from recent experience, when he had been worried that his ability to compose had left him.

300. To Nancy Bush[1]

25 September [1938?]

From R. Vaughan Williams,
The White Gates,
Westcott Road,
Dorking.

Sept 25

Dear Mrs Bush

Many thanks for sending me the poem – I fear I entirely disagree with the idea of making such a music meeting the vehicle for propaganda of any kind.[2]

If children learn to love beauty wherever they may be they will grow up to hate ugliness – But the one thing we do not want is for them to associate the arts with all the political strife which unfortunately later on they will be obliged to partake in

Yrs sincerely
R. Vaughan Williams

[1] Wife of Alan Bush.

[2] Alan Bush's wife had written to VW on 10 Sept. asking him to provide a test piece for the annual contest of affiliated choirs to be mounted by the London Cooperative Joint Education Committee in May 1939. She enclosed a poem by Sylvia Townsend Warner to be set as the test piece for female choirs, of which VW appears to disapprove of the content.

301. To Ursula Wood

[4 October 1938]

From R. Vaughan Williams,
The White Gates,
Westcott Road,
Dorking.

My Dear

What a lovely picture – though not half pretty enough of course (this is truth – I always tell you the truth). It will require a cupboard all to itself!

Well we seem out of the mess at the moment.[1] The truth is we are being really xtian & giving the other cheek etc & realizing that the ungodly do prosper & that if we are to try & be civilized ourselves it can only be at the expense of letting the ungodly prosper. All very horrid.

I'm glad you liked the symph. I did rather myself after many years. It is really war time music – a great deal of it incubated when I used to go up night after night in the ambulance wagon at Ecoiv[r]es & we went up a steep hill & there was a wonderful Corot-like landscape in the sunset – its not really Lambkins frisking at all as most people take for granted.[2]

Take care of yourself my dear & forgive all my vagaries. I am sending back the poem – rather too personal to show round, though I like it (and your hair)

Yrs
RVW

[1] A reference to the Munich Agreement.

[2] The *Pastoral Symphony* had been given at the Queen's Hall on 29 Sept. at a concert to which VW had taken Ursula. Part of this letter is printed in *RVW*, 121.

302. To Henry Wood

9 October [1938]

From R. Vaughan Williams,
The White Gates,
Westcott Road,
Dorking.

October 9

Dear Sir Henry

Many thanks for your kind letter. It was indeed a privilege to be able to take a share in expressing the gratitude of all of us to you for what you have done for music.[1]

That evening at the Albert Hall was a great occasion. We have to thank Lady Wood and yourself for entertaining us so splendidly after the concert.

I should like very much to be present at the recording when it takes place.

I do hope you are having a rest and a holiday now.

Yours very sincerely
R. Vaughan Williams

[1] Wood had written on 7 Oct. thanking VW for the *Serenade to Music*, *CW* 1938/2.

303. To Gerald Finzi

14 October [1938[1]]

From R. Vaughan Williams,
The White Gates,
Dorking,
Surrey.

Oct 14

Dear Gerald

The exhortation was beautiful – & I thought well sung.[2]

I like the obvious ones best – Ditty & When she sighed – though I like the apple man very much – though is he a bit too sinister?

I want to give a lecture one day on the English song – showing how you & Gurney & Robin & one or two others have at last found the musical equivalent of English poetry only that w[d] mean an intensive study of all your songs which my natural laziness boggles at.

My love to Joyce

Yrs
RVW

[1] The date of this letter is uncertain. The letterhead precludes it having been written in 1933 at the time of the first publication of Finzi's song cycle. Ivor Gurney (1890–1937) and Robin Milford (1903–59) were both students of VW at the RCM.

[2] *A Young Man's Exhortation*, for tenor and pianoforte.

304. To Henry Wood

15 October [1938]

From R. Vaughan Williams,
The White Gates,
Westcott Road,
Dorking.

October 15

Dear Sir Henry

Very many thanks for showing Rachmaninoff's delightful letter.[1] I am most gratified that he should have approved of my 'Serenade'.

I return his letter herewith. I hear that the recording is to be next Saturday at 10.0. I will be there.

Yours very sincerely
R. Vaughan Williams

[1] The letter is now with Sir Henry Wood's papers in the British Library (Add. MS 56421, fo. 117).

305. To Ursula Wood

[18 October 1938]

From R. Vaughan Williams,
The White Gates,
Westcott Road,
Dorking.

Tuesday

My Dear

I hope you didn't mind my sending your poems to R. C. Trevelyan. He is a most cultured and well read man & a good critic & a very good poet himself – though too literary for my taste. So you may like to see his opinions.

Yrs
RVW

306. To Ernest Newman[1]

13 November [1938]

From R. Vaughan Williams,
The White Gates,
Westcott Road,
Dorking.

Nov 13

Dear Mr Newman

I hope you will forgive my troubling such a busy man as you.

I have received a letter from Mr Hutchings,[2] enclosing a letter to the press about Bloch which he tells me you are willing to sign and asking me, and others, to sign as well.

I cannot help feeling the letter would be unwise:

(1) It refers to another letter published in a magazine which nobody except professional musicians has ever heard of.[3]
(2) The real case seems to be the supposed refusal of the B.B.C. to perform Bloch on political grounds – this obviously cannot be referred to in the letter – therefore the argument falls to the ground.

(3) I am a great admirer of Bloch's music – but I cannot find that he is unduly neglected in this country in comparison with other composers – one could, I believe, make out a similar case for every contemporary composer (except Sibelius) – and even include Elgar in the list if it were not for the three Choirs festival.

(4) I always feel, when I see the public declaration that a composer is 'unduly neglected' that there is something suspect about him. Such a declaration, I believe, creates *distrust*, e.g. the strong prejudice created against Van Dieren by the unwise propaganda of some youthful enthusiasts.[4]

(5) I believe much more can be done by private work than by letters to the press.

Therefore, in spite of the authority given the letter by your signature, I feel that I cannot subscribe it.

I am sending a copy of this letter to M[r] Hutchings.

Yours sincerely
R. Vaughan Williams

[1] Ernest Newman (1868–1959), writer on music (largely on opera) and one of the most eminent English music critics of his time. For most of his career he was attached to the *Sunday Times*.

[2] Arthur Hutchings (1906–89), composer and writer on music. He later became Professor of Music at the University of Durham, 1947–68 and at the University of Exeter, 1968–9.

[3] The letter in question has not been identified.

[4] A reference to Philip Heseltine (Peter Warlock) and Cecil Gray, who both crusaded strenuously for recognition of Bernard van Dieren's music.

307. To Miss Townsend[1]

15 November [1938][2]

From R. Vaughan Williams,
The White Gates,
Westcott Road,
Dorking.

Nov 15

Dear Miss Townsend

I wonder if you would be so good as to play for me at my Toc H.[3] concert tomorrow week (Wednesday Nov 23rd) – the rest of the programme consists of a conjuror! Also Miss Hilda Bertha (the conjuror's wife) who does 'songs at the piano'.[4] This lady tells she is a very good accompanist & has played for Melba – are you willing to trust her? If not, there are several good accompanists in Dorking.

Perhaps if you get this in time you c[d] give me a ring – so that I may announce you in tomorrow's programme.

The time of the concert by the way is 7.30 & goes on till 9.0. You might send me your repertoire for me to choose suitable pieces – I think two 'tunes' of about 7 or 8 minutes each would be right.

Yours sincerely
R. Vaughan Williams

[1] An instrumental player, probably a violinist, living at Holmwood.

[2] The date on the letter reads Nov. 12 but this must be an error for Nov. 15 because of 'tomorrow week' being 23 Nov., a Wednesday in 1938.

[3] Toc H was the charity which was founded in a building renamed Talbot House (Toc H in signaller's code) at Poperinge in Belgium during the First World War. On VW's work for the charity see no. 474.

[4] The concerts were a series held on Wednesdays for troops. See *VWD*, 17.

308. To Robert Müller-Hartmann[1]

18 December [1938]

From R. Vaughan Williams,
The White Gates,
Westcott Road,
Dorking.

Dec 18

Dear Mr Müller-Hartmann

(Forgive me for making you out an academic[2])

I hear that you have written some delightful pianoforte pieces – would you play a short group from them (about 10 minutes) at one of our Wednesday concerts? It would give everyone much pleasure I am sure.

You will probably tell me that you are not a virtuoso pianist – my answer is that I am sure you would play your own music better than anyone else.

May I leave the date doubtful for a short time – it will probably be either Feb 18 or March 4.

Yours sincerely
R. Vaughan Williams

[1] A German composer who came to England in 1937 and was recommended to VW by Imogen Holst. At this time he was living in Dorking with Yanya and Genia Hornstein, friends of the VWs. See *New Grove*.

[2] In a previous letter VW had addressed him as Dr Müller-Hartmann.

309. To Alan Bush

7 January [1939]

From R. Vaughan Williams,
The White Gates,
Westcott Road,
Dorking.

January 7

Dear Mr Bush

I fear I could not possibly get anything ready by February – but besides this, as far as I can make out from your prospectus, 'the people' are only those who happen to agree with the opinions of the committee (many of which opinions I probably also agree with –)

But to give a true and just account of the peoples music one must represent the people as celebrating in song many things which we doubtless deplore such as battles and kings and coronations & highwaymen and kind squires etc – Unless you include these things in your scheme you are to my mind giving a *false* impression of 'the peoples' music.[1]

Yours sincerely
R. Vaughan Williams

[1] Bush had written to VW on 4 Jan. asking him to write a piece of music for the Festival of Music for the People, a three-day event beginning with a pageant in the Royal Albert Hall on 1 Apr. 1939.

310. To Gerald Finzi

[9 January 1939]

From R. Vaughan Williams,
The White Gates,
Westcott Road,
Dorking.

Dear Gerald

We listened to your 2 songs yesterday. You *have* hit the nail on the head – it ought to be spread abroad that here is the exact equivalent of Hardy & to a certain extent of all English poetry of the post-classical period.

When is 'Dies Natalis' – I am excited to know – especially as I have had a mysterious letter about it from Captain Gyde (Sophie Wyss' husband).

I sent S.W.[1] a sheaf of songs by various English composers which I thought she ought to know – especially as she only seemed to know the wrong-note variety. I included Y.M.s exhortation.[2]

Now Gyde writes to me and says 'she thought that Finzi's work stood out by its self & that she would endeavour to give it in Birmingham and perhaps a London Broadcast. I now see . . . that this work has been accepted for . . . Hereford next year . . . As she told him when she met before this choice was made she would always sing it for him anywhere.'

I am thoroughly puzzled

Love to Joyce

Yrs
RVW

[1] The singer for whom Benjamin Britten wrote *Les Illuminations*.

[2] i.e. Finzi's *A Young Man's Exhortation*, Op. 14.

311. To Adrian Boult at the BBC

30 January [1939[1]]

From R. Vaughan Williams,
The White Gates,
Westcott Road,
Dorking.

Jan 30

Dear Adrian

I heard bits of the S S[2] being floated on the air from Stockholm between shouts from Rome and howls from Paris – from what I could judge it was a fine performance – Thank you very much.

I wish I c[d] come to hear the record on Thursday, but I fear it will be impossible.

Yrs
RVW

Please thank Mrs Beckett[3] for keeping me so well informed.

[1] Year taken from context in file.

[2] *A Sea Symphony* (*CW* 1909/3).

[3] Gwen Beckett, Boult's secretary.

312. To Maud Karpeles

[beginning of February 1939[1]]

From R. Vaughan Williams,
The White Gates,
Westcott Road,
Dorking.

Dear Maud

I hate writing begging letters – I know in my bones that you have already done more than your share for refugees – Here is a case – I just send it for what it is worth.

Love from
RVW

Dr Fuchs (Jew) is an Architect from Carlsruhe – was in a concentration camp for two months – was then released and obliged to leave. He made arrangements to go to New Zealand. The Authorities there required that he should bring £1000 for himself, wife and 2 daughters. This, at the time he had, but by the time he reached England the Nazis had left him only £300. His passage is already booked for Feb 17 but unless he can get the money he will have to forfeit it as it was paid in German money.

He has now managed to raise £600 and it seems to me that it would be tragic if he could not sail to New Zealand where there are good prospects for him because of this.

He is a fully qualified architect with all the German diplomas & incidentally an excellent musician & a charming cultivated man with a very nice and capable wife. Owing to the fact that he came to England at the private invitation of some friends in Dorking he is debarred from any of the public refugee funds.[2]

[1] Maud Karpeles's reply is dated 5 February.
[2] In her reply Maud Karpeles promised to make a loan of £50.

313. To Hubert Clifford[1]

[early 1939[2]]

From R. Vaughan Williams,
The White Gates,
Westcott Road,
Dorking.

Dear Clifford

Will the enclosed screed be any use to you – If so I suggest you should have it typed & I will correct the type script before it goes to the printer

I have been much interested in the book & think it excellent – I have spotted one or two apparent misprints.

& one point I should like you to elaborate about – the inexperienced conductor. It is my own experience but I have never seen it mentioned in any of the text books. When I first waved a stick I felt like playing the piano or organ & went on moving my stick *till I heard the sound* – Now of course the sound comes to the conductor's ear a fraction late & the music got slower & slower.

– I think it is important to point out to the conductor that he must go on to the next beat as soon as ever he reaches the point where he thinks the sound *ought* to come whether *to his ears* the sound *has* come or not.

Yrs
R. Vaughan Williams

PREFACE

In this book Mr. Clifford preaches the gospel, to which I cordially subscribe, that if the art of a country is to be vital, we must be doers of the word and not hearers only.

We owe much to the Radio and the Record, but these wonderful inventions have their comcomitant dangers. I once examined a candidate for a musical scholarship. I asked him: 'What is your favourite piece of music?' – he answered, 'The Prelude to Tristan', but he was unable to play or even hum the opening phrase. His knowledge was entirely obtained from sitting in his armchair and smoking his pipe while he turned on the gramophone. Now in my young days our only method of studying great music was to strum out the score for ourselves, preferably by means of the now neglected art the pianoforte duet, or to join an amateur orchestra. Those who have studied the great masters from the humble position of last desk in the 2nd violins of an amateur orchestra get to know them in a way which the gramophonist can never achieve.

If all the world is content to listen there will soon be nobody left to listen to. At present we still have with us great artists both to delight our ears and to set a standard for the humble amateurs respectfully to imitate; but expert performers are not like old soldiers; they will, alas one day die and their places will have to be filled up. Whence can the recruits be enlisted better than from the school orchestra? This is not to say that every school boy is a budding Kreisler, but that where the embryo genius exists the school orchestra will find him out, such cases are by no means uncommon in the experience of school music teachers.

There is a well known 'Punch' picture of a cynical old gentleman listening to an amateur quartet. 'Do you get any pleasure out of your playing?' he asks, 'Oh, yes' is the enthusiastic reply. 'That, I suppose, is some compensation for the pain you must cause others.' The conductor of a school orchestra must not expect in his early stages that the mere listener will get pure aesthetic pleasure out of the result, nor, indeed should this be his object. It is the players themselves who count; if they obtain spiritual exaltation from their communion with the classics, however imperfect, provided the desire for perfection is there, then the battle is won and the listener, if he has ears to hear, will find something which the most expert performance, listened to in the purely critical spirit, will not give him.

Mr. Clifford's book is at once idealistic and practical. He aims at the highest but he does not shirk the various makeshifts which are inevitable in amateur music. The aesthete may be appalled, but I believe that Beethoven or Schubert, and certainly Bach, would not have made any objection to the transference of their horn parts to saxophones, to the eking out of the violas by violins, to the occasional simplification of an awkward passage, to a discreet euphonium helping the double basses, to the presence of the harmless pianoforte to strengthen the inner parts, as long as the true spirit of the composition remained unimpaired. All art is a compromise and some of the greatest strokes of genius have arisen from the necessities of an imperfect instrument.

A great man does not appear suddenly out of the sky, he is the product of his surroundings. If we want perfect music in England it will only come as the final result of a great mass of imperfect music. The great composer nearly always springs from artistically humble circumstances. Verdi first learnt his art by hearing his first efforts played on the band of his native town. Dvorak's early compositions were written for the village band organized by his father the local butcher. In England today after a dark period we are gradually winning the battle of music, our Waterloo will be won in the music rooms of our schools.

R. Vaughan Williams

[1] Australian composer and teacher, who settled in the UK. He taught at the County School for Boys at Beckenham, 1930–40, and was author of *The School Orchestra: A Comprehensive Manual for Conductors* (Winthrop Rogers edition, London, 1939), to which he had asked VW to provide this preface.

[2] The book was deposited in the British Museum and stamped on 7 June 1939.

314. To Hermann Fiedler

25 June [1939][1]

From R. Vaughan Williams,
The White Gates,
Westcott Road,
Dorking.

June 25

Dear Professor

Can you help me with a literary problem?

I remember being told some years ago that when Schiller wrote his Ode 'An die Freude' (9th Symphony) he intended originally to put 'Freiheit' but the 'Freedom' being in Germany as unpopular then as it appears to be now he was obliged to alter it to 'Freude'.

Can you tell me anything about this and/or could you tell me of any books which I could consult?

If we could prove it it would make the English version much easier since 'Freedom' is two syllables like 'Freiheit' and 'Joy' is only one syllable – Also an ode to Freedom would be something much more inspiring than an ode to Joy –[2]

My love to Herma

Yrs
R. Vaughan Williams

Have you any news of Masefield?[3]

[1] Printed in *RVW*, 226.

[2] VW was preparing a performance of the symphony at the Leith Hill Musical Festival, which did not take place because of the outbreak of war. VW makes no mention of the 'Freiheit' possibility in the essay he wrote on the symphony later in the year, published in *Some Thoughts on Beethoven's Choral Symphony with Writings on Other Subjects* (London, 1953).

[3] John Masefield had been awarded the Shakespeare Prize in Hamburg the year after VW.

315. To Alan Bush

13 July [1939]

From R. Vaughan Williams,
The White Gates,
Westcott Road,
Dorking.

July 13

Dear D[r] Bush

You put me in rather a difficult position because, as you know, I do not care about mixing propaganda and art and I do not quite see that the people who hold particular political views should arrogate to themselves and none others the title of 'Workers'.[1]

On the other hand I am always glad when I hear of any Society or Club turning from its nominal object and doing something that is worth while – but that something seems to me to be something much too big and eternal to be made the handmaid of quarrels between people who want to turn the world each his own way. I am very glad, for example, when I hear of Selfridges starting a choral society, but I should much disapprove if all the music they sang was an advertisement of Selfridge's goods – and it seems to me almost equally bad to advertise through music any particular brand of political opinion, even if those opinions are to my mind admirable.

As a matter of fact I hold all political opinions to be good or bad according to the nature of the people who hold them.

But since I hope that in spite of all this these societies may help people to realize what is in the long run worth while I will guarantee the sum of £100 as you suggest up to December 31st 1939. Please write the exact form of words I should send to your bank.

Yours sincerely
R. Vaughan Williams

[1] VW had been asked by Bush to provide a guarantee of up to £100 for the Workers' Music Association to cover any overdraft that might arise.

316. To Ursula Wood

[26 July 1939][1]

From R. Vaughan Williams,
The White Gates,
Westcott Road,
Dorking.

My Dear

This is splendid about Noyes – you will soon be appearing in the Sketch and Tatler 'Ursula Wood the well known poet and friend'.[2]

Douglas has now written to say that he cannot get up Epi[thalamion] by Oct 28th and if we do it it will be 'under-rehearsed' – & there is no later date that is possible for him. So I have told him that I cannot urge him to do it under those circumstances and that I never urged him to do it unless he was keen & that he himself chose the date. I am so sorry my dear but what else is to be done.[3]

Love from
RVW

[1] Douglas Kennedy had written to Ursula in the same vein on 25 July and therefore this must have been written a day or so later.

[2] Ernest Rhys had shown UW's poems to Alfred Noyes, the poet, and had taken her to tea with him.

[3] Douglas Kennedy wrote to UW on 25 July: 'I am worried to death about the question of rehearsal and also over the programme. Amy Stoddart in writing to me about her Schubert Trio asks for a lot of rehearsing and for space for the rehearsals here at awkward times. The response to my invitation to dance in the Ballet is only mildly successful and I am in a real flap now about whether we can do it in the time. I wouldn't mind if it was just Epi[thalamion] but the problem of dealing with Amy Stoddart's Ballet as well fusses me. I think it is partly that I don't like the Ballet very much and rather resent having it in the programme and yet that seems so ungrateful and unhelpful considering our position!! I see there is a danger of a General Election on October 25th. That would put the "Kibosh" on the whole scheme, for I know that many dancers are terribly political.'

317. To Ursula Wood

[30 July 1939][1]

From R. Vaughan Williams,
The White Gates,
Westcott Road,
Dorking.

Sunday

My Dear

I got your express last night. The boy came twice – because the first time he'd forgotten it.

I thought the only thing to do when I got Douglas' letter was definitely to cry off for that date, so I wrote [to] all my people & told them so. I c^d not keep them shilly-shallying any longer. So Oct. 24th is off any how. It rather goes against my grain to let Amy[2] do it later, but if Douglas made the suggestion we might consider it.

My dear, I feel so sorry about it – not so much for my music, which if it is good can wait its time & if it is bad had better not be heard, but for you and the whole thing. You know I think I wrote it because I'm fond of you (though appearances were against that theory!) & because I like the idea of you, me and Douglas all working together. If that cannot be achieved I do not feel inclined to push it. You know, my dear, I can never and will never push my work – if people want my stuff they must ask for it & that applies to other people pushing for me. We might get pushed into the wrong box. If Ninette[3] ever did it, your share w^d go – my share (except the music) w^d go & probably my music w^d be played all at the wrong tempo. That may be its fate, but we won't ask for that. I know I suffer from inertia in these matters, but I can't do otherwise. I was willing to work like billy-o for our original scheme – but now!

It will be lovely to see you at Hereford.[4]

I like the sonnet. But I suppose you w^d not consider transposing the last two lines to make more climax. Shall I challenge Noyes for betraying a lovely woman?

The local farmer has just said he will take our derelict hay – so I am sweating at piling it up.

Love yrs
RVW

P.S. What we must face is that Douglas does not want to do it – his mood is full of America. He wishes he could say so openly – I gave him a chance saying 'Do you want to be out of this? I shall understand'

[1] This seems the most likely date, since the letter clearly follows closely Kennedy's letter to UW of 25 July.

[2] Amy Stoddart.

[3] Ninette de Valois.

[4] At the Three Choirs Festival due to take place on 3 September. The outbreak of war intervened.

318. To Douglas Lilburn

postmark: 31 July 1939

From R. Vaughan Williams,
The White Gates,
Westcott Road,
Dorking.

Dear Lilburn

This is splendid news – & I congratulate you.

I wish I c^{d} have heard your overture – perhaps I shall one day.[1]

I was in Skye on a 'reading party' in 1894!! It was a good place – we were in a farm house at Tothardor (Struan) – & we walked once to the Cuchullin hills and climbed Skur-na-Gillean & got lost in a fog.[2]

Have you seen Loch Coruisk – a wonderful place

Also if they have one of their big open air prayer meetings you should go to that – a wonderful sight & sound – all good wishes to Gundry[3] – & tell him I want to see his variations

Yrs
R. Vaughan Williams

1 Lilburn had won the Cobbett Prize, the Farrar Prize, and the Foli Scholarship at the RCM. The overture to which VW refers would have been the Festival Overture, of which George Dyson had conducted the premiere that year at the RCM.

2 In current cartography, the Cuillin Hills and Sgùrr nan Gillean. According to UVW on this walk G. E. Moore discovered he was vertiginous and when the fog cleared had to be flanked by someone on each side so that he couldn't see the steep falls.

3 Inglis Gundry (1905–2000), Cornish composer who had been a fellow pupil of VW with Lilburn at the RCM; see *New Grove*.

319. Completed registration form for cultural national service[1]

[summer 1939]

NATIONAL SERVICE

a) Surname	*Vaughan Williams*
b) Christian names	*Ralph*
c) Literary pseudonym (if any)	–
d) Permanent address	*The White Gates, Dorking*
e) Telephone number	*Dorking 5055*
f) Sex	*Male*
g) Age	*66*
h) State of health	*Good*

i) Married or single — *Married*

j) ~~Number of children under 18 years of age (if any)~~

k) Nationality — *British*

l) Professional or Academic Qualifications (if any)

Doctor of Music

m) Practical experience in spheres other than literature, drama or music (*e.g.*, lecturing, broadcasting, teaching, farming, etc.)

Lecturing on music

n) Titles and character (*e.g.*, fiction, educational, etc.) and names of publishers of books of which you are the author

National Music (Lectures) O.U. Press

o) Titles and particulars of plays which you have written and names of theatres in which or companies by which they have been performed.

p) Titles and character of musical works of which you are the composer or author and names of publishers. Which, if any, of such musical works have been broadcast or recorded?

Too many to enumerate

q) Particulars of books or periodicals which you edit or have edited. Please give sale or circulation figures.

r) Subjects of articles which you have contributed to periodicals and names of periodicals which published such articles

s) Names of periodicals which have published short stories you have written

t) Titles and particulars of films that have been made of any of your books or plays

u) Have you any and if so what technical experience of writing (a) for the screen; (b) for broadcasting?

No

v) Particulars of foreign languages which you (a) write; (b) read; (c) talk fluently

French (fair)

Brief general particulars likely to be of interest, *e.g.*, political views, attitude to conscription, military service, etc.

[1] This form was perhaps connected with the initiative undertaken by Paul Nash from Apr. 1939 under which lists were to be drawn up of artists, and particularly of writers, who might be employed in War Service. See John Betjeman, *Letters*, ed. Candida Lycett Green (London 1994–5), i. 225–6. VW's answers to questions are in italic.

4

The Second World War: September 1939–May 1945

THE arrival of war again on 3 September 1939 found VW in a not dissimilar situation to that in August 1914. He was not happy that events were such that war had become inevitable, but, given this was so, he again wanted to 'do his bit'. At the age of 67 there was little formal war service he could do, though he profoundly disagreed with pacifism once war was a reality. He was certain that the musician cannot divorce music from real life: while he agreed with Iris Lemare, who had referred to this 'wretched war' in a letter to him, he said 'if we look on it merely as a bore we shan't push through with it, as we've *got* to do now unless we want to live perpetually in the state we are living now'. A year later he wrote to Michael Tippett, a conscientious objector, that he felt it was the duty of artists to do all they could to preserve the world they inhabited from destruction and help to create 'a world where creative art will be a possibility'. In addition to these more general concerns he also felt that everyone had a first duty to care for their immediate responsibilities, in his case Adeline.

Like many others, VW undertook practical measures: gardening both at The White Gates and on an allotment (he appears to have prized his potato patch); keeping hens; fire-watching, and collecting salvage in a handcart. However, it was as a musician that he felt he could help especially. As Adrian Boult summed it up in an internal BBC memorandum of 1947, based on briefings from Dorking residents:

> he collected a choir from former Leith Hill Festival adherents and rehearsed them every week regularly. They gave two concerts each year and in addition five annual performances of the St Matthew Passion. He also organised a large number of concerts at Toc H [which had a branch at Dorking] for troops, and had a great deal to do with what was called 'An Informal Hour of Music'. These events were fortnightly and went on for many years.

The concerts had started in 1938, and finding performers was a continual preoccupation.

On top of the concerts, there was his work with Jewish refugees, which fell into two separate fields of endeavour: he had been chairman of the local refugee committee for some time, and through it had come to know and make a lasting friendship with the Hornsteins and the Müller-Hartmanns. However, with the war came internment of such refugees as enemy aliens and their plight, especially of those who were musicians, affronted him to such an extent that he spearheaded a campaign for their release. The Home Office agreed to set up an advisory committee, of which VW accepted the chair, to advise on which internees were of such eminent distinction in music and had made such a contribution that they should be released. Some of those released later became household names in music.

However, the genesis of the war had one telling effect on VW's political outlook: he became an ardent supporter of Federal Union, a movement which survives to the present day. It advocated a union 'of free peoples under a common government' with the ultimate aim of the 'prevention of war, the creation of prosperity and the preservation and promotion of individual liberty'. VW started a branch of the movement in Dorking but references to 'F.U.' seem to occur much less after the end of the war and, writing to Boult in 1955, he said he would never again enter into politics; when he had done so in the past he had always regretted it.

Whatever his feelings and uncertainties about politics, he was never in any doubt about stating his mind publicly should there in his view be a palpable injustice to be put right. His relations with the BBC, which had normally been good, are a case in point: he castigated the Director-General of the BBC soon after the beginning of the war about its duty to preserve the cultural well-being of the nation. This object, he told him, was not best achieved by broadcasting hours of second-rate music (much of it on the cinema organ) and by the wholesale cancellation of professional engagements for musicians, since there was a danger that they might be driven to other professions and thus not be there in the future when they were needed. He returned to the fray again when the broadcaster announced a ban on the compositions of Alan Bush, on the grounds of his publicly stated political opinions. While VW declared himself strongly opposed to his views, insofar as he knew them, he could not as a matter of principle condone such victimization and underlined his stand by withdrawing his choral song 'England, my England', which had been commissioned by the BBC, and returning the commission fee.

On a happier note, VW became engaged in a form of war work as a member of the Council for the Encouragement of Music and the Arts. This body was the predecessor of the Arts Council of Great Britain, to be an important strand in the future of post-war British music. The secretary at the time was the composer Elisabeth Lutyens. On accepting membership he was promptly invited to be chairman. He firmly turned the offer down but nonetheless played a full role in the Council's efforts to encourage musical performances in the regions. In fact sitting on committees was a major way in which VW found himself making a contribution to the war effort. At one point he found he was sitting on ten of them, and wryly remarked, when writing in 1942 to an old friend and RCM contemporary, Fritz Hart (who had made his career in Australia but had then moved to be Professor of Music in the University of Hawaii): 'As Hugh Allen said the other day "our war work is forming *quorums*". At all events for that one does not require a brain, only a behind.'

Hart was not the only correspondent connected with the Antipodes with whom VW kept in touch during these years: there were two of his recent RCM students, both from New Zealand, with whom he started a regular correspondence that he maintained for the remainder of his life. Douglas Lilburn and Frederick Page became extremely influential in New Zealand musical life; indeed Lilburn has been described as 'The Grandfather of New Zealand music'. VW was intensely proud of both of them and characteristically followed their careers with close interest. Other regular correspondents of course continue: Gerald Finzi, Herbert Howells, Adrian Boult, Elizabeth Maconchy, and especially Ursula Wood. Ursula's arrival on the scene made a marked difference. She was admitted into the closely protected mental inner sanctum where discussion of his compositional work in progress was allowed. He would tell her in his letters what he was working on and her literary enthusiasms were called on to help him find texts for setting. We find her introducing him to previously unencountered poets such as Emily Dickinson, while on a more practical front, VW took advantage of her typing abilities. As we have seen, work on his opera *The Pilgrim's Progress* seems to have been diverted into work on the Fifth Symphony, which was well on the way to completion when war broke out. However, that diversion was only a temporary respite from the opera project, which he seems to have continued to mull over in the background. Certainly by November 1939 Ursula had typed out a fair copy of his draft of the complete libretto.

The war brought more insistent demands for music of a patriotic nature. *Six Choral Songs to be Sung in Time of War* are settings of passages from Shelley, some of which Ursula had been enlisted to help him find. The work was intended for the 1940 Proms season, but this was curtailed, due to air raids, so that they were not performed until a broadcast the following December.

Another work in the same vein was the BBC commission *England, my England*, a setting of part of W. E. Henley's poem *Pro Rege Nostro*, which, as already mentioned, was the work which VW withdrew from the BBC. Once the BBC had settled its dispute and agreed once again to broadcast the music of Alan Bush, *England, my England* was eventually performed by BBC forces under Adrian Boult in December 1941. Also, as a sort of war service, VW became involved with film music, writing the scores for a series of works with a wartime background: *49th Parallel*, *Coastal Command*, *The People's Land*, and *Flemish Farm* among them. He enjoyed the strict discipline involved in getting timings right to the nearest second. With the comparatively recent phenomenon of the DVD, films such as *49th Parallel* have become accessible once again; hitherto the music was not available in its original form and context but only through derivative works (such as the song 'The New Commonwealth', based on the prelude to *49th Parallel*).

In the background to these minor compositions, work continued on the Fifth Symphony, the central pillar of his symphonic output. The symphony was sufficiently far advanced by December 1941 to be tried out before a few friends on two pianos, played by Hubert Foss and Alan Richardson. However, it continued to develop in his mind for a further fifteen months (perhaps with some uncertainty, since in 1942 he refers more than once to needing to learn to compose: 'I seem to get worse rather than better') before he felt it was ready to be heard. It was only in February 1943 that he was ready to offer it to Sir Henry Wood for the Proms. Wood accepted it at once and it received its first performance on 24 June that year. Adrian Boult for one found it 'completely satisfying in these times and shows, as only music can, what we must work for when this madness is over'. Certainly the work is a point of repose between the two fiercer symphonies which came before and after it, and for many it is the crowning achievement of VW's oeuvre. For his closer friends, the serenity of the symphony was perhaps testimony to the role which Ursula was now playing in his life.

That life had not been unscathed by the war. On a personal front there was a series of deaths: Dorothy Longman, wife of his Bach Choir colleague Robert Longman, in memory of whom VW wrote his moving motet *Valiant for Truth*; Adeline's sister Emmeline, the wife of R. O. Morris (who subsequently went to live with Ralph and Adeline at The White Gates); and especially hurtful was the death in an air raid on London of Honorine Williamson, R. O. Morris's niece, who had lived with them helping Adeline ever since the move to Dorking. She had been married to the trumpeter Bernard Brown for only six months. For Ursula, there was the tragedy of the loss of her husband Michael from a heart attack, about which Ursula has given an account in her autobiography. Adeline and Ralph gathered her in at once following the news in the hope that the quiet life at Dorking would be helpful in her bereavement.

VW's distress at these events is evident from his correspondence, but it does not make itself evident in the even course of the symphony. The two major works which followed drew on material originally intended for other purposes: the String Quartet No. 2 in A minor, dedicated to Ursula's great friend Jean Stewart, violist in the Menges Quartet, is in the scherzo thematically connected with the film music for *49th Parallel*, while the Oboe Concerto draws on material intended for, but not used in, the Fifth Symphony. The concerto was apparently complete by 1942, as we learn from an internal memo of that year in the Oxford University Press archive, but was not offered for a Prom performance to Henry Wood until May 1944, following much revision.

The internal OUP memo of 1942 was in effect an assessment of VW's attitude to his publisher following the departure of Hubert Foss, with whom he had worked so closely. Foss had become frustrated by the limitations on publishing imposed by the war and by the fact that his department was relocated to Oxford. This had led to depression and drinking problems to an extent that it was agreed that he should tender his resignation. Though upset at the loss of Foss, VW did not allow this development to impair his good relations with OUP, which continued as before until the end of his life. At the same time he remained close friends with Foss, who became involved in a number of projects involving the composer and published a book about him in 1950. Foss eventually died in 1953.

As it became possible to envisage the end of the war, VW was asked in 1943 by the Director of Music at the BBC, now Arthur Bliss, to write a 'Victory Anthem', which he was happy to do. It was sad that earlier difficulties with the BBC were not laid to rest in this commission but rather compounded. The score (requiring soloist, speaker, large chorus, chorus of children, full symphony orchestra, and large organ) was sent to the BBC early in 1944 but, apart from a brief acknowledgement from Bliss, VW heard nothing more until August. Then Boult asked VW, to the latter's fury since the score had been with the BBC for months, whether he had written the work yet! The work had then to be tidied up in a great hurry for recording against the eventual day of victory. There was also confusion over the title, which, at the BBC's request, was changed from 'Victory Anthem' to 'Thanksgiving for Victory'. Good relations between the composer and the corporation were, however, restored by a fine performance of the Fifth Symphony broadcast shortly after VE day.

As ever with VW, his musical imagination couldn't remain still for long. Since 1944 a new symphony had been taking shape in his mind which would reflect the tribulations and losses of the war years.

320. To Ursula Wood

[6 September 1939]

From R. Vaughan Williams,
The White Gates,
Westcott Road,
Dorking.

My Dear

This is to thank you for your love and send you mine. You are lucky to have a job – I daresay I shall get one in time – but I feel my first duty is to my own belongings & I don't want to do anything that will interfere with that. I hope that they, also, serve who only stand and wait.[1]

Yrs
RVW

[1] Quotation from Milton's sonnet on his blindness.

321. To Douglas Lilburn

postmark: 18 September 1939

From R. Vaughan Williams,
The White Gates,
Westcott Road,
Dorking.

Dear Lilburn

I am very sorry I shall not be teaching at the R.C.M. this term – it has been decided that only those who live in or quite near London are to come. But I should much like to look at your work occasionally – I shall probably be in London from time to time – or if you cared to come down here one day I should be pleased to see you

Yrs
R. Vaughan Williams

P.S. It is up to you young people to keep the cultural side going so that we may not sink entirely to the level of animals.

322. To Imogen Holst

September [1939]

From R. Vaughan Williams,
The White Gates,
Westcott Road,
Dorking.

Sept

My Dear Imogen

I was thankful to know you are back in England.[1]

I am not going to RCM this term as it was decided that only those who lived in or quite near London should do the teaching this term.

I am coming up for an EFDS C[tee] meeting tomorrow Tuesday week – & might look in then if you were in London.

Do you think you can help me about Goldsmith – His copying has of course all gone under – But he tells me that he had 6 years office experience as a young man & can do shorthand & typing – & he might be able to replace a called up man. – But don't worry about him – at all events till you have found your own job! & then not much – I think he will find something.[2]

Our love to Isobel & you.

Uncle Ralph

[1] Imogen had been in Switzerland and had returned earlier than planned.

[2] Until she eventually found a job in Jan. 1940 as a travelling music organizer in the South West area for the Pilgrim Trust Music Travellers scheme (later taken over by CEMA), Imogen Holst first went apple-picking in Essex and then worked for the Bloomsbury House Refugee Organisation. S. O. Goldsmith was a copyist used by VW—and was recommended by VW to others, such as Ina Boyle. He lived in Luxemburg Gardens.

323. To Myra Hess

5 October [1939]

From R. Vaughan Williams,
The White Gates,
Westcott Road,
Dorking.

Oct 5

My Dear Myra

Of course use my name & let me do anything else I can to help.[1]

One suggestion – would it be better to pay the nominal fee, as you suggest, to the artists, & then divide the profits (?) up between them – & *not* give it to the Mus: Ben:[2] (they could pass it on themselves if they wished) – but I daresay you have thought it all out.

One more thing *please* don't 'Doctor' me – most of the young women of my acquaintance call me 'Uncle Ralph' when they wish to be respectful, 'V.W.' when otherwise inclined. Won't you do one or the other according as you consider me a man or a mouse.

Yrs
RVW

[1] VW is writing in response to a request for advice about the famous series of concerts which Myra Hess was to run throughout the war in the National Gallery.

[2] The Musicians Benevolent Fund, which received the profits from the National Gallery Concerts.

324. To Elizabeth Trevelyan

received: 10 October 1939[1]

From R. Vaughan Williams,
The White Gates,
Westcott Road,
Dorking.

My dear Bessy

I saw the lady conductor of Forest Green[2] yesterday and she tells me that it is quite untrue what you were told and what you told me that the hut had been taken over by the W.O.[3] and was empty.

(1) It has not been taken over by the W.O. but by the Y.M.C.A.
(2) That it is being used by the village in the ordinary way simply with the proviso that in the (unlikely) event of troops coming to the neighbourhood the Y.M.C.A. would then take it over for the troops.

If you have told any body else this I hope you will take the trouble to put it right. The poor W.O. has so many true accusations to put up with that it is important that no false accusations should be made.

With regard to our conversation over the BBC and German music it occurs to me that many musical and sensitive people who love German people and German music might for that reason find it an unbearable pain to listen to German music – because it would remind them so forcibly of what Germany had been, what it might have been – & what it still may be – & contrast this with what it is.

A true musician cannot divorce music from real life. So perhaps the BBC had this in their mind if (which I doubt) they deliberately abjured German music for a week or so.

You know we English are not always quite so stupid and so evil intentioned as our candid friends in the New Statesman and elsewhere try to make out.

Yrs
RVW

[1] According to a note on the original.
[2] Miss E. Etté. See Leith Hill Musical Festival, *Music Won the Cause*, 145.
[3] War Office.

325. To Vally Lasker

12 October [1939]

From R. Vaughan Williams,
The White Gates,
Westcott Road,
Dorking.

Oct 12

My Dear Vally

Thank you very much for remembering my 102nd birthday.[1]

On my 103rd perhaps we will meet round our last patch of potatoes (which I shall have planted) and drink each other's health in blackberry juice.

Yrs
RVW

[1] A wry twist—it was in fact his 67th birthday.

326. To Herbert Howells

12 October 1939

From R. Vaughan Williams,
The White Gates,
Westcott Road,
Dorking.

Oct 12 1939

Dear Herbert

How good of you to write and send me all the messages from all my friends – to whom I request you to send my love with suitable actions.[1]

As to me there is nothing to report – I try to make myself useful in the small ways that come my way committees etc & starting the village choirs going (they are all *keen* to carry on).[2]

I am also 'digging for victory' – preparing a potato patch for next year when it will probably be all we shall have to live on.

Also an essay on the 9th symphony!![3] How are you? Has all this hit you very hard materially? Urge the young people to keep their music going – so that they shall be there to carry on when we return to sanity.

The latest bee in my bonnet is 'Federal Union' (Have you read Streit's 'Union Now' – you should[;] it is I believe the only solution). I am trying to get a branch started in Dorking.[4]

Yrs
RVW.

[1] Howells had apparently written with 67th birthday greetings from VW's friends at St Paul's Girls' School. The actions were probably kisses.

[2] Although the LHMF had ceased in the First World War, in the second it continued to take place.

[3] VW's essay 'Some Thoughts on Beethoven's Choral Symphony' was eventually published in his collection of writings under that title in 1953.

[4] A meeting of the Federal Union organization had just been held in London on 4 Oct. and had declared the following general aim: 'I believe in a Federal Union of free peoples under a common government elected by and responsible to the people for their common affairs, with national self-government for national affairs as a first step towards democratic self-government for the prevention of war, the creation of prosperity and the preservation and promotion of individual liberty.' The book, by Clarence K. Streit, was *Union Now: A Plea for a Union of the Democratic Nations* (London, 1939).

327. To the Director-General of the BBC[1]

19 October [1939[2]]

From R. Vaughan Williams,
The White Gates,
Westcott Road,
Dorking.

Oct. 18

Dear Sir

I hope you will not think I am taking a liberty in writing to you on the subject of the BBC musical programmes.

It seems almost an impertinence to mention to you the obvious truth that the BBC have a great responsibility in the matter of the cultural well-being of the country, but as the whole of this letter hangs on this point I hope you will forgive my putting it down in black and white.

It appears to me that one of the things we are fighting for is a free as opposed to a regimented culture. In that case we must prove that we have a culture worth fighting for.

I believe that in times of stress such as these when peoples' purpose & determination need special encouragement that only the best & most vital art is of any use. Anything else is enervating & discouraging and I believe that the 'ordinary man' will respond to the stimulus in a way which in normal times he possibly would not do.

It has, I think, been a great pain to many people to find that in the early days of the war it was apparently the opinion of your programme makers that the English people when their hearts & minds were strung up to great endeavour only wanted to listen to the loathsome noises of the so-called cinema 'organ'. Later on I admit the programmes began to get better, but to judge from this weeks 'Radio Times' things have taken a turn for the worse again & the so-called 'serious' programmes are filled with second rate material which *nobody* wants.

In times like these when so many people are looking for comfort & encouragement from music, among them those who have probably never attended to music before, surely we ought to give them something that will *grip*. I believe that really great music, especially if it is familiar, will grip every body (in a category of great music I include a Beethoven Symphony, a Schubert song and a fine marching tune). I admit that very bad music does grip certain minds but this halfway-house stuff grips *nobody*. The result of this policy has I believe been that the discriminating listeners are tuning in to *Germany* for their spiritual sustenance while the undiscriminating are perforce falling back on the unspeakable Mr Sandy Macpherson.[3]

Are we not missing a great opportunity which may never recur?

I venture to add to this already overlong letter one more point. It is not for me to doubt the necessity of the BBC policy in cancelling all engagements except for a few artists but the result is that many musicians have been thrown out of work. It may of course be argued that it is not the business of the BBC to provide incomes for musicians, but to provide entertainment & instruction for listeners – but, taking a long view, even on these grounds may we not argue that if incomes are not provided now for musicians & especially the younger musicians, those of them who can will turn to other professions & when in the future we again need them they will not be there & we shall indeed be 'a land without music'.

I venture to think that we ought to provide for the needs of future listeners as well as for those of the present.

Would it be *ultra vires* for the BBC to use the money which would have been spent on these cancelled engagements for organizing non-broadcast concerts so as to keep up the supply of performers which in the future we shall so badly need?

Once more pardon me for putting my views at such length.

Yours faithfully
R. Vaughan Williams[4]

[1] Frederick Ogilvie, who had succeeded Sir John Reith in 1938 as second Director-General of the BBC. He remained in the post until 1942.

[2] Date taken from context.

[3] The cinema organist who was a regular performer on the BBC right through the war and afterwards.

[4] He received the following reply, dated 23 October, from the Controller (Public Relations):

'I am asked by the Director-General to thank you for your letter of October 18th, and to assure you that the trouble you have taken in letting him have this full statement of your views is warmly appreciated. The sense of our cultural responsibility which you describe is very present in our minds, and we are constantly endeavouring to effect in our arrangements a wise balance between programmes of a serious nature on the one hand and the need for light entertainment and relief on the other.

Considerations of national security have for the present robbed us of our principal means to such an end—the alternative programme. We now have to attempt to satisfy all our listeners during the course of the day with only one programme at our disposal, but that we are anxious not to neglect the requirements of those primarily interested in serious music is I think shewn by our present programmes. A glance at the "Radio Times" of this week will show that there are seven performances by the B.B.C. Orchestra playing under Sir Adrian Boult or his deputy in addition to a number of other concerts and recitals.

We can readily sympathise with your suggestion that the concerts by professional musicians should be organised by the B.B.C. not necessarily for broadcasting, but we are not I am afraid in a position to say whether this would be possible. The B.B.C. is, however, alive to the difficulties which wartime conditions have imposed upon the musical profession, and is anxious to do what it can to compensate for them.'

VW promptly sent a copy of this reply to Boult in disgust: see no. 328.

328. To Adrian Boult at the BBC

24 October [1939[1]]

From R. Vaughan Williams,
The White Gates,
Westcott Road,
Dorking.

Oct 24

Dear Adrian

I wrote to the D.G.[2]

Here is his substitutes deputies[3] answer.

You will see he has not even troubled to find out what my grievance was, which was, as you know, not that there was not a certain amount of 'serious' music but that the *quality* of the 'serious' music was so half hearted.[4]

Yrs
RVW

[1] Year taken from context.

[2] Director-General (of the BBC). For the letter see no. 327.

[3] i.e. substitute's deputy's! The reply came from the Controller (Public Relations).

[4] VW had sent a copy of his original letter to the Director-General to Boult and was now reporting the result. Boult wrote privately to VW on 26 Oct.:

'Thank you for your second letter. I return your B.B.C. reply. I did not write sooner because I have been moving about and I wanted to think over your letter a little more carefully. I think you will realize that in a post mortem of this period I do not intend to be unvocal, and I think you will guess how I feel about the whole matter. I have perhaps been too easy-going in the past and only occasionally put forward the plea that I am the only broadcasting Director of Music in any broadcasting organization who is not absolute master of his own programme policy. Between these four walls I can tell you that I am saying it pretty forcibly at the moment, but I do not think resignation would be any use or threats of that kind because I have reason to believe, though I have not been officially told, that a certain amount of the instructions that come to us in regard to these emergency programmes both at the present time and when they were planned some time before the crisis, had emanated from Whitehall, and I do not think Whitehall, or that part of it that is capable of giving instructions that the public is to be amused at all costs even when they have just been told that a battleship has been sunk, cares whether A.C.B or X.Y.Z. is Director of Music of the B.B.C.

I do not want to make any excuses, but it is a fact that between September 2nd and 11th nine symphonies were performed by the following composers, Haydn, Beethoven, Dvorak, Mendelssohn, Mozart, Schubert, i.e. one a day. Did you realize this? I admit that many of them were at impossible times to listen, but, rightly or wrongly, we have assumed (no doubt here again under instructions) that most of Britain had gone on a shift system and would be listening at all times of the day. Did you see that delightful letter from Manchester in last week's Radio Times about the eight o'clock Concerts? It made me want to do one every day.

In regard to the enclosure, which I return, I have taken steps to see that the Director-General personally sees your letter. He has been travelling a good deal, and it may have been passed on in his absence.

ACB'

329. To Elisabeth Lutyens

6 November [1939]

From R. Vaughan Williams,
The White Gates,
Westcott Road,
Dorking.

Nov 6

Dear Mrs Glennie[1]

(or do I on these formal occasions call you Elisabeth Lutyens?) I am most anxious to help and w^{d} be glad to give my name to your Council[2] if I can be sure that it is not merely overlapping & creating yet another body of which there are already too many. You have doubtless envisaged these – but in case you have not – I mention a few which have all written to enlist my sympathy

(1) I.S.M. 'Concerts in wartime'
(2) Federation of rural music (Miss Ibbetson 106 Gloucester Place W.1)

(3) Society of Women Musicians Concert parties
(4) 'Council of Music' (or some such name with rather high falutin' terms of reference with T. Beecham at the head & John Goss for Secretary)

There are also, of course, the various rural community councils, the ATNS (or whatever it is for concerts to troops[3]) & the National Council for Social Service.

Would it not be a good plan to get into touch with one or more of these & work with them rather than start a new organization? But I daresay you have already thought this all out.

By the way you ask for an immediate reply & your letter is dated Oct 28 – but it did not reach me till Nov 3rd or 4th.

Yours sincerely
R. Vaughan Williams

[1] Elisabeth Lutyens was married to Ian Glennie, until they divorced in 1940.

[2] The Council for the Encouragement of Music and the Arts, later (1948) the Arts Council of Great Britain.

[3] VW is probably thinking of ENSA (Entertainments National Service Association).

330. To Ursula Wood

[7 November 1939]

From R. Vaughan Williams,
The White Gates,
Westcott Road,
Dorking.

My Dear

What a lovely copy of P.P.[1] Do you really want the original? I will save it [for] you if you do.

I think your suggestion of masks for the fair just right. About Apollyon I am not quite sure. I do not think I want any movement on the stage. I know the passage in Wisdom[2] – it is very wonderful – some of it has been used by Elgar in 'The Kingdom'.[3]

I don't know whether you made a carbon of P.P.; in case you did I send a list of such corrections – many of them my fault.

With all my love
RVW

P.S. I think it perfectly marvellous what you've done with my script. The Act II sc 2 takes place next day.

[1] UW had typed out the libretto for *The Pilgrim's Progress*.

[2] The passage in question was Wisdom of Solomon 2: 5–8: '(5) For our time is a very shadow that passeth away; and after our end there is no returning: for it is fast sealed, so that no man cometh again. (6) Come on therefore, let us enjoy the good things that are present: and let us speedily use the creatures like as in youth. (7) Let us fill ourselves with costly wine and ointments; and let no flower of the spring pass by us. (8) Let us crown ourselves with rosebuds, before they be withered.'

[3] In fact v. 7 is used by Elgar in *The Apostles*.

331. To Cedric Glover[1]

28 November [1939]

From R. Vaughan Williams,
The White Gates,
Westcott Road,
Dorking.

Nov 28

Dear Glover

I hope you will forgive my sending you the enclosed.[2]

I know it is a difficult time to cry for help, what with taxes and increased prices. Nonetheless these refugees are our responsibility – we can't (if we would) send them elsewhere till the war is over.

Yours sincerely
R. Vaughan Williams

[1] See no. 141 n. 1.

[2] A prospectus for the Dorking & District Refugee Committee.

332. To Elisabeth Lutyens

[13 December 1939[1]]

From R. Vaughan Williams,
The White Gates,
Westcott Road,
Dorking.

My Dear Miss Lutyens

I shall be happy to do what I can on your council – but not as Chairman please.[2]

For one thing I do not live in London and therefore cannot be sure of frequent attendance.

Secondly, I do not know really enough of the details of the working of the society.

Thirdly, I belong to the C^tee of several other societies and if they came into conflict my choice of loyalties w^d be more difficult than merely as a member of your Council.

Honestly I think I shall be much more useful to you as an ordinary member.

Yours sincerely
R. Vaughan Williams

[1] See n. 2.

[2] Lutyens had invited VW to take the Chair of the Council for the Encouragement of Music and the Arts. He had sent a telegram on 13 Dec. 1939 declining the position and promising this letter of explanation.

333. To Ursula Wood

26 December [1939]

From R. Vaughan Williams,
The White Gates,
Westcott Road,
Dorking.

Dec 26

My Dear

I spent an hour over the lovely poetry book, and found quantities I did not know – but that is not strange for an illiterate person like me.

By the way who is Emily Dickinson – and also can you search Shelley for me for some more lines to set – I want a series of war time songs[1] – I've done P. Unbound[2] last 9 lines ('Song of Victory') and a number of earlier lines 'Love from its . . . healing wings'[3] (Song of Healing) – I want some more 'Courage' 'Hope' etc – but they must be 'settable' e.g. the next lines starting 'Gentlemen' are quite unsettable – can you find me some?

Love from
RVW

[1] These were published as *Six Choral Songs—To Be Sung in Time of War*, CW 1940/1.

[2] *Prometheus Unbound*, the play in four acts by Shelley published in 1820.

[3] 'Love, from its awful throne of patient power / In the wise heart, from the last giddy hour / Of dread endurance, from the slippery, steep, / And narrow verge of crag-like agony, springs / And folds over the world its healing wings.' *Prometheus Unbound*, Act IV, ll. 557–61.

334. To Fritz Hart[1]

25 February [1940]

Feb 25

Dear Fritz

Many thanks for your two letters. We keep cheerful & confident here and prepared for anything and to withstand anything. Outwardly life seems to go on much as usual except we've all changed our jobs.

I am too old to do any of the real jobs so I go about picking up scraps. (Incidentally I conduct a rehearsal of the Messiah every Saturday).

We are full of hope here – but know we've got to go through a hard time. It is magnificent the way the English speaking races are automatically federating.

My love to Marvell.

Yrs
RVW

[1] Fritz Hart (1874–1949) had been a friend and contemporary of VW at the RCM; after a period composing and teaching in Melbourne, Australia, he was currently Professor of Music at the University of Hawaii. He had married Marvell Allison in 1937.

335. To Ursula Wood

[February 1940]

From R. Vaughan Williams,
The White Gates,
Westcott Road,
Dorking.

My Dear

I went and got a Lear[1] at once – it is a good book – but I wish he[2] w[d] not call them 'Limericks' – I feel sure he w[d] have hated the word – a Limerick is an indecent poem in the same metre as the Lear nonsense rhymes.

I'd often thought of setting the Pobble[3] to music – its one of the most mysteriously romantic poems I know.

Have you read the prose nonsense story[4] – its superb – I did not know it before.[5]

The wedding[6] is next Sat. wk – I am told the bridegroom has a pretty sister so I am all agog.

Love from
RVW

[1] According to *RVW*, 233 this was a paperback edition of some of Edward Lear's writings. It was possibly *Edward Lear's Nonsense Songs, with the Author's Own Illustrations*, an edition published by Chatto & Windus in 1938.

[2] i.e. the editor, not the author.

[3] i.e. 'The Pobble who has no toes'.

[4] 'The story of the four little children who went round the world'.

[5] As far as here is quoted in *RVW*, 233.

[6] Honorine Williamson, who had lived with the VWs ever since the move to Dorking, was to marry Bernard Brown, a trumpeter.

336. Talk on folk-song music for the BBC[1]

BBC Military Band
Programme: 27th March,
1940, 9.35 p.m.

FOLK-SONG MUSIC – 2
Script by R. Vaughan Williams

Last time I had the pleasure of speaking to you we heard some splendid marching tunes, all of them good for singing – tunes which really belong to us because they have been sung for generations of our forefathers. I promised you then that if I was allowed I could show you a lot more, and here they are – nothing precious about them – tunes with real blood in their veins and real muscles in their limbs. I don't believe that you could help stepping out to them even when you are tired after a long day's march.

There is not only the quick step march to be thought of, but also the slow march and the double. The first piece to be played to you tonight, 'The Running Set' is all at the double. The 'Running Set' is a dance with a series of traditional tunes to it, some of which are well known. I remember in my Army days how we were sent for a route march at 7 o'clock every morning, except Sundays, and part of that route march was always at the double. How we hated it! And how we longed for a good tune to help us through the ordeal.

First, then, Major O'Donnell[2] and his players will give you 'The Running Set'. Now we have what I have called a 'Folk Dance Medley'. It was originally arranged for a festival of the Folk Dance Society at the Albert Hall. You will see that the tunes often run into each other, so that the end of one tune is found to be the beginning of the next one. The Albert Hall dancers, who of course knew the tunes very well, were therefore continually finding that they were off on one dance before they had finished the last.

I have introduced one tune which is not a dance at all, but a song 'The Seeds of Love'. I introduced this partly because I liked the tune, and partly for sentimental reasons. This was the first tune which Cecil Sharp collected in Somerset. Perhaps if he had not by accident heard this song being sung in the fields he would not have been led on to rescue from oblivion that wonderful collection of melodies which he has bequeathed to us.

We will finish up with three march tunes which I have put together into a little Suite. The first tune is the 'Blue-eyed Stranger', a tune which the Morris men dance to – I do not know what the words are, so I cannot tell you what the sex of the stranger was – but I like to think that she had flaxen hair as well as blue eyes.

Then comes a man-of-war song, 'On board a '98'. This was sung to me in King's Lynn by an old sailor. I spent many happy mornings with him and his friends listening to their almost inexhaustible stock of splendid tunes.[3]

1 This talk, though not strictly speaking a letter, is included since it does not appear to survive elsewhere.

2 B. Walton O'Donnell, who had been conductor of the BBC's Military Band for some years.

3 Neither the 'Folk-dance medley' nor the three march arrangements (VW doesn't give the name of the third tune) is listed in *CW* and may now be lost. On *The Running Set*, see *CW* 1933/3.

337. To Harry Farjeon[1]

12 April [1940[2]]

From R. Vaughan Williams,
The White Gates,
Westcott Road,
Dorking.

April 12

Dear Mr Farjeon

I venture to write to you about Daniel Jones (late Mendelssohn Scholar).

I heard he was in a bad way & had no work. So I wrote to him asking for his credentials. He sent me among other things a very excellent testimonial from you.

He seems a most gifted young man all round.

Do you think we can do anything for him?

He is, so I believe, at his last gasp financially.

Yrs sincerely
R. Vaughan Williams

1 English composer and professor of composition at the RAM, 1878–1948. See *Grove* 5. Daniel Jones had been his pupil for composition.

2 A letter from VW to Daniel Jones now in the National Library of Wales is dated 1940.

338. To Robert Longman

[2 June 1940]

From R. Vaughan Williams,
The White Gates,
Westcott Road,
Dorking.

Dear Bobby

I want to say so much and cannot.[1]

Only my love – and I do thank her for her beautiful life and for your beautiful life together.

It has been happy I know and has made others so happy.

Perhaps there will be no more happiness or peace for any of us now and we must be thankful for what has been.

God bless you
Ralph.

[1] Bobby Longman had telephoned the previous day to say that his wife Dorothy had died.

339. To an unidentified correspondent

12 June 1940

June 12 1940

Dear Sir

In reply to your kind invitation I feel much honoured by your letter but I want to make it quite clear that I am *not* an authority on F.U. only a *layman* who strongly believes in it – if you would care for me to come and give you my reactions as 'a man of the street' in favour of F.U. I shall be proud to do so.[1]

But I have not the power to give the correct answer to all questions & objections & I find that my questioners often know more than I do.

If all this is clearly understood & you still wish to honour me with your invitation I shall be pleased to accept – But if after this letter you think better of it I shall quite understand. I note the date: July 16th at Reigate.

Yrs sincerely,
R. Vaughan Williams

[1] On VW and the Federal Union see no. 326.

340. To Ursula Wood [early July 1940[1]]

My Dear

I am so sorry about your foot. Do take care and don't move – that is essential with a poisoned foot – they kept me in bed *10 weeks* though I was quite well.

Your bit of news was very exciting – but was it wise to write it – I am tearing that bit into small pieces.[2]

I went and practiced fire fighting the other day – they stage a real fire with lots of smoke & I had to creep along on my stomach with an axe in one hand & the nozzle of the hosepipe in the other!

I heard from Maud[3] today & she has had her op. & says she goes on well.

Yrs
RVW

[1] The letter is written on the reverse of a communication to VW from the Society of Authors dated 28 June 1940.

[2] UW had told VW that she had seen the French destroyers which had escaped from Oran (Mers-el-Kebir) arriving in the Solent.

[3] Maud Karpeles.

341. To Ursula Wood [July 1940[1]]

My Dear

The flowers are lovely – & the arrangement is a real sonnet.

Thank you for the warning – the queer things[2] arrived yesterday & we have been practising – I have been fully sandbagged & digging the garden.

Yrs
RVW

[1] Written on the reverse of a letter from the Oxford University Press dated 19 July 1940.

[2] Gas masks.

342. To Robert Müller-Hartmann

6 August 1940

From R. Vaughan Williams,
The White Gates,
Westcott Road,
Dorking.

Aug 6th 1940

Dear Dr Müller-Hartmann,

It was a great pleasure to meet your daughter yesterday – I thought she was looking well though naturally depressed, but I feel that now there is great hope & I cannot but believe for what I think a great wrong will be put right.

I had such pleasure in your lecture at Burchett House[1] the other day. I hope very soon that you will be again able to contribute to our National Culture by your studies in English music.

I feel sure then, in spite of all, you will still continue to believe in English freedom. The Government were in a terrible emergency and had to adopt all [of] a sudden whole sale measures which wanted enquiries on many perfectly innocent people. May you soon be free to work for the country of your adoption and for the cause we all have at heart.

Yours sincerely
R. Vaughan Williams

[1] Run by the Dorking Refugee Committee for Jewish refugees.

343. To Granville Bantock[1]

21 August [1940]

From R. Vaughan Williams,
The White Gates,
Westcott Road,
Dorking.

August 21

Dear Bantock

I feel that it is time that British musicians got together and looked for the release of their fellow musicians which are interned.

Musicians do not appear to come under any category in the 'White Paper'[2] and this makes it difficult for us, but perhaps by a joint letter we could persuade the authorities to broaden their interpretation of 'work of national importance' (see 'White Paper' Section 8) and to point out that to fructify the life of the country is of national importance and the fact that artistic and intelligent people who will spread the gospel of anti-Nazism are an asset to the country.

Perhaps you have read Professor Rosenberg's report on the appalling conditions in his internment camp. This does not of course affect the injustice or otherwise of internment, but it does make it imperative, unless conditions have enormously improved, to release those, who ought to be released immediately. Could we have a meeting to discuss the question?

I am sending a copy of this letter to:

Dyson	Walton
Marchant	Berners
Edric Cundell	Lambert
Allen	Colles
Whittaker	Newman
Walford Davies	
Boult	
Dunhill[3]	

Yours sincerely
R. Vaughan Williams

[1] Composer and, until 1934, Peyton Professor of Music at Birmingham University.

[2] *Civilian internees of enemy nationality: categories of persons eligible for release from internment and procedure to be followed in applying for release*, Cmnd 6233, July 1940.

[3] The recipients were Sir Hugh Allen, Lord Berners, Sir Adrian Boult, H. C. Colles, Edric Cundell, Sir Walford Davies, Thomas Dunhill, George Dyson, Constant Lambert, Stanley Marchant, Ernest Newman, William Walton, and W. G. Whittaker. They constituted perhaps VW's view of the British musical establishment in 1940.

344. To Granville Bantock

28 August [1940]

From R. Vaughan Williams,
The White Gates,
Westcott Road,
Dorking.

Dear Bantock

Thank you for your answer to my letter. Can you come to a meeting at the Royal Academy of Music at 2.30 on Wednesday Sept 4?

I have had a promise from Sir Cyril Asquith[1] that the case of musicians shall be 'sympathetically considered' – So I suggest that we now meet and discuss action & among other things draw up a list of interned musicians. Could you bring your contribution to such a list as complete as possible in detail – If you cannot come would you send your list to me?[2]

Yrs sincerely
R. Vaughan Williams

[1] Sir Cyril Asquith (1890–1954), later (1951) Baron Asquith of Bishopstone, was at this time a judge of the King's Bench Division and for six months in 1940 served as chairman of the advisory committee on aliens.

[2] As a result of his initiative about internees, VW was invited to chair an advisory committee for recommending interned musicians for release on grounds of having made an outstanding contribution to music. See Cobbe, 'Vaughan Williams, Germany and the German Tradition', 93–4.

345. To Adrian Boult at the BBC [about 4 September 1940[1]]

The White Gates,
Dorking.

Dear Adrian

I wish I'd known of this 6 months ago – because in a way I feel I've already shot my bolt & the M.O.I. are a way behind the fair[2] – I sh[d] love for the B.B.C. to have had the enclosed which I think w[d] have just filled the bill – But as they did *not* ask me for anything I offered them to the Proms (who *did* ask me) & they are to be done on the 10th.[3]

Then the Bach Choir asked me & I refused them because I felt I had done all the occasional music I can – so if I do anything more it must be B.C. before the B.B.C. – But perhaps a commission w[d] make me start writing which I feel quite incapable of at present.

So will you send me more details – I do not understand at present what you want

Is it (so to speak) the 'Jerusalem' brand or the 'Blest pair of sirens' brand that you want?

As regards words I should probably want to go to the old masters – But if the BBC like to send me any contemporary poems I w[d] consider them – but not promise to use them.[4]

Yrs
RVW[5]

[1] Written in response to a letter from Boult dated 2 September.

[2] Boult had written on 2 Sept.: 'At the instigation of the Ministry of Information, the B.B.C. has asked me to approach you and ask you whether you would consider the acceptance of a commission to compose a "Song or lay hymn" with orchestral accompaniment on a patriotic (but not necessarily war-like) theme; the lyric to be chosen by you from existing lyrics, or from poems which would be commissioned from certain

living poets. I won't enter at this point into further detail until I know whether you are interested enough to consider a proposal of this sort. Needless to say, I very much hope you will be, as it is *you* we want.'

[3] *Six Choral Songs—To be Sung in Time of War* (*CW* 1940/1). Their first performance was planned for a Promenade Concert on 10 Sept., but the Proms season was cancelled from 7 Sept. due to air raids and so the songs were eventually first performed by the BBC SO and BBC Chorus under Leslie Woodgate in a broadcast concert on 20 Dec. 1940. In 1940 and 1941, because of a disagreement between the BBC and the lessors of the Queen's Hall, the Promenade Concerts were managed by Keith Douglas operating under the auspices of the Royal Philharmonic Society rather than by the BBC, so that offering a work for the Proms was not tantamount to offering it to the BBC, as would have been the case before or after that period. See Doctor and Wright, *The Proms*, 116 ff.

[4] Boult had asked VW to compose a patriotic song. The work eventually written in response to his request was a setting entitled *England, my England*, of W. C. Henley's poem *Pro Rege Nostro, CW* 1941/1. See no. 350.

[5] Printed in Moore, *Music and Friends*, 132.

346. To Ursula Wood

[23 September 1940]

From R. Vaughan Williams,
The White Gates,
Westcott Road,
Dorking.

My Dear

Thank you for the timely present & for your father's address which may be very useful.[1]

I know the Blake poems well – but I've never felt tempted to set him. I do not expect you ever got my letter[2] written to you c/o Maud to tell you that we have lost our beloved Honorine – she was killed in an air raid on London about a 4[t] night ago.

I know she had a very happy 6 months married and that is what I wanted for her so much.

Love fr
RVW

[1] UW's father, Major-General Sir Robert Lock, was working in the Ministry of Supply in Ottawa and was in a position to help with problems over interned musicians. See *RVW*, 237.

[2] Not included in the present collection.

347. To Ursula Wood

[after October 1940]

The White Gates,
Sunday morning 7.30

My Dear

I've not taken umbrage (I don't know quite what it is – but I certainly haven't taken it – but if it is anything which belongs to you I should like to have it [)]. I didn't get any large batch of verse – only 'Soliloquy' which I like very much.

My dear don't escape from Bude – everywhere is deadly now – and you have your job (as we all have) of looking after those who belong to you which I believe is the *first* thing to do (here endeth [the lesson])[1]

Have you heard anything from the Abinger Chronicle – the last number was so bad that I thought of giving it up – But then I thought 'No they'll say say it's because they haven't put in Ursula's poems' – Then they asked me to write something more – & I refused – but wondered afterwards if I ought to have said 'I will write for you on condition you put in something by Ursula' – But I did neither.[2]

Take care of yourself my dear & write a lot more beautiful poetry and keep your beauty – my goodness what wonderful things to possess – to have beauty & to be able to make beauty. The Nazis can't destroy that.

Love from
RVW

I've been re-reading 'Soliloquy' – I think it is beautiful – one or two things I am doubtful about

'Record, not guide, is all past history'

and

'masks all the world beyond a stage & decoration'[3]

RVW

[1] Michael Wood was at Bude in Oct. 1940 spending six weeks at a Radar unit; UW had accompanied him there.

[2] However, it is clear from a letter to UW not included in the present collection that the paper did eventually publish a poem of UW's alongside poems of Max Beerbohm and Robert Trevelyan.

[3] 'Soliloquy' was published in UW's collection of poems *No Other Choice* (Oxford, 1941), 45. The first line criticized by VW does not appear in the published version, but the second survived intact!

348. To Iris Lemare

4 October [1940]

From R. Vaughan Williams,
The White Gates,
Westcott Road,
Dorking.

Oct 4th

My dear Iris

There seem to be several shadowy schemes – but nothing seems to materialize.

(1) I believe the I.S.M. were setting up a scheme – about which Eames[1] consulted me – but nothing seems to have come of it yet.
(2) Then there is the ANSC or whatever it is called.[2]
(3) There is a grand scheme in the air for co-ordinating everybody & everything – but again it has not materialized.

But all these things will take some time to get going – so don't let your backer slip through your fingers too soon.

Why not try & organize some concert in *your district* with professional musicians from Newbury, Reading etc – that would avoid railway fares. Meanwhile you are lucky to be able to milk a cow – most of us can't even do that.

If your orchestra materializes in London I will try & arrange a concert for you in Dorking – But the difficulty, as you know, is

(1) Hall
(2) Police regulations

Don't talk about this 'wretched' war – it is wretched – but if we look on it merely as a bore we shan't push through with it – as we've *got* to do now unless we want to live perpetually in the state we are living now.

There were only 2 things to do

(1) Let Hitler have his way unchecked & hope he would hang himself with his own rope – this is what I believe Chamberlain wanted (the only true pacificism). But the so-called 'peace bloc' wanted war – & called Chamberlain traitor etc for wanting peace – Now we've got our war & we've got to see it through – & further decide what to do at the end of it.

I hope for a United States of Europe to which all nations (including Germans) who do not believe in force will belong. *Not* a *league* of sovereign nations – but a *Union* to which all nations will give up part of their sovereignty – preserving their individuality & nationality for their own affairs.[3]

Forgive this rigmarole – & give my love to Joyce & Gerald.

Yrs
Uncle Ralph[4]

[1] Frank Eames, General Secretary of the Incorporated Society of Musicians.

[2] This may be the same unidentified body as 'ATNS' which VW is groping for in no. 329. It was probably ENSA.

[3] An allusion to his enthusiasm for Federal Union. This paragraph seems to be the second of VW's '2 things to do'.

[4] Iris Lemare has provided a comment on this letter: 'This is obviously a very interesting letter – I have always wanted to ask someone who can decipher the handwriting *what* he felt about the war—but the letter was put away with the others. It was at the time of the "phoney war" – I had done farming in Cornwall until October when a 2nd hand was not needed. Back in London we were all asked to get out if we could. I went to Newbury to Gerald and Joyce. Nothing happened! I went back to London the night before the blitz started.'

349. To E. J. Dent

21 October [1940]

From R. Vaughan Williams,
The White Gates,
Westcott Road,
Dorking.

Oct 21

Dear Dent

Many thanks for your book.[1] I did not write before because I wanted to read it carefully more than once. It seems to me a very good practical guide for beginners. It seems to me however that you do (in common with all other writers on fugue except Gedalge[2]) not give enough attention to the *episode* which to my mind is the real value of fugue as a training – the power of *going on* and covering long stretches as Bach can do and not be merely perfunctory as Handel usually is (e.g. the episodes in 'He trusted in God').

Incidentally I wish you had mentioned Higgs' book which I think is one of the best – I know he commits the unpardonable sin of praising Bach and holding him up for a model.[3]

By the way you lay great stress on the emotional value of fugue – and then advise not to study Bach – and expect them to achieve the emotional side of fugue from those dull perfunctory affairs in Mozart's masses and the purely mechanical developments in Handel. – I admit that many of the 48 are not fugue except in name but what about Book I No I, Book II no II and the great E major.

You never suggest a way I believe in of taking say the E major and analysing it and writing a parallel fugue on the same model.

I am sorry you bow the knee to the fashionable 'denigreeing' of Bach – it is the old story – as soon as a great man becomes popular he is put on the Index Expurgatorius – & it is ridiculous to insinuate that he has been galvanised into life by the efforts of a few people – That will never make an unpopular man popular (e.g. the frantic efforts of certain people to boost e.g. Van Dieren[4] or Berlioz).

Incidentally do we really still call Mendelssohn 'respectable' & Brahms 'academic'? I thought all of them died in the 19th century.

Now, having said all the nasty things I can think of I end by saying that I shall certainly use your book as a basis for teaching fugue to beginners if I ever have to again (which Heaven forfend) & I hope every one else will do so – only as it is not published how are they to get hold of it?

Yrs
R. Vaughan Williams

[1] Dent had apparently sent VW the typescript of *Notes on Fugue for Beginners* (Cambridge, 1941); see the final paragraph.

[2] André Gédalge, whose *Traité de la fugue* (Paris, 1901) is described in *New Grove* (1980) as unsurpassed.

[3] James Higgs (1829–1902) taught harmony at the Royal College of Music from 1884 and later became Professor of Organ until his retirement in 1901. His book *Fugue* was published by Novello in 1878. Together with Sir Frederick Bridge he prepared an edition of Bach's organ works for the same firm which remained standard in Great Britain for many years.

[4] For a similar comment see no. 306.

350. To Adrian Boult at the BBC

26 October [1940[1]]

The White Gates,
Dorking.

Oct 26

Dear Adrian

Here is a suggestion for the patriotic song.[2] Please criticize it [as to]

(1) Its artistic merit if any
(2) Its popularity & singability

It *must* hit the nail on the head and be able to be picked up by ear – For that reason I made it as square as possible – possibly to the detriment once or twice of its quality – for example in my original sketch line 2 ran –

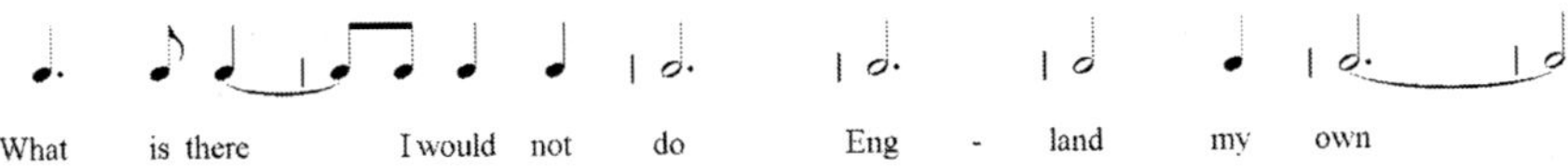

Again at line 5 I originally had

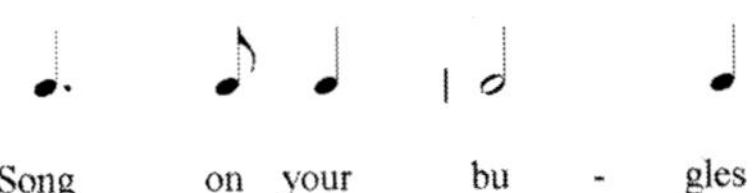

but this seemed to me to pull it out too much – On the other hand

is 'Song on your' too much of a gabble? In subsequent verses I have been obliged to make slight note alterations to fit the words but this is the case also in 'Jerusalem' which does not seem less singable on that account.

If you think this sketch is possible I would suggest the following arrangements of it

Verses 1 & 2 Baritone Solo with chorus coming in at 'England'

Verse 3 Harmonized chorus

Verse 4 Everybody in unison with a descant

But as an alternative unison chorus throughout.

Would you please pass this copy letter on to Walford for his criticism – I am also sending copies to Colles & Foss for suggestions – Gustav used to say that he always asked for advice but never took it. I always say to my pupils that there are 3 things to do with advice (1) to reject it blindly – this is bad. (2) to accept it blindly – this is worse. (3) to let it sink in and suggest a 3rd course – this is good.

Yrs
RVW

P.S. Show it to any one you like for further opinions – could not you get some of the more *un*musical of your staff together to try it out & see how well they picked it up.[3]

[1] Year taken from context. Also inserted above the date is the following note to Walford Davies from Boult: 'Dear Walford, This explains itself. I have acknowledged & criticised, & so you can (if you like) send it straight back to Ralph Yrs Adrian 30/10/40.'

[2] *England, My England* (*CW* 1941/1), commissioned by the BBC. See also no. 345.

[3] Printed in Moore, *Music and Friends*, 133–4.

351. To Imogen Holst

postmark: 31 October 1940

The White Gates,
Dorking.

Dearest Imogen

It was dear of you to write – we don't quite realize she has gone yet[1] – one keeps on thinking that she may come in any minute as of old – we old people would not mind going.

I read all about your work in the RCM Magazine – we've got to keep the musical flag flying – it is the only thing left us[2] – My only contribution at present is organizing quite low brow concerts for soldiers in Dorking!

By the way can you tell me anything about Nicolo Draber[3] (Flutist)? He has written to me asking me to help him get release. The only 'terms of reference' of my committee is 'musicians of eminent distinction who have made outstanding contributions to art'. Could N. Draber by any stretch of the imagination come under that category?

Will you give my Committee your candid opinion (in confidence of course)?

Much love from us both
Uncle Ralph

[1] Honorine Williamson, who had been killed in an air raid on 2 September.

[2] Imogen Holst, 'Rural Music', *R.C.M. Magazine*, 36/3 (Sept. 1940), 78–9. See no. 322.

[3] After leaving Berlin, where he had been a flautist with the Berlin Philharmonic Orchestra, Draber had gone to Moscow and eventually to England. He subsequently settled in Aldeburgh and changed his name to Nicholas Debenham (see the obituary in the *Aldeburgh Parish Magazine*, Sept. 1987).

352. To Ursula Wood

[about October 1940]

Dorking.

Sunday

My Dear

I never answered your last letter. I really have been rather busy – with internees & evacuees & low brow concerts for the troops!

How sad about the flat[1] – what memories. But there must be another flat and more memories.

I thank you so much for the Canadian documents.[2] I have written twice to Rosemary now – and had no answer yet.

The tall beauty still comes once a week for a 6^{d} stamp. She takes my advances in rather a perfunctory spirit 'All in the day's work' – still she doesn't reject them.

I wonder where and how you are – I am very well & the carrots and turnips flourish.

Love from
RVW

PS Müller-Hartmann is home again.[3]

[1] UW had sublet the flat in Thayer Street.
[2] VW had possibly been trying to arrange for a refugee to emigrate to Canada.
[3] On Robert Müller-Hartmann see no. 308 n. 1.

353. To Mary Glasgow[1]

2 November [1940[2]]

The White Gates,
Westcott Road,
Dorking.

Nov 2

Dear Miss Glasgow

Many thanks for your letter.

I have already had a talk with Mr. [Tom] Harrison and have written him a letter which I have asked him to pass on to you. I shall be happy to help all I can[3] – The difficulty at Dorking at present is a hall. I think we can get one of the cinemas for a Sunday afternoon. I am waiting to hear from the manager about it. I like the idea of an orchestral concert with a singer. Would December 15 be a possible date – or is that too short notice? Otherwise I think we should have to wait till after Xmas. My suggestion is that you sh[d] send down the orchestra, soloist etc – also bills & posters for distribution and we will secure a hall if possible & see to the local advertising & ticket selling. I am all for cheap seats & I personally would like to let the troops in free, but I believe that does not come into your scheme.

Yours sincerely,
R. Vaughan Williams

[1] Secretary-General of CEMA (Committee for the Encouragement of Music and the Arts).
[2] Year taken from context.
[3] CEMA was trying to provide music for Surrey, which had a high number of evacuees and troops stationed there during the winter of 1940.

354. To Percy Scholes

received: 7 December 1940

The White Gates,
Dorking.

Dear Scholes

I was very glad to get your letter – It carries me back to very early days when we used to meet in London – I didn't listen in the other night – I didn't dare to – Alas I find I can seldom listen to music. I find more & more that modern music means nothing to me – (I hope it means something to the younger generation – if so then it is all right—but does it?) And the older music reminds me too much of old far off unhappy things[1] – I liked the Purcell the other night & Haydn *passim* & Byrd in New College chapel – & the finale of the 9th Symphony tonight—which confirmed my opinion that the Finale is potentially the most magnificent of the 4 movements – That vulgar march with the drunken Welshman singing a Penillion to the tune is superb.[2]

Thank you very much for writing – it does one good to know that one's life has not been quite useless – though it seems so nowadays.

Yrs
R. Vaughan Williams

[1] An allusion to Wordsworth's *The Solitary Reaper*: 'Will no-one tell me what she sings? / Perhaps the plaintive numbers flow / for old, unhappy, far-off things, / and battles long ago.'

[2] In his essay 'Some Thoughts on Beethoven's Choral Symphony', written a year earlier in 1939 (but not published until 1953), VW writes of this passage in the symphony: 'Then, against the march tune, a man's voice is heard singing – probably a drunken soldier... He is without doubt a Welshman, for he is obviously singing a "Penillion" to the principal melody, though he probably has not obeyed all the rules for Penillion singing. Gradually his companions join in and the song culminates in a lusty shout.'

355. To E. J. Dent

13 December [1940[1]]

From R. Vaughan Williams,
The White Gates,
Westcott Road,
Dorking.

Dec 13

Dear Dent

We recommended Gellhorn[2] for release about 3 weeks ago. I have written to tell him so – But I do not in the least know whether any attention is paid to our recommendations – I am so sorry you have been ill again.

Yrs
R. Vaughan Williams

[1] Year assumed from the fact that Gellhorn took up his post at Sadler's Wells (see next note) in 1941.

[2] Peter Gellhorn, who had been Music Director at Toynbee Hall until 1939 and, following his release from internment, became Assistant Conductor at the Sadler's Wells Opera. See *IWWM*[12].

356. To the Director-General of the BBC

9 March [1941[1]]

From R. Vaughan Williams,
The White Gates,
Westcott Road,
Dorking.

March 9

Sir

I learn from the 'Times' of March 8 that the British Broadcasting Corporation has banned the musical compositions of Dr Alan Bush on account of his political opinions.

So far as I know Dr Bush's political views I am strongly opposed to them. Nevertheless I wish to protest against this victimization of private opinion in the only way possible to me. You may remember that the British Broadcasting Corporation has lately done me the honour to commission from me a choral song.[2] I now beg leave to withdraw my offer of this song to the British Broadcasting Corporation.

I return the fee which was paid me and ask you to give directions that all manuscript material of the song be returned to me. I will, of course, be responsible for the expenses incurred in its production.

I am sending copies of this letter to Sir Adrian Boult and to the 'Times'.

Yours faithfully
Ralph Vaughan Williams[3]

[1] The letter was noted on receipt: 'VERY URGENT B.M. D.S. will you pl. handle? F.C.O. 10/3.'

[2] *England, My England* (*CW* 1941/1).

[3] The greater part of the letter is printed in *RVW*, 239. The letter was acknowledged by 'MGF' on 14 Mar.: 'It was with deep regret that we received your letter of 9th March and the cheque for £21 which accompanied it. You will perhaps have seen in "The Times" today the B.B.C.'s statement on its attitude towards those who contribute to its programmes in war-time.' The statement is reproduced as no. 357 below.

357. BBC Public Statement

The Times, 14th March, 1941

B.B.C. AND FREEDOM OF EXPRESSION

ANTI-WAR AGITATORS ONLY BANNED

The B.B.C. issued last night the following statement on its attitude towards those who speak or perform in its programmes in war-time: –

The sole criterion is that no one is invited to the microphone who has taken part in public agitation against the national war effort. Beyond this one limit the Corporation is jealous to preserve British broadcasting as an instrument of freedom and democracy. The B.B.C. does not withhold invitations or engagements from persons because of their political views or because their views on the conduct of affairs do not coincide with those of the Government or of any particular political party. Controversy will be allowed, as it always has been, and critics will no doubt continue to protest every time a view they do not themselves happen to hold is heard at the microphone.

Broadcasting is a vital part of the war effort, and is used at home and overseas to urge the successful prosecution of the war. The B.B.C. believes it to be wrong that anyone living under the protection of the armed forces and benefiting from the sacrifices of the merchant navy should be free to express publicly opposition to the war effort and yet be allowed to share in the publicity and profits of broadcasting.

There has been over the People's Convention, as the Minister of Information stated in the House of Commons, some confusion. The B.B.C. is reviewing the matter and taking steps to ensure that there shall be no withholding of engagements unless it is quite clear that the persons concerned come within the category stated.

MISUSE OF B.B.C. TALKS

Mr Hely-Hutchinson is to ask the Minister of Information in the House of Commons: –

Whether he is aware of the injury to our united war effort arising out of the propagation on the British Broadcasting Corporation, in war-time, of highly controversial political doctrines which many men and women are unwilling to receive; whether he is aware of the growing misuse for this purpose of the religious talks, preceding the 8 a.m. news, by anonymous speakers claiming the support of high authority in the Churches for their views; and whether he will take power to control this abuse of public confidence.

358. To Myfanwy Jones[1]

31 March [1941]

From R. Vaughan Williams,
The White Gates,
Westcott Road,
Dorking.

March 31

My Dear Myfanwy

Of course I remember you well (I never forget a pretty face!) & I remember also very well our drive in the car & also an afternoon we spent together at Osborne Row when we made great friends I hope. It is very sweet of you to write to me about the BBC business – I've had letters of all sorts – but I like to have some nice ones.

I was much interested to hear of your activities – I wonder if we shall ever meet again in Newcastle – the last time was a rather riotous evening at Osborne Row after a concert.[2]

Have you heard that Steuart (and most of the other professors) have resigned from the Curtis as a protest against the dismissal of Randall Thompson & some show-fiddle put in his place.[3]

Love from
Uncle Ralph

[1] VW had met the recipient while staying with Steuart and Mary Wilson.

[2] A performance of *Five Tudor Portraits* conducted by VW on 29 Mar. 1939.

[3] Steuart Wilson, the English tenor, had been a teacher at the Curtis Institute of Music, Philadelphia, since 1939. The chief benefactor of the Institute, Mrs Bok, had taken against the Director, Randall Thompson, the American composer (see *New Grove*; he eventually became Professor at Harvard) because of some of the reforms he had introduced. Thompson had reportedly carried his resignation in his pocket at all times so as to forestall Mrs Bok in dismissing him. She had also withdrawn support from Steuart Wilson, whose pupils were all informed that they must re-audition for the Institute. The 'show-fiddle' was Ephraim Zimbalist, whom Mrs Bok married shortly after this episode. R. O. Morris had briefly been Professor of Composition at the Curtis Institute.

359. To Ursula Wood

[8 April 1941[1]]

My Dear

What a lovely poem – I will wait till the last minute for a fine day (Middleton's[2] advice).

But today I dropped 400 potatoes into holes under directions of the gardener – & shall do the rest tomorrow.

I actually listened in to part II of Matt: Pass yesterday afternoon!

Love from
RVW

Another lovely card with the little man sowing!

[1] Note in UW's hand.
[2] C. H. Middleton gave gardening talks on the BBC Home Service on Sunday afternoons. He launched the 'Dig for Victory' campaign.

360. To Gerald Finzi

postmark: 11 May 1941

The White Gates

Sunday

Dear Gerald

Your distressing news about poor Robin[1] is most heart breaking – certainly the only thing for him is to get right away from associations.

I daresay you saw in the Times that Emmie (Mrs R.O.[2]) died last week – she had been ill for a long time & we expected it for some weeks.

I think R O will live on here.

Love from Adeline and myself to both of you

Yrs
RVW

[1] Robin Milford's young son Barnaby had been run over and killed by a car just outside his house.
[2] i.e. Adeline's elder sister Emmeline, wife of R. O. Morris.

361. To Lord Kennet[1]

20 May 1941

From R. Vaughan Williams,
The White Gates,
Westcott Road,
Dorking.

May 20th, 1941.

Dear Kennet,

I apologise for the delay in answering – you sent your letter to my cousin Roland[2] – it was forwarded twice to him and then on to me. Also I wanted to think the whole thing over, which took some time. I fear my letter has developed into an essay – so I enclose [it] on separate sheets.

I am delighted if I can do anything to help your son – both for our old friendship and for his sake.

Yours sincerely
R. Vaughan Williams

I understand that when your son says he wants to go in for music he means first and foremost he wants to be a composer.

I presume he will have to earn his living; even if it is not absolutely necessary he will probably think it desirable.

Now composing 'serious' music is very seldom a paying proposition, at all events in the early stages of one's career.

Very few of the Great Masters earned their living by their compositions – Bach was a schoolmaster and organist – Beethoven lived partly by giving pianoforte lessons and partly by a pension – Schubert and Mozart lived in miserable poverty and died early – Wagner was a conductor at the Dresden Opera till he was about 30 and sponged on his friends for the rest of his life – Brahms was approaching middle age before he was able to give up concert playing etc.

It may sound very egotistical, but I think it may help you if I tell you a little about myself. I am now making a good income by my compositions, though they are not of the 'popular' order. But I did not achieve this until I was about 40 and it is quite precarious and may stop any minute. So except for the fact that I was born with a very small silver spoon in my mouth I could not financially afford to devote my whole time to composition – from the age from about 20 to 30 I supplemented my income by playing the organ (very badly) and teaching and lecturing.

The upshot seems to be that a composer of serious music must at the beginning of his career, at all events, have some other means of livelihood – either musical, in the technical, but alas, not often in the true sense of the word, or something outside music (1) He can be an executant but to be a performer nowadays demands a very high standard: an ordinary student at the Royal College can do technical feats which 50 years ago would have been considered the province of a virtuoso. It is rather late at the age of 17 to start acquiring the necessary co-ordination of muscle and brain to achieve this. So I think the chances are against his being able to achieve sufficient professional skill as a performer. There are, of course, exceptions – Pugno,[3] I believe, started his professional career at 40 but he was already a skilled amateur pianist. A wind instrument, I think, is more possible but I do not know that to be an orchestral trombonist is an attractive career. (2) A School job – This requires more general musical knowledge and less special virtuosity, but the music master at a Public School is usually expected to be a competent organist. In a job like this I think that a general educational background like the history tripos would be a help. (3) He might become one of the young men at the B.B.C., but again unless he has special qualifications as conductor or performer it is rather a dim job. One young friend of mine started as a conductor at a provincial B.B.C. He was very musical but I think not sufficiently technically skilled and now, as far as I can make out he is acting as a sort of superior messenger boy at the B.B.C.

The snag about all musical jobs is that they involve a lot of unmusical work. On the one hand you do not get right away from music in your working hours as you would do if you were a solicitor or a scientist. You have to spend a lot of time playing and conducting music you hate, teaching unwilling and unmusical pupils etc. This leaves you just as little leisure for real music as being in an office but, unlike being in an office, you have 'music' of a sort in your mind and in your ears all day long: therefore you do not come fresh when the work is over to the music which is in your soul. People of very strong character can fight against this – Gustav Holst for some years earned his living as a trombone player in a dance band dressed up as a 'blue Hungarian', but it was a desperate struggle.

There is much then to be said for earning your living outside music and being a 'spare time' composer. On the other hand it is essential for a composer to be in touch with practical music – playing in an orchestra – singing in a chorus – conducting and teaching – doing all the odd jobs of arranging, orchestrating etc. by which composers eke out their livelihood, all this helps the composer keep the necessary proportion between the world of facts and the world of dreams – Wagner I am sure would not have achieved his mastery over the orchestra if he had not been for some years conductor of the Dresden Opera, Brahms would have obtained a surer touch if he had not refused the post of conductor at Düsseldorf (?) – Delius would perhaps have had more backbone in his music if he had gone down into the arena and fought with beasts at Ephesus instead of living the life beautiful in a villa in France.[4]

On the whole – but with many doubts I vote for history – your son says that music will take up his whole time. By this I guess he means composing music.

Now my advice to young composers is 'don't'. I know by personal experience that the young composer thinks that what he is writing is what the world is waiting for – and I should not think much of him unless he did think so – but he also thinks that it must be done here and now and that tomorrow will be too late – not realizing that if he studies and learns now the masterpiece will come later – and that at the age of 17 he has got all his life before him.

I think it was Smetana who as a young man realized this and set to work on his intensive study of the Great Masters. This study, it seems to me, can to a certain extent, be combined with History lectures. Let him not despise the humble counterpoint exercise – not necessarily with a master. Let him one day look at a bit of Palestrina and try and write something if only a dozen bars that sound more or less like it. Let him look at the Bach Inventions and then experiment in what we call 'bad Bach'. He should always have a miniature score in his pocket and look at it in trains and buses and hear as much music as possible. All this – it seems to me – can be spare time work.

Your son raises the question of where to study after the war and queries Leipsig [*sic*]. I do not know the answer with regard to executive music though I believe that except for virtuoso training here is as good as anywhere and Heaven forfend that any one should go to Germany and learn to make a noise like German Oboists, Clarionetists and Horn players. However I do feel pretty certain that creative work must grow out of its native soil. My opinion is that the elements of composition can be taught better in this country, partly because less pedantically than abroad. I think it most important that the young composer should mature himself and find his direction in his own surroundings – then when he knows his own mind is the time to go to foreign countries and compare fresh views, to broaden his outlook and fructify his inspiration. Perhaps taking a sort of finishing course with some good foreign teacher, always remembering the attitude of Foreign to English musicians is unsympathetic self-opinionated and pedantic. They believe that their tradition is the only one (this is especially true of the Viennese) and that anything that is not in accordance with that tradition is 'wrong' and arises from insular ignorance.

Almost all the British composers who have achieved anything have studied at home and only gone abroad when they were mature – Elgar, Holst, Parry, Bax, Walton. Stanford is an exception, but he was by no means a beginner when he went to study abroad and as a matter of fact never quite recovered from Leipsig. On the other hand I have known many young musicians with a genuine native invention who have gone to Germany or France in their most impressionable years and have come back speaking a musical language which can only be described as broken French or German. They have had their native qualities swamped and never recovered their personality.

This is especially true now when there is so much talk about 'new paths' in music. All these young composers do is pick up a few shibboleths of the new language without understanding it, whereas if they were first thoroughly grounded in their native culture they would be able to assimilate anything that was worth while in these supposed new ideas into their own organism.

I am much elated to find that so many young people with the public school tradition are finding that music is a possible means of self expression.

But we must remember – and you of course must know this as well or better than I do – that one cannot tell whether a boy of 17 has the creative impulse or not. At this stage they are bitten by music and naturally they burn to 'do it too'. They write out pages of Sibelius, Hindemith or Delius and imagine they are composing. This is an inevitable stage in artistic development, even among the great artists – sometimes the personality emerges, sometime it does not – sometimes the flicker of invention disappears when they eat of the fruit of the tree of knowledge – so we must be prepared for disappointments.[5]

[1] Edward Hilton Young, 1st Baron Kennet (1879–1960), was a Privy Councillor, a writer, and a businessman. His son Wayland Hilton Young (b. 1923) did not follow a career in music but, following wartime service in the Royal Navy, pursued a career as a politician.

[2] Roland, son of VW's uncle, Sir Roland Vaughan Williams.

[3] Raoul Pugno (1852–1914), French pianist. He resumed a concert career in 1893 having been organist and later choirmaster of the Paris church of St Eugène-Ste Cécile for twenty years.

[4] 1 Cor. 15: 32: 'If after the manner of men I have fought with beasts at Ephesus, what advantageth it me, if the dead rise not? Let us eat and drink; for to morrow we die.'

[5] Printed in full in *RVW*, 240–3.

362. To Hubert Foss at OUP

13 June [1941]

The White Gates,
Dorking.

June 13

Dear Foss

I think you had better deal with enclosed – if you do not mind – Walford asked me to write these a long time ago – & I had quite forgotten about them. The fee seems very good as they are never more than ten bars long each. But in case the O.U.P. ever wished to publish then I suggest that we should get clear with the B.B.C. over publication rights

I think they had better send me a copy (or to you) as I have quite forgotten what they are like & I wrote them in a great hurry.[1]

By the way you have not sent me a copy of 'l'Alouette' yet.[2]

Yrs
R. Vaughan Williams

[1] The copyright section of the BBC had written to VW saying that they understood he had written nine Introits which they hoped to broadcast from time to time; that they had discovered that the PRS would not pay the royalties due on performances within religious services and therefore they proposed that they should pay an outright fee of 8 guineas each for the right to perform, record, and broadcast them whenever they desired. Walford Davies had been on the advisory staff of the BBC in 1927–39. The works were listed as:

All nations whom thou hast made shall come
Be strong all ye people of the land
I heard a voice from heaven saying unto me
Jesus said, Inasmuch as ye did unto me
Jesus said, Upon this rock will I build my church
Nations shall come to thy light
Jesus said, Blessed are they that mourn
There were great voices in Heaven saying
Thou wilt keep him in perfect peace

OUP wrote to the BBC on VW's behalf accepting the fee of 8 gns but reserving all rights other than that to broadcast in religious services and asking for a copy of each introit. These scores do not appear to have been ever sent nor have the original scores been discovered at the BBC. For VW's recollection of the whole matter see no. 548, a letter to Foss commenting on the work-list in his book on VW.

[2] VW planned to include the song in the film *49th Parallel* (*CW* 1940/3).

363. To Arnold Bax

[about June 1941]

The White Gates,
Dorking.

Dear Arnold

I had hoped to see you on Tuesday & to congratulate not indeed you but those who had the good sense [to] show publicly their appreciation of your work. I know that 'honours' mean little to you – but they are the only way of telling the world how your music is admired by your fellow countrymen including of course

Yrs
RVW[1]

[1] Written on Bax's appointment as Master of the King's Musick.

364. To Hubert Foss at OUP

3 August [?1941]

From R. Vaughan Williams,
The White Gates,
Westcott Road,
Dorking.

Aug 3rd

Dear Foss

Do come over one day – it would be nice to have a talk. Would M[rs] Foss come down too – that w[d] be a great pleasure. I thoroughly enjoyed my days at Denham – & am quite prepared to do another film provided (1) I like the subject (2) I get good money (3) I have a say as to when & how the music should come in – By the way I've had no money for 49th / /l yet – I forget when the 1st wodge of cash is due![1]

Yrs
R. Vaughan Williams

[1] The film *49th Parallel*, *CW* 1940/3, was first shown in Oct. 1941. On the stimulus provided by writing for films see *WVW*, 258 ff.

365. To Fritz Hart

14 August [1941]

From R. Vaughan Williams,
The White Gates,
Westcott Road,
Dorking.

Aug 14th

Dear Fritz

I was very glad to have news of you. We plug along here & are prepared for anything. My latest war work is to write music for a propaganda film.[1] Writing in seconds to the stop watch is rather fun & composing & *scoring* extra bars during the rehearsal interval (5 minutes).

My love to Marvell

I cannot read your address, I print mine.

Yrs
RVW

[1] See no. 364 n. 1.

366. To Frederick Page[1]

5 September [postmark: 1941]

From R. Vaughan Williams,
The White Gates,
Westcott Road,
Dorking.

Sep 5

Dear Page

Your letter has just arrived (3 months!). I was very glad to have it and to have news of you

We all keep cheerful and confident here – but realize that a lot of hard work has to be done & difficulties & danger met yet. N.Z. is doing bravely.

I am glad you are teaching – & you couldn't do better than with R.O.M.'s books[2] – he is a great man. He is now living with us since his wife died a few months ago. Give my love to Lilburne – & tell him he must try & combine farming and music.

Please give a message to the 'Harmonic'[3] that I hope they will do the B minor.[4]

The great difficulty is the high trumpet parts – I always *double* these by clarinets which steadies their notes (the clarinets are also useful for thickening Bach's oboe & flute part which do not balance with the large modern chorus & orchestra).

If you have only the ordinary B♭ trumpets I should give the trumpet parts as they stand to clarinets (including an E♭ or D clar) (doubled if possible) & make a faked part for the 3 trumpets. But I daresay you know all this already.

Yrs
R. Vaughan Williams

P.S. You say nothing about your *own* compositions. I should like to hear favourable news of them.

RVW

[1] New Zealand pupil of VW at the RCM 1935–7 and at the time of this letter a teacher in the music department of Canterbury University College (later Canterbury University), New Zealand. He went on to be lecturer and then Professor of Music at Victoria University College (later Victoria University of Wellington).

[2] R. O. Morris.

[3] The Harmonic Society in Christchurch, New Zealand, which favoured Bach works. See J. M. Thomson (ed.), *The Oxford History of New Zealand Music* (Oxford and Auckland, 1991), 106–7.

[4] J. S. Bach's Mass in B minor.

367. To Hubert Foss at OUP

12 September [1941]

From R. Vaughan Williams,
The White Gates,
Westcott Road,
Dorking.

Sep 12

Dear Foss

I have received a letter from Dennis Van Thal[1] suggesting he should act as my agent in film music & asks for an interview.

I have been and am perfectly happy with you as my 'agent' in these matters and am very grateful for all you have done & am perfectly content to let things remain as they are. So unless *you* think it a good plan I will not go on to negotiations with him.

Or w^{d} it be a good plan for *you* to represent me with him, or at all events be present at our interviews.

I will not answer him till I hear from you & get your advice.

Yrs
R. Vaughan Williams

P.S. I am waiting to acknowledge the cheque for 49th//1 till I hear from you I can acknowledge it as a final settlement.
P.S. I always meant to go for Tovey about his dictum that great masters never have to get out of holes because they never get into them. The great masters are *always* getting into holes – it is the Saint Saens & Goldmarks & Stanfords who keep out of holes.

1 Of Christopher Mann Ltd, a firm of artist's agents.

368. To Ursula Wood [postmark: 16 October 1941]

Thursday

My Dear

I am spending the day in bed as the cold has aggrandized – not bad but I thought this would be the quickest way of getting back to normal – I have a lot to do Saturday & Sunday – I have been reading through the Gardener's Calendar[1] again. I think it is lovely – it reminds me of Virgil sometimes. I like October v. much & I see metrical experiments in November. March is v. good. I quite disagree with May! What I like about it all is that the poetry grows out of real knowledge.

It's great fun you [are] going to be [at] Shiffolds[2] – Bessy is very intelligent & cultivated but quite homely in her domestic methods. I feel sure they don't dress for dinner if that is what you were wondering.

Make Bob show you Leith Hill Place.

Love from
RVW

1 Written by UW for RVW.
2 Shiffolds was the house of R. C. Trevelyan and his wife, Bessy. See no. 324.

369. To Hubert Foss[1]

6 November [1941]

The White Gates

Nov 6

Dear Foss

This is sad news indeed – how shall we get on without you? I did not realize how much I counted on you – 'Ask Foss' advice' – 'Ask Foss to see to it' or 'I'll ask Foss to play it over to me at Amen House' – But perhaps it is not all over as regards all that – and any way it is a selfish and material way of looking at things – and I ought to think only of how grateful we all are for all you have done for music (and incidentally musicians; so many people who think they are doing a lot for music seem to forget that music is made by musicians). But you must have a glow of satisfaction when you think of Walton & Milford & Van Dieren – & if in the two latter cases (in the first (Milford) I think wrongly and the second (Van D) rightly) the horse has refused to drink – it is in spite of you not having merely led him to the water but positively shoved his nose in it.

As regards myself I know that I owe any success I have had more to you (except H.P.A.[2] who insisted on shoving the S.Symph down people's throats after it was a complete flop at Leeds) than to anyone.[3]

Well the next lot of people who get the advantage of your energy & insight will be lucky and though your official relations with music & musicians may cease I know that you will continue to keep a fatherly eye on even those of us who are really old enough to be *your* father.

I always admired the way in which you took an interest in even the humblest of music makings – choral competitions school music etc – realizing the profound truth that without that foundation the Elgars & Waltons can't exist.

Well good luck to you in any new ventures & congratulations to those who get you for a co-operator.

Yrs
R. Vaughan Williams

[1] Written on his resignation as head of the Music Department at the Oxford University Press, a post he had held since he had founded the Department in 1923. He had been VW's publisher from that date (though a few works appeared with other firms later, e.g. *Three Choral Hymns* with Curwen in 1930). This letter is printed in part in *RVW*, 244–5.

[2] Hugh Percy Allen; see no. 98 n. 1.

[3] The first performance of *A Sea Symphony* at Leeds had not been a flop by any means. Herbert Thompson described the performance as a 'wonderfully good one' and *The Times* critic reported that it had been warmly received (see *WVW*, 98–9).

370. To Myfanwy Jones[1]

30 November [1941]

From R. Vaughan Williams,
The White Gates,
Westcott Road,
Dorking.

Nov 30th

My dear Myfanwy

What splendid news. And how romantic to be engaged by cable. I wish you could also be married by cable – This long dreary waiting will be terrible for you both. But directly he comes home don't wait a moment.

Middle age creeps on even when you are as young as you are & passion declines – so take your love at its height and damn the consequences. Your Charles will be a lucky man to have such a sweet and pretty wife. But I expect you are lucky too because from what I know of your character you could not love anyone who was not first rate.

How abominably Steuart[2] has been treated. I fear he must be having a bad time – & must long to be back home – But he and Mary have great courage & I know he will pull through.

All my love
Uncle Ralph

[1] This letter is printed in part in *RVW*, 244.

[2] Steuart Wilson. VW is referring to his dismissal from the Curtis Institute of Music in Philadelphia. For an account of the episode see no. 358 n. 3.

371. To John Ireland

[about November 1941]

From R. Vaughan Williams,
The White Gates,
Westcott Road,
Dorking.

Dear John

Thank you for 'Sarnia'[1] – I think No 1 is beautiful and I liked the simplicity of No 2 so much – I hope you don't think it cheeky of me to say all this. No 3 I did not make so much of first time – partly because the pianistic brilliancy of it prevented my seeing the wood for the trees.

I used to feel the same with Elgar's Symphonies – the actual orchestral virtuosity prevented me seeing the music behind it – all my own fault as I realise now.

Yrs
RVW

[1] *Sarnia*, three pieces for piano, composed 1940–1 and deposited in the British Museum in Nov. 1941.

372. To Stanford Robinson at the BBC 5 December [1941]

From R. Vaughan Williams,
The White Gates,
Westcott Road,
Dorking.

Dec 5

Dear Stanford Robinson

I am sorry for my delay in writing to thank you & your colleagues for the P.K.[1] Many of my friends have told me how much they enjoyed the performance

My only criticism is that the singers took it all a little too seriously – I suppose they thought that a Mus. Doc. could not possibly intend to write light music.

Yrs
R. Vaughan Williams

[1] There had been a broadcast performance of *The Poisoned Kiss* (*CW* 1936/4).

373. To Gerald Finzi 10 December [postmark: 1941]

The White Gates,
Westcott Road,
Dorking.

Dec 10

Dear Gerald

Foss & A Richardson[1] have kindly promised to play on 2 pianos [a] sketch for a new symphony[2] to see if I like it well enough to go on with it. Your criticism w[d] be much valued, if you c[d] come. *Date* Tuesday (next) Dec 16 *Place* Trinity College (Mandeville Place) *Time* 3.30 p.m.[3]

Yrs
RVW

[1] Alan Richardson, later married to the oboist Janet Craxton.
[2] The Fifth Symphony. A number of piano sketches are preserved in the British Library (Add. MS 50427).
[3] VW apparently asked only Herbert Howells in addition to Gerald Finzi to this play-through.

374. To Michael Tippett

17 December [1941]

The White Gates,
Dorking.

Dec 17

Dear Tippett

Here is something for you to show which is the best I can do.

I will not argue with you about your pacifist scruples which I respect though I think they are all wrong.

But I *do* join issue with you in the idea that it is anyone's business at a time like this to sit apart from the world & create music until he is sure he has done all he can to preserve the world from destruction and helped to create a world where creative art will be a *possibility*.

If your house was on fire you would not ignore it & go on writing until you had helped to put it out and saved the inmates – if for no other reason because if your music paper was burnt you would not be able to go on composing.

There is a great danger of our spiritual music paper being burnt – we must save it *now* so that creative art may flourish later.

This does not apply, of course, to using one's craft for a definite useful purpose (e.g. arranging Xmas carols for the troops in Iceland which I did the other day[1]).

I certainly can't feel that peace of mind which is necessary for composing until I have done all the little jobs which I believe will help us out of our present terrible dilemma (too few, alas, for me with my advanced years and circumstances[2]).

I remember when I was a small boy reading a story of a saint who vowed to spend so many hours a day in solitary meditation. One day the calls of kindness & charity & distress were so insistent that she failed to keep the appointed number of hours – But she realised that in spite of that her vow had been kept.

Another point – you are not the only composer in this predicament. What about Rubbra & Finzi & Bush who have all temporarily given up their creative work & gone on to various kinds of 'war-work'. If you are to be exempted so as to carry on your composition, why not they?

However wrong & dreadful we think war (and we all do) – here it is & we can't blink it – & surely we can all do a little bit to try & bring it to an end.

Yrs
RVW

[1] Twelve carols, of which nine were published as *Nine Carols for Male Voices*, *CW* 1942/4. The arrangement had been completed in Nov. 1941 (see no. 382), a fact which provides a date for the present letter.

[2] The circumstances were largely that Adeline was crippled with arthritis and VW didn't like to be away from home for very long at a time.

375. To RVW from Robert Longman

21 December 1941

35, Lansdowne Road,
London, W.11.

21.12.41

My dear Ralph,

'When he understood it, he called for his friends'. Though at the time I did not know it, I feel that Dorothy did understand & I thank God that you came to her on that Wednesday, 3 days before she 'passed over'; from that evening until the end it was too late for she knew no one.[1]

It was you and Fanny[2] that she most wished to see & both of you came.

She wd: wish for no better memorial than 'Valiant for Truth'[3] & when Marriott[4] (who will not play it to me until she has learned it) has played it this particular copy will go with certain letters which I keep.

I always hoped that Dorothy might have some memorial like this & my wish is fulfilled; thank you, dear old friend, from the bottom of my heart.

May you all at White Gates have all that is possible at this Christmastide.

Yours
R.G.L.

[1] The phrases in quotation marks are taken from Bunyan's text, which VW used in the motet.

[2] Frances Farrer (later Dame), for many years secretary of the Leith Hill Musical Festival.

[3] The motet was written as a memorial to Dorothy Longman, who had died on 1 June 1940. *CW* 1940/2.

[4] Marriott Longman, the writer's daughter.

376. To Adine O'Neill

28 December 1941

From R. Vaughan Williams,
The White Gates,
Westcott Road,
Dorking.

Dec 28 1941

Dear Mrs O'Neill

The professional musicians of Dorking and district have instigated a series of 'Informal hours of music' on Wednesday afternoons. The admission is 1/- and the room holds about 150. The performers just pocket the 'takings' large or small as the case may be (less 10% for overhead expense). Up to the present we have had 3 very successful concerts and are encouraged to go on in the new year – would you honour us by playing at one of them? Either a whole programme or sharing it with a singer or violinist – I suggest the date Wednesday March 4 at 3.0 p.m. White House Assembly Room Dorking – the programme to last about an hour.

If you graciously concur, I have yet another request to make – we want composers as well as performers represented – There is living in Dorking a distinguished German composer, Robert Müller-Hartmann – He has written some short pfte pieces which I am told are very good – would you play a short group of these? (about 10 minutes)

As regards the instrument, we have been lent a very good Blüthner – not a full concert grand, but what I think is called a drawing room grand. Murdoch[1] has played on it and pronounces it satisfactory.

I wish we could see you here one day and talk over old times, but communication is so difficult nowadays.

With [wishes for] as much happiness as is possible for the new year.

Yrs
R. Vaughan Williams

[1] The Australian pianist William Murdoch (1888–1942), who lived nearby at Holmbury St Mary.

377. To the editor, *Civil Liberty*

31 December 1941

Draft

From R. Vaughan Williams,
The White Gates,
Westcott Road,
Dorking.

Dec 31 1941

~~Dear~~ Sir

I have lately received vol 5 of so called 'Civil Liberty' – I resent strongly your 'stop press' resolution about Greece – You might at least have waited till the full facts were revealed by Churchill – we ~~nearly lost~~ risked losing the war in early days by sending to the aid of Greece troops which were badly needed in Africa. We have fed ~~them~~ the Greeks, we have driven out the Germans – we have put in our troops to protect the decent citizens & true democrats against some ruffians who have not the decency to wait till the war is over to put their 'views' forward in an orderly manner – If this is 'civil liberty' heaven defend us from it.

I propose as an amendment to your resolution the following

(1) That the government be censured for allowing Mr Churchill to waste his time & risk his life for a people utterly unworthy of him.
(2) That the British troops be withdrawn & leave the Greeks to the tender mercies of the Germans – they will then probably learn what 'civil liberty' means.

Unless your present 'resolution' is withdrawn I shall feel it my duty to resign from your association & find some other body which will protect civil liberties in reality.

Yrs fai
R. Vaughan Williams

378. To Stanford Robinson at the BBC

4 January [1942[1]]

The White Gates,
Dorking.

Jan. 4th

Dear Stanford Robinson,

Many thanks for your letter.[2]

I wish you could find me a first class librettist. The really good playwriters won't write libretti. I recoil with horror from the hack librettist however much he may know about stage business. (Have you ever read in cold blood, the libretto of 'Merrie England'[3]?)

Three of my operas have at all events good libretti

(1) Sir John in Love
(2) Riders to the Sea
(3) The Shepherds[4]

Yours
R. Vaughan Williams

[1] Year taken from stamp of receipt.

[2] The letter may have been connected with broadcast performances of *Hugh the Drover* (*CW* 1924/2), which took place the following May.

[3] The comic opera by Edward German.

[4] The libretto of *Sir John in Love*, *CW* 1928/3, was drawn from Shakespeare; *Riders to the Sea*, *CW* 1936/6, was a setting of the play by J. M. Synge; The text of *The Shepherds of the Delectable Mountains* (*CW* 1922/6) was taken from John Bunyan's *The Pilgrim's Progress*. It is significant that VW did not include *Hugh the Drover* (librettist: Harold Child) or *The Poisoned Kiss* (librettist: Evelyn Sharp) in this list.

379. To George Parker[1]

11 January 1942

The White Gates,
Dorking.

Jan 11 1942

Dear Parker

I am delighted to hear from Miss Cullen[2] that you will kindly sing for us at Dorking March 21 & 28.

We make several cuts.

Your numbers will be

28 'The Saviour'
29 Gladly would I
63 (choral) 1st verse – solo 4[tet]
74 At evening
75 Make me clean (1st part only)
77 & Now the Lord

Would you also take the parts of Judas, Peter, High Priest, Pilate etc.

Miss Cullen tells me that you would rather have taken the *Christus* (we have engaged Cranmer for that[3]). To my view the bass solos are equally important (and I believe actually longer than the Christus part).

Would you, however, like to try an experiment?

March 21 Christus Cranmer, solos Parker
March 28 Christus Parker, solos Cranmer!

If you would like this and Cranmer has no objection I should be quite willing.

Thank you once again

Yours sincerely
R. Vaughan Williams

[1] George Parker, a baritone, sang in the Dorking performances of the St Matthew Passion on a number of occasions. He knew a number of composers of the period such as Moeran, Ireland, etc.

[2] Margery Cullen, Honorary Secretary of LHMF 1939–64.

[3] Arthur Cranmer; see *RVW*, 246.

380. To George Parker

26 January [1942]

The White Gates,
Dorking.

Jan 26

Dear Parker

(I think we need not M[r] and D[r] each other any more)

On mature thought I think it better to stick to the original plan & for you to sing the arias on *both* occasions.

I hope I shall have the pleasure of hearing you take the Christus part on some other occasion.

Yours sincerely
R. Vaughan Williams

P.S. I am shortly sending you a 'cut' copy which will show you exactly what we are doing.

381. To George Parker

[January 1942]

Dear Parker

Many thanks for your letter – I have been trying to find the ideal 'Christus' & as yet have failed – that is why I am trying a different singer each year – each has his points but none satisfy me.

Yours sincerely
R. Vaughan Williams

382. Memorandum from Norman Peterkin to Humphrey Milford[1]

24 April 1942

Sir Humphrey S. Milford.

April 24th 1942

VAUGHAN WILLIAMS

I had hoped to see him round about Easter but he expressed a wish to leave it until after the 18th of month.

He phoned me last Monday to ask could he come and see me next day as he wished to lodge some MSS with us and could also discuss other matters. This I thought typical of him for a Walton would either march in without warning in advance or simply phone to say he was on the way.

Vaughan Williams spent some considerable time with me, looking more like an Ancient Briton than ever, but perceptibly aged since I met him last. This would be well before the Foss business of last July though of course I have frequently talked with him on phone.

I do not think Foss's departure has made any difference at all to Vaughan Williams' feelings about the O.U.P. or his relations with us. I am sure he has not the least intention of going to any other publisher, even if he were approached, which I gather has not been the case. Indeed he assured me of this himself. This too is borne out by the fact that on several occasions he has referred B.B.C and other bodies, and also conductors to me in matters connected with his works, unpublished and published, and told them they must secure necessary permissions from me.

Naturally Foss was mentioned and V.W. said he had written to him a very nice letter at the time of his resignation; and that he had been extremely sorry over what had happened, but that he supposed Foss would be sure to get a good permanent job.

To my complete astonishment he remarked that he had always thought the partnership (his word) of Foss and myself in the Music Department as the ideal one; of me as the elder brother and steadying influence, and what a great pity the partnership had come to an end. I share the view, but was surprised for I had no idea that V.W. had ever given a thought to my existence or function in the department, or that he had any inkling that I had some share in building it up.

From remarks he dropped he undoubtedly had been given the impression that we would not be publishing, or scarcely at all, till the war was over. This came out when I mentioned that I had just sent him the first proofs of his arrangement of Meyerbeer's 'Blessing of the Swords' (a work accepted by Foss) and said I was sorry it had taken so long to get them through. He at once expressed surprise and said he had taken it for granted we would not be getting it out at all and that it would have to wait.

I assured him we would continue to get out what was possible within the limits imposed on all publishers by the paper quota and the manufacturing difficulties, and that there certainly was no change in the policy of the department.

He left with me for safe keeping various works in MS, saying he did not want to consider their publication as yet, and I notice that most of them are marked 'for revision'.

Concerto for Oboe and Strings (not performed to my knowledge)[2]
Epithalamium–Ballet–Edmund Spenser (the spelling is that of V.W. not mine)
Double Trio for Strings. (performed about 2 years ago)
The Lake in the Mountains (Piano Solo)[3]

He also told me the score of an unfinished symphony was in Foss's hands and that he was asking him to send it on to me.[4]

I think this must be the work that Foss mentioned to me some time after his resignation, and about which for some obscure reason he was most mysterious. Foss said V.W. did not want its existence known (he would not tell me the name of it); but that V.W. earlier on had asked him to arrange to run through a piano duet version of it before a few personal friends. Foss said he would try and get me invited to the hearing! When later I referred to the matter Foss maintained his secretive attitude and I do not know if the hearing ever came off.

V.W. mentioned also a 'Hymn for Airmen' he had done and asked had it been sent to me. He said Sir Hugh Allen had wanted to have it saying he would approach the O.U.P. about publishing it. V.W. rather dryly said that seemed hardly necessary, but as Allen had asked and I had heard nothing of it he said he expected to get it back from Allen and would send it in to me.

On my side I raised the question of now doing something with his 'Household Music – Three Preludes on Welsh Airs'. This is music so written as to be playable by String Quartet or any other alternative wind or brass instruments available. This fairly recent work was of course known to Foss but was not available for publication, since following his usual custom V.W. likes to get performances first, put aside and revise before printing.

It was written for the Blech String Quartet and they have given several performances and broadcast it. Now the Griller Quartet, probably the finest English group, are to do it at a Boosey-Hawkes Concert on June 1st and it is again to be broadcast. It has been excellently reviewed and we have had very many inquiries for it. It is not a big work and I suggested to V.W. that we should try and print the score but produce the parts for both strings and alternative wind by lithographic process as we could save using paper from our quota by this means, as we have the special paper needed and have just secured further supplies as it is non quota material.

V.W. remarked that Foss always produced beautiful scores but did not pay sufficient attention to the parts which in his view were more important, and that he would rather see good engraved parts got out. It is true that some of our lithographed parts are deplorable, but when I showed V.W. the parts done in the opalograph machine by Mr Negus for the Rathaus String Quartet he agreed they were excellent, and is quite ready to leave matter[s] to me. It may be possible to do both Score and Parts by this method and I am to go into this and will bring it before you in due course.

The other work I was holding is a set of 10 or 12 carols – chiefly from the Oxford Carol Book – arranged by V.W. for male voice chorus at the request of the British Council for performance by H.M. Forces in Iceland.

When this cropped up first last November, V.W. left the business end of the matter in my hands and I fixed things with the British Council reserving all rights to the composer and O.U.P.

The Council have recently returned the MS to me after the Iceland performance and are most anxious to have printed copies from us. I told Miss Henn Collins we would certainly try and put them into print in good time for next season, and I intended to discuss first with V.W. then place [the] matter before you. V.W. is keen himself on getting them out and has taken the MS for final look through.

There is not any doubt in my mind that both 'Household Music' and the Male Voice Carols will do well and be bread and butter Vaughan Williams for the O.U.P.

In conclusion I think Vaughan Williams was pleased with our talk, and he certainly was most pleasant to me. Whilst he was with me Walton arrived at Soho Square, as usual not having warned me. The Show Room girls told him I was engaged with V.W. and reported later that Walton remarked 'I suppose the old buffer is going to monopolise him all morning'. He then sent through a message that he would come back in half an hour to see me.

He had apparently been waiting a few minutes when I took V.W. out. I left them talking together and afterwards heard that when V.W. learned Walton had been waiting to see me apologised to him for keeping me engaged. According to the girls V.W. was far nicer to W, than W was to him, and W is not considered to be a gentleman I gather!

Walton came into my room remarking 'well the old pussy cat has gone at last'. I suppose I must have shown some astonishment for he went on to say that 'of course V.W. was a really big pussy with very sharp claws', and was 'the biggest intriguer of the lot'; that it was astonishing how nobody realised it (except W.W. apparently) and how he managed to get away with it as a result.

I simply cannot comment on this for it runs completely counter to my conception of V.W. But I have seen but little of him.

N.P.

[1] Publisher to the University.

[2] *CW* 1944/1. The fact that the concerto was ready as early as 1942 may imply that it was written rather earlier than Kennedy indicates in *WVW*, 285.

[3] *CW* 1947/4, an arrangement of music written for an episode in *49th Parallel*, eventually published in 1947.

[4] The Fifth Symphony, *CW* 1943/2.

383. To Harold Child

18 May [1942]

The White Gates,
Dorking.

May 18

Dear Harold

Here is the 49th //l tune with a nonsense verse attached to show the metre and suggested rhyme scheme.[1]

To fit the time we want something rather high falutin' 'noble & sentimental' – like about Canada or Unity of Nations ('Parliament of man the federation of the world') – I suggest 3 verses – I do hope you will feel like it – It might be a popular success.[2]

Yrs
RVW

1 2 3 4 1 2 3 & 4 123
1 4/4 Now I have | made a beast-ly | tune, A

4 <u>123</u> 2 3
2 4/4 You'll | 3/2 probably hate it |. B

12 3 4 1 2 3 & 4 123
3 4/4 May be t'will | prove a pre-cious | boon A

4 1 2 3
4 4/4 To | 3/2 you and me | C

1 2 3 4 1 2 3 & 4 123
5 4/4 When the fat | cheques keep moun-ting | up D

4 1 and a 2
6 4/4 We'll | 3/2 dine and sup D

3 1 23 4 1 2&3 4 1 2 3
7 3/2 And | 4/4 bless that whose | fate it was to | earn so soon A

4 12 34 1234 °
8 4/4 Such | £. s. | d.°

[1] i.e. The *49th Parallel*. Harold Child had been asked to write a song to music adapted from the Prelude. He wrote 'The New Commonwealth'. See *CW* 1940/3/3.

[2] The words were as follows:

See where the beacon fires of Faith
  Fling glory to guide us.
There lies man's upward way o'er death,
  O'er hate and fear.
Trust we the light that burns so dear,
  And lift our eyes
Whose Faith sees what heavenly host of great allies
  March on beside us.

Hope we have won from our despair
  And joy out of pining.
Fast anchored safe in waters fair
  We've lain at rest.
Hark from afar on wider quest
  Life calls us now.
Then up anchor, spread the sails
    and point the prow
  Where hope is shining.

384. To Beryl Lock[1]

27 June [1942[2]]

From R. Vaughan Williams,
The White Gates,
Westcott Road,
Dorking.

June 27

Dear Mrs Lock

I hope you will forgive my writing to you – I want your help & first let me introduce myself as a friend of your daughters Ursula & Rosemary.

There is a refugee lady in Dorking (Austrian) Mrs Sternbach – Her husband is a scientist in Toronto and is earning a good living but, as you know he cannot send any money to his wife here. Up to a short time ago she was earning her living as a domestic servant to keep herself & her daughter aged 16, but some months ago she broke her leg & is now only able to do light work & is therefore very badly off. As she says herself her husband is 'moving heaven & Earth' to get her to Canada, but she tells me that the Canadian authorities will not allow this. Do you think you could see your way to help her? or advise me about any steps I could take? His name and address is

Dr Karl Sternbach
University of Toronto
(Dept of Hygiene)

Her address would be

Mrs Sternbach
at The White Gates
Dorking.

Again forgive me for troubling you & believe how grateful I should be if you could help.

Yours sincerely
R. Vaughan Williams

[1] Mother of UW. Her husband, Major-General Robert Lock CB, was working in the Ministry of Supply in Ottawa and in a position to help with problems over interned musicians. See *RVW*, 237.

[2] The date may be wrong because VW does not mention Michael Wood's death on 8 June 1942.

385. BBC internal memorandum from K. A. Wright, BBC Music Department

29 June 1942

29th June, 1942.

As you know, Vaughan Williams will be 70 on the 12th October, and the Home Service plans a week's celebration – one programme each evening, ending on the Saturday with a broadcast of the Celebration Concert by the Royal Philharmonic Society. How are you planning to reflect this on the Red Network? Would it be convenient for us to change the 'Music of Britain' ('Homespun', Scotland) into a Vaughan Williams concert, which we could easily do. My only feeling is that the occasion calls for a half hour in all services, rather than merely a quarter.

If it comes back to 'Music of Britain' I suggest that we think of Vaughan Williams not so much as a composer, as a quarter hour can carry very little which is representative of his wide range, but rather as a great personality in believing in and helping to develop the music of the people, whether in his work for folk music, festivals, or writing music for homely choirs and bands. This is an angle that would have wide appeal in the Dominions.

K. A. Wright

386. To Eveline Reed

5 July [1942]

From R. Vaughan Williams,
The White Gates,
Westcott Road,
Dorking.

July 5

My Dear James[1]

You know I am thinking about you now with great love and sympathy.[2]

What a wonderful friend he was – all his great musicianship always at our disposal to help us in our difficulties – they are too many to tell – But may I just tell you one story – I was trying to conduct my 'Pastoral Symphony' – got stuck over a difficult bar – & Billy (who had played in Dorking[3] for 4 years) said 'last time you did it like this' – His great musicianship, his wonderful memory & his kind heartedness all in that short sentence.

All my love
Uncle Ralph

No answer of course.

[1] W. H. Reed's wife, Eveline Dreyfus, was 'known to her friends as "James"'; see Wulstan Atkins, *The Elgar–Atkins Friendship* (Newton Abbot, 1984), 206.

[2] The English violinist W. H. Reed (1876–1942) had died on 2 July. He was leader of the LSO from 1912 until 1935 and had become a close friend of Elgar, whom he advised on his Violin Concerto. He had been guest leader of the LHMF orchestra in their 1934 performance of *The Dream of Gerontius*.

[3] At the Leith Hill Musical Festival.

387. To Beryl Lock

14 July [1942]

The White Gates,
Dorking.

July 14

Dear Mrs Lock

Thank you very much for your letter – Ursula has been quite wonderful[1] – she has determined to make a new life for herself and not let the past take possession of her – and I believe that she will succeed. She has been down here twice now – the second time to help rest her bad toe – poor child – (I think it is mending well now) – she fitted in so wonderfully to our rather hugger-mugger household – & did not mind having to sleep on a sofa in our rather crowded house. I am so glad that Rosemary is here so that they can see each other.

You know that we shall love doing all we can to help her – & she has many other good friends – she has such a genius for making friends.

Yours sincerely
R. Vaughan Williams

[1] Michael Wood had died of a heart attack on Monday 8 June 1942. See *PR*, 114–15.

388. To Ursula Wood

[July 1942[1]]

My Dear

I write on this fine note paper out of economy!

I am so thankful your foot is getting better – I could not bear to think of your pretty foot all swollen[2] & I was afraid it might develop into something worse. But what a hard time you've had – Yes we will meet soon & drown our cares in beer.

I am pleased with the film music[3] on the whole – though it was all rather against the collar.[4] Of course I will take you to it my dear.

Is dill a sort of feathery plant? If so some of it is coming up.[5]

Hens do an average of 2 a day which I suppose is all one can expect. Today I've been spreading their droppings out in the sun to dry.

I've been reading Patmore[6] lately in a certain place – v good and each poem takes about the right time.

[No signature]

[1] Written on the reverse of a letter from Boosey & Hawkes dated 16 July 1942.

[2] UW had had a broken needle removed from her foot.

[3] UVW's note says *The Loves of Joanna Godden* (CW 1946/2) but *Coastal Command* (CW 1942/1) seems more likely for 1942. The film was to receive its premiere in October.

[4] A ploughing metaphor.

[5] UW had given the VWs some dill seeds.

[6] Coventry Patmore, the Victorian poet (1823–96).

389. To Norman Peterkin at OUP

9 August [1942]

The White Gates,
Dorking.

Aug 9th

Dear Peterkin

I was very much upset by all this trouble with Stainer & Bell – but we must not judge the rights and wrongs of the case because Howard was bad mannered.[1]

It seems to me that on 2 points we put ourselves in the wrong:–

(1) In not originally asking S & B for leave to include the 3 carols in my Iceland M.S.[2]
(2) In not finding out about the terms on which the O.C.B. obtained leave to print those carols.

My point of view is:–

(1) I owe a lot to Stainer & Bell who published big works of mine when I was comparatively unknown long before the O.U.P as music publishers existed.
(2) Howard has always been very friendly to me and has never shown any grudge against me for deserting him 1st for Curwen & then for O.U.P.
(3) The carols in their original arrangement *do* belong to them so it seems logical that they should have the male voice arrangement.

So I propose, as we agreed, over the telephone that we should omit the 2 (or 3) carols from the O.U.P. book.

Then comes the problem. Howard may say (and with some justification) 'Here are these carols already arranged – you cannot publish them elsewhere – why not with us?'

Am I to say 'no' – that would surely be a very 'dog in the manger' policy.

I think I must ask Sir Humphrey in this instance (supposing always Howard asks me for them) to let me off my 'gentleman's agreement' with him.

You say that O.U.P are my 'exclusive' publishers – but in this case it is not a new composition that Stainer & Bell would publish, but a rearrangement of a work which is clearly their property and could not anyhow be the exclusive property of the O.U.P. You may rest assured that I shall not *offer* these carols to Stainer & Bell – But supposing they *ask* for them I must be prepared with my answer. I should be glad if you would show this letter to Sir Humphrey.[3]

Yours sincerely
R. Vaughan Williams

[1] Peterkin had written on 21 July to Stainer & Bell asking for permission to include in OUP's proposed *Twelve Carols for Male Voices*, new male-voice versions of 'The truth from above', 'On Christmas night', and *Yorkshire Wassail*, the tunes originally published in 1919 by that firm in *Eight Traditional English Carols*, edited by VW (*CW* 1919/5) and later included, with Stainer & Bell's permission, in *The Oxford Book of Carols*. Ellis Howard, Managing Director of the firm, had refused permission and turned down a later proposal that they be published jointly by S&B and OUP.

[2] For an internal OUP report from Norman Peterkin to Sir Humphrey Milford about these carols, amongst other matters, see no. 382.

[3] In the end, it was agreed to omit the three carols in which Stainer & Bell had an interest and OUP proceeded to publish the set as *Nine Carols for Male Voices CW* 1942/4. The manuscripts of the three disputed carols were returned to VW.

390. To Ferdinand Rauter[1]

16 August [1942]

The White Gates,
Dorking.

Aug 16

Dear Dr Rauter

Your letter has opened up a great problem.

I find it difficult to state but I want as a preface that nothing contained in this letter affects my *personal* affection for my many Austrian friends; nor my admiration for their art.

The great thing which frightens me in the late peaceful invasion of this country by Austria is that it will entirely devour the tender little flower of our English culture. The Austrians have a great musical tradition, and they are apt to think that it is the *only* musical tradition and that everything which is *different* must be *wrong* or *ignorant*; they think moreover that they have a mission to impose their culture wherever they go as being the only one worth having.

Now this seems to me to be all *wrong*.

We cannot swallow the strong meat of your culture whole (even if we wished to) our stomachs are not strong enough – indigestion & finally artistic putrefaction would result.

To try and make England, musically, a dependency of Austria could kill all the musical initiative in this country – destroy all that is vital and substitute a mechanical imitation of your great art – which will have no vitality, no roots in the soil and no power to grow to full stature.

What do I suggest therefore? – We want your art and we want your help – Become Englishmen – try to assimilate our artistic ideals and then strengthen and fertilize them from your own incomparable art – But do not force a 'Little Austria' on England – keeping itself apart from the 'untouchables' and having its own musical life without any reference to the life going on around. This would not only be of no value to our country but would actually be a disservice – because people seeing this little body of musical aristocrats with their art perfected by generations of artistic endeavour would think that was the only art worth having and that they could reap without sowing by a mere mechanical imitation of Austrian music.

As you must already know from your sojourn in England that there is a tendency, clearly, among English people to take it that 'Schmidt' is musical – while Smith is *ipso facto* unmusical. You must not stand apart and say 'Schmidt is musical – you are not. Your only chance is to become musical Schmidts' – You must help Smith to realise that he *is* musical, help him to discover where his artistic nature lies hidden and to help it to grow to a full flower

Yours sincerely
R. Vaughan Williams

[1] An Austrian musician (1902–87) who had settled in London in the later 1930s. He had been interned and, in due course, released on the recommendation of VW's committee. He published a number of collections of folk songs in cooperation with the Icelandic singer Engel Lund, whose accompanist he was, and with Ursula Vaughan Williams. He founded the Anglo-Austrian Music Society and this letter was written in response to his invitation to VW to become its Patron. After the war he entered the field of music therapy and was awarded the Goldene Ehrenzeichen by the Austrian Chancellor in 1977. See *Österreicher in Exil: Großbritannien 1938–45. Eine Dokumentation* (Vienna, 1992), 449–52, etc.

391. To Reginald Thatcher at the BBC[1]

25 August 1942

The White Gates,
Dorking.

Ref: P/RST.

Aug: 25. 1942.

Dear Thatcher,

I think that you had better describe in more detail the 'special' programme which you propose before Mr Halliwell comes to see me: for if it is anything like some of the programmes about great men that I have heard on the wireless, I would rather not be connected with it.[2]

Yours sincerely,
R. Vaughan Williams

P.S. I am free Aug: 31 Sept: 1, 3, 4, but not Sept 2, or 5.

[1] Deputy Director of Music at the BBC.
[2] VW had been asked to participate in a radio programme concerning Gustav Holst.

392. BBC internal memorandum to Arthur Bliss from Adrian Boult

15 September 1942

BBC Internal Circulating Memo

From: Sir Adrian Boult
To: D. M.[1] (London)
Subject: Dr. Vaughan Williams – Anniversary Programmes
September 15th 1942

I know it is too late to do anything about it, but I venture to think that something a little more suitable might have been done for my Concert of October 13th in the Vaughan Williams' Week.

It is surely common knowledge that Harriet Cohen's performance of the Vaughan Williams Pianoforte Concerto caused it to be completely dropped since it was first performed. The work (very stupidly as it was *written* for Harriet Cohen) was laid out for a pianist of the Busoni calibre, and though she made a very valiant effort, she could get nowhere near the spirit of it or even the notes in many passages.

Frederick Grinke played 'The Lark Ascending' quite recently with us in the Studio, and we all agreed that the poor lark never left solid earth. Marie Wilson plays it infinitely better.

It is easy to be wise after the event, and I am continually saying that things must not be held up in an effort to consult me here in Bedford when I am out of reach, but in the one case the matter has been common property for 8 to 10 years, and in the other the performance was so recent that the reports must surely be fresh in the minds of a good many people – I know I myself wrote one to such an effect.

I am indeed sorry that the only contribution that I am making to the Vaughan Williams' Week with our own Orchestra should consist of these two works.

But I have really dictated this in order to repeat, what A.D.M.[2] has already in mind, my request to be allowed to do a number of the other big works during the autumn in the studio.[3]

A C Boult

[1] i.e. Director of Music, Arthur Bliss.

[2] The Assistant Director of Music, at this time Julian Herbage.

[3] Bliss replied on 16 Sept.: 'I am sorry that you have been landed with these two soloists on October 13th. During the illness of Herbage, I asked Hubert Foss to arrange the week's scheme; He suggested Grinke for 'The Lark Ascending', as he had just heard a fine performance by him. I am afraid it is too late to alter that as Grinke has been approached by Music Bookings Manager. With regard to Harriet Cohen, it was the special wish of Vaughan Williams himself that she should play his work if it were included, and Arnold Bax came to tell me, so I feel we can make no change there either. Of course you must have an opportunity of doing a large orchestral work of Vaughan Williams later. We will make a point of this. Congratulations on the magnificent playing of the orchestra last Sunday. I feel it is again nearing its pre-war form. Arthur Bliss.'

Boult returned to the fray on 13 Oct. 1942: 'Looking at it dispassionately do you not think you have treated me rather badly in this little matter of Vaughan Williams? I have of course got the "Pastoral Symphony" on a Wednesday, but otherwise I have been fobbed off with one inefficient soloist to-day; a provincial choir with two female choruses on Thursday; and absolutely nothing else. May I in all humility remind the great of the Music Department of the B.B.C. that "Job" is dedicated to me; that I conducted the first performance of the F minor Symphony; that I was intimately concerned with the first performance of "The Shepherds of the Delectable Mountains"; that "Sancta Civitas" is Vaughan Williams' favourite work; and that Tertis has urgently asked me to allow him to take part in a performance of "Flos Campi". A. C. Boult.'

393. To Hubert Foss

23 September [1942]

The White Gates
Dorking

Sept 23

Dear Hubert

I have lost a letter from you asking me I think to write out something to broadcast to the Dominions.

Here is a bit of hot air which I hope will do –

Music is the one thing which defies bombs and blitzes

Music is the one thing which binds together those who live at opposite ends of the globe

Music is the one thing which makes friends of those who have never met, and perhaps will never meet except through the power of the greatest of the arts.[1]

Yrs
RVW

[1] A message in connection with his 70th birthday celebrations—perhaps to be included in Foss's radio talk?

394. To Ferdinand Rauter

29 September 1942

The White Gates,
Dorking.

Received: 29. Sept 42

Dear D[r] Rauter

I thank you for your far-seeing and eloquent letter.[1]

I must explain that I thought it fair that you should know what my attitude was before I accepted the honour you do me – so that you might withdraw, if you wanted to, while there was still time.

I need hardly say that if there is any danger of the tradition which produced Haydn, Mozart & Schubert disappearing we must make every effort to preserve it.

So if my 'patronage' can be of any use to you please command me.

Yours sincerely
R. Vaughan Williams

[1] Rauter had replied to no. 390 on 26 Sept. that there was indeed some truth in the idea that Austrians tended to impose their culture on other countries. This was because of their failure to appreciate that other traditions had different cultural roots than their own and because of the lack of opportunities in Austria to hear English music. The proposed Anglo-Austrian Society was an attempt to correct the balance and also to organize and unite exiled Austrian musicians in the face of the present threat to old Austrian traditions at home. Inviting VW to be Patron was an expression of gratitude for his role in obtaining release for internees. See Cobbe, 'Vaughan Williams, Germany and the German Tradition', 94–8, where Rauter's letter is printed in full.

395. To Armstrong Gibbs

1 October [1942]

Dorking.

Oct 1st

Dear Armstrong

Your splendid letter revives many pleasant memories – If I have succeeded, when normally unhelpful, in helping you to realize yourself more and to achieve all the good things you have done then my 70 years will not have been altogether wasted.

But I wish I could have taught myself how to compose – I seem to get worse instead of better.[1]

Yrs
R. Vaughan Williams

[1] Gibbs had apparently sent a letter of good wishes to VW for his 70th birthday.

396. To Fritz Hart

11 October 1942

The White Gates,
Dorking.

Oct 11 1942

My dear Fritz

I am one behind in my letters.

We keep well – and at my advanced years I try to do one or two little things to help the war – but it is rather playing at it. As Hugh Allen said the other day 'our war work is forming *quorums*'. At all events for that one does not require a brain, only a behind.

I believe I sit on 10 committees now. Heaven knows what we do. I am so glad your music goes on – it['s] astonishing here how everyone *hungers* for music.

My love – & from both of us to you both.

Yrs
R. Vaughan Williams

397. To Gerald Finzi

13 October [postmark: 1942]

The White Gates
Dorking

Oct 13

Dear Gerald

The apple was much admired both for appearance, magnitude and taste – it fed 5000 & there are some broken pieces left.

Thank you very much for the Garlands[1] – I wish I could hear them on Sunday (perhaps I shall) – I feel certain about Fidele & Mistress mine – fairly sure of Come away and Greenwood Tree – not yet about Sylvia – but I shall go through her quietly. I feel very unhappy about the 6tet[2] – it sounded dreary & muddled – partly the room because I *didn't* feel that when I heard it rehearsed in a small room. But the more I hear my own stuff the more I dislike it – where I shall be at the end of the week I don't know – & I shan't have the courage not to listen.

My love to Joyce

Yrs
RVW

[1] *Let us Garlands Bring*, Op. 18, dedicated to VW. It had been first performed the day before at the National Gallery.

[2] The Double String Trio, *CW* 1938/5. The first performance of the revised version had been given at the same concert by the Menges Sextet. Howard Ferguson, who was present, bore out VW's concern. The work was withdrawn and eventually rewritten as the Partita for Double String Orchestra. See *CW*, p. 163.

398. To Harriet Cohen

postmark: 14 October 1942

The White Gates,
Dorking.

My Dearest Harriet

Thank you for your beautiful playing yesterday – I don't like the work – but that is a different question[1]

Thank you also for the telegram.

Love from
RVW

[1] Cohen had played VW's Piano Concerto at the BBC concert conducted by Adrian Boult (see no. 392).

399. To Herbert Howells

19 October [postmark: 1942]
Dorking

Oct 19

Dear Herbert

Thank you so much.

What I want to do now is to wipe the slate clean & try to learn how to compose music.

Do you think there is still time?

Yrs
RVW

400. To Hubert Foss

20 October [1942]
Dorking

Oct 20

Dear Hubert

Thank you both for your friendship & your good wishes.

Thank you also very much for all you have done for me anent the BBC. I listened to everything – though sometimes I wish I had had the courage not to – I think I get more & more incompetent as a composer. My later things seem to come off *much* worse than my earlier – so it is certainly time I retired.

Your extravagant praise alarmed me – & might cause the enemy to blaspheme – but thank you all the same, because I know you meant it.[1]

Yrs with much Gratitude
R. Vaughan Williams

[1] The BBC had asked Hubert Foss to organize the season of VW's major works to celebrate his 70th birthday (see *WVW*, 260), on account of Julian Herbage's illness. As part of it he gave a talk on VW and his music. VW alludes to 2 Sam. 12: 14: 'Howbeit because by this deed thou hast given great occasion to the enemies of the Lord to blaspheme . . .'.

401. To Benjamin Britten

22 October [1942]

Dorking

Oct 22

Dear Britten

Thank you very much for your kind good wishes.

Yours sincerely
R. Vaughan Williams

402. To John Tindall Robertson[1]

24 October [1942]

The White Gates,
Dorking.

Oct 24

My dear Tindall Robertson

But I must just say 'thank you' to my old companion of the Maresfield Hut for remembering my birthday – I often look back on those days with pleasure and largely because of the friends I made there – I wonder what has happened to them all – Do you remember the man next to me who every morning sang

'I often lie awake and think what an awful thing is work'

– But I am getting garrulous a clear sign of old age.[2]

Yrs
R. Vaughan Williams

[1] A cadet with VW at the Royal Garrison Artillery Cadet school at Maresfield and later at Bordon. See *RVW*, 127–8.

[2] The unheaded paper indicates a wartime birthday, probably VW's 70th. Tindall Robertson had presumably asked VW not to trouble to reply.

403. To Roger Quilter

24 October [1942]

Dorking

Oct 24

Dear Quilter

Thank you very much.

– I value it very much when my fellow craftsmen wish me well – because you know how things are done & must so often be amazed at my want of 'metier'.

In that in spite of this you find something to praise in my works gives me great pleasure – especially from one like you who have the whole craftsmanship of your exquisite art at your fingers ends.

Yrs sincerely
R. Vaughan Williams

404. To RVW from Steuart Wilson

9 November 1942

From Steuart Wilson,
23, Chepstow Villas,
W.11.

9 Nov. 1942

My dear Ralph

There can't be anyone else who has got so much out of you who could be so slow in writing to you on this anniversary year; don't put it down to any cause but laziness to get down to a pleasure.

I didn't hear the broadcast & I wasn't in London for the Nat. Gallery but I did hear the Albert Hall concert; and over the Sea Symphony I lived again the days of 1909, 10 & 11 when your music was the great excitement and stimulus of my life, it has never ceased to be that, but when I was young and 'exposed' to it for the first time the effect was naturally more than it could ever be in pure *excitement*; so I heard again the phrases 'Flaunt out visible as ever' and the old mysteries of 'Mocking Life', and the hard places & the glorious places all coming in together again to make me feel that it had been worth while to have been young while *that* music was young too and that *I* could not be so old while *it* was still so full of beans.

Dona Nobis still enthrals & I can hear it with the calmer appreciation of middle age! But do you know that you've left a more valuable thing to us of this generation than your music, and that's your personal character and your integrity and 'guts'. Your 'all this' won't mean anything in 100 years unless people can divine it in your music but it has meant everything to us, that we could admire without reserve a man who could write such music and who could stand like a rock when he wanted to. Perhaps I should have put my own rock facing a little differently some times, but what a thing it has been to have a rock in these days. That's the biggest service you have given to music in your generation – and in that respect we are all your pupils and should be your followers.[1] I can't judge whether music is immortal or not and I don't care. But I do know that character in music is immortal in its influence on people, and That Means You.

All the way through Sea Symphony I was haunted by Jim McInnes' voice – I don't think anyone will ever sing it so well again. And Agnes Nicholls – but I'm not so clear in my remembrance there.[2]

I have now to break it to you that I've joined the B.B.C. staff in a minor capacity with hopes of preferment. We haven't even got a hatchet left to bury now.[3]

Mary was with me too & sends her love and excitement at the music. We couldn't burst our way through the ranks on Saturday & salute you – it looked like a Wedding Reception.

Yrs
Steuart – Mary

[1] This paragraph to this point was printed in *RVW*, 252.
[2] Campbell McInnes, as principal baritone at the Leeds Musical Festival that year, had sung the baritone part in the first performance of *A Sea Symphony* in 1910 and again in the first London performance on 4 Feb. 1913, when the soprano soloist was Agnes Nicholls.
[3] This is an allusion to the fact that Adrian Boult, Conductor of the BBC Orchestra and, until recently, Director of Music at the BBC, was married to Ann, Steuart Wilson's first wife.

405. To Gerald Finzi

postmark: 12 December 1942

Dear Gerald

I am thoroughly ashamed of myself. I was waiting to thank you for the music till I had been able to go through it again.[1] – But I haven't had time (Gustav used to say that really busy people never say they haven't time, so I can't be really busy). The truth is that I am 'with Film' (as E. N.[2] w^{d} say) once more – the gestation period of a film composer seems more like a cat than a human.

Yrs
RVW

[1] *Let us Garlands Bring*.
[2] Ernest Newman, the music critic.

406. To Herbert Howells

17 December 1942[1]

The White Gates,
Dorking.

Dear Herbert

Ruth Dyson & her 4^{tet} played your pfte 4^{tet} today – I heard it I am ashamed to say for the first time. It is *most beautiful* – Gerald[2] & others had often told me about it & said how good it was but I had fought shy of it – I don't like pfte 4^{tets} usually & thought this w^{d} be the same – But I feel this is *all* that

I should have liked to have done & have never succeeded in doing. – When you people who know your job *do* get the right sow by the ear by Jove you *do* get it – but some how I believe your very competence somehow prevents you often perceiving which the right sow is and leaves it to us bunglers to get hold of it by accident. But when you *do* get hold (of it?) you get it by the right ear all right while we so often get it by the *wrong* ear.

I daresay you are annoyed at having the 'sins of your youth' praised – I feel the same when people single out the 'Sea Symphony' or rather I feel that perhaps all the rest of my life has been wasted – perhaps it is true of both of us & we have never got back the 'first careless rapture' of our early works – but you have this advantage that you already knew your job in 1918.[3]

Yrs
RVW.

[1] Date provided on a transcript in the hand of UW.
[2] Gerald Finzi.
[3] Howells's Piano Quartet was written in 1916.

407. To Robert Lock

14 January [1943]

From R. Vaughan Williams,
The White Gates,
Westcott Road,
Dorking.

January 14

Dear General Lock

Thank you very much for your kind letter. Forgive my delay in answering, but we could not get Mrs Sternbach to make up her mind. She has now decided she would rather stay in England until her daughter has completed her school examinations in July.[1]

I am very sorry you have had all this trouble with so little result, but we are none the less grateful to you and Mrs Sternbach shares our gratitude.

I am so glad that we have been able to be of some help to Ursula in her trouble[2] – she has been wonderfully brave.

Yours sincerely
R. Vaughan Williams

[1] See no. 384.
[2] Michael Wood had died on 8 June 1942.

408. To Henry Wood

5 February 1943

From R. Vaughan Williams,
The White Gates,
Westcott Road,
Dorking.

Feb 5 1943

Dear Wood

I have come to the conclusion that my new Symphony[1] must now go forward 'for better, for worse' – So would you like me to send it to you & see if you would like to do it (The orchestration may want a little revision (I am taking it to Gordon Jacob for that purpose, as usual)).

It plays about 35 minutes – & though not technically difficult will I am sure want a good deal of rehearsal to make it 'come off' – so perhaps for that reason if for no other, you may not think it suitable.

I am delighted that you approve of Gundry's[2] Suite.

Yours sincerely
R. Vaughan Williams

[1] Symphony No. 5 in D.

[2] Inglis Gundry, a pupil of VW; see no. 318 n. 3. The suite referred to is *Heyday Freedom*.

409. To Henry Wood

9 February [1943]

The White Gates,
Dorking.

Feb 9

Dear Wood

I am honoured that you will put my symphony into your programme without seeing it! As regards conducting it – Of course I shall be pleased & proud if you did it – on the other hand if it w^{d} take a burden off your shoulders I will willingly do it myself & though no conductor I think I have sufficient experience not to let you down.[1]

Yours sincerely
R. Vaughan Williams

[1] In the event VW did conduct the work on 24 June as Wood was ill.

410. To Henry Wood

22 February [1943]

The White Gates,
Dorking.

Feb 22

Dear Wood

Many thanks for your letter of Feb 15.
'Symphony in D' is all I want by way of title.

Yours sincerely
R. Vaughan Williams

411. To Adrian Boult at the BBC

1 May 1943

From R. Vaughan Williams,
The White Gates,
Westcott Road,
Dorking.

May 1st 1943

Dear Adrian

You may remember that you adumbrated that you might be able to run through my symphony at Bedford some time before July – At last with great difficulty I have had the parts copied and they will be ready by next week – does your offer still hold good? – It seems curmudgeonly, but I had better tell you the days on which I am *not* free – any other day I would of course come with stones in my shoes if necessary – the *unfree* dates for me are

May 5, 7, 8, 9, 12, 15, 16
June 4,

By the way the orchestration is

2 Fl (Picc) 1 ob, 1 c. ang. (doubling 2nd oboe), 2 clar 2 fag
2 horns 2 Trt 3 Tro (*no* tuba) Timp strings

Yrs
RVW

412. To Gwen Beckett at the BBC

21 May 1943

The White Gates

Received: May 21st 1943

Dear Mrs Beckett

At the request of Sir Adrian I send you a list of those I am inviting to Maida Vale on May 25.[1]

Mr. Hubert Foss
Mr. Gerald Finzi
Dr. Howells
Mrs. Wood
Miss Farrer
Miss Stewart
Mrs. Curle
Mr. Bernard Brown
Miss Cullen
Miss Ivy Herbert
Mr. Eric Gritton
Mr. Gordon Jacob
Mr. Frank Howes
Miss Karpeles
Mr. Muir Matheson

Yours sincerely
R. Vaughan Williams

[1] For the play-through of Symphony No. 5 (*CW* 1943/2). The proposed list of guests is a good indication of those who were musically closest to VW at this time. Of those not previously encountered in these letters: Miss Stewart was Jean Stewart, viola player in the Menges Quartet; Margery Cullen and Ivy Herbert had performed an early play-through of the 5th Symphony on two pianos at Dorking (see *RVW* 253); and Muir Mathieson was at this time directing film music for the Ministry of Information.

413. To Elizabeth Maconchy

[7 June 1943]

Dearest Betty

– I thought the 4tet was *fine*

– I confess I got no idea of it looking at the score

– Yours is nearly the only 'wrong note' music I see any point in (Burkhardt is another[1])

– ~~it does not sound~~ yours does not sound *dreary* like most of it.

I think your notation in the 1st & last movements is all wrong – I think it shd be quavers & crotchets (or even semiquavers & quavers)[2]

much love
Uncle Ralph

P.S. I will send the score as soon as I can find an envelope big enough.

[1] For VW's championing of the music of Willy Burkhard, see no. 294.

[2] The letter is about Maconchy's String Quartet No. 4 and was written around 7 June 1943; it is referred to in a letter from Maconchy to Grace Williams of 6 July 1943.

414. To Sir Henry Wood

25 June [1943[1]]

From R. Vaughan Williams,
The White Gates,
Westcott Road,
Dorking.

June 25

Dear Wood

I cannot tell you how touched I was by your letter & how I felt about Lady Wood coming all the way to the Albert Hall to give it to me. But, you know, it was very wrong of you – you have to spend every ounce of your energy getting well quick to come back and feed your hungry sheep at the Albert Hall. The orchestra were splendid – and as I made no serious mistakes we had a very fine performance.

Yrs
R. Vaughan Williams

[1] The letter refers to the first performance of Symphony No. 5 in D Major, which had been conducted by VW himself on 24 June in the absence of Sir Henry Wood through illness.

415. From Adrian Boult

27 June 1943

Peaslake

27 June 1943

Dear Ralph

You may like to hear that one or two people thought it a lovely broadcast.[1] Everything seemed clear and well balanced, & I thought the orchestra played very finely: on the top of their form (which doesn't often happen nowadays). I thought too that first things seemed foremost all the time which is a quiet achievement in broadcasting & it must have reached most listeners faithfully. It isn't for me to judge compositions but Ann & I both feel that its serene loveliness is completely satisfying in these times & shows, as only music can, what we must work for when this madness is over.

I look forward to another performance & to the privilege of doing it myself sometime soon.

believe me,
Adrian

No answer of course

[1] Of the first performance of the Fifth Symphony.

416. To Mary Glasgow[1]

31 July [1943[2]]

The White Gates,
Dorking.

July 31
Confidential

Dear Miss Glasgow

Here is my promised cantankerous letter.

It concerns a letter which was sent in your name to Miss Sybil Eaton[3] and, presumably, to other of our travellers besides and Miss Eaton has given me full leave to comment on it.

You already know, of course, that she has sent in her resignation as a result of this letter. She was chiefly upset by the sentence 'The Council will not expect the Music Advisers to take very much part themselves as performers at Cema concerts'.

Miss Eaton considers and I think rightly that unless she can take part as performer in the scheme she is being reduced to the position of a mere concert agent.

I challenged Dr. Jacques[4] when I met him with the sentence and he told me that in her case 'it meant nothing'. But if it means nothing why write it?

The next sentence starting 'how far it will be possible' etc seems to suggest that those travellers who do not fit in with some new scheme, not yet clearly defined, will receive their Congé. Miss Eaton also tells me that she has had instructions that 'Cema concerts must be made to pay' and that in consequence the pioneer concerts in remote villages which obviously cannot pay and in which the services of the traveller as performer would be particularly valuable, must be discontinued. Unless Miss Eaton has also misunderstood this part of her instructions this policy seems to me to be drifting in the direction of 'window dressing' rather than of fostering art, and reducing CEMA to little more than a commercial concert agency. These symptoms may be unimportant in themselves and would not trouble me so much if they did not coincide with the policy which our new Chairman appears to me to advocate in all his pronouncements.

Yrs sincerely,
R. Vaughan Williams

[1] Secretary General of CEMA.
[2] Year taken from context.
[3] Violinist (b. 1897). She had been the first music traveller for CEMA and after this episode became a music traveller for the Rural Schools Music Association.
[4] Reginald Jacques (1894–1969), organist and conductor. He was first Director of CEMA.

417. To Fritz Hart

8 August [1943]

The White Gates,
Dorking.

Aug 8

Dear Fritz

I have taken a long time in answering your last letter. Also I have been reading your account of Gustav in the R.C.M. magazine which took me back so many years.[1]

You always have been faithful to Hurlstone.[2] I never could get hold of him till lately when I have been much struck by some music of his. (Of course I always knew that he had extreme dexterity – but I c[d] not see anything beyond). I agree with you that not only America but all the world ought to have a strong dose of 16th century music. I've been hearing some American music lately. I admired Copland but not Piston – also I loved Gershwins Pfte Concerto – just a series of intriguing tunes – but why not?[3]

Thank Marvell very much for her message – I send her a respectful embrace.

Yrs
RVW

[1] 'Early Memories of Gustav Holst', *RCM Magazine*, 39 (1943), 43–52, 84–9.
[2] William Hurlstone, a fellow pupil of Stanford at the RCM. His music had considerable success but he died in 1906.
[3] Aaron Copland (1900–90); Walter Piston (1894–1976); George Gershwin (1898–1937). His Piano Concerto dates from 1925.

418. To Mary Glasgow

15 August [1943[1]]

The White Gates,
Dorking.

Aug 15

Dear Miss Glasgow

Thank you for your helpful answer to my letter.[2]

We shall probably discuss these things at our September meeting.

Yrs sincerely
R. Vaughan Williams

[1] Year taken from context.
[2] See no. 416.

419. To Charles Moody[1]

17 September 1943

The White Gates,
Westcott Road,
Dorking.

17.9.43.

Dear Dr Moody,

It would be a terrible thing if the Cathedral tradition were to disappear, and I hope very much that you will win your fight with the Dean and Chapter.[2] These people do not seem to realise that music also has its nobilities and indecencies. I wonder what they would say if it was suggested that a chapter from a pornographic novel should be substituted for the first lesson? or that the Lord's Prayer should be rewritten in the style of American journalism? And yet they permit, and even encourage, such indecencies in music for the sake of 'bringing people to church'.

I admit, and I know that you agree, that the people should have a share in the service, but there is no more reason why they should join in the anthem and canticles than in the Absolution or the 'comfortable words'. And further I think the idea of a choir service is a noble one, where the people come only to listen and meditate. Would not a practical solution be to have a Choir Service every Sunday at 10am and 3pm, and a congregational service at 11am and 6pm?

We must beat this ecclesiastical totalitarianism somehow, but we can only do so by confining ourselves to what is really noble in our cathedral repertory. You know of course that many of our Canticles and Anthems are vicious, theatrical, mechanical or intolerably smug. Unless we can root those out of our services we shall give the enemy cause to blaspheme.[3]

Please make any use you like of this letter.

Yours sincerely
R. Vaughan Williams

[1] Organist of Ripon Cathedral 1902–1954.

[2] In a note to UVW (3 June 1959) Moody explained that, supported by the Royal College of Organists, he had been opposing the Dean and Chapter in the High Court. 'Ignoring the Cathedral statutes, they proposed to do away with settings of the Canticles on Sundays. I had no alternative but to fight them, & I am glad to say I had the backing of almost all leading musicians, and a good many dignitaries of the Church, my own bishop among them.'

[3] As in no. 400, an allusion to 2 Sam. 12: 14.

420. To the Revd John W. Welch at the BBC[1] [23 October 1943[2]]

The White Gates,
Dorking.

Dear Mr Welch

Only today (when your letter arrived) I was about to send you a revised version of the Victory Anthem[3] words – the same succession of ideas, and some of the same words – but more often rather less familiar words which have been set less often.

I have been carefully through your suggestions & will consider whether I sh[d] like to incorporate them.

The music is beginning to shape itself around the words as I send them to you.

We must be careful not to let the anthem develop into a *sermon* – that is the business of the preacher – not the singer.

As regards the spoken words (I propose to have other passages beside the Henry V spoken). My reason is purely practical – the sung words over the wireless are *never heard* unless they are well known – & I want to make sure that certain key passages in the anthem *are* heard.

Yrs sincerely
R. Vaughan Williams

Blessed art thou, O Lord God of our Fathers
Blessed is thy Holy and Glorious name
Blessed art thou in the temple of thy Holy Glory
Blessed art thou on the glorious throne of thy kingdom

Refrain (after each verse)
And to be praised and exalted above all for ever

O give thanks unto the Lord for he is gracious
and his mercy *endureth* for ever

(song of the 3 children)

O God thine arm was here
and not to us but to thine arm alone
ascribe we all
Take it O God for it is none but thine

(Henry V)

Thine O Lord is the greatness
and the power & the glory
Thine is the victory and the majesty
Thine is the Kingdom O Lord

(Chronicles)

The spirit of the Lord is upon me
Because the Lord hath anointed me

To proclaim liberty to the captives
And the opening of the prison to them that are bound
To comfort all that mourn
To give them beauty for aches
The oil of joy for mourning
The Garment of praise for the spirit of heaviness

(Isaiah chap 61)

Go through, go through the gates
Prepare ye the way of the people
Cast up, cast up the highway
Gather out the stones

Lift up a standard for the people
And they shall call them the holy people
The redeemed of the land
And thou shalt be called
'Sought out', a city not forsaken
(chap 62)

And they shall build up the old wastes
They shall raise up the former desolations
And shall repair the wasted cities
The desolations of many generations
Lift up thine eyes round about & see
They gather themselves together
They come to thee
Who are these that gather as a cloud?
And as doves to the window?
Surely the isles shall wait for
thee, and the ships, to bring
thy sons from afar.
They shall bring their gold and silver with them
Unto the name of thy Lord God
Because he hath glorified thee.
Violence shall be no more heard in thy land
Wasting nor destruction in thy borders
But thou shalt call thy walls salvation
and thy gates praise
The Lord shall be thy everlasting light
and the days of thy mourning shall be ended
(chap 60)[4]

[1] Director of Religious Broadcasting at the BBC. See *RVW*, 261.

[2] Note on original.

[3] *Thanksgiving for Victory*, renamed *A Song of Thanksgiving* in 1952, *CW* 1944/4. See *CW*, p. 187 ff.

[4] These passages from Scripture differ in some ways from both the Authorized Version and the work as published.

421. To Elizabeth Maconchy

20 December [?1943]

The White Gates,
Dorking.

Dec 20

Dearest Betty

Thank you & Billy for remembering me. It takes me back to old times & your lessons & I said 'Study Purcell or Bartok' & you chose Bartok.

All love
Uncle Ralph

422. From Jean Stewart

18 December 1943

7½ Thayer Street:
W.1.

18:XII:43

My beloved Uncle Ralph,

The shortest day and the longest night – so of course I write you a letter anyhow. Even if there were nothing special to say you would get a letter. This time there is something special to say & I don't know any more than I did on Sunday how to say it. You have made me so happy that I am walking on air. Without exaggeration this Quartet is the most lovely thing that has happened to me in my life, & it will continue to be a joy to me as long as I live. I am longing to get my teeth into it & for you to come & hear it with the Quartet, and then to work it & really get to know it. It's so lovely when you're learning something new how you rehearse it & something goes on inside you & it develops by thinking of it & sometimes even by sleeping on it!

Oh we are going to have a great time with 'my' Quartet bless you! Incidentally it has been lovely having it in instalments because I have had twice the thrill of getting it. When will you be in town with time to spare when we could have a session on the viola part (& all that ??). In case these are any use to you I am at present free during the day time on Jan. 1, 3, 5 & 7 (I am away from Thursday – back next Monday).[1]

Bless you & bless you & thank you & thank you. I wish I could tell you how deeply moved I feel and how happy.

All my love
Jean.

[1] VW had finally delivered to Jean Stewart, whom he had met through Ursula Wood, the third and fourth movements of the String Quartet No. 2 in A minor inscribed 'For Jean on her birthday' (*CW* 1944/2). The earlier movements had been given to Jean the previous February. The quartet was first performed on 12 Oct. 1944 at a National Gallery concert by the Menges Quartet in which Jean Stewart played the viola.

423. To Norman Peterkin at OUP

1 January 1944

The White Gates,
Dorking.

Jan 1/1944

Dear Peterkin

As usual the BBC are careless and ignorant.

As you say, the words in my Anthem are not from 'Recessional' but from 'Puck of Pooks Hill'. I took the words from the text as given in 'Songs of Praise' 488.[1]

I have omitted 2 or 3 verses –

It occurs to me that the people to apply for permission to use the words should be the BBC themselves. They have done me the honour to ask me to write an Anthem for the celebration of what will be, I suppose, one of the most important events in the history of the world. I can hardly imagine that Kipling's executors would face the public scandal of refusing a request by the Governors of the BBC to make use of his words on such an occasion.

If they insist on the whole poem being printed we can print the extra verses with the direction that they are not to be sung.

Would it be worth your while to find out on what terms the O.U.P were allowed to use the words for Songs of Praise.

Yours sincerely
R. Vaughan Williams

[1] *Thanksgiving for Victory*, later *A Song of Thanksgiving*, *CW* 1944/4.

424. To Vaughan Williams from Michael Tippett

[?January 1944]

Whitegates Cottage
Oxted

Sat

Dear V.W.

Goehr[1] was very touched by your speaking to him at the Committee in London some days ago (which I could not get to). He told me I was rather to blame in not having spoken to you at some time of the oratorio which he is to do in March for me.[2] The real reason is that I have been hanging on waiting for the printed vocal scores which have been held up at the printers, & one of which I want to send you. I expect they will be available any week now. Meanwhile I send you the letter press of the affair which will interest you I think. *If* you feel like coming to the performance you shall be put in what the LPO call the 'Royal Box'! I'll get Tom Russell to write you properly nearer the time.

I think its a work you will like – even the spirituals, I was going to say, are somehow brought within the tradition. The music is so direct & moving that one is not offended by the vernacular speech within it.

I have had no opportunity to thank you for all you said at Oxted in June[3] – & which I did not merit. I was rather unmanned the other day by what seemed to be the start of another official prosecution – but not only have I regained my small moral courage, but I gather it is not certain that the wheels will turn round to the end this time – or that we won't be able to bring pressure to stop them – it being not customary (tho legal) to re-imprison on my charge. For myself I am so sentimentally tied to the world's outcasts that I was quite at home among the 800 of them in the Scrubbs. A great sense of comradeship & a sweet tolerance overriding the general social tragedies. I was a general favourite of course – found myself even giving advice to a Welsh warder how to educate his little daughter to music! But nevertheless the experience is a deep-going one. I grieve for that strange community – & I grieve for all the coming nations of outcasts. It will need, in those of us who are sensitive, a tolerance, an understanding springing from depths 'too deep for taint' as Wilfred Owen put it during the last war[4] – & which did not obtain then. I know of no duty more binding on myself than this increase of understanding – I can well believe that voluntary prison is a way through for people like myself, meaning much more than the negative withdrawal from general acts which one cannot take part in, but a positive searching for that deep level from which even criminals are our brothers. I might remark that with some of the older ones, long-term married men & some of the soldiers who had destroyed human life & wondered at it, there were occasional moments of spiritual apprehension we shall never forget. The ways of God are very curious.

Kind regards

Yours sincerely
Michael Tippett

[1] Walter Goehr, conductor and father of the composer Alexander Goehr. See *New Grove*.

[2] *A Child of Our Time* was to be given its first performance on 19 March.

[3] Tippett had been sentenced to three months' imprisonment on grounds of his uncompromising stand as a conscientious objector in a hearing at Oxted Police Court in June 1943. VW had spoken in his support. See also no. 374.

[4] The phrase comes from Wilfred Owen's poem 'Strange meeting'.

425. To Elizabeth Maconchy

18 February [1944]
Dorking

Feb 18

Dearest Betty

You have been good to Jasper[1] – I will write to H.J.W.[2] when J. has sent his work in.

Now about you – I do feel it very bad that you do not get your stuff done – Have you anything *new* you could send in to the proms? If so let me know *at once* & I will write to H.J.W. at the same time as about Rooper – I have tried to persuade B.B.C. to do the Land again – but as usual they hedged.[3]

I fear we must confess that you are *not popular* – I know though theoretically that is a very noble aspiration practically, it is galling

But dearest Betty, you are still young – I was about 30 before I ever heard even a *song* of mine done in public – so your time may come – so push on and one day perhaps the key will turn in the lock.

I loved the photograph of Anna[4] – we must meet one day before she's too grown up.

My love to Billy & all you want for yourself

from
Uncle Ralph

[1] Jasper Rooper, a student of RVW and contemporary of Maconchy.

[2] Sir Henry Wood.

[3] RVW wrote to the BBC about Maconchy's suite of 1929, *The Land*, in Nov. 1943 and to Henry Wood; see no. 426.

[4] Maconchy's elder daughter.

426. To Henry Wood

25 February [1944]

The White Gates,
Dorking.

Feb 25

Dear Wood

You will hate me for worrying you – but I have just heard that another ex-pupil Elizabeth Maconchy has sent in a work for the Proms 'Puck Fair'. I do not know the work, but from what I *do* know of her I think it ought to be worth consideration.[1]

Could you find time to glance at it & see if it is likely to suit you?

Do not answer this please.

Yours sincerely
R. Vaughan Williams

[1] A ballet written in 1940 from which Maconchy made a suite which was first performed at the Proms by the BBC Symphony Orchestra under Adrian Boult on 5 Aug. 1944. The ballet as a whole was first performed in Ireland. See nos. 425 and 433. There is a note on the letter in Wood's hand: 'Already seen & included'.

427. To Henry Wood

29 March [1944]

From R. Vaughan Williams,
The White Gates,
Westcott Road,
Dorking.

March 29

Dear Wood

I am almost ashamed to be always worrying you – but that is the inevitably penalty of your kindness of heart.

This time it is about Jelly d'Aranyi.[1] It would, I am sure, give pleasure to her many friends and admirers if you could give her an appearance at the Promenade concerts or elsewhere. I believe that at one time – largely owing to family sorrows – her playing declined for a bit, but I understand that now she is playing as well as ever.[2]

What would give *me* the greatest pleasure would be to hear her and her sister, either in the Bach double concerto or in those delightful Spohr duets of which – so far as I know – they were the only exponents.

Yours sincerely
R. Vaughan Williams

P.S. On no account is this to be answered.

[1] Jelly d'Arányi (1895–1966), a great-niece of Joachim. She was the dedicatee of Bartók's two violin sonatas, Ravel's *Tzigane*, and VW's *Concerto Accademico* (*CW* 1925/7). She often played with her elder sister, Adila Fachiri. See also no. 246 n. 5.

[2] This letter was followed two days later by a formal joint letter to Wood signed by Sydney Cockerell, Lord Howard of Penrith, Neville and Sandra Lytton, Philip and Irene Noel-Baker, and Desmond MacCarthy asking for her to be given an engagement, which she was on 26 July. Wood's draft reply to VW remarks 'There is no doubt dear Jelly is a great artist – but the last time she appeared at a Promenade Concert the B.B.C. decided definitely it was her last – I agreed for there was not a note in tune and she seemed to have gone right off the rails. I believe now that she suffered horribly over [her brother-in-law] Fachiri's illness and death'.

428. To John Ireland

10 May [1944]

From R. Vaughan Williams,
The White Gates,
Westcott Road,
Dorking.

10th May

Dear John

I want to thank you for your beautiful work,[1] both for my self and the choir who loves and admires it – They were a little frightened at first, but soon realized that here was something whose idiom was theirs and which meant something especially to them. I think they sang it well – they certainly knew it.

We had, alas, only strings organ & timps. But Cole[2] did wonders on the organ, the strings were largely professional & all very good players – they tackled the difficulties gallantly. We spent 3 hours rehearsing them & finally they mastered it – only in one place the 2nds came unstuck for a few bars.

Yrs always
RVW

[1] *These Things Shall Be*, performed at Dorking in 1944.

[2] William Cole, who succeeded VW as Festival Conductor in 1954. Owing to the pitch of the organ, wind instruments could not be used and VW rescored works accordingly. See *And Choirs Singing*, 24.

429. To Douglas Lilburn

22 May [postmark: 1944]

The White Gates
Dorking

May 22

Dear Lilburn

I was very glad to get your long and interesting letter and to have news of you and especially to be able to thank you for the fine present which you and Page sent me a long time ago.

Your account of music in N.Z. is rather deplorable. I remember that about '38 when refugees began to leave Germany that the whole of the Berlin Philharmonic applied for leave to come in a body to N.Z. – my advice was unofficially asked & I was against it – I thought that if they went as a body they would remain a 'foreign body' & that a process of 'infiltration' was better – a few to fill up gaps & so gradually form a 'national' orchestra – But I fear I was wrong! However I hope now that they realize that having a real live composer among them they must have real live material for him to work on.

I heard your 'Aotearoa'[1] a little while ago – I did not quite get hold of it at first hearing but I see it is down on the BBC programme again this week & I hope I shall be able to hear it.

Inglis[2] is having a little success at last – he had a work done at the Proms last year and I *think* is down for another this year. He has had a hard and strenuous time in the Navy and deserves all the luck he can get.

I had forgotten that you were a friend of Tom Harrison[3] – I may be seeing him soon and will remind him of your existence.

Remember me to Page – they seem to have behaved disgracefully to him[4]

I am much interested to hear of the violin sonata – I hope we shall hear it over here one day

Yrs ever
R. Vaughan Williams

P.S. R. O. Morris sends his kind remembrances.

[1] An overture written by Lilburn in 1940. The title means 'Land of the long white cloud' – the Maori name for New Zealand.

[2] Inglis Gundry.

[3] Actor and producer, *inter alia*, of *The Abinger Pageant* in 1934, *England's Pleasant Land* in 1938, *Sir John in Love* at Birmingham in 1949 and at Stratford in 1951. He lived near Dorking.

[4] Frederick Page, having served as a temporary lecturer in Canterbury University College, had been passed over for a permanent appointment. See Page, *A Musician's Journal*, 79–80.

430. To Henry Wood

31 May [1944]

The White Gates,
Dorking.

May 31

Dear Wood

At last I am able to send you a fair copy of my oboe concerto.[1]

I am so sorry for the delay which is due (i) to the fact that when I had, as I thought, finished it I began to re-write it and (ii) my copyist fell ill in the middle.

It is most kind of you to be willing to conduct it. I hope you will receive the score from O.U.P. simultaneously with this.[2]

Yours sincerely
R. Vaughan Williams

[1] VW had offered his Oboe Concerto, CW 1944/1, to Henry Wood for the 1944 Proms season in the preceding January, but Wood initially turned it down on the grounds that it would not work in the Albert Hall. However, he later changed his mind since no other new VW work was available.

[2] On the letter Wood has drafted the substance of a reply: 'Many thanks. I am going to find much pleasure in doing this & hope you will be kind enough to run through it with me prior to rehearsal.' In fact the concerto was not done by Wood that season since the Proms were cancelled.

431. To Margaret Keynes[1]

3 June [postmark: 1944]

The White Gates,
Dorking.

June 3

Dear Margaret,

Thank you very much for your letter. I am glad you liked Leith Hill Place – but I think the old life there can never be relived – & it had better go – but I hope worthily of her.[2]

Hervey lent me your delightful life of Leonard & Mildred[3] – Thank you very much for it.

Yrs
R. Vaughan Williams

[1] A Darwin cousin, married to Geoffrey Keynes, and sister of Gwen Raverat.

[2] VW refers to his mother, who had lived at Leith Hill Place from the death of her husband until her own death in 1937. VW's brother Hervey had lived at Leith Hill Place since 1933 and, having inherited the house on Hervey's death, VW was offering it to the National Trust.

[3] Leonard Darwin (1856–1945), fourth son of Charles Darwin, who married as his second wife Mildred Massingberd (1868–1940).

432. To Elizabeth Trevelyan

1 August [1944]

The White Gates

August 1

Dear Bessie

I shall certainly stipulate – if and when the National Trust accept Leith Hill Place[1] – that the public shall have rights of access to the woods & some of the fields. Anyhow you & Bob and your friends must feel yourselves free to walk in the woods as you always have done.

The Kitchen Garden may go to keep up the estate – So it is up to me, and you as neighbours, to try and find a tenant who at the same time, is desirable and rich – Some form of community is possible, but I think I should prefer a private tenant as they are likely to be more human in their relations with the cottagers and workmen – and I want to keep up the great tradition in that respect set up by my Grandfather, my mother and Hervey himself.

The house will be let partly furnished – the valuable pictures, china and furniture will be gone, but there will remain a good lot of 'utility' stuff with the house – or may be let out to a market gardener which I think could be the best as it has great potentialities – but I want to make it quite clear that the National Trust have not definitely accepted it yet.

Yrs
Ralph

[1] The National Trust eventually accepted the house, with an endowment of £4,000, in a letter dated 15 Nov. 1944. By that time it had been agreed that the house would be let to VW's cousin Ralph Wedgwood.

433. To Elizabeth Maconchy

13 August [1944]

The White Gates,
Dorking.

Aug 13

Dearest Betty

I listened to Puck – & have been waiting to coordinate my ideas about it. – I feel I am going to like much of it – but I feel baffled at present – the atmosphere does not seem clear at present. I do not know whether you want it to be gay or sinister – at present it seems rather to fall between 2 stools. The Goat I definitely like straight away & the Lovers – the tinkers seems to me definitely too short and not to have time to say any thing – do make it into a larger piece. Evening seems to me not worthy of the rest in distinction of style.

But, dearest Betty, you know how impossible it is to judge of a brand new work absolutely on first hearing. So we want to hear it several times.[1]

All my love
Uncle Ralph

[1] The suite from Maconchy's ballet *Puck Fair* had been performed at the Proms on 5 Aug. 1944 by Boult and the BBC Orchestra. Puck Fair is a traditional event which takes place each year in Killorglin, Co. Kerry. Maconchy had grown up in Ireland and the full version of the ballet was first performed there. See no. 426.

434. To Kenneth Wright at the BBC

18 August [1944[1]]

The White Gates,
Dorking.

August 18

Dear Mr. Wright

I received the score of the 'Victory' Anthem yesterday Aug 17, enclosing a letter from Boult dated Aug 12![2]

It will save time if I send you my own copy of the score and I will keep your copy and correct it at my leisure for my own use. I hope to let you have it by Monday. I have had to make a good many revisions. You must remember that when I sent it to Arthur Bliss some months ago I asked him to go through it with Welch and see if it was suitable. He contented himself with a brief acknowledgement and some formula to the effect that 'they were proud to have it'. Since then I have been waiting for some further sign of life, but nothing happened till the other day when I had a telephone call from Boult asking me when I was going to send it!

This brings me to another point: On the title page I made certain demands as to what was required for the performance. I feel strongly that a historic occasion like this requires an imposing personel [*sic*] whatever the value of the music may be which the BBC have done me the honour to ask for.

I took it for granted that having stated my requirements and these not having been refused, that silence gave assent, but it now occurs to me that as the music was apparently put away unread these requests have never been brought to the notice of the officials. So I think I had better repeat what I asked for –

1. A soprano with a powerful dramatic voice but no wobble. (I should prefer Florence Austral).
2. A chorus of about 200. (The BBC professional chorus with their highly individualised voices would be entirely wrong except as part of a larger chorus.)
3. Chorus of 100 children (NB *not* choir boys).
4. Full symphony orchestra including 6 trumpets.
5. A large organ.
6. A speaker.

Please show this letter to Boult when he comes back – also to anyone else that you think ought to see it.

Yours sincerely
R. Vaughan Williams

1 Year taken from stamp of receipt.
2 *Thanksgiving for Victory* (*CW* 1944/4).

435. To Ursula Wood

19 August [1944[1]]

From R. Vaughan Williams,
The White Gates,
Westcott Road,
Dorking.

Aug 19th

Dear Ursula

Thank you for shewing me our film script – your part is excellent and often beautiful. But the whole is, to my mind, entirely spoilt by the additions made, I understand, by your colleague in which he seems deliberately to have distorted history to fit in with his political bias.[2]

I notice in particular four points:

(1) It is I believe contrary to the known facts to suggest that all the lords were devils and all the villeins angels.
(2) The account of the death of Wat Tyler is I think pure invention, manufactured so as to make it an act of treachery which it was not.
(3) There is, I feel sure, no justification for the suggestion Richard's famous 'I will be your leader' was a deliberate trick and not, as is generally supposed, the impulsive speech of a generous hearted boy, who was afterwards over persuaded by his counsellors who perhaps even acted without consulting him.
(4) The worst historical falsification to my mind is the scene where Richard leads a slaughtering party against the Peasants. This is I believe historically impossible even if it were not psychologically false.

Please, as a writer of repute, disassociate yourself absolutely from this attempt to back up a weak case by dishonest means.

Pick out your own excellent sections and offer them to some honest film-maker – the rest will I hope & believe go where it deserves, the waste paper basket.

Yrs
R. Vaughan Williams

[1] This letter is dated 1944 on the assumption that the question of a film on the Peasants' Revolt and Richard II was in the air following VW's completion of incidental music for a radio performance of *Richard II* (*CW* 1944/3) in the first part of the year, which in the end was not used.

[2] UVW does not mention this film project in *Paradise Remembered*.

436. To Alan Smith

19 August [1944]

From R. Vaughan Williams,
The White Gates,
Westcott Road,
Dorking.

August 19

Dear Mr Smith

I was much interested in your letter. I can imagine how hungry you must be for music 'out there'.[1] I wonder if the struggle between the 'classical' and the 'popular' music will ever be resolved – I sometimes feel that we must eventually find some kind of music which will satisfy both sides.

As regards my new symphony I suppose it's a good record – but records never satisfy me so I hope you will be able to hear it in 'real life' or even over the wireless before you hear the record.

I enclose a photograph – It's your own fault – you asked for it!

Yours sincerely
R. Vaughan Williams

[1] Alan Smith was on military service in Italy at the time.

437. To the Revd John W. Welch

8 September [1944]

From R. Vaughan Williams,
The White Gates,
Westcott Road,
Dorking.

Sept 8

Dear Dr Welch

I am glad to understand that you approve of the words of my Victory Anthem.[1]

May I venture to make one or two suggestions about the music for the rest of the Service? I hope we shall have 'O God our help' and 'All people' and I hope the Old Hundredth will be sung in its proper version with the long notes at the end of each line. I would not mention this but for the fact that at St Paul's Cathedral at a Thanksgiving service a few years ago the tune was sung in its square form – all minims. This caused me much dismay. Nor would I mention the matter of hymns at all to you, but for something that happened, I am sure without your sanction, on the day of our invasion of Normandy. The hymn chosen after the 7.55 am sermon on that day was not played through as usual but was sung with great pomp by a full choir and the hymn sung was 'Ein' feste Burg'![2] I could hardly believe my ears.

Yours sincerely
R. Vaughan Williams

[1] Sent to Welch on 23 Oct. 1943; see no. 420.

[2] The Lutheran hymn usually translated as 'A stronghold sure'.

438. To RVW from J. W. Welch at the BBC 12 September 1944

Please reply to:
Kingsley Hotel, Bushmead Avenue, Bedford.

12th September, 1944.

Dear Dr Vaughan Williams

Many thanks for your letter of September 8th. We are all very excited about the Victory Anthem[1] and much looking forward to assembling our musical resources for rehearsal and to making a record. We thought it best to make a record, in case victory came suddenly and we were unable to collect the children, the chorus and the orchestra at the same time – besides there may be occasions when we wish to broadcast the Anthem by itself if necessary. Our present intention is to have the first broadcast of the Victory Anthem in the Sunday morning service following Victory Day. I believe the Oxford Press has now printed copies, and I am looking forward to seeing one this week.

Thank you for your suggestions for the music in the rest of our services; we shall almost certainly have the *Old Hundredth* to 'All people that on earth do dwell' or to 'Before Jehovah's awful throne', and Thalben Ball or Leslie Woodgate will certainly have it sung to its proper version with the long notes at the end of each line. We shall also have 'O God, our help' to *St. Anne*.

If ever we meet I should very much like to have your mind on the whole question of our using German music in broadcast religious services. We do not, e.g. ever broadcast Haydn's *Austria*,[2] because listeners in occupied Europe, not knowing the English language, would be conscious only that we were broadcasting the old German national anthem; so my colleague Taylor has written a very good alternative tune called *Abbot's Leigh*. But I must confess that *Ein Feste Burg* seems rather different: it is essentially in Church history the hymn of believers in freedom struggling against tyranny, and when the Nazis dismissed the leading Norwegian pastor and put a quizling in charge of the Church, the congregation assembled outside the Cathedral with the dismissed pastor, and sang to the Nazis' dismay and anger *Ein Feste Burg* in Norwegian. What would you think, e.g., of our singing 'Now thank we all our God' on victory day? That comes from the same tradition of Church history, the Lutheran proclamation of freedom against what was thought to be the tyranny of the Roman Catholic Church. The B.B.C. in its broadcasts of orchestral music has not allowed the German origin of great music to weigh against our broadcasting it, and I am just wondering whether you think that in a religious service people's feelings are more sensitive and that we ought to feel 'all things are lawful, but all things are not expedient'. Our general impression is that the average listener doesn't know where tunes like *Ein Feste Burg* and *Nun Danket* come from, and the people who do know feel that great Church music is the possession of the whole Church and not of any one nation. Still, I must confess that I am puzzled about all this, and when next we meet I should be grateful for your views.

We have just finished a three-day meeting going through the B.B.C. hymn book, and I hope our suggestions of tunes will be ready to send to you in the early spring.

Yours sincerely,
Rev. J. W. Welch[3]

[1] *Thanksgiving for Victory* (CW 1944/4).

[2] Haydn's tune had been (and is again) the German and Austrian national anthem as well as the tune (called 'Austria') used for the popular hymn 'Glorious things of thee are spoken'. Cyril Taylor's 'Abbot's Leigh', written specifically to avoid the use of Haydn's tune in wartime, has remained a popular alternative to 'Austria' ever since.

[3] This letter was written in response to no. 437.

439. To Robert Müller-Hartmann

2 January 1945

From R. Vaughan Williams,
The White Gates,
Westcott Road,
Dorking.

Jan 2nd 1945

Dear Mr Muller Hartman

I do not know whether you would care to undertake a task which is chiefly copying – but involves a certain amount of scholarship. It is no less than to copy out the voice parts of Bach's Mass in B minor in the most correct edition available.

I have been preparing a version of the mass adapted to the English liturgy. – so in addition to all you would have to decipher my rough notes! – though this is not really so formidable since you would get the notes from the printed copy & as to the words you could check my hieroglyphics from a printed prayer book.

There is no hurry about the work as there is no chance of it being printed till after the war. I could lend you a B.G.[1] and a Novello copy corrected.

Would you care to undertake it? I suggest as a preliminary a fee of £50.0.0 – which could be adjusted later.

Yours sincerely
R. Vaughan Williams

[1] i.e. the Bach Gesellschaft edition.

440. To Alan Bush

10 January [1945]

The White Gates,
Dorking.
Tel 3055

Jan 10

Dear Mr Bush

I enclose a letter which you can send to any one you like except a Newspaper.

I don't think, if I did write to the 'Times' they would put it in.

If all the hard cases in the Army were the subject of letters to the Times there would be little else to read in that paper.[1]

Yours sincerely
R. Vaughan Williams

From R. Vaughan Williams,
The White Gates,
Westcott Road,
Dorking.

January 10 / 1945

Dear Sir

I venture to write to you about Private A. D. Bush R.A.M.C. I understand that in May P[te] Bush applied for admission to the Army Education Corps but that owing to some mistake for which he was not responsible, though he was accepted, his posting never went through.

I hear that he is now due to sail very shortly to a hospital in the Far East. As you doubtless know M[r] Bush is a distinguished musician and in my opinion he is wasting his time as a medical orderly whose duties he doubtless does quite well but not better than hundreds of others, while his services to Army Education would be most valuable. I believe that M[r] Bush has already lectured to H. M. Forces and he has been described by the Regional Committee for Education as the best musical lecturer on their panel.

I much hope, before it is too late, his services may still be secured for this very important work.

Yours faithfully
Ralph Vaughan Williams

[1] Bush had written to VW on 9 Jan. explaining his predicament over a posting and enclosing a draft letter which he asked VW to sign and send to *The Times*. The outcome is not fully clear from the papers. In his acknowledgement Bush undertook not to send the letter to any newspapers.

441. To Adrian Boult

7 February [1945]

The White Gates,
Westcott Road,
Dorking.

Feb 7

Dear Adrian

Thank you so much for your letter – I wish I c^{d} have heard the D Symph[1] on Sat – but I had my choir – Adeline listened & said it was fine & beautifully clear & all the Tempi just right.

I will make a note of the C.A.[2] & cello places when the proofs come in. I am rather upset by what P. Beard says about the string parts – I ought to have had them vetted before they were played the first time – but I thought they were all right. I wish he'd told us before – after all he's played it about 6 times & has never said a word to me!

I am writing to him to ask if he could mark a part with *constructive* suggestions – If so I will get the OUP to send him a V I Part.[3]

There is one part which worries me over a broadcast performance – that opening C (cello & bass) is all but inaudible – I think for *wireless* it ought to be mf or even start fp – But of course this would spoil a concert performance.

As regards Paddy[4] & the end – I have already lengthened it by several bars from the first sketch – & I don't feel I want any more – But perhaps a bigger rallentando & a longer final pause especially on the last 2 bars (where the inner parts all move for 1st two crotchets) w^{d} do the trick.[5]

Thank you so much for all you do for my music—you make it live.

Yrs
RVW

[1] The Fifth Symphony, *CW* 1943/2. The full score was published in 1946.
[2] Cor Anglais presumably.
[3] i.e. 1st violin.
[4] Patrick Hadley (1899–1973), English composer and pupil of VW who became Professor of Music at Cambridge in 1946, had apparently suggested that the ending of the symphony should be extended.
[5] The final bars in the published score are marked *Molto rit.* but the pause is only on the final bar.

442. To Eugene Kilinski[1]

25 February [postmark: 1945]

The White Gates,
Dorking.

Feb 25

Dear Mr Kilinski

At present I am very busy but perhaps one day I shall have the pleasure of meeting you – but I thought I ought to warn you that I never discuss my music with anyone but my most intimate friends.

With kind regards

Yours sincerely
R. Vaughan Williams

[1] A private in the 761st American Air Force Band. In 1963 he was Assistant Professor of Music at Western Reserve University, Cleveland, Ohio.

443. To Gerald Finzi

postmark: 13 March 1945

Dear Gerald

Thank you very much for Farewell to Arms.[1] But don't call it 'small beer' because it isn't & you know it isn't. If you did think so you ought not to have published it ~~but I know you dont & hope~~ But I hope you take a proper pride in your own work – which is quite a different thing from the modesty which sees the vast difference between the final result & what we all feel of our work it *might* have been – so don't *denigré* your own work.

My love to Joyce

Yrs
RVW

[1] For tenor and small orchestra, Op. 9.

444. To Cordelia Curle from AVW [9 May 1945]

Wednesday

Belov Boo

Dork[ing] behaved very sedately yesterday – The church bells pealed at intervals – now & then a megaphone brayed outside the Star – & in the evening there were searchlights & fire works & excited cries of children.[1]

I sat out under the lilac w^{h} still is full of scent & we had a young American for tea who has something to do with radio in the Azores. A nice lad. Morris[2] brought back news of London's thunderstorm – a house in Addison Road was struck – and what happened in Chelsea? We had no storm here.

How nice to have had Racy and Mungo. I shall I suppose hear something from Bob after tonight's supper at Ursula's – or of him from her.

Have you both – I mean Bernard & you – any plans for weekend – you ought to hear our 2 challenging cuckoos – or is the tumult in London too fascinating to leave?

I wonder if R's 'Thanksgiving' will be heard on Sunday – No word has come about it. He has been digging & now is at his compo – his Pilgrims Progress so nearly finished.

To go back to the great happenings yesterday I admired the King's speech so much –

Churchill wasn't at his best in his statement? I didn't care for 'Advance Britannia' but I loved 'Dear Channel Islands' & his 'its your day' to the crowd – perfect – and their quick answer.

A

[1] The final surrender of the German forces had been formally signed in Berlin on 8 May. Cordelia was Adeline's sister, married to Richard Curle. AVW wrote to her very often with daily news.

[2] R. O. Morris, who had lived with the VWs since the death of his wife.

445. To Victor Hely-Hutchinson at the BBC[1]

14 May 1945

The White Gates,
Westcott Road,
Dorking.

May 14th 1945.

Dear Hely Hutchinson

Thank you very much for your courteous telephone call. I am sorry I was out. It was an excellent recording[2] and came through very well.

Nevertheless I think you ought to know the whole history of the negociations [*sic*], especially as you only came into the saddle near the end of the proceedings, and it may be useful to you for another time, to know what is likely to happen when one has dealings with your fellow BBC officials.

The history is as follows: – About the end of 1943 (I am, I fear, vague as to dates,) I had a letter from Arthur Bliss asking me to write a 'Victory Anthem' to be ready to put on at a moments notice if victory suddenly came upon us.[3] I had, I think, some negociations with Dr Welch about the words, and in a fairly short time I sent Bliss a *sketch* as a 'basis of discussion', and asked that he and Dr Welch should look it through, and tell me if the idea was suitable: I could then go ahead and finish it. I also asked them to make a copy of my sketch, and return me my original. I had a perfunctory letter of thanks from Bliss, and my copy was in due course returned, but with no further letter.

I then waited and wondered what was happening, and I am afraid improper pride came into the question: I had done my bit, and it was up to the BBC to make the next move.

About June 1944 I had an agitated telephone call from Adrian Boult. 'How about that Victory Anthem? It may be wanted any minute, please get to work on it.' I replied 'You've already had it for nearly six months.' So a hue and cry was made, and it was, I believe, found forgotten in a drawer. So then after wasting six idle months, I had to revise, partly rewrite, and wholly orchestrate the work all in a hurry, which was the one thing I did not want to do for a great occasion. However it got finished fairly soon. I went to Bedford and we had a very successful recording.

While I was there I talked with some BBC officials and the objection was raised that this was *not* an anthem, and would I change the title? This I willingly did, and called it 'Thanksgiving for Victory'. I understood, at the same time, that it was to be made into a big feature, (this was strengthened by the handsome cheque which I presently received!). I had discussions as how best to announce it in the Radio Times, whether the words could be printed, etc. from which I gathered that the BBC did the honour to consider it a work of some importance. Did the BBC Authorities change their minds and come to the conclusion that it was not worthy of the occasion? In this case they should have told me so, and given me a chance to withdraw it. What happened was, as you know, the announcement was shoved away in a corner at the end of the ordinary 9.30am service, where it was only by accident that I noticed it; just the bare title without explanation or comment. Even the title was wrong, 'Victory Anthem.'

I understand that, owing to your kind offices, the title was corrected in the spoken announcement, but the young lady with a plum in her mouth still persisted in calling it an Anthem, directly contrary to the express wishes of the BBC. There was no preliminary explanation as is usual when a work is specially written for the BBC of the nature and peculiar features of the work: eg. there was no mention of the speaker, or the children singing Kipling: after the broadcast a friend said to me, 'I liked your music, but why did they allow that fellow to butt in with his talking?'

For myself I do not mind, I have heard two very fine performances, and the BBC have kindly given me a record. But I think the O.U.P. may feel themselves badly let down: they have issued an edition, and I imagine a large one, on the understanding that it would have a big send-off at the Victory celebrations.

Yours sincerely,
R. Vaughan Williams.

[1] Hely-Hutchinson had succeeded Arthur Bliss as Director of Music at the BBC in 1944.
[2] *Thanksgiving for Victory* (*CW* 1944/4), recorded in Nov. 1944, had been broadcast on the previous day.
[3] In fact the invitation came from Boult on 17 Aug. 1943.

446. To Victor Hely-Hutchinson at the BBC — 25 May [1945[1]]

The White Gates,
Dorking.

May 25

Dear Hely Hutchinson

I hear there was a very fine performance of my D. Symph[2] yesterday for which I am grateful – I have decided to omit the 'motto' which is part of the title of the 3rd movement.[3] Would you be so good as to instruct the announcer at any future performances (if any!) that this quotation from 'Pilgrims Progress' is *not* to be read out. – I find it leads to misunderstanding.

Yrs sincerely
R. Vaughan Williams

[1] Year taken from stamp of receipt.

[2] The Fifth Symphony (*CW* 1943/2).

[3] 'Upon this place stood a cross, and a little below a sepulchre. Then he said: "He hath given me rest by his sorrow, and life by his death."' Taken from *The Pilgrim's Progress* by John Bunyan.

5

From the Second World War to the Move Back to London: June 1945–15 September 1953

THE end of the war found VW with two major projects in hand, one a new symphony, the other his opera *The Pilgrim's Progress*, which had been maturing since 1906. Parts of the music had manifested themselves in incidental music to the pageant at Reigate in that year, then again in *The Shepherds of the Delectable Mountains* of 1922, then as he struggled towards the final objective of the complete opera, music spun off into the Fifth Symphony and the incidental music written for a radio adaptation of the work by Edward Sackville-West broadcast in 1943. Already in 1945 he was showing the libretto of the opera to Gerald Finzi, asking whether he thought that incorporating *Shepherds* more or less whole into the opera would work. Throughout this period the final work takes shape and negotiations move forward towards a possible performance. The Arts Council became involved in 1948 and the work was eventually staged by Covent Garden. Both these developments were due to his old friend Steuart Wilson, who had moved from the Arts Council to the BBC as Director of Music in 1948 and was to become Deputy General Administrator of Covent Garden in 1949. The correspondence with both Ursula Wood and Gerald Finzi bears ample testimony to the difficulties he encountered over the dramatic structure of the work, problems which led to further adjustments after the first production. Perhaps with *Pilgrim* more than any other work we can see from letters and the manuscripts how long and hard VW wrestled to get it right. The work was in effect a regular companion on his musical journey for nearly half a century.

From 1944 to 1947, however, there was another work vying to occupy the forefront of his attention—the Sixth Symphony. This came to be seen, in a way that the Fifth was not, as an expression of the trauma of the war, the loss of friends, the deprivations suffered by refugees, and the final fear of eerie devastation. VW himself, as ever, firmly denied any such associations and protested when he heard it referred to as the 'war symphony'—as with the Fourth, the symphony simply wrote itself that way—but as the composer himself maintained, the musician could not divorce himself from real life, and real life for those who went through the war had been hard and destructive, albeit alleviated by a sense of comradeship and common purpose. The letters bear eloquent witness to VW's own reaction to what was going on around him and many of those who heard the Sixth felt it embodied his summing up of that.

It was with the Sixth that VW started to make use of Roy Douglas, a young musician who had been suggested to him in 1944 by Norman Peterkin at the OUP as someone who might help with the preparation of a reduced score of *Thanksgiving for Victory* for performance purposes. A close working relationship between VW and Douglas began in earnest early in 1947 when VW asked him to go through the score of the new symphony and, as the composer put it, 'wash its face', by making a legible and correct copy and advising VW where he was uncertain, because of his deafness, about matters such as balance in the orchestration. Thus was established a working friendship which lasted for the rest of VW's life. Douglas became expert at deciphering VW's atrocious hand and was able to produce scores which were not only readily legible by conductors but more authoritative than the original manuscripts since his scores incorporated corrections, where readings might be doubtful, which had been discussed fully with and were thus authorized by the composer. In his book *Working with Vaughan Williams* Douglas has left a fascinating account of the minutiae of the couple's dealings which provides a vital insight into the genesis of the works of VW's last decade. VW's reliance on such people as Douglas and Gordon Jacob to help him with technical matters probably arose from feelings of uncertainty such as those expressed to Richard Walthew in 1947, when Douglas was working with him closely. Remembering their time as fellow students at the RCM, he says: 'you must have thought me a mere amateur – & I have been so, more or less, all my life – I seem to have had no natural techniques – but have had to hammer out everything from the facts of the case.'

VW, as ever, moved ahead on more than one front: at the same time as the Sixth was being prepared for its first performance and while the opera was still being tidied he became involved in another project which was to be the crowning achievement of his work on film scores. *Scott of the Antarctic* was the second of the film scores he wrote for his fellow Old Carthusian, Ernest Irving, who was Music Director at Ealing Studios, the first being *The Loves of Joanna Godden*. The new film, with its promise of desolate Antarctic wastes, immediately conjured up in VW's mind's eye musical ideas which, one suspects, chimed in with the preoccupations evident in the last movement of his newly finished symphony. The use of a wordless soprano part was reminiscent of the *Pastoral Symphony* and its echoes of the desolation caused by an earlier war and of his opera about the bleak west coast of Ireland, *Riders to the Sea*. Of all the film music he wrote this was the only work which reached towards an inner core to the extent that when the film was finished and on release, he felt the need to rework some of the music into symphonic form in what became *Sinfonia Antartica*, dedicated to Irving. There were, and remain, differences of opinion amongst critics as to whether the *Sinfonia* is truly symphonic and not just a suite of rechauffé music from the film.

Alongside the central symphonic spine of VW's creative life, works of more ephemeral nature continued to be provided when asked for. Two examples from this period are the Romance in D flat for Harmonica and small orchestra written for Larry Adler and, preceding it, a setting of words by Ursula Wood, *The Sons of Light*, written for performance by massed choirs of the Schools Music Association. This work worried him (though he had thought it satisfactory at the time of writing it) to the extent that he was uncertain whether to scrap it or not. Finzi persuaded him to leave it alone, even though he agreed with VW that it was not of the first water, and a recent recording assures the hearer that this was the right advice: the work was not as inferior as VW feared.

If Roy Douglas was now assisting VW along the tortuous path between the first draft of a composition and the final fair copy full score ready for performance, there had been changes at OUP too. After the war, Norman Peterkin's former post as music editor was taken by a returning member of staff, Alan Frank, and it was he who became VW's main point of contact with his publisher for the rest of his life. Frank was a keen clarinettist and his wife was Phyllis Tate, the composer, which made him well equipped to understand and respond to VW's needs, especially after he became head of the department in 1954. Peterkin's predecessor, Hubert Foss, was of course still very much a figure in VW's life and played a role in planning and advising on the celebrations of both the major anniversaries falling within this period, the 75th in 1947 and 80th in 1952. However, the difficulties that had led to his leaving OUP remained and VW was the tactful figurehead of a campaign on the part of some of Foss's friends, coordinated by James McKay Martin, which raised the money to enable Foss to spend some time in the purlieus of Buckfast Abbey for recuperation. For his part, Foss had written a monograph on VW's music published in 1950 and later in 1951 tried to persuade VW to be filmed for television in connection with his 80th birthday, in which he failed. The book was the first major monograph to be devoted to VW's music, but earlier in 1948 VW had been asked by Percy Young to comment on the draft of a similar book, which eventually appeared in 1953. In both cases VW firmly refused to do anything other than correct points of fact, on the grounds that he didn't want to run the risk of being suspected by readers of having directly inspired favourable comments and of having censored any unfavourable ones.

Moving away from his own music, we find regular correspondents continue. Elizabeth Maconchy still sought his advice and support as her family grew. His old friend Edward Dent continued as a reliable confidant, joined in the campaign to help Hubert Foss, and took a very close interest in *The Pilgrim's Progress*. VW made friends with Katharine Thomson, the daughter of his Cambridge friend, the French scholar H. F. Stewart. She ran a choir in Birmingham, the Clarion Singers, who had pleased VW greatly by performing *Sir John in Love*. There were new young composers who sought his advice: Arthur Benjamin, of whose Symphony and opera, *The Tale of Two Cities*, VW became a stout advocate, and Arthur Butterworth, whose surname had a strong resonance for him and to whom he sent some particularly sound advice. His correspondence with his Bristol admirer Arnold Barter continued and a new Bristolian was added to the flock: Herbert Byard was a lecturer in music at the university and conductor of the Bristol Madrigal Choir. The two found special common ground over the issues which VW confronted in his annual performances of Bach Passions at Dorking. They supported each other in resisting the pressures for 'authentic baroque performance practice', some aspects of which they found repugnant—for example VW was quite unabashed about using a piano as his continuo instrument.

In 1946 VW was characteristically pleased to receive an enthusiastic letter from a young 20-year-old admirer serving in the navy called Michael Kennedy. Kennedy was soon invited to dinner at The White Gates. They met further at concerts after Kennedy had become northern music critic for the *Daily Telegraph*. They were all at the first performance of *Sinfonia Antartica* in Manchester and so a firm friendship was established which continued thereafter. VW found in Kennedy someone with whom he could discuss musical matters without having to bear in mind all the time that he was talking to a fellow composer. He found the views of the percipient critic stimulating.

In the correspondence of this period, we can see VW's political stance in clearer terms. He told Fritz Hart that overall he felt that compared with the days of their youth at the RCM the rich were possibly not so rich but the poor were definitely less poor and that was a good thing, but he became very exercised over 'peace' campaigns and entered into heated correspondence with Rutland Boughton on the subject. He regarded such movements as being inspired by the Kremlin and in refuting Boughton's arguments he gave a clear account of his political history as a Labour voter on all occasions except one. He was kinder to the pianist Frank Merrick, who also asked him to support a 'peace' campaign with a message, but remained wary and insisted that his message could only be a musical quotation of two bars of 'Dona nobis pacem' with those words only underlaid. If he was wary of peace movements, he also had his own bees in his bonnet: he did his best to stir up a campaign against a new translation of the Bible. Though an agnostic, he was deeply devoted to the language of both the Authorized Version of the Bible and the *Book of Common Prayer*. For VW, as for many of his contemporaries, the resonances of these works were an integral point of reference, alongside Shakespeare. This is evident from turns of phrase throughout his correspondence. VW's case against a new translation did not hold theological water, but it was a concise apologia for those who, like him, treasured the traditional language of the church.

It is clear from the letters that came in from admirers and friends that VW's major birthdays were red-letter days in the musical calendar now that he was the undisputed doyen of British composers. It was to him that the authorities naturally turned when music was required for national purposes —*Thanksgiving for Victory* and pieces commissioned for the 1953 Coronation ceremony (the motet *O Taste and See* and his arrangement of *The Old Hundredth Psalm Tune*) are examples. Whatever his role on the national stage, though, life and music at Dorking continued with VW unwilling to be away from home for any length of time because of Adeline's frailty. Many of his performances had perforce to be listened to on the radio or on record. With radio reception a somewhat uncertain quantity because of foreign interference, VW went to some trouble to consult EMI to see if more elaborate equipment would ameliorate this, but without striking success; VHF was still some years away. When he did go away, Ursula was able to accompany him to ensure that all went well for him—and on this account she had Adeline's blessing. Notwithstanding, Adeline and The White Gates remained the base to which he returned as quickly as he could—at home they were a devoted elderly couple. But Adeline's health had been deteriorating and there were bouts of illness; her handwriting, hitherto VW's passport to legibility, became a tremulous scrawl and, eventually, on 10 May 1951, she died peacefully in her sleep.

VW wrote at once to his cousin, Ralph Wedgwood, now the National Trust's tenant at Leith Hill Place, to give him the news and a few days later responded to a letter from Bessy Trevelyan, whose husband Robert had died a few weeks earlier: 'We are both alone now. I go on with my work as usual which is what she wants I feel sure.' Ralph's feeling of loss must have been enormous: Adeline had been there quietly but firmly all his life since they married in 1897, supporting him in the background, taking a close interest in his music, and writing to his dictation those letters which needed to be readily legible. She seemed happy that he had the companionship of Ursula Wood when she was unable to be there. She was, as one friend put it, a 'wise woman'.

The fact that Ralph could go on with his work after Adeline's death was largely due to Ursula being there to support him. She had become a constant collaborator, especially so in the preparations for the production of *The Pilgrim's Progress*, for which she had typed out the libretto in 1939. She attended the lighting rehearsals on his behalf and when, afterwards, it became clear that the Vanity Fair scene needed to be longer, it was she who wrote a song to be sung by Lord Lechery. Now, joined in the immediate aftermath of Adeline's death by Cordelia Curle, Adeline's sister, she rallied round to ensure that VW was able to carry on with work: he was looking over his symphonies ahead of a series of performances by the Hallé Orchestra under John Barbirolli; he dealt firmly with mutterings amongst the members of one of the local choirs about the perceived impropriety of the words of Holst's 'Tomorrow shall be my dancing day'; and he continued to work on *Sinfonia Antartica* in readiness for its first performance in January 1953. In 1952 there was music to be written for the Coronation the following year and his 80th birthday celebrations in October were in preparation. In all of this Ursula was by him and it came as no surprise to their close friends when they received a postcard at the beginning of February 1953 announcing that they had decided to marry. The marriage took place quietly on 7 February, with Gil Jenkins as best man, and was described by Ralph, when thanking him, as 'one of the best weddings I have been to'.

When VW had moved to Dorking because of Adeline's increasing infirmity he had missed being able to participate fully in London life. He had made up for this to some extent by encouraging music-making in Dorking and by conducting the annual performances of Bach Passions and the Leith Hill Musical Festival. It now seemed natural to him and Ursula to move back to London and to continue to be involved with Dorking music from there. He was in any case ready to resign from being conductor of the festival after forty years because of increasing deafness, though he planned to continue to conduct the annual Passions. Ursula found a house in Hanover Terrace, in Regent's Park, on which they signed a twenty-one-year lease; they moved there on 15 September 1953 and so the final phase of VW's life began.

447. To Ralph Wedgwood

21 July [1945]

The White Gates,
Dorking.

July 21

Dear Randolph

I am going to make a very bold request. Is there any chance that you would be willing to come & speak to our Dorking branch of FEDERAL UNION – We like so much to have someone to talk to us who views the Bees in our Bonnet from outside.

– The difficulty is (if otherwise you would be good enough to be willing to come) how to announce you & the lecture – The lecture must be given under the auspices of the F.U. – but it must also be made clear that you are not a member and not necessarily in agreement – can you see any solution to this problem?[1]

My love to Iris.

Yours
R.V.W.

[1] Wedgwood politely turned down VW's invitation.

448. To Gerald Finzi

4 September [postmark: 1945]

The White Gates
Dorking

Sept 4

Dear Gerald

I have discovered a set of parts of the Concerto (3.3.3.3.2.).[1]

I should like to *give* these to you if they are any use.

The only thing is, we must not be unfair to the O.U.P. So I suggest that each time you give a public performance with those parts you sh[d] pay a hire fee to the O.U.P. (incidentally I shall get a fraction of that).

If you approve of the scheme, let me know & I will put it before Peterkin.[2]

My love to Joyce

Yrs
RVW

[1] Finzi had asked for a set of parts for VW's Violin Concerto, *CW* 1925/7.

[2] Norman Peterkin, formerly Assistant Editor and now in charge at the OUP Music Department, following Hubert Foss's resignation. For VW's letter to him see no. 449.

449. To Norman Peterkin at OUP

9 September [1945]

Extract[1]

9th September

Concerto Academico:

Now another matter. My friend, Gerald Finzi, wants to do my Violin Concerto, but he wants to buy parts as apparently his orchestra rehearses each Work for several years, and mark their parts, but I understand that you can only *hire*. Now I have a set of parts (3.3.3.3.2.) which were given me when the Work was first published. I should like to give these to Mr. Finzi, but in fairness to you I have suggested that he should pay you a hire fee for each public performance. If you think this a good suggestion, I will send him the parts and ask him to communicate with you.[2]

[1] From a letter on other matters—the remainder not found.

[2] See no. 448. Peterkin wrote to Finzi on 11 Sept. agreeing to the scheme. Finzi replied on 14 Sept.: 'Your cooperation over the V.W Concerto Academico is very much appreciated & of course I agree to pay a hire fee for each public performance we give. As by far the majority of our performances are non-profit making (in churches, village halls etc) may I suggest that on any such occasions we pay 10/6 & in cases where money is taken at the door, or we get our expenses paid, then we sh[d] pay you a Guinea. I presume this arrangement sh[d] hold good so long as the work remains on hire only & the parts are not purchasable, but I sh[d] in any case, be very glad to pay for the parts which you have offered to let us have.' On 17 Sept. Peterkin accepted the proposal.

450. To Gerald Finzi

8 November [postmark: 1945]

The White Gates
Dorking

Nov 8

Dear Gerald

Thank you very much.[1] Your criticisms give food for thought – Bruce Richmond[2] also objects to By ends. I feel he is wanted as the 3rd obstacle on the Pilgrims way (Physical force – temptation – ½ hearted sympathy) – but I *do* agree then that we must avoid after By ends exit picking up *exactly* where we were – that can easily be done.

(By the way years ago I saw a dramatic version of PP where By ends came in just there – & I thought it was good.)

I think I want the Epilogue for the very purpose of bringing us back to earth (by the way the new end is quite different from the 'shepherds'[3]). If you cut the Epilogue you must also cut the prologue.

– But as you say without the music one can only detect glaring impossibilities – & that is all I asked.

Now as regards singers

Captain Aylwyn Best RM
Buff's Close Camp
Faringdon
Berks

– he is *not* a very good timer but his words & voice are excellent.

How about the enclosed?

Love to Joyce

Yrs
RVW

[1] Finzi had sent VW some comments on the libretto of *The Pilgrim's Progress*, saying that it was difficult to judge it without the music (for example the libretto of Britten's *Peter Grimes* alone gave no idea of the force of the opera). He was puzzled by the proposed treatment of Pilgrim's fight with Apollyon through lighting; the Vanity Fair scene was exciting but the scene with Mister and Madam By-Ends was an anti-climax after it. The incorporation of *The Shepherds of the Delectable Mountains* worked well but he felt that the Epilogue at the end with Bunyan was a 'barbarous intrusion' after the alleluias and the trumpet.

[2] Editor of the *Times Literary Supplement*.

[3] VW incorporated his 'pastoral episode' *Shepherds of the Delectable Mountains* of 1922 almost unaltered into *The Pilgrim's Progress*.

451. To Geoffrey Keynes

17 November [?1945[1]]

From R. Vaughan Williams,
The White Gates,
Westcott Road,
Dorking.

November 17

Dear Geoffrey

Your letter puts me in rather a difficulty because I have nearly finished the sketch of an opera on the same subject[2] which incorporates the scene of the Delectable Mountains which was performed as a one act opera years ago and is possibly to be revived at Sadlers Wells this season. On the other hand, though I says it as shouldn't, anyone else would make a complete mess of the music to the proposed Masque. On the 3rd hand if there were such a thing – if I used up some of my opera music for the Masque it might [hamper][3] its chances, if there ever were any, of its being performed as an opera – So there you are!

I send you a copy of the libretto of my opera in case it would interest you to glance at it.

My love to Margaret

Yrs
R.V.W.

[1] VW sent the libretto of *The Pilgrim's Progress* to Gerald Finzi in Oct. 1945 for comment and had heard back on 5 Nov. with some suggestions. The work was therefore much in VW's mind at this time.

[2] It is not clear what Keynes was suggesting in his letter to VW.

[3] Supplied word missing in original.

452. OUP File note on VW's English version of Bach's B minor Mass by Norman Peterkin

20 November 1945

20.11.45

Vaughan Williams came to discuss his Bach B minor mass scheme[1] with NP. Foss' report of Oct 29th was read out to him & a copy given him to take away & consider. I also passed to him Foss's personal list of music suggestions.

Vaughan Williams realised, probably for the first time, the magnitude of his scheme, especially when NP told him that a moderate edition of the vocal score, chorus parts, orchestral score & parts would probably cost anything from £2000 upward. He was astounded & had thought £400 or so would cover the cost which he was prepared to meet himself. NP made it clear that quite apart from the question of the expense involved we simply could not tackle the project because of the lack of paper & the acute manufacturing difficulties involved – As Foss advised in his report, there is not a printer in England who would undertake the job in the conditions now prevailing. This applies even if V.W. ignored the larger implications as to a definitive English edition & wanted it produced for the Leith Hill Festival only. V.W. seemed greatly impressed with Foss's views, even tho he disagrees in some directions, & accepted the position that we can't do anything with the scheme. He says he will probably collect a number of copies of the Novello Ed. of the B mi Mass from friends & choral societies, & get his friend Miss Gritton to underlay his English text to the music so that material will be provided for a performance by his Leith Hill people. On the large question of a definitive edition of the Mass, working with a committee, he absolutely refuses to consider any such co-operation. His edition is the work of a very long period, & he says it is as he wants it for his purposes, & he is not in the least prepared to alter or revise to suit the view of any committee. He adds that in any case any such committee would never reach any unanimous view about what the edition should be. NP thereupon told him that naturally as far as V.W.'s own version is concerned, the question of any co-operation or working to produce it with a committee would be abandoned, as VW was against it.

Vaughan Williams also has some curious idea that he does not want his edition of the Mass, if ever it reaches print, to be copyright. He wants it to be free to everybody etc. Yet at the same time he is scared that if Novello's heard of his idea of the Mass using the English Church Services they would steal the idea & rush out the edition themselves!!! NP told him he felt there was not the slightest chance of Novello's doing any such thing. In any case it is far too big a thing for *any* publisher to embark on in the present conditions & it will be years before it is practical & economic to consider any further edition of the Mass.[2]

[1] See no. 439.
[2] VW's version of Bach's B minor Mass was eventually performed at the Leith Hill Musical Festival on 18 Apr. 1947.

453. To E. J. Dent

11 December [*c*.1945?[1]]

The White Gates
Dorking

Dec 11

Dear Dent

Very confidential

I have had a visit from Professor Santos[2] & his wife – she sings Spanish folksongs delightfully – very beautiful tunes to which he had added quite competent but not very distinguished accompaniments. The only other work he showed me was an early pfte sonata – just student work – quite well done but with absolutely no character – just a hotch potch of early Chopin & Liszt. He has composed nothing recently as far as I can make out – & I told him that if he wants help with his composition he must get to work and write something first (I suggested a fantasia on some of those Portuguese folksongs).

Then I w[d] suggest his taking his work for criticism to *several* people – especially *you* & after you Arthur Bliss – & I said that whenever he liked to show me a work I should be pleased to discuss it – I suggested strict cpt[3] with R.O.M.[4] – but he said he wanted to do 'modern' cpt whatever that may mean.

I hope you will be able to see him and advise him. But (more confidential than ever!) I have grave doubts *as to whether he is a composer.*

Yrs
R. Vaughan Williams

[1] Hypothetical date based on the wartime unheaded paper.
[2] So far unidentified.
[3] i.e. counterpoint.
[4] R. O. Morris at the RCM—Adeline's brother-in-law.

454. To Ursula Wood

[sometime between 1943 and 1946]

My Dear

I opened the book at random today and found

'You walk unaware of the slender gazelle
that moves as you move
and is one with the limbs that you have'.[1]

That is you my dear – & then the poem this morning – which has [moved] me to a ribald rhyme.

A line that is long
and a skirt which is short
10 feet for a thought
– and 2 for a song
– the thought shows 10 feet
But the song – oh how sweet
~~shows 2 of the fairest~~
shows 2 lovely limbs
therefore my hymns.

Love
RVW

[1] The opening of 'To Maeve' by Mervyn Peake, which was included in an anthology compiled by Walter de la Mare, *Love* (London, 1943), 17, a book which Ursula had sent to VW.

455. To Douglas Lilburn

15 January [postmark: 1946]

The White Gates
Dorking

Jan 15

Dear Lilburn

I had already guessed it was you and wrote accordingly – Now, your welcome letter has come – & I thank you & your helper once more. Please remember me to D^{r} & Mrs Page – I expect great things of his professorship.[1] I hope that you are writing something bigger than incidental music – But as you say the natural tendency is to write in terms of the available material.

– I think the BBC ought to do more music from N.Z. & Australia. I think the American broadcasts were largely political – but I heard a lot of music I enjoyed very much – As regards Britten I find great power and character in his music – he is undoubtedly very exploited by B & Co[2] – but up to the present he has stood up well to it.

All good wishes for new year

Yrs
R.Vaughan Williams

[1] At Victoria University College, Wellington.
[2] Boosey & Co., Britten's publishers.

456. To John Ireland

7 February 1946

From R. Vaughan Williams,
The White Gates,
Westcott Road,
Dorking.

Feb 7 1946

Dear John

That is a fine work – one of your best – & it is the best [of] you all the way through – so many works by most composers only transcend themselves & thereby become their *real* selves in patches – but this seems to me to be your real self all through.[1]

I think they played it well – & the audience were evidently impressed

Yrs
R. Vaughan Williams

[1] Probably Ireland's *Fantasy-Sonata* for Clarinet and Piano, composed in 1943, published in 1945. The British Museum copy was deposited in Jan. 1946.

457. To Gerald Finzi

5 May [postmark: 1946]

The White Gates
Dorking

May 5

Dear Gerald

My committee believing as I do that a conductor as much as a tenor or a double bass is worthy of his hire wish with my complete concurrence to send you a small 'expenses' fee. This is merely a matter of our own conscience and has really nothing to do with you. My only trouble is that it is entirely inadequate – but I hope you will take the will for the deed – but of course it has nothing to do with our gratitude to you for your masterly conducting & a beautiful work.[1]

Yrs
RVW

[1] VW had invited Finzi to conduct a concert at the LHMF on 4 May at which the tenor Bainbridge White sang Finzi's cantata *Dies Natalis*.

458. To RVW from Jean Sibelius

18 June 1946

Järvenpää

June 18th, 1946

Dear Dr Vaughan-Williams,

Through the British Council I have these days received a full-score edition of your Symphony in D-major which you kindly have dedicated to me. Please accept my most cordial thanks for your great kindness which I consider a great honour to me. I am very happy that this honour has been shown me by an English composer as my music has many friends in Great Britain.

I have heard your Symphony in the Radio and now it has been a great pleasure to study it more closely. It is a well-rounded, harmonious and vivid work. Moreover I have seldom heard anything that is more English. I do not mean that you were influenced by British folk songs but the symphonic grip seems to me to be English.

Thanking you once more, I remain, with admiration and friendship,

Yours sincerely,
Jean Sibelius.[1]

[1] Writing to her sister Cordelia on 2 July, AVW said '[Ralph] had a letter from Sibelius, type written in English – R w[d] so much have preferred a scrawl in Finnish in his own hand [–] not that the letter wasn't a very cordial one but Sib doesn't know enough English to write it—when R met him he spoke French.'

459. To Alan Frank at OUP[1]

3 August [1946]

The White Gates,
Dorking.

Aug 3

Dear Frank

Herewith the 4[tet] proofs[2] – forgive delay but I have had them checked by Michael Mullinar & the parts were all checked from their own parts by the players – The 1st violin part is in a pretty good mess. Chiefly owing to the vagaries of your copyist who shoved in 8[ves] promiscuously without (so far as I remember) any authority from the 'master' copy. The result was almost impossible to read. It's a great pity I have to have those copies made for the engraver – a new crop of mistakes come up each fresh copy. In future if this has to be done the copy must be properly checked before going to the engraver. I must see another proof please of every part and the score. Also please let me see the title page before it is engraved (all the trouble over my symphony came from this being omitted).[3]

I enclose a draft of the way the title page should be set.

By the way I hear that GOLDSMITH has left his war job & w[d] be glad of copying – He has just lost his wife – so apart from financial considerations some work would be very good for him.

His address is

S O Goldsmith
10 Brandon Road
Norwood Green
Southall
Middlesex

Yrs sincerely
R. Vaughan Williams

Quartet in A minor
for Jean on her Birthday
by
R. Vaughan Williams

Note This complete title should be printed in every programme etc

[1] Music Editor in succession to Norman Peterkin (1947); Head of Music at OUP from 1954 until his retirement in 1975.

[2] Of the String Quartet in A minor, *CW* 1944/2.

[3] It is not clear what the problem with title page of the Fifth Symphony was; it may have had to do with the placing of the dedication.

460. To Fritz Hart

24 August [?1946[1]]

The White Gates,
Dorking.

Aug 24

Dear Fritz

I was very glad to get your last letter though I was a long time answering it. I wonder if things are *mentally* so very different now to what they were when we were young. I believe the things we talked about at Wilkins[2] were much the same as what our followers at the modern equivalent of Wilkins say now & that the clever young men who write in modern journals are saying exactly the same clever foolish things that the young men said in 1896 and old B. Shaw says *exactly* what he said in the 'Saturday Review' in the 90's.

One thing however I *do* believe – the world (or at all events England) is *not* less prosperous in essential things and indeed *more* prosperous than in the so called 'prosperous' '80's and 90's – the rich people are not so rich but the poor people are not so poor – And if the present slump (like that of 1931) means that a few millionaires are ruined and a few stock-exchange-gamblers commit suicide so much the better for us all.

My love to Marvel.

Yrs
RVW

[1] This date is suggested because of VW's reference to 1896, which would have been fifty years earlier —but this was also the year he was at the RCM and much in Wilkins'.

[2] A café near the RCM where VW and his friends, including Holst, Ireland, and Fritz Hart, used to gather. See *WVW*, 20, and also John Ireland's short memoir in the *Musical Times* for Oct. 1958, 535–6: 'We used to frequent a teashop in High Street Kensington, then known as Wilkins', where we could sit for hours in animated discussions.'

461. To Harriet Cohen

24 August [1946[1]]

The White Gates,
Dorking.

Aug 24

Dear Harriet

I am sorry you feel cross about the concerto – But, you know, you had it all to yourself, I think, for a year – most people for whom I have written things are content with a first performance – & then are willing to have it thrown open.[2] Since that time many other pianists have played it (including Cyril Smith himself) – & you know you c[d] not have played it by yourself on 2 pftes (one hand on each?) any more than if I had arranged it for organ and ukelele.

At the time of the first performance many people urged me to rearrange it for 2 pftes – they thought it to[o] heavy going for one – But I held on so as to give the 1 pfte a good send off before I did anything.

Have a good time in U.S.A. and bring back plenty of dollars – I am so glad about the recording of the Gibbons – I shall probably rearrange that for 4 bass tubas & a banjo.[3]

Love from
RVW

[1] Presumably written about the time that the first performance of the two-piano version of the concerto by Cyril Smith and Phyllis Sellick, on 22 Nov. 1946, was announced.

[2] On the question of Harriet Cohen's exclusive use of the concerto, see no. 248.

[3] Printed in *WVW*, 292.

462. To Michael Kennedy[1]

29 August [postmark: 1946]

The White Gates
Dorking

29th August

Dear M[r] Kennedy

I was much touched by your letter – one of the advantages of putting down black dots on paper is that it forms a means of communication and sympathy with people whom we may never meet in life (though I hope we may one day) I am glad you like the end of the slow mov[t] of my F minor symph.

It may interest you to know that records of my 'Job' are now out & 'Flos Campi' very soon[2]

Please write again if you feel moved to

Yours sincerely
R. Vaughan Williams

[1] Addressed to Commander G. M. S. Kennedy, 19 Mess, H M S Ulysses, c/o F. M.O., Devonport. Michael Kennedy, born 1926; northern editor 1980–6 and (since 1950) staff music critic (Joint Chief Critic since 1987) for the *Daily Telegraph*; Chief Music Critic of the *Sunday Telegraph* 1989–2005; writer on music. He became a close friend of both Ralph and Ursula Vaughan Williams and advocate of his music. VW named him as his music biographer, and he eventually also took on the chairmanship of the RVW Trust and RVW Ltd, the bodies set up to administer VW's estate. According to *RVW*, 317 Kennedy and VW started corresponding in 1945, but the date of this letter indicates that it was in fact 1946. VW's use of the title 'Commander' in addressing him was based on a misinterpretation of the abbreviation Cdr, which in Kennedy's case in fact meant 'Coder'. VW's promotion of Kennedy became a joke between them as their friendship grew. The Kennedys remained close friends with VW until his death and with Ursula until her death.

[2] Both from HMV conducted by Boult, *Flos Campi* with William Primrose.

463. To Herbert Byard[1]

1 September [1946[2]]

The White Gates
Dorking

Sept 1

Dear Mr Byard

Many thanks for your letter – I have not heard from Jacques[3] – but anyway I fear I could not come – Oct 12th is my birthday & I should want to spend at least part of it at home. Yr programme seems v. good – certainly include Greensleeves if you like.[4]

– Perhaps you would like to quote verse 6 in your programme

'Thy crimson stockings all of silk
with gold al wrought above the knee
Thy pumps as white as was the milk
And yet thou woulds't not love me'

Yrs ever
R. Vaughan Williams

[1] Organist, lecturer at Bristol University, and conductor of the Bristol Madrigal Society. Possibly VW had met him through Arnold Barter. VW and Byard maintained a lively correspondence, mainly about Bach, from 1946 onwards.

[2] According to a note on the original.

[3] Reginald Jacques, founder of the Jacques Orchestra.

[4] *Fantasia on 'Greensleeves'*, adapted from *Sir John in Love*, *CW* 1934/1.

464. To Gerald Finzi

postmark: 18 September 1946

My Dear Gerald & Joyce & all my friends on the postcard (I feel sure all the young women whose names are signed & whom I don't know are as pretty as those I do).

so thank you all – but I am glad I was not there as if I had been I sh^d have had to conduct my tune[1] myself – & that performance under G.D.[2] which everyone (you included) says was so fine w^d not have come off.

Yrs
RVW

[1] A performance of VW's *Benedicite*, *CW* 1929/1, had been given at the Three Choirs Festival at Hereford, conducted by George Dyson. See *RVW*, 269.

[2] Sir George Dyson (1883–1964), Director of the RCM.

465. To Gerald Finzi

postmark: 27 September 1946

Dear Gerald

I'm sorry about the music – I will return it. (I think Miss Cullen[1] has the Purcell.)

Quite at *y^r leisure* I sh^d like the Parry which I sent by mistake.

As regards y^r choice of music

Why not do King Arthur (Novello's shortened version – which leaves out a lot of good things but makes it of reasonable length). When we did it Fanny Farrer wrote a splendid connecting story (embodying a good deal of Dryden) which Steuart[2] declaimed with great effect. (I think I could get a copy for you.) Otherwise I suppose you could not bea[t] (A) Meistersinger selection (Curwen) (B) Phaudrig Crohoore (Boosey).[3] The choirs *love* them. I suppose you are beyond Orpheus Act II[4] & 'Spring'[5] – By the way we once did Autumn & Winter – lovely – & great fun when the sportsmans gun goes off & the young woman sings what is supposed to be an improper ballad with punctuations by the choirs of Ha! ha! ha!

My love to Joyce.

Yrs
RVW

PTO & PS[6]

[1] Margery Cullen, Hon. Sec. of LHMF and conductor of various choirs in the LHMF at various times, but mainly Mickleham. See *And Choirs Singing*.

[2] Steuart Wilson.

[3] By Stanford.
[4] By Gluck.
[5] From Haydn's *Seasons*.
[6] The postscript does not survive.

466. To Alan Frank at OUP

5 October [1946]

The White Gates,
Dorking.

Oct 5

Dear Frank

In answer to your letter (NP/ACP/2008D & 119)

(1) Mullinar – I gave him I think £5-5-0 for the arrangement of the oboe concerto – I feel he ought to have his share of the moneys received from sale of copies so I suggest that you pay him an estimated share of my royalties in one sum & put it against my royalties (This is I think what you suggest).[1]

(2) Cooper – I shall of course pay him the arranger's fee according to the musician union scale – But I feel that he ought also to have a share of performing fees – So I must estimate that as best I can & capitalize it[2] – This brings up the whole question of the PRS about which I have already spoken to you in the case of Muir Mathieson[3] – It is a scandal that the PRS should arrogate to themselves the right to say whether a man is a 'composer' or not – They are just a collecting agency & every-one who has a work performed should automatically become a member of the PRS & get a share of the fee – in these cases where the composer or arranger is not a member of the PRS where does the money go to?

Echo answers 'where'?[4]

Yrs
R. Vaughan Williams

[1] Michael Mullinar had made the orchestral reduction for the published score of the Oboe Concerto, *CW* 1944/1. VW was always concerned that those who contributed in such ways should be adequately recompensed. Frank had proposed an outright fee rather than a continuing share in VW's royalties from sale of the published copies.

[2] Joseph Cooper had reworked the solo part of the Piano Concerto (*CW* 1931/3) for two pianos.

[3] Mathieson had arranged a suite from VW's music for the film *Coastal Command*, *CW* 1942/1.

[4] An allusion to the lines in Byron's *The Bride of Abydos*, c. ii, st. 27: 'Hark to the hurried question of despair / "Where is my child?" An echo answers "where?".'

467. To Gerald Finzi

8 October [postmark: 1946]

The White Gates
Dorking

Oct 8

Dear Gerald

I entirely disagree about Boult's B.P.[1] I thought it noble and moving & tears were (literally) in my eyes at the end. Such a relief after a terribly jaunty performance under M.S.[2] which I heard the other day. Even then it came out top.

Yrs
RVW

[1] i.e. *Blest Pair of Sirens* by Parry.
[2] i.e. Malcolm Sargent.

468. To Boris Ord[1]

25 December [1946?]

The White Gates,
Dorking.

Christmas Day

Dear Boris

Thank you very much for your letter which warmed my heart – I am so glad you are back at music again.

As regards an evening service – the atmosphere of smugness has so settled on those canticles that it seems almost impossible to lift the pall & get at the essence. I fear the service I wrote for Xts Hospital w^{d} be no use to you.[2]

Now it seems ungracious after your splendid letter to make a grouse – but I have meant to do this for years – indeed every Xmas – but have never done it.

I deplore the almost entire absence of English carols in your King's College service. I think every English carol service ought to start with God Rest you merry & end with 1st Noel – then what about

The Lord at first
Virgin unspotted
Cherry Tree
Tomorrow shall be my dancing day
This is the truth
On Xmas night & many more

I only find London Waits, God rest you (I think that is new this year) & Holly & Ivy (which I am glad to see is not now called French in your programme) among the traditional carols – a small proportion to my mind.

I spoke about this to Darke[3] last year & he did not know which were English and which were not!

Yrs with much gratitude
R. Vaughan Williams

[1] Boris Ord (1897–1961), organist and Master of the Choristers at King's College, Cambridge, 1929–57. The letter is based on a transcript made by UVW and is printed in *RVW*, 272, omitting Darke's name.

[2] Services in D minor, *CW* 1939/1, dedicated to C. S. Lang and his singers at Christ's Hospital.

[3] Harold Darke, organist of St Michael's, Cornhill, 1916–66.

469. To Elizabeth Maconchy

13 January [1947]

The White Gates,
Dorking.

Jan 13

Dearest Betty

(a) I am so glad about the 4^{tet} – I will certainly listen if the interfering gentlemen from Latvia will allow it.
(b) I am very glad about the baby – there ought to be one for each 4^{tet} – then 'the works of nature would keep pace with the works of art'.[1]
My love to Billy.

Much love to you
Uncle Ralph

[1] Maconchy's String Quartet No. 4 was to be performed at a BBC Chamber Concert on 20 Jan. 1947 (and broadcast on the Third Programme, with its heavy interference from Radio Latvia). Maconchy had also announced that a second child was on the way—Nicola Lefanu was to be born in Apr. 1947.

470. To Roy Douglas[1]

13 February [1947]

The White Gates,
Dorking

Feb 13

Dear Douglas

I have been foolish enough to write another symphony.[2] Could you undertake to vet and then copy the score?

If in the course of this you have any improvements to suggest I would receive them with becoming gratitude.

On March 10 Michael Mullinar is playing through the sketch at room 46 Royal College of Music at 11.30 & 2.30 – could you (if you are able to undertake the work) come & hear it one of those times?

Yrs
R. Vaughan Williams[3]

[1] A young musician who had been recommended to VW as a helper and copyist by OUP. He became VW's closest musical collaborator for the rest of his life. His book about this, *Working with Vaughan Williams* (2nd edn., London 1988), gives a good insight into VW's later working methods.

[2] The Sixth Symphony, *CW* 1947/3.

[3] This letter is printed in *WWVW*, 9.

471. To John Lowe at the BBC[1]

21 February [1947]

The White Gates,
Dorking.

Feb 21

Dear Mr Lowe

PLEASE do NOT have specially written works for your celebration – they are always duds – choose a programme of all the best works of our own and other countries (especially ours) starting with that wonderful mass by an unknown English composer which was done at John's College Cambridge a few years ago (I wish Mr Tippett would do more of that kind of thing instead of being seduced by his foreign companion into wasting his efforts over that dreary Monteverdi stuff[2]).

Then you could do Maurice Greene 'Lord let me know mine end' & Blest pair[3] which will again I expect come out top if it is conducted by Adrian – then Sullivan 'To a garden full of posies' (from Ruddigore) a quite lovely song.

– The Britten boy is born – also 1st rate performances & thoroughly rehearsed by the controllers as well as by the performers. Also Britten's 'Boy is born' which is much better than Ceremony of Carols.[4]

As regards your other query: If you want to give me real pleasure you will organize a performance of my 'Sancta Civitas' with all the balances of distant trumpets & chorus & semi-chorus etc beautifully proportioned. It is my favourite among my own choral works – every one else hates it.

By the way Kirby & his Croydonians[5] are sing[ing] at the concert at Dorking somewhere about Oct 12 – & I *must* go to it – so please don't clash.

Yours sincerely
R. Vaughan Williams

[1] Head of the music for the BBC Third Programme. He had asked for advice about the forthcoming celebration of the first anniversary of the Third Programme.

On 19 February he had written: 'Since Dr Hely-Hutchinson invited me to take over Anthony Lewis's work in the organisation of music in the Third Programme here I have been looking forward to the opportunity of meeting you – if you can spare the time – to talk about one or two plans which I have in mind. My old friend Steuart Wilson with whom I stay from time to time suggests that you might be able to do with me if I were to come out Leith Hill way one Saturday, and if that would be convenient to you it would be a great pleasure to me. The first idea I have in mind to ask you to think about is this: on September 29th the first anniversary of the inauguration of the Third Programme will occur and on that date we propose to have a full choral and orchestral concert of works specially written for the occasion – either orchestral, unaccompanied choral or choral and orchestral. Might you feel inclined to honour us by writing something for this important occasion? Apart from the big choral and orchestral concert it will also be possible to plan one or two recitals or chamber music concerts of new works written for the occasion during the same week in case you have anything of that kind in mind.

The other question is your own 75th birthday. During that week I feel it my duty to recommend Third Programme to pay particular attention to your own works, orchestral, choral and chamber music. If you could do with me to come and visit you I should like first to find out your views as to the works – not necessarily the best known ones – which ought to be heard. Of course if you ever have a free lunch time or dinner time when you are in London I should be only too delighted to have the pleasure of entertaining you and we could perhaps talk about these matters then.'

[2] This probably refers to a performance of the Monteverdi Vespers in an edition by Walter Goehr, done by Morley College under Michael Tippett's direction, which VW attended at the Central Hall, Westminster.

[3] Parry's *Blest Pair of Sirens*, a work much loved by VW (see no. 467).

[4] Apparently VW's mind was distracted and he had forgotten the mention just before.

[5] Alan Kirby conducted the Croydon Philharmonic Society and the London Symphony Orchestra in a performance of the *Sea Symphony* and *Five Tudor Portraits* on 11 Oct. at Dorking Halls in celebration of VW's 75th birthday. See *RVW*, 278.

472. To Gerald Finzi

[early March 1947]

The White Gates
Westcott Road
Dorking

Dear Gerald

On Monday, 10th March, MULLINAR will play through the sketch of a new symphony[1] by me.

Place: Royal College of Music, Room 46.

Time: 11.30 and 2.30 (by kind permission of the Director).

It would give me great pleasure if Joyce & you could come and hear it.

Yours sincerely,
Uncle Ralph

[1] Sixth Symphony, *CW* 1947/3.

473. To Ralph Wedgwood

[? Spring 1947[1]]

From R. Vaughan Williams,
The White Gates,
Westcott Road,
Dorking.

My Dear Randolph

I am delighted to have the 'Robins Nest'. I wish I could remember the year I wrote it – Adeline is really on the mend now & sends you her love.[2]

Yrs
Ralph

[1] 'Adeline had been ill again early in the spring . . .' (*RVW*, 276) but this could be the severe illness in late 1945, though VW was not using headed paper for this kind of letter at that time.

[2] 'The Robin's Nest' was written in 1878 (see *CW* under that year) and is VW's first extant composition. The manuscript, apparently owned by Wedgwood but returned to VW, is now British Library Add. MS 54186.

474. Internal BBC memorandum to the Home News Editor from Adrian Boult

18 April 1947

Dr R. Vaughan Williams, O. M.

April 18th 1947

I happened to be asked to go down and give away the prizes at the revival of the Leith [Hill] Music Festival, which has been conducted by Vaughan Williams for, I believe, something like 30 years. I was particularly asked to give the audience some idea of what he has done during the war and the whole list is so impressive that I venture to pass it on to you in case anyone who reads this may feel that it may be useful in any celebrations of his 75th birthday.

He kept on composing, of course. A great deal of work was done on two symphonies, the magnificent 'Thanksgiving for Victory', which our religious Broadcasting Department commissioned, a number of smaller works, and I believe some films were all in his war contribution. He also collected a choir from former Leith Hill Festival adherents and rehearsed them every week regularly. They gave two concerts each year and in addition five annual performances of the St Matthew Passion. He also organised a large number of concerts at Toc H for troops, and had a great deal to do with what was called

'An Informal Hour of Music'. These events were fortnightly and went on for many years.[1]

Apart from music, he did a good deal of fire-watching. Incidentally I believe he translated Bach's B minor Mass into English while doing this. He went round with a hand-cart collecting salvage. He also took on a weekly War Savings' collection. Besides this there was a good deal of extra gardening, fire-fighting classes, Chairmanship of a Refugee Committee, and several days devoted to helping with the organisation of the evacuees at the outbreak of war.

This is, I think, an immense record for a man who in a few months will be 75. One is tempted to think of certain of his colleagues both in this and former wars who simply shut themselves up and went on with their music.

Adrian Boult
ACB/GB

[1] On Toc H see no. 307.

475. To Arnold Barter

20 April 1947

The White Gates,
Dorking.

April 20 1947

Dear Barter

I have delayed answering your letter before till our own festival was over which we ended on Friday with a really triumphant performance of the B minor mass – adapted to the English liturgy by RVW.[1]

You know (perhaps you don't know) but *we* know that you & a few others like you are the salt of the musical earth – you work without reward (except that of artistic triumph) & without recognition – but it is *you* & not the international stars who are making (or rather re-making) England into a land of music.

Thank you.

Yrs
R. Vaughan Williams

[1] VW's English version of the Gloria, Sanctus, and Agnus Dei of Bach's Mass in B minor had been performed at the LHMF on 18 Apr. 1947.

476. To Gerald Finzi

postmark: 13 May 1947

The White Gates.
Dorking. 3055

The postponed play through of my Symphony[1] by Michael Mullinar will now take place on Thursday June 5 at 11.30 & 2.30 at the Royal College of Music by kind permission of the Director. I hope you both can come.

R. Vaughan Williams

[1] The Sixth Symphony, *CW* 1947/3.

477. To Katharine Thomson[1]

31 May 1947

From R. Vaughan Williams,
The White Gates,
Westcott Road,
Dorking.

31st May, 1947.

Dear Mrs. Thomson,

I do not quite know what to say about a work of mine. I think good amateurs could do 'Riders to the Sea', but it requires an expert orchestra. On the other hand, my 'Shepherds' has been done in a very moving manner by school boys with a partly amateur orchestra. I do not see much point in *scenes* from 'Sir John'.

I suppose you would not like a real low-down comic opera, 'The Poisoned Kiss'; all these are published by the Oxford University Press.

Yrs sincerely
R. Vaughan Williams

[1] Musical Director of the Clarion Singers in Birmingham. She was daughter of the Cambridge French scholar H. F. Stewart.

478. To Ernest Irving[1]

3 July 1947

From R. Vaughan Williams,
The White Gates,
Westcott Road,
Dorking.

3rd July, 1947

Dear Irving,

Thank you very much for your letter about Stanley Bate.[2]

As regards the Scott film, I think before finally deciding, I should like to have a conference with you and the producer, or director, whichever it is – I never know which is which – and see whether your his and my ideas agree as to the sort of music required. I have very definite ideas and if they do not agree with his, it might be rather difficult.

Yours sincerely
R. Vaughan Williams

[1] Ernest Irving (1877–1953), Director of Music at Ealing Studios and a fellow Old Carthusian.
[2] Stanley Bate (1911–59), composer and pianist, who had studied with VW at the RCM.

479. To RVW from Ernest Irving

9 July 1947

9th July, 1947.

Dear V-W,

Regarding the Scott film, Charles Frend, the Director, has now returned intact from Switzerland where he has been photographing people falling into and being hauled out of crevasses, and would be delighted to confer with you at any time to suit your convenience. I would suggest early next week. Could you come to Ealing, or have you any other suggestions?

I am not surprised that you have definite ideas about the music; that is what we expect and welcome from you. I would suggest that you insist on a definite agreement as to the points when music can be used in full volume without admixture, and if a contract is made that it should include a stipulation that alterations must receive your consent or mine, and that no third person should be brought in to amplify or replace your work. That is, of course, assuming you find me trustworthy in those respects.

yours ever
Ernest Irving.

480. To Adrian Boult at the BBC

30 July 1947

The White Gates,
Westcott Road,
Dorking.

30th July, 1947.

Dear Adrian,

Of course I only meant a message about rehearsal for the secretary. I thought, if necessary, it might strengthen your hand but I never meant it to be passed on to you.

I welcome with great gratitude your idea of running through the Symphony[1] when the parts are ready, which ought to be before Christmas. Then I shall be able to find out whether any or all of it wants rewriting. The O.U.P., quite rightly, I think, do not want to make copies of the score till I am quite sure that it is correct and I cannot do that until I have heard it.

So they are refusing all bookings for the present. Therefore, the sooner we get this trial trip through the better.

Yrs
R. Vaughan Williams

[1] The Sixth Symphony (*CW* 1947/3).

481. To Robert Müller-Hartmann

7 August 1947

The White Gates,
Westcott Road,
Dorking.

7th August, 1947

Dear Müller-Hartmann

I am so glad you like the idea of May Harrison playing your work. I think it would be nice if you wrote to her yourself, here is her address

647 Nell Gwyn House,
Sloane Avenue,
London S.W.3.

Meanwhile here is something I should like you to do for me if you feel inclined. The young man who writes my music for me[1] is at present away on holiday, will you do it? What I want you to do is to correct any mistakes before I send it to the copyist and also tell me of any places where you think I have made any error of judgement. The work is a suite for string orchestra. I should be very grateful if you would do this for me.[2]

Yrs
R. Vaughan Williams

[1] Roy Douglas, who at this time was working hard preparing a full score of the Sixth Symphony. See *WWVW*, 11 ff.

[2] The work in question is the *Partita for Double String Orchestra*, *CW* 1938/5a, a reworking of the 1938 Double Trio for string sextet. The *Partita* is dedicated to Robert Müller-Hartmann.

482. To R. W. Fenn[1] 1 October 1947

1st October 1947

Dear Mr Fenn,

I enclose the draft agreement. My only doubts are the words 'or Mr Irving'. I think that the word 'or' ought to be 'and' because although Mr. Irving and I are not likely to disagree yet I don't want any alteration made in my work without my permission as well as Mr Irvings.[2]

For example, if he retires I might not at all be in agreement with his successor.

Yours sincerely
R. Vaughan Williams.

[1] Of Linnit & Dunfee Ltd, who had sent VW a draft contract for writing the music for *Scott of the Antarctic*.

[2] The discussion refers to clause 3 of the contract, which eventually read 'but no alterations shall be made in the music without your consent and that of Mr. Ernest Irving'. However, Irving did, in a letter to Fenn dated 6 Oct., say that as a matter of expediency it would be necessary for VW to grant him an 'omnibus' permission to authorize necessary cuts and minor changes to fit the picture, with an assurance that his wishes would be respected 'down to the last tail on the last quaver'. See no. 485.

483. To Adrian Boult 4 October 1947

Oct 4th 1947

Dear Adrian

Very confidential

I hear a rumour that my *pianoforte* music is going to be talked about on Sunday week. Could this be stopped as it is quite an unimportant part of my work.

If not could you possibly vet: the script so that nothing shall be said that I could possibly object to?

Yrs
R

484. To Michael Mullinar

4 October [?1947]

From R. Vaughan Williams,
The White Gates,
Westcott Road,
Dorking.

October 4th

My dear Michael

It was wonderful on Thursday – your splendid playing, I hope, did not throw dust in the eyes of your audience – so that when they admired the playing they thought they were liking the music. I hope that the enclosed will at all events cover your expenses.[1]

My love to Mary

Yrs
RVW

[1] The letter possibly refers to a play-through of the Sixth Symphony.

485. To Ernest Irving

8 October 1947

From R. Vaughan Williams,
The White Gates,
Westcott Road,
Dorking.

8th October, 1947

Ernest Irving, Esq.
Ealing Studios,
Ealing Green,
London, W.5

Dear Irving,

Of course you can do exactly as you like without consulting me. I only thought that in a formal document my rights over the music ought to be maintained.

I will let you know when they are rehearsing my Symphony[1] and will be pleased if you could come.

Could I have the score of 'Joanna' back[2] – you promised it me a long time ago! Also Mr Frend promised me some books about Scott which I shall be very glad to have.

Yrs
R. Vaughan Williams

P.S. I want to make it quite clear that you have had my absolute permission to do what you like with my music, but this is not official.

[1] The Sixth Symphony.
[2] Music for the film *The Loves of Joanna Godden*, *CW* 1946/2.

486. To G. E. Moore

[13 October 1947]

The White Gates,
Dorking.

My dear Moore

I was delighted & surprized to get your good wishes for my birthday[1] – It carries me back to old days when you used to sing 'Adelaide' & play Beethoven sonatas.

Yrs
R. Vaughan Williams

[1] VW's 75th birthday on 12 October. Moore sent messages for VW's 80th and 85th birthdays, the latter being acknowledged in almost exactly similar terms—see no. 724.

487. To the conductors of the choirs of the Leith Hill Musical Festival

[October 1947]

Could this be typed and sent now to the conductors of the choirs –

I want to thank you all for the beautiful wireless set and for the lovely flowers for which my wife wants me to send especial thanks. The wireless is a splendid one & when my wife has to stay in her room is a great blessing.[1]

R. Vaughan Williams

[1] This thanks the choirs for a gift marking his 75th birthday (12 Oct.).

488. To Richard Walthew[1]

18 October 1947

From R. Vaughan Williams,
The White Gates,
Westcott Road,
Dorking.

Oct 18th 1947

Dear Walthew

I do not suppose I can make you understand what a pleasure it was to get your letter.

I owe you such a lot from those early days – you taught me so much (and not only about music; we discussed Browning, theology & all sorts of other strange subjects). Do you remember taking me to 'Carmen' & I being then an insufferable young prig went prepared to scoff but remained to pray – & that when you asked me to your home & we played pfte duets (or rather you played & I followed after as best I could) – these are all fragrant memories for which I am grateful.

You know, you must have thought me a mere amateur – & I have been so, more or less, all my life – I seem to have had no natural techniques – but have had to hammer out everything from the facts of the case.

I wish we ever met now –

Do you remember that?—I *think* I have got it right.[2]

Always yours
R. Vaughan Williams.

[1] A fellow student with VW at the RCM. VW often played piano duets with him. See 'A Musical Autobiography' (*NM*, 182–3), an essay which was first published three years after the date of the present letter and echoes some of its phraseology. Richard Henry Walthew was about three weeks younger than VW and spent much of his life as an opera and piano teacher at the Guildhall School of Music and Drama. His most successful compositions were in the field of chamber music. He died in 1951. There is an article on him in *Grove 5*.

[2] The opening of Walthew's cantata *The Pied Piper*, a work which was performed by the Highbury Philharmonic Society in 1893 and was presumably heard then by VW. The quotation is a good example of VW's musical memory.

489. To Cedric Glover

10 December 1947

The White Gates,
Dorking.

10th December, 1947

Dear Glover

Thank you very much for your letter.

I have written to the two players you suggest, Mrs. Forrest and Miss Jordan.[1]

In engaging professionals I hope you will give first chance to our 'Old stalwarts', – I think I sent you a list of those who were practically essential and those who had often played for us, – before, so to speak, 'second strings'. I think your engagements ought to come from these two lists before you go outside, but I am quite glad to have Mrs Pike.

In your letter you mention four amateur horns. Now, I don't want any amateur horns – they are rather too dangerous. Also we have no horns, as you know, in the 'Passion'.

I enclose a letter in answer to my own from Josiah Wedgwood.[2]

Yours sincerely
R. Vaughan Williams

Major Glover,
Rotherwood,
Holmbury St. Mary,
Dorking.

[1] Marjory Jordan, vet to the VW cats.

[2] VW enclosed a letter from his cousin Josiah Wedgwood, apparently in response to a request from VW, saying that he had invited Miss Glover (Cedric Glover's daughter, Rowena) to lunch at the works and hoping that she would like the North Staffs. Workers Educational Association job; there were quite a few nice people connected with it.

490. To Fritz Hart

[?1947]

The White Gates,
Dorking.

My dear Fritz

I was very glad to hear from you again and to know that all goes well with you. We've been hearing quite a lot of young American music here. Barber and Roy Harris seem to me to come out best.[1] Copland in spite of his wrong notes seems to have something there though I cannot always get at it.

My love to Marvell.

Yrs
R. Vaughan Williams

[1] Samuel Barber (1910–81); Roy Harris (1898–1979).

491. To RVW from Ernest Irving 9 January 1948

9th January, 1948.

Thank you for the scores which I devoured with avidity.

Regarding the main titles, there should be no difficulty whatever in making these sound exactly as they look. Considering that you have placed yourself in Statu pupillari the orchestration is most promising. In fact, I could not have done it better myself. I should like to record them on February 6th in the afternoon at Denham, also the vocal section which follows. Will you please let me know who you would like to sing the solo and how many voices you would like in the choir?

Major Meade can remain for you a name as the Indian Chanty has disappeared from the opus and the Major's co-operation with it. For your information, he is a very nice man and a great authority on matter Persian, Turkish and Arabian, besides being a middle ranking minor poet.

I quite agree with your point about the military march. 'Land of Hope & Glory', however, would be wrong for the situation, which demands a bright 6/8. I cannot think of any English march of the period sufficiently well known to the present generation of filmgoers to immunize you, but as the band is in dim perspective, we can photograph them to the rhythm of 'The Queen's birthday'. Then, if you disapprove of the result, we can dub any 6/8 march of which everybody approves, or, alternatively, you could write one yourself if you feel in light hearted or penguinesque mood.

Regarding the timings, I am afraid no amount of bullying on my part will produce measurements of film that has not yet been shot, so you will be 'walking in darkness' (though not necessarily in B minor[1]) for some while yet. It is quite likely that when the film is cut, you may wish to synchronize some of the happenings a little closer than it is possible to do before shooting. This may involve, beside the carpentry and juggling which I can bring to your aid, some structural alterations which will need your personal attention, but we cannot deal with that for some months and it is a good thing to get all the music we can into the score.

[1] The key of the well-known aria in *Messiah*.

492. To VW from Ernest Irving

[20 January 1948[1]]

Ealing Studios Limited
Ealing Green
London W 5

Una vox et praeterea nihil.[2]

I very much regret to state
Your scheme for treating No. 8,
Has pulled us up with quite a jerk,
Because we fear it will not work.

Miss Mabel Ritchie's off-stage tune,
Besides annoying Miss Lejeune,[3]
Would cover, blur, confuse and fog
Our most expensive dialogue.

Unfriendly Charles[4] will cry 'Aroynt',
V.W. and his counterpoint,
The public wish to hear, sobs Cole
Why Scott, the ass, pursued the Pole.

Failure they meet, and ruin black,
Who mix two voices on one track;
Choose then a horn or cello which
Have different timbres, weight and pitch.

Your programme would, as you aver,
Astound and shock the chronicler,
But so, I must admit with pain
Did Casca, Crippen, Cromwell, Cain.

You would not wish with siren tones
To deafen fans of Odeons
Who, listening to Miss Ritchie's A,
Would miss what Kathleen[5] has to say.

The frequencies her voice employs
Should be kept free from other noise,
Your tune should be of different hue,
And run below, or soar the blue.

Forgive me, Maestro, if I seem
To hold the voice in small esteem
Its use like oboe, trumpet, flute,
Is when the characters are mute.[6]

[1] Pencil note on Irving's carbon copy.

[2] An adaptation, included in Brewer's *Dictionary of Phrase and Fable*, of a phrase taken from Plutarch who told that it was used by a Spartan of a nightingale he had just plucked: 'Vox tu es, et nihil prӕterea' ('You are a voice and nothing else').

[3] C. A. Lejeune, film critic of *The Observer*.

[4] Charles Frend, director of *Scott of the Antarctic*.

[5] Scott's wife.

[6] Irving was worried about VW's plan to include a wordless soprano solo in the music for the film *Scott of the Antarctic* in case it distracted attention from actions or speech. In the end it was made to sound so disembodied that there was no difficulty.

493. To *The Musical Times* 27 February 1948

The White Gates,
Dorking.

February 27th. 1948.

To: The Editor of the 'Musical Times'[1]

Sir,

The Article on Hubert Parry in your issue of February 1948 appears to one who had the privilege of being a pupil of that great man, as inept, inaccurate and impertinent (I note the article is not signed).[2] We are told, for example, that Parry is not quite so unworthy of remembrance as – Paolo Tosti and Augusta Holmes!

If your contributor's object was merely to insult Parry's memory, which according to him is already non-existent, why write about him at all? The frequent performances of 'Blest Pair'[3] and the fact that 'Jerusalem' is becoming our second National Anthem are apparently of no account. It is true, of course that many people do not like 'Jerusalem'. There are also people who do not like 'Land of Hope and Glory' but that does not mean that either of these are forgotten.

We are told in this article that because the more intelligent critics of Parry's day took the trouble to explain why they admired his music they did not *really* admire it; they ought, apparently, to have said, 'This music gets me, I cannot tell you why'. But in those days the better writers on music thought it necessary to give a reason for the faith that was in them. The modern 'sensitized plate'[4] style of criticism had not yet been made fashionable by the Manchester school.[5] Your contributor asks, 'Was his music ever really loved?'. I can only speak from my own small experience. I have had the honour to conduct 'Job' with a country choir more than once and they are always asking for it again and their enthusiasm for it, probably regretfully uncritical, showed itself in their emotional singing. Luckily for them they do not have to analyse their appreciation, and passages which we professional prigs may condemn as Mendelssohnian or Brahmsy are eagerly and uncritically swallowed by them. The truth is that Parry's genius was not, as this writer suggests, 'clean and bright and making no smoke', but was like a smouldering fire, often obscured by smoke and dust but occasionally bursting forth in a great flame as in, for instance, the Prelude of 'Job' or the superb choral passage starting 'Then shall God also confess'.

Some of us will remember a performance of Parry's '1914' Symphony at the Balfour Gardiner concerts in that year – We all felt that here was something very great and portentous struggling for expression like a lion in a cage, but which the inhibitions of what one supposes must have been an inadequate technique, refused to set at liberty.

The chief fault of Parry's orchestral writing is usually held to be his bad scoring and this is partly true; he had a moral repugnance to what he called 'mere colour'; but what about that magical horn note just before the entry of the voices in 'Blest Pair of Sirens'? The style is the man and we cannot fundamentally alter Parry's orchestration without also taking away that individuality which is essential to a work of art.

I was once sitting next to Elgar at a rehearsal of Parry's 'Symphonic Variations'. I commented on the curious spiky sound of the orchestra which fascinates me though it may repel others. I said to Elgar, 'I suppose this would be called bad scoring though personally I do not think so'. He turned on me almost fiercely and said, 'Of course it's not bad scoring; that music could not have been scored anyhow else'. Elgar probably recognised this profound truth when he tried, at the request I believe of Sir Hugh Allen, to smarten up the orchestration of 'Jerusalem' with the result that the music seemed to lose much of its character.

Parry suffered all his life from bad performances, owing partly to the inadequate preparation of Festival conditions, partly it must be admitted, owing to a certain hurry and carelessness which prevented him giving the finishing touches of marks of phrasing and expression to his work, partly to his extraordinarily bad conducting and to his good nature which prevented his insisting on adequate rehearsal. Is it not time that new editions of his work were prepared, carefully and accurately edited? This would make the music glow once again with fresh life and vigour. I see that the B.B.C. are performing 'Job'. Let them follow it up with the still finer 'De Profundis' and let them be carefully prepared and intelligently understood performances and not merely barren acts of piety to be got through somehow as a dreary duty.

Ralph Vaughan Williams

[1] This letter was not published.

[2] 'Hubert Parry' in the *Musical Times*, 89 (Feb. 1948), 41–2 was an unsigned centenary assessment of Parry's music and achievement. While VW was disposed to take issue with the approach taken by the writer, the article was in general admiring of Parry.

[3] *Blest Pair of Sirens*.

[4] A reference to photography, in which Adeline was much interested, having been taught by her aunt, Julia Margaret Cameron.

[5] Perhaps a reference to the critic Neville Cardus.

494. To Fritz Hart

25 March [1948]

The White Gates,
Dorking.

March 25

Dear Fritz

I was glad to get your letter and will try to perpetrate a few bits of local news. The chief seems to be the proposed 1951 festival for which commissions and competitions are flying about everywhere – Opera, large small & medium, Ballet, symphony, concerto, unison song and what-not. I fear the result will be, as usual, still-born.

Do you remember Dunhill's series of your '2nd performance' concerts which were labelled by some wit 'last performance concerts'.[1]

There is to be also an Elgar festival quite soon. Have you seen Bernard Shores new book '16 Symphonies' – it is very good.[2]

I am recovering from a performance in Dorking of the Matthew Passion – last Saturday. We had 85 children to sing the ripieno in No.1 so *they* were heard – & we had 8 flutes for 'let him be crucified' so *they* were heard.

I have just finished a very interesting book about Delius by Hutchings.[3] He argues that the fact that Delius never went down into the Arena and fought with beasts, but lived a (fairly comfortable) 'life beautiful' at Gres had no influence on his music. I feel that some of Gustav's struggles w^{d} have added *strength* to his undeniable beauty.[4]

My love to Marvel.

Yrs
RVW

[1] These were founded in 1907. See *New Grove*.
[2] Bernard Shore, *Sixteen Symphonies* (London, 1947).
[3] Arthur Hutchings, *Delius* (London, 1948).
[4] VW expresses a similar opinion about Delius in no. 361.

495. To Alan Frank at OUP

25 March 1948

The White Gates,
Dorking, Surrey.

25th March, 1948.

Dear Frank,

Here are my answers to your letter.

The 'Partita' takes about twenty minutes.

The reference to Henry Hall only means that after hearing one of his more nostalgic pieces I was moved to write that Intermezzo.

Personally I think the performance was extremely good. They had worked hard at it.[1]

As regards programme notes, I am sending you a copy of the notes which I have written for the Philharmonic. I should like this to be used whenever programme notes are wanted. I suppose the Philharmonic would give leave? I will send the musical illustrations when I get a proof.[2]

As regards the Saxophone – it is essential to the work. I am tired of boiling down my work so that it can be played by two banjos and a harmonium, and surely all clarinetists * [*sic*] double the saxophone now. If they cannot run to a Saxophone I fear they cannot do the Symphony. You might as well play it without double basses.[3]

The Tudor Singers were rather previous. I have not written a new work for them, but they are giving the first concert performance of my Motet 'The Souls of the Righteous', which I wrote for Westminster Abbey.[4]

Yours sincerely,
R. Vaughan Williams

* except of course Alan Frank

Encl.

Alan Frank, Esq.,
Oxford University Press.

[1] Frank had written on 22 Mar. saying that he heard the first performance of the work 'with great interest' though the performance had struck him as being not too assured in places; the reference to Henry Hall [the Intermezzo has the subtitle 'Homage to Henry Hall'] had eluded him.

[2] In his letter of 22 Mar. Frank had asked for information about when VW had been working on the Sixth Symphony, *CW* 1947/3, and for any other vital points of interest to anyone writing a programme note.

[3] Frank had asked whether VW would permit the tenor saxophone part to be played on a bass clarinet when no saxophone was available, fearing otherwise that potential performances might be lost.

[4] Frank had told VW that the Tudor Singers had sent him a programme announcing a new work by VW in their concert on 30 Apr. and he would much like to see it if it existed. VW had offered them the first concert performance of *The Souls of the Righteous*, *CW* 1947/1, in lieu of a new work. The Tudor Singers and their conductor Harry Stubbs had close links with VW and gave the first private performance of *An Oxford Elegy* in November the following year at The White Gates. Frank was a keen clarinettist.

496. To John Barbirolli

8 July 1948

The White Gates,
Dorking,
Surrey.

8th July, 1948.

Dear Barbirolli,

It was a fine performance at Cheltenham, and it came through very well. Thank you and your orchestra very much.[1]

The first movement was wonderfully clear, as also was the third. I liked the slow opening of the slow movement. The only thing I find not quite happy (and perhaps that was only the wireless) was the reiterated trumpets. I originally put dots over the notes and that made them sound too perky altogether, so I changed these to stress marks and now that seems to have taken some of their fierce quality away. I do not quite know what the solution is, but it may be only over the wireless.

I hope I shall hear you do it again one day. Perhaps not over the wireless.

Thank you also for your postcard from abroad which gave me great pleasure.

I also listened to Arthur Benjamin's Symphony which impressed me very much. I think the Second Movement is the most completely satisfactory. The beginning and the end of the Third Movement are fine, but it seems to fall to pieces a little in the middle.

The First Movement I did not altogether get hold of and in the last movement I could not hear all the tunes he promised us but that may have been the wireless reception.

Please give my kind regards to your wife and thank her for her share in the postcard.

Yours sincerely,
R. Vaughan Williams.

John Barbirolli, Esq.,
Hallé Concert Society,
Manchester.

P.S. Your letter just arrived; many thanks for it.

[1] Barbirolli had conducted a performance of the Sixth Symphony.

497. To Arthur Benjamin[1]

16 July 1948

The White Gates,
Dorking,
Surrey.

16th July, 1948.

Dear Benjamin

I shall of course be proud to be the dedicatee of your Symphony and I should like to hear the records very much.[2] The only trouble is that we have an old-fashioned gramophone and it does not take anything but the commercial wax records. If yours are of the very thin kind they might not do on our machine. At all events we should have to have special needles ('trailer' I think), so it might be better if I heard them one day when I was in London.[3]

Otherwise I am free all week after next except July 29th.

R. Vaughan Williams

Arthur Benjamin, Esq.,
3, Gloucester Gate Mews,
London, N.W.1.

[1] Australian/British composer (1893–1961).
[2] Presumably of the performance which had just taken place at Cheltenham.
[3] Recordings taken from broadcasts were made on acetate discs, on which normal commercial steel needles could not be used.

498. To Alan Frank at OUP

5 August 1948

The White Gates,
Dorking,
Surrey.

5th August, 1948.

Dear Frank

Here are the facts with regard to my undertaking to the National Federation of Women's Institutes.

They have asked me to do a choral suite for women's voices, founded, I think, entirely on folk songs. There will be about sixteen songs in all, some for elementary choirs, some for more advanced, some for massed singing and some for unaccompanied singing. I have undertaken to do this, though it seems to me that April 1949 is rather early since I understand the concert actually will not take place until 1950. Still I will do my best.[1]

They asked me about [a] fee and I said that they had better arrange that with you. I presumed some fee was usual in the case of a commissioned work, and I think this is right, though probably I should give it back to them as a donation; but still, on principle, they ought to give it to me, or any other composer.

That is all I can tell you about it at present. Indeed I have hardly begun to think about it, I have so many other things I want to get finished first.

Thank you very much for your paragraph about 'P.P.' I received one or two telephone rings, but not many. I see there have been a few press notices which were just what I wanted, but no offers of a performance![2]

Yours sincerely,
R. Vaughan Williams

Alan Frank, Esq.

[1] *Folk Songs of the Four Seasons*, *CW* 1949/1, was completed in vocal score by Jan. 1949 and being orchestrated by Jan. 1950.

[2] *The Pilgrim's Progress*. OUP had apparently published the news that VW was working on the opera.

499. To Steuart Wilson at the BBC[1]

12 August 1948

The White Gates,
Dorking,
Surrey.

12th August, 1948.

Dear Steuart

Yesterday I sent to you by Registered Post, vocal score and libretto of my 'Pilgrim's Progress'. Even if you do not feel inclined to go further with it I should be very grateful for any criticisms that you, or any other expert that you like to show it to, has to make.

Of course the obvious criticism is that it is not 'dramatic' – but then it is not meant to be. Whether this is a good excuse I do not know. It is more of a ceremony really than a drama. This applies especially to the end of Act I. I do not know whether Act I of 'Parsifal' is any precedent for this, but even here there is a certain amount of what dramatic experts call 'conflict' when Amfortas makes his rather melodramatic interruption. On the other hand my ceremony only takes about seven minutes whereas Wagner's takes over half an hour.

Perhaps the initiation scene from the 'Magic Flute' is a nearer parallel.

As regards James Robertson's objection, it seemed to be chiefly the apparent large size of the cast, but perhaps he did not realise that there is a different cast for each Act, and the parts can be doubled, trebled or even quadrupled.

Also many of the small parts, especially in 'Vanity Fair', which consist only of one or two sentences could be sung by members of the chorus.

It would want a full orchestra but nothing abnormal.

Yrs
RVW

[1] Wilson had recently been appointed Director of Music at the BBC.

500. To T. Tertius Noble[1]

4 September 1948

The White Gates,
Dorking.

4th September, 1948

Dear Noble

Thank you so much for writing and sending the press notice.

I had hoped to see you in England again this year. We had a very pleasant but such a short meeting last time.

I always tell my friends that I have the distinction of being the only person whom Walter Parratt and yourself entirely failed to teach the organ to.

Yours
R. Vaughan Williams

Dr T Tertius Noble
Old Garden Road
Rockport,
MASS, U.S.A.

[1] 1867–1953; English organist and composer of mainly liturgical music. He was organist of St Thomas's, Fifth Avenue, New York from 1912 to 1947. He was organist at Ely Cathedral at the time VW was at Cambridge.

501. To Arnold Barter

15 September 1948

The White Gates,
Dorking.

Sept 15 1948

Dear Barter

Very Confidential

You know how much I admire your work & I know how much you must feel that you are often frustrated from perfection by lack of funds – I should therefore be very glad if I might help – only my name must be kept *right out of it* – To every one else it must be an 'anonymous donor' *through* me – this may be necessary as the cheque is in my name & your treasurer & banker will see it. One other thing so as to avoid a scandial [*sic*] (though I leave you quite a free hand) that no part of the money shall be spent on any concert in which a work of mine appears.[1]

Yrs
R. Vaughan Williams

[1] This letter is a very good example of VW's habit of doing good by stealth. See further no. 502. The condition that his gift should not be used for any concert including a VW work was a forerunner of one of the conditions under which the RVW Trust was to operate.

502. To Arnold Barter

[19 September 1948[1]]

From R. Vaughan Williams,
The White Gates,
Westcott Road,
Dorking.

Sunday

Dear Barter

I think the best way (I ought to have thought of it before) is *not* to pay the cheque into the Philharmonic a/c *at all*. But to keep it in your own bank as *yours* – to be used by *you* at *your* discretion in the interests of the Philharmonic[2]

– Then you will have *entire* control over the money & the society need not know anything about it unless you chose – & in that way my name need not be even mentioned.

Yrs
RVW

[1] The letter is marked by the recipient 'Recd. Sept 19/48' and by VW 'Sunday'. As 19 Sept. 1948 *was* a Sunday it was apparently delivered the same day. Probably Barter, like VW, was at Worcester for the Three Choirs (*RVW*, 286).

[2] i.e. the Bristol Philharmonic Society.

503. To Percy Young[1]

20 October 1948

The White Gates,
Dorking.

20th October, 1948.

Dear Dr. Young,

I make it a rule never to read anything written about myself before publication, otherwise I could hardly pass anything I did not like, and I might be held guilty of inspiring anything I did like.

Of course any facts you want to know I shall be delighted to help you with, but I am afraid you will find me very shaky as to dates, &c.

I look forward with great interest to your book when it comes out.[2]

I have today had a letter from Eric Greene.[3] He tells me you are great friends.

Yours sincerely,
R. Vaughan Williams

Dr Percy M. Young,
Wolverhampton & Staffs Technical College,
Wolverhampton.

[1] Percy Young (1912–2004), writer on music. He was best known for his work on Elgar.

[2] *Vaughan Williams* (London, 1953).

[3] A tenor, who often sang the Evangelist in RVW's annual performances of the St Matthew Passion at Dorking. See *Grove* 5.

504. To Derek G. Smith

20 October 1948

The White Gates,
Dorking.

20th October, 1948.

Dear Mr. Smith,

I was interested in your letter.[1] I fear that your search for English music of the type of lullabies or laments or instrumental pieces would be difficult. Folk music, as I daresay you know, is always applied music, either a tune to fit the words of a song or the steps of a dance.

The songs, according to their nature, are sometimes sad and romantic but the dance tunes are nearly always energetic and lively, and we occasionally find slow and romantic song tunes such as 'Newcastle', 'Greensleeves' and a carol tune, the name of which I forget, converted into dance tunes by livening up the rhythm.

You tell me that you are interested in the structure of the folk tune. I gather from your letter that you have already read Cecil Sharp's 'English Folk Song, Some Conclusions'. I am also sending you a little pamphlet on the same subject which I wrote some years ago. I would also advise you to read the opening chapters of Hubert Parry's 'Evolution of the Art of Music'.[2]

I fear the local branch of the E.F.D.S. would not be much use to you. They seem to be entirely occupied organising dance parties, but you might write for advice to the Librarian at Headquarters:

Miss Dean-Smith,[3]
Librarian,
Cecil Sharp House,
London, N.W.1.

I am glad to hear that you are progressing with your composing. I feel sure the study of our own folk music forms a very sound basis on which to build.

Here are the names of one or two song tunes of the more romantic kind, which you may not know:

'Sheep Shearing'　　both from Cecil Sharp's collection
'The Cuckoo'

'My Bonny Boy' 'Lazarus'	from 'English County Songs'
'She's Like a Swallow'	from 'Folk Songs from Newfoundland'

Yours sincerely,
R. Vaughan Williams

Derek G. Smith, Esq.,
39, Newlyn Drive,
Western Boulevard,
Nottingham.

[1] Smith had written asking for information about English folk music.

[2] A second edition of Sharp's book had been published in 1936. VW's pamphlet *English Folk-Songs*, the text of a lecture, had been published in 1912 and a 10th edition of Parry's book had been published in 1931.

[3] Margaret Dean-Smith was remembered as being rather formidable, with an encyclopedic memory for her subject. She was author of *A Guide to English Folk Song Collections 1822–1952*, published by the EFDSS in 1954.

505. To Ernest Irving

26 October [1948]

From R. Vaughan Williams,
The White Gates,
Westcott Road,
Dorking.

Oct 26th

Dear Irving

V. good – only are not Main Titles & End Music too much alike [?] – but just as you think best. How about one of the 'snow marches'? I presume that the 'prologue' includes Mabel.[1]

I suppose it is just possible that I am down for an invitation to the Command performance[2] – please see that my name is *deleted*. It w^{d} be difficult to refuse & I c^{d} not face it.

My love to Una.

Yrs
RVW

[1] Margaret Ritchie, who performed the wordless soprano solo in the film *Scott of the Antarctic*.

[2] This took place on 29 Nov. 1948.

506. To Eric Walter White[1]

4 November 1948

The White Gates,
Dorking,
Surrey.

4th November, 1948.

Dear Mr. White,

I am sorry I cannot come to the Music Panel Meeting.

Would it be in order to suggest to you that brass bands should be included in the 1951 festival?[2] As I daresay you know they are the most popular form of music in England and their technique is wonderful; their taste shocking. Perhaps if we admitted them into the fold it would help them in that matter.

Yours sincerely,
R. Vaughan Williams

Eric White, Esq.,
Arts Council of Great Britain,
4, St. James's Square,
S.W.1.

[1] Assistant Secretary of the Arts Council of Great Britain, 1942–71.

[2] The Festival of Britain.

507. To Eric Walter White

18 November 1948

The White Gates,
Dorking,
Surrey.

18th November, 1948.

Dear Mr. White,

Thank you very much for your letter. I have also had one from Miss Glasgow, and though your letters flatter me they rather alarm me, because as I have already explained to her this will be in no sense a performance. The work is not really finished yet and it is partly for this reason that I want to go through it with some experts before I do put the final touches.[1]

I should like to ask a few friends including, of course, Steuart Wilson[2] and anybody he wants to bring and perhaps somebody from Sadlers Wells, and of course Miss Glasgow, yourself, Mr. Dennison[3] and anybody else from 4 St. James' Square, but anybody who comes must clearly understand what they are in for. So I have suggested to Miss Glasgow perhaps you will want to withdraw your kind offer on hearing this. If not, the question of dates will be a difficulty.

Up to Christmas all dates are free for me and Michael Mullinar except November 26th (evening), November 27th, November 30th, December 1st, 4th, 5th, 8th (evening), 12th, 15th, 16th, 17th, 20th and 21st. These are dates on which I am not free. Also you must not choose a date on which Steuart Wilson cannot come, because he is one of the important people.

Will you thank Mr. Dennison very much for his suggestions about the singers, but I do not think that is practical.[4]

I shall have, I hope, about four or five copies of the libretto which I can hand round at the time and a few people can look over the music. Other people I should like to ask because I have mentioned [it] are Hubert Foss, Alan Frank, Edmund Rubbra, Gerald Finzi, Inglis Gundry and a few others.

I am very grateful to you for all you are doing.

Yours sincerely,
R. Vaughan Williams

Eric White, Esq.,
Arts Council of Great Britain.

[1] The work referred to is the opera *The Pilgrim's Progress* (*CW* 1951/1).

[2] Steuart Wilson was, at this time, Director of Music at the BBC, but in 1949 he went to be Deputy General Administrator of the Royal Opera House, where *Pilgrim's Progress* was eventually to be performed.

[3] John Denison, music director of the Arts Council, 1948–65.

[4] Denison had said that if VW wanted two or three singers for some of the airs, he could probably arrange to pay them a small token fee.

508. To S. P. Waddington[1]

15 December [1948]

From R. Vaughan Williams,
The White Gates,
Westcott Road,
Dorking.

Dec 15

Dear Waddington

You may have seen in the Times before this reaches you that our dear friend R. O. Morris died early this morning. A sudden heart attack and he was only ill a few minutes.

I am not writing to many people but I want to tell you personally – I am sure you know in what affection he held you and how much he admired you.[2]

Yrs
R. Vaughan Williams

[1] Sydney P. Waddington (1869–1953), composer and teacher at the RCM. He conducted the first private performances of *Hugh the Drover* there and was greatly admired by VW, who said of him that he was the finest sight-reader he had ever met.

[2] Waddington and Morris had been colleagues at the RCM.

509. To Ernest Irving

16 December 1948

The White Gates,
Dorking.

16th December, 1948

Dear Irving

This letter is already out of date owing to our telephone talk – so read no further.

I should like it very much and I feel sure the O.U.P. will agree.[1]

The only trouble to my mind is – will it prevent me later on writing an 'Antartic Symphony'[2] using the same themes, which I have slowly revolving in my mind, though it may never come to anything?

I will do my best to come to the H.M.V. on December 30th. 10 o'clock, I presume? But you do not say.

I do hope you will be better by then or even before.

Yrs
RVW

Ernest Irving, Esq.,
Ealing Studios
Ealing, W.

[1] Irving appears to have suggested that a suite should be made of the music of *Scott of the Antarctic*.

[2] VW suffered some confusion about the spelling of Antarctic—subsequently he varies between Antartic Symphony and Sinfonia Antarctica until eventually the correct *Sinfonia Antartica* was adopted. See nos. 580 and 597.

510. To Douglas Lilburn

29 December 1948

The White Gates,
Dorking,

29th December, 1948.

Dear Lilburn

Thank you so much for your wonderful parcel. You are one ahead of me with the honey because I have only just started on the tin you sent before.

I must tell you that R. O. Morris died just before Xmas. I think that both you and Page were pupils of his. Certainly those who came under him have had the privilege of being under one of the best teachers there have ever been, and I think the most distinguished musical theoritician [*sic*] in this country, but people do not entirely realise his quality as a composer, and of course he made no effort to make his work known – in fact he did his best to prevent it.

I have been urging the BBC to give a programme of his work so that people may realise its unobtrusive beauty and the wonderful clarity of its texture, especially, I think the suite and the short pieces for string quartet and also a delightful choral work 'Corinna', which we did at Dorking two years ago.

Please give my kind remembrances to Page when next you see him.

Yrs
R. Vaughan Williams

Douglas Lilburn, Esq.,
Victoria University College

511. To Hubert Foss [1948[1]]

Dear Hubert

Many thanks for interesting programme – I am again in the film way (9 months does not seem to apply in this case) – & I am rationing my visits to London – I am sending you my 'musical influences' in a few days.[2]

Yrs
RVW

[1] According to note by UVW.

[2] Foss was preparing his book on VW, *Ralph Vaughan Williams: A Study* (London, 1950), which included a piece by VW, 'A Musical Autobiography', later reprinted with slight revisions in *Some Thoughts on Beethoven's Choral Symphony with Writings on Other Musical Subjects* (London, 1953) and again in *NM*.

512. To Eric Walter White 9 February 1949

The White Gates,
Dorking,
Surrey.

9th February, 1949.

CONFIDENTIAL.

Dear Mr. White,

Thank you very much for your letter. My first re-action to your suggestion is that my Opera[1] is absolutely theatrical and could not be played anywhere outside a theatre. Certainly if I had written with a view to a performance in a Cathedral I should have done it very differently. For instance, in the nave of a cathedral any procession or entrance would take about three times as long and would want three times as much music. Also it should be much more of a pageant.

Secondly, I cannot see my opera without scenery and a curtain to rise and fall. The scenery could be the merest suggestion but, for instance, in the scene where the stars come out, the whole scene demands some form of realism there. Also the orchestration, which is now finished, pre-supposes the acoustics of a theatre, and I very much doubt whether it would be successful in a big building like a cathedral.

However, as you suggest it seems to be either that or nothing, so I do not want to absolutely turn it down and I should very much like to have a talk with the theatrical producer who has actually produced drama in a cathedral and see if, as it stands, it is possible.

Further, I feel that if it is first done in a Church it will remain there for evermore and will never get to a theatre.

If it is done in a Cathedral at all I think I should prefer Chichester as being much easier of access for me.[2]

Thank you very much for all the trouble you are taking.

Yours sincerely,
R. Vaughan Williams

[1] *The Pilgrim's Progress* (CW 1951/1).

[2] It is interesting that the persistent suggestion that *The Pilgrim's Progress* was more suited to a church performance than to the theatre was being made as early as this. VW continued to resist the idea: see no. 555 to Dent and no. 560 to Foss.

513. To Eric Walter White

28 February [1949[1]]

The White Gates,
Dorking.

Feb 28

Very confidential

Dear Mr. White,

Thank you for your letter. I cannot make up my mind about Mr. Guthrie[2] – All I know about him or his work firsthand is that he once sent me a libretto which seemed to me to be very bad and I was horrified by the newspaper accounts of the new production of Carmen at Sadlers Wells – and other people tell me that he thinks too much about Guthrie and too little about the work he is producing –

On the other hand I know him to have great experience and skill and he might be able to point out a great many weak places in my opera[3] which I had not noticed – But from what people tell me I should feel so frightened that he would use my opera just as a peg on which to hang his own fantastic notions and if I tried to pin him down he would probably lose interest –

This is my first reaction to your suggestion – but of course I may be all wrong – Other possibilities which I have in my mind are Clive Carey or Jooss[4] – I happen to know that Jooss saw the production of my 'Shepherds'[5] in Brunswick and was impressed by it.

In my present state of mind I do not think it would be a good plan to interview Guthrie before March 8th – [6]

Yrs sincerely
R. Vaughan Williams

[1] Year taken from context.
[2] Tyrone Guthrie (1900 – 71), theatre director.
[3] *The Pilgrim's Progress* (*CW* 1951/1).
[4] Kurt Jooss (1901–79), German choreographer who had fled Germany in 1933 and returned there in 1949.
[5] *The Shepherds of the Delectable Mountains* (*CW* 1922/6).
[6] The reason for not interviewing Guthrie until after 8 Mar. is not clear. In any case Nevill Coghill was eventually engaged to produce the opera.

514. To Katharine Thomson

9 March 1949

The White Gates,
Dorking.

9th March, 1949

Dear Mrs. Thomson

Mrs. Wood and I got home safely after a really thrilling day on Sunday.

I thought, for a company mostly young and all, I believe, amateur, without stage, scenery, property, costumes or orchestra, to hold our attention rivetted for the whole afternoon, was a wonderful feat.[1]

Their vitality and enthusiasm was astonishing.

I was sorry not to have had the pleasure of meeting your husband again. I fully thought from what he said, he was coming with you. I should like so much to have made his further acquaintance.

I send a sheet of suggestions for you to pass on if you wish to Mr. Harrison or Professor Lewis. There are very few of them and these are not really criticisms but only suggestions for still further improvement, but the Producer and Musical Director must decide, of course, whether they pay attention to them or not.[2]

Yours sincerely
R. Vaughan Williams

Mrs. Thomson,
84, Oakfield Road,
Selly Park, Birmingham.
Encl.

[1] A rehearsal for *Sir John in Love* to be performed by the Clarion Singers on 18 and 19 Mar. at the Midland Institute, Birmingham. See *RVW*, 289.

[2] VW's sheet of suggestions for the producer, Tom Harrison, and the conductor, Anthony Lewis (Peyton and Barber Professor of Music at Birmingham 1947–68), listed 16 places where he felt the tempo or some other aspect was not quite right.

515. To Leonard Smith[1]

21 March [1949[2]]

From R. Vaughan Williams,
The White Gates,
Westcott Road,
Dorking.

March 21

Dear Mr Smith,

I have now had the Radiogram you kindly sent me on trial, for a week and I think you will like to have a report on it. The Gramophone part seems to be very satisfactory and gives my wife and myself great pleasure.

I do not feel so happy about the radio part – The chief part of my desire to try your machine which had been so highly recommended to me by Sir Malcolm Sargent was that I hoped that a more selective machine would eliminate the interference from foreign stations on wave length 514 (3rd programme) but I am sorry to say that the interference is just as bad as on my present much smaller set.

I have also tried 3rd programme on wave length 202, but here though there is no foreign interference there is a most unpleasant <> effect like a concertina. I ought to add that the switch 'radio selective' does not seem to help at all.

As regards the tone of the instrument this of course is a matter of opinion but I feel that the rather 'fruity' tone prevents clearness of articulation in quick passages. Also, though I like plenty of bass, this instrument seems to 'boom' excessively and I cannot cure this, though I have tried the 'tone switch' in every position. I wonder if it would be better if I contented myself with the gramophone which you originally – as you may remember – sent me in error.

Yours sincerely,
R. Vaughan Williams

[1] A member of the Artistes Department of the Columbia Gramophone Company with whom VW dealt over audio equipment.

[2] Year from stamp of receipt.

516. To Herbert Byard

24 March 1949

The White Gates,
Dorking,

24th March, 1949.

Dear Mr. Byard,

Thank you so much for your letter. I wish I had seen you on Saturday, and we could have talked things over. I have quoted your kind words in a letter I have written to my choir.

As regards the question of the end of No. 67.[1] I know that the B.G. edition[2] has the figured bass, but whenever I have heard the work it has been pure unison – even a performance in Amsterdam, so far as I can remember, which was supposed to be very correct and had all the horrors like harpsichord and other pedantries. I suppose if the harmonies were put in at all they were put in on the organ. I think one is quite justified, however, in leaving them out. In the same way I always leave out the harmonies that have a pure bass in the accompaniment to 'Eli, Eli' if possible on the organ only.

I should very much like a criticism of my realisation of the figured bass in the Evangelist part.

I remember the very interesting letter you wrote to the 'Times' some time ago condemning what you call the 'plops' in the ordinary pianoforte scores. I cannot believe that is what Bach meant and I venture to think he meant something more like what I wrote out for Gritton to play. Some people, however, strongly object to it and say it is not Bach, and other people go so far as to say that it is like a pianoforte concerto.

I should very much like to know what you think about this?

Yours sincerely
R. Vaughan Williams

H. Byard, Esq.

[1] i.e. of the St Matthew Passion in the edition by Elgar and Atkins: 'And when they came unto a place' (recitative for tenor and chorus).

[2] i.e. the complete edition of the works of J. S. Bach published in forty-six volumes by the Bach Gesellschaft 1851–1900.

517. To the conductors and the choirs of the Leith Hill Musical Festival

24 March 1949

The White Gates,
Dorking.

24th March, 1949.

Dear Conductors and Chorus,

As you know, I was rather disheartened at the early rehearsals of the 'Passion' this year. Well – I ought to have known better. I ought to have remembered that you never let down either L.H.M.F. or J.S.B.

Not only was the performance technically the best we have given, but it had a quality of flow in the phrases and an understanding of the real meaning of the music greater than we have formerly achieved. A friend, who is also a very fine musician writes: 'I have never heard a performance of the "Passion" in which the chorus seemed to have caught its spirit better, but not only had they caught the spirit of the work but they were technically equal to it.'[1]

When next you meet I want you to tell your Conductor what you feel about going on next year. Now we have got so far it seems a pity to take our hands from the plough. In a way the work will be easier because we shall know it better, but from another point of view harder, because more will be expected of us.

I am now 76 years old and the time must come before long when I shall have to relinquish the honour of conducting you, but I feel sure that you will show, through my successor, the same loyal devotion that you have always shown to great music and its greatest composer.

I like to think that our performance of the 'Passion' will never cease and that when you in your turn are unable to cope with your high Soprano A's and low bass D's, that the younger generation will be there, ready to step into the ranks from which you have reluctantly fallen out.[2]

Yours sincerely,
R. Vaughan Williams

[1] Herbert Byard. VW's response to his letter is no. 516.

[2] On the background to this letter see *RVW*, 290. The choir had performed both the St John and St Matthew Passions and VW was feeling tired and ill.

518. To Leonard Smith

31 March [1949[1]]

From R. Vaughan Williams,
The White Gates,
Westcott Road,
Dorking.

March 31

Dear Mr. Smith,

Reference A 7/7/ML

Thank you for your letter – I do not want to trouble your experts to come down for nothing and I feel pretty sure – and I think it is also the opinion of your representative – that it was impossible to get the 3rd programme in this district without interference – and as I, doubtless wrongly, prefer the tone of my present set I must reluctantly return the set you kindly lent me – However I understand that you have a gramophone without the radio and if I liked that I should be glad to have one.

I suppose you have a show room in London – Could I call in one day and hear it before making up my mind?

Yours sincerely
R. Vaughan Williams

[1] Year from receipt stamp.

519. To Herbert Byard

6 April 1949

The White Gates,
Dorking,

6th April, 1949.

Dear Mr. Byard,

Many thanks for your second letter. There is only one point I want to answer – that is the question of the pianoforte going on all through the solos.

If Bach wanted that why did he have strings occasionally and then drop them at certain moments, unless he meant the key-board to take it up there? Also I feel that the pianoforte continuo right through would sound very monotonous, and of course the harpsichord would sound unbearable.

I was very much interested in all your quotations which I did not know. I wish you would write an article for 'Music & Letters' about filling in continuo.

You say your pupils often ask you how they can best give Bach exactly as he meant it. The answer, to my mind, is in the famous words of 'Punch' – 'don't'.[1] We want to give Bach and every other composer as the music appeals to us at the moment. As you say, the tone of all instruments and the conditions being so different, we cannot give it as Bach meant it, even if we wanted to. The question is whether he will bear transference to modern conditions. A great many of the eighteenth century composers will not bear the transposition and therefore had better be left alone; but Bach obviously can.

Yours sincerely
R. Vaughan Williams

H. Byard, Esq.

[1] Mr Punch's advice to those about to marry was invariably 'Don't'.

520. To Gilbert Murray[1]

19 April 1949

The White Gates,
Dorking,

April 19th, 1949

Dear *Professor Murray*

I expect you have seen with concern, as I have, the proposal to make a new translation of the Bible.

Of course if a few scholars helped by some literary hacks choose to convert the Bible into scholarly journalese I suppose it cannot be helped, but does not this new scheme mean more than this? Will not the new version be officially adopted and 'appointed to be read in churches'? If so, goodbye to our glorious heritage of English thought and language, founded on the authorized version. As it is we are having a hard tussle with Americanized newspaper diction and the English Bible is one of our stoutest bastions of resistance.

It is said that the Bible as it stands is no longer read, but will not the doubtful morality and still more doubtful history of the Old Testament make an even weaker appeal to the ordinary man if it is no longer clothed in magnificent language?

Promoters of this new scheme do not seem to realise that a thought and its expression are indivisible: if you take away the beauty of the expression the beauty of the thought will disappear also. The language of the English Bible has created thoughts in the minds of English people, different, no doubt, from the thoughts expressed in the Hebrew original, but it is these thoughts that have formed much that is best in the English character and it is these thoughts, or at all events, the most forcible expression of them which are, as I have said, one and the same of which these Wiseacres propose to deprive us.

We hear much about the so-called 'mistranslations'. Now much of the moral fibre of the English character is built up on these very mistranslations. Let me quote two examples:–

(1): Job's 'I know that my Redeemer liveth'. Even without Handel's music these words have been a stand-by to troubled minds for generations. Do our reformers propose to substitute 'Avenger', which I am told is the correct translation?

(2): In St. Luke XI.14 the English version has 'Goodwill toward men' which has surely always been the watchword of all right-thinking people, but the Vulgate, as you know, has 'Hominibus bonae voluntatis' which is a sentiment only worthy of the Soviet Republic. Are we to destroy all that three centuries have taught us to hold as true and of good report because it is now supposed that a few primitive Easterns thought differently?

I wonder if the translators will dare to alter the words of the Lord's Prayer or such phrases as 'Man goeth to his long home' or 'For there the wicked cease from troubling and there the weary are at rest', words which have engraved themselves indelibly on our consciousness.

If the translators keep these and others like them and 'modernise' the rest, the result will be an intolerable patchwork.

Will you not use your influence to stop all this? Perhaps you and other men in your position would write a letter to the 'Times' to set the ball rolling and you may be sure that all right-thinking people will back you up.

I am writing a similar letter to *the Master of Trinity College Cambridge.*

Yours sincerely
R. Vaughan Williams

[1] This letter refers to what resulted in the *New English Bible*, the first new translation since the King James version. It was sent in identical terms to G. M. Trevelyan. VW probably wrote to Murray and Trevelyan as fellow members of the Order of Merit but was unable to enrol either of them in his crusade. In 1951 he further wrote to Veronica Wedgwood in the hope of arousing her interest in the matter, as editor of *Time & Tide*—see no. 547. Italicized passages are added in VW's handwriting to the typed text.

521. To Arthur Butterworth[1]

25 May 1949

The White Gates,
Dorking.

25th May, 1949

Dear Mr Butterworth

Thank you very much for your letter. Your name means much to me because one of my greatest friends was George Butterworth, the composer. If you become as good a composer as him you will indeed do well.

I am glad to think that my music means something to you. If it did not mean anything to anybody why, indeed, write at all.

You say that the influence of certain composers on you changes as you get older. This is a natural element of development. If you did not change your opinions with more experience you would indeed be in a bad rut, and if your opinion of me changes with the course of years, as I daresay it will, you must not mind or think anything about 'disloyalty'. It only means that you are moving on to something better. I, myself, when I was quite young was an intense admirer of the music of Hubert Parry, but now that I am old, though I admire a great deal of his work very much, I no longer swallow him whole and can see obvious faults and weaknesses which I did not see when I was young.

On the other hand, do not be frightened by being influenced by other composers when you are young. Think of Brahms and Schumann, of Wagner and Weber and of Sibelius and Tschaikovsky. Indeed Sibelius' First Symphony was described by some humorist as the best symphony Tschaikovsky ever wrote. Again, this is a necessary part of development. I think it was Emerson who said that the most original genius was the most indebted man.

You say that you want to be a conductor and composer. Well nothing can be better training for both of these than to be an orchestral player, so do not leave that before you feel that you have got all you can out of it. I always wish I had been an orchestral player myself. I am sure it would have taught me a lot.

All that you say about my work only makes me wish it was better.

I was much interested in your idea for [the] trumpet part in my 'Pastoral Symphony'. I shall certainly keep your letter and make a note of your suggestion. I am afraid that at present trumpeters use their ordinary trumpets, and one of them confessed to me that he 'faked' the natural B flat and D by playing them a little bit flat or a little bit sharp as the case might be.

You may be interested to know how the idea of using those notes came to my mind. When I was in the army in the first war I was stationed at Bordon and every morning in the woods about half a mile off I used to hear a young trumpeter practising – and he was always (by accident of course) landing on that natural B flat, which as you know is not a recognised note in military trumpet calls; but the note fascinated me. As to the D, which as you know is slightly sharp in the tempered scale, it comes in the Trumpet Reveille and the notes C, D and E in the true scale have an extraordinary exhilarating effect which you do not get in the tempered scale.

At the first performance the trumpet part was played by Herbert Barr on his own trumpet and we could not find an E flat-pitched trumpet, but after the last rehearsal Mr Barr was passing a second-hand shop and he actually saw a natural E flat trumpet and he bought it for £5 and played on it that very evening. I afterwards bought it from him but unfortunately it was blitzed in the war.

If ever you come south let me know. I should like to see some of your work.

Yours sincerely
R. Vaughan Williams

[1] British composer, born in 1923. He studied in Manchester and became principal trumpet in the Hallé Orchestra.

522. To Gerald Finzi

5 June 1949

The White Gates,
Westcott Road,
Dorking.

June 5/49

Dear Gerald

Dictated

In my will which I made a few years ago I appointed Morris and Bliss as my literary executors. I should feel so happy if you could now undertake it with Arthur Bliss.

Your duties would be to look at all my unpublished manuscripts and decide what is to be done with them ie – either to be destroyed – kept in manuscript or published. All that you think ought to be published will be handed over to the Butterworth Trust to whom I am leaving all my copyrights and royalties.[1]

I do hope you will do this for me. Perhaps you will like to know also that I am leaving you Beethoven's tuning fork[2] which was left to me by Gustav Holst to be passed on to anyone I considered worthy.

Love to Joyce.

Yrs
RVW

[1] As matters turned out, VW's marriage to Ursula Wood in 1953 meant that it was she who was entrusted with the responsibilities that VW envisaged at this time might be held by Finzi and the Butterworth Trust.

[2] In fact Finzi died before this provision could take effect and in the end Ursula Vaughan Williams presented it to the British Library in 1992.

523. To Gerald Finzi

8 June 1949

The White Gates,
Dorking.

8th June, 1949

Dear Gerald

Thank you so much for saying you will do it.

I ought to have explained that you will not function until after both our deaths, unless of course one of us wishes to consult you unofficially.

As regards your two points:

1. You would, by my Will, have an absolutely free hand to do what you liked with all my manuscript works. As regards publication, that would rest with the Butterworth Trust – i.e.: they need not publish even if you do recommend it, but they could not publish unless you recommend it.
2. As regards the scattered manuscripts – I do not think there are many of them, and I do not think they are worth worrying about. I do not think they can be published or printed without the leave of my Executors.

My love to Joyce.

Yrs
RVW

Gerald Finzi, Esq.,
Ashmansworth,
near Newbury, BERKS.

524. To Cedric Thorpe Davie

15 June 1949

The White Gates,
Dorking,
Surrey.

15th June, 1949.

Dear Cedric

Please quote the whole Symphony if you feel inclined to, but whatever you do, do not make acknowledgments.

Dear Robin Milford is always plastering his printed works with notes such as 'This C natural is taken from Vaughan Williams' Symphony', or 'The D flat in the third bar is a quotation from Elgar's Gerontius', or 'I wish to acknowledge my indebtedness to Dr. R. O. Morris for the bar's rest on Page 27'.

I am glad the Snobopolis Festival is recognising its own country at last.[1]

My love to Bruno.

Yrs
RVW

[1] For the 1949 Edinburgh Festival Davie made arrangements of folk music for Allan Ramsay's *The Gentle Shepherd* (*New Grove*). This pastoral drama of 1725 was usually staged as a ballad opera with Scots airs (*CGLE* under Ramsay). He had also contributed incidental music to the 1948 Edinburgh Festival.

525. To Frank Howes[1]

10 August 1949

The White Gates,
Dorking,

10th August, 1949.

Dear Howes,

Confidential

I see in the 'Times' that the notice of my Symphony calls it 'the War Symphony'.[2]

I dislike that implied connection very much. Of course there is nothing to prevent any writer from expressing his opinion to that effect in a notice, but it is quite a different thing, this reference to a supposed title, as if it was official on my part.

Yours sincerely
R. Vaughan Williams

[1] Chief music critic of *The Times*.

[2] Presumably a notice for the Sixth Symphony.

526. To John Ireland

[14] August [1949]

From R. Vaughan Williams,
The White Gates,
Westcott Road,
Dorking.

Aug

My Dear John

I have only just discovered that your birthday was yesterday so these words of admiration and affection are a day behind the fair – but none the less sincere for that.[1]

– My mind goes back to very early days at the R.C.M. when we each heard our first orchestral works – how I admired your technical power! and how I felt (and still do) my almost amateurish bungling.

– You have always had the (apparently) masterly ease of expression (though I know it really comes from hours of hard labour) which I have always envied.

I wish you w[d] write another choral work – my people loved 'These things shall be'.

Well you have now reached the allotted span – but I feel sure that you have years of inspiration before you. I have already passed the limit by 6 years and am evidently becoming a garrulous old gentleman – so it is time I stopped

Yrs
R. Vaughan Williams

[1] John Ireland was born on 13 Aug. 1879.

527. To E. M. Tillett[1]

14 September 1949

The White Gates,
Dorking,
Surrey.

PERSONAL

14th September, 1949

Dear Mrs. Tillett,

Confidential

I hope you will forgive my taking the liberty of asking you for some advice which I know you are able, and I hope willing to give.

I am writing a piece for pianoforte and orchestra which will probably be done at one of the provincial Festivals and I want Michael Mullinar to play the pianoforte solo part; but it occurs to me that it might damage his chances as an accompanist if it was supposed that he had set up as a solo pianist, and it is as an accompanist that he has to earn his living, since as you know better than I do, only a few people like Myra Hess or Solomon can make their living as solo pianists.[2]

I shall be very grateful for your opinion on this problem.[3]

Yours sincerely
R. Vaughan Williams

Mrs. Tillett,
124, Wigmore Street,
W.1

[1] Director of the agents Ibbs & Tillett.

[2] The work in question was *Fantasia (Quasi Variazione) on the 'Old 104th' Psalm Tune*, CW 1949/3, first performed in public by Mullinar with the LSO conducted by VW at the Three Choirs Festival in Gloucester Cathedral on 6 Sept. 1950.

[3] Mrs Tillett responded on 16 Sept. saying that in her opinion Mullinar's appearing as a soloist would enhance rather than damage his reputation as an accompanist.

528. To G. E. Moore

9 November 1949

The White Gates,
Dorking,
SURREY.

9th November, 1949

Dear Moore,

I hope you will forgive an old friend writing to you though it is years since we met, and I want to write to you about another old friend of ours, Bob Trevelyan. He has done such splendid and unrecognised work that I feel we ought to bestir ourselves to get him some public recognition. Though, of course he never suggests that he wants anything of the kind, yet I cannot help feeling that it would please him, especially now when family troubles and a complete loss by fire of his 'complete edition' are tending to depress him.

The obvious thing to my mind would be a LL.D. of Cambridge or D.C.L. of Oxford.

Perhaps you can tell me whether it is possible to offer a Cambridge man a Cambridge Hon. degree, then I shall know how to proceed, and perhaps if you approve of the plan you could suggest some names to whom I could write who would be influential in arranging it. It must not, of course, be a sort of hole in the corner degree, but done properly at the big function in the summer when all the grandees get their honorary degrees.

Yrs
R. Vaughan Williams

Professor G. E. Moore,
Trinity College, Cambridge.

529. To Mary Glasgow

9 November 1949

The White Gates,
Dorking,
Surrey.

9th November, 1949.

PERSONAL AND CONFIDENTIAL.

Dear Miss Glasgow,

I noticed in one of the Minutes of the Arts Council – I cannot for the moment remember whether it was Council, Executive, or Music Panel, that there was a question of performing my 'Pilgrim's Progress' at Covent Garden.

As there seems to be a good deal of misunderstanding about this I fear I must inflict on you an account of what exactly happened.

You will remember that some months ago you kindly allowed Mr. White[1] to arrange a play-through of the Opera at 4 St. James' Square to which, among others, Mr. Webster and Mr. Rankl of Covent Garden were invited.[2] At the end of the performance they made a few perfunctory remarks like 'very interesting' and I heard no more for about two months. I naturally then came to the conclusion that they did not want the Opera and so I approached the Arts Theatre at Cambridge. They, as you know, are very keen on the idea and are determined to do it if the financial side can be arranged.

A little later on I had a letter from Mr. Webster asking if he could see the score of the Opera. I sent it to him but told him that the first performance was already promised to Cambridge if they wanted it. I heard no more for some time. Then Mr. Webster asked me to go and see him and from what he said I could only gather that he wanted me to withdraw my offer to Cambridge and offer it to Covent Garden instead. I told him there was honour even among musicians and that if Cambridge wanted the Opera they must have it.

Mr Webster then suggested that he should write to the Cambridge Arts Theatre and ask them if they really did want it. This, I pointed out to him was tantamount to telling Cambridge that I repented of my bargain, and I asked him not to write.

So please understand that there can be no performance of my 'Pilgrim's Progress' until after it has been produced for the first time at Cambridge.

The Minute I refer to did not seem to make this clear.

Yours sincerely,
R. Vaughan Williams

Miss M. C. Glasgow, C.B.E.,
Secretary General
Arts Council of Great Britain.
(Personal & Confidential)

[1] Eric Walter White, Assistant Secretary of the Arts Council; see no. 506.

[2] David Webster, General Administrator, and Karl Rankl, Music Director, of the Royal Opera House, Covent Garden.

530. To the Provost of King's College, Cambridge[1]

16 November 1949

The White Gates,
Dorking,
SURREY.

16th November, 1949

Dear Provost,

I venture as a stranger, to write to you about Robert Trevelyan. Do you think there is any chance that he would be given an Hon. LL.D. at next summer's ceremony?

You know, probably even better than I do, what fine work he has done, his original poems and his translation of Lucretius, Catullus and of the Oresteia. He has done all this work without much hope of public recognition, but now I think, towards the end of his life some token that he was appreciated would be very gratifying to him.

He was about to publish a complete edition of his works but this was destroyed during the war, which I think was a great blow to him.

I was advised to write to you by Professor Moore of Trinity College, who I think is also writing to you himself, and I feel sure that other authorities like Desmond McCarthy and E. M. Forster would back my request.[2]

Yours sincerely
R. Vaughan Williams

The Provost,
King's College, Cambridge.

[1] Sir John Sheppard, Provost of King's College 1933–54.
[2] VW's efforts on behalf of his old friend and neighbour came to nothing.

531. To J. M. Martin[1]

28 December 1949

The White Gates,
Dorking,
Surrey.

28th December, 1949

Dear Martin

Thank you so much for your interesting but painful letter.[2] I wonder what we can do? That week you describe in Gloucestershire seems to be the right thing. I wish we could extend it to six months. If there is any question of a fund to help on that idea let me know what can be done about it. Also if there is anything else I can do?

Our friend has always been so helpful to me that I should like very much to be able to do something for him.

Yours sincerely
R. Vaughan Williams

J. M. Martin, Esq.,
21 Norland Square Mansions,
London, W.11.

[1] James McKay Martin, a former student of VW at the RCM and participant in the LHMF. He was also a friend of Hubert Foss and played a central role in organizing the campaign to help him in his illness. He wrote a short article, 'Recollections of R.V.W.', *Musical Opinion* (July 1984), 303–5.

[2] About Hubert Foss, who had resigned as Head of the Oxford University Press Music Department in 1941 (see no. 369) and was now in bad health due to stress.

532. To Douglas Lilburn

28 December 1949

The White Gates,
Dorking,
SURREY.

28th December, 1949.

Dear Lilburn

Thank you so much for your Christmas letter.

I have also heard from Page and he promises to play me your new works when he comes to England.

I was much touched by all you said about our lessons. Personally I can only look back with shame when I think of the little I did for you, but after all everyone has to find his own salvation, and you evidently have done this.

Your honey was wonderful and we have not finished the last jar yet.

Yrs
R. Vaughan Williams

Professor Douglas Lilburn,
c/o Victoria College,
Wellington,
NEW ZEALAND.

533. To Herbert Byard

3 January [?1950]

The White Gates
Dorking

Jan 3

Dear Mr Byard

I added the extra scene to 'Hugh' because we were told it was too short – that in the provinces they 'wanted their moneys worth!'.[1]

But it was never a success both dramatically & musically it is poorer & an addition entirely spoils the dramatic effect of the sudden hush at the old beginning of Act II coming straight after the noisy finish of Act I. So I never want to hear it or see it again!

Yrs ever
R. Vaughan Williams

[1] *Hugh the Drover*, *CW* 1924/2. The request possibly came from the publishers, Curwen.

534. To Margery Cullen

8 March 1950

The White Gates,
Dorking,
Surrey.

8th March, 1950

Dear Margery

I feel it is now time that I gave a detailed answer to your and Mr. Bixley's letter.[1]

I need hardly say I am much touched by your request and in a way wish I could agree to it; but do you think you are going the right way to work? For one thing you are rather late in the day, because I have promised so many other things and refused many more. You may say, if I have promised to other people why not to us? But the things I have promised were special cases; – for instance, the 'Concerto grosso' for the Rural Music people and the masque music for Charterhouse.[2]

But in this case it does seem to me it would be much better if you wanted to do something of mine to do something which has already been tried and proved. Or do you not think that anything already written is good enough? In that case it is hardly likely that a work which is done rather in a hurry in the middle of other occupations would be likely to be any better.

Surely there are many works of mine which have not been often, or even ever, done by L.H.M.F. I do hope, if you want to do anything of mine, you would consider one of those.

I fear that, like Brahms, I have no sympathy with the mere desire for novelty and the fact that you can say that it was specially written for this occasion. All I can promise is that if later on when you have to make up your programmes finally, I have something ready or nearly ready, I could offer it to you. Or possibly some work like my 'Voice from the whirlwind' which at present is only accompanied by the organ, could be orchestrated for this purpose.

I do not want to appear churlish, but at the present moment I am feeling rather tired and cannot face the idea of promising a new work. You know you cannot write a new piece of music like you can make a suit of clothes – just sit down and do it. The actual writing is often nothing; it is the mental preparation beforehand which counts.[3]

Yrs
RVW

Miss Cullen
Northacre
Westcott

[1] VW had been invited by George Bixley, as secretary of the Surrey Philharmonic Orchestral Society, to be President of the Society for the season 1950–1, during which it was proposed to give joint concerts with the LHMF choir as part of the Festival of Britain. The present letter is in response to a subsequent invitation to provide a new work for one of the concerts.

[2] *Concerto Grosso* for string orchestra, *CW* 1950/1, was written for the massed orchestra of the Rural Music Schools Association and performed the following November; *Solemn Music for the Masque of Charterhouse*, *CW* 1950/4, was written for performance at the school the following July.

[3] In the event the concert in Dorking Halls on 16 June 1951 included the cantata *Dona Nobis Pacem*, *CW* 1936/5, and, as he had suggested, *The Voice Out of the Whirlwind*, *CW* 1947/2, with the accompaniment specially orchestrated by the composer for the occasion. The soloists were Elsie Suddaby and Gordon Clinton. Other works in the programme were Gordon Jacob's *Sinfonietta* and Elgar's *Enigma Variations*. VW conducted his own works.

535. To Hubert Foss

15 March 1950

The White Gates,
Dorking,
Surrey.

15th March, 1950.

Dear Hubert

I hope you already know what affection and admiration your friends have for you and your work. Now some of us want to show it in a practical way:

We understand that you are feeling overworked and in need of a rest to enable you to have that quiet leisure to help you to concentrate on this new book which we hope and believe you are planning. Therefore we ask you to become our guest at some quiet and sympathetic place where you will have the necessary surroundings for your work.

We hope to be able to make arrangements by which you will become our guest at Buckfast Abbey for a month or six weeks directly after Easter. I do hope you will see your way to accept an invitation which will give great pleasure to your friends. You will later receive a formal letter from them. Meanwhile you may like to know a few of their names:

Arnold Bax.	Stanley Roper.
Patrick Hadley.	Edward Dent.
Gordon Jacob.	J. M. Martin,

and others.

I need hardly add that I also wish to be associated with this invitation.[1]

Yrs
RVW

Hubert Foss, Esq.,
60, Corringham Road, N.W.11.

[1] This letter was the result of a campaign started by J. McKay Martin to raise funds amongst Foss's friends to enable him to spend a period at Buckfast Abbey. See no. 531 and further correspondence.

536. To J. M. Martin

22 March 1950

The White Gates,
Dorking,
Surrey.

22nd March, 1950

Dear Martin

It seems to me that we can go ahead now, though it is not, to my mind, quite satisfactory, because I fear that this guest house will be not much more than an ordinary boarding house.

I wonder if he will have a quiet room in which he can work, or whether they will allow him to go up to the monastery[1] to use their library &c. I think we might find out about this and also to suggest that if they could take him into the Monastery at the first possible opportunity it would be a good plan.

We can afford six weeks, but the question is whether we had better try only for a month first and see how we get on. I would suggest, when we do settle, sending the money in advance. Of course there will be the question of fares and so on and coupons. Will you have time to see to all that and really pack him off safely?

I do not think, as they are so anxious to take him and there seems no objection the other end, that we need have a doctor's opinion. What do you think?

Perhaps you could kindly some time send me the names and full initials of all the participants? Then I will get a proper letter typed out with all the names typed underneath and spaces in between for the actual signatures. I do not think it need be a long letter, and will you trust me to do it on my own?

R. Vaughan Williams

J. McKay Martin, Esq.,
21 Norland Sq. Mansions, W.11

[1] Buckfast Abbey.

537. To Katharine Thomson

24 May 1950

The White Gates,
Dorking.
SURREY.

24th May 1950.

CONFIDENTIAL.

Dear Mrs. Thomson,

I believe that I am supposed to know nothing about the proposed visit of you and your singers to Dorking, and for that reason I have kept right out of all the discussions in the early stages.[1]

I was, of course, much flattered and touched by the idea, but I was always rather apprehensive and now that I have heard more details (and I hear you even propose three performances) I feel I must speak out and beg of you to reconsider the matter.

I know Dorking audiences. They do not even come in great numbers to our own Festival, except for the 'Passion'. The local Dramatic Society is seldom well patronised and the visits of the London Philharmonic Orchestra have been given to half empty halls. So I cannot hope that your visit will be anything but a failure in the matter of audiences, and to speak quite frankly I think that the 'snob' value of my name has been overworked lately.

The idea is prevalent in Dorking that you have been invited to give this performance. Is this so? In addition I understand that all the arrangements at this end have been handed over to Miss Cullen. She is very keen and capable but is already overworked and in her enthusiasm is apt to undertake more than she can manage and it is essential that her energies should be kept for what is really her chief job – that is, the Festival.

I also hear that a local choir is to be recruited and trained by Miss Cullen to help in the choruses. These will inevitably be drawn from our own local choral societies. These singers have already as much to do as they can manage and 'speaking as a fool',[2] though I know they would do anything to help me, I feel I cannot be a party to overworking a willing horse.

You know what affection I have for your singers and how much I admire their work and I want to save them from disappointment; also I cannot help feeling that to take a long journey and perform in a strange hall on a strange stage and to strange audiences with a strange orchestra would almost certainly prevent them from doing themselves justice.

So may I repeat that I advise you most strongly to abandon the project. I say this with great sorrow because personally it would give me great pleasure to welcome you here and hear your performance, which as you know I have only heard at present in the rehearsal stages.

Yours sincerely,
R. Vaughan Williams

Mrs. Thomson,
84, Oakfield Road,
Selly Park,
BIRMINGHAM.

[1] It had been suggested by Tom Harrison that the Clarion Singers should give a performance of *Sir John in Love* at Dorking. VW had attended rehearsals for a Birmingham performance in Jan. 1949. See no. 514.

[2] VW was fond of this allusion from 2 Cor. 11: 23: 'I speak as a fool . . .'.

538. To Ralph Wedgwood

24 May 1950

The White Gates,
Dorking,
Surrey.

24th May, 1950

Dear Randolph

I have heard a rumour that the National Trust are cutting down trees rather freely in the Leith Hill woods. Do you think they are overdoing it? I should be glad of your opinion on this matter.[1]

According to my Deed of Gift there is a stipulation that no trees should be cut except to improve the amenities and in the interests of good forestry.

Yours
R.V.W.

Sir R. L. Wedgwood, Bart.

[1] Wedgwood had become the tenant of the National Trust at Leith Hill Place, following VW's gift of the estate to the Trust in 1944 (see nos. 431 and 432).

539. To Roy Douglas

12 July 1950

The White Gates,
Dorking,
Surrey.

12 July, 1950.

Dear Roy Douglas

I enclose herewith what I hope is the correct fee for your expert advice about the orchestration of 'Hugh'.[1]

I have finished it now according to your suggestions and sent it back to the Publishers.

As regards my Opera, I have a feeling that you do not want to do it, and it occurred to me the reason was that you wanted time for your own composition. If you have any inspiration floating about it would certainly be blasphemy against the Holy Ghost to interfere with it, and I should not like to be a party to that; so think it over very carefully before you decide.[2]

Yrs
R. Vaughan Williams[3]

[1] VW had sought Douglas's advice when revising the orchestration of some passages in the opera. See *WWVW*, 20.

[2] In fact Douglas decided to undertake work on the score of *The Pilgrim's Progress*. See ibid. 21–2.

[3] This letter is printed ibid. 21.

540. To Hubert Foss

26 July 1950

The White Gates,
Dorking,
Surrey.

26th July, 1950

Dear Hubert

First, forgive a typewritten letter because I want you to be able to read this. I am quite overpowered by the affection and thought in your book. I feel hopelessly unable to live up to it. Indeed I owe you rather a grudge because I had a hoped for the rest of my life, to be able to live comfortably following my lower instincts, without ideals. Now everybody will be able to refer to your book to find out what I ought to be like! But, alas, I am not and I shall have to try and live up to my (or rather your) ideals.

I will not try to thank you any more. I am sure you will understand.

Just one small point. It looks rather like 'looking a gift horse in the mouth', but I have found a slight misprint on Page 33 – the word printed 'snuggery', should of course be 'smuggery'.[1]

Well once again, my affection and admiration

Yrs
RVW

Hubert Foss, esq.,
60 Corringham Road,
London, N.W.

[1] 'the second accusation is made by people who affect to scorn what is "folky" because it does not come within the ken of their airless snuggeries', from 'Musical Autobiography' as printed in Foss, *Ralph Vaughan Williams: A Study*, 33, para. 2, line 3. The spelling is corrected in the second impression (1952) and in the later versions in *Some Thoughts on Beethoven's Choral Symphony* and *NM*, 189, but 'snuggeries' would not have been wholly inappropriate.

541. To E. J. Dent

9 August 1950

The White Gates,
Dorking,
Surrey.

9th August, 1950

Dear Dent

Thank you very much for your long and interesting letter.

I ought to perhaps have explained that the idea of having a young man to conduct the Opera[1] was originally mine. The Impresario first suggested getting a well-known man like Barbirolli or Boult to do the first performance, and then hand it over, but I said I would rather that whoever conducted the subsequent performances (if any) should conduct the first performance also, and as I had some doubts about the head man,[2] although I did not say so, I suggested perhaps giving it to one of the younger conductors, who would be very keen to make his name through a good performance.

I think the young conductor in question has had some experience on tours, and has also conducted things like 'The Firebird' for the American Ballet, and I think, if he can conduct that he can conduct anything.[3]

I put Alan Frank on his track and he hears very well of him, and says that the orchestra thought well of him, which is very important.

Yrs
R. Vaughan Williams

Professor Dent,
Lion Hotel,
Cambridge.

[1] *The Pilgrim's Progress*, *CW* 1951/1. Dent was closely involved in the revision of this work, before, as here, but particularly after the first performance on 26 Apr. 1951. See the correspondence published in *CW*, 208–18.

[2] Karl Rankl. See *New Grove*: 'he was considered difficult with singers, orchestras and producers'.

[3] Leonard Hancock.

542. To Elizabeth Trevelyan

1 September 1950

The White Gates,
Dorking.

1st September 1950

Dear Bessy,

I had not seen anything about the proposed closing down of the Third Programme. I believe they have means of telling how many people are listening in at any given moment. I feel myself that their programmes must improve a lot before we really make serious efforts to retain them. I find there is almost as much music as I want to listen to on the Home Service and even occasionally on the light[1] as there is on the third.

The Third Programme people are much too fond of dreary 17th and 18th Century music which may be very interesting to the antiquarian and the musicologist but has no real artistic value. As to their talks – they won't be much use to me until the speakers learn the elements of English elocution, by which I mean merely learn to speak so that they can be heard. They ought to take lessons from Desmond McCarthy or Gilbert Murray.

I was very interested to know that you used to play Raff's 'Cavatina' also when you were young. Of course I played the opening phrase all on the G string, and a horrible noise I must have made.

Yrs
Ralph

Mrs Trevelyan,
The Shiffolds,
Holmbury St. Mary

[1] The BBC Light Programme.

543. To Arnold Barter

15 November 1950

The White Gates,
Dorking,
Surrey.

15th November, 1950.

Dear Barter

Thank you so much for your invitation. I was hoping to come but I have an engagement I cannot miss now on the same day. So there it is!

May I send you my little personal contribution to the expenses of your performances – I am afraid not so much as formerly, but this year I have to give an extra large Christmas Box to the Chancellor of the Exchequer.

Yrs
R. Vaughan Williams

Arnold Barter, Esq.,
9, Hurle Crescent,
Clifton, BRISTOL.
Encl.

544. To Anthony Scott[1]

29 November 1950

The White Gates,
Dorking,
SURREY.

29th November, 1950

Dear Scott,

I was very glad to hear your work[2] and I think it is going to be extremely good, but please do not take my advice – it is always a mistake to take advice. What you have got to do is to see for yourself what you think of my suggestions. If you reject them then you will be all the stronger in your own opinion, which will be to the good. But never take anybody's opinion unless you find you entirely agree with it. After all you know more about the work than I do.

Please give my kind regards to your wife and I hope that one day we shall meet again.

Yrs
R. Vaughan Williams

Anthony Scott, Esq.,
The Cedars,
Horton,
near Slough, BUCKS.

[1] Anthony Scott (1911–2000), composer and organist. He was a pupil of Herbert Howells at the RCM. He and his wife, Ruth, were close friends of the Finzis (he had also studied privately with Gerald Finzi) and became close friends of the VWs.

[2] According to a note on the original, this was a Violin Concerto.

545. To Roy Douglas

30 November [1950]

From R. Vaughan Williams,
The White Gates,
Westcott Road,
Dorking.

Nov 30

Dear Douglas

I am going to be a nuisance (which you probably are not surprised at!)

Here is an 'appendix' for Act I (I expect the opera[1] will suffer from a good deal of appendicitis before we have done with it) It consists of a few additional bars before fig 10 of Act I scene 2 which may or may not be put in as the producer decides. The question is shall we put at the end of the act or in its place in the score? – I incline to the latter if it will not upset your pagination too much – because chiefly of the band parts, where it wd be obviously better to put it in at its proper place & then cross it out if not wanted than for the players to have to scrabble over to the end of the act and probably knock the music over in doing so.

The score may want a little modification because I am not quite sure how if will fit (e.g. I cannot remember whether it is cor anglais or oboe 2 just there – oboe 2 will do just as well as cor anglais just there). Perhaps this bit of copying ought to have precedence so that when the act is ready the parts can be copied.

Sorry to be such a nuisance.

Yrs
R. Vaughan Williams[2]

[1] *The Pilgrim's Progress.*
[2] This letter is printed in *WWVW*, 23.

546. To Rutland Boughton

20 December 1950

The White Gates,
Dorking,
Surrey.

20th December, 1950.

Dear Rutland

Please forgive a typewritten letter, as otherwise I am rather illegible, and thank you for your letter.[1]

My memory of our conversation is not quite the same as yours. As I remember it – just when we were going into a meeting of the Composers' Guild (I think) you met me and asked me in the most innocent manner, whether I was in favour of peace, to which I naturally replied 'Yes'. Then you asked me to sign a manifesto, but did not explain what the manifesto was. Luckily I had already been approached on the same subject and forewarned was forearmed. When I refused to sign you again said, 'But surely you are in favour of peace'. Then the conversation had to stop.

I cannot help feeling that your approach to me in this matter was, to say the least of it, disingenuous, as I was almost tricked into signing something which you felt sure I should disapprove of if I knew all the facts.

As I say, luckily I did know the facts, because I had already been approached with a request to sign this bogus Russian 'peace' manifesto, which we most of us guessed at the time and now know through Russia's own newspapers, was simply a means to sow dissension and want of will among the Western countries.

As I say, the Russians have by now admitted that this so-called 'peace' manifesto was designed to weaken the resistance to their nefarious designs of tyrrany [*sic*] and imperialistic aggression.

I suppose that those who tried to get others to sign the manifesto adopted their method of technique from the Russians, who have shown at Lake Success that they have no regard for truth or justice but only for expediency in their own favour, with the result that they behave like selfish, dishonest and petulant children – e.g: when they refused to attend a meeting and then declared that the decision made there was invalid because they were not present. Or again, after talking all this hot air about 'peace', refused to sign a request to the forces in Korea to cease fire.

Their whole conduct would be comic if it were not so tragic.

If we have to negotiate with the Chinese it will indeed be a triumph of might over right.

As regards my Opera, might I ask you, at all events to read the libretto before you criticise it or me for writing it, and as to what you accuse me of – i.e. 'redressing an old theology', it seems to me that some of your ideas are a good deal more moribund than Bunyan's theology:– the old fashioned republicism [*sic*] and Marxism which led direct to the appalling dictatorships of Hitler, Stalin and Mussolini, or your Rationalism, which dates from about 1880 and has entirely failed to solve any problems of the Universe.

You know how much I admire your energy, your honesty of purpose and your wish to give up everything for what you believe to be a good cause, but please do think whether it is not time, even now to enlist under the banner of democracy and freedom rather than the dictatorship of Moscow.[2]

Yrs
R. Vaughan Williams

Rutland Boughton, Esq.,
Kilcot,
Newent,
Gloucester.

[1] Boughton had written on 8 Dec. accusing VW of having refused to sign a peace petition in 1949, on the grounds that Russia refused to allow free intercourse between Russian and British nationals, and of now having written an opera 'redressing dead theology without at the same time actually opposing those evils which would not exist if that theology had developed as a reality'. VW's letter is printed in full in *RVW*, 303–4.

[2] Boughton replied on 8 Jan. 1951 disputing VW's memory of events, expressing surprise that VW should feel the need to be forewarned against Peace, and suggesting various books which he ought to read.

547. To Veronica Wedgwood

17 January 1951

The White Gates,
Dorking,
Surrey.

17th January, 1951.

Dear Veronica

A few years ago I tried to stir up George Trevelyan and Gilbert Murray about this awful scheme for a translation of the Bible into 'Daily Mail' English. I could get no sparks out of them.[1]

It now occurs to me that you might possibly be the person to take up the crusade, with which your wonderful pages about the English Bible in your new book convince me you are in sympathy.[2]

I enclose a copy of the letter I wrote to these two. Could you not start a crusade in 'Time and Tide' about it?[3]

Yrs
R. Vaughan Williams

Miss C. V. Wedgwood,
22, St. Ann's Terrace,
London, N.W.8.
Encl.

[1] For VW's letter to Gilbert Murray, see no. 520.
[2] *Seventeenth Century English Literature* (London, 1950).
[3] She was Literary Editor of *Time & Tide*, 1944–52.

548. To Hubert Foss

7 February 1951

The White Gates,
Dorking,
Surrey.

7th February 1951

[Dear Hubert]

I have been through the book carefully, as you asked, and I have found a certain number of misprints and mistakes, which you have doubtless already discovered yourself, but in case not I send them herewith:[1]

Page 20: Surely 'insisted' and not 'insists'.
Page 30: 'Smuggeries', not 'snuggeries'.
Page 84: 'Soul' not 'semi'.
Page 93: 'Flag' not 'half'.
Page 107: 'Grow slack' not 'go slack'.
Page 183: 'Lob' not 'Nob'.

Also the following mistakes:

Page 13: 'Vicar' not 'rector'.
——13: After the word 'Bruch' add 1897.
——24: The 'Willow Song' is a part song.
——44: 'Sound Sleep' is by Christina Rossetti. (See also Page 80)
——73: 'Easter Wings'. Surely this arrangement of the words is meant to suggest wings, not hour-glass.
——84: 'Willow Wood' was written before 'The House of Life'.
——116: The Tallis Fantasia was first performed at the Gloucester festival in 1910. I conducted it myself. It has never, so far as I know, been conducted by Beecham. Are you not mixing it up with 'The Fen Country' which

was produced by Beecham at
Queen's Hall in, I think, 1909.

—143: The last revised version of
the Pianoforte Concerto ends quietly.

—157: 'Flos Campi' was not written
for Tertis, though it was first
performed by him. The 'Viola Suite'
was composed for him.

—164: 6 clarinets, not 16.

—202: Same mistake about Tallis.

—204: There is now only one Norfolk Rhapsody;
the other two are scrapped.
Fantasia on a theme by Tallis—again 1910.

—209: 'O Vos Omnes'. A version
with English words of this
has lately been issued by Curwen.

—211: 'On Christmas Night' is still in manuscript.

As regards 'Songs of Travel'. It was originally written and sung as one cycle. The order was quite different from what it is as now published and included 'Whither must I wander', which had already been published, but not by Boosey's though Boosey's have it now. Boosey's originally refused to publish the whole cycle and chose three – then published the others later.

I don't know whether it is worth while doing anything about that.

With regard to your queries: The history of the 'London Symphony' has no *musical* interest, therefore I don't think it comes into your scheme. I do refer to it in my autographical [*sic*] chapter when I am talking about Butterworth.

Page 204: 'The Wasps' suite is published complete
by Curwen and I think is still in print.

—205: 'Folk Song Suite' for military band
and March of Seasongs also for
military band published by Boosey.
These both have orchestral arrangements
by Gordon Jacob.
'Suite for Pipes' published by O.U.P.
'Fantasia on Sussex Folk Songs' scrapped.
'Fantasia on Old 104th Psalm tune', 'Concerto Grosso', 'Folk Songs of the Four Seasons' all published by O.U.P.

I do not think we need bother about the background music done for the B.B.C., but if you want them, they are, as far as I can remember, as follows:

Incidental Music to 'Pilgrim's Progress', a lot of which I have used in the Opera.

Incidental Music to 'Richard II' paid for, but as far as I can make out, never used.[2]

A series of very short motets written for Walford Davies. These were also paid for, but whether the B.B.C. ever used them I do not know.[3]

I think that is all. Sorry for so long a letter, but you asked for it.

R. Vaughan Williams

Hubert Foss, Esq.
60, Corringham Road,
London, N.W.11.

[1] Hubert Foss, *Ralph Vaughan Williams* (London, 1950). The mistakes appear in the first edition; a corrected reprint was issued in 1952. VW had already pointed out one of the mistakes to Foss in no. 540 when he first received his copy.

[2] See *CW* 1944/3.

[3] Walford Davies was on the advisory staff of the BBC, 1927–39. The motets do not appear to have survived but the file copy of the contract is preserved in the BBC archives and some correspondence in the OUP archives (see no. 362).

549. To the children of the Parents' Union School, Ambleside[1] February 1951

February, 1951

A small girl was once having a music lesson. Her teacher gave her a new piece to learn, which she explained was composed by a well-known musician who had lately visited the school. 'But', said the little girl, in great bewilderment, 'I thought all composers were dead.'

Have we really been taught that all composers are dead? Then indeed our art is dead. Vital art must be creative.

It has been said that we should stand in the present with one eye on the past and one on the future. Let us by all means build our house on the foundations of the great masters, but let us remember that the composers of our own time and of our own country have something to say to us which even the greatest masters of the past age cannot give us; that is the only way we can build a great future for our music.

We must not let the dead lion swallow up the living dog.

R. Vaughan Williams.

[1] Enclosed in a letter dated 19 Feb. 1951 from (?) the music mistress, Elizabeth Molyneux, to Cedric Glover, who apparently asked VW for a message on the school's behalf. In the letter she says: 'I am delighted with the result of your approach to Dr. Vaughan Williams on our behalf and I am sending you a copy of his message to the children which will certainly convey the impression that we are studying a living composer!'

550. To Gilmour Jenkins[1]

8 March [1951]

The White Gates,
Dorking.

March 8

Dear Gil

I was much moved by your letter – I know what knowledge and practical experience underlay it. Well I know that we all were on tip-toes to do our best – & that must have an effect however much the technical side is missing.

We had about 6 of our best basses away through influenza etc which accounts for a little weakness there.

As regards 'Truly this was' I know that it was whispered by a few soldiers – But I always imagine that at that moment we get away from Golgotha & the whole world joins to affirm its belief.[2]

You know that I value your opinion & I trust you in future to tell me all your *adverse* criticism as well.

Yrs
R. Vaughan Williams

[1] Sir Gilmour Jenkins (1894–1981), a successful senior civil servant, at this time Permanent Secretary at the Ministry of Civil Aviation. VW had first met him when Gerald Finzi had worked for him during the war. Jenkins became a close friend of both VW and Ursula and was Best Man at their wedding in 1953. See *DNB*.

[2] Jenkins had clearly been at the performance of the Matthew Passion on 3 Mar. at Dorking Halls.

551. To Ursula Wood

postmark: 12 March 1951

Many thanks to the Lady of Shallotts.[1]

RVW

[1] Presumably UW had brought some shallots or onions as a present and this had inspired the Tennysonian allusion.

552. From Ursula Wood

[mid-April 1951[1]]

A LONG LETTER
Suitable reading for
you-know-where.

My Dear

I do want you to know *before*, & *above* all, that I was more than ever moved and excited by the music. I feel that there is so much new-to-opera in this opera; that the stage has not fulfilled its partnership. *Never* that the music is too long, or too anything – but often that the staging lags.

Appolyon [*sic*]: I don't think blackouts work if App. is represented by lights & starts by winning. I believe the answer might be this—as the Pilgrim dashes in to fight him the lights (set low of course, not coming, as now, from above) start to flicker (flicker machine) they dim at the first words, flicker furiously again, & get brilliant for 'surely I have thee now' – and flicker again, & dim to almost nothing, & then fade as the Pilgrim wins, & the doleful creatures slink away. *Sword clashing would go with this* – & P. could, if you like, also sing *off* – at least one of his lines.

I said all along I should like to keep the direction the same. It seems to be diagonal, except for Act 2. sc. 2 & Act 3. sc. 1. Its not a big alteration, but I think it would be a good one (see diagram enclosed).

Other points

House beautiful. Lighting *awful*. They left the colonades transparent on one side so the chorus *off* could be seen. They also introduced a horrid purple at one point.

I'm not happy about the chorus. They do stand about so. I think as you are not using the sepulchre it could go and would give more room.

Abolish candles.

Watchful Lights *bad*.

Appolyon Lighting rehearsal with creatures and Pilgrim *essential*.

Vanity Fair

Chorus movements untidy. It wasn't a real surge round as it used to be, & that must be replaced – or else, & *better* – what you really wanted – their only coming to life when something happens. However this will all have to be re-produced with new music, & can wait.

Prison

Gils contribution. The Key has to unlock both handcuffs, & door – key-holes

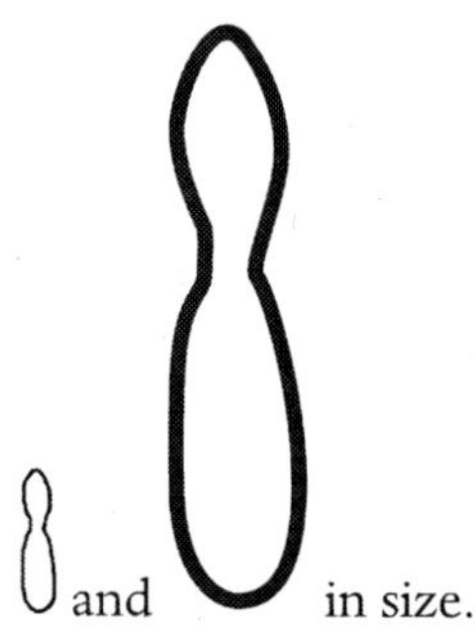

It *must* therefore be a magic key, & he should not use it to *unlock* in a practical way, but to *touch* the locks, so that they fly open, and make this apparent to the audience.

Lighting here could be *much* more imaginative with a little work.

Act IV

River of Death lighting started too soon, before backcloth of Delectable Mts flew away. It also went on much longer, but as this gave the effect of the waters of death washing round the foot of the heavenly city I thought it rather good. But its tricky timing, & could easily damage Heaven if not under control.

The fade out was not absolute – they left the angel in full light at the end. Not so good as before I thought.

[1] The letter seems to have been written after a lighting rehearsal for *Pilgrim's Progress* at which VW was not present.

553. To Beryl Lock, her mother, from Ursula Wood

[21 April 1951[1]]

Saturday

. . .

Thank you so much for the heavenly flowers – they really do the gardeners credit. I brought some down here.

Life has been hectic. Covent Garden rehearsals going full out, & the Dorking Festival, & Mrs V.W. frightfully ill – no-one can discover what it is, but she has temperatures varying between 102 and 97, & has lost the use of her hands – it's wretched for her, particularly just now.[2] Ralph is managing well, though this week has been rather too much of a good thing – leaving the house at 8.40 – Rehearsals 10–1.30, sandwiches in the car, conducting rehearsals from 2.45 – 5.30, & then an evening concert – but now its only Covent Garden. Of course it's thrilling, & exasperating and satisfying & unsatisfying – but it's doing pretty well, & not too unlike what he intended – the orchestra is good, & the singers know their music, but he wants more acting.

The major worry just now is Appolyon [*sic*], whether he can possibly fall dead in a 3 ft mask, & if so how to get him off stage without ruining his wings! It's all set for Thursday, Ralph, Gil, & Mrs Curle[3] will dine with me first, (his party) & we are going to a party given by the management afterwards. Then you shall have your evening coat back! I have been grateful for it.

I wore my blue American (Hattie Carnegie[4]) dress to make my speech in. It went well, & I enjoyed doing it – in fact I think public speaking may be a taste as easily acquired as a taste for gin – & everyone was very nice about it. I was on the Milton – Handel night, so the matter was easy.

Gil came to dinner here – so did Kathleen Long,[5] who was playing – frightfully pleased with herself as she had made her own dress – so I had plenty of support, & Ralph was pleased with me.

All these activities have rather interfered with gardening. I don't know how that was so – but everything is so behind this year.

The Martels were in London on Monday, so I had them & their parents to dinner – not a word of English among them.[6] There were 6 of us, & 7 of them, & then dancing & singing, all very gay & bilingual – but I did rather tremble for the floor!

No news otherwise.

Thank you so much –

Love
U

[1] Date deduced from postmark 22 Apr. 1951, which was a Sunday. The beginning of the letter has been omitted

[2] Adeline died shortly afterwards on 10 May.

[3] i.e. Sir Gilmour Jenkins and Adeline's sister, Cordelia Curle.

[4] Hattie Carnegie (1889–1956), well-known Viennese-born New York dress designer.

[5] Kathleen Long (1896–1968), English pianist.

[6] The Martels were possibly refugees and presumably friends of both Ursula and her mother.

554. To Steuart Wilson[1]

27 April [1951]

April 27 (7.15 A M)

My Dear Steuart

Personal

My mind goes back 40 years – also on a musical occasion when I first met you & ever since then my music & any success I have in it has been connected with you – & now comes the climax. I know that I owe last night to you (probably in face of strong opposition) & I do hope you do not feel that you have backed the wrong horse. It was, everyone says, a splendid performance & I feel most grateful to everyone – & I have entirely lost my heart (not for the first time) to the woodcutter lad.[2]

My love to Mary

Yrs
R. Vaughan Williams

No answer of course.

[1] At this time Deputy General Administrator of the Royal Opera House, Covent Garden. The letter was written the morning following the first night of *Pilgrim's Progress* and is printed in *RVW*, 308.

[2] Iris Kells, first wife of the conductor Leonard Hancock.

555. To E. J. Dent

30 April [1951]

The White Gates
Dorking

April 30

Dear Dent

I was much moved by your letter.[1] You know how I value your judgement & to have your approval is something I am very proud of.

I agree with you how all taking part seemed to 'dedicate' themselves to a work which containing as it does none of the ordinary ingredients of opera must have been disconcerting. Nevertheless I believe that it is 1st & foremost a stage piece & do not want it (at all events yet) relegated to the cathedral – If it once gets there it will never get back to the stage & will be put in the same semi-amateur category as 'Everyman' & 'Eager heart'.[2]

Now as you have shown a friendly interest in the work may I ask your advice on one or two points

(1) Is 'Vanity Fair' too *short* (I don't usually wish to lengthen my own works!) but I had a feeling that it was over before the audience had time to find out what it was all about.[3]
(2) The Fight with Apollyon was quite unsatisfactory – the truth is that the producer came to the conclusion that my scheme (see libretto) would not work & at the last minute we had to patch up a 'pis aller' (including sacrifice of near ½ the music).

I still believe that my original scheme w[d] work – if not then we must scrap it & do something quite new (it's no good patching). I am sending you a libretto in case you have time to look at it.

Yrs
R. Vaughan Williams

[1] Dent had written on 27 Apr.: 'I hope you were pleased with the performance of the *Pilgrim* last night, and with the way in which the audience were completely absorbed by it and gave it the tribute of a definite silence at the end. I felt very conscious all the time of the audience's tense concentration on the work. As I have myself a deep-rooted inherited Quakerism (though I have never been able to live up to it!) I can very willingly make a complete surrender to a work of that kind, although most of my friends would not think it possible. The performance last night was a great deal better than the rehearsal the day before. What impressed me very deeply was the complete sense of what the Germans call "Weihe" on the stage – a thing they know well and respect in the theatre, whereas Italians have no sense of it at all and Viennese hardly any; it is the utter self-surrender and self-dedication of all the performers to a great work of art. English people are fully capable of it, but we only get it in the theatre at Oxford and Cambridge, never (until last night) in the professional Opera House. It has a practical and technical result too, for it produced really beautiful singing from everybody and a surprisingly clear and intelligent enunciation of the words, such as I have never heard at Covent Garden before. I felt indeed thankful to escape from the influences of Milan and Vienna!' He went on to praise the conductor and the orchestra. The letter is printed full in *CW*, pp. 196–7. Responses from Dent to this letter were sent on 2 and 6 May also printed in *CW* (pp. 197–204). A further letter to Dent from VW (printed by Kennedy on p. 204) does not survive in the Dent archive at King's College.

[2] *Everyman*, the 16th-c. morality play; *Eager Heart*, the Christmas mystery play by Alice Buckton.

[3] The scene was lengthened for the performances from Feb. 1952 with the addition of a song for Lord Lechery and the quartet of witnesses to words by Ursula Wood.

556. To Ralph Wedgwood

10 May [1951]

From R. Vaughan Williams,
The White Gates,
Westcott Road,
Dorking.

May 10

Dear Randolph

Adeline died today in her sleep – It was not a surprize to me as she had been very ill for some weeks. I wanted to tell you before you saw it in the paper.[1]

Yrs
Ralph

[1] It is clear that Wedgwood was amongst the first people he felt he must tell of Adeline's death on 10 May, just as he had been one of the first people with whom VW shared news of his engagement to Adeline in 1897.

557. To Dorothy Wallis[1]

11 May 1951

From R. Vaughan Williams,
The White Gates,
Westcott Road,
Dorking.

May 11th 1951

My Dear Dorothy

This is to welcome you to England – Not a very gay welcome on my part. My wife died yesterday – she was wanting so much to meet you – and now it will not be. All the same I sh^{d} like it so much if you could find time to come down here for an afternoon – I am wanting so much to see you in real life.

Love from
Uncle Ralph

[1] A young Australian admirer who had sent the VWs many food parcels during the war.

558. To E. J. Dent

15 May [1951]

The White Gates
Dorking

May 15

Dear Dent

Thank you very much. One wants letters from one's friends at these times.

Yrs
R. Vaughan Williams

559. To Gilmour Jenkins

postmark: 16 May 1951

The White Gates,
Dorking.

Dear Gil

It was very good of you to write and express your friendship which I value so much.

Both Ursula and Mrs Curle are with me and are wonderfully helpful – indeed I soon shall be able to do nothing for myself!

Yrs
R. Vaughan Williams

560. To Hubert Foss

17 May 1951

The White Gates,
Dorking,
Surrey.

17th May, 1951

[Dear Hubert]

I have never answered your long and most interesting letter. I was on the whole very much pleased with the production, and I think I ought to tell you so.

There are one or two things I disagreed with. I still believe that the Apollyon fight could be done on my lines. Of course the fight as it appeared on the first night was a patched up affair at the last minute, which was a pity.

I still feel it is essentially a stage piece and not for a Cathedral. To start with it would have to be about twice as long for a Cathedral. It probably takes about six bars of moderate time for a procession to cross the stage at Covent Garden, but it would take about 100 bars for a procession to walk down the nave of (say) Salisbury Cathedral, and the whole thing would have to be on a much larger scale.

I am lengthening 'Vanity Fair'. I am sure it is too short at present. I am making one or two slight alterations. The end of the Arming scene, Act II Scene I wants altering. This also was a last minute affair. In my original version, as you will see the Pilgrim goes off singing and his voice is gradually lost in the distance, but we found that on the big stage at Covent Garden he was quite inaudible directly he got off the stage, and so we had to alter it; but I am altering it again now. They did not seem to realise it was not a 'Curtain' in the ordinary sense of the word.

What I wanted was a gradual black-out and then an Act Drop Curtain to prepare for the next scene, instead of which they dropped the House Curtain, which to my mind was a mistake.

I may begin to think of more to say to you later on, in which case I shall worry you again.

Thank you so much for writing.[1]

Yrs
RVW

[1] It is curious that VW does not mention Adeline's death a few days earlier.

561. To Elizabeth Trevelyan

21 May [1951]

Dorking.

May 21

Dear Bessy

It was dear of you to write.

We are both alone now – I go on with my work as usual which is what she wants I feel sure.[1]

Yrs
Ralph

[1] Written In response to a letter of sympathy following Adeline's death. Robert Trevelyan had died a few weeks earlier on 21 Mar.

562. To Rutland Boughton

[?21 May 1951[1]]

From R. Vaughan Williams,
The White Gates,
Westcott Road,
Dorking.

Monday

Dear Rutland

Your long and interesting letter would take several weeks to answer properly so I will content myself with a few points – the music is not published yet because I wanted to hear it to make some revisions – & I am glad I did – mostly purely technical questions. Even the libretto (enclosed) is by now out of date (the 'nocturne' with 'Watchful' is not there).

I left out Valiant for Truth – one had to leave out many people (e.g. Faithfull) as his great speech w^d^ not have gone well in the mouth of the Pilgrim – (as a matter of fact I once made a musical setting of Valiant's speech[2]).

I, on purpose, did not call the Pilgrim 'Christian' because I want the work to be universal and apply to any body who aims at the spiritual life whether he is Xtian, Jew, Buddhist, Shintoist or 5th [*sic*] day Adventist.

As regards the Cathedral – it is, to my mind essentially a *stage* piece & I said I w^d^ not allow it in a hall or church till it was fully established on the stage.

Thank you so much for writing.

Yours sincerely
R. Vaughan Williams[3]

1 Boughton's letter was dated [Saturday] 12 May (and is printed in *WVW*, 312), so the date of the present letter is likely to have been the following Monday week. It is notable that again VW does not mention Adeline's death on 10 May, especially seeing that he wrote a number of acknowledgements of letters of sympathy on 21 May.

2 *Valiant for Truth*, *CW* 1940/2.

3 This letter, and Rutland Boughton's to which it is a reply, are printed in *WVW*, 312–14.

563. To Gerald Finzi

3 July [1951]

Hythe
As from: The White Gates,
Dorking,
SURREY.

July 3rd

Dictated[1]

I had a letter from Bernard Rose & it requires thinking about. Anyway I shall have to change the title[2] so that people shall not think that I am trying to run counter to the Oxford Requiem man. This is as you see from Hythe where Ursula has conducted me for my holiday. A real lower middle class existence with ice creams on the beach in the morning, & a trip in a motor boat.[3]

(Also went up the tower of Rye Church ladders!! U.)

Yrs
R. Vaughan Williams

[1] To UW.

[2] The letter refers to *An Oxford Elegy*, *CW* 1949/2, written in 1949. The first public performance took place the following year at Queen's College, Oxford, on 19 June, conducted by Bernard Rose. Rose had pointed out that the title of VW's work was very similar to that of a work by Bruce Montgomery, *An Oxford Requiem*, which had been given its first performance by the Oxford Bach Choir on 22 May. Despite that the title of VW's work was not changed.

[3] UVW commented to the editor very firmly that she had wished to go to France—Hythe was entirely RVW's idea.

564. To Roy Douglas

10 September [1951]

The White Gates,
Westcott Road,
Dorking.

Sept 10

Dear Roy

As there seem to be about to be a good many performances of my symphonies I think they ought to be overhauled. I am sending you 'pastoral' & 'No. 5' – will you help me by going through them carefully & suggesting alterations in any places where in your opinion the texture (& especially the orchestration) does not 'come off'.

It is often difficult to decide whether one ought to score for the wireless, the concert room, or the Albert Hall – also I am getting deaf & things which are probably all right sound all wrong to me: e.g. No. 5 V. 1 & 2 p. 2 figure 1. I often over the wireless have literally *not heard* the violins & even in the concert room I have only just heard it – yet it *looks* all right!

Of course if you kindly undertake this it will be as between you & me & not between you & the publisher.

The red ink corrections already in the pastoral are already in the parts – those in No 5 are not

How is the opera going – Act III is ready for you whenever you want it

Yrs
R Vaughan Williams[1]

[1] This letter is printed in *WWVW*, 30.

565. To John Barbirolli

6 October 1951

The White Gates,
Dorking.

Oct 6 1951

Dear John,

I am sending you under separate cover scores of my Pastoral & No 4 – If you approve will you ask the librarian to put it[1] in the parts (Though of course you will not have time to think about it yet with all your 'garden' work).[2]

In No 4 I have altered the last note of the slow movement from F to E♮ – I always felt the F was wrong – but c[d] not make out what the right note was –

Score of No 5 will follow shortly.

I am not sending the score of Sea Symphony – but I think that with my fairly full direction your librarian will be able to find his way.

The London Symphony is past mending – though indeed with all its faults I love it still – indeed it is my favourite of my family of 6.

Yrs
R. Vaughan Williams

[1] i.e. corrections in the full scores.

[2] VW had written to Barbirolli on 12 Sept.: 'Now, as regards myself, I see that you are doing me the great honour of performing all my Symphonies during your season, and this seems to me a good opportunity to overhaul them, and I have already started doing this. Do tell me, quite frankly, any points either in construction, orchestration or anything else that occur to you which want alteration or revision. With

all your experience you must know rather more about it really than I do.' Barbirolli was conducting regularly at Covent Garden.

566. To John Barbirolli

17 October 1951

The White Gates,
Dorking,
Surrey.

17th October, 1951.

Dear John

It is wonderful of you to have time to think about my music when you have so much on your mind.

All your suggestions are most useful except, I fear, one, and that is the transferring of the tune in the trio of No. 3 in the Fourth Symphony from tuba to trombone. I cannot help feeling that it is essentially a tuba tune. Somebody said to me once it sounded like Falstaff and it wants that slightly fat oily sound which the tuba gives. I put the bassoons in just to steady the tone of the tuba, but that can be left out if you prefer it and have a bare solo for the tuba.

By the way, if you give the opening of the fugue to the trombone it seems to me that the entry of the three trombones in the answer will be rather spoilt.

Otherwise your corrections are splendid.

Yrs
R. Vaughan Williams.

Sir John Barbirolli,
Columbia Concerts, Ltd.,
127a Oxford Road,
Manchester 1.

P.S. I have just received your copy of No. 5 – I am also making some corrections including adding Flute and Clar[inet] to that place in the slow mov[t] – the only way out of the difficulty I think.

567. To Joyce Hooper[1]

31 October 1951

The White Gates,
Dorking,
Surrey.

31st October, 1951.

Dear Mrs. Hooper,

I am amazed to hear that some members of your choir have taken exception to the beautiful words of Holst's 'Tomorrow Shall be my Dancing Day', apparently on the grounds firstly that dancing and religion are something apart and ~~consequently~~ secondly that it is wrong to use the words 'This I have done for my true love' in connection with a statement of the central doctrines of Christianity.

I had hoped that the killjoy and lugubrious view of religion which once obtained was now happily dead, but I fear there are still some people who have a degraded view of the dance and connect it only with high kicking and jazz, but the dance in it's highest manifestations shares with music, poetry and painting, one of the greatest means of expression of the very highest of human aspirations. The dance has always been connected with religious fervour – that is, orderly and rhythmical movement surcharged with emotion.

What are the great Church ceremonies but a sublimation of the dance? What about the 150th Psalm, 'Praise Him with the timbrel and dances'? Surely Bunyan's 'Pilgrim's Progress' is full of the highest religious fervour and he makes Mr. Ready-to-Halt celebrate his deliverance by dancing.

One of the most beautiful books of the Apocrypha, the Gospel of Niccodemus, contains in 'The Hymn of Jesus' an apotheosis of the dance, 'divine grace is dancing, dance ye therefore'.

As regards my other point, human love has always been taken as a symbol of man's relationship to divine things. The Song of Solomon has been treated in all the Churches as a symbol of the relationship of God to man. And what about Isaiah and his 'beloved's Vineyard'? And is not the Church in the Book of Revelations always symbolised as the bride?

Let me conclude with a practical suggestion. I should advise all those who do not feel themselves worthy to sing the beautiful words of this carol, to vocalise, and to leave the words to those singers who have not this inhibition. But if they do this they will miss a great spiritual experience.

Yours sincerely,
R. Vaughan Williams.[2]

Mrs. Hooper
18, Ridgway Road,
Redhill, Surrey.

[1] At this time conductor of the Dorking Oriana Choir, one of the participants in the Leith Hill Musical Festival.

[2] This letter is printed in *WVW*, 315–16. The work was performed on 2 May 1952.

568. To Hubert Foss

14 November [1951[1]]

The White Gates,
Dorking.

Nov 14

Dear Hubert

I remember a great many years ago (early '90s) that the 'Strand' Magazine started the fashion of personal interviews & sent round a questionnaire to several eminent composers – Hubert Parry's reaction was 'I'm damned if I'll tell those fellows whether my bottom is painted blue'.[2]

I feel the same with the BBC snoopers trying to get a factitious interest in my music by telling people what I eat for breakfast and what sort of lavatory paper I use.

– If my music cannot stand on its own bottom, I have no desire for it to stand on mine.

Of course I sh[d] love to have you write about my music – but you have already done that.[3]

I'm sorry but there it is!

Yrs
RVW

[1] Clearly written after the publication of Foss's study in 1950 and the first performance of *The Pilgrim's Progress*.

[2] Foss had written to VW saying that the BBC had asked him to persuade VW to reconsider his decision against allowing a short television documentary film about him which would represent music in a series that also included Henry Moore and Augustus John. Foss felt that the film could include shots of Wenlock Edge, Gloucestershire, Leith Hill, Cambridge, and Dorking, with VW himself depicted at The

White Gates smoking his pipe. Such a film might well open the door, he suggested, to a television production of *The Pilgrim's Progress*. The commentary would be written by Foss himself.

[3] *Ralph Vaughan Williams: A Study* (1950).

569. To Hubert Foss

5 December 1951

The White Gates,
Dorking,
Surrey.

5th December 1951

Dear Hubert,

I am so glad you are writing about Constant.[1] Have jotted down a few reminiscences which may be useful to you.

Constant Lambert came to me as a pupil straight from school. I think he was about sixteen then and all who had to do with him realised at once his brilliant qualities and some of us insisted that he must be given a scholarship.

The first works he showed me were perfectly delightful tunes, songs, I think and pianoforte pieces very much in the folk song style. I wish they were extant still, but I expect he destroyed them as he soon became ashamed of them, and as he got to know more about French music got more and more away from the folk-song idiom. Indeed, at one of his early lessons he took me to task seriously for being influenced by folk song and told me I was all wrong. I took his rebuke quite meekly and kept my own opinion to myself.

The first work which he showed me with the 'New look' was a very remarkable piece for clarinet solo without accompaniment. Again, I do not know what happened to that.

Though he was so brilliant he was difficult to teach because he knew what he wanted and did not see the point of going through the ordinary mill, and I preached him a sermon once and told him that later on he would find the want of the 'stodge' which I was trying to make him do, and would then come back and ask me or someone else to teach him, which he countered with the invincible argument, 'Well won't that be the time to do it?'. I was non-plussed.

Lambert conducted the first performance of my ballet 'Job', and wonderfully he did it, because his work included cutting down the orchestra to the then dimensions of Sadlers Wells. I remember he got over one difficulty when he added in a bass part for the harp, which was extremely effective. These rehearsals were the only occasions on which I knew him really worried and nervous. Rehearsal time was short, the orchestra was difficult, the clarinet said he could not, according to his trade union rules, double clarinet and saxophone & so on, but he triumphed over it all.

Though nominally he was a pupil of mine I was really much more a pupil of his. I feel sure it was he who pointed out to me that the introduction to my 'London Symphony' was a clean crib of Debussy's 'La Mer'. But he denies he ever said this.

As we all know, he hated Brahms and once told me that he longed to push as if by accident that plaster cast of Brahms which decorates one of the passages at the R.C.M. and smash it for ever.

I do not think his music was easy to get at straight away. I remember when I heard his 'Summer's last will' for the first time I did not care about it. It was only at a later performance that I realised what a fine work it is. When I wrote and told him so he gave me a characteristic and delightful answer.

If I think of anything more to say I will tell you later.[2]

Yrs
RVW

Hubert Foss, Esq.,

[1] Constant Lambert (1905–51), composer, conductor, and writer on music. He had died the previous August.

[2] Foss had written an appreciation of Lambert for the *Musical Times* (92 (1951), 449–51), but his planned biography was never completed. See Hinnells, *An Extraordinary Performance*, 37.

570. To Hubert Foss

postmark: 6 December 1951

I made a slip in my letter. It was the first *stage* performance of 'Job' which C.L. conducted.

RVW.

571. To Gerald Finzi

18 December 1951

The White Gates,
Dorking,
Surrey.

18th December, 1951.

Dear Gerald

Will you thank Mr. Court for his very kind letter.

I very much fear that on March 5th. I shall be right in the middle of my own festival preparations but I will keep the date in mind in case I can possibly come.

Now another matter – I think I have persuaded Boyd Neel to do some young English composers at some of his concerts and I have suggested Tony Scott and Leighton.[1] Which Leighton shall I suggest? It ought not to be too long; say twenty minutes to half an hour and be for strings only unless there is a solo instrument involved.

Would you make suggestions to me? If I recommended a work by any young composer I would be responsible for any additional band parts which were wanted, but I should have to ask the composer to check them very carefully and make quite sure that they were correct and legible.

My love to Joyce.

Yrs
RVW

Gerald Finzi, Esq., Ashmansworth, near Newbury, Berks.

[1] Boyd Neel (1905–81), conductor of the Boyd Neel Orchestra (later to become the Philomusica of London), for which Britten had written *Variations on a Theme by Frank Bridge*. On Anthony Scott see no. 544 n. 1. Kenneth Leighton (1929–88) at this time was studying in Rome with Goffredo Petrassi, having won the Mendelssohn Scholarship.

572. To Hubert Foss

2 January [1952]

The White Gates
Dorking

January 2

Dear Hubert,

I am dictating this letter, not from want of affection but because I want to be legible.

I am so sorry to hear you are ill in hospital.[1] I shall be in London for a few days this week & I will ring up the hospital to see if there is any chance of paying you a visit.

I am up chiefly for the first night of Wozzeck – up to the present Berg has merely bored me – but I went to a bit of a rehearsal the other day and I was so intrigued by the stage that I did not bother to listen to the music: which perhaps is the best way of listening to it, and what the composer meant.[2]

I wonder how you are getting on with your life of Constant? There is one very amusing story which he told me which I fear you cannot put in –

How, before being finally passed for his scholarship at the R.C.M. he had to be medically examined and the doctor demanded a specimen... which he duly brought down to college, but could find no instructions as to where to leave it & had finally, so far as I can remember, to carry it about all day in his music case.

There is a fine comedy part for Parry Jones in Wozzeck.[3]

Yrs
R. Vaughan Williams

[1] Foss was in University College Hospital for the removal of a tumour from his lung. See Hinnells, *An Extraordinary Performance*, 37.

[2] This was not VW's first encounter with *Wozzeck*; AVW reported to Ann Boult that they had listened to a broadcast of it in Mar. 1945.

[3] The tenor. He sang the Captain; see *New Grove*.

573. To Alan Frank at OUP

2 January 1952

The White Gates,
Dorking,
Surrey.

2nd January, 1952.

Dear Frank,

So far as I can remember I answered direct to Mr. Woodworth of Harvard to say that I was very doubtful if I could get anything done. I fear now it is impossible, I have so many other things on hand. Would you mind telling him that? I return the letter.[1]

This reminds me. I am writing a piece for Larry Adler to play on his harmonica. I do not know whether you would care to handle it or not. The trouble is I do not see how it can ever be played on any other instrument because the harmonica is the only wind instrument that plays c[h]ords, and I have made full use of that.[2]

Will you let me know what you think?

Yours sincerely,
R. Vaughan Williams

[1] G. Wallace Woodworth (1902–69), American choral conductor and music teacher. He was university organist and choir director at Harvard from 1940 and successor to Archibald Davison as James Edward Ditson Professor of Music there from 1954 until his death. He had presumably asked for a work by VW.

[2] The Romance in D Flat for Harmonica (*CW* 1951/4) was published in 1953 in an arrangement for harmonica and piano.

574. To Alan Frank at OUP

16 January 1952

The White Gates,
Dorking,
Surrey.

16th January, 1952.

Dear Frank,

It is most kind of you to lend us your room for January 25th. It will be quite a small meeting my idea being to gather together a few experts whose judgment I trust, to give me what will amount to a composition lesson, and advise me whether I shall go on with the work which is still in sketch form, or scrap it.[1] Therefore I do not want a large crowd and I do not want it to be known that this is taking place, otherwise quantities of people will be offended at not having been asked.

The company will consist besides yourself of E. J. Dent, Gerald Finzi, Arthur Bliss, Ernest Irving, and Roy Douglas, who will be playing.

I am so glad you can come to lunch with Mrs. Wood afterwards.

R. Vaughan Williams

[1] The work in question is *Sinfonia Antartica*, which was first performed in public a year later.

575. To Alan Frank at OUP

19 February [1952]

The White Gates,
Dorking.

Feb 19

Dear Frank,

Herewith Larry's piece which you said you w[d] like to look at – I fear it w[d] be very little practical use to you as I cannot see how it can arrange for any other instrument & Larry is the only person who plays this kind of music on that queer instrument – I have given him a copy of the pfte score.[1]

Yrs
RVW

[1] Romance in D flat for Harmonica, accompanied by an orchestra of strings and pianoforte, *CW* 1951/4, written for Larry Adler. Frank replied that OUP would happily prepare performing material and control

performances but would wait to see how the piece was received (it was to be given its first performance in New York on 3 May 1952) before deciding on publication. A score for harmonica and piano accompaniment was published in 1953.

576. From Ernest Irving

7 March 1952

Ernest Irving
4, The Lawn,
Ealing Green, W.5.

7th March, 1952

Dear V-W

The score of 'Antarctica' arrived this morning.[1] I have had, you may be sure, an exciting time reading it through. It will take, of course, some days to digest it but at first reading it gives an unmistakable impression of power, magnitude and colour. The tunes seem to me to stand up nobly to their new symphonic responsibilities, including the penguins!!

I am afraid the Intermezzo will become popular.

I am certain John Barbirolli will be delighted with it, and revel in rehearsing and conducting it. Its epic style and colourful illustration will suit him down to the ground – or I should say, down to the ice-floe. It is the first time that film music has been really raised to the loftier level of symphonic poetry, and it will be the first Symphony ever written that schoolchildren will enjoy as much as their elders.

I am really too excited to write any more, so will close with respect and affection.

Later, 4 p.m. I have read the score through again and though I naturally find it difficult to dissociate the music from the visuals of the film I feel confident that the music can stand by itself. One must remember that it was inspired by actual history and composed before the film was made and though it was applied ad hoc it possesses I think sufficient character and individuality to put it in the first rank.

It is not easy to compare it with VI because it is impressionistic and even descriptive, whereas VI was absolute and metaphysical. It has more unity of style with the Pastoral, which by the way, I am trying to get into the Phil[2] programme for next season. I expect there will be a few half-blind critics who will imagine nothing good can come out of the Kinema but its strength, forthright style and simplicity of outline will I am sure find recognition from the great body of music-lovers, including naturally

Yours ever
Ernest Irving

P.S. Will write again later.

[1] The symphony was dedicated to Irving and was clearly newly completed. Its first performance was in Manchester on 14 Jan. 1953 given by the Hallé Orchestra under John Barbirolli.

[2] i.e. the Royal Philharmonic Society, which gave the first London performance on 21 Jan. 1953 with the same forces.

577. To Michael Kennedy

3 April [1952[1]]

The White Gates,
Dorking.

April 3

Dear Mr Kennedy

It was a great pleasure to meet you & your sweet wife in Manchester & I hope to do so whenever I visit there. Curiously enough when I came home & was looking over some old papers I came upon the letter you wrote me some years ago.[2]

I was delighted & amused at the account of your wedding hymn.[3] I hear you wrote a criticism of my 'S.S'[4] in a Manchester paper – May I see it?

Yrs sincerely
R. Vaughan Williams

[1] Year taken from postmark.

[2] VW was in Manchester to conduct two performances of *A Sea Symphony* with the Hallé Choir. VW's earlier letter to Kennedy is no. 462.

[3] The Kennedys had chosen 'For all the Saints', sung to VW's tune *Sine Nomine*, as a change from the more usual 'Come down O Love Divine' sung to VW's *Down Ampney*.

[4] i.e. *A Sea Symphony* (*CW* 1909/3).

578. To Roy Douglas

23 April 1952

The White Gates,
Dorking,
Surrey.

23rd. April, 1952.

Dear Roy

I feel I have done all I can now with the S.A., so it must now take its chance. I think Barbirolli will do it at the beginning of the New Year, but I think it ought to be ready for a try-through in the Autumn. As you know it wants its face washing badly. Will you undertake this? If so I will send you the score, but as you see, there is no hurry – that is to say, do not put off other work for it. Let's make the date, say October 30th by which date the score [and] parts will be ready. You will see whether that is possible or not.

As regards the 'Folk Songs of the Four Seasons' I enclose a letter from Miss Karpeles suggesting the orchestra required; but of course that would depend entirely on you. What you will go by is the number of strings which I imagine cannot be altered, but the rest of the instruments can be left entirely to you. I should imagine that four horns are unnecessary.[1]

Will you get in touch with Miss Karpeles or the Secretary of the Boyd Neel Orchestra and tell them what orchestra you think is necessary?

Yrs
RVW[2]

[1] Roy Douglas was making a suite for small orchestra from *Folk Songs of the Four Seasons*; see *CW* 1949/1.

[2] This letter is printed in *WWVW*, 42.

579. To Michael Kennedy

22 May 1952

The White Gates,
Dorking,
Surrey.

22nd May, 1952.

Dear Mr Kennedy,

Thank you so much for your letter. It was a great pleasure to meet you both again.

I think you are right in suggesting that to attach 'meanings' to music is a mistake. Each person may attach their own meaning if they like, but it does not follow that their meaning will have the same meaning to anybody else – music is too universal for that.

I hope we shall meet in Manchester in January for the first performance of the S.A.

Yours sincerely,
R. Vaughan Williams.[1]

Please give my love to Eslyn if I may venture.

[1] This letter printed in part in *WVW*, 382, with additions from a letter not included in this collection.

580. To Alan Frank at OUP 24 May 1952

Incomplete

From R. Vaughan Williams,
The White Gates,
Westcott Road,
Dorking.

May 24th 1952

Dear Frank,

Dictated

First: welcome home. And now to answer numerous letters, both from you and Foote.[1]

1] *Sinfonia Antarctica*.[2] This is the correct title. I have never numbered my symphonies. This has been done by other people for me. As regards the connection with the Scott film – would it be honest not to refer to this at all? If it is absolutely nescessary, then I suggest that we should merely say that some of the themes are taken from the music which I wrote for Scott of the Antarctic. Otherwise people will think that it is a mere bit of carpentry. – which as a matter of fact, it largely is; but don't tell anybody this.[3] Will it matter that some of the music has already been issued – in a commercial record – rather against my will? There is no connection so far as I know between the Scott music and my sixth symphony. As a matter of fact, some of the music of that symphony was suggested by music I wrote for 'Flemish Farm'. This, again, is confidential.[4]

2] Orchestration 12 woodwind, 4 horns, 3 trumpets, 3 trombones, timpani, any amount of percussion, glockenspiel, xylophone, celesta, wind machine, vibraphone, pianoforte, harp, organ, soprano solo, small S.A. chorus, & strings. Approximate length, I believe, 40 minutes.
First performance. January 14th. in Manchester – & I believe in London, January 21st.

3] 'In the Spring'. I enclose a letter from the Barnes Society – could we do anything about presenting them with a few copies when it is out? And foregoing performing fees when it is performed at their official meetings? I should like to know your opinion of the best key. Foote favours D & I believe he is right. Certainly so for community singing – but as I have told them the words seem to me quite unsuitable for community singing.[5]

[1] Guthrie Foote was Production Manager at the OUP Music Department. The part of the following letter about *Sinfonia Antartica* was written in response to a letter from Alan Frank of 22 May:

'I gather that your new Symphony has been announced in the Press in connection with JB's performance. Do you by any chance have a copy of what appeared, or better still, can you give me the following information, please? What is the exact title, and is it to be numbered, as No. 7; can you perhaps be kind enough to give me a note of the orchestration and approximate duration? How is the connection with the Scott film to be mentioned in the Press, if at all? And incidentally, is there some indirect relationship between the last movement of the *Sixth* Symphony and the Scott film? Between ourselves, I heard in a roundabout way that Ernest Irving had hinted at such to a certain music critic, and it would be greatly interesting to me to know if there is something in this: and in any case to know your wishes as regards statements that may be made in the Press about both works.'

[2] *CW* 1952/2. UW, in whose hand the letter is, follows VW's incorrect spelling of the Italian title. On the orthography see also nos. 509 and 597.

[3] The connections between the music for the film *Scott of the Antarctic* (*CW* 1948/2) and *Sinfonia Antartica* are discussed in *WVW*, 359 ff.

[4] On the use of some music from *Flemish Farm* in the Sixth Symphony (*CW* 1947/3), see *CW* 1943/4.

[5] 'In the Spring', *CW* 1952/1, a setting of words by William Barnes, had been commissioned by the Barnes Society. It is not clear whether there is a further part of the letter which is missing. In his reply on 26 May Frank confirmed that OUP would not issue any statement about the symphony and its connection with the Scott film and that he would know what answer to give to any questions about it. He suggested a private letter from VW to Ernest Irving to clear matters up about connections between the film music and the Sixth Symphony, which VW sent. Finally he agreed that D was the best key for 'In the Spring'.

581. To the Editor, *Bournemouth Daily Echo*

published 24 June 1952

Sir,

A wise man once said that he would prefer to be Socrates discontented than to be a hog contented. The Town Council of Bournemouth evidently would like us to be contented. But contented with what? One of your councillors is reported to have said that of course we must spend money on necessities like the Health Service rather than on music. But is not music a necessity for our spiritual health?

Have any of your councillors ever been into a school and perceived the exaltation created in the children's natures when they sang good music? When they grow up, this spiritual exaltation will die away and fade into the light of common day unless we see to it that this splendid vision of the ultimate realities is preserved for them.

It is this vision that I understand one of your councillors had the impertinence to describe as an expensive toy.

Up to the present, largely owing to its Symphony Orchestra, Bournemouth has been a civilised town. Is your Council prepared to let their names go down to posterity stigmatised with the disgrace of allowing the town, for whose welfare, spiritual as well as material, they are responsible, to lapse into barbarism?

Ralph Vaughan Williams.[1]

The White Gates,
Westcott Road,
Dorking.

[1] The letter, engendered by a threat to close the orchestra, is printed in *RVW*, 322.

582. To Rutland Boughton

25 June 1952

The White Gates,
Dorking,
Surrey.

25th June, 1952

Dear Rutland

Mr. Dunsman kindly sent me his notice of my Opera. I am sorry he should see in it any particularising to certain political views in my work. Of course everyone has the right to apply the generalisations of music to their particular views, but I do not like to be pinned down to 'meaning' anything in particular, like Bernard Shaw's ridiculous degradation of Wagner's 'Ring' into political propaganda.

All right-minded people are in theory communists insofar as they believe that everything ought to be done for the common good, but when Socialism in practice means the unholy mess which the late government made of things and when Communism in practice means tyranny, double dealing and insincerity by Russia, one cannot join with its present manifestation.

Yrs
R. Vaughan Williams

Rutland Boughton, Esq.,
Kilcot,
Newent,
Gloucester.

583. To Rutland Boughton

9 July 1952

The White Gates,
Dorking,
Surrey.

9th July, 1952

Dear Rutland,

This is really too bad![1] To accuse me of not being able to speak my mind because of my official position. To start with, I have no official position.

I am afraid I am now going to imitate St. Paul and 'speak as a fool'. I have always refused all honours and appointments which involved obligations to anyone in authority – (The O.M. involved no such obligations). My fault is probably that I have been always too much in opposition. When I was a boy at school I and another boy stood out as Radicals (as we were called then) against all the other boys. When I got to Cambridge in '93 I and a few friends read the Fabian tracts, and in opposition to the majority of undergraduates, became socialists. (This was probably before you were born.[2])

The truth is, I think, that when I am with Conservatives I become socialistic and when I am with Socialists I become true blue Tory.

Now the pendulum has swung right round and it is fashionable to be a Socialist or 'Kremlinist' – (I will not defile what ought to be a fine name 'Communist' by calling the present creed by that name), I have the courage to criticise and dissociate myself with the present manifestations of what used to be a fine creed, and I am not afraid to have the finger of scorn pointed at me because I refuse to be taken in by all these bogus 'peace' moves, which I think have also even duped you.

Ever since I had a vote I have voted either Radical or Labour except once, after the last War when I was so disgusted by what I considered the mean tricks of the Labour party in forcing an election.

I voted Labour in the last election though in my heart of hearts I wanted the Tories to get in, but the old spirit of opposition crept up and with all the County shouting for the Tories I determined to be on the other side; so I assure you my spirit remains what you call 'generous'. I believe in freedom and that is why I will not be bullied by Nazis, Fascists and Russians.[3]

Yours sincerely
R. Vaughan Williams

Rutland Boughton, Esq.,
Kilcot,
Newent,
Gloucester.

[1] Boughton had responded to VW's previous letter on 3 July accusing VW of turning his back on the live legacy left behind by such writers as Whitman, Blake, and Bunyan, 'whose (dead) hand you have taken', and urging him to live up to the liberalism of his nature and not cause those shades to laugh at him.

[2] VW was born on 12 Oct. 1872 and Rutland Boughton on 28 Jan. 1878!

[3] This letter is printed in *RVW*, 322–3.

584. To Herbert Howells

9 July 1952

The White Gates,
Dorking,
Surrey.

9th July, 1952.

Dear Herbert

I return your list. Of course I would not dream of cutting out any names, even if personally I do not want them.[1]

By way of additions, would you consider Mr. and Mrs. Finzi, and I should also be very glad if invitations could be sent to Alan Bush as representing the W.M.A.[2] and Rutland Boughton – what he represents I do not quite know, but I have lately had rows with each of them, so if it could be stated that they were invited at my special request I should be very grateful.

I am glad you are having no music. I wish you would have a conjuror – that is my favourite form of entertainment. When you say 'no music', do you not think that we ought to start dinner with the 'Non Nobis'? Surely a company of musicians ought to be able to sing it. Would it be a good plan for me to issue you with a number of cards which Novello issue with the 'Non Nobis' printed on them. If it was not too many I should be delighted to do so. Otherwise I think a special choir ought to be arranged to sing it.[3]

Yrs
RVW

Dr. Herbert Howells,
3, Beverley Close,
Barnes, S.W.13.

[1] Guests to be invited to the dinner given by the Incorporated Society of Musicians in honour of VW's 80th birthday on Monday, 6 October.

[2] Alan Bush was President of the Workers' Music Association from 1941 until his death in 1995.

[3] 'Non nobis domine', variously attributed to William Byrd and others, had been published on a card (together with a grace by E. A. Price) by Novello in 1904.

585. To Alan Frank at OUP

9 September [1952]

Imperial Hotel
Hereford

September 9th

Dear Frank,

I wrote to Hochhauser about the Concerto & here is his answer.

In his former letter to me he said he had made every possible enquiry to find if the work had been done before. To which I replied that if he had applied to the O.U.P. he would have been told about it. What I really mind is about Jelly. By the way, he ought to have guessed that from the printed dedication to her that she had played it in public.

Besides the performance in 1925 at the Aeolian Hall, unless my memory fails me, [she] played it under me at Queen's Hall a few years later.[1]

I hope you heard Larry the other night? He was splendid.[2]

Yours sincerely,
R. Vaughan Williams

[1] In the handbill for Menuhin's 1952 performance of the Violin Concerto, Victor Hochhauser, the concert promoter, had announced it as the 'first public performance in London'. In fact the concerto was dedicated to Jelly d'Arányi and she had given the first performance on 6 Nov. 1925, as VW states, at the Aeolian Hall. See *CW* 1925/7. She was still alive, though not now playing very much, and VW was obviously concerned that her feelings would be hurt by this announcement.

[2] Larry Adler had given the first London performance of Romance in D flat for Harmonica at the Albert Hall on 6 September. See *CW* 1951/4.

586. To Cedric Glover

17 September 1952

The White Gates,
Dorking,
Surrey.

17th Septr. 1952

Dear Cedric

Thank you so much for your invitation, but I don't think I can face 'Electra'. I remember being taken to it years ago by Beavis Ellis[1] and I thought the opening bars were from the wrong Opera and must be by Macfarren, and it sounded to me like that all the way through.

Yrs
RVW

Cedric Glover, Esq.,
The Aldermoor,
Holmbury St Mary,
Dorking.

[1] F. B. Ellis, at one of whose concerts of modern orchestral music the *London Symphony* received its first performance in 1914. He was killed in the war.
[2] Printed in *RVW*, 315.

587. To John Tindall Robertson

[October 1952?]

From R. Vaughan Williams,
The White Gates,
Westcott Road,
Dorking.

Dear Tyndal Robertson

It was very nice to get a letter to remind me of the old days at Maresfield – you were a boy then and I was middle aged – now you are middle aged and I am old & toothless – But it doesn't seem to make much difference.[1]

Yrs ever
R. Vaughan Williams

[1] On Tindall Robertson see no. 402.

588. To John Ireland

5 October [1952[1]]

From R. Vaughan Williams,
The White Gates,
Westcott Road,
Dorking.

Oct 5th

My Dear John

I was very much touched and very grateful to you for your characteristic and generous letter.

I remember well that occasion at the College when 3 of us (You, N.C. Gatty and I) had our tunes tried over – Yours though possibly immature had real mastery and a sure touch – N.C.G's was probably the most mature – his 'boat was small but he rowed well in it'.[2]

– Mine was a horrible amateurish business now happily lost – it so happened that its style fitted in for the moment with C.V.S's[3] prejudices.

You know I have always envied your mastery of your method. I fear that I am only just beginning to conquer my amateurish awkwardness – now probably that it is too late.

Please can we have another 'Things shall be'.[4]

Yrs with great affection
R. Vaughan Williams

[1] The letter is presumably answering one from Ireland of a month or so earlier in which he congratulated VW on his approaching 80th birthday and reminisced about their time together at the RCM.

[2] An unidentified quotation. The rehearsal was probably one on 21 march 1901 when Ireland's *Symphonic Prelude* and VW's *Heroic Elegy CW* 1900/1, were tried through.

[3] Charles Villiers Stanford, teacher of all three at the RCM.

[4] VW had conducted *These Things Shall Be* at Dorking in 1944.

589. To Gerald and Joy Finzi

14 October 1952

The White Gates,
Westcott Road
Dorking.

October 14th 1952.

Dear Gerald and Joyce,

I have eaten your pears for three days without stopping now, they are delicious.

I have looked at your Magnificat[1] between the letters, and I like the look of it very much, but I shall go through it thoroughly when this tyranny is overpast.[2]

It was wonderful of you to come to both concerts.[3]

Love from Uncle Ralph

[1] *Magnificat*, Op. 36, for chorus and organ.

[2] Another allusion to Ps. 57: 1. Here VW has in mind his 80th birthday celebrations.

[3] Held in celebration of VW's 80th birthday at Dorking and the Royal Festival Hall. See *RVW*, 326–8.

590. To Hubert Foss

14 October 1952

From R. Vaughan Williams,
The White Gates,
Westcott Road,
Dorking.

October 14th 1952

My Dear Hubert

A personal thought from you is a better present than all the marble clocks and Purdoneums in the world.[1] I cannot hang up anything so laudatory for my friends to see, so I shall keep it in a drawer, where I keep my other valuables.[2]

Yrs
RVW

My love (if I may be so bold) to M[rs] Hubert.

[1] VW refers to an elaborate form of coal scuttle invented by a Mr Purdon.

[2] Foss had written a sonnet to VW on his birthday and had had it calligraphically written out by Henry Ball and framed.

591. To G. E. Moore

15 October [1952?[1]]

From R. Vaughan Williams,
The White Gates,
Westcott Road,
Dorking.

Oct 15

Dear George

Thank you over & over again for your telegram.

It seems all wrong that my job should command more publicity than yours.

always yours
RVW

[1] Clearly written in connection with the 80th birthday celebrations.

592. To Gerald Finzi

19 October 1952

The White Gates,
Westcott Road,
Dorking.

October 19th 1952.

Dictated to Ursula.

Dear Gerald,

There are three things to do with S.O.L.[1] –

A. Leave it to its fate. But is this right? there is no room in the world for second rate work, and if this is really second-rate it had better be put out of its misery by the vet. The more so because Ursula's words which are certainly worth preserving are already in print in her new book, QV.

B. I could revise it. But is it worth revising? In which case I had better

C. Scrap it.[2]

The funny thing is that

(1.) I got excited and liked it while I was doing it and thought the tunes very good. But when I heard them they all seemed to be still-born.
(2.) The part I liked best is part I, especially the horses of the sun, and this is the part which most people seem to like least.
(3.) The chorus seemed tame and bored, but to excuse the work on these grounds is like a bad workman complaining of his tools.

What really worries me is that this flop, if it is one, has made me lose my self-confidence. For the last two months I have been writing away hard, and thinking it all very good, but now after this interval, I am sure I shall say 'Am I deceiving myself? and losing my power of self-criticism?'

Now I want you, and my other friends, to tell me, like the policeman did to Mrs Sheldon Amos at Piccadilly Circus,[3] when I ought to go home as being too old for this job. This probably will not prevent me going on writing but I can keep it all confidential.[4]

There, that is all I have got to say at the present.

Ursula and I laughed till we cried over the free milk.[5]

My love to Joyce.

Uncle Ralph

[1] *The Sons of Light* (*CW* 1950/3), first performed at the Albert Hall on 6 May 1951.

[2] This would have been difficult, since it had been published the previous year by OUP.

[3] Sarah McLardie Amos (1840–1908), a political activist especially concerned with women's rights. She was the mother of VW's Cambridge contemporary and friend Maurice Amos, from whom VW may have heard this story.

[4] Finzi replied the next day saying that in all artists' output there were good and less good works and if VW had stopped writing at the time of earlier second-rate examples such as *Old King Cole* or *The Poisoned Kiss* then a number of truly great works would never have been written.

[5] Finzi seems to have told VW a funny story to do with something like the government's provision of free milk to schoolchildren.

593. To Frank Merrick[1]

27 October 1952

From R. Vaughan Williams,
The White Gates,
Westcott Road,
Dorking.

October 27th 1952.

Dear Merrick

Your letter puts me in a difficulty. I thoroughly mistrust these so-called 'Peace' movements. I know that your 'Peace' organisation is run by honest and single-minded people: (indeed in early days I think I joined it myself) but I think there is a great danger that you are *too* simple minded and will become dupes of the nefarious designs of the kremlinists. On the other hand I cannot well refuse to allow any statement of mine in favour of peace to be used by you. But I must insist that it take the following form and have nothing else added, unless indeed the OUP. insist on having it put down that it is used by their permission, which I hope they will not do.

The form must be as follows: – *and nothing else*

(R. Vaughan Williams)

It seems to me that a much simpler solution to the problem would be to use either the Bach B Minor Mass or the plainsong for your quotation. This would obviate all difficulties about permissions etc.

I am sending a copy of this letter to the O.U.P.[2]

Yrs
R. Vaughan Williams

[1] Pianist, composer, and teacher (1886–1981). He and VW had been colleagues at the RCM for many years.

[2] Alan Frank of OUP had written to VW saying that the Musicians Organisation for Peace had asked if they could reproduce a fragment of *Dona Nobis Pacem, CW* 1936/5, from either the manuscript or the printed score, on their annual Christmas card for 1952. OUP were not keen but would assent if VW agreed to the proposal.

594. To William McKie[1]

24 November 1952

The White Gates,
Dorking,
Surrey.

November 24th 1952.

Dear McKie,

I find I never answered your letter about the anthem.[2] I do not quite understand whether you only want the words you quote set, which, without several repetitions will not last more than thirty seconds; or do you want the whole thing, with the bit about the lions?[3] or will that run too much into Sir John Goss?[4] I hope you will be able to put the Old Hundredth through.

Yours sincerely,
R. Vaughan Williams

[1] Organist of Westminster Abbey 1941–63.

[2] McKie had asked VW to write an anthem for the coronation of Queeen Elizabeth II, who had succeded George VI on 6 Feb.The result was *O Taste and See* (*CW* 1952/3).

[3] The setting does not proceed to verse 10: 'The lions do lack, and suffer hunger.'

[4] Sir John Goss, organist of St Paul's Cathedral 1838–72, also wrote an anthem 'O Taste and See'.

595. To William McKie

17 December 1952

The White Gates,
Dorking,
Surrey.

17th December, 1952.

Dear McKie

I am glad you liked the little Anthem. I have an informal agreement with the O.U.P. that I offer everything first to them, so will you get into touch with them for making the necessary arrangements?[1]

I hope you will persuade the Archbishop[2] to have two verses of the hymn sung by a choir only. For the last verse I should very much like to use the version of a tune in my 'Hundredth Psalm', but this involves Fanfares between the lines and I am afraid would upset the congregation. Will you let me know what you think? I will send you a copy if I can find one.[3]

Yrs
R. Vaughan Williams

Dr. William McKie,
33, Greycoat Gardens,
London, S.W.1.

[1] *O Taste and See* (*CW* 1952/3) (a setting of Ps. 34: 8), written for the Coronation of Queen Elizabeth II on 2 June 1953. It was first published in the service book for the coronation, which was published by Novello's, so it was necessary for them to arrange copyright clearance with OUP.

[2] Geoffrey Fisher, Archbishop of Canterbury 1945–61.

[3] VW had written *The Hundredth Psalm* in 1929 for the Leith Hill Festival Chorus and orchestra (*CW* 1929/2) and did indeed make use of the music in his arrangement of the hymn 'All people that on earth do dwell', *The Old Hundredth Psalm Tune*, for use at the Coronation (*CW* 1953/2).

596. To William McKie

24 December 1952

The White Gates,
Dorking,
Surrey.

24th December, 1952.

Dear McKie

About the arrangement of the 'Old Hundredth', I think you are right that it is too elaborate. Besides if the congregation are going to start singing Verse 4 after the choir will sing alone, we shall have to give them a good start.[1]

I think the Archbishop is liturgically wrong not to have an 'Amen' after the Doxology, but of course he must have his way.

Yrs
R Vaughan Williams

Dr. Wm. McKie,
33, Greycoat Gardens,
London, S.W.1.

[1] See no. 595.

597. To Alan Frank at OUP

31 December 1952

The White Gates,
Dorking,
Surrey.

31st December, 1952.

Dear Frank

I think we will stick to 'Antarctica', even if it is bad Italian. It ought to be good and it is their fault if it is not. I named it 'Sinfonia' on the lines of the 'Sinfonia Domestica',[1] though I hope the work has no other likeness to that![2]

Thank you so much for sending the score up to Manchester. That is by far the best plan. I shall be at the Grand Hotel. I think it had better be sent there.

As regards your second query. I cannot quite remember when the idea of making the music into a Symphony occurred to me. Almost always when I write film music I have an ulterior idea of a concert version in my own mind.

I remember Ernest Irving once saying to me, 'You composers always write with one eye on the concert room' and I said to him, 'I will tell you why – because in the concert room we are pretty sure we shall not have half the music cut out and the rest inaudible.'[3]

Could you pass an order on from me for your sales dept to send all the P.P.[4] songs to Keith Falkner[5] – for *me* of course

address Keith Falkner
Music Department
Cornell University
Ithaca, N.Y. U.S.A.

R. Vaughan Williams

[1] By Richard Strauss.

[2] Frank had written on 23 Dec. saying that 'the pundits at the Radio Times say, and I feel they are probably right, that Sinfonia Antarctica is no known language! 'Sinfonia' is Italian and 'Antarctica' is Latin, the Italian being 'Antartica' without the 'c': while the Latin for Symphony is 'Symphonia'. I said I thought you would probably stick to the present title, but promised to put it to you. It doesn't worry me either way.' Despite VW's dismissal of the suggestion here, he was quickly persuaded to approve the change and on 6 Jan. 1953 Frank sent a message to the New York office with the instruction that the title was now spelt *Antartica* with one 'c'. The question of the title's orthography had arisen earlier in nos. 510 and 580.

[3] Frank had asked in his letter: 'While I am writing to you, may I ask one small question out of personal interest: was it before, during, or after composition of the film score for Scott that you conceived the idea of this Symphony? I imagine that it was during it, but I really don't know.'

[4] *Seven Songs from 'The Pilgrim's Progress'* (*CW* 1951/1a).

[5] On Falkner see no. 227.

598. To Gilmour Jenkins

1 January 1953

From R. Vaughan Williams,
The White Gates,
Westcott Road,
Dorking.

Jan 1st 1953

My Dear Gil

Ursula & I have decided to marry. I don't quite know when but probably shortly. I hope & believe that we have your blessing. It makes me very happy & I hope it makes her happy also. For the present life will go on just as ever – your room will always be there – & when & if we move house there will also be a room for you. You know how we both love & admire you – indeed I believe you have become indispensable to both of us. You will soon receive a formal announcement – till then mums the word – on the day I hope Mumm will be the word.[1]

Love from
RVW

[1] Mumm refers of course to the well-known champagne. In his reply Jenkins said 'Indeed you have my blessing, my very warm blessing and congratulations. I am sure it is absolutely & completely right for both of you. You already make one another supremely happy and you can preserve and enhance that by being married.'

599. From Gerald Finzi

22 January [1953]

Ashmansworth
Nr Newbury
Berks.

Jan 22nd

Dear Uncle Ralph

The Oxford performance[1] was good, but having heard the Manchester broadcast, & again, last night, the Phil, it's quite clear that the organ is missed a lot when its not there. Also the curtains & flys in the New Theatre absorbed a lot of sound, so that although one got great clarity of playing there was never a real *fff* with a bite to it. There was a huge audience and standing room only. As with Marie Lloyd – hundreds turned away![2] The original run through with piano was fairly well fixed in my mind & whatever the alterations you made it was generally what one expected, except for the extraordinary & fantastic sounds, chiefly in W.W & 'extra' departments. I loved them.

The arguments about whether its a Symphony or not are just what one expected – from Dyneley Hussey who has no doubts that it is, to the musicians who have.

I can't help feeling very strongly that its a work apart. Great big work that it is, it's not in the line of the Symphonies. This isn't because of the 5 mvts, or the opulence of the score, but more on account of the episodic material. Your 'Sinfonia' leaves the critics and announcers open to call it 'his 7th symphony', but it seems like calling 'Flos Campi' 'his viola concerto'. Well perhaps you'll produce Symphony no 7 before long, which will clear matters up. It will probably be for a Haydn-Mozart orchestra, now that everyone is expecting you to get bigger and bigger, & will have a number, just because its always presumed that you never number them!

Well, all this ought to show you how little significance there was in the fact that 'The Sons of Light' wasn't up to the best.

Congratulations & love & thanks from us both.

Yrs
Gerald

[1] Of *Sinfonia Antartica* between the first performance at Manchester and the London performance on 21 January.

[2] The famous music hall singer.

600. To Michael Kennedy

27 January 1953

The White Gates,
Dorking,
Surrey.

27th January, 1953.

Dear Michael

Thank you so much for the photographs.[1] The one of John and I meeting looks just as if one of us had just been telling an improper story; but do I really look like a sick dog when I am listening to music?

With love to Eslyn

Yrs
RVW[2]

Michael Kennedy, Esq.,
3, Moorwood Drive,
The Avenue, Sale.

[1] Taken at the premiere of *Sinfonia Antartica* in Manchester.

[2] This letter printed in part in *WVW*, 382.

601. To Gerald and Joy Finzi

postmark: 1 February 1953

Printed card signed

Ursula Wood,
57, Gordon Mansions,
Torrington Place, WC1

R. Vaughan Williams,
The White Gates,
Dorking,
Surrey.

Dear Gerald & Joyce

YOU WILL, WE THINK, NOT BE SURPRISED TO HEAR THAT WE HAVE DECIDED TO MARRY SHORTLY.

OUR ADDRESSES WILL BE AS ABOVE FOR THE PRESENT, TILL WE FIND A SUITABLE HOUSE.

PLEASE GIVE US YOUR BLESSING.

(no flowers!)

Love from
Ursula
Uncle Ralph[1]

[1] This printed card, which was sent to many of their friends, is reproduced in Moore, *Vaughan Williams*, 104. The wedding took place on 7 February.

602. To Gilmour Jenkins

1 February 1953

From R. Vaughan Williams,
The White Gates,
Westcott Road,
Dorking.

Sunday, February 1st. 1953

Dear Gil

Will you really be my best man? Ursula tells me that you kindly suggest paying the fees...£5 to the vicar with the balance to go to church expenses, and one pound to cover tips to Pew-openers and general hangers-on.

Yrs
Ralph

603. To William McKie

4 February 1953

The White Gates,
Dorking,
Surrey.

4th February, 1953.

Dear McKie

(may we stop Doctoring & Mistering each other?)

I send herewith a sketch of my proposed arrangement of the 'Old Hundredth'. I do not think the fanfare at the beginning and end will upset the congregation, but if you still think so I will cut them out.

I have noted the tune in crotchets and minims instead of minims and semibreves, because I think this will be easier for the orchestra to understand, but this does not mean that it is to go any quicker, in fact the slower the better. I have marked it, as you will see

Crotchet = 66

I should like all the extra fanfare trumpets to play in the introduction and before the last verse. Could you tell me the size and composition of your orchestra and then when you have approved this (if you do) I will start scoring it.

Now, will you ask the Archbishop two things?

The earlier version of words say 'mirth' instead of 'fear', which is a much better version of 'Serve the Lord with Gladness'. Also, I think 'folk' is preferable to 'flock'. The original edition had the word 'folck' which was misread in later editions as 'flock' but obviously meant 'folk'. Also it is a much better version of 'We are His People'.

Can you persuade the Archbishop to allow this?

I enclose a copy herewith

Yrs
R. Vaughan Williams

Encl.
Dr McKie.

604. To S. P. Waddington[1]

[about 5 February 1953]

The White Gates
Dorking.

My dear Waddy

Thank you so much for your letter which comforted me very much. I wish you were back in London. I feel lost without you or Gustav to look over my things & tell me where I get off – Nobody else has *both* the skill & the patience to tell me what I want to know.

As an awful result of your letter I am sending you one or two scraps which I have produced during the last 2 years – it's a shame to pester you.

I am so sorry you have been ill.

Yrs
RVW

[1] See no. 508.

605. To Gilmour Jenkins

8 February 1953

8.2.53[1]

Dear Gil

You are certainly best man there is. It seemed a shame for you to have to do all the clearing up – But you insisted. I didn't even give you a proper good-bye. It seemed to me that it was one of the best weddings I have been at.

Yrs
Ralph

[1] In the hand of the recipient. The wedding had taken place the day before.

606. To Michael and Eslyn Kennedy

15 February 1953

From R. Vaughan Williams,
The White Gates,
Westcott Road,
Dorking.

February 15th 1953.

Dear Eslyn and Michael,

Thank you from both our hearts.[1]

Let me see your article on Antartica[2] when it comes out. It is chiefly ~~owing~~ to that work that we owe our friendship with you, which, if for no other reason, makes it a *Good Thing*.

Love from
Uncle Ralph

[1] The Kennedys had written a letter of congratulation in response to the announcement by VW and Ursula of their wedding (see no. 601).

[2] Written on *Sinfonia Antartica* (CW 1952/2) for the *Hallé Magazine*.

607. To Guthrie Foote at OUP

[about 28 February 1953[1]]

Herewith proofs of old 100th. Please let me see a revise.

I am troubled about the question of l. c. or cap: for 'his' and 'him' when referring to the Deity. I prefer l. c. following the practice of the Bible, Prayer book, English Hymnal & S. of Praise.[2]

H. A & M[3] on the other hand has caps:

I suppose we must follow the lead of the whole book and not be different.[4]

RVW

[1] Written in response to a letter of 26 Feb. from Guthrie Foote enclosing first proofs of *The Old Hundredth Psalm Tune*, CW 1953/2.

[2] *Songs of Praise*.

[3] *Hymns Ancient and Modern*.

[4] The music was to be included in the Coronation Service book being published by Novello's.

608. To Adrian Boult

18 March 1953

The White Gates,
Dorking,
Surrey.

18th March, 1953.

Dear Adrian

It was wonderful of you to come the other night, and your praise has been a great stimulus.[1]

As regards standing up to sing, of course I do not hear all the clatter and noise from where I stand and I feel, during a long session like that people like to stand up occasionally. I do not think they would join in so well if they sang sitting down, but I admit the clatter and interruption is annoying.

As regards how I do the different chorales, I am afraid I have no principles but do what I think is going to sound best. There are one or two considerations, however. I can only ask the audience to join in the ones they know well; I am gradually adding to the number, and some of the more meditative ones I feel can be sung softly unaccompanied. You mention, 'Thy will be done'. This [it]' seems to me ought to be meditative and soft, not an agonised shout like ''Tis I', and the same applies, of course, to the very soft chorale 'Be with me, Lord'.

Sometimes the effect was meant to be purely musical as when, in the chorale with two verses, I have the first verse sung solo quartette and then answered by the whole body of people. Sometimes the reason is dramatic as in the chorale after 'Let Him be crucified', which obviously has to stand out as something different from the shout that has gone before it. If I had sufficient singers I would detail a small semi-chorus to sing that off-stage, but by singing with only half the choir very softly we nearly get that effect.

I hope I am gradually improving the general conception of the thing and I shall think over all your ideas very carefully.[2]

Thank you again so much for coming. I shall tell my singers of your praise.

My love to Ann.

Yrs fr both
RVW[3]

Sir Adrian Boult,
South Hawk
Woldingham, Surrey

[1] Boult had attended a performance of the St Matthew Passion at Dorking.

[2] On 23 Mar. Boult replied: 'How very kind of you to answer so fully. I am afraid I must have said something stupid because I felt that every one of the chorales was completely and splendidly appropriate, and am quite sure that those in Part II were equally so. It was just that I jibbed at the interruption even when the Choir only stood up after "Thy Will be done". I see no reason why some should not be sung unaccompanied. It was a great performance and the further off it is, the greater it seems – you know what I mean!'

[3] Letter and reply printed in Moore, *Music and Friends*, 157–8.

609. To Mrs Monier Williams[1]

25 March 1953

The White Gates,
Dorking,
Surrey.

25th March, 1953.

Dear M[rs] Monier Williams

You cannot be more sad than I am, at resigning or partly resigning from the Festival. Please do not think it was a sudden decision; I have thought about it for at least four years now and I think I explained that to Miss Cullen. For one thing I am getting very deaf and doubt how long I can go on conducting at all. Secondly, it is obviously better for me to retire now than suddenly have to give up owing to being unable to do it, and it is really time someone else took on.[2]

I will conduct the Passion next year if I may and will remain your President if you will allow me to.[3]

I hate, on an occasion like this to make stipulations, but my undertaking to conduct the Passion must depend on your Committee being able to allow an adequate orchestra and adequate rehearsals. Having reached such a high peak as we did at the last performance we cannot now descend from it.

Yrs sincerely
R. Vaughan Williams

Mrs. Monier Williams,
Downside,
Epsom, Surrey.

[1] Chairman of the LHMF.

[2] Probably a major reason for resigning the conductorship of the LHMF was the VWs' plan to live in London.

[3] VW continued to conduct performances of the Passions until 1958.

610. To Michael and Eslyn Kennedy

20 April 1953

From R. Vaughan Williams,
The White Gates,
Westcott Road,
Dorking.

April 20th 1953.

Dear Michael and Eslyn,

Thank you so much for your letter. Yes, after forty years, I think it is time to resign from the Leith Hill Festival before my hair comes off and the rest of my teeth drop out. But I will go on conducting the Passion if they ask me.

I enjoyed your article about Antartica[1] very much; didn't I write and tell you so? I know that the wind machine must remain. I know it's not a musical sound but nor is the side drum, and no-one objects to that. The most satisfactory version is in the record made of some of the music as actually used in the film. The Manchester one didn't satisfy me entirely. The horns were my suggestion; you may remember that at one of the Manchester rehearsals one of the horns started whistling through his instrument and that gave me the hint; and when I didn't like the little tin trumpets that Malcolm Sargent produced, I suggested the horns, and they seemed alright at rehearsal. But for some reason at performance, at all events over the wireless, they didn't seem right.

Do you know Haydn's 'Imperial' Mass?[2] A magnificent work. We did it at our Festival last week.

I sympathise with your doubts over Larry's Piece.[3] I was surprised myself when it turned out a 'best seller'.

I too am sorry that the Howells work is so difficult, I rather think that the double chorus is quite unnecessary; we couldn't possibly do it here at Dorking.[4]

I am glad you like the new Barnes song.[5]

We are leaving for London in July, so you must come and see us there.[6]

Love from us both to you both,

Yrs
RVW[7]

[1] i.e. *Sinfonia Antartica* (*CW* 1952/2)

[2] *Missa in Angustiis*, Hob. XXII/11, better known in the UK as the 'Nelson' Mass.

[3] i.e. Larry Adler, and the Romance in D Flat for Harmonica (*CW* 1951/4).

[4] *Hymnus Paradisi* had been written in 1938 after the death of his son, but was not performed until VW urged him to allow it to be given at the Three Choirs Festival, Gloucester in 1950. See Boden, *Three Choirs*, 192–3.

[5] *In the Spring*, *CW* 1952/1.
[6] In fact the VWs moved to Hanover Terrace in September.
[7] This letter printed in part in *WVW*, 382–3.

611. To Michael and Eslyn Kennedy

postmark: 26 May 1953

The White Gates,
Dorking,
Surrey.

Dear Eslyn & Michael,

Thank you so much for your letter, which I will try and answer. I also have not heard the final record of my Pastoral Symphony and Mass.[1] I am so glad you like Sancta, it is, on the whole, the one o[f] of my own choral works that I like best.

Fancy Antartica getting into a popular concert![2] I must try and come up for the recording, and we *must* get the wind machine right. The only satisfactory version at present of that is the record of the original film.

Here is the history of 'The Bridal Day'; about fifteen years ago a lady called Ursula Wood, then unknown to me, wrote suggesting a ballet or Masque on Spenser's Epithalamion. We had an interview and the result was we made this Masque together. It was originally intended for the E.F.D.S. . . Indeed rehearsals had started then the war intervened and it had to be dropped. Now, with certain additions and alterations, it is going to be televised on June 5th. I do hope you will be able to listen or look or what ever it is you do with a television. Of course the scenario has had to be much altered from the original stage version.

I am sending you a copy of the Oxford Elegy. I agree that E.N.[3] probably really wanted to show how much he knew about the poem.

I never saw the controversy about the Old Hundredth in the Telegraph. I am rather proud of having persuaded the Archbishop to put it in, but I am afraid that the Viscounts will only know the equal note version, and with British Doggedness will stick to it through thick and thin.

I fear I cannot sympathise with 'Dorabella's' effusions. She seems to think that hers is the only variation, and to my mind it is the worst and the weakest of the lot.[4]

I'm afraid we shall not be at Cheltenham . . . I suppose you will not be passing here on your way there or back?

As regards Elgar and the 5 T. Ps[5]. . . The story is as follows: I was talking to Elgar and a great friend of his, Colonel Isaac, and Isaac suggested a very fine poem, rather more like Donne than Skelton, which I have since set.[6] But Elgar said: 'No, don't do that, you make an oratorio out of Elinor Rumming'.

My love to you both. I do hope that you, Eslyn, are getting better.

Yours
RVW[7]

Love from the typist.[8]

[1] The recordings were by Decca—the symphony conducted by Boult and the Mass sung by the Fleet Street Choir.

[2] The symphony had been included in the Hallé Sunday Series of concerts.

[3] Ernest Newman had written about the *Oxford Elegy* in his weekly piece in the *Sunday Times*.

[4] A reference to the book by Dora Powell (the 'Dorabella' of Elgar's *'Enigma' Variations*): *Edward Elgar: Memories of a Variation* (London, 1937), of which a second edition had been issued in 1947.

[5] i.e. *Five Tudor Portraits* (*CW* 1935/5).

[6] *Prayer to the Father of Heaven*, *CW* 1948/1, a setting of words by Skelton.

[7] This letter printed in part in *WVW*, 383.

[8] i.e. UVW.

612. To the Editor of *The Times* published 18 June 1953

From R. Vaughan Williams,
The White Gates,
Westcott Road,
Dorking.

'GLORIANA'

Sir,

I do not propose, after a single hearing to appraise either the words or the music of *Gloriana*. The important thing to my mind, at the moment, is that, so far as I know, for the first time in history the Sovereign has commanded an opera by a composer from these islands for a great occasion. Those who cavil at the public expense involved should realize what such a gesture means to the prestige of our own music.[1]

Yours faithfully,
RALPH VAUGHAN WILLIAMS.

[1] *Gloriana*, commissioned from Benjamn Britten as a part of the coronation celebrations, had had a controversial premiere on 8 June at Covent Garden. On the opera's critical reception see Robert Hewison, '"Happy were he": Benjamin Britten and the *Gloriana* Story' and Antonia Malloy, 'Britten's Major Setback? Aspects of the First Critical Response to *Gloriana*', both in Paul Banks (ed.), *Britten's Gloriana: Essays and Sources* (Woodbridge, 1993).The letter is printed in *RVW*, 335.

613. To Rutland Boughton

21 June 1953

From R. Vaughan Williams,
The White Gates,
Westcott Road,
Dorking.

June 21st 1953.

Dear Rutland,

It was a great pleasure to hear *The Immortal Hour* again;[1] there are some lovely things in it, and you are not afraid of writing a tune. On the whole I like the first Act better than the second except for the druid's song; and as to the luring song, it is like the Marseillaise or the National Anthem, 'hors de combat'.

I first heard it with you playing magnificently on the pianoforte years and years ago at Glastonbury when you gathered together a noble company of young enthusiasts. I so well remember that we took ourselves too seriously to be frightened of relaxing in the evening when Clive Carey and Johnstone Douglas used to improvise duets on two pianofortes which were slightly out of tune with each other and Fellowes was there with his new found madrigals, and Bernard Shaw propounding truisms from Cherubini, imagining that he had discovered them himself; and Katie and Bee Larpent set up a restaurant which they called 'Cramelot' which rather shocked the more pure minded of your audience.

Well, we were all young then, but I believe you remain young still.[2]

Yrs
RVW

[1] It had been performed at Sadler's Wells.
[2] Printed in *RVW*, 335–6.

614. To Mr Barnes

2 August 1953

From R. Vaughan Williams,
The White Gates,
Westcott Road,
Dorking.

August 2nd 1953

Dear Mr Barnes

I do not usually send my autograph to strangers as I consider autograph hunting is a bad habit. But I hope you are not a mere autograph fiend, but have a genuine love of music, so here is my signature at the bottom of this letter.

Yours sincerely
R. Vaughan Williams

615. To Roy Douglas

10 August 1953

From R. Vaughan Williams,
The White Gates,
Westcott Road,
Dorking.

August 10th, 1953.

Dear Roy,

Further to our telephone conversation, I have written a Christmas Cantata called *Hodie*[1] which David Willcocks wants to hear before deciding whether to do it at Worcester in 1954. The playing through on your part will involve faking up the thing to include solo and chorus parts where nescessary [*sic*]. There is, or will be, a pianoforte arrangement nicely copied by Gus,[2] and an illegible full score by me: you can use which you like

As we arranged the playthrough shall take place at 2.45. on Thursday September 3rd. at the R.C.M. if available, if not probably at the O.U.P. We ought to run it through privately beforehand. There are several things I want to hear at the morning Gloucester rehearsal which means that I should not be available till 12.30, I think we could get in an hour, and have time for lunch between 12.30 and 2.45, but if you happen to be coming to London on Monday, Tuesday or Wednesday I should be available, except on Tuesday between 10.30 & 2.45. Of course if you cared to come here on Sunday August 30th if would be a great pleasure to see you, and if your sister would care to come with you she would be welcome.

Do you think that a fee of five guineas would be adequate?

Yrs R V W[3]

[1] *This Day (Hodie)*, *CW* 1954/3.

[2] Gus de Mauny, a copyist used regularly by VW at this time.

[3] This letter is printed in *WWVW*, 58.

616. To Elizabeth Trevelyan

12 September 1953

The White Gates,
Dorking.

Sept 12th, 53

Dear Bessie

How dear of you to write such an affectionate letter. I am still here – Ursula will not have me in London till all is ready! So here I sit & do my job as if nothing had happened – the removers come and take me and the rest of the moveables on Tuesday!

We have not had an invitation to Birkbeck yet – I hope we shall get one.[1]

Yrs affectionately
Ralph

[1] Perhaps a party when Robert Trevelyan's library was handed over to the University of London.

617. To Roy Douglas

12 September 1953

From R. Vaughan Williams,
The White Gates,
Westcott Road,
Dorking.

September 12th 1953.

Dear Roy,

Have you any criticisms or suggestions about Hodie? *before* I start revising it? Gerald & David have two, which they both made quite independantly [*sic*] of one another.

A. That the third verse of the Three Kings, the one about myrrh, is not good enough.
B. That the chord F Natural, A, C sharp, E flat, is weak, conventional and out of the picture. You may remember that it comes very often in the Gloria in Excelsis. I should be very grateful if you will also give me your

reactions to these points, as well as any other criticisms. You know that, like Gustav Holst, I ask everybody's advice and take no ones.

Yrs R V W[1]

[1] This letter is printed in *WWVW*, 60.

618. To Michael Kennedy

postmark: 12 September 1953

Postcard

From September 15th 1953 our address will be
10, HANOVER TERRACE, REGENTS PARK,
LONDON, N.W.1.
Telephone: AMBassador 8200

URSULA VAUGHAN WILLIAMS
RALPH VAUGHAN WILLIAMS

6

From the Move Back to London until VW's Death: 15 September 1953–26 August 1958

THE decision to move back to London was not a hurried one. It had been twenty-one months since Adeline's death before VW felt himself ready to remarry, despite a close friendship with Ursula of some thirteen years. Doubtless he needed that time to adjust to Adeline's absence and to Ursula's constant presence and support. But when the marriage did take place it heralded a time in his life when he was possibly more content and carefree than at any other time. The move to London was a great success. The house in Hanover Terrace was central and Ursula saw to it that they had a busy social life seeing old friends, to whom he was once more readily accessible, and there were regular madrigal parties which they christened 'singeries'. Ursula became integral to every aspect of his life, providing poems for him to set and typing many of his letters, occasionally with curious orthography, and usually with a postscript of her own. She took close care of his needs, ensuring that he came to no harm, for example by insisting on using taxis, and that there was nothing to worry him. They were both very happy.

This is especially evident from the fact that they now engaged in regular foreign travel. Hitherto VW had not often been in a position to go abroad as Adeline's health deteriorated but now, despite his eighty years, he and Ursula spent a holiday in northern Italy in May 1953, before the move to London, another a year later in central Italy (Florence, Siena, and Rome), and then they had a busy but stimulating autumn in North America when VW was made a visiting Professor for a term at Cornell University at Ithaca, New York. This was a happy arrangement put in place by the English baritone Keith Falkner, who was professor of singing there. Once his lectures had been delivered, they tackled, quite undaunted, a challenging itinerary which took them to Toronto, Niagara, Ann Arbor, Chicago, Bloomington, Los Angeles, Santa Barbara, the Grand Canyon, and back to Cornell. From there they went on to Buffalo, New

York City, Yale (just for an evening to collect a prize and give a lecture), and finally enjoyed a stormy voyage home on the *Queen Mary* in December.

Thereafter there were no comparably adventurous journeys—when invited to New Zealand in 1956 by his pupil Frederick Page, he firmly replied: 'I wish I could accept your invitation to New Zealand, but I am getting rather old for long distance travelling.' However, journeys in Europe were still practical: in September 1955 there was an extensive Hellenic cruise followed quickly by a journey to Ireland to give, at Harriet Cohen's request, the first Arnold Bax lecture at University College Cork, where Bax had died in 1953. In 1956 their autumn excursion was a month on Majorca, where Ralph made progress with the Ninth Symphony; and in 1957 there was an early holiday in Austria and Bavaria (Innsbruck, Salzburg, Munich), during which VW felt somewhat unwell, it turned out because of the effects of prostate cancer. Their last foreign holiday just after Easter 1958 was a trip to Naples and on to Ischia, where they spent a month in April and May in a villa belonging to William and Susana Walton.

While Ursula's organization of a more active social life and regular foreign travel enhanced life greatly for the VWs, her greatest contribution for posterity was ensuring that VW had time to compose. It is very striking just how productive the years following Adeline's death were: few would have expected in 1952, after *Sinfonia Antartica*, that he would write two further symphonies as well as a number of other works which entered into the standard repertory, such as the Tuba Concerto and the *Ten Blake Songs* for voice and oboe. The letters about the two symphonies bear testimony to the most obvious characteristics of each work. In the case of the Eighth it is the inclusion of 'all the 'phones and 'spiels known to the composer'; these included three tuned gongs in D, E, and A 'as used in Puccini's *Turandot*', which were added, at a late stage when the work was almost complete, because VW was much taken with their effect when he heard a performance of the opera on 9 November 1955. In the case of the Ninth, it was the use of the sombre tone of the flügel horn, which, if UVW is to be believed, he heard by accident on the Königsee near Salzburg in June 1957, but which a letter to Anthony Scott indicates was in his mind much earlier than that, in 1955, not very long before work on the composition was started. But the fact remains that no more now than in earlier years does VW allow his friends anywhere near the inner workings of his mind. He once said that while it mattered enormously to the composer what he was thinking of when he wrote a particular work, it mattered not a jot to anyone else. Accordingly there is little in his letters or writings about what lay behind this symphony—his own programme note explains cheerfully what happens but not why. Uncharacteristically, though, VW when approached by Alan Frank about a possible exhibition of the autograph scores of his symphonies, to be shown at the Royal Festival Hall when the Ninth was first performed on 2 April 1959, suggested that only the Ninth be shown, but that it should be accompanied by all 'scaffolding' in the form of notebooks and drafts. This was a surprising suggestion on the part of VW because study of these sources and the scribbled notes therein would reveal that the underlying programme with which he had started out composing the symphony was connected with Salisbury, Stonehenge, and Hardy's *Tess of the d'Urbervilles*, a programme which he otherwise went to some lengths to conceal.

The fact that we know about the plans for this exhibition comes from his correspondence with Alan Frank at OUP. Frank worked closely with VW, as one would expect, given that VW was the most eminent contemporary composer on his department's list, so the surviving correspondence between VW and Frank and colleagues at OUP, taken together with that between VW and Roy Douglas, gives a closer insight into the practical aspects of VW's composing in his last decade than at any other time.

Another casement through which we can gain some idea of VW's distilled experience of eighty years is his correspondence with the young Kennedys. The rapport struck up by VW and Ursula with them at the first performance of *Sinfonia Antartica* in 1952 became ever stronger. As VW wrote to Kennedy in 1956: 'Our friendship has not been long – at all events to an octogenarian like me – but I believe it is firm & lasting and strong. I consider it a lucky day when I first met you both in Manchester.' Kennedy's questions evoked from the composer memories and thoughts on a number of matters which would otherwise not now be recorded. For his part Kennedy found the older man's advice important—such as at the time when Kennedy was wondering whether to leave Manchester. VW advised against it, and so he never did. VW for his part was able to ask Kennedy about aspects of contemporary music such as serialism, by which he was frankly puzzled, and to expect an explanation in terms which he could understand.

A further new arrival in the VW circle was a young writer, Simona Pakenham. She had become so enthused by VW's music that she had written about the experience of getting to know it and had sent him the script of her book in April 1956. As ever VW refused to comment, other than to point out factual errors, but he did go so far as to admit that in reading it he had found much with which he did not agree. Nonetheless Ursula warmly welcomed the new friend into their circle. In 1958 Simona asked him to set a libretto she had written for a charity performance entitled *The First Nowell*. Before that she had touched a sensitive spot, by asking him, in connection with a radio series she was preparing, about the original words attached to the folk tunes which VW had adapted for use in his hymn books. She drew a blank because VW was always alarmed that prudish people would be put off good tunes if they realized they had originally been associated with louche words (his letter to Joyce Hooper in 1951 (no. 567) was a case in point), in the same way that he felt some of the earthiness of the Bible in its original languages needed to be disguised in the decent clothing of the Authorized Version rather than be laid bare by modern, accurate translation.

It is not in any way surprising that there is a Janus-like dimension to the letters of VW's final years. He looks back and remembers the past for the benefit of the younger generation; for example, he was happy to talk to the Composers Concourse in November 1957, not of course about his own music but about his teachers, Parry and Stanford, who seem to shine ever more brightly in his memory as he bemoans their neglect in the present day. The present was demanding: composition remained his primary concern, whatever other distractions might beckon, and the performance of his own music and that of younger contemporaries provided the VWs with a busy engagement diary. But the future was increasingly casting its shadow before it. He became concerned to ensure first and foremost Ursula's financial security after his death, and at the same time to do something to promote the well-being of new British music. Such concerns doubtless received a strong impetus from the death of Gerald Finzi in 1956 and from the discovery in 1957 that he himself was suffering from prostate cancer, a fact which was not made widely known at the time.

He had often been asked to give financial assistance for the performances of works by other, usually younger, British composers, and when he received money unexpectedly his first instinct was to pass it on, with as little fuss as possible, to a worthy musical cause, such as the Leith Hill Festival or Gerald Finzi's Newbury String Players. When he and Ursula were assured by their accountant that they had more money coming in than they needed for themselves, he abandoned his former intention of leaving his copyrights and royalties to the Butterworth Trust and made the characteristic decision to institute an R.V.W. Trust to put his performing rights income to use for the altruistic purposes which he set out very clearly in a memorandum in October 1956. In effect this was putting on a formal footing something he had done quietly throughout his life—coming to the financial rescue of his friends and their music when there was need. It was a generous and visionary move, and the Trust he set up continues to carry out his intentions over fifty years later. He had hoped that Gerald Finzi would play a key part both in the Trust and in sorting out his own musical affairs, just as he saw him in some ways as the torch-bearer of the next generation of composers, but Gerald's death frustrated that. VW then looked to Edmund Rubbra to carry the torch. He thanks him for the dedication of a work because 'it gives a feeling of continuity to the great art which we serve and will insure that the line goes on unbroken from generation to generation'. But for his own affairs he turned to Ursula and to Michael Kennedy to take care of the practical aspects of his estate.

All of this was put in place in 1956, when he still had the best part of two busy years ahead of him, which would include the extensive celebrations of his 85th birthday in October 1957 and the completion of his last symphony, to be given its first performance not quite five months before his death. This was an Indian summer in which he and Ursula felt very content. Fierce letters about political issues do not occur (except when the EFDSS, of which he was President, was slighted by the Director-General of the British Council), and even his relations with Rutland Boughton become imbued with sweetness and light. He continued to compose and sat for a second portrait by Gerald Kelly, which is now in the National Portrait Gallery. Kelly had painted a portrait of VW for the RCM in 1952 but said he now found him 'much more beautiful' than before and wanted to paint him again. VW thought the result very good.

Another of VW's activities reached a culminating point in 1958. He had conducted annual performances of Bach's St Matthew Passion at Dorking since 1942 which had remained separate from the competitive festival. VW had conducted the work regularly with the Bach Choir in the 1920s and had formed a deep emotional attachment to it, which he brought to bear in Dorking. We have seen that he refused to bow to pressures from those who derided, for example, the use of the piano rather than a harpsichord as a continuo instrument, and the fairly florid part he wrote for it (a matter on which the Festival eventually caved in, in 1963). However, even his critics could not deny the emotional force of his interpretation, achieved by familiarizing his choirs ever more closely with it over a period of eighteen years. It is a great benefit that his final 1958 performance of the Passion at Dorking was recorded and, now available on CD, enables posterity to share in his vision. Critics have compared the intensity of his interpretation favourably with more anaemic performances where every feature is rigorously authentic. His 1958 performance was the pinnacle of a contribution to Dorking music-making, which had started with the foundation of the LHMF in 1905 and, as he put it when writing to thank them, the choirs covered themselves with glory. Not long after the performance, in May, he decided that he should conduct the work no more and wrote to the Secretary of the Festival accordingly: 'I have consulted my doctor (Rowntree) and he agrees that it is time to give up. I can't tell you how much I feel it: but it had to come some time, and I think now is the time, after the glory of that splendid, recorded performance.'

After that there was then a lightning day's journey around Lincolnshire in June, including Gunby, the home of his Montgomery-Massingberd cousins, where he had written *Happy Day at Gunby* in 1892. There was a further operation on his prostate in July, which entailed a brief stay in the Middlesex Hospital, performances of *Sir John in Love* by the New Opera Company, a Prom performance of the Ninth Symphony, and then in August a week with Joy Finzi which was spent revisiting some of VW's favourite Dorset country. When VW went to bed on 25 August there were two works very much under way: the music to Simona Pakenham's libretto, *The First Nowell*, was almost complete; and the preliminary draft piano score of a new opera planned by VW and Ursula together, *Thomas the Rhymer*, on which he had put in much work at Ischia, was ready for the next stage of development. But both works became loose ends, one to be tied up by Roy Douglas and the other to remain unfinished when VW died peacefully of a heart attack in the early hours of 26 August.

The Indian summer of his marriage to Ursula had been fulfilling, productive, and above all clearly very happy. The shadow cast by his cancer did not have time to lengthen before nature suddenly and decisively intervened. VW had achieved almost four score and six and was pre-eminent in his field; Ursula, aware of what the future could well hold for him, felt that his death was right and 'at the right time'. For her part, she had devoted herself entirely to his well-being in the five years of their marriage, just as she was to devote herself thenceforward to the well-being of his music and his reputation.

619. To Roy Douglas

24 September 1953

10, Hanover Terrace, N.W.1.

September 24th 1953.

Dear Roy,

Thank you so much for your letter. I have altered 'the chord that nobody loves' except in one or two places. This has meant a good deal of re-writing, since the new chord sometimes involves a new progression. As regards the title, are you afraid people will call it 'Howdy'? But I will think it out, and ask Alan Frank about the selling value of a new title. Nativity Cantata seems to run into Maunder Simper & Toop;[1] and the Birth of Christ into Berlioz. I know the baritone solos are close together, but I do not see how it can be helped. I tried to put as much variety as I could into the choir boys, though after all it has got to be much the same thing. I don't think I can put anything 'merry and bright' in the middle. I am, as a matter of fact, adding another song for tenor, but this, again, won't be merry and bright. It is meant primarily for a church but I should like it also to be done in concert rooms. I fear that in spite of you I am going to add another verse to the worse-than-Delius-&-almost-as-bad-as-Barnby choral.[2] I hope that Ursula will do one.

We are beginning to settle down, though most of the things I want are lost. Thank youso mucg. (Effecet of moving on typist is, alas, only too evident.)[3]

Yours.
R V W

[1] John Maunder (1858–1920), Caleb Simper (1856–1942), and their contemporary Augustus Toop (1869 to after 1939) were all composers of church music which had a vogue in its day but is now largely forgotten.

[2] Joseph Barnby (1838–96), another composer of church music well known in its day.

[3] The typist was of course UVW. The letter is printed in *WWVW*, 61.

620. To Rupert Erlebach[1]

11 October 1953

10 Hanover Terrace. N.W.1.

October 11th 1953.

Dear Erlebach

I'm afraid your screed won't do. I cannot remember saying a good deal of it, & much of it is incorrect. I think the only thing to do is to have one short paragraph as follows:–

Dr Vaughan Williams, in a short speech, referred to Stanford's distinction as composer, teacher, and conductor. He gave reminiscences of his personal experiences of Stanford, and also some he had learned, by hearsay, of earlier years. His opinion was that a composer of Stanford's calibre, if he had been German or Italian would have been celebrated in every opera house in his country. But in England, instead of *Much Ado* and *Shamus O'Brien*, we were content to resuscitate *Norma* and *Samson and Delilah*.[2]

This is, as far as I can remember, some of what I did say. It will be found more fully in my new book.[3]

Yours sincerely
R. Vaughan Williams

[1] Secretary to the Royal Musical Association. VW had contributed to the discussion following a paper given by Herbert Howells entitled 'Charles Villiers Stanford (1852–1924): An Address at his Centenary', *Proceedings of the Royal Musical Association*, 76 (1952–3), 19–25.

[2] Printed, slightly edited, ibid. 31.

[3] 'Charles Villiers Stanford', in *Some Thoughts on Beethoven's Choral Symphony with Writings on Other Musical Subjects* (London, 1953). The piece was originally written for a broadcast on the General Overseas Service in Sept. 1952, to mark the centenary of Stanford's birth.

621. To Beryl Lock

15 October [1953]

From R. Vaughan Williams,
10, Hanover Terrace,
Regents Park,
London, N.W.1.

Oct 15

My dear Ursulas Mother

How dear of you to remember my birthday – you know how much Ursula means to me.

Love from
Ralph

622. To Margaret Keynes

20 December 1953

From R. Vaughan Williams,
The White Gates,
Westcott Road,
Dorking.[1]

December 20th 1953

My dear Margaret,

I think it very unfair to label people like this on such very slight evidence. But I fear I did not know her[2] well enough to bring any evidence to the contrary. I was quite young when she died, and before that she had been an invalid, chair-ridden and bed-ridden, for many years. I very seldom saw her, and I expect she became difficult in extreme old age. My nurse used to tell me that she was rather de-haut-en-bas with the servants, but my nurse was a complete red, and therefore not a trustworthy witness on these matters. But two good things about her I do remember, one, that she taught me to read out of 'Cobwebs' when I was quite a small boy, which I used to enjoy very much.[3] And my mother told me that my grandmother before she married, did very good social work in Shrewsbury. I am sorry I cannot be more helpful.

I always remember a delightful supper party about Job at your house where I met Lilian Bayliss and while discussing ways and means, she said that the Job scenery could be kept in a store and used afterwards for 'heavens'.

I hope now that we are living in London we shall both have the pleasure of meeting you and Geoffrey.

Yrs
R. Vaughan Williams

P.S. We have got the copy of Cobwebs, and it is affectionately annotated in very pretty writing, 'Ralph read as far as this aged 4½'. I think it speaks well for both teacher and scholar.

[1] In fact the Vaughan Williamses had moved to Hanover Terrace the previous September—VW was using up old paper.

[2] VW's maternal grandmother Caroline Wedgwood, a sister of Charles Darwin.

[3] Eleanor Fenn, *Cobwebs to Catch Flies; or, Dialogues in Short Sentences, Adapted for Children from the Age of Three to Eight Years* (new edn., London, 1837). VW's copy is still extant.

623. To Alan Frank at OUP

26 December 1953

From R. Vaughan Williams,
10, Hanover Terrace,
Regents Park,
London, N.W.1.

December 26th 1953.

Dear Frank,

About the Houseman [*sic*] Songs:– I am a little bit worried about Joan Stuart; it must be someone with a sense of humour, and also beautiful diction, almost like a diseuse. I still hanker after Nancy Evans: if there is only one note which is too high I will be willing to put an alternative: I have looked through them to see.[1]

Yrs
R. Vaughan Williams

P.S. I find that except in one song the compass is 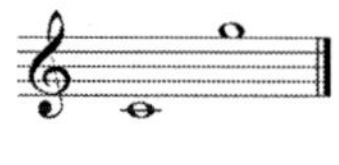

– In that song there is one 

but I w^d find an alternative for that

RVW

[1] VW is writing about *Along the Field*, *CW* 1927/1, his cycle of Housman songs for voice and violin written in 1927 but not published until 1954. The recording was eventually made by Nancy Evans and Leonard Hirsch but not issued.

624. To Elizabeth Trevelyan

10 January 1954

From R. Vaughan Williams,
10, Hanover Terrace,
Regents Park,
London, N.W.1.

January 10th 1954

My dear Bessie,

It was very nice to hear from you and I hope we shall see you here one day. We love our new house, and Ursula has made it beautiful.

I am sending you a copy of one of my arrangements of Greensleeves from which I think Philip Erasmus[1] can pick out the tune. I have to confess that it is a 'cento'. There are several versions of the tune and I took the best bits out of each version. I feel I am quite justified.

Love from us both,
Ralph.

[1] Philip Erasmus Trevelyan, Elizabeth Trevelyan's grandson.

625. To Mr Chandler[1]

14 January 1954

From R. Vaughan Williams,
10, Hanover Terrace,
Regents Park,
London, N.W.1.

January 14th 1954.

Dear Mr Chandler,

Thank you very much for the photograph. I cannot remember the circumstances, but apparently I was very rude, and you have heaped coals of fire.

I do not know much about records, I do not care about them much, and therefore did not even know that Herbert Howells had not been recorded. He certainly ought to be and I will see what I can do. I think the British Council should be the first people to approach, or Novellos, or both. But of course recording [a] choral work is a much tougher proposition than that of an orchestral composition as I know by experience. It has taken forty three years to achieve a recording of my Sea Symphony! But I hope we shall succeed in doing something for the Hymnus.[2]

Yours sincerely,
R. Vaughan Williams

[1] The recipient of the letter has not been identified.

[2] *Hymnus Paradisi* was a work which VW admired—and which gave rise to his dedication of *Hodie* to Howells; see *RVW*, 347. The sort of request for assistance to which VW is responding may have helped put the idea in the VWs' mind of establishing the RVW Trust to assist fellow composers.

626. To Michael Kennedy

10 February 1954

From R. Vaughan Williams,
10, Hanover Terrace,
Regents Park,
London, N.W.1.

February 10th 1954.

Dear Michael,

Thank you both so much for your wedding good wishes.[1] We celebrated with lots of drink and a visit to a French film about an unhappy marriage!

Your article made me blush, but I enjoyed it very much.

I agree with you that P. Young's book is awful, and he hasn't even taken the trouble to get his facts right.[2]

As regards the piano pfte concerto, the only thing that is published is the one piano pfte version, with the orchestra arranged for 2nd pfte. This is confusing, as some people think that this means the 2 pfte version, but it does not: to do the two pianoforte version with the pfte arrangement for the orchestra wd require 3 pftes! And to add to the confusion, I have altered the end since it was printed. I think both 1 pfte and 2 pfte versions are occasionally played, any way in America.

Give our love to Eslyn. It will be lovely to see you both at Cambridge, and possibly at Dorking: leaflets enclosed.

In answer to your P.S. *This Day* (Hodie) is a Cantata for Christmas, down for the Worcester Festival this year. It is now with the printers, and I will send you a copy as soon as it is out.

Yours,
RVW[3]

P. S. I have not got a leaflet of St. John; it is Feb 27 7.0 pm Dorking church

[1] For VW's and UVW's first wedding anniversary.

[2] Percy Young, *Vaughan Williams* (London, 1953). VW had written to Young listing some of the errors having declined to comment on the text itself—see no. 503.

[3] This letter printed in part in *WVW*, 383.

627. Foreword for a brochure issued by the Society for the Promotion of New Music[1] [about March 1954]

Foreword

by

DR. RALPH VAUGHAN WILLIAMS, O.M.

How are we to find the diamond hidden in the dunghill? Only by trial and error; and as the heroine of A. P. Herbert's novel said about her amorous entanglements, 'The more the trial the less the error'.[2]

This is the principle which the S.P.N.M. has adopted. Every work which, at all events, makes sense (and, it is whispered, even some which to the ordinary ear did not make sense) is set down for performance, and so far as time and funds allow, is put to the supreme test of a hearing.

The pundits may tell us that they can judge a work by the eye only. This is not true. They may be able to see that the orchestration is competent, that the form is logical, and can see whether a harmony obeys or (according to the temperament of the beholders) disobeys the text-books' rules, but no one can tell whether the essential and elusive spark of inspiration is present without actually hearing the work.

If you come to our experimental rehearsals expecting to find a masterpiece you will be disappointed. That is not our object. Our motto, in plain language, is 'Let 'em all come', and your duty as audience is to spot the winner.

On the whole we have been lucky and the proportion of the diamonds has been surprisingly big. We beg all those who are interested in music to come to our recitals remembering Bach, Beethoven and Wagner were once beginners and had to face the verdict of an audience to whom their work was entirely new. Especially we appeal to those omniscient supermen who can stroll into a concert room and pronounce judgment, and not only pronounce, but print it, on a new and difficult work without turning a hair. We shall be grateful for their praise, but equally we shall appreciate their blame.

Finally, we owe thanks to all those artists who have helped us for the minimum of material reward, and we thank also those public bodies and individuals who, by their donations, have made all this possible.

[1] The SPNM produced a brochure in 1954 introducing its aims and objects, setting out the composers and works supported by the Society over the previous ten years since its foundation. VW, as President since its Foundation, provided a foreword. He also wrote to Alan Frank in Mar. 1954 asking him to sponsor a SPNM concert.

[2] Topsy was the heroine of three novels based on a column in *Punch* by A. P. Herbert, of which the first was *The Trials of Topsy*, published in 1928. In letter xvi, 'The case for the defence', Topsy writes: '*nearly* all soul-mates find each other in the end by *trial* and *error* and the more *trial* the less *error* . . .'. All three novels were combined and published in 1949 as *The Topsy Omnibus*. The reference was probably intended by VW as a discreet tribute to the energetic secretary of the SPNM, Topsy Levan.

628. To Michael and Eslyn Kennedy — 2 March 1954

From R. Vaughan Williams,
10, Hanover Terrace,
Regents Park,
London, N.W.1.

2nd March 1954

Dear Michael and Eslyn,

I can hardly tell you what pleasure your letter has given us both. If you had been, like we were, at the earlier rehearsals, you would have been even more amazed at the almost miraculous final result.[1] I am so glad about what you say, that it is essentially a stage work, and I am so frightened of it finishing up in the Parish hall. But this was a stage performance, in the best sense of the word, though not conventionally of the stage.

It was such a pleasure to see you again, and I feel more touched than I can say that you both should have taken that long and arduous journey in order to hear a tune by me.

We had a very good performance of St John on Saturday. The chorus howled like Whipsnade[2] where necessary.

Here are your St Matthew tickets. It will be splendid to see you again at Dorking.

Love from us both
Uncle Ralph

P. S. I saw Marianne on Saturday, and she said that you had made Manchester absolutely lovely for her, and that she was enjoying her life tremendously thanks to you both.[3]

Love U.

If you want a meal in Dorking, we can heartily recommend the *Star*, in West Street, just opposite the Fire Station. It has fine food going on all day, and is very warm, and very friendly.

Not Star & Garter

You will be sitting next to Anthony Asquith (14, 15)[4]

[1] i.e. of the Cambridge production of *The Pilgrim's Progress* (*CW* 1951/1). Ursula had confided to them a month earlier that as far as they could tell from the rehearsals, it would not be a good performance.

[2] i.e. like the animals at Whipsnade Zoo.

[3] Marianne, the daughter of Yanya and Genia Hornstein, had been doing teaching practice in Manchester and UVW had asked the Kennedys to look after her.

[4] Anthony Asquith was a friend of VW's associated with London Films, but, according to Kennedy, didn't turn up. This letter printed in part in *WVW*, 383.

629. To G. E. Moore

14 March 1954

From R. Vaughan Williams,
10, Hanover Terrace,
Regents Park,
London, N.W.1.

March 14th 1954

Dear George

Here is a photograph of the Log Book.[1] I am sending one to each representative of the party.

The work was done as a friendly act through a friend of ours and I think the photographer would like to have a letter of thanks signed by all of us. I am sending this to George Trevelyan, and asking him to send it on to you, and you to be good enough to stick on the label enclosed, for Ralph Wedgwood.

George Trevelyan thought that we might give the original to Trinity Library, if you approve of this idea will you tell him?

Yrs
RVW

[1] The log book of the reading party at Seatoller, Easter 1895. Trevelyan, who held the original at this time, gave it to UVW in 1959 and she in turn presented it to the British Library in 1995, where it is MS Mus. 163.

630. To Michael Kennedy

4 April 1954

From R. Vaughan Williams,
10, Hanover Terrace,
Regents Park,
London, N.W.1.

April 4th 1954.

My dear Michael and Eslyn,

I read your splendid notices in the Daily Telegraph. You are right certainly in saying that the singers feel the Passion[1] in their hearts as well as in their minds now.

It is wonderful to think you are coming to hear the Five T.Ps.[2] I hope they will do it well, but they are finding it very difficult and rather out of their usual run.

As to Gloriana,[3] I can't pretend I got much out of it, and I think that dramatically, to include such a scene as that in the Queen's bedroom, on such an occasion as the Gala, if it was not meant for a deliberate insult was a gross piece of insensitivity.

All love from both to both,

Yrs
RVW

[1] Kennedy had reviewed the Dorking performance of Bach's St Matthew Passion in the *Daily Telegraph*.

[2] i.e. *Five Tudor Portraits* (*CW* 1935/5), to be done during the LHMF at Dorking. It was in the event a 'dashing performance' (*RVW*, 345).

[3] On the critical reception of Britten's *Gloriana* see no. 612.

631. To Margery Cullen

11 May 1954

From R. Vaughan Williams,
10, Hanover Terrace,
Regents Park,
London, N.W.1.

May 11 1954

Dear Miss Cullen

Will you please give all the choirs my affectionate greetings and thank them all for their beautiful singing. I was so glad to hear my 'Three Choral Hymns'[1] again, which I had not heard for a long time – last time I heard it in Dorking it was sung by the *first* division and it was considered rather difficult for *them*; we have come on since those days!

I hear that the first division found my 'Toward the Unknown Region' difficult. All I can say is that their beautiful and assured singing made it *sound* easy – theirs is truly the art which conceals art.

The '5 Tudor Portraits' one [*sic*] are [a] hard nut to crack and at early rehearsals I wondered if the kernel was going to emerge. But with indomitable perseverance and artistic insight they finished up with a really splendid performance.

I am no longer the official conductor – but my successor has shown that he has it in him, if loyally supported by all concerned, to lead the LHMF on from strength to strength.[2]

Yrs ever
R. Vaughan Williams

[1] *Three Choral Hymns* for baritone (or tenor) solo, mixed chorus and orchestra, *CW* 1929/3.
[2] VW's successor was William Cole, who also bought The White Gates.

632. To Beryl Lock

22 August 1954

From R. Vaughan Williams,
10, Hanover Terrace,
Regents Park,
London, N.W.1.

August 22nd 1954

Dear Beryl

I felt that you wanted to see Ursula so much that I must spare her for a day or two. I know how much you liked having her, and I know how glad I am to have her back. She had a very comfortable journey.

Thank you very much for the good wishes for our journey.[1]
Your peaches tasted lovely

Love from
Ralph

[1] The VWs were to leave shortly for the United States, where VW was to be Visiting Professor at Cornell for the autumn term, an arrangement instigated by Keith Falkner.

633. From John Ireland

22 August 1954

Rock Mill
Washington
Sussex

August 22nd 1954

My dear V.W.

I was delighted to get your greetings telegram on my 75th. My mind always returns nostalgically to our early RCM days, with Dunhill, Holst, and the others – our meetings at 'Wilkins' – and when we first heard Brahms No 4, and sang[1]

And your joke about Judas Maccabeus –

'Hoary Tory, O, You 'dnot mak' a bee-us!!' O, happy days.[2]

Now, you and I are the sole survivors of that happy carefree group. You have reached well-deserved world fame – all honour to you.

You say 'please write a lot more music' – but I was a *minor* composer, and I say to myself (to paraphrase a wartime caution) – 'Is your music really necessary'???[3]

Anyhow, *far too much music* (?) is being written, performed and published in these times.

But I'm getting a garrulous old man, and will close. Thanking you, dear V.W., very affectionately for your kind thoughts,

Your friend as ever,
John Ireland

[1] The first two bars of the Scherzo from Brahms's Symphony No. 4. Thomas Dunhill also recalls this story; see *WVW*, 20.

[2] Ireland wrote a fuller version of the story in his obituary appreciation of VW in the *Musical Times* for Oct. 1958 (pp. 535–6): 'Vaughan Williams, who even then we called V.W., had a somewhat naive sense of humour, his favourite tale or joke was "Why does an oratorio remind you of an elderly Conservative?" Answer being Judas Macabeus. The interpretation being "Hoary Tory, O, you just mak' a bee- 'us" (bee-house).'

[3] An adaptation of the wartime injunction: 'Is your journey really necessary?'

634. To Herbert Byard

2 September 1954

From R. Vaughan Williams,
10, Hanover Terrace,
Regents Park,
London, N.W.1.

September 2nd 1954.

Dear Byard,

Thank you so much for your letter. If I remember right the Bell effects in Parsifal include a grand pianoforte and a gong, and the deep bell, made especially for the Huguenots[1] for the Paris Opera weighs 6 tons. So I fear 2 of those is out of the question.[2]

I expect that Bach's predecessors are all right on the bubble-and-squeak organ because they are definitely period music, but Bach, to my mind, and I believe to yours, belongs to no period and must be treated as such.

With kind regards to you both,

Yours,
R. Vaughan Williams

[Note added by UVW]
And I must add my best wishes for your holiday.

UVW

[1] Meyerbeer's opera. VW's memory about *Parsifal* is not correct—there is no piano or gong in the orchestration; perhaps they had been used to substitute for the bell effects in a performance heard by VW.

[2] At this time VW was at work on his eighth symphony, the last movement of which contains 'all the 'phones and 'spiels known to the composer', including '2 tuned gongs as used in Puccini's *Turandot*' (see no. 665). He had presumably consulted Byard about bells and gongs.

635. Internal OUP memo by Lyle Dowling 21 September 1954

21 September, 1954

The President

Vaughan Williams Agenda

Saturday, 25 September. He arrives on the Parthia (with Mrs. Vaughan Williams). I am trying to get Tony Rundall's help in seeing him through customs and all that. Dr. Donald J. Grout, head of the Music Department at Cornell, and Keith Falkner, on the music faculty there, are coming by motor to New York on that day and will also meet the Vaughan Williamses. They will stay at the Cornell Club (Barclay hotel). To 'A Midsummer Night's Dream' at the Met, if the people are not too tired.

Sunday, 26 September. A small luncheon. Later, the V.W.'s want to be left free to go and see friends here.

Monday, 27. They will go by car (two cars) to Ithaca. (I should have preferred a train for them – however...)

27 September–6 October. At the Cornell Residential Club in Ithaca; lectures at the university.

7 October. To Toronto.

8 October. Lecture in Toronto.

9 October (probably). Return to Ithaca.

12 October. Lecture at University of Michigan, Ann Arbor.

14 October. Lecture in Chicago.

15 October. Lecture in Bloomington, Ind.

20 October. Lecture in Los Angeles.

21 October–2 November. Returning to Ithaca, stop-off in Arizona to visit friends.

The remainder of the time is not entirely planned yet, but on 4 December they sail for home, again on the Parthia.[1]

Dr Vaughan Williams writes me that he has never given interviews to the press and doesn't intend to begin now. Too bad.

[1] UVW's account of the journey is in *RVW*, 348–58.

636. To Cordelia Curle

24 September [1954]

Cunard Line
RMS Parthia

Sept 24th

Dear Cordelia

That is splendid news about the infant. It was good of Bernard to wire us.

We are having a very hymnious [*sic*] journey – fellow passengers dull except for Gerrald [*sic*] Moore and his wife and a delightful elderly Anglo-American Miss Skume and about 3 passably pretty girls – so not much doing there. We had a good start – but then it got very stormy & Ursula lay low for 24 hours – but she is quite well now – only bored as we both are with nothing to do but eat & sleep at which we both do plenty!

We shall not arrive in New York till Sunday morning at 8.0 – It is lovely weather now with a lot of sun & wonderful glacial sea

Love to all from us both

Yrs
Ralph

637. To Luther Noss

2 November 1954

The Cornell Heights Residential Club
One Country Club Road
Ithaca,
New York

November 2nd 1954

My dear Dean,

Thank you for your kind letter. I need hardly enlarge on the honour which I feel in being awarded the Howland Prize by Yale University.[1]

Thank you for the details, which I have noted, namely, a late afternoon lecture followed by a dinner. I think on the whole it would be more convenient for us to return to New York the same evening. Nevertheless, my wife and I thank you very much for so kindly offering us the use of your house while we are at the university.

As regards the title of my lecture I propose 'Making your own music' – should you approve of this? I am giving a short talk on more or less the same subject for Toronto but I do not think that need affect the question.[2]

Perhaps you could tell me, at your convenience, how long you would like the lecture to be; also whether it should be afternoon or evening dress?

Yours sincerely
R. Vaughan Williams

P.S. Please forgive delay. I am only just back from California.

[1] On 28 Oct. 1954 Luther Noss, Dean of the School of Music at Yale, had written to VW:

Dear Dr. Williams:

The Secretary of the University has informed me that you have been sent an official notice of the action taken by the Corporation in awarding you the Howland Prize. This, at last, frees my hand so that I might write to you expressing the great pleasure which this brings to all of us here at the University.

Mr Falkner has perhaps told you something of our plans for December first on which day the award will be made. We are anxious that they be completely at your convenience and have, therefore, made tentative arrangements for a late afternoon lecture, the award to be given at the same time followed by a small dinner in your honor. We understand that you will be in New York and that it would be possible for you to come to New Haven for the afternoon and early evening. You could plan to return to the city after dinner if you wish, for it is but an eighty minute journey by railroad.

My home is located in the center of the University, and we would be happy to have you use it while you are here. It is perhaps too early for you to indicate any specific plans, but if it is possible for you to send us the title for your lecture, we would appreciate it in order that we might make the proper public announcements.

Yale is this year celebrating the completion of one hundred years of music instruction at the University, and we are especially honored that you will join us in commemorating this important chapter in our history.

Very sincerely yours,

Luther Noss
Dean

The Henry Elias Howland Memorial Prize at Yale had been established in 1915 as an award for distinguished achievement in the fields of literature, the fine arts, or the theory of government and politics. The recipient received a sum of money and a Howland Medal. It had been awarded for music to Gustav Holst in 1924 and Paul Hindemith in 1940; it was to be awarded subsequently to Aaron Copland in 1970 and Virgil Thomson in 1986.

[2] His lecture formed the basis for the chapter entitled 'Epilogue' published in *NM*, 237 ff.

638. To Michael and Eslyn Kennedy from UVW

postmark: 12 November 1954

UVW
Cornell Heights Country Club
Ithaca NY. USA

My dear Eslyn & Michael,

Thank you so much for your letter – I will bring the record with pleasure.[1]

We are having a splendid time – Ralph's lecture tour took us all across Toronto with Boyd Neel & Niagara thrown in, so to speak – Ann Arbour [*sic*] (Huron river county) Chicago, Bloomington, & Los Angeles. We looked out of the train window for two* nights & two days, & ended up under palm trees & hibiscus – a climate entirely my cup of tea. Then a weeks holiday by the sea at Santa Barbara – 2 days by the Grand Canyon, & back here. All the lectures were a terrific success – & Ralph was much enjoyed and appreciated. We even found a student performance of Riders to the Sea going on in Santa Barbara! He has conducted the Buffalo orchestra here, & it, with Krips[2] are doing Sancta Civitas next week in Buffalo. Then there is a concert here with the student orchestra, & that's all, besides our present job of preparing lectures for the press.[3] New York on the 26th, and a lecture at Yale on the 1st. Sail on 4th. Ralph is terrifically well, & bouncy – & *thrives* on milk shakes & butterscotch sundaes.

We look forward to going home now – & to seeing our friends – & the dear cats.

Fond love from us both.
Ursula

*Actually we had very comfortable bunks, but we did get up to see dawn in the deserts.

[1] Kennedy had asked the VWs to obtain for him the only available recording at the time of the two-piano version of the Piano Concerto, *CW* 1931/3, played by Rae Robertson and Ethel Bartlett. In the event they failed to find it.

[2] i.e. Josef Krips, conductor of the Buffalo Philharmonic.

[3] i.e. for publication as a series of essays called *The Making of Music*.

639. To Elizabeth Maconchy

16 November 1954

R. Vaughan Williams,
Music Department, Cornell,
Ithaca, N.Y. U.S.A.

November 16th 1954.

Dearest Betty,

Thank you so much for your letter and good wishes. I had my birthday at Ann Arbor on the Huron river, when we were touring. We have had a fine time, seeing the sights – Niagara, including dressing up in oilskins and going down to the foot of the falls all among the spray, and in the little ship – and the Grand Canyon. We went right across the continent by train, through the most astonishing scenery, and after lecturing at Los Angeles, had a week's holiday by the sea at Santa Barbara among palm trees and pelicans. Lovely weather and swimming, so it was a bit of a shock to return to eight inches of snow! That has vanished now, and its bright autumn weather. We have a week more here, two concerts, one in Buffalo, where one goes in a small plane like a bus, and then a week in New York, and home. It has all been very exciting and interesting, and we have met a lot of nice people. But we are looking forward to going home all the same.

I do hope Nicola is quite recovered now. I am glad they let you stay with her.

Love from
Uncle Ralph

640. To Alan Frank at OUP

23 November [1954[1]]
[Ithaca, NY]

November 23rd

Dear Frank,

Please send a full set of P.P. songs[2] to Miss Balmforth, Walsingham House, the Cottage, Ely; with my compliments.

Thank you for your letter about Kipling & Rostand. As regards Rostand – I think we can do without a translation, because what we want to do, if at all, is to adapt the play freely as an opera: & I daresay this will not be allowed![3]

We are having a very good time but almost too hectic.

Very good performance of Benedicite[4] at Cornell on Wednesday. By the way, the full score they sent me to conduct off is a *scandal*!

Yours,
RVW

[1] Year taken from context.

[2] *Seven Songs from 'The Pilgrim's Progress'* (*CW* 1951/1a).

[3] VW had earlier asked Frank (a) about obtaining permission on behalf of an American pianist in connection with a setting of a Kipling poem by Charles Ives and (b) to find an English translation of Edmond Rostand's *Les Romanesques*, but none was found to exist.

[4] *Benedicite* for soprano solo, mixed chorus, and orchestra (*CW* 1929/1).

641. Address by Luther Noss

[1 December 1954]

Presentation of Dr Ralph Vaughan Williams to President A. Whitney Griswold by Dean Luther Noss.

'Mr President

Twenty-five years ago a friend and compatriot of our distinguished guest today spoke from this same platform on 'The Teaching of Art'. Gustav Holst remarked in concluding his talk that 'a picture, a poem, a symphony, a dance, a dress, or even a dinner must spring from a tradition and yet bring something fresh to the world if it to be a work of art'.

It is our privilege today to be honoring one who for over sixty years has uncompromisingly followed this ideal – indeed one who has himself become one of the great musical traditions of our time. His music has touched the lives of all of us, whether it be his hymn-tunes, his songs, his choral music, or his symphonic masterpieces. Wherever music is heard in the Western world his name is respected as a symbol of all that we hold to be true and good in our art and in our profession.

One biographical account relates that he has, for the most part, characteristically avoided all honours. I am especially pleased therefore, Mr President, that I am permitted to present to you as candidate for the Henry Elias Howland Memorial Prize,[1] Dr Ralph Vaughan Williams.'[1]

[1] On the prize see no. 637.

642. To Michael Kennedy

13 January 1955

From R. Vaughan Williams,
10, Hanover Terrace,
Regents Park,
London, N.W.1.

Jan 13 1955

Dear Michael

I have put off answering your letter because I thought it a good plan to ponder & see if I could find useful advice.

My advice for what it is worth is to stay in Manchester – you will soon be king of the castle there & in London at first at all events only one of a crowd – & what a crowd! You have not such a great *quantity* of music in Manchester – but what quality! – But I quite understand your wanting to come to London—and it w^{d} be lovely to have you.[1]

Thank you so much for what you say about 'Hodie' especially the 'Kings' (which was an afterthought!)[2]

I am glad you like Ursula's poems – so do I![3]

As regards Delius – I think anyone who could write the wedding scene from Romeo & Juliet (*not* the Paradise Garden) entitles Delius to be a great composer – for the rest he smells rather too much of the restaurant.

I liked your 'best man' photograph so much – Eslyn looked prettier even than usual (please tell her this from me).[4]

All I know about Birmingham is that it starts at 6.25 – but where I do not know.[5]

All our love to both of you.
RVW

[1] Kennedy doesn't recall this episode and maintains he never wanted to move to London.

[2] *Hodie, CW* 1954/3, was to have its first London performance on 19 January. The 'March of the Three Kings' is no. 14.

[3] Nos. 14 and 15 (second verse of 'Choral') of *Hodie* are settings of poems by UVW.

[4] Kennedy had been Best Man at the wedding of Eslyn's brother.

[5] The VWs were going to Birmingham to hear a performance of the *Sea Symphony* by the CBSO.

643. To Stanley Godman

14 January 1955

From R. Vaughan Williams,
10, Hanover Terrace,
Regents Park,
London, N.W.1.

Jan 14 1955

Dear Mr Godman

Thank you very much for your letter and interesting account of Burstow.[1] He was not I think really a folk singer in the technical sense of the word (like my Mr Verrall[2] or the landlord of the Inn at Rusper who sang 'Turtle Dove'[3]) he was much more a collector like you and me & judged the matter rather from the outside – but he had a wonderful store of songs. I have in my M.S. book several more of Burstow's songs – unfortunately I have deposited them in the EFDS library[4] & the Librarian is away. I cannot remember what happened to the records (they were of course phonograph cylinders not Gramophone discs) – many of them have perished – what were worth keeping are also in the EFDS library.

Thank you for your interesting account of Ham Fair.

I expect you know the excellent account of her uncle[5] by Miss Lucy Broadwood in her Traditional songs & carols (Boosey).[6] A dictionary is no use unless its facts are correct – If it is wrong about John Broadwood it may be equally wrong about Joh Bach!

Are you any relation to the Godmans of Merstham? – one of them married my cousin Tom Harrison who was killed in the 1914 war (he was a sailor).

Yrs sinc
R. Vaughan Williams

[1] Godman had sent VW a copy of his article 'Henry Burstow: The Horsham Singer and Bellringer', *Sussex County Magazine*, 28 (1954), 519–22. On Burstow see also *CW*, p. 261.

[2] Peter Verrall of Monk's Gate and later Horsham. See *CW*, p. 267, etc.

[3] Mr Penfold, landlord of the Plough Inn, who sang this tune to VW on 4 May 1906. See *CW*, p. 281.

[4] VW's folk song notebooks are now in the British Library (Add. MSS 54187–91, 59535–6, and 57294D,F).

[5] The Revd John Broadwood, to some extent the founder of the English folk-song revival.

[6] *English Traditional Songs and Carols* (1908).

644. To Michael and Eslyn Kennedy

17 January 1955

From R. Vaughan Williams,
10, Hanover Terrace,
Regents Park,
London, N.W.1.

January 17th 1955.

My dear Michael & Eslyn

I want to ask you a lot about John South.[1] Firstly, as regards finance: owing to a surprise packet from the P.R.S.[2] I have about £250 eating its head off in the stable. Do you think a loan of that would be useful or necessary to him? Could you find out? Second, as regards his compositions: can you find out if there is any chamber music, or any songs which you consider good. If so I would send them to Anne Macnaghten to see if she could put them into one of her concerts.[3]

Thank you also for the rest of your letter but I will stick to business in this one.

Love to you both from us both.
[RVW]

P.S. I saw that Mr Milner[4] said that neither Rubbra or I had learnt the new chaos and that it was excusable for me owing to my advanced years – but that there was no excuse for Rubbra.

& P.S. (U).
Where did Martin Cooper say that R. should go to Russia?[5]

[1] John South was a young composer. VW gave him some money and, according to Kennedy, this episode may well have been another example which encouraged him towards the eventual founding of the RVW Trust.

[2] Performing Right Society.

[3] Anne Macnaghten and Iris Lemare had founded the Macnaghten Concerts Society in 1931 to perform the works of young or little-known British composers. See no. 220.

[4] Anthony Milner, composer and teacher. At the time, he was a London University extension lecturer. The article RVW refers to appeared in the *Musical Times* (Jan. 1955), 29.

[5] Martin Cooper, chief music critic for the *Daily Telegraph*, may have made the suggestion in one of his Saturday articles. This letter is printed in part in *WVW*, 384.

645. To Margery Cullen

30 January 1955

From R. Vaughan Williams,
10, Hanover Terrace,
Regents Park,
London, N.W.1.

January 30th 1955

Dear Margery

Here is the song, original – I have sent copy to OUP. I have come to the conclusion that I should like to give the L.H.M.F. not only the song, but the thousand copies, and these will be given, not sold, to the singers. I am seeing Alan Frank tomorrow, and if the O.U.P. wants to print it, I should like them to do so. I shall explain to them that I have given it to the L.H.M.F., and it is their property, will be marked 'privately printed' and no one else will be allowed to sing it. The O.U.P. are not printers, so I expect they will not want to undertake it. In that case you will go ahead with Novello, or any one else you choose, and you can tell them to send the account to me.

Love from
Uncle Ralph
pp Ursula

P.S. Some of the letter does not apply. I have sent it to Alan Frank as I definitely want O.U.P. to print. The question of copyright must be settled & will write again about it when I hear from Alan Frank.

Song for a spring Festival

What is the meaning of spring
~~on~~ this gay spring morning?
Bells in the Easter air,
swallows returning,

new leaves on branches
where frost has been,
young grasses in fields,
green light on green:

plumage of yaffle and dove,
cowslips and violets grow
by orchards blossoming
and the blackthorn's snow:

morning of daffodil air
and migrants bringing
spring home with flowers and songs
and choirs singing.[1]

[1] VW set these words by UVW with the same title for mixed chorus, *CW* 1955/1. He gave the work to the LHMF under the terms set out in the letter.

646. To Michael Kennedy

24 February 1955

From R. Vaughan Williams,
10, Hanover Terrace,
Regents Park,
London, N.W.1.

February 24th 1955.

Dear Michael,

Thank you for sending me your article which I like very much, with the exception of two places. You have already discovered that it was I who conducted the first performance at Norwich.[1] Secondly, I do not like the idea of calling the bird's requiem in Jane Scroop 'a parody'. Jane and I both take it quite seriously...she believed that her sparrow had a soul, and we have no proof that she is wrong.

My love to Eslyn,
RVW

P.S. My love to you both, too.

U.

[1] The first performance of *Five Tudor Portraits* (*CW* 1935/5) was at the Norwich Triennial Festival on 25 Sept. 1936.

647. To Alan Bush

20 March 1955

From R. Vaughan Williams,
10, Hanover Terrace,
Regents Park,
London, N.W.1.

March 20th 1955.

Dear Bush,

(May we stop Doctoring each other? at all events when we are not engaged in political controversy, so you may tell, if you get a letter from me, starting dear Dr Bush, I am going to be nasty. But now let us turn to the real things of life.)

Thank you very much for the programme and the account of the concert. It was splendid of you to advance the cause of your fellow English musicians in this way.[1]

I wish I could hear your opera: it is a scandal that so many fine operas, like yours and Arthur Benjamin's Tale of Two Cities, to mention only two, do not take their rightful place on the stage of our national theatre, when they are welcome abroad. At the Stanford centenary, when in France or Germany every opera house would have put on a Stanford opera – had he belonged to them – we in England ignored Shamus O'Brien at Sadlers Wells (was this for political reasons?!) and Much Ado about Nothing at Covent Garden (one would have thought in this case that the words 'about Nothing' would have saved the situation.) Let us hope for better things soon.[2]

Yours sincerely,
R. Vaughan Williams

[1] Bush often included VW's and other British compositions in concerts he conducted in East Germany and the USSR.

[2] Bush had also told him of a performance his opera *Wat Tyler*. VW eventually heard a performance of the work at the Camden Theatre on 9 Dec. 1956.

648. To Alan Frank at OUP

27 March 1955

From R. Vaughan Williams,
10, Hanover Terrace,
Regents Park,
London, N.W.1.

March 27th 1955.
2nd letter.

Dear Frank,

You may possibly know that I am President of the Society for the Promotion of New Music. I understand that they have requested you to sponsor one of their Studio Recitals; may I second their request? I think they are doing very good work. Of course a lot of rubbish passes through our hands, but as A. P. Herbert's Topsy says of her amourous [*sic*] entanglements 'It is all a question of trial and error, and the more the trial the less the risk of error'.[1]

Yrs
RVW

[1] OUP were apparently unable to do as he asked. On Topsy, see no. 627 above.

649. To Frank Howes

18 April 1955

From R. Vaughan Williams,
10, Hanover Terrace,
Regents Park,
London, N.W.1.

April 18th 1955.

Dear Howes,

Thank you very much for your letter, and for coming to hear my new tune.[1] As you say, though I do not accept yours, or anyone's advice blindly, I assure you it makes its affect. On the main point, however, I am not taking your advice. I feel the thing IS a symphony and it is going to remain so. But a lot of your suggestions about detail I am going to think over hard, and probably adopt. However I shall probably do nothing till I have let it 'mature in bond' for a bit.

Thank you once again.

Yrs
R. Vaughan Williams

[1] Symphony No. 8, *CW* 1955/3. See *RVW*, 358, where this letter is printed.

650. To Iris Lemare 21 May 1955

From R. Vaughan Williams,
10, Hanover Terrace,
Regents Park,
London, N.W.1.

May 21st 1955.

My dear Iris,

I enjoyed very much working with you again after so many years. I thought you and your colleagues secured some fine performances. I fear that Anne has a notion of giving up, but I am trying to persuade her not to.[1]

Love from
Uncle Ralph

[P.S. in UVW's hand]
And you, dear Iris, looked so radiant, as well as making all sound splendid. Thank you.

[1] Iris Lemare explained to UVW: 'The letter refers to the concert in the "Arts Council Drawing Room" which was *intended* to be the *end* of Anne [Macnaghten]'s Post War series of concerts she called "The Macnaghten New Music Group". She asked me to come and conduct it. It was the occasion of the "Little Basket" – the RVW "Diableries". Ralph tried – (and succeeded) in halting the closure of the concerts. It was the start of the named *"Macnaghten Concerts"*. Anne herself and all of us (I think you too?) became the *Council* of the new series—and Ernest Chapman took over the organisation.'

651. To Albert Sturgess[1] 9 June 1955

From R. Vaughan Williams,
10, Hanover Terrace,
Regents Park,
London, N.W.1.

June 9th 1955.

Comments on Mr Sturgess's Memorandum.

Page 1. Though my income from Royalties and performing fees is now large, in my opinion it has reached its peak and will soon begin to go down, perhaps steeply.

As regards Estate Duty, is it possible to pay this in installments? Will the duty be calculated on our joint income or only on mine? I have recently made over to my wife about 30 thousand pounds: after five years that is, say, about three years from now, this will, I understand be free of estate duty.

Page 2. & 3. The statement about my income is not quite clear and I should like some more explanation. I find that I never, as yet, have had to sell out to pay income surtax: though I have occasionally have [*sic*] had to overdraw for a few months.

Page 3. continued. It is the opinion of this memorandum that by handing over my performing fees to the Mus. Ben. I should loose [*sic*] £1630 and should be left with about £3500 spendable income.

My expenditure in 1953 & 1954 was over £4000, not including taxes or payments under covenant, and not including my wife's expenditure out of her income. I admit this was rather a heavy year, but I do not see how I can afford to loose [*sic*] £1600. According to the memorandum my death duties would be over £60000 and this would absorb my whole invested income. But would not this be payable out of the £70000 which I earn by royalties and performing fees and leave my invested income intact? I am most anxious that the payment of death duties shall not leave Mrs Vaughan Williams in any difficulty. But except for the first year, I do not see how it could be so. This is all on the supposition that I do not adopt the proposed scheme of making over my performing fees to the Mus Ben.

I shall ask for a little more explanation of page 5. My ignorance of financial affairs is abysmal.

Page 6. I do *not* like the idea of making over my fees to the Mus Ben. without restriction. Of course I throughly [*sic*] trust Mr Thistleton and his colleagues, but we do not know who will follow them. The paragraph about the assignment of performing fees wants a little more explanation.

Finally, I am not interested in money, except as a means of not having to think about it, and though naturally, I do not want to have too little, I should feel equally burdened if I had too much. I repeat what I said at the beginning, the payment of income and surtax has never been a worry to me, and I have always found it possible to live on the income which remained. This therefore makes me doubtful as to the wisdom of starting this new scheme. I have shown the memorandum to Sir Gilmour Jenkins and have asked him to make some comment on it.[2]

[1] VW's accountant, known to all as Bert Sturgess.

[2] This document enshrines VW's first (rather cautious) reaction to proposals which were eventually to culminate in the establishment of the RVW Trust and RVW Ltd.

652. To Benjamin Frankel

20 June 1955

[From R. Vaughan Williams,
10, Hanover Terrace,
Regents Park,
London, N.W.1.]

20th June 1955

Dear Mr Frankel,

I am, at the present moment, simply bursting with ill-gotten gains from the P.R.S. I feel that others, more deserving, should share some of them.

After your victory in the Courts and your shocking treatment by the jury I hope I may be allowed to count you as one of them.

I am no politician and I am sorry that politics entered into the case as this will make it difficult to have any public expression of our regard for you.

May I therefore have the pleasure of sending you the enclosed as a personal expression of our personal esteem.[1]

Yours sincerely,
Ralph Vaughan Williams

When we saw you at Glyndebourne we had no idea how soon this was to be and we followed the report each day with passionate interest. May I add my love to you both.

Ursula

[1] Frankel had just successfully defended a case of slander, in connection with Clark's management of the ISCM, brought against him by Edward Clark. For the details see Meirion and Susie Harries, *A Pilgrim Soul: The Life and Work of Elisabeth Lutyens* (London, 1989), ch. 12. Many musicians and composers subscribed to a fund to enable Frankel to pay his share of the costs of the case, though VW's contribution does not appear to have been made public at the time because of his concern at the political overtones in the case: much of the evidence was concerned with the alleged communist sympathies of Clark and his chief witnesses, Christian Darnton and Bernard Stevens.

653. To G. O. May at OUP

1 July 1955

From R. Vaughan Williams,
10, Hanover Terrace,
Regents Park,
London, N.W.1.

July 1st 1955.

Dear Mr May,

We must try and do something about Mrs Child. I am not quite sure whether the £300 was for words and music, or only for the music, but as I suppose we could now get nothing for the words from America, we had better divide the £300 into two halves. I suggest that I should send her £150 myself, explaining the circumstances. This would not upset your accounts and would be simpler. I shall then see if I can get her elected as a member of the P.R.S. They are so ridiculously pompous in all their methods; after all, they are merely a collecting agency, but they treat membership of their society as a sort of Holy Brotherhood to which one can only be initiated by Bell Book and candle. Let me know if you approve of my scheme & I will then act immediately.[1]

Yours sincerely,
R. Vaughan Williams

[1] Harold Child, the librettist of *Hugh the Drover*, had also written the words for *The New Commonwealth* and had died in 1945. This letter concerned a payment from the Performing Right Society concerning *The New Commonwealth*, *CW* 1940/3. May replied that the payment was in respect of the music only. He approved of VW's proposal to send £150 to Harold Child's widow and offered to contact the PRS about her being accepted as a member.

654. To Alan Frank at OUP

24 July 1955

From R. Vaughan Williams,
10, Hanover Terrace,
Regents Park,
London, N.W.1.

July 24th 1955.

Dear Frank,

Now for your second letter (ACF:119 F). I think you will agree with me that the answer to the Cincinatti [*sic*] people who want to do bits of Pilgrim's Progress, probably in concert form, & without orchestra, is NO. Let us wait for a real slap-up performance in America, which I think is still not beyond the bounds of possibility.

Now there is something more: I daresay you have seen that Evelyn Sharp has died? Would it be a good plan to try to buy the complete rights of the text of Poisoned Kiss from her Executors? Such rights to include adding, omitting and altering as we want? I met a man at Cheltenham last week who is toying with the idea of doing it at the Grammar School there: unfortunately I never got his name, but I told him to write to you.[1]

Yrs
RVW

[1] This performance did indeed take place.

655. To Anthony Scott

30 July 1955

From R. Vaughan Williams,
10, Hanover Terrace,
Regents Park,
London, N.W.1.

July 30th 1955

Dear Tony,

Thank you so much about the Tuba.[1] I am now having a flirtation with her young cousin the flugel horn whose acquaintance I first made in the Salvation Army Band: she has more or less the same compass as the Cornet, but is much more mellow, though not so active. I need hardly say that, she being a Salvationist, I do not use the word mellow in its technical sense.[2]

Our love to Ruth,

Yrs
RVW

[1] Presumably a letter about the Tuba Concerto, *CW* 1954/2.

[2] This passage perhaps indicates that VW had started work on the Ninth Symphony, with its prominent part for the flügel horn. He had first used it in the *Prelude on Three Welsh Hymn Tunes*, *CW* 1955/2, written for the Salvation Army, but according to UVW it was hearing it played on a boat on the Königsee near Salzburg while on holiday there in June 1957 that prompted him to make use of it in the new symphony (see *RVW*, 381).

656. To the Choirmaster and members of the Budo Festival Choir

29 August 1955

[From R. Vaughan Williams,
10, Hanover Terrace,
Regents Park,
London, N.W.1.]

29 August 1955

Dear Choirmaster and Members of the Budo Festival Choir

It gave me great pleasure to receive your very nice letter, especially as it contained all your signatures and your photograph.

I am glad you enjoyed singing my motet.[1] I am a great friend of Dr Harold Darke, and I am glad he heard you sing.

I wish you many happy years of singing, and that you will go on from strength to strength. Perhaps one day my wife and I will have the chance of hearing you sing – perhaps over the wireless, which would be better than nothing.

Thank you once again for your letter.

With kind regards from both of us,

Yours sincerely
R. Vaughan Williams

[1] The choir at Budo in Uganda had sung *O Taste and See*, *CW* 1952/3. The motet was the test piece in the Namirembe Music Festival, which the choir had won.

657. To Laurence Taylor[1]

2 October 1955

From R. Vaughan Williams,
10, Hanover Terrace,
Regents Park,
London, N.W.1.

October 2nd 1955

Dear Mr Taylor

My advice to you is as follows:– and I think it is the advice which would be given by any composer, whether they are bi-tonal, poly-tonal, or any other kind of tonal:–

You will not be wasting your time if, for a time you neglect free composition and make a *thorough* study of strict counterpoint, classical harmony, fugue and strict sonata form. You will then be fully equipped, your tools will be sharp and of tempered steel, ready for whatever use you wish to put them to.

I am glad you approve of the alteration of the last note in the slow movement of my number four. I had long felt that the original last note was wrong, and I fear I must confess, that I behaved like the lady in the Lost Chord, and tried out every possible note till I hit on the right one.

If you want to study books I suggest those written by R. O. Morris, *Sixteenth Century Counterpoint* – this of course is not a text book, but a treatise – published by Macmillan, but you will found [*sic*] excellent text books on harmony, counterpoint and form by him and H. K. Andrews published by Oxford University Press. There is a tendency at present to despise Cherubini; I entirely disagree, I think every composer ought to go right through him.

Yours sincerely
R. Vaughan Williams

[1] A young American composition student who had written to VW asking for guidance and encouragement. He gives an account of the circumstances of this letter and of a visit to the VWs in Aug. 1958, a week before the composer's death, in 'RVW Remembered: An Afternoon with Ralph Vaughan Williams', *Journal of the RVW Society*, 15 (June 1999), 7.

658. To Alan Bush

2 October 1955

From R. Vaughan Williams,
10, Hanover Terrace,
Regents Park,
London, N.W.1.

October 2nd 1955.

Dear Bush,

Please forgive my delay in answering: I have only been back a few hours from a month in Europe, and no letters were forwarded.[1]

As regards your kind invitation, if you wish it – I feel that I cannot say no, though I admit that I had hoped to be able to work quietly for the next few months, except for a few already-made engagements. But the question arises, am I the right person? I am a great admirer of Stanford, both as composer and teacher, but I was not for long a pupil of his, and I think that the real influence on my work has been Parry. Now, it seems to me that the man who really imbibed all the good of Stanford's teaching was Herbert Howells; and last year he gave an excellent talk to the Musical Association about Stanford, his work and his teaching.[2] May I venture to suggest that he should give the lecture and that I should, if you wish, add a little on the more general question on nationality in music?[3]

Yours sincerely,
R. Vaughan Williams

[1] Bush had asked VW to speak on Stanford as a teacher to a meeting of the Composers' Concourse on 17 Nov. The VWs had been in Greece.

[2] Howells's lecture to the Musical Association was published in *Proceedings of the Royal Musical Association*, 79 (1952–3), 19–25. See no. 620.

[3] In the event Howells was not free and VW spoke on Parry and Stanford, with Gerald Finzi in the chair.

659. To Alan Frank at OUP

9 October 1955

From R. Vaughan Williams,
10, Hanover Terrace,
Regents Park,
London, N.W.1.

October 9th 1955.

Dear Frank,

The only trouble about the symphony is that it is *just* possible though very unlikely that I might want to rescore it after hearing it with the orchestra. Therefore the Hallé people ought not to make too much fuss about it till after Feb. 13th.[1]

As regards Antartica, I heard my alterations, I admit over the wireless only, and liked them. It made the tunes come out better, and I have no use for my music, or anyone else's, unless the tunes come through. Has John got a set of parts of his own? If so I would allow him to play it unaltered, if he prefers it.[2]

Yrs
RVW

[1] Frank had written on 30 Sept. saying that the first performance of the Eighth Symphony (*CW* 1955/3) would be on 2 or 3 May in Manchester and Barbirolli wanted the performing material to be ready in February as he was giving VW a private run-through on the 13th. In his reply to VW's point Frank said that he still thought it in order for the symphony to be announced since VW was unlikely to want to rewrite the whole work as a result of the run-through.

[2] Frank had also said that John Barbirolli disapproved of the late revisions in *Sinfonia Antartica* (*CW* 1952/2) and would not use them.

660. To Arnold Barter

13 October 1955

From R. Vaughan Williams,
10, Hanover Terrace,
Regents Park,
London, N.W.1.

October 13th 1955.

My dear Barter,

Thank you so much for remembering my birthday and for the lovely flowers.

I remember well my first correspondence with you over the Sea Symphony, 1911, and then later I came and conducted it and made a fearful mistake in the last movement.

We did not go to Hereford this year as we had planned a visit to Greece, and the programme did not attract me. This does not mean that I was not in thorough sympathy with putting me and other old fogeys such as Gerald and Herbert Howells on the shelf! But in the first draft of the programme our place had not been taken by the younger English generation as it should have been. This was partly rectified later, but they ought never to have done Huber. I heard the orchestral rehearsal and it seemed deadly to me.[1] We enjoyed our trip in Greece very much.

I hope we shall soon meet again.

With kind regards from us both,

Yrs
R. Vaughan Williams

[1] Under Meredith Davies's direction, the Festival that year was aiming at a new look. English music included Berkeley's *Four Poems of St Teresa of Avila*, Bliss's *Colour Symphony* and *Meditations on a Theme by John Blow*, and Geoffrey Bush's choral suite *In Praise of Mary*. The notice of the festival in *Musical Opinion* noted 'Apart from one unfortunate venture (Huber's *The Prodigal Son*) the Festival may be reckoned an important success'. Paul Huber's work received its first British performance.

661. To Michael Kennedy

15 October [postmark: 1955]

From R. Vaughan Williams,
10, Hanover Terrace,
Regents Park,
London, N.W.1.

Oct 15

Dear Michael

When I got your letter it made me unhappy for a bit because I thought of the sort of man that all that wonderful praise of yours would really fit & this made me wish I could start life all over again and really become, approximately at all events, the sort of person you describe.[1]

Nevertheless I loved having your letter because the affection of a good man is worth having any how.

As regards the new symphony[2] – I hope it is going to be all right – but I feel rather nervous – at all events it is simple and sets no problems – but at my age ('I speak as a fool')[3] I cannot afford to let out anything 2nd rate – which is not really straight from the fountain-head.

I think May 24 is the date in Manchester – but I believe John is going to allow me a private run through in Feb which will settle its fate.[4]

We went to B'ham on Tuesday & had fine performances of my F Minor & Serenade[5] (the former with Schwarz[6] who also did a fine performance of Beethoven No 7).

Who is Wallenstein?[7]

All our love to Eslyn

Yrs
RVW[8]

[1] Kennedy had written for his 83rd birthday.

[2] No. 8 (*CW* 1955/3), which was approaching completion. See no. 662.

[3] 'I speak as a fool': a much-favoured echo from 2 Cor. 11: 3.

[4] John Barbirolli and the Hallé Orchestra in the event gave the first performance of the Eighth Symphony on 2 May 1956. There was indeed a run-through on 7 Feb., which Kennedy attended.

[5] i.e. Symphony No. 4 (*CW* 1934/13) and the *Serenade to Music* (*CW* 1938/2).

[6] Rudolf Schwarz, Musical Director of the City of Birmingham Symphony Orchestra.

[7] Alfred Wallenstein, American conductor and cellist, who had either recorded or conducted a piece of VW's.

[8] Kennedy noted 'wonderful letter' on the envelope of this letter, which is printed in part in *WVW*, 384.

662. To Roy Douglas

28 October 1955

From R. Vaughan Williams,
10, Hanover Terrace,
Regents Park,
London, N.W.1.

October 28th 1955.

Dear Roy,

Many thanks for first movement, which I return under a separate cover.

I think I have noted all your corrections. Now for your special points: (1) I have never put numbers to my symphonies yet and I don't want to start now. After all, Beethoven wrote a D major and a D minor, & nobody seems much the worse and it won't do much harm if they do play number five instead of number eight! (2) Trombones; I have decided to add 3, instead of your 1, at the end of the first movement. This involves altering the horns in one or two places. I hope you will approve. It was really pure willfulness [*sic*] which made me leave them out in the first movement because I determined to do without them, though the necessity stared me in the face. You may remember that the original version of the last movement also had no trombones. (3) Harps: I don't want two harps if I can help it. Impressarios [*sic*] do not seem to mind how much percussion they engage, but I only know of 2 performances of my Sea Symphony in 45 years in which the second harp was used, so I suggest using your second emendation for the end of the first movement – the one with one harp part only, [marginal note: LH to double RH 8ve lower] and I have marked certain places, harp to be doubled if possible. In the last movement I w^{d} have 2 harp parts if you think it is absolutely unavoidable, but the second harp MUST be marked ad. lib, & so arranged that we shan't mind much if its not there.

Yrs
R V W[1]

[1] This letter is printed in *WWVW*, 81.

663. To Eugene Goossens

30 October 1955

From R. Vaughan Williams,
10, Hanover Terrace,
Regents Park,
London, N.W.1.

October 30th 1955.

Dear Goossens

I listened with much interest to your Apocalypse last night, especially as I once set some of these words myself.[1] Of course Spohr has done the same thing, and Elgar told me that he was intending to do the same himself – so I am in good company.

I admired your four horsemen very much and also a choral number to, I think, Alleluia, which came soon after. Of course there can be no question of your skill and of your knowledge of choral and orchestral sounds which came through wonderfully, even over the wireless. I suppose you deliberately avoided the more spiritual aspect of the words which doubtless has often led us astray into sentimentality; you occasionally suggested Blake to me, but more often Hieronymus Bosch; after all they are both great masters.

I have to confess to disappointment with your setting of the Holy City – again you may accuse me of being a sentimentalist.

I hope you will forgive my setting down these few impressions while they are fresh in my mind. Thank you and the BBC for letting us hear it.

No answer is expected of course.

Yours sincerely
R. Vaughan Williams

[1] In *Sancta Civitas*, *CW* 1925/6.

664. To Adrian Boult

30 October 1955

From R. Vaughan Williams,
10, Hanover Terrace,
Regents Park,
London, N.W.1.

October 30th 1955.

Dear Adrian,

I do not want to say in public that I have had differences of opinion with Stanford. I did quote once, in print somewhere, some reminiscences of my lessons with him in which he disapproved of my flattened sevenths in harmonizing folksongs.[1] But he is not the only person who has done so, and I do not want this small episode to be magnified into a 'difference of opinion'. So please may we leave it alone?[2]

Yrs
RVW

[1] In *A Musical Autobiography*, reprinted in *NM*, 187.

[2] This was to do with the Composers' Concourse at which VW spoke about Parry and Stanford as teachers. See no.658 and *RVW*, 367–8. It took place on 17 November.

665. To Roy Douglas

10 November 1955

From R. Vaughan Williams,
10, Hanover Terrace,
Regents Park,
London, N.W.1.

November 10th 1955

My dear Roy,

Here is the second movement returned with all your corrections noted. I think I have marked the metronome rather too quick, I think ♩= 100 would be more right.

It would be angelic of you to come to Manchester, but as you are apparently going to be an angel at home as well you will be an angel either way. No date is fixed for the run-through yet. I imagine that John is waiting till he hears the score and parts are ready.

Now there are two things that worry me: ought we to vet the vibraphone part in the first movement before we put it into the score? Would it be a good plan to have the vibraph. part copied out and get a vbrphnst to play it through? I imagine its a bit experimental.

Secondly, I went to Turandot yesterday and they used a set of tuned gongs, chromatic scale, which sounded superb, much better than tubular bells. Of course they could not do a glissando. Do you think it would be worth while to put them into the score as an alternative to the tubular bells? – keeping those for the glissando.[1]

Yrs
R V W

[1] See no. 634. This letter is printed in *WWVW*, 82.

666. To the EFDS

12 November 1955

Address to the AGM of the EFDS.

November 12th 1955.

We have it on the authority of the Master of the Rolls sitting in judgement, and as good citizens of course we loyally accept it, that Folk Dance is not a fine art.[1] But without officially challenging his decision I think we may allow ourselves in private to examine his reasons. He bases his judgement, so far as I can make out, on three points. That folk dance is not creative, that it does not use the mind, that it gives no aesthetic pleasure to the beholder.

The master only knows, as far as I can make out, two folk dances, Sir Roger de Coverley, (country dance), and the Lancers, (square dance) and one singing game, Oranges and Lemons. He has apparently never heard of the Morris or Sword Dance. Nor has he realised that Folk Song as well as dance, plays an important part in our scheme. Folk song, which on no less authority than Hubert Parry, contains specimens of supreme art.

Let us take these three points in turn. First, that folk dance is not creative: but all executive art must be creative, and to dance a folk dance well is as much an act of creation as to play the violin well.

The second point is that it gives no aesthetic pleasure. As I have already said, the Master does not seem to know of the existence of the Morris or the Sword which are definitely by experts designed to give aesthetic pleasure. To my mind the Morris especially can be as truly called high art as the Parthenon or the ninth symphony or Michaelangelo's Night and Day. The country dance is of course primarily for personal enjoyment. But who can doubt that the figures and steps, when well done, are a source of intense aesthetic pleasure. I need hardly refer again to the artistic quality of many of our beautiful folk songs.

Now is the question of the use of the mind in the folk dance: our Director insists, quite rightly, on the sub-conscious quality of the best folk dancing. But I think he would be the last person to deny that this must be preceeded [*sic*] by conscious artistry. To my mind our finest folk dancer was, and indeed still is, the Director himself,[2] and I cannot believe that he achieved this supremacy without a gruelling course of technique. I fear that many of our dancers have misunderstood this question, and imagine it does not matter how badly they dance so long as the solar plexus is working alright. I feel sure that the Director would be the last person to insist that mind is not an important part of the folk dancing equipment.

The issue is now officially settled, and has been settled against us; and officially we bow to the Master's decision. But might we not persuade him, purely as a private individual to pay us a visit and find out what Folk dancing really is, and whether it is not after all, a fine art.

Of course we must do our part and make sure that our art does not fall from its high position. We must not be content just to jump about and enjoy ourselves. If we set out to enjoy ourselves we shall fail to achieve much enjoyment. If we set out to practise our art, and learn how to practice [*sic*] as well as we can, then, and then only, we shall achieve the highest enjoyment.

Are we still practising a fine art, as we certainly used to or have we fallen from our high estate[?] I cannot believe it – But it is a serious problem and must be faced.

[1] The EFDSS had appealed against a rating assessment, claiming exemption from rates on grounds that it was a society instituted 'for purposes of . . . the fine arts exclusively'. In the Court of Appeal the Master of the Rolls, Sir Raymond Evershed, had, in his judgment, pronounced that 'the activity or "art" (if it is properly so called) of folk dancing and singing is not in any sense creative . . . In the case of folk dancing and singing the purposes of the Society are not to create anything . . . but rather to encourage the performance by as many persons as possible of the old and traditional dances and songs in an old and traditional manner. The Society does not claim to appeal to the mind, or even, as I understand, to the faculty of taste.' The society had lost the appeal. See *English Dance and Song*, 20/1 (Sept./Oct. 1955).

[2] Douglas Kennedy.

667. To Michael Kennedy

22 January 1956

From R. Vaughan Williams,
10, Hanover Terrace,
Regents Park,
London, N.W.1.

January 22nd 1956.

Dear Michael,

With regard to the last movement of my No 6. I do NOT BELIEVE IN meanings and mottoes as you know, but I think we can get in words nearest to the substance of my last movement in

'we are such stuff as dreams are made on, and our little life is rounded by a sleep'.[1]

Love to Eslyn
RVW

[1] From Shakespeare's *The Tempest*, Act IV, Sc. i. See *WVW*, 302, where Kennedy discusses VW's response to his question.

668. To John Barbirolli

10 February 1956

From R. Vaughan Williams,
10, Hanover Terrace,
Regents Park,
London, N.W.1.

February 10th 1956.

Dear Glorious John[1]

I expect it was really your magic, but if you approve, I propose not to scrap the symphony. I can't thank you enough for all you and your players did.[2]

We send our love to Evelyn and to you,

Yrs
RVW

[1] An accolade derived by VW from Walter Scott's *The Pirate*, where Claud Halcro addresses the poet John Dryden thus, and from Borrow's *Lavengro*, where Lavengro addresses the publisher John Murray similarly. See Roger Savage, 'Three Glorious Johns', *Journal of the RVW Society*, 32 (Feb. 2005), 5–6.

[2] Barbirolli and the Hallé had run through the Eighth Symphony, *CW* 1955/3, for nine hours for VW while he was in Manchester preparing the St Matthew Passion; see *RVW*, 369.

669. To George Trevelyan

15 February 1956

From R. Vaughan Williams,
10, Hanover Terrace,
Regents Park,
London, N.W.1.

February 15th 1956.

Dear George,

I think it may amuse you to have a copy of my opera which you can glance at from time to time when nothing more serious intervenes. I have marked the copy showing what we do and what we leave out.[1]

We must try and meet while we are in Cambridge.

Yrs
R. Vaughan Williams

[1] The Cambridge Opera Group were performing *Sir John in Love*. In the end the VWs were unable to attend because of VW having caught a cold. See *RVW*, 369. VW also wrote in similar terms to his other great Cambridge friend, G. E. Moore.

670. From John Barbirolli

17 February 1956

Grand Hotel
Leicester

Friday 17/II/56

My dear Ralph,

I have been wanting to write ever since we spent that wonderful day with N° 8, but we have had a continuous run of concerts & travelling since then, which I have unfortunately had to face with a severe bronchial chill and to cap it all, '*lumbago*' for the last 3 days.[1] So every spare moment I have had to try & rest a little. Last Tuesday was rather a 'black' day, when lo, your adorable inimitable letter arrived, & I was enabled to set forth again in renewed strength. Ralph, I feel rather shy in the face of all the honour you have done me, & my lack of words must measure the depth of my gratitude for the Symphony, the M.S. & your faith & confidence.[2] We have had quite a V-W. week, since the 7th. Two performances (Bradford and Wolverhampton) of 'Wenlock Edge' (Richard Lewis) & Tallis last night (Leicester).

'Wenlock' sounded magical I think with orch': (the texture is most lovely and appropriate & never too thick if properly played). Richard sang most beautifully & it had the greatest success. Parts were full of wrong notes but all is correct now I hope.[3] We do it again in Manchester April, & wld like to record it if you consent. N° 8 is I am sure going to be a great success & we are all working for May 2 & 3. Hanley, Newcastle & London follow immediately.

Best love to you both.

Ever
John.

P.S. Must congratulate Roy and O.U.P. on the extraordinary accuracy of the Parts of N° 8.

[1] Barbirolli had devoted a day in early Feb. to running through the Eighth Symphony, *CW* 1955/3, to try it out—the first public performance was not until 2 May.

[2] VW had presented the autograph score to Barbirolli with an inscription to 'Glorious John'. It is now in the British Library.

[3] The orchestral version of *On Wenlock Edge*, *CW* 1909/1, prepared in the early 1920s, was not widely performed and was published only in 1995.

671. To Alan Frank at OUP

19 February 1956

From R. Vaughan Williams,
10, Hanover Terrace,
Regents Park,
London, N.W.1.

February 19th 1956.

Dear Frank,

I will answer your question about printing the symphony in a few days. Meanwhile I am writing to ask Roy what my opinion about it is.[1]

Yrs
RVW

[1] Frank had written to VW on 17 Feb. asking if it was safe to start engraving the full score of the Eighth Symphony (*CW* 1955/3), or whether VW still wished to wait until after the first performance in case he wanted to make further revisions. The Symphony had received a run-though a few days previously.

672. To Roy Douglas

19 February 1956

From R. Vaughan Williams,
10, Hanover Terrace,
Regents Park,
London, N.W.1.

February 19th 1956.

My dear Roy,

I have had a letter from Alan Frank asking me whether the symphony is ready to print, or whether I want to wait to hear another performance. I feel, at present, that I can pass it with those alterations we made in the train, and one addition; namely in the scherzo, the bassoon tune *ff*, with third bassoon ad lib. and the rest *pp*. But you know my mind by this time and do you think it likely that I shall, or do you yourself want, other revisions?

Yrs
RVW

[added by Ursula:]
P.S. What a good thing it was that you took your degree in Foretelling, crystal gazing and Cultivation of Second Sight at Salamanca.

U.[1]

[1] This letter is printed in *WWVW*, 87.

673. To Gerald Finzi

13 April 1956

Regents Park,
London, N.W.1.

April 13 1956

Dear Gerald

Some time ago an American society wanted to shut me up in a cage & not let me out till I had written a symphony – When I refused this honour they converted it into a grant of $500 (about £175) to [be] used by me for any worthy purposes – I think your orchestra ought to share in the spoil.

Love to Joyce

I have made the cheque personal to you to avoid audit worries.

Yrs
RVW

674. To the Treasurer, LHMF

13 April 1956

From R. Vaughan Williams,
10, Hanover Terrace,
Regents Park,
London, N.W.1.

April 13th 1956

Dear Mr. Treasurer,

A short time ago an American Society offered to shut me up in a cage till I had written acceptance. When I refused the honour they converted into a grant of $8,500 (= I am told about £1750) to be used by me for such worthy purposes as I thought best. I should like LHMF to share in the spoil.[1]

Yours ever,
R. Vaughan Williams.

[1] It is curious that VW wrote on the same day to two potential recipients of his largesse but mentioned the American grant as having been a different sum in each letter. Perhaps he set it at the figure he was proposing to give to the beneficiary to whom he was writing.

675. To Simona Pakenham[1]

17 April 1956

From R. Vaughan Williams,
10, Hanover Terrace,
Regents Park,
London, N.W.1.

April 17th 1956

Dear Simona Pakenham,

Thank you very much for sending me your book.[1] At first I intended not to read it as that would involve approval or requests for alteration,[2] but I changed my mind and was fascinated. Of course there is a lot I disagree with, but you put your own point of view most forcibly, and with an intimate knowledge of my music. In fact you often know it better than I do myself! For example I had to verify your example from my fourth symphony!

Officially, then, I have not read the book, and I send you no criticism. But I have made a list of facts which should be corrected, and which you may find useful.

Perhaps we can meet one day?

Yours sincerely
R. Vaughan Williams

I wonder if you could come to tea with us on Saturday, Sunday or Monday? (21, 22, 23rd). About 4. We should love it if you could.

Ursula V.W.

Corrections

Page 18. Gwen Raverat was granddaughter of Charles Darwin, and daughter of George Darwin by his marriage with Maud Dupuis of the U.S.A. Her husband was a French artist who died many years ago.
Page 20. too, not to.
Page 21. Bryn Mawr College, Pennsylvania. Not a university.
Page 25. Who wants the English composer
Page 33. Toward, not towards, (and elsewhere, also p. 34)
Page 42. Tallis Fantasia, first performed Gloucester Festival, 1910, but not published till some years later.

Page 48. Principal, not principle.
Page 49. Soloist, not soloists.
Page 64. Liturgy I think, not anthology.
Page 72. Note, not chord. (unless you call an octave a chord)
Page 103. Discord, not dischord. (and elsewhere.)
Page 131. Scherzo, not slow movement.
Page 153. I admire Uranus very much, it is Mercury that I do not care for.
Page 154. – and elsewhere. Second repetition, not third.
Page 164. After Cecil Day Lewis, add 'who became'. He was not Oxford Professor of Poetry at that time.[3]
Page 164. 'far as the eye can pass ...'
Page 165. Matthew Arnold, not Meredith.

[1] Simona Pakenham, a writer, had been introduced to the VWs by their friend Jill Balcon, wife of Cecil Day-Lewis, because she was writing about VW. Her book was published as *Ralph Vaughan Williams: A Discovery of his Music* (1957).

[2] VW clearly felt that if he were to suggest alterations it would imply that he approved of everything else in the book. He had taken the same line with Percy Young in no. 503.

[3] See *Ralph Vaughan Williams: A Discovery of his Music*, 155, which refers to VW's 80th birthday concert at Dorking in Oct. 1952 and describes Day-Lewis, the speaker in the performance of *An Oxford Elegy*, as being Professor of Poetry at Oxford. VW is wrong here since she was correct in doing so: Day-Lewis was elected to the Chair in 1951 for a five-year term.

676. To Frank Callaway[1] 26 April 1956

April 26th 1956.

Dear Mr Callaway,

Thank you for your interesting letter. Please give your performers my affectionate greetings. I believe that music prepared and performed in common is a sure way of getting to its real meaning.

I feel very proud that my music should form part of the substratum of your splendid communal effort. In your desire to find out the meaning of contemporary composers, do not forget to hitch your waggons to the great stars, Beethoven, Bach and Mozart.

Yours sincerely,
R. Vaughan Williams

[1] Professor of Music at the University of Western Australia, who had informed VW of performances there of the *Sea Symphony*.

677. To Simona Pakenham

6 May [1956]

From R. Vaughan Williams,
10, Hanover Terrace,
Regents Park,
London, N.W.1.

May 6th

My dear Simona,

It was most sweet of you to give me that delightful fiddler.[1] I wish we had seen more of each other in Manchester – the 2nd performance was even better than the 1st.[2]

We had great difficulty over trains back owing to cup tie[3] – finally had to take a car, us and our two friends from Dorking.[4] How did you fare?

See you, I hope, at singery tomorrow.

All love
Ralph

[1] Simona Pakenham had given the VWs an etching by Walter Sickert.

[2] The VWs had been in Manchester for the first performance of his Eighth Symphony, which had taken place on 2 May.

[3] See *RVW*, 372. Manchester City had been playing in the Cup Final.

[4] In fact one friend only, Genia Hornstein.

678. To Michael Kennedy

13 May 1956

From R. Vaughan Williams,
10, Hanover Terrace,
Regents Park,
London, N.W.1.

May 13th 1956.

Dear Michael,

Thank you so much for your fine notice of the concert.[1] I am still worrying a little about the last movement. I think the critics perhaps thought there were no tunes, because they could not hear them! So I am thinning down the percussion a bit – if John will allow me to, because it may be the Hittites[2] who obscure the tunes, and a few bars less of phones and spiels won't do any harm.

Love to Eslyn.

Yrs
RVW[3]

[1] Kennedy had written a notice of the first performance of the new symphony in the *Daily Telegraph*.
[2] A term (with Charterhouse overtones) which VW was using at this time for percussionists. See also no. 680, where VW discusses his changes with Herbert Byard.
[3] This letter reprinted in part in *WVW*, 385.

679. To Alan Frank at OUP

16 May 1956

From R. Vaughan Williams,
10, Hanover Terrace,
Regents Park,
London, N.W.1.

May 16th 1956.

Dear Frank,

Thank you for your letter. As regards the two points:

1. My experience of conductors is that they always make commas into pauses. I think even John made it too long, and really all I want is a comma there: but I expect most of them will make it into a pause, so we will leave it as it is.[1]
2. I do not see any reason to alter the sentence about the xylophone: it is heard in this episode, though some of it is cut out.[2]

There is one more alteration that I am sorry to say that I have to make: at page 40, figure 17, the trumpets and horns obscure the tune, also the side drum. I want *pp* added on the second beat of the bar at 17, crescendo two bars later. *f* on the second beat of the 5th bar – see enclosed slip. I am also writing to Roy about this. Perhaps he could get in touch with the Hallé librarian and get this addition put into the parts?

Yrs
RVW

[1] Frank had written about two points which needed settling in connection with the engraving of the score of the Eighth Symphony (*CW* 1955/3). The first was about the comma at the double bar-line seven bars before the end of the work—he said that several conductors felt this to be insufficient and proposed replacing it with a pause mark.
[2] Frank's second point was to do with the programme note where the second episode of the last movement was described as being 'characterised by the voice of the xylophone'. Since two of the three passages had been cut out he suggested that this was no longer fully correct.

680. To Herbert Byard

20 May 1956

From R. Vaughan Williams,
10, Hanover Terrace,
Regents Park,
London, N.W.1.

May 20th 1956.

Dear Byard,

May we stop mistering and doctoring? I am glad the symphony came through well. I think the second performance was better, because I had dispensed with some of the 'Hittites' in the last movement, which I think came out too strongly over the wireless. I agree that the spiels and phones cannot play a tune, and for that reason I always double them with strings or other instruments. Indeed, in the last movement I added the trumpet to the bells after hearing it at rehearsal.[1]

I am so sorry I cannot accept your delightful invitation to talk to you at Bristol, but as our old friend Cyril Rootham used to say, even as it is 'I am not a composer, I'm a clerk' – and rightly or wrongly, I want to spend more time putting down black dots on bits of paper.

I had not heard of Stanton's wife's death: the few times we both met her my wife and I both liked her so much.[2]

I am so glad to have good news of Arnold Barter; what *astonishing* news of Rutland Boughton.[3]

Kind regards from us both,

Yrs
R. Vaughan Williams

[1] The Eighth Symphony had had its second performance on 14 May at the Royal Festival Hall. In his programme note VW said 'Also there is a large supply of extra percussion, including all the 'phones and 'spiels known to the composer'.

[2] Dr W. K. Stanton was Professor of Music at Bristol. See *RVW*, 314.

[3] Boughton had abandoned the Communist Party on account of the Russian suppression of the Hungarian uprising. *RVW*, 378.

681. To Cedric Glover 20 May 1956

From R. Vaughan Williams,
10, Hanover Terrace,
Regents Park,
London, N.W.1.

May 20th 1956.

My dear Cedric,

Thank you so much for your letter. You know I like being appreciated, and make no pretence about it! As regard[s] printing the miniature score beforehand – I may tell you that a lot of alterations were made at the rehearsals ...[1]

Yrs
RVW

[1] The letter is in response to one of congratulations following the first London performance of the Eighth Symphony. Glover had observed that it would be nice if a published score were available at the same time. VW was usually anxious not to allow the engraving of the score of a major work to begin until after rehearsals and the first performance, in case he decided upon alterations in that period. The letter is printed in *RVW*, 372.

682. To Michael Kennedy from UVW 22 May [postmark: 1956]

From R. Vaughan Williams,
10, Hanover Terrace,
Regents Park,
London, N.W.1.

May 22nd

Dearest Michael

I don't think I've ever had a letter that gave me more pleasure than yours. It was always quite impossible that Ralph & I should have a life together, & I feel in a sense, that the gods have a bet on us – lets see what happens to a person who has all they ever wanted – and I hope the test case will be a precedent for making them give the same richness to other mortals.[1]

How lovely for you two to have been married for nine years. I wish you 999 more, as I am sure life gets better all the time – for the best people, anyway. Ralph *loved* your telegram, & we had a *most* happy time with John & Evelyn – I like to think of them in Venice now.

We have to water the garden every day, & the green fly are with us – but it looks gay. We've had a BBB weekend[2] – doing the income tax – relieved on Saturday by a charming visit from the Morris dancers, who danced in the terrace & came in after for quarts of cyder & Perry.[3]

Our dearest love to you both – we look forward to Cheltenham

Ursula

Thank you again.

[1] Kennedy had written to UVW following the performance at Manchester, remarking on how much happiness she had brought VW.

[2] 'bloody, bloody, bloody'.

[3] Pear cider.

683. To Gerald Finzi

31 May 1956

Regents Park,
London, N.W.1.

May 31st 1956.

Dear Gerald,

On the advice of my accountant I have decided [to] use the money coming from my performing fees to endow a fund for the benefit of music and musicians to be administered by a special Committee under the general auspices of the Musicians Benevolent Fund.[1]

I should be very grateful if you could consent to be a member of this Committee. Arrangements are not yet finally completed, and may indeed take some further time. In the meanwhile I should be grateful if you would not mention the arrangement to anyone else. I do not anticipate that the Committee would have to meet very often.

Yours,
Ralph Vaughan Williams

[1] This became the RVW Trust.

684. To Sir Adrian Boult

2 June 1956

From R. Vaughan Williams,
10, Hanover Terrace,
Regents Park,
London, N.W.1.

June 2nd 1956

My dear Adrian,

I am so sorry we cannot after all come either on the eighth or the ninth: we have had a delightful invitation from the Finzis for those nights: I have important things I want to talk over with Gerald, and in addition to that I very much want Ursula to have two days in the country to refresh her after a fortnight's overwork. I think you have all my new corrections in No 4 but I am now quite sure about the final note of the second movement. I always felt F was wrong, & the Lord came down one day and told me it ought to be E natural: see enclosed slip.

Our love to Ann.

Yrs
RVW

Symph No. 4 2nd movement last 4 bars flute

E♮ not F

685. To Cedric Glover

10 June 1956

From R. Vaughan Williams,
10, Hanover Terrace,
Regents Park,
London, N.W.1.

June 10th 1956.

Dear Cedric,

The other day Gerald made my flesh creep by an account he had had from you of the parlous state of the Purcell Society: and when I said I should like to help, he said that he wasn't sure that it wasn't too late already. This does not agree with the very optimistic typed report I have just received saying that Novellos have taken over and all is well – as far as I can make out. If help is really wanted I should very much like to do my bit; a small sum now, and later on, in a few months time, I may be able to tap a fund which will enable me to give some more. But I AM NOT KEEN ON PUTTING MONEY INTO NOVELLO'S POCKET![1]

If I decide to send a cheque, will you tell me to whom I ought to send it?

Yrs
RVW

[1] The fund VW had in mind was probably the RVW Trust, which he was in the process of setting up. The Purcell Society had been established in 1876 to publish all the works of the composer, which was achieved in thirty-two volumes in 1965. Novello & Co. published the music on the society's behalf. VW had himself edited two volumes for the society in 1905 and 1910.

686. To Cedric Glover

14 June 1956

From R. Vaughan Williams,
10, Hanover Terrace,
Regents Park,
London, N.W.1.

June 14 1956

Dear Cedric

Many thanks for your letter – I will willingly sign any letter of which I approve – Meanwhile I find to my horror that I have *never* been a subscriber – I sh^{d} like to put that right now if I can get in touch with the treasurer. As I say later on I think I would join any subscription list which he's started.[1]

I return the letter

Yrs
RVW

[1] See no. 685; the appeal in question was for the Purcell Society.

687. To Michael Kennedy

1 July 1956

From R. Vaughan Williams,
10, Hanover Terrace,
Regents Park,
London, N.W.1.

July 1st 1956.

My dear Michael,

I am dictating this from my bed. I am perfectly well, but the doctor says I must not put my foot down till I am cured of the phlebitis – or whatever it is I have got.

You discuss so many interesting things and ask so many pertinent questions in your letter that I will take them in order.

Have you got a copy of the Aeroplanes?[1] If not I will send you one. There was very little in the press about it.

Merry Wives: This is altogether delightful. I think it is the best of the operas on the Falstaff saga. There is a splendid Buffo duet for Falstaff and Ford, a delightful quintet with Fenton & Ann making love in the middle of the stage, and the rival lovers hiding behind bushes and making incidental remarks.[2]

Do you happen to know if John ever got a copy of my Partita for string orchestra? I left it for him in the artist's room at the Festival Hall, but it may have been forgotten.

With regard to Parry and Stanford, I think Howes and the other critics are so frightened of not being up to date: but I believe they will come back into their own.[3] Do you know an early choral work by Parry, *The glories of our blood and state*?[4] It is a bit Brahmsy, but, I think, very fine. There is an interesting story about it which I believe is true. It had been put down in the programme of the Bach Choir in 1887: then it occured to one of the Committee that it would hardly do, seeing that the Royal Family were among the Patrons of the Choir, for them to sing a piece about Thrones and Crowns toppling down in the year of Queen Victoria's Jubilee. So a friend, I think Stanford, went to Parry and asked him to write something else: whereupon, he wrote Blest Pair of Sirens. We must not judge, with all respect to you, the vitality of a composer entirely from the Press. Parry and Stanford, may, according to Howes, be historic relics; but it would take a good many fingers of a good many hands to count up the number of annual performances, even now, of Blest Pair, Songs of the Fleet,—not to mention a large number of part songs and other smaller works which continually appear on programmes.[5]

I fear I cannot put Mackenzie on a level with Parry and Stanford. He was a sound craftsman, and his Benedictus for violin solo, is, I imagine, still popular but that is all.[6] As regards Bax, I am beginning to feel rather doubtful. He had, perhaps, more musical invention than any of his contemporaries, but, as you say, it was quite undisciplined. I wish he had had some gruelling lessons from Stanford. But probably they would have quarrelled, and nothing would have come from it. I agree with you that No 3. is the best, and the last one, No 7, I cannot remember for the moment.

Your story about Sibelius and Berg, reminds me of a bon mot about Sibelius' own first Symphony, namely that it was the best symphony Tchaikowski ever wrote.[7]

You ask if my likes and dislikes change as I get older: certainly they do. I could see no point in Beethoven when I was a boy, – and I am still temperamentally allergic to him. But I am beginning to find out that he is nevertheless a very great man. I used to enjoy Schumann's sentimental songs very much when I was young, but I can't bear them now. Schubert has also gone off the boil as far as I am concerned. But Bach remains![8]

I hope very much when we meet at Cheltenham we can have a long talk about all these things.

I am so glad to hear about the cricket. I never could bear it myself, but I had to play when I was a boy, and one day I was out in the field and thinking about something else, when a ball suddenly hit me hard on the shins. I awoke from my dreams to enthusiastic cries of 'well fielded sir', and got a reputation as a cricketer!

Love from us both to you both,

Yrs
RVW[9]

[1] *A Vision of Aeroplanes* (*CW* 1956/1).

[2] VW much admired *The Merry Wives of Windsor*, by Otto Nicolai.

[3] Frank Howes was music critic of *The Times*.

[4] *The Glories of Our Blood and State*, a choral setting of the dirge from *The Contention of Ajax and Ulysses for the Armour of Achilles* by James Shirley completed in 1883, revised in 1908 and 1914.

[5] This passage has as background the lecture given by VW on 17 Nov. 1955 to the Composers' Concourse on 'The Teaching of Parry and Stanford', which had been broadcast on 1 January. It is printed in a shortened version in *HR*, 94–102 (but misdated to 1957).

[6] VW had been an adjudicator when, in 1922, Alexander Mackenzie's (Scottish composer and conductor, 1847–1935) opera *The Eve of S John* had been turned down for inclusion in the Carnegie scheme for the Publication of British Music.

[7] Sibelius had remarked that he thought Schoenberg's best composition was Alban Berg, a story well calculated to amuse VW.

[8] This last phrase is handwritten (the rest of the letter is typed).

[9] This letter reprinted in part in *WVW*, 385–6.

688. To Evelyn Barbirolli

22 July 1956

From R. Vaughan Williams,
10, Hanover Terrace,
Regents Park,
London, N.W.1.

July 22nd 1956.

My dear Evelyn,

It was wonderful of John to send us that splendid telegram. I am so glad you were with him, and you know what we all know how essential it is that he should have a good rest and get quite well to go on with his great work: and if anyone can make him, you can. Also, you have got to keep well yourself, dear Evelyn, and go on playing beautifully. We listened to your record the other night, and it is lovely. I cannot imagine anything better in the way of a performance. Thank you again.[1]

I hear on all sides how splendidly they all played under their inspirer – not only in my tune, but in everything. I listened in to most of it. A wonderful performance of Beethoven 7. and the other works had fine send-offs, though I can never judge of the quality of a new work at first hearing.[2]

Love from us both to you both,

Yrs
Ralph

[1] Evelyn Rothwell (Barbirolli) had recorded the VW Oboe Concerto.

[2] A further performance of VW's 8th symphony, *CW* 1955/3; the Hallé had given the first performance at Manchester on 2 May and a London performance on 14 May.

689. To Michael Kennedy

29 July 1956

From R. Vaughan Williams,
10, Hanover Terrace,
Regents Park,
London, N.W.1.

July 29th 1956.

Dear Michael,

Your letters were splendid. I will not attempt to answer them, but I want to ask you to do something for me. I find I am entirely ignorant of all the jargon of the wrong note school: could you give me a short resume? Telling me especially what the twelve tone scale means and what a tone row means.[1]

Our love to Eslyn
RVW[2]

POSTAL TUITION IN THEORY AND PRACTICE OF WRONG NOTERY: CONVERSATIONAL SUCCESS GUARANTEED. LEARN WHAT ALL THE LEARNED REVIEWERS MEAN: BE CONTEMPORARY! ENROL TODAY AS A KENNEDY STUDENT!

[1] According to Kennedy, VW liked to pronounce 'tone row' to rhyme with 'cow'.
[2] This letter reprinted in part in *WVW*, 386.

690. To Michael Kennedy

18 August 1956

From R. Vaughan Williams,
10, Hanover Terrace,
Regents Park,
London, N.W.1.

August 18th 1956.

My dear Michael,

I have much to thank you for. Firstly for the book.[1] I have tried several rounds with Mr Wilson, and have bitten the dust each time up to the present. But I am going to try one more bout, bloody but unbowed! He is apparently writing about existentialism, and he never explains what it is, and as I do not know, I feel I am fighting with one hand tied behind my back. At present the book seems to me almost entirely scissors and paste, with unexplained allusions to novels, most of which I do not know, and most of which, judging from the quotations, I do not want to know. But there! I am an old fogey, and it has apparently been much admired though Edith Sitwell's praise is blame indeed.

Secondly, thank you for your lucid explanation of the tone rows. If that is really all there is to it, it seems to me the most astonishing bit of mechanical pedantry which has ever been dignified by the name of art. I think I must try a tone row myself and see what happens. But apparently one must not use any succession of notes which sounds agreeable to the cultivated ear. I remember Charles Wood giving a lesson to a young modern at the R.C.M. who thought he was going to show the old dry-as-dust how to do it. Wood looked at his work and said, 'It's all right, but it seems to me rather tame, why didn't you do something more like this?' & sat down at the piano and played some outrageous stuff that the poor young man had never even dreamt of.

Evelyn very kindly brought a record of the new symph. Some of it seems a muddle to me, but then most records do, and both Ursula and Gil said it was splendid.

Poor Eslyn and her tooth. Give her our love and tell her that I am sure it was a sweet tooth.

Yrs
RVW[2]

[1] Colin Wilson's *The Outsider* (1956), which Kennedy had given to VW to test his reaction.
[2] This letter reprinted in part in *WVW*, 386–7.

691. To Juanita Berlin[1]

28 August 1956

From R. Vaughan Williams
10, Hanover Terrace,
Regents Park
London N.W.1.

August 28th 1956

Dear Juanita,

Thank you for your delightful letter and all the songs, which are all interesting and some of them beautiful: did you get them out of printed books, or purely orally? I ask, for if the latter, I would with your leave send them to the journal of the English folk-song society. But if they are already printed, of course there is no point.

I am sending you a little quantity of ruled music paper so that next time you won't have to rule your own lines – though you do it so beautifully.

I do hope we shall hear your programme before too long.

Our greetings to Mr Sven,

Truly
R. Vaughan Williams

[1] Wife of Sven Berlin, a painter. They lived in a caravan in the New Forest, claiming to be gypsies. See *RVW*, 362–3 and also Roger Savage, 'Vaughan Williams, the Romany Ryes, and the Cambridge Ritualists', *Music & Letters*, 83 (2002), 417.

692. To Herbert Byard

[August 1956]

From R. Vaughan Williams,
10, Hanover Terrace,
Regents Park,
London, N.W.1.

Dear Byard

I am sorry you are not going to Dartington – your account of it sounds most depressing – I have never heard of Richard Halse – I hope he is not one of those people who think that wrong notes are the *only* music – If it means anything *really* to people by all means good luck to them – To my mind it only sounds *dreary* not solemn or gay or even vulgar but just *dreary*.[1]

Yrs
RVW

[1] Byard had applied to be Head of Music at Dartington but was not successful.

693. From Joy Finzi

28 September [1956]

Ashmansworth

September 28th

Dearest Uncle Ralph,

I wish I could bear this news gently to you.

Two years ago Gerald had a small growth in his neck diagnosed as a fatal deasease [*sic*] the least drastic of a series of reticulosis – because of the vigour of his constitution the authorities said he might live ten years.[1] It was unpredictable. This was a nightmare to him & only endurable if no-one knew. Two years ago owing to the dangerous condition of his blood (x-ray treatment on the glands which checks them produces aenemia [*sic*]) they decided to remove his spleen to check the production of white blood cells. This was removed (we found appendix an appropriate alternative). The operation was entirely successful & after a long treatment of x-ray the glands subsided. We have had two wonderful years & his blood condition had actually improved. On Chosen Hill we went into the Sextons cottage – we naturally ignored the recent chicken-pox. G^{d} developed acute shingles 12 days later – a week later acute chicken-pox appeared all over. Three days ago he became mentally disconnected & quickly sank into oblivion. The day before yesterday after having experts from Oxford (where fortunately for us a very distinguished man runs the finest research department for this in England) I took him in an ambulance to Oxford – he just knew this & was contented – oblivious when I left him. I returned yesterday & was comforted exceedingly by knowing he was out of pain. Shortly after I left his bedside he had a sudden convulsion – died. The spleen being removed he had not sufficient forces to fight the chicken-pox virus which had attacked his brain. We who knew of what might possibly be his end can only be relieved to know it came without any sense of its coming & without him impaired. He just knew of your happy letters from Majorca, but this correspondence with the London Philharmonic I withheld from him.

I am returning them to you – as under the circumstances I think you would prefer to deal with it yourself – and on your return – We heard this morning from the L.P.O

Dear Mrs Finzi

December 10 Concert (Holst)

All the answers I wanted have arrived from R.V.W. I believe he has sent you a copy of his reply.

Thank you very much for your help

Yours sincerely
Alan Gregory.

I hope this reaches you before the wireless & papers. Gill[2] wanted to wire, but I preferred to be able to now tell you the whole story. We are having a private cremation tomorrow after the post mortem – We felt that if his many friends wished to gather together – he w[d] prefer it in some musical way. Tomorrow we are cancelling the string rehearsal (Kiffer took it very well last week[3]) & next week we shall continue to work for the next 3 concerts we have undertaken. This was one of G's most urgent wishes.

Christopher Bunting & the Hallé under Georges Tzipaine gave a very fine performance of G's cello concerto on Wednesday. Gerald wasn't able to listen in – but we ordered several tapes –[4]

Our love to you both
Joy

Forgive pencil.

[1] In fact GF had been diagnosed in 1951.

[2] Gilmour Jenkins.

[3] Kiffer was the family nickname for the Finzis' elder son Christopher.

[4] Georges Tzipine had conducted a studio broadcast of the work.

694. To Joy Finzi from UVW

[29 September 1956]

Hotel Bendinat
Palma de Mallorca

Saturday

Dearest Joy

Since [Gil's?] letter came early this morning we have thought about you all the time.[1] It seems to me that you have made something between you that has enriched many people. We were so happy with you, and so glad that we had those lovely few days, & that drive onto the downs, – and that's only one, of many many times, for which we are glad. And Gerald – 'all that I do is me, for this I came'[2] could be most truly and wholly said of him. We shall be home next Sunday, and if you'd like to come to us and if I could help you with letters – or in any other way please let me.

We were going out today – & we sat in a remote hermitage high on a mountain with the island & the sea below us in a pale blue haze, & Ralph dictated the letter he is sending to the Times.[3] It all seems very fitting, & there were swallows – perhaps some of yours on their way south.

Nothing counts much just now, but when you want us, we are here.

Love to you all

Ursula

[1] Gerald Finzi had died on 27 September.

[2] A misquotation from Gerard Manley Hopkins, 'As kingfishers catch fire':

> Each mortal thing does one thing and the same:
> Deals out that being indoors each one dwells;
> Selves—goes itself; *myself* it speaks and spells,
> Crying *Whát I do is me: for that I came.*

[3] An appreciation of GF which appeared on Wednesday, 3 Oct.; see no. 696.

695. To Joy Finzi from RVW

[29 September 1956]

Dearest Joyce

You know how great a friend he was and what a staunch adviser – I always came to him for advice & help.

I am thinking of those days which we have spent with you & him – they are bright spots in our memory framed in that lovely view of the downs.[1]

All love to you and the boys

From Ralph

[1] The VWs had spent the weekend of 18 and 19 Aug. with the Finzis at Ashmansworth.

696. An appreciation of Gerald Finzi 3 October 1956

The Times, Wednesday October 3 1956

MR. GERALD FINZI
A MANY-SIDED MAN

Dr. Ralph Vaughan Williams writes:–

Gerald Finzi's last new work was the cantata *In Terra Pax*. This work is significant not only for its intrinsic beauty but because it seemed to give us hope of even better things to come. These hopes will not be fulfilled. *In Terra Pax* is characteristically founded on a poem by Robert Bridges. Finzi's music shows an extraordinary affinity with this poet and with Thomas Hardy, both their language and their thought find an absolute counterpart in his settings.

No mention has been made in your obituary notice of Finzi's work as a musicologist. He was convinced that the English eighteenth-century composers were under-rated, so he brought his imaginative scholarship to bear on the British Museum and other libraries where he discovered and made known to the world many hitherto hidden treasures.

Visiting the Finzis' house, with its wonderful view of the distant downs, was a happy experience. Gerald had a wide and critical knowledge of English literature, his wife is an accomplished artist and his two sons are fine musicians, so that a feeling of beauty without any self-consciousness has always pervaded the atmosphere of their home, in which there was always a welcome for their many friends and where the discussion and hospitality flowered. Finzi had strong views on all that was going on in the world, with which I did not always agree; and he expressed them in vigorous and clear-cut language. His interests were varied; he was, for instance, an enthusiastic fruit grower; indeed he was almost as keen on reviving forgotten varieties of apples as on reviving forgotten English composers.

Finzi had a great sense of the social responsibilities of the artist. This led him, during the war, to found the Newbury String Players, a small body of amateur musicians, who, with a little professional help, have continued ever since to bring good music to the small villages of the neighbourhood which otherwise would have been without any such artistic experience.

Finzi's compositions range from the slightest of songs through the noble cantata *Dies Natalis*, to the large scale choral work *Intimations of Immortality*. He also wrote much purely instrumental music, including concertos for clarinet, violoncello and pianoforte. In all these works we find something absolutely personal, and in my opinion they will last on when other more showy but less truly original compositions are forgotten.

697. To Tom Whitestone

9 October 1956

From R. Vaughan Williams,
10, Hanover Terrace,
Regents Park,
London, N.W.1.

Oct 9th 1956

Dear Tom

Sir John Barbirolli has sent me your letter to him – I am glad you like Haydn; he is a very great man & wrote beautiful tunes.

I must one day try to write a tune which you will like.[1]

Yrs affectionately
R. Vaughan Williams

[1] This letter was sent to the OUP by the mother of the writer for use by UVW in *RVW*. Tom Whitestone, a young boy, had been at the first London performance of the Eighth Symphony and had written to JB advising him to stick to Haydn, and avoid composers such as VW.

698. To Herbert Howells

13 October 1956

From R. Vaughan Williams,
10, Hanover Terrace,
Regents Park,
London, N.W.1.

October 13th 1956.

Dear Herbert

I suppose you have heard of the proposed Holst concert, to be given by the L.P.O. on December 10th, which Adrian and I are organizing? We very much want the programme notes written by those who understand and like his work. Would you be one of them? If you will, could you undertake The Choral Fantasia and Ode to Death? When, as I hope, you accept, I will tell the L.P.O and they will send you a formal invitation.[1]

Thank you so much for your birthday good wishes. We look forward to meeting soon.

Yrs
Ralph

[1] This concert was funded by VW through his newly formed R.V.W. Trust. The programme notes were written by Scott Goddard, Edmund Rubbra, and Howells. The full programme was: *A Fugal Overture*, Op. 40 No. 1 H151, *The Morning of the Year*, Op. 45 No. 2 H164, *Ave Maria*, Op. 9 H49, *Assemble All ye Maidens*, Op. 44 No. 7 H162, *Egdon Heath*, Op. 47 H172, *A Choral Fantasia*, Op. 51 H177, *Ode to Death*, Op. 38 H144, *A Fugal Concerto*, Op. 40 No. 2 H152, and the ballet music from *The Perfect Fool*, Op. 39 H150. See *RVW* 377–8. A similar letter was sent to Edmund Rubbra and, presumably, to Scott Goddard.

699. To Paul Henry Lang[1]

18 October 1956

From R. Vaughan Williams,
10, Hanover Terrace,
Regents Park,
London, N.W.1.

October 18th, 1956

Dear Mr Lang

I have been sent your notice of my eighth symphony in which you suggest that the opening of the slow movement was taken from the Passion Chorale. This is to a certain extent true: I was thinking about the slow movement and how I wanted a cello tune, an[d] it suddenly occur[r]ed to me how lovely that chorale would sound on the cellos, so, as far as I can remember, without deliberately adopting it, the two themes got mixed up in my mind with the result you know. I am quite unrepentant!

Yours sincerely
R. Vaughan Williams

[1] 1901–91, Professor of Musicology at Columbia University 1939–69. He was author, *inter alia*, of *Music in Western Civilization* (New York, 1941), Chief Music Critic of the *New York Herald Tribune* 1954–63, and editor of the *Musical Quarterly* 1945–73.

700. To Arnold Goldsbrough[1]

18 October 1956

From R. Vaughan Williams,
10, Hanover Terrace,
Regents Park,
London, N.W.1.

October 18th 1956

Dear Arnold

Thank you so much both of you for remembering my birthday. I wish we could have met at Gloucester.

I hope your letter does not mean that you have given up music and taken to pig keeping? Lots of people can keep pigs quite nicely but very few can practise music in the way that you can.

Please give my love to Jo: I often think of you both when Dorking Festival comes round.

Yrs
RVW

[1] On Arnold Goldsbrough see no. 263.

701. To Michael and Eslyn Kennedy 20 October 1956

Oct 20 1956

Dear Eslyn & Michael

It was wonderful to get your letter – If anything in my life – music included – has enabled anyone to have a fuller enjoyment of life – then I feel I have not lived in vain – & is this not especially true with dear friends like you – I hope people feel this but so few of them take the trouble to say so – certainly not in the wonderful way you have said it.

Our friendship has not been long – at all events to an octogenarian like me – but I believe it is firm & lasting and strong. I consider it a lucky day when I first met you both in Manchester.

But on the other hand your letter makes me feel my inadequacy – I wish I could be all you think & say I am – but it gives me an ideal to live for.

You write of being true to oneself – that is a thing I always try for & hope I may sometimes achieve it.

Our love to both of you & thanks for a good friendship

Yrs
R. Vaughan Williams

P.S. Forgive the scrappy letter – I thought it was going to be a rough copy – but I think you will be able to read some of it with a magnifying glass.[1]

[1] The letter is written on lined paper torn from a spiral notebook. Kennedy added a note on the envelope: 'This letter is my greatest treasure MK'.

702. To Alan Frank at OUP

25 October 1956

From R. Vaughan Williams,
10, Hanover Terrace,
Regents Park,
London, N.W.1.

October 25th 1956.

Dear Alan,

I am sorry to have to write a complaining letter: I very seldom have to do so. Ursula brought home to day a reprint, – so I understand – of the catalogue of me. I have marked the mistakes as you will see. But the worst thing is on Page 18. I have already explained that I have NOTHING TO DO with Tony Scott's Almighty Word, except that he found the tune, I believe, in the English Hymnal. The melody is by Tallis and the harmony, where it is not also by Tallis is by Tony Scott. Tony is very much upset about this, naturally, and so am I because I do not like taking credit for what I have not done. I have spoken about this before, and I understood that it was to be altered. I think you ought to put in an errata slip correcting what amounts to a mis-statement. One other small point, on page 13, I think 'to be sung in time of war' ought to be deleted, and the word (unison) added.[1] Ursula also wants to say that she did NOT write the words of Epithalamion, – but wishes she had.[2]

Yrs
RVW

[1] A reference to *Six Choral Songs* (*CW* 1940/1).

[2] UVW had chosen the words for *Epithalamion* from Spenser's poem of the same name.

703. To the Committee of the R.V.W. Trust

29 October 1956

October 29th 1956

<u>*CONFIDENTIAL*</u>

This trust is the invention of my friend and accountant, Mr. Sturgess, who I am glad to say is here today to explain the business side of things – of which I am quite incapable.

This trust is not an act of generosity, but of common sense. Donations to charity are, I understand, free of income tax so that if I can arrange to give a portion of my earnings to musical charity I shall not have to pay on that portion. In fact I shall be merely robbing Peter to pay Paul: and though

I have no desire to rob Peter of his dues, I wish, in the words of John Bright, to be 'sorry five pounds' for Paul. To this end we applied to the Musicians' Benevolent Fund and they, through their Secretary, Frank Thistleton, have kindly agreed to sponsor a Trust to be administered under their aegis. Mr Thistleton will be Secretary, and the gentlemen who are down on your list have agreed to form a Committee. As you see this consists partly of musicians and partly of laymen.

Now, as to the objects of the trust: these will combine all the objects which come under the terms of reference of the Musicians' Benevolent Fund, but especially, the following, in which I have a great interest:–

(Before giving you the list, I must tell you that the Funds of the Trust will be the total amount of my earnings under the P.R.S. Last year these came to about £18,000 and as the amount has been steadily rising year by year, we may expect at least as much this year, though we shall not know the exact figure until December, when the chief amounts come in. The sums therefore in the following lists are calculated on the £18,000 basis, but as Mr. Sturgess will explain to you later it is not advisable to make them so large the first year. Here then is the list of what I consider desirable objects, and the sums opposite them I propose should be annual until further notice except where particularly remarked.)

A. The financing of public performances of musical works which are not likely to be profitable.
Concert of Holst's music by the L.P.O. under Adrian Boult on December 10th Guarantee: (single payment) £1500.
New Opera Society. Tale of Two Cities. Guarantee £500.

B. Financing of copying or publication of music which is not likely to have a ready sale: say £250.

C. Financing of books and magazines of educational value.
Music and Letters £100.

D. Grants to Musical Festivals.

Leith Hill Festival £500
Federation of Musical Festivals £250.
St Cecilia's Day Church Festival £100.

E. The advancement of public education in music.
(This is rather a vague term, but includes most things that cannot be got in elsewhere.)

English Folk Song and Dance Society.		
	General Purposes	£500.
	Library.	£500.
The McNaughten New Music Society.[1]		£50.
International Council of Folk Music		£500.
Royal Philharmonic Society		£250.
Dorking Bach Choir.		£100.
St. Michael's Singers.		£100.
Newbury String Players		£100.
Arnold Foster Choir.		£100.
South Western Arts Society (single donation)		£50.
Oxford Orchestral Society		£50.
Society for the Promotion of New Music		£250.
The Cygnet Company (Children's Plays)		£50.
Various small donations, e.g. Surrey Philharmonic Society, say, about		£50.
Composers' Guild		£50.
Renaissance Singers		£50.
Rural Music Schools		£50.
Purcell Society (single donation)		£500.

F. Assistance to musicians and students of music to further musical education.

Morley College Music Department.	£100.
Geoffrey Shaw Fund.	£250.
Butterworth Trust	£500.

G. The relieving of poverty among musicians.
I am not in favour of spending much on this, as I think it is already well provided for.
But I would like to consider particular cases, and I have three in my mind at present.

Mrs. Holst (1956 – £50)	£250
Dr. Martin Shaw	£250.
British Musicians' Pension Fund	£250.

> [I am not in favour of granting scholarships, except in particular circumstances as this is well cared for elsewhere, nor would I wish the fund to be used to augment the income of teaching colleges.]
>
> I would ask the Committee not to make any single allocation of £100 or over without consulting me.

The sums given above amount to about £8,000 or less. But Mr. Sturgess warns me that for reasons he will presently give you that this will have to be scaled down for the first year. The Holst Concert however will require immediate payment.

Now there is one other point about our income that we must consider. My performing fees have lately been increasing, but these, as you know, depend entirely on the whim of a fickle public, and they may at any time begin to decline, and even go down to nothing. I am therefore advised that we ought to invest some of our money. I agree to this, within limits, nevertheless in my opinion, the money is there primarily to be spent and not hoarded.

Finally, I wish to thank all my friends who have helped me with their knowledge and experience in forming this trust; and also those who are so kindly giving their skill and their time to this Committee.[2]

R. Vaughan Williams.

[1] *Recte* Macnaghten.

[2] This letter sets out the main guidelines which the R.V.W. Trust was to follow for next fifty years. The only point he does not make is an instruction he later gave to the Trust that he did not wish it to support any performances of his own work.

704. To Rutland Boughton — 9 December 1956

From R. Vaughan Williams,
10, Hanover Terrace,
Regents Park,
London, N.W.1.

December 9th 1956.

Dear Rutland,

First, I am so glad to hear about the copies of your operas. Also, thank you for all you say about my number 8.

I feel much touched at your taking the trouble to explain your new position to me. It seems to me that all right minded people are communists, as far as the word means that everything should be done eventually for the common good. But communism has got to mean now so much more other than that, which I, for one, cannot subscribe to. Myself, I see no reason why the Russian atrocities should prevent your remaining a communist in the ideal sense of the word. The Russians are a strange mixture of artistic ideals and barbarism, and the barbarians seem to come out top, whether they call themselves Czarists, Karenskiists or Stalinists.

I hope we shall soon meet again

Love to both of you from us both
Ralph Vaughan Williams[1]

[1] Printed in *RVW*, 379.

705. To Michael and Eslyn Kennedy 23 December 1956

From R. Vaughan Williams,
10, Hanover Terrace,
Regents Park,
London, N.W.1.

December 23rd 1956.

Dear Eslyn and Michael,

Your selection of poems is splendid. I am especially glad that you have introduced the Tennyson lines about the full juiced apple, which I sometimes think, are, for pure beauty of sound, among the best things in poetry. But I don't know if I shall ever be able to get to your selection. I do not know whether I dare to set Hardy![1]

The Holst concert was, I believe, a success: excellent performances, the house not full, but not painfully empty. I hear that there were a lot of quite young people there who were much excited. I am confirmed in my opinion that the Ode to Death is his finest choral work. Egdon Heath is gradually clarifying in my mind – it is still a bit of a puzzle. Christopher Finzi, as representing the younger generation, admired it most of all. Then there is Assemble all ye maidens, which I had not heard since I conducted it years ago. It is very lovely. The morning of the year is a strange mixture – I like the tunes very much, and I like the choral part when I can forget the words – but the two don't seem to fit. I am glad we did the choral fantasia, which again, takes some knowing, as I believe it is fine.[2]

I am glad to hear John is back in harness. I hope to goodness he has learned his lesson.[3]

I went to St Martins to hear the new Stravinskys, and they, frankly, bored me.[4]

We had a very nice carol party here the other night – we sang all REAL carols, no Wenceslasses, or silent nights: we started at half past eight, had half an hours break at about ten and finished up with the first Nowell about 12.30 then more drinks.

Did you know the First Nowell goes in canon? Perhaps some people thought we sang it like that as a result of the very potent cup we had been imbibing. One thing we sang which was not traditional was the splendid tune sung to While shepherds Watched in the west country. (See English Hymnal Appendix 8)[5]

Your Christmas card is lovely, and when I have finished the book I am on, I am going to go for the scrolls. You ought to read the Lost Steps, translated from the Spanish, by Carpentier. You will see something about it by me in next weeks Sunday Times.[6]

Our love to you both,

Yrs
RVW[7]

[1] Kennedy had compiled a collection of English poems on autumn which he hoped VW might set. The Tennyson lines come from the third stanza of the Choric Song in *The Lotos-Eaters*: 'Lo! sweetened with the summer light / The full-juiced apple, waxing over-mellow, / Drops in a silent autumn night.' See also no.16.

[2] On the Holst concert, which VW had funded through the Trust he had set up, see no. 698.

[3] Barbirolli had been ill due to overwork.

[4] Stravinsky's *Canticum Sacrum* and his orchestration of Bach's canonic variations on *Vom Himmel Hoch* had been performed at St Martin's-in-the-Fields on 11 December.

[5] A tune ascribed by VW to A. Northrop with the note 'Tune often sung in Cornwall'.

[6] Alejo Carpentier, *The Lost Steps* [*Los Pasos perdidos*], translated by Harriet de Onís, published by Gollancz in 1956. VW contributed occasionally to lists of well-known figures' favourite books of the year.

[7] This letter reprinted in part in *WVW*, 387.

706. To Dorothy Howells 23 December 1956

From R. Vaughan Williams,
10, Hanover Terrace,
Regents Park,
London, N.W.1.

December 23rd 1956

My dear Dorothy,

If anything I can do will help Herbert to write still more of his beautiful music I shall feel amply repaid. As a matter of fact – I loose [*sic*] nothing – it is the Chancellor of the Exchequer who looses.[1]

I am so sorry we could not meet at the Barnes Music Club, we had a delightful evening. Thank you all for the lovely card, and love from us both,

Yrs
Ralph

[1] The R.V.W. Trust had apparently made a grant to Howells.

707. To Michael Kennedy

26 January 1957

From R. Vaughan Williams,
10, Hanover Terrace,
Regents Park,
London, N.W.1.

January 26th 1957.

Dear Michael,

I was so glad to get your letter, though I find some of it difficult to answer. Your question of who is the greatest man in my life time, is very difficult to say. I don't think Churchill, somehow, but a few names, taken at random would include Brahms, Walt Whitman and General Booth. But it is an almost impossible one to answer[1]... and of course there is also Sibelius. It took me some time to get accustomed to his number 6, but I rather believe now that it is his greatest. I am sorry I missed the broadcast.

I have no particular use for Bruckner. I have never got over the first symphony I heard of his, in which 4 Wagner Tubas played what sounded like old English glees.

I am glad you like my oboe tune.[2] Evelyn gave a wonderful performance of it. We shall be so glad if you can come to hear the John.[3] We haven't been to hear the Britten ballet[4] yet – it is rather difficult to find a night – but we intend to. Our next excitement is the Finzi concert tomorrow. Carol Case is singing a hitherto unheard Hardy cycle by him.[5] This seems rather a catalogue, but you ask me so many questions and I enjoy answering them so much. My love, and three kisses please to Eslyn, but perhaps she is la Belle Dame sans merci, in which case it must be four.[6] And all love from us both,

Yrs
Ralph[7]

You must read

In a Great Tradition by the Community at Stanbrook

and more exciting, but a good follow – Time out of Mind by Joan Grant

& finally, most exciting of all – The Third Eye, Lobsang Rampa.[8]

[1] Original reads with a typing error: 'an almost one impossible to answer'.

[2] Evelyn Rothwell (Barbirolli) had given a performance of VW's Concerto for Oboe and Strings (*CW* 1944/1).

[3] VW was to conduct a performance of Bach's St John Passion at Dorking on 23 February.

[4] *The Prince of the Pagodas*, which was first given on 1 Jan. at the Royal Opera House, Covent Garden.

[5] A concert of works by Gerald Finzi was given on 27 Jan. at the Victoria & Albert Museum by the Chamber Music Society with Eric Greene, John Carol Case, Kathleen Long, and Howard Ferguson and the Kalmar Chamber Orchestra conducted by John Russell. The programme contained Richard Mudge's 4th concerto for strings (edited by Finzi), the first performances of *I Said to Love*, a setting by Finzi of six Hardy poems for baritone and piano, and of the Eclogue for piano and strings, and ended with *Dies Natalis*.

[6] Reference to the Keats poem: 'and there I shut her wild wild eyes / with kisses four'.

[7] This letter reprinted in part in *WVW*, 388.

[8] This entire last passage is a postscript from UVW enclosed on a separate sheet of writing paper. The books she recommends were all newly published in London in 1956: *In a Great Tradition: Tribute to Dame Laurentia McLachlan, Abbess of Stanbrook, by the Benedictines of Stanbrook*; Joan Grant, *Time out of Mind* (an autobiography); Lobsang Rampa, *The Third Eye: The Autobiography of a Tibetan Lama*.

708. To Michael and Eslyn Kennedy 15 February 1957

From R. Vaughan Williams,
10, Hanover Terrace,
Regents Park,
London, N.W.1.

February 15th 1957.

My dear Michael and Eslyn,

I had already got a record of Nielsen 5, and had not made much out of it, but hearing it under John[1] was quite a different thing and we both admired it very much though the first movement is perhaps rather too much what Tovey used to call a prelude-to-a-prelude-to-a-prelude. (But what I really liked most of all was the Haydn: absolutely heavenly U.) We also heard the Walton, a fine work, finely played.[2] John is much pleased because you have chosen a composition by his second trumpet for Cheltenham.[3] I don't think he looks at all well, and Evelyn evidently did not think so either.

As regards Gerald's new songs – the first and the last hit the nail in my head first away, the others I should like to hear again, but this does not mean, as it usually does, that I do *not* want to hear them again![4] If, as I hope, you do come to St J. at Dorking, show the enclosed chit to one of the sidesmen and he will lead you to a reserved pew.[5]

Love to you both
RVW[6]

[1] John Barbirolli.

[2] Kennedy thinks this was Walton's *Partita*.

[3] The First Symphony of Arthur Butterworth.

[4] See no. 707. The odd language is very likely to be a misreading by UVW, when typing, of 'hit the nail on the head right away' in VW's draft.

[5] The performance of Bach's St John Passion at Dorking was to be on 23 February.

[6] This letter is printed in part in *WVW*, 388.

709. To Michael and Eslyn Kennedy

3 March 1957

From R. Vaughan Williams,
10, Hanover Terrace,
Regents Park,
London, N.W.1.

March 3rd 1957

My dear Michael and Eslyn,

I am so glad that you were able to come to the St John and that you approved of it.[1] I think it was the best performance that we have given: I believe that it is our tenth year!

I should like to see your article on The Apostles[2] very much. I am afraid that I have never cared about it, except the final Alleluias which are beautiful. I always feel that he was oppressed by the fact that he was writing for the Church of England and could not get rid of the bombazine and bonnets of the Anglican Sunday morning service. On the whole I like the Kingdom[3] better, though of course there is nothing so bad in the Apostles as the 'Lord's prayer'. This is all for your ear *only*, please!

I think we shall probably not go to Cheltenham after all this year – though we may change our minds.

Our love to Eslyn.

Yrs
RVW[4]

[1] The Kennedys had been at the performance of the St John Passion at Dorking on 23 February.

[2] Kennedy had written a piece on Elgar's oratorio for the *Hallé Magazine*.

[3] The 1906 oratorio by Elgar intended as the second work of a trilogy after *The Apostles*.

[4] This letter is printed in part in *WVW*, 388.

710. To Ross Lee Finney[1]

29 March 1957

From R. Vaughan Williams,
10, Hanover Terrace,
Regents Park,
London, N.W.1.

March 29th 1957.

Dear Mr Ross Lee Finney,

I listened to your cello sonata last night, played by Mr Jelinek and Miss Bates (who kindly sent tickets for the recital at your request) – a fine performance of a fine work.[2]

I was reminded of our delightful visit to you at Ann Arbor, and your visit to us.

Please let us know when you have performances in this country, we should so much like to have a chance to hear more of your work. The sonata is original without being excentric [*sic*], and I need hardly say most skillfully written for both the instruments. You seemed to have escaped from the Boulanger virus which is being rather a colorado beetle in American music at the moment. This work makes me feel like Oliver Twist – I want more! With kind regards to you both.

Yours sincerely
R. Vaughan Williams

Mr Ross Lee Finney
2015 Geddes Avenue
Ann Arbor
Mich.U.S.A.

[1] American composer (1906–97). He was Professor of Music at the University of Michigan, Ann Arbor and had had entertained the VWs during their visit there in the autumn of 1954.

[2] The American cellist Jerome Jelinek became a professor at the University of Michigan in 1961 and recorded a number of Finney's works.

711. To Ian Parrott[1] 11 April 1957

From R. Vaughan Williams,
10, Hanover Terrace,
Regents Park,
London, N.W.1.

April 11th 1957.

Dear Dr. Parrott,

I am so glad the opera went well.[2] I hope I shall hear it one day.

I did not intend my fourth symphony to have any 'meaning', – that is a meaning which can be expressed in words; of course music has a meaning, but I think that can only be expressed in terms of music. I know that some people try to narrow the effect of music to something visual or verbal. To my mind, when they do so they make a horrible mess of it.

Yours sincerely
R Vaughan Williams

[1] At the time Gregynog Professor of Music at the University College of Wales at Aberystwyth.

[2] Ian Parrott's opera *The Black Ram*, which had been performed in a concert version by the Welsh Region of the BBC on 28 February. VW had made a contribution to the cost of publishing the vocal score by Curwen.

712. To Roger Fiske at the BBC 4 May 1957

From R. Vaughan Williams,
10, Hanover Terrace,
Regents Park,
London, N.W.1.

May 4th 1957.

Dear Mr Fiske,

Thank you very much for inviting me to talk about Elgar; I am sorry not to be able to accept. I think I said most of what I have to say about him, and, as I have to be away a good deal this month, and I am going abroad for most of June, I do not feel that I have time to spare to think of, and prepare the sort of material I should wish to use for such a talk. I say again, I am so sorry.[1]

Yours sincerely,
R. Vaughan Williams

[1] VW was in fact persuaded to contribute to the Elgar centenary tribute. The producer, Charles Parker, sent a script (see no. 713) to UVW in 1959 recalling: 'at first he was very reluctant to be recorded, although of course when he finally agreed to do so he was quite superb and I in fact used the recording for the very end of the programme.'

713. Elgar Centenary [May 1957]

'The Fifteenth Variation': Transcript of VW's contribution to Elgar Centenary Programme on the BBC taken from the recording[1]

My first knowledge of Elgar's music was a performance – shortly before 1900, of the *Variations*. I had been advised by a friend to go to a Richter Concert and hear a work by Dohnanyi, of all people. So I went. The Dohnanyi was all right. But the *Variations*: Here was something new, yet old: strange, yet familiar: universal, yet typically original and at the same time typically English.

Well, having heard the *Variations*, I was pining to find out more; and I journeyed to Birmingham to hear the first performance of *Gerontius*. And I have to confess, perhaps to my shame, that at first I was bitterly disappointed. I now know I was wrong. Not that I am yet reconciled to the opening, or to the Demons – in spite of their virtuosity: but that the beauty of the rest more than outweighs those places.

Stanford was wiser than me, and on the strength of *Gerontius* obtained an honorary degree for Elgar at Cambridge; and travelled up to Leeds to press for a performance at the next Festival.

The first time I ever addressed Elgar personally was not by word of mouth, but by a 'Dear Sir' letter, early in the 1900s, when I wrote and asked him to give me some lessons in composition; and received a polite answer from Lady Elgar saying that her husband was too busy at the moment, and advising me to apply to Bantock.

The first time, I think, that I actually had a conversation with Elgar was at a performance of his Violoncello Concerto, when he approached me rather truculently and said – 'I am surprised, Dr Vaughan Williams, that you care to listen to this vulgar stuff!' The truth was, I think, that he was feeling sore over an accusation of vulgarity made against him by a well-known musicologist who, Elgar probably knew, was a friend of mine.[2]

I did not meet Elgar again for some years, and then he was always gracious and friendly. He came to hear a performance of my *Sancta Civitas*, and gave it generous praise. He told me that he had once thought of setting those words himself 'But I shall never do so now' he said. To this I could only answer that this made me sorry that I had ever attempted to set the words myself.

Now I will, if I may, finish off with a technical point: in the introduction to Elgar's First Symphony, the melody is given to fairly heavy woodwind and violas. The violoncellos and double basses play the bass *détaché*, while the inner harmony is left to two soft muted horns. Well I think if a student had brought that score in to any composition teacher, he'd have put his blue pencil through it and said: 'This will not be heard'. And to my mind, when I look at it still, it looks all wrong, but it sounds all right. Here indeed we have a mystery and a miracle.

[1] This transcript has been taken directly from the recording of the broadcast by Jerrold Northrop Moore and differs in some respects from the transcript in UVW's possession, sent to her by the programme's producer, Charles Parker (see no. 712 n. 1).

[2] This was Edward Dent.

714. To Michael Kennedy — 9 May 1957

From R. Vaughan Williams,
10, Hanover Terrace,
Regents Park,
London, N.W.1.

May 9th 1957.

My dear Michael,

First, my fondest love and kisses sweet and twenty to Eslyn. I am so sorry to hear that she has been ill, and do hope she is getting better now, but well or ill she is always lovely. Now, to answer as far as I can, some of the points in your letter.

The Parry, Glories of our Blood and State, which I heard last week in Dorking again, is I think, a fine work: though a bit Brahmsy. In case you don't know it I tell you the story of its connection with the Bach Choir. It had been put down for performance in 1887 by the Bach Choir: then it occurred to one of the Committee that it would not be very polite to H. M. who was President... and whose Jubilee it was to sing a work all about Crowns and Thrones tumbling down; so Stanford asked Parry to write something else instead. Whereupon he wrote Blest Pair! So, it's an ill wind, etc.[1]

With regard to that aria in the Matthew P. about bearing the Cross. I was told that at the first performance, under Mendelssohn this was the hit of the evening – apparently then, they used to encore things they liked at these early performances.

I have an idea that I will put it in to my next performance. But it will have to [be] re-arranged for three cellos. I WILL NOT HAVE a viol da Gamba inside the building. I assure you we used to come to grief in early days over 'he is guilty of death'. It went right at rehearsal because I made the Evangelist sing the leading in phrase in strict time, and then at performance he forgot. But they know it so well now that they would come in right even if the Evangelist sang the tune the old cow died of.[2]

Yes, you are quite right, I had lunch in the presence of the P.M.[3] the other day, who was very pleasant and amusing after his 6th glass of port.

As regards Third Programme, I do not quite understand network 3, or whatever it is called. I entirely agree that the Third Programme wants improvement, but to shorten it will probably mean that the young pansies who run the BBC will cut out all that we think worthwhile, and have entirely Telemann and Blacher.[4]

I have heard of Stanley Pope but never met him.[5] I am so glad to hear John is better. You asked me about Richter and Elgar. I think I only heard him conduct Elgar twice, first the Variations, when I was absorbed by the music, and naturally being the first time I heard it, did not know if it was being done well or badly. And then came that extraordinarily bad first performance of Gerontius*, which nearly killed the work. But it was not Richter's fault that the semi-chorus consisted of second rate professionals from Birmingham and district, that the choir got hopelessly flat at the end of Part 1, that Plunkett Greene lost his voice, that Marie Brema had none to lose, and that Edward Lloyd sang it like a Stainer Anthem in the correct tenor attitude with one foot slightly withdrawn.[6]

I like having your letters; for one thing, they really make me sit up and think, which I am too lazy to do usually.

Love once again to Eslyn

Yrs
RVW[7]

*Ursula can do everything except spell – she did not deliberately make Gerontius rhyme with louse.[8]

Love to you both from me too

Ursula.

[1] VW had already told Kennedy this story in no. 687.

[2] A colloquialism for an old, bad tune.

[3] The Prime Minister, Harold Macmillan.

[4] Boris Blacher (1903–75), German composer.

[5] Stanley Pope, English conductor.

[6] Kennedy at this time was writing a history of the Hallé Orchestra, published as *The Hallé Tradition* in 1960, and had asked VW for any memories he had of Hans Richter, who had been the principal conductor from 1899 to 1911.
[7] This letter is reprinted in part in *WVW*, 388–9.
[8] UVW had first typed 'Gerontious' but W corrected it by hand; she did not like the work.

715. To Robin Ivison[1]

16 May 1957

From R. Vaughan Williams,
10, Hanover Terrace,
Regents Park,
London, N.W.1.

May 16th 1957

Dear Mr Ivison

It gave me great pleasure to receive your interesting letter, which showed, among other things, that the more elaborate music ought to grow out of the simpler. You tell me that you first got to know my music through a simple hymn tune and a simple song (by the way, Linden Lea is not a folk song – that was a mistake on the part of an ignorant publisher). If I can feel that my more elaborate music has grown out of the simpler I shall feel that I have achieved something. For instance, I myself can get an inkling of what the later Bartok is all about because I can see in it the same mind that invented the simple children's pieces.

May I be allowed to send my respectful greetings to your Gillian, and good wishes for your wedding? And your choice of hymns. By the way, I hope you will use the true version of the Old Hundredth, with the long notes at the ends of lines, thus:

You may remember that at the coronation the magnificent effect of the Old Hundredth was partly spoiled because all the Dukes and Viscounts sang the wrong version![2]

Yours sincerely
R. Vaughan Williams

[1] Ivison had written to VW to thank him for his music and had mentioned that his mother sang 'Linden Lea' to him as a child and asked if it was a folk song.
[2] VW had been afraid of this when preparing for the service; see no. 611.

716. To the Editor of *The Times* [19 July 1957[1]]

From R. Vaughan Williams,
10, Hanover Terrace,
Regents Park,
London, N.W.1.

Sir,

I understand that the Third Programme is the admiration and envy of all foreign listeners. Is that why the authorities propose to emasculate it? Or is it a question of finance? Has the Third Programme got to be a 'paying proposition'? We do not apply that test to education, religion, or justice in this country, and does not our Third Programme partake of all these essentials? Is war a paying proposition? We spend millions of pounds every year in finding out how to kill people, and in destroying all that many people think worth having in life. Is it not worth while to spend a small proportion of our wealth in increasing the value of our life?

Yours faithfully
Ralph Vaughan Williams

[1] Date taken from the Times Index.

717. To Ursula Vaughan Williams [about 24 July 1957]

From R. Vaughan Williams,
10, Hanover Terrace,
Regents Park,
London, N.W.1.

Wednesday

My Dear

I can't write love letters – but you know its there
(Here is a line for you to read between)

I slept well – though Betty is right in saying that I feel lost without you.[1] But I managed my safety razor all right & made tea for the young people.

All said it was a fine performance last night – But I am glad I did my work.[2]

Take great care of yourself my dear – Come back when you can. Give my love to your mother.

All love[3]

Here are a few dull letters

[1] Elizabeth Maconchy.

[2] Of *The Poisoned Kiss* (*CW* 1936/4) at the Royal Academy of Music in early celebration of VW's 85th birthday. It was the first performance with the new version of the libretto prepared by UVW.

[3] UVW was with her mother following the death of her father, Major-General Sir Robert Lock.

718. To Roy Douglas

4 August 1957

From R. Vaughan Williams,
10, Hanover Terrace,
Regents Park,
London, N.W.1.

August 4th 1957.

Dear Roy,

I think I told you, though it is still a secret, that I am having a flirtation with a symphony. Will you, and can you give me your usual help? There are two movements ready for your inspection, and I am going to ask you first to play them through to me off a fairly legible pianoforte score, (there is also a fairly illegible full score) I can't play it myself at all, and I am not sure what some of it sounds like. Having done that, will you make a real pianoforte arrangement [*sic*] with a view, when the wole [*sic*] thing is finished, to making a private recording. However, I have an idea that you said you hated playing for recording: but anyway, I should like you to make the pianoforte arrangement. I am free the rest of this month, except a few days for London rehearsals for Three Choirs: if you are coming to London naturally any day perhaps we could arrange a session.

Yrs
RVW[1]

[Dear Roy, the sooner the earlier, I am so agog. Love U.]

[1] This letter is printed in *WWVW*, 89–90.

719. To Michael Kennedy

20 August [postmark: 1957]

From R. Vaughan Williams,
10, Hanover Terrace,
Regents Park,
London, N.W.1.

Dictated.

August 20th

My dear Michael,

As regards Old Hundredth – would it be possible to print the tune – or at all events explain its true form? – with the long final notes at each phrase? The effect in the Abbey was largely spoiled because all the Dukes & Viscounts, who probably had not copies of the music – & anyway could not have read it, – sang the old all-equal version, steadily, against the whole chorus & orchestra.[1]

As regards the London Symphony, & Fritz Busch – so far as I can remember, it was Tovey who asked me to send it to him.[2]

Tallis: you might point out that the harmonisation of the first statement is Tallis's own. I agree with you about the scoring of the Ninth Symphony[3] – there are magnificent & unexpected things in it, especially among the trombones; but there are some errors of judgement

My love to you both
Ralph

[1] VW, in *The English Hymnal*, had favoured the early version of the hymn tune with double value notes at the beginning and end of each phrase over the version with all notes of the same value, which had become customary in the 19th c. (see no. 171). His coronation setting of the hymn, *CW* 1953/2, absolutely required the early version to be used.

[2] VW sent the autograph score of *A London Symphony* to Fritz Busch, but it was never returned. It had to be reconstructed by friends working from the separate orchestral parts. Kennedy was writing a programme note for the birthday concert in Manchester.

[3] Of Beethoven.

720. To Michael Kennedy from UVW 20 August [postmark: 1957]

From R. Vaughan Williams,
10, Hanover Terrace,
Regents Park,
London, N.W.1.

August 20th

My dear Michael,

Lovely to hear from you – & I'm so glad you like John Hersey. I didn't know you'd been to Hiroshima etc. How strangely awful it must have been.

We've had a hell of a week, as they suddenly felt R. ought to have an operation – indeed quite inevitable, so into hospital he went, & had it on Saturday. Everyone most helpful and kind, & though it was quite a big do *he* rang *me* at 8 am the next morning to see if I was all right! He's been astonishing everyone with his vitality, & has been working yesterday & today, & today was up for a bit. He'll be in hospital for another 10 days I expect, & no Worcester for us, either, but we are going to Spain on the 10th–23rd. He's looking very well, cosy & serene, & has started something by kissing *all* the nurses – who adore it. Last week was dreadful, but all is happy now. We've *managed* to keep it dark from the press so far, but now we've had to tell Worcester we cant come – so Im telling our friends as well dont worry at all.[1]

All love
Ursula

At the time only Jean (& George, who was implicated) & Genia & Yania & Gil knew, & my mother – so it made it all much easier.[2]

P.S. Party after the concert on Oct 9th [3]
P.S. We can't come up till 27th as theres Brass Band Festival on 26th. Hell![4]

U

[1] The operation was to remove a cancerous prostate.

[2] Jean Hadley, George Hadley (as a surgeon the matter would have been discussed with him), Genia and Yanya Hornstein, Gilmour Jenkins, and Beryl Lock.

[3] The Royal Philharmonic Concert celebrating VW's 85th birthday at the Royal Festival Hall.

[4] A birthday concert at Manchester including *A London Symphony*. See *RVW*, 385.

721. To Arnold Barter

28 August 1957

From R. Vaughan Williams,
10, Hanover Terrace,
Regents Park,
London, N.W.1.

August 28th 1957.

(Dictated)[1]

Dear Arnold,

I think after nearly 50 years this is allowable.[2]

The great thing which would incline me to come to Bristol would be for my wife & I to have the pleasure of seeing you & your brother. But I fear I ought not to do it – October & early November are always great productivity times with me – and October, as you know will be nearly full of champagne and birthday cakes.[3] So I must keep the rest of the time free for my work.

I often think of those early days when I met you at Kingsway Hall & you had just been doing the Sea Symphony. And all the other episodes of a long friendship. Do you remember how I came down a few years later to conduct the S.S – made a mistake which nearly brought the last movement to grief – but the chorus & orchestra made a soldiers victory of it?

But [I] could go on for ever with these reminiscences. I am so sorry the doctor will not allow me to come to Worcester, though I am feeling quite well. But perhaps sometimes you come up to London – if you do, let me know & we'll arrange a meeting.

Give my affectionate greetings to your brother

Yrs
Ralph

P.S. Ralph is getting on splendidly & will be home next week – the doctors say he'll be 100% +++ – but he must take the next few weeks gently.[4]

1 To UVW.
2 i.e. the use of first names.
3 i.e. for the celebration of VW's 85th birthday.
4 The postscript is by UVW.

722. To Adrian Boult

1 October 1957

From R. Vaughan Williams,
10, Hanover Terrace,
Regents Park,
London, N.W.1.

Oct 1st 1957

Dear Adrian,

This is most sad for all of us & especially for Ursula and me – Do take care of yourself – & I shall have fragrant memories of early rehearsals of Pastoral – when you were so wonderful & C.V.S. came & rehearsed & was very kind but rather a nuisance – & told somebody afterwards that it was fluff (I think that was the word).

Did I ever tell you that C.V.S. took the RCM orchestra through it with many of the instruments away & the parts not yet checked & I very nearly withdrew it!

– and then there was Job –

B. Cameron is very very good and useful and has worked like a Trojan & has got hold of it all very well – but I did want you![1]

All love to you both from us both

Ralph

[1] This letter was written in response to a letter from Boult telling VW that he could not conduct his 85th birthday concert because of illness. The programme included the *Pastoral Symphony* and *Job* (together with the orchestral version of *On Wenlock Edge*)—thus these particular reminiscences. See *RVW*, 383.

723. To Imogen Holst

13 October [1957[1]]

From R. Vaughan Williams,
10, Hanover Terrace,
Regents Park,
London, N.W.1.

Oct 13

Dearest Imogen

I love those songs & love hearing them. I believe I conducted the 1st performances of 'Assemble' with the Bach choir – the solo was sung by Dora Labette – I do not suppose you remember her – Not only had she a beautiful voice & style but her diction *when she sang* was perfect – but when she spoke!! At rehearsal she sang her opening 2nd phrase beautifully – words *perfect* – but the choir were [a] little flat leading up to her so she turned to me and said 'Look 'ere if thaose wimmen cain't sing in toon, 'ow the dooce am Oi to kem in'![2]

All love dear Imogen

Yrs
Uncle Ralph

[1] Year added by Imogen Holst.

[2] Gustav Holst's *Seven Part-songs*, Op. 44 H162, were written in 1925–6. 'Assemble, all ye maidens', the last of the set, was first performed by the Bach choir under VW on 24 May 1927 at the Queen's Hall. Dora Labbette (1898–1984) was an English soprano who sang opera as Lisa Perli.

724. To G. E. Moore

14 October [1957[1]]

From R. Vaughan Williams,
10, Hanover Terrace,
Regents Park,
London, N.W.1.

Oct 14

Dear George

How good of you to think of me on my birthday – It carries me back to very old days when you used to sing Schubert & play Beethoven to us after Hall. I've had a splendid present from Timothy in the shape of a composition.[2]

My love to Mrs George

Yrs
R. Vaughan Williams

[1] This letter is most probably connected with VW's 85th birthday in 1957.

[2] On Timothy Moore, George Moore's son, see no. 289.

725. To Edmund Rubbra

16 October 1957

From R. Vaughan Williams,
10, Hanover Terrace,
Regents Park,
London, N.W.1.

October 16th 1957.

Dear Edmund

Thank you for your composition of Friday. It gives me great pleasure to think that the younger composers wish to connect my name with one of their inspirations. It gives a feeling of continuity to the great art which we serve and will insure that the line goes on unbroken from generation to generation.[1]

Yrs
R. Vaughan Williams

[1] Rubbra's setting for SATB of Louis Macneice's *The Givers*, Op. 96, was one of the new works written by ex-pupils and friends in honour of VW's birthday and performed at a Macnaghten Concert on 11 Oct.; see *RVW*, 384.

726. To Frederick Page and Douglas Lilburn

18 October [postmark: 1957]

From R. Vaughan Williams,
10, Hanover Terrace,
Regents Park,
London, N.W.1.

Oct 18

My dear friends

– it was good of you to remember my birthday – I am glad to think that old pupils of mine are carrying on the torch.

Yrs
R. Vaughan Williams

727. To John Barbirolli

25 October 1957

From R. Vaughan Williams,
10, Hanover Terrace,
Regents Park,
London, N.W.1.

October 25th 1957.

Dear Glorious John

First, thank you a thousand times, once again, for leading your forces to such a superb victory.[1]

Second, give our fond love to Evelyn, who was so nice to us, and as usual, looked lovely.

Third, that was a wonderful supper, and the wine was so good that we, neither of us, had any hangover.

Fourth, I must apologise for telling a lie. Not indeed, to you, but to one of the guests, who asked me if I was writing a new symphony, and I said No, or rather, prevaricated. As a matter of fact – I have a new symphony 'in preparation' – whether it will go any further I shall settle soon. When you did me the honour to accept my number 8 for first performance Malcolm Sargent, almost at the same time, asked me for a new symphony for Edinburgh. I told him that I had already promised one to you, and that I was incapable of twins at my age! Now, the Royal Philharmonic Society has asked Malcolm to conduct one of their concerts and to include in it the first performance of a new work by me if there is one available. So, if Malcolm likes my new tune he shall have it for this purpose. I do hope that you and your wonderful men (and women) will one day give one of your superb performances of it.[2]

Love from us both to you both.

Yrs
RVW

[1] The VWs had been to Manchester for the opening concert of the Hallé's 100th season on 16 Oct., for which VW had written the *Flourish for Glorious John*, *CW* 1957/3. He was there again on 27 Oct. for a concert of his works to mark his birthday, at which the *Flourish* was played for him as an encore (see *RVW*, 385 and *WVW*, 338–9).

[2] The Ninth Symphony, *CW* 1957/4, received its first performance on 2 Apr. 1958 at the Royal Festival Hall.

728. To Gerald Kelly[1]

20 November 1957

From R. Vaughan Williams,
10, Hanover Terrace,
Regents Park,
London, N.W.1.

November 20th 1957

Dear Sir Gerald

I have been laid low with a ridiculous disease called phlebitis, and the doctor says I must keep my leg up for a week or two: so I fear that I cannot come to you to put my hand right until the doctor has put my leg right. As a matter of fact, I think the portrait, hands and all, very good as it stands.[2]

Yours
R. Vaughan Williams

[1] Gerald Kelly had painted VW for the RCM in 1952, but had asked to paint him again. The hands were never quite finished and had to be completed from photographs after VW's death. The portrait is now in the National Portrait Gallery.

[2] Covering note from UVW: 'Dear Sir Gerald, I wonder if it can wait? I do hope so – the doctor thinks this won't be a very long business. I should think (and hope) a fortnight will see Ralph on his feet again. I wish we'd seen your programme. We don't have television, & usually we are thankful, but this time, sorry. Greetings to you both, Ursula Vaughan Williams.'

729. To Paul Sinker

22 December 1957

December 22nd 1957.

Dear Sir,

Mr Douglas Kennedy, Director of the English Folk Dance and Song Society, of which I have the honour to be President, has passed on to me your extraordinary reply to his invitation to Sir David Kelly to serve on a Committee for our Library Endowment Fund Appeal. The flippancy of your letter addressed to such a Society as ours seems to me little short of an insult.

You appear to take for granted that it is necessarily a misuse of public money to send English Folk dancers overseas. I should like you to know that our Society, which has many distinguished members, considers that Folk music and dance are an essential part of our national culture of which it is our duty to inform other nations. It astonishes me that the British Council should pay any attention to the ignorant attacks of what you yourself describe as an irresponsible section of the press.

The library, for which our appeal is made is often used by folklore and other ethnological experts of all nations and its complete educational value is only hindered by lack of funds.

You say in your letter that your Chairman cannot accept this invitation to serve on a special Committee: if this is an expression of his views as well as your own I should like him to know that I can only be glad of his refusal.

Yours faithfully
[RVW][1]

[1] Douglas Kennedy, Director of the EFDSS, had written to Sir David Kelly, Chairman of the British Council, inviting him to join a special committee for celebrating the 60th anniversary of the founding of the Folk Song Society in 1897 and launching an appeal to raise an endowment for the Library at Cecil Sharp House. The Director General, Sir Paul Sinker, replied that Kelly felt unable to join the committee because of an impression that had got abroad that the Council spent 'considerable sums of public money on sending English Folk Dancers overseas'.

730. To Alan Bush

31 December 1957

From R. Vaughan Williams,
10, Hanover Terrace,
Regents Park,
London, N.W.1.

December 31st 1957.

Dear Bush,

Of course I want to be in this celebration of Rutland, and if you think a dinner is the right thing I should like to attend. Personally, from what I know of him, I should have thought that a real slap-up dinner, with waiters and champagne would be distasteful to him, – besides, is he not a vegetarian and teetotaler? I should have thought that we ought to spend any money we can collect on the performance of one of his operas.[1]

I am sending on your letter to the R.V.W. Trust, they will be having a meeting soon, and I should like to put the case to them. Could you let me know what you estimate the production [costs] of such a production would be, and any other particulars that you think would be useful.

Would it be worth your while to try co-operation with the New Opera Company? (c/o Leon Lovett, 40 Haslemere Avenue Hounslow W. Middx) I suppose that Steuart Wilson is in on this? For, as you doubtless know, he is a great friend and admirer.

Yrs
R. Vaughan Williams

[1] Bush had written to VW about plans for marking Rutland Boughton's 80th birthday on 23 Jan. 1958, asking him to join the organizing committee. Boughton had been, like Bush, a member of the Communist Party. The proposal was to give Boughton a dinner in either London or Gloucester and to stage one or more of his operas, possibly his last works *Sir Galahad* and *Avalon*. The plan for the production of the two operas came to nothing and they remain unperformed.

731. To Margery Cullen

28 January 1958

From R. Vaughan Williams,
10, Hanover Terrace,
Regents Park,
London, N.W.1.

January 28th 1958.

My dear Margery,

Things are rather piling up for me – there is going to be a run-through of my new symphony on March 21st, to which you will get an invitation – on April 2nd is the first performance, to which I hope you can come: on May 16th I have to go to get an Honorary degree at Nottingham, and between those dates we have been offered one of the Walton villas in Ischia.[1]

We shall both badly want a holiday then, and it is an opportunity, which both for my own sake and for Ursula's I cannot miss. This means I fear, that we shall have to miss the Festival this year. I am very sorry for our own sake, but I think it is quite a good plan to show that we are not essential there, and that Bill can get on very well by himself.[2]

Love from us both – till Thursday

Ralph

[1] The Ninth Symphony, *CW* 1957/4, was to be given its first performance at the Royal Festival Hall on 2 Apr. by the Royal Philharmonic Orchestra under Sir Malcolm Sargent. It was revised between the run-through on 21 Mar. and the first performance.

[2] This probably marks the culmination of the gradual handing over of the direction of the Festival by VW to William Cole.

732. To Simona Pakenham

3 February 1958

From R. Vaughan Williams,
10, Hanover Terrace,
Regents Park,
London, N.W.1.

February 3rd 1958

Dearest Simona

I ought to have explained that I have made a rule never to give the titles or words of my folk tunes which I have made into hymn tunes;[1] for instance, I've often been asked what the tunes in my Te Deum are, and I've never told anybody yet. The reason being that a lot of narrow minded people refuse to use the tune if they think it has Sexular (i.e. secular!!) associations. I think that Hymns A&M still refuse to admit the magnificent tune Helmsley for Lo he comes, because it is derived from a comic song called Where's the mortal can resist me? I should love to help you, but I'm afraid I cannot allow Wilfrid Brown[2] to sing the tune with the original words.[3] So sorry. I hope this won't prevent you employing him as you suggest.

Love
Ralph

[1] She was working on a series entitled 'Sacred & Secular' for the Religious Broadcasting Department of the BBC, about hymn tunes with secular origins.

[2] Wilfrid Brown, tenor and dedicatee (with Janet Craxton) of *Ten Blake Songs*.

[3] Pakenham had asked if Brown could sing 'Our Captain calls all hands on deck' as an introduction to 'He who would valiant be'. As no. 733 shows, VW agreed to help by starting off the series with a talk about his work for *The English Hymnal*. The series was illustrated by the St Martin Singers conducted by W. D. Kennedy Bell; Brown was the principal tenor.

733. To Simona Pakenham

9 February 1958

From R. Vaughan Williams,
10, Hanover Terrace,
Regents Park,
London, N.W.1.

February 9th 1958

Dearest Simona

I am sorry if I didn't explain myself – I'd love to help you by talking about folk song into hymn tune, – the only thing I can't do is to quote the original words (Ursula thinks I am silly about this). I don't think Helmsley appeared in a C of E Hymn Book till I put it into the E.H. in 1906. Of course I don't DISapprove of your scheme as a whole[1] – and to prove this I give you the following as a present... Jesu meine Freude was originally a love song, Flora meine Freude.

I believe that Margery Cullen is going to ask you to do a write-up of the Matthew Passion (no fee) for the Dorking paper. I should love you to do it if she asks you – you can say anything you like, but there must be no comparison between the two performances.[2]

Love
Ralph

[1] A series of BBC programmes entitled 'Sacred & Secular'.

[2] The first performance was to be conducted by Sir Thomas Armstrong, the second by VW.

734. To Alan Frank at OUP

15 February 1958

From R. Vaughan Williams,
10, Hanover Terrace,
Regents Park,
London, N.W.1.

February 15th 1958.

Dear Alan,

With regard to your first letter of February 10th, – as you know, I had nothing to do with the words of the Oxford Carol book, so I fear I cannot help Mr Attwater solve his problem, so I return his letter.[1]

In answer to your second letter, February 14th, I can tell you very little about the MS of my symphonies. Sea Symphony is probably Breitkopf & Hartel – or Stainer and Bell. London Symphony was sent to Fritz Busch at Aachen, just as war broke out in 1914, and never returned. A new score was made from the parts by various friends, including George Butterworth, but very little of it is in my handwriting: I imagine it is with Stainer and Bell. Pastoral I think must be with Adrian Boult. Four was dedicated to Arnold Bax, and I think I sent it to him: I expect Harriet Cohen could tell you. Five, according to your letter is at the R.C.M. 6 was dedicated to Michael Mullinar, so I think he has it. 7, Antartica was given to Ernest Irving, and I think he gave it to the BM. 8 – Barbirolli.[2]

My own feeling is that we ought only to show the MS. of the new one, 9, – but who ever does that I should like them to show the whole of the scaffolding, so to speak, including about 12 rough notebooks and a rough full score, 2 rough copies in some cases. Then the final, so-called fair copy, which Roy Douglas used. This will not be available till after March 21st, when I shall probably want it for myself. As I say, with regard to this no 9. its a case of all or nothing: I usually destroy my rough copies, but I have kept these as I thought it might be useful to show the scaffolding. It is dedicated, as you know, to the Phil – personally, I would prefer to give it to the FitzWilliam Museum, Cambridge.[3]

I will try and get some programme notes done before the end of the month, but it is rather difficult without a fair copy of the full score. At present I only have two movements with me.

Yrs
RVW

[1] The words of the *Oxford Book of Carols* had been edited by Percy Dearmer.

[2] There had been a suggestion that there should be an exhibition of the autograph scores of all VW's symphonies at the Royal Festival Hall at the time of the first performance of the Ninth Symphony. All the autograph full scores of the symphonies are now in the British Library with the exceptions of that of *A*

London Symphony, which has never come to light in Germany, and of the Fifth Symphony, which is at the RCM. In fact Ernest Irving gave the score of *Sinfonia Antartica* to the Royal Philharmonic Society, from whom it was acquired by the British Library.

[3] The Ninth Symphony is dedicated to the Royal Philharmonic Society. Most of the preliminary sketch material which VW describes is now, together with the autograph full score, in the British Library.

735. To the Editor of the *Daily Telegraph*[1] 20 February 1958

London N.W.1

20th February 1958

Sir—

First let me thank your critic for his kind and appreciative notice of the performance of the St. John Passion by the Dorking Bach Choir on Feb. 15.[2] I only wish to take exception to one sentence; he seems to consider the use of the pianoforte instead of the harpsichord for continuo as a jarring factor.

To my mind to use the harpsichord or viol da gamba for continuo seems to reduce the St. John Passion to a museum piece to be put in a glass case. Surely this work should be produced in such a way as to give modern hearers the same emotional and spiritual effect which Bach himself produced on his contemporaries.

I have no doubt that if the grand pianoforte of our day had been available to Bach he would have used it in preference to the harpsichord. This I believe was the opinion of Donald Tovey.[3]

Opinions may differ as to the intrinsic beauty of the harpsichord, but there can be no doubt that the pianoforte, with its infinite gradations of tone, from the almost orchestral fortissimo to an almost inaudible pianissimo, performs the function of a continuo much better than the harpsichord with its hard, unyielding tone.

The same applies to our oboes with their lovely tone, which no one hesitates to use instead of the coarse-sounding oboes of Bach's time; why make an exception of the harpsichord, which is now fashionable?

It seems to me that to use the resources which we now possess reverently, and with true musical insight, is right; not only in the interests of the performers and hearers of our own time, but also as the highest tribute we can pay to the greatest composer the world has yet produced.

It is well known that Bach was dissatisfied with his orchestral resources and was often obliged to put up with what he could get. A striking example of this occurs actually in the St. John Passion where the wonderful lute obbligato may, according to the composers' footnote, be played also on the organ!

I believe it is our privilege and our duty to use all the improved mechanisms invented by our instrument makers to do full justice to this immortal work.[4]

Yours faithfully
Ralph Vaughan Williams

[1] Published on p. 8 of the issue for 20 Feb. 1958 under the heading 'Harpsichord or piano: a word to purists from Dr. Vaughan Williams'.

[2] John Warrack had written a notice of the performance in the *Daily Telegraph* of 17 Feb., p. 10, which, though otherwise laudatory, included the statement: 'Accustomed as we now are again to harpsichord tone, the piano sounds oddly in the recitatives and certain other things are bound to jar a little.'

[3] In 1914 Tovey wrote in an essay 'On the Performance of the St Matthew Passion' (most recently published in D. F. Tovey, *The Classics of Music*, ed. M. Tilmouth (Oxford, 2001), 691): 'Should one wish to insist that the modern pianoforte is not a proper substitute for a genuine harpsichord, one would immediately find oneself at odds with the view of Bach's son, Carl Philipp Emanuel, who quite definitely preferred a piano for continuo purposes. The reasoning behind this opinion is even more apposite today with modern instruments and conditions of performance than it was in his time: we perform in larger concert-halls and hence require instruments with an even greater volume of sound . . .'

[4] On 22 Feb. the paper published a letter from Walter Emery in response, making the points that (1) there was no need to argue between the harpsichord and pianoforte since the normal continuo instrument would have been the organ; (2) the piano might well be able to play fortissimo but 'one thing known for certain about 18th c. organ continuo playing is that it was done unobtrusively on one or two quiet stops'; (3) the only 18th c. oboe he had heard 'did not sound coarse. Its tone was smooth and perfectly acceptable.'

736. To Herbert Ellingford[1]

23 February 1958

From R. Vaughan Williams,
10, Hanover Terrace,
Regents Park,
London, N.W.1.

February 23rd 1958.

Dear Dr Ellingford,

Thank you so much for your letter. My mild little letter to the Telegraph seems to have lit a candle that shall not easily be put out. I am glad to think that an organist of your eminence disapproves of the 'bubble and squeak' organ.[2]

Am I not right in thinking that in very early days, before you rose to fame, you were organist of St Barnabas South Lambeth, in succession to me?[3]

Yours sincerely,
R. Vaughan Williams

[1] Former organist of St George's Hall, Liverpool. He had been a contemporary of VW at the RCM.

[2] See no. 735. VW alludes to Hugh Latimer's remark to Nicholas Ridley in 1555, made as they were both about to be burnt at the stake for heresy: 'We shall this day light such a candle as by God's grace in England (I trust) shall never be put out.'

[3] Ellingford replied on 25 Feb. that it had not been him—nor had he ever taken a D.Mus. (however, in an earlier letter to him of 1930 (not included in this volume) VW remembered him as having once deputized for him at the church). His objection to Baroque-style organs was their lack of foundation tone. This was not what he remembered of organs he had played in Leipzig in 1938.

737. To John and Evelyn Barbirolli

6 March 1958

From R. Vaughan Williams,
10, Hanover Terrace,
Regents Park,
London, N.W.1.

March 6th 1958.

Dear John and Evelyn,

We had what I believe to be the finest performance we have ever given at Dorking of the Matthew. It must have been the result of your dear telegram.[1]

Our fondest love to you both,

Yrs
RVW

[1] On the performance see *WVW*, 342 and *RVW*, 389. It was recorded by Christopher Finzi and Noel Taylor and was eventually issued on CD in 2000.

738. To Herbert Howells

8 March 1958

From R. Vaughan Williams,
10, Hanover Terrace,
Regents Park,
London, N.W.1.

March 8th 1958.

Dear Herbert,

Now the Passion is over – though very tired I went through the clavichord pieces, or tried to: naturally I can't play them, or always understand them, so you must come and play them to me. It is all nonsense to say you can't! THANK you a thousand times for the Pavane and the Galliard. I love the pavane – I haven't got hold of the Galliard quite, yet, that is chiefly because I can't play it, and as you know I can't read music, so you simply must come and play them to me, and also the Mass and the beginning of the Concerto.

You are a busier man than me, so will you suggest a date – I think not till after the 21st – and even then I may have to rewrite the symphony in ten days!

Love to you both from us both
Ralph

Old Toast

If you 2 doesn't love we 2
as we 2 loves you 2
then here's us 2 & no more.
But if you 2 does love we 2
as we 2 loves you 2
then here's to us 4.

739. To the performers in the LHMF Passion

16 March 1958

From R. Vaughan Williams,
10, Hanover Terrace,
Regents Park,
London, N.W.1.

March 16th 1958.

To all those who took part in the performance of Bach's St Matthew Passion on Wednesday, March 5th 1958.

You covered yourselves with glory, having to follow that fine, but very different, performance by Dr Armstrong without special rehearsal. I thank you heartily. You were assisted by a fine orchestra and by the inspiring and helpful continuo playing by Dr Cole and Mr Gritton. It is difficult to describe what both the conductors and performers owe to these fine artists. We also had the advantage of what I believe to be the best sextet of singers we have ever had.

Thank you once again: and may we repeat our triumph next year.[1]

[1] The letter is printed in *WVW*, 342. VW decided later in May not to conduct the Passion again. See no. 746.

740. To Michael Kennedy

29 March 1958

From R. Vaughan Williams,
10, Hanover Terrace,
Regents Park,
London, N.W.1.

March 29th 1958.

My dear Michael,

Thank you so much for liking the new Symph.[1] I have made a few alterations in the scoring and in the metronome marks – and specially the last movement where I have speeded it up a bit all through and made a short cut, of about fifteen bars in the middle, I am sure it is an improvement.

I do hope that long and tiring expedition was not bad for Eslyn.

I wonder if you disliked the Carmelites[2] as much as we did? We must meet on Wednesday, at the party if not at the concert.[3]

Love from both of us to both of you.

Love
R
& U[4]

[1] Kennedy had attended the run-through of the Ninth Symphony on 21 March.

[2] The VWs had recently heard Poulenc's *Dialogues des Carmélites* (1957) and had found it had 'no tunes worth having', as UVW wrote to Kennedy. He did not agree.

[3] The first performance of the symphony.

[4] This letter is printed in part in *WVW*, 382.

741. To Margery Cullen

[about 8 April 1958[1]]

From R. Vaughan Williams,
10, Hanover Terrace,
Regents Park,
London, N.W.1.

To the L.H.M.C. Choirs.

We are very sorry for our own sakes that we cannot be with you for the Festival.

I shall miss you, – but you need not miss me; you have an excellent and experienced Musical Director, & a splendid Secretary[2] – what more do you want?

So, good luck to you, and sing beautiful music beautifully. This after all is what our Festival is for.

R. Vaughan Williams

as from
Villa Drina, Forio d'Ischia, Italy.

[1] i.e. just after Easter but before VW and UVW went to Italy to stay on Ischia in a villa belonging to the Waltons, where they arrived on 14 Apr. and stayed until 14 May. LHMF was on 15–18 April.

[2] William Cole and Margery Cullen.

742. To Anthony Scott

8 April 1958

From R. Vaughan Williams,
10, Hanover Terrace,
Regents Park,
London, N.W.1.

April 8th 1958.

Dear Tony,

Thank you so much for writing, and I won't pretend that I am not pleased that you liked it. The Flugel man showed me at rehearsal that unless I allowed a minimum of vibrato, the tone would sound hard, rather like a bad horn. The valve trouble caused him to miss a few notes, but the trumpet, who was sitting next to him, gallantly came to the rescue and played them for him: so that I, at all events, did not know that anything had gone wrong!

I am delighted to hear about the opera – I understand it is about an organ tuner. I hope you introduce the whole tone scale?[1]

Love from us both,

Yrs
RVW

[1] Scott's entry in *IWWM* lists two one-act operas but without title or other detail.

743. To Cedric Glover

8 April 1958

From R. Vaughan Williams,
10, Hanover Terrace,
Regents Park,
London, N.W.1.

April 8th 1958.

My dear Cedric,

Thank you so much for liking my new tune.

Sancta Civitas was a very good performance also – the only fault, as usual, was with the balance & control who continued their bad habit of making every thing into a harp concerto. I like it the best of my own choral works.[1]

Thank you about your interpreter, but I'm afraid we cannot expect him to travel from Trieste to Ischia for us!

Love from us both,

Yrs
RVW

Alan Frank will let Eric Greene have a copy of the Blake songs in plenty of time for the party.[2]

U.

[1] *Sancta Civitas* had been broadcast on Good Friday, 4 April. See *RVW*, 391.

[2] *Ten Blake Songs*, *CW* 1957/5, written for the film *The Vision of William Blake*. The work was not performed publicly until Oct. 1958. The party, not mentioned in *RVW*, would have been at Dorking, connected with the LHMF.

744. To Adrian Boult

8 April 1958

From R. Vaughan Williams,
10, Hanover Terrace,
Regents Park,
London, N.W.1.

April 8th 1958.

Dear Adrian

It was a fine performance of Sancta by you and your singers and players the other night – the tempi, the balance, – everything, was just right as far as you were concerned, but of course the balance & control people made their usual mistake, and did their best to make it sound like a harp concerto. But as often the harp part is not strong enough, this did not hurt. Thank you and all your forces heartily from me, if you have an opportunity. Clinton was splendid, and the tenor excellent.[1]

Thank you once again, and our love to Ann,

Yrs
Ralph[2]

[1] *Sancta Civitas*, *CW* 1925/6, had been broadcast on the Home Service on Good Friday, 4 Apr. from St Andrew's Hall, Glasgow; see *RVW*, 391. Boult had conducted the BBC Scottish Choral Society and the Scottish National Orchestra; the soloists were Mitchell Hodge, tenor, and Gordon Clinton, baritone.

[2] UVW added a note: 'I thought it was absolutely radiant, and most moving. I do love it, and it was perfect hearing it again after what seems too long always, though the grammar seems to have gone astray . . . emotion is too much for my parts of speech. We are going to Italy on Friday, and shall be away for five weeks. Thank you, and love.'

745. To Michael and Eslyn Kennedy from UVW and VW

postmark: 15 April 1958

Postcard

Villa Cristabella (*Not Drina* – the postman understands[1])

We had a bumpy flight, saw a very bad opera – a new one – in the ravishing opera house at Naples, and went to Herculaneum. This is a lovely house, terraces, hills covered with broom in flower, cyclamen & grape hyacinths – but very cold, & little sunshine – however we are going to enjoy all, we keep warm with wine, wood fires & jerseys in bed! Ralph seems very well again

The opera is said to be founded on Sardinian folk songs. If that is so God help the Sardines!

R[2]

[1] UVW had given the address to friends in advance as Villa Drina.

[2] This letter is printed in part in *WVW*, 391.

746. To Margery Cullen

26 May 1958

From R. Vaughan Williams,
10, Hanover Terrace,
Regents Park,
London, N.W.1.

May 26th 1958.

My dear Margery,

I have made the very sad decision that the performance of the Matthew Passion this year ought to be my last. I am getting blind and deaf, and I find that to do the Passion on top of all the other things I am doing, is a little too much for me. I have consulted my doctor (Rowntree) and he agrees that it is time to give up. I can't tell you how much I feel it: but it had to come some time, and I think now is the time, after the glory of that splendid, recorded performance.

I need hardly say that I shall always be here as a standby, and I will listen to rehearsals and performance, and can even take some of the Saturdays if you would like me to.

I know that with Tom Armstrong, and Bill Cole standing by, the Passion will go on and prosper. It is a great wrench to stop after so many years, but this is one of the great penalties of old age, and one has to face it. The one person we cannot get on without is you, so please don't you get old, – but I don't think you ever will.

You can read this letter out to the Committee if you wish, but if you read it, you are to read it *ALL*

Love from Ralph

747. To Michael Kennedy

postmark: 16 June 1958

From R. Vaughan Williams,
10, Hanover Terrace,
Regents Park,
London, N.W.1.

Dear Michael

Richter[1]

When I was young the only orchestra concerts (except the Phil: which did not count) were Manns[2] (Crystal Palace) or Richter with Henschel a little later – so we had no real standard of comparison. But I felt that at all events in Wagner & Beethoven you heard not an 'individual reading' – but the music itself – and that's what mattered both for Richter & audience – I felt with him as with no other conductor that he never got between you and the composer. It was always straight-forward with no monkey-tricks and intensely satisfying – a feeling which no other conductor has given me.

He used the old fashioned walking-stick baton for a straight-forward business-like beat

I only once remember his using any showmanship when he used to let the orchestra play the $\frac{5}{4}$ Tschaikowsky without (manually) beating[3] – of course he did a good deal of conducting in the movement with his eyebrows & little finger – but the audience thought it wonderful. I'm sorry I have so little to tell you – it's more than 50 years ago

My love to Eslyn – it will be lovely to meet at Cheltenham

Yrs
RVW[4]

Just back from a lovely flash round the Fens – Lincoln, Tattershall, Gunby, Boston, Spalding, Crowland & Thorney ending with Peterborough Cathedral & a folk dance festival & home on the 8.30 train – we felt as if we'd had a fortnight in the country & it was just 24 hours. It all looked lovely, & was *all* new to me. R is nice & brown!

Love
U.[5]

[1] Kennedy was at this time working on his history of the Hallé Orchestra, of which Hans Richter had been the director from 1899 to 1911, and had asked VW for his memories of the conductor.

[2] Sir August Manns (1825–1907), conductor at the Crystal Palace.

[3] VW is referring to the second movement of Symphony No. 6 (*Pathétique*).

[4] This letter is printed in part in *WVW*, 391.

[5] Postscript written on the back of the envelope by UVW.

748. To Eugene Goossens

24 June 1958

From R. Vaughan Williams,
10, Hanover Terrace,
Regents Park,
London, N.W.1.

June 24th 1958.

Dear Eugene,

I am so sorry but this ridiculous phlebitis of mine has come back, and the doctor says I must keep my foot up for a few days. We are both desolated to miss meeting you. I hope we shall meet again soon.

Our affectionate greetings

Yrs
RVW

749. To Rosamund Strode

29 June 1958

From R. Vaughan Williams,
10, Hanover Terrace,
Regents Park,
London, N.W.1.

June 29th 1958

Dear Rosamund,

Will you come to Dorking, St Martin's Church, on Saturday, February 14th and sing the soprano solos in Bach's St John Passion? Rehearsal 2.30. Performance 7pm. This is a small private show, and nothing to do with the Festival and we cannot offer a fee of more than 10 guineas.[1]

Do hope you can come

Love from
Uncle Ralph

[1] Rosamund Strode, a young friend of Imogen Holst, had taken over the soprano solo part in the St John Passion at Dorking at short notice owing to the illness of Nicola Darwin on 27 Feb. 1954. VW had of course died by the time of the performance on 14 Feb. 1959 which was in any case to be conducted by William Cole, following his retirement as conductor (see no. 746). However he was evidently putting in place well in advance arrangements for the performance (which it may be assumed he was financing). Subsequently Strode did much work indexing VW's folk song notebooks, now at the British Library, and then became Curator of Manuscripts and Archivist at the Britten–Pears Library, and also Chairman of the Holst Foundation.

750. To E. A. Barber, Headmaster of Swaffham Primary School

10 July 1958

From R. Vaughan Williams,
10, Hanover Terrace,
Regents Park,
London, N.W.1.

July 10th 1958.

Dear Mr Barber,

I feel much honoured that you propose to name one of your houses after myself. I enclose a message to the boys and girls for you to read out, and frame, if you so wish.

Yours sincerely,
R. Vaughan Williams

To the boys and girls of The Primary School Swaffham.

I am very much pleased to think that one of your houses is going to bear my name. I am myself a musician, and I believe that all the arts, and especially music, are necessary to a full life. The practical side of living of course is important, and this, I feel sure is well taught in your school: such things teach you how to make your living. But music will show you what to do with your life. It is necessary to know facts, but music will enable you to see past facts to the very essence of things in a way which science cannot do. The arts are the means by which we can look through the magic casements and see what lies beyond.

Ralph Vaughan Williams.[1]

[1] Printed in *RVW*, 397.

751. To Michael and Eslyn Kennedy from UVW

27 July 1958

From R. Vaughan Williams,
10, Hanover Terrace,
Regents Park,
London, N.W.1.

July 27th 1958

Dearest Michael & Eslyn,

In case it gets abroad I want to tell you that Ralph is in the Middlesex for a *very* few days, having had a very minor operation. The waterworks department again, but it was all decided on Saturday morning, & he was in the hospital by 12, operated on by 2, & hopes to be out on Tuesday for Sir John. Its meant his missing the dress rehearsal, which has *infuriated* him, but its made spending pennies a comfortable occupation for spare moments again, not a full time job! The surgeon is very pleased with him, the nurses as sweet as ever, & we feel tolerably at home in the hospital – I spend $^3/_4$ of the day with him, so its not too bad! We'll cancel Kings Lynn, so we'll have Friday evening with you, which will be lovely.[1]

All love to you both –

U.

Terribly thrilling about the cadillac in which I suppose yr next visit will be made.

[1] VW was undergoing a further operation in connection with his cancerous prostate.

752. To Alan Frank at OUP

10 August 1958

From R. Vaughan Williams,
10, Hanover Terrace,
Regents Park,
London, N.W.1.

August 10th 1958.

Dear Alan,

Good.

If you hear any reports of Vancouver we'd love to know. We shall be at Joy Finzi's – Ashmansworth, Nr Newbury, till the 18th.[1]

Yrs
RVW

[1] There was the possibility of a performance of the Ninth Symphony (*CW* 1957/4) in Vancouver.

753. To Michael and Eslyn Kennedy from UVW

postmark: 14 August 1958

Joy took us for a glorious trip round Dorset, Stonehenge remade en route – & Yarnbury. Then Shaftesbury & this glorious giant[1] on his sunny hill, & over wild downs. We found a remote thatched pub in the quietest village I've ever met. Then down to the sea on the Chesil bank yesterday – a visit to Sylvia Townsend Warner & home in the rain via Sarum. Here by Monday. Thank you for HWN[2] & the cutting. All well & lots of love to you both from us both.

U

[1] The postcard depicts the giant at Cerne Abbas, Dorset.
[2] Kennedy had sent the VWs an article he had found about H. W. Nevinson.

754. To Simona Pakenham

24 August 1958

August 24th 1958

Dearest Simona

Very M U C H A G A I N S T M Y W I L L I have arranged to orchestrate for an orchestra of 32. I understand there will be plenty of room for them, including a bulky thing like a harp. Of course its no good putting the players in a pit where there won't be room for them to play... this applies specially to the strings with their bow-arms. In detail, the orchestra will be Strings: 6, 4, 3, 3, 2, total 18. Woodwind, 2 flutes, (flute doubling piccolo), 1 oboe, 1 clarinet, 1 bassoon. Total 5. Brass, 2 horns, 2 trumpets, 2 trombones. Total, 6. 1 harp, 1 timp, (ad lib.) this makes 1 or 2. Grand total 31 or 30. This means a certain amount of re-writing but I will do my best.[1]

Love
Ralph

[1] VW was writing about *The First Nowell*, see *CW*, p. 254 (1958/3) and was responding reluctantly to the constraints imposed by the orchestra pit at the Drury Lane Theatre, where the work was to be given at a charity matinée. It was a condition for using the theatre that the layout for 'My Fair Lady', which was then showing there, should not in any way be disturbed. Work on the score was found to be about three-quarters complete when VW died not quite two days later. The work was finished by Roy Douglas on the basis of his sketches; see *WWVW*, 102 ff.

755. To UVW from Steuart Wilson

27 August [1958]

Beguildy,
Knighton,
Radnorshire

Wed 27 Aug.

My dear Ursula,

Mary and I are in the depths of Wales and by the merest accident were in the local pub when the morning news came on. How happy an ending – the tide just ebbs and the great life goes out with it.[1] How happy I am to think of the near 50 years during which he was everything I admired most in a man and in music – and all the time he was endlessly kind to me and I have never been able to show it openly.

There have been few people ever in the world who have asked so little for themselves and given so much to other people.

We go back to B'ham for two nights and then back to Wales, but we are always obtainable at short notice through the School.

And you know we are both of us ever your friends.

Steuart & Mary

[1] VW had died suddenly early in the morning of 26 Aug. of coronary thrombosis. In many ways this was a mercy since the cancerous prostate, though removed in Aug. 1957, threatened a bleak future. UVW has told friends that because of that, his death was right and 'it was time'.

756. To Ursula Vaughan Williams from Benjamin Britten

28 August 1958

The Red House,
Aldeburgh,
Suffolk.

August 28th 1958

My dear Mrs Vaughan Williams,

I should like to send my deepest sympathy to you on the death of your husband, a very great man. He has been such a tremendous figure to me, all my musical life, that it is hard to realise he is no longer with us. We all miss him sadly – above all, his wonderful, uncompromising courage in fighting for all those things he believed in – things which I personally believe to be some of the most important things in life.

You have the warmest thoughts of the countless people who loved him with you at this terrible moment.

Yours sincerely
Benjamin Britten[1]

[1] This letter was presented to the BPL by UVW in Nov. 1990.

757. To Vera Mackenzie and Molly Hodge from UVW[1]

4 September 1958

10, Hanover Terrace,
Regents Park,
London, N.W.1.

Sept. 4, 1958

Dear Vera, & Molly, & all,

I wanted to write to you at once, but there has been so much to do, so much to think of, & so many letters to read that I've not been able to before.

Ralph died very early in the morning, and as simply and quietly as he had lived. Our great friend Gil Jenkins and the doctor, who is also a friend, were there, as he'd been restless and unable to sleep, & had difficulty breathing – but the doctor gave him an injection which relaxed all the tension, and he slipped away, with his head on my shoulder, and his hand in mine. I opened our window to the dawn, and after a time I played his pastoral symphony – and the music flowed quietly and serenely out into the still morning. He stayed there, untouched by anyone but me, lying quietly in his room, so that I could be in and out of it – which was wonderful – & right. And the house was full of roses brought by his friends, and there was a feeling of a birthday – a gentleness and lovingness that filled the whole place. The cremation was a putting away of beautiful clothes that cannot be used again, and there was a blazing and magnificent thunderstorm raging over the whole country – all as it should be.

I took his ashes to the Abbey, and they let me carry them myself through the cloisters, passed [*sic*] the graves of the Norman priors, through the Poet's corner, to the tiny early chapel of St. Faith, where they stay till the service on the 19th. For that the music is some he loved best, and some of his own – and after it all the Abbey bells will ring across London and across history.

I wonder if there is any chance of your hearing the service broadcast – its 11.30 A.M. Greenwich time. I should love to feel you were all there.

We have had a particularly lovely summer, doing things we loved to do, and spending, not long ago, a week in the country driving over Dorset and Berkshire, all very golden now – a most happy and serene last time. I don't think there have been many people who were so happy in their time together, or so lucky. That serenity is still with me – a magical and unexpected content.[2]

Molly's letter was the first real news of Vancouver. It came the morning Ralph died, but I was so glad of it. That morning too, Adrian recorded No. 9.

Will you thank Joy for her letter? I have had so very many and all must be answered in time. They are so personal and glowing I can't at all send even the nicest printed form – so I'm buried under envelopes at the moment – though lots of our closest friends come in, & then I can stop writing for a little and talk!! Please will you also thank Kenneth & all for their telegram – for the time being?

This brings all my love

Ursula

[1] Daughters of Ursula's uncle, Perceval Lock. They both lived in Vancouver.

[2] Writing in similar vein to Adeline's cousin Margaret Keynes a few days later, UVW said: 'Ralph & I had a most golden summer & did so many lovely things, that I can only feel that we were most fortunate in this too, & he died in a time of great serenity, and completion, and as simply as he lived.'

LIST OF SOURCES

Letters which do not appear on the following list are either held in the collection of the late Ursula Vaughan Williams (in original form or as a photocopy) or remain in private hands. The collection of Ursula Vaughan Williams will in due course be transferred to the British Library.

BBC Written Archives Centre
File 910, VW artist: 242, 254, 336, 391, 474, 712
File 910, VW composer: 194, 196, 202, 206, 222, 224, 236, 249, 250, 253, 311, 328, 345, 350, 356, 357, 372, 378, 385, 392, 411, 412, 420, 434, 445, 446, 471, 480, 483, 499
Programme Correspondence Section, File R41/241 PCS (Misc. files: RVW 1939): 327
Birmingham City Archives MS 135: 14, 15, 19, 33
Birmingham Reference Library: 13
Bodleian Library
MS Eng. c.3269: 84, 108
MS Eng. misc.c.453: 98
Finzi papers (photocopies): 138, 165, 166, 168, 198, 209, 231, 261, 265, 280, 303, 310, 360, 373, 397, 405, 443, 448, 450, 457, 465, 467, 476, 522, 523, 563, 571, 589, 592, 601, 673, 683
MS Fisher 74: 276
Fisher additional papers: 636
MS Gilbert Murray 19: 72, 73, 74
MS Gilbert Murray 82: 281, 283
MS Gilbert Murray 99: 520
MS Gilbert Murray 116: 67
Bristol University: Special Collections, Arts and Social Sciences Library: Arnold Barter papers: 66, 68, 81, 475, 501, 502, 543, 643, 660, 721
British Library
Add. MS 56422: 302, 304, 408, 409, 410, 414, 426, 427, 430
Add. MS 59814: 650
Add. MS 63547: 470, 539, 545, 564, 578, 615, 617, 619, 662, 665, 672, 718
Add. MS 65143: 379, 380, 381
Add. MS 69816: 113, 146, 306, 691, 728
Add. MS 70935: 42, 44, 56, 124
Add. MS 71064: 620
Add. MS 71105 A: 557
Add. MS 71536: 477, 514, 537
Add. MS 71700: 3, 4, 22, 32, 38, 123, 319, 337, 447, 473, 538, 547, 556, 593, 614
Add. MS 72624: 170, 245, 273, 608, 684, 744
Cup.404.c.1/11: 323
MS Mus. 158: 2, 5, 20, 21, 25, 26, 27, 39, 52, 96, 97, 100, 101, 105, 114, 115, 130, 140, 154, 189, 211, 213, 215, 223, 230, 246

BIBLIOGRAPHY

Adams, Byron, and Wells, Robin, *Vaughan Williams Essays* (Aldershot, 2003).

Banfield, Stephen, *Gerald Finzi: An English Composer* (London, 1997).

Blezzard, Judith, 'Holst and Vaughan Williams Manuscripts at Liverpool Cathedral', *Transactions of the Historic Society of Lancashire and Cheshire*, 139 (1990), 161–87.

Boden, Anthony, *Three Choirs: A History of the Festival* (Stroud, 1992).

Boyes, Georgina, *The Imagined Village: Culture, Ideology and the English Folk Revival* (Manchester, 1993).

Cobbe, Hugh, '"My dear Elgar": The Letters of Elgar and Vaughan Williams', in John Norris and Andrew Neill (eds.), *A Special Flame: The Music of Elgar and Vaughan Williams* (Rickmansworth, 2004), 85–98.

—— 'Vaughan Williams, Germany, and the German Tradition: A View from the Letters', in Alain Frogley (ed.), *Vaughan Williams Studies* (Cambridge, 1996), 81–98.

Cohen, Harriet, *A Bundle of Time: The Memoirs of Harriet Cohen* (London, 1969).

Day, James, *Vaughan Williams*, 2nd edn. (Master Musicians; Oxford, 1998).

Doctor, Jennifer, 'Working for their Own Salvation', in Foreman (ed.) *Vaughan Williams in Perspective* (London, 1998), 181–201.

—— and Wright, David (eds.), *The Proms: A New History* (London, 2007).

Douglas, Roy, *Working with Vaughan Williams: The Correspondence of Ralph Vaughan Williams and Roy Douglas*, rev. and enlarged edn. (London, 1988).

Elgar, Edward, *Letters of a Lifetime*, ed. Jerrold Northrop Moore (Oxford, 1990).

Ferguson, Howard, *Music, Friends and Places* (London, 1997).

Finzi, Gerald, and Ferguson, Howard, *Letters of Gerald Finzi and Howard Ferguson*, ed. Howard Ferguson and Michael Hurd (Woodbridge, 2001).

Foreman, Lewis, *Bax: A Composer and his Times*, 3rd edn. (Woodbridge, 2007).

—— *From Parry to Britten: British Music in Letters 1900–1945* (London, 1987).

—— (ed.), *Vaughan Williams in Perspective* (London, 1998).

Foss, Hubert, *Ralph Vaughan Williams: A Study* (London, 1950; corrected reprint 1952).

Fox Strangways, A. H., with Karpeles, Maud, *Cecil Sharp* (London, 1933).

Frogley, Alain, 'Vaughan Williams and Nazi Germany: The 1937 Hamburg Shakespeare Prize', in Guido Heldt and Christa Brüstle (eds.), *Music as a Bridge: Musikalische Beziehungen zwischen England und Deutschland 1920–1950* (Hildesheim, 2005), 113–32.

Heffer, Simon, *Vaughan Williams* (London, 2000).

HINNELLS, DUNCAN, *An Extraordinary Performance: Hubert Foss and the Early Years of Music Publishing at the Oxford University Press* (Oxford, 1998).

——'Vaughan Williams's Piano Concerto', in Foreman (ed.), *Vaughan Williams in Perspective*, 118–63.

HOLST, IMOGEN, *Gustav Holst: A Biography*, 2nd edn. (London, 1969).

——A *Scrap-book for the Holst Birthplace Museum* (East Bergholt, 1978).

——*A Thematic Catalogue of Gustav Holst's Works* (London, 1974).

HOWES, FRANK, *The Music of Ralph Vaughan Williams* (London, 1954).

KENNEDY, MICHAEL, *A Catalogue of the Works of Ralph Vaughan Williams* (London, 1964); rev. edn. (London, 1982); 2nd edn. (Oxford, 1996; corrected repr. 1998).

——*The Works of Ralph Vaughan Williams* (London, 1964; 2nd edn. 1980).

LEITH HILL MUSICAL FESTIVAL, *And Choirs Singing: An Account of the Leith Hill Musical Festival 1905–1985* (Leith Hill, 1985).

——*Music Won the Cause: 100 Years of the Leith Hill Musical Festival 1905–2005* (Leith Hill, 2005).

LEVY, PAUL, *Moore: G. E. Moore and the Cambridge Apostles* (London, 1979).

LLOYD, STEPHEN, 'Vaughan Williams's *A London Symphony*: The Original Version and Early Performances and Recordings', in Foreman (ed.), *Vaughan Williams in Perspective*, 91–117.

LUNN, JOHN E., and VAUGHAN WILLIAMS, URSULA, *Ralph Vaughan Williams: A Pictorial Biography* (London, 1971).

MCVEAGH, DIANA, *Gerald Finzi: His Life and Music* (Woodbridge, 2005).

MOORE, JERROLD NORTHROP, *Music and Friends: Seven Decades of Letters to Adrian Boult* (London, 1979).

——*Vaughan Williams: A Life in Photographs* (Oxford, 1992).

The Oxford Book of Carols, ed. Percy Dearmer, R. Vaughan Williams, and Martin Shaw (London, 1928).

PAGE, FREDERICK, *A Musician's Journal* (Dunedin, 1986).

PAKENHAM, SIMONA, *Vaughan Williams: A Discovery of his Music* (London, 1957).

RAVERAT, GWEN, *Period Piece* (London, 1952).

ROPP, ROBERT S. DE, *Warrior's Way* (Nevada City, Nev., 1992).

SHARP, CECIL, *Country Dance Tunes* (London 1909–22).

——*English Folk-carols* (London, 1911).

——and CAMPBELL, O. D., *English Folk-songs from the Southern Appalachians* (London, 1917).

SHAW, HAROLD WATKINS, *The Succession of Organists of the Chapel Royal and the Cathedrals of England and Wales from c.1538* (Oxford, 1991).

SHORT, MICHAEL, *Gustav Holst: The Man and his Music* (Oxford, 1990).

TAWASTSTJERNA, E., *Sibelius*, iii: *1914–1957*, trans. R. Layton (London, 1997).

VAUGHAN WILLIAMS, RALPH, *National Music* (London, 1934).

——*National Music and Other Essays*, 2nd edn. (Oxford, 1987).

——*Some Thoughts on Beethoven's Choral Symphony with Writings on Other Musical Subjects* (London, 1953).

——*Vaughan Williams on Music*, ed. David Manning (New York, 2008).

——and HOLST, GUSTAV, *Heirs and Rebels: Letters Written to Each Other and Occasional Writings on Music*, ed. Ursula Vaughan Williams and Imogen Holst (London, 1959).

VAUGHAN WILLIAMS, URSULA, *Paradise Remembered: An Autobiography* (London, 2002).

——*R. V. W.: A Biography of Ralph Vaughan Williams* (London, 1964).

Vaughan Williams in Dorking: A Collection of Personal Reminiscences of the Composer Dr. Ralph Vaughan Williams O.M., ed. Celia Newbury, Local History Group of the Dorking and Leith Hill Preservation Society (Dorking, 1979).

WILSON, DUNCAN, *Gilbert Murray OM* (Oxford, 1987).

YOUNG, PERCY M., *Vaughan Williams* (London, 1953).

INDEX OF WORKS BY RALPH VAUGHAN WILLIAMS

GENERAL INDEX